The tradition of excellence that began with
African-American Almanac ...

"An entire reference shelf between two covers."

> — *Wilson Library Bulletin*

"The many biographical sketches on prominent blacks is reason enough to own this massive work. Highly recommended."

> — *Book Report*

"It remains the most complete single-volume reference work about blacks available today."

> — *American Reference Books Annual 1990*

"An outstanding reference source and a necessary purchase for all libraries."

> — *Library Journal*

Continues and flourishes with
African America: Portrait of a People ...

"*African America: Portrait of a People* continues the tradition of excellence that has been established by its predecessors, by its editor, and by its publishers, and I am honored and pleased to commend it to all who would investigate and learn the history —the trials and the triumphs—of people of African descent."

> — Jean Currie Church
> Chief Librarian
> Moorland-Spingarn Research Center
> Howard University

African America

Portrait of a People

African America

Portrait of a People

Kenneth Estell

DETROIT • WASHINGTON D.C. • LONDON

African America: Portrait of a People

Cover painting "Family" by Romare Bearden courtesy of National Museum of American Art, Washington, DC/Art Resource, N.Y.

Published by Visible Ink Press™
a division of Gale Research Inc.
835 Penobscot Building
Detroit, MI 48226-4094

Visible Ink Press is a trademark of Gale Research Inc.

Most Visible Ink Press books are available at special quantity discounts when purchased in bulk by corporations, organizations, or groups. Customized printings, special imprints, messages, and excerpts can be produced to meet your needs. For more information, contact Special Markets Manager, Gale Research Inc., 835 Penobscot Bldg., Detroit, MI 48226. Or call 1-800-877-4253, extension 1033.

ISBN 0-8103-9453-7

10 9 8 7 6 5 4 3 2

ADVISORY BOARD

CONTRIBUTORS

Stephen W. Angell
Associate Professor of Religion, Florida A&M University

Robin Armstrong
Adjunct Lecturer, University of Michigan, Dearborn

John Cohassey
Writer and Researcher, *Contemporary Black Biography*

Allen G. Harris
President, Air Force Association, General Daniel James Chapter

Donald Franklin Joyce
Director, Felix G. Woodward Library, Austin Peay State University

Kwame Kenyatta
Detroit Board of Education, New African People's Organization

Mark Kram
Sportswriter, *Philadelphia Daily News*

Ionis Bracy Martin
Lecturer, Central Connecticut State University

Dan Morgenstern
Director, Institute for Jazz Studies, Rutgers University

Wilson J. Moses
Professor of History, Pennsylvania State University

Richard Prince
National Association of Black Journalists

Nancy Rampson
Writer and Researcher, *Contemporary Black Biography*

Michael D. Woodard
Director, Los Angeles Institute for Multicultural Training; Visiting Scholar, UCLA Center for Afro-American Studies

CONTENTS

Provides a sweeping overview of Africans' early explorations in the Americas, the rise of slavery and of anti-slavery movements, and the status of black citizens after the Civil War, as well as detailing the lives of notable African Americans who helped shape the history of the United States, including slave-ship mutiny leader Joseph Cinque; newspaper publishers William Lloyd Garrison and Frederick Douglass; and underground railroad conductor Harriet Tubman.

From pre-Civil War movements, through the massive protests of the mid-twentieth century, to the current status of African Americans. Important rights activists include Martin Luther King, Jr., Daisy Bates, Stokely Carmichael, Angela Davis, W.E.B. DuBois, Fannie Lou Hamer, Jesse Jackson, Thurgood Marshall, and Booker T. Washington.

Explores black nationalism from its inception in the late eighteenth century to its applications in modern society. Examines the lives and teachings of Marcus Garvey, Elijah Muhammad, Malcolm X, and Louis Farrakhan.

the first black-owned publishing enterprise, to currently successful publishing companies such as the Third World Press and Just Us Books; from Freedom's Journal, the first black newspaper, to popular magazines such as Ebony and Essence. Also profiles the careers of radio and television personalities, including Bryant Gumbel, Carole Simpson, Ed Bradley, and Oprah Winfrey.

From the days of minstrelsy to comedians on "Saturday Night Live," covering drama, musical theater, television, film, dance theater, and stand-up comedy; includes such talented artists as Alvin Ailey, Josephine Baker, Redd Foxx, Whoopi Goldberg, and James Earl Jones.

Chronicles the rich musical heritage of African Americans as it has developed from music composed in the time of slavery to current compositions; details the achievements of singers Kathleen Battle and Marian Anderson, conductors Dean Dixon and James Anderson DePreist, and composers Scott Joplin and Helen Hagen.

Records the history of jazz, from ragtime to swing, from bebop to avant garde, and the African-American composers and performers who made jazz one of the most popular forms of music worldwide, including Louis Armstrong, Ella Fitzgerald, Duke Ellington, Branford Marsalis, Billie Holiday, and John Coltrane.

Examines the wide variety of musical styles that constitute black popular music—gospel, country, rhythm and blues, funk, soul, and rap— and the performers who contribute to these genres, like James Brown, Tina Turner, Jimi Hendrix, Ice Cube, Aretha Franklin, and Prince.

The lives and works of not only fine artists, but also architects, craftspeople, fashion designers, illustrators, and automobile designers, including Romare Bearden, Jean-Michel Basquiat, Willi Smith, Gordon Parks, and Augusta Savage.

Outlines accomplishments in scientific fields from the first patent held by an African American to the latest achievements in technology and medicine.

INTRODUCTION

African America: Portrait of a People illustrates nearly 400 years of black American history and achievements through enlightening essays, inspiring biographies, and more than 300 photographs. Eighteen chapters, each written by an expert in the field, cover current and historic issues and events surrounding the civil rights movement, African-American literature, religion within the black community, advances in science and medicine, and many other areas of key interest to students of African-American culture.

African America continues the tradition of excellence established by its acclaimed predecessor, the exhaustive, award-winning *African-American Almanac*. First published as *The Negro Almanac* in 1967, *The African-American Almanac* has been hailed as the most comprehensive reference work of its kind by the American Library Association. *African America* condenses this wealth of information and inspiration, creating a unique and valuable reader devoted to illustrating and demystifying the moving, difficult, and often lost history of black life in America. With insight and passion, *Portrait of a People* connects that history to the issues facing the African-American community today.

Each chapter opens with a series of informative essays, then describes numerous leaders and other individuals noted for their contributions to the field. Although the individuals featured in *African America* represent only a small portion of the African-American community, they embody excellence and diversity in their respective fields of endeavor. Many notable persons have made a great impact in more than one field (Angela Davis and W.E.B. DuBois, for example, have contributed mightily to both civil rights and literature); such figures are profiled in detail in one of the appropriate chapters, then addressed briefly in the others. References throughout the book to individuals and various subjects can be found through the index.

Acknowledgments   The editor wishes to gratefully acknowledge the contributions of the advisors, writers, copy editors, and designers who assisted in the compilation of *African America*. Special thanks are also due *Black Enterprise* magazine and the NAACP Legal Defense and Educational Fund, Inc., for their assistance.

This edition was shaped for Visible Ink Press by Christa Brelin and Judy Galens. Mark C. Howell designed the pages and Art Chartow the cover. Typesetting was supplied by Marco DiVita and the Graphix Group. Susan Stefani was responsible for copywriting. Barbara Wallace and Margaret Chamberlain provided patience and photo management. Roger Jänecke is thanked for his ability to simultaneously prod, push, and pull.

Kenneth Estell

African America

Portrait of a People

Africans in America

The presence of the first Africans in the Americas is a point of contention among historians. Some scholars assert that Africans established contact with the Americas prior to the Europeans, arguing from archeological, anthropological, botanical, and linguistic evidence that Africans were present in pre-Columbian America; the work of Ivan Van Sertima is notable in this regard. Others mark the advent of the African presence as coinciding with the presence of the Europeans. Pedro Alonzo Niño, an explorer and companion to Christopher Columbus on his exploratory journey of 1492, appears to have been of African extraction; and it is known that an African named Estevanico accompanied the Spanish explorers Panfilo de Narvaez and Alvar Nuñez Cabeza de Vaca on trips throughout the American southwest during the 1500s. Several other European explorers, including Vasco Nuñez de Balboa and Hernán Cortés, also had African members in their parties.

EXPLORATION AND THE FIRST SETTLEMENTS IN THE AMERICAS ♦

In 1496 Santo Domingo was established as the first permanent European settlement in the Americas. Indigenous Carib Indians were at first used as laborers; however, they were ill suited to the rigors of the European system of slavery and died in large numbers from either disease or the constant pressure of forced labor. Portuguese explorers first visited the west coast of Africa in the fifteenth century and found that slave trading was an established institution. West Africans had for some time sold each other to Arabic traders from North Africa. By the early sixteenth century the Portuguese and Spanish were supplying newly established colonies in the Americas with African slave labor, and by the seventeenth century several other European nations had entered the trade. African slaves proved to be a relatively cheap and inexhaustible source of labor, and from about 1501 they were increasingly used as slaves, replacing the dwindling Indian labor pool.

SLAVERY IN COLONIAL AMERICA: 1619–1787 ♦ ♦ ♦ ♦ ♦ ♦ ♦ ♦ ♦

The Emergence of Slave Status

Twenty Africans accompanied the Europeans who landed at Jamestown, Virginia, in 1619. These people were not slaves but indentured servants, and upon completing their contracts they were free to enjoy the liberties and privileges of the "free laboring class." By 1650 there were about three hundred Africans in the American colonies, most of whom were indentured servants and some of whom eventually became property holders and active citizens. The first African American born in the colonies, William Tucker, shared with the other settlers the common birthright of freedom. The slave Anthony Johnson apparently became free about 1622 and had by 1651 amassed enough wealth to import five servants of his own, for which he obtained two hundred and fifty acres from the colonial government; the African-American carpenter Richard Johnson imported two white servants in 1654 and received one hundred acres.

It is unclear when the first African slaves arrived in the North American colonies. From the 1640s Africans were increasingly regarded as chattel (or persons regarded as fixed items of personal property). In 1641 Massachusetts became the first state to make perpetual bondage legal, and the institution gradually spread among the original thirteen colonies. Rhode Island had an anti-slavery ordinance, but this was openly violated, and only Pennsylvania maintained a sustained opposition to slavery. By the 1650s Africans were commonly sold for life, and in 1661 the Virginia House of Burgesses formally recognized the institution of black slavery. The erosion of African indentured servitude in Maryland was finalized with the slave law of 1663, which stated specifically that "All negroes or other slaves within the province, [and] all negroes to be hereafter imported, shall serve *durante vita*."

As white indentured servitude gradually disappeared from the colonial labor market, the flow of African labor into the colonies was accelerated, and planters rigidly institutionalized the perpetual servitude of Africans. One practical reason for this system was that slaves of African origin could be more easily detected than whites should they escape. And among the common rationalizations for the enslavement of Africans was reference to their non-Christian status; it was asserted that Africans were primitive and savage, and fit for nothing better than a life of unbroken labor. Even after African Americans became Christianized, their slave status was not altered; in 1667 the Virginia legislature enacted a statute that proclaimed that "baptism doth not alter the condition of the person as to his bondage or freedom."

In recent years archeologists have come to believe that early humans, Hominidea, originated in Africa some two to three million years ago and migrated to other continents. Sophisticated societies developed early in Africa, including the Kush, Ghana, Kanen, Mali Songhai, and the Haissa states.

The Trans-Atlantic Slave Trade

The Dutch West India Company began to provide slave labor to the American colonies in 1621. By the late seventeenth century the Royal African Company, an English company whose most profitable commodity was slaves, began to exert powerful influence within the English court and parliament. The British government in turn exerted great pressure upon the American colonies to develop attitudes and laws that would support a slave economy. The influence of the Royal African Company contributed to William Penn's decision to overrule the objections of fellow Quakers and permit slavery in Pennsylvania. The company also drew the shipping industry of New England into the slave trade. By the time the Royal African Company lost its monopoly on the West African slave trade in 1696, the sea captains of New England were participating in the massive slave incursions into Africa.

The majority of Africans who were transported to the Americas as slaves came from the area comprising the modern nations of Senegal, Gambia,

A group of African slaves disembark in America.

The diversity of Africa's people is underscored by the existence of more than 2,000 languages and dialects. Some fifty major languages are spoken by groups of one million or more people.

Guinea, Sierra Leone, Liberia, Upper Volta, Ivory Coast, Ghana, Togo, Benin, Nigeria, Cameroon, Gabon, and the Republic of the Congo. The number of Africans who reached the Americas is estimated at between ten and twenty million. About six hundred thousand Africans were brought during the sixteenth century, two million in the seventeenth century, five million in the eighteenth century, and three million in the nineteenth century. In addition to those who reached the Americas must be added the enormous number who died in passage. It is estimated that 15 percent of those who were shipped to the Americas died of disease on the over-

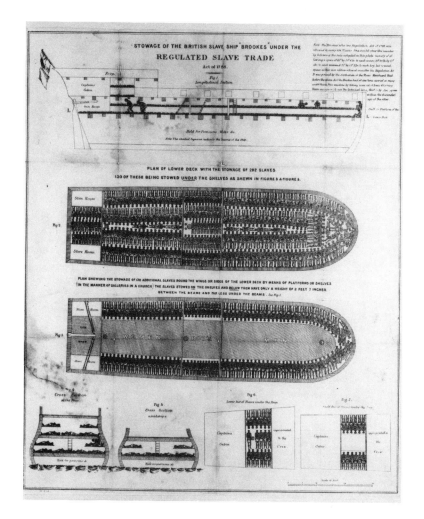

Diagram illustrating the layout of a slave ship.

crowded boats of the "Middle Passage," and that another 30 percent died during the brutal training period faced in the West Indies before shipment to the American mainland.

The Growth of Slavery in Colonial America

The colonies of New England played a principal role in the slave trade, despite their having little local need for slave labor. By 1700 African Americans of New England numbered only one thousand among a population of ninety thousand. In the mid-Atlantic colonies the population comprised a

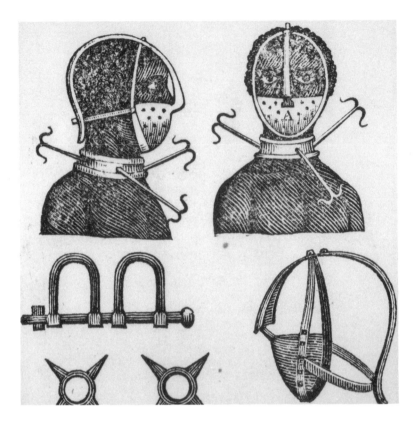

Slave catching and trading apparatuses.

larger percentage, as small slaveholdings employed slaves as farm laborers, domestics, and craftsmen. In New York slaves comprised 12 percent of the population during the mid-eighteenth century. The Quakers of Pennsylvania protested that slavery violated the principles of Christianity and the rights of man, and passed laws prohibiting the slave trade in 1688, 1693, and 1696, but the British parliament overruled these statutes in 1712. Most slaves lived in the South. The southern colonies were divided between the tobacco-producing provinces of Virginia, Maryland, and North Carolina, and the huge rice and indigo plantations now comprising Carolina and Georgia. Tobacco tended to be grown on family farms around the Chesapeake Bay area, and because of this the slave population was not as concentrated as it was on the plantations further to the south.

James Derham, born a slave in Philadelphia in 1762, became the first African-American physician in the United States in 1783. Derham purchased his freedom in 1783 and developed a thriving practice with both black and white clientele.

The growth of a plantation economy and the concentration of a large number of African Americans in the southern states led first Virginia (1636) and then the other states to form all-white militias. The terror of slave uprisings led the slaveholders to institute ever harsher slave codes. Ultimately, a slave could not own anything, carry a weapon, or even leave

TO BE SOLD, on WEDNESDAY 3d AUGUST next,

By COWPER & TELFAIRS,

A C A R G O

Of 170 prime young likely healthy

GUINEA SLAVES,

Laft imported, in the Bark Friends, William Rofs Mafter, directly from
Angola. Savannah, July 25, 1774.

To be Sold at Private Sale, any Time before the 18th of
next Month.

THE PLANTATION, containing one hundred acres, on which the
fubfcriber lives, very pleafantly fituated on Savannah River in fight
of town. The terms of fale may be known by applying to
July 21, 1774 RICHARD WYLLY.

W A N T E D,

AN OVERSEER thoroughly qualified to undertake the fettlement of
a River Swamp Plantation on the Alatamaha River. Any fuch
perfon, who can bring proper recommendations, may hear of great encouragement by applying to NATHANIEL HALL.

THE fubfcriber being under an abfolute neceffity of clofing his concerns without de-
lay, gives this laft publick notice, that all perfons indebted to him by bond,
note or otherwife, who do not difcharge the fame by the firft day of October next,
will find their refpective obligations, &c in the hands of an Attorney to be fued for
without diftinction. It is hoped thofe concerned will avail themfelves of this notice.
PHILIP BOX

RUN AWAY the 10th of May laft from John Forbes, Efq.'s plantation in St.
John's parifh, TWO NEGROES, named BILLY and QUAMINA, of the
Guiney Country, and fpeak good Englifh. Billy is lufty and well made, about 5 feet
10 or 11 inches high, of a black complection, has loft fome of his upper teeth, and
had on when he went away a white negroe cloth jacket and trowfers of the fame.
Quamina is ftout and well made, about 5 feet 10 or 11 inches high, very black,
has his country marks on his face, had on when he went away a jacket, trowfers
and robbin, of white negroe cloth. Whoever takes up faid Negroes, and deliver
them to me at the above plantation, or to the Warden of the Work-Houfe in Savannah, fhall receive a reward of 20s. befides what the law allows.
DAVIS AUSTIN.

Poster advertising a slave sale.

his plantation without a written pass. Murder, rape, arson, and even
lesser offenses were punishable by death; small offenses were commonly
punished by whipping, maiming, and branding. In the area where 90 percent of colonial African Americans lived, a slave had no rights to defend
himself against a white, and as far north as Virginia it was impossible for a
white to be convicted for the murder of a slave.

The large slave revolt in New York City in 1712 and the public paranoia
over the alleged slave conspiracy of 1741 led to the development of slave

codes that were in some cases as severe as those in the South, but in general the North was a relatively less oppressive environment. In Pennsylvania the Quakers allowed African Americans a relative degree of freedom, and in New England the slave codes tended to reflect Old Testament law, maintaining the legal status of slaves as persons with certain limited rights.

African-American Military Service before and during the Revolutionary War

Records of King William's War (1689–1697) relate that the first to fall in Massachusetts was "an Naygro of Colo. Tyng," slain at Falmouth. During Queen Anne's War (1702–1713), African Americans were drafted and sent to fight the French and the Indians when white colonists failed to provide the number of requisitioned men. Many armed African Americans fought at Fort William Henry in New York. Slaves sought freedom as their payment for fighting, and those who were already free sought the wider benefits of land and cash payments. The colony of Virginia ended its policy of excluding African Americans from the militia by 1723, and in 1747 the South Carolina Company made slaves eligible for enlistment in the territorial militia according to a quota system in which a 3:1 ratio was maintained between whites and blacks, thus abating the whites' fears of insurrection. African Americans also fought for the British in the French and Indian War.

African-American Patriots

In the years leading up to the Revolutionary War it became apparent that, despite the growth of slavery, at least some African Americans were willing to fight alongside white Americans. On March 5, 1770, an African American named Crispus Attucks was one of the first men killed in the Revolutionary War, when British troops fired on a crowd of protesters in the Boston Massacre. Many African-American Minutemen fought at the defense of Concord Bridge: among them were Lemuel Haynes, a gifted speaker and later a prominent Congregationalist minister, and Peter Salem, who had received his freedom to enlist. Other figures of the Revolutionary War include Pomp Blackman, Caesar Ferrit and his son John, Prince Estabrook (who was wounded at Lexington), Samuel Craft, and Primas Black and Epheram Blackman (who were members of Ethan Allen's Green Mountain Boys).

The Move to Disarm African Americans

A major issue during the Revolutionary War was whether African-American slaves, and even freemen, should be permitted to bear arms. On May 29, 1775, the Massachusetts Committee of Safety, in a move that reflected their desire to strengthen ties with southern states, proclaimed that the

Crispus Attucks was one of the first men killed in the Revolutionary War.

enlistment of slaves "was inconsistent with the principles that are to be supported, and reflect[ed] dishonor on the colony." On July 9, 1775, Horatio Gates, the adjutant general of the Continental Army, issued from General Washington's headquarters the order that recruiting officers should not accept "any stroller, Negro, or vagabond."

The enormous slave populations of certain southern states meant that many whites lived in perpetual fear of slave uprisings. In South Carolina slaves outnumbered whites, and in Georgia the population was above 40

Lemuel Haynes, who served during the American Revolution as a Minuteman in Connecticut, became the first black minister with a white congregation in 1786.

In setting forth the number of representatives to be accorded each state in the lower house of Congress, the Constitution originally counted the African slaves as "three-fifths of all other persons." This clause augured the history of the African American in the United States: the black American would share less in the promise of the new nation. That clause, though no longer effective, proved to be prophetic.

percent slaves. To minimize the risk of slaves arming themselves, Edward Rutledge of South Carolina introduced a measure in Congress to discharge all African Americans (whether free or enslaved) from the Continental Army. Although the proposal was rejected, General George Washington's own council of war decided to terminate all African-American enlistment two weeks later, and on October 13, 1775, Congress passed the law. Colonial generals like John Thomas argued that African Americans soldiered as well as whites and had already "proved themselves brave" in action, but their protests went unheeded. At the close of 1775 it was extremely difficult for African Americans to join the revolutionary forces at any level.

As the leaders of the Revolution realized that there were inadequate numbers of white troops, they brought an end to their racially exclusionary policy. Local militias that were unable to fill their muster rolls won the quiet agreement of recruiting boards and the reluctant acceptance of slave owners as slaves were substituted for those white men who bought their way out of service. As the war progressed slaveowners were compensated for the enlistment of slaves, who were then made free. During the course of the Revolution many colonies granted freedom to slaves in return for military service. Rhode Island passed the first slave enlistment act on February 2, 1778, raising a regiment that participated gallantly in many important battles. In 1780 Maryland became the only southern state to enroll slave troops, while South Carolina and Georgia refused altogether to even arm their slaves. While slave conscripts were at first assigned to combat support, in the heat of battle they were often armed. African Americans were often enlisted for longer terms than whites, and by the latter years of the war many of the most seasoned veterans were African-American troops.

AFRICAN-AMERICAN STATUS IN THE NEW REPUBLIC ♦ ♦ ♦ ♦ ♦

Slaves and Freemen After the Revolution

At the end of the war about five thousand African Americans had been emancipated through military service. In the following years the northern states abolished slavery: Vermont in 1777, Massachusetts in 1783, Connecticut and Rhode Island in 1784, New York in 1785, New Jersey in 1786, and Pennsylvania in 1789. In the mid-Atlantic state of Virginia, Thomas Jefferson convinced the state legislature to allow slaveowners to manumit their slaves in 1783. In 1790 there were 757,208 African Americans comprising 19 percent of the population of the United States: 697,681 were slave, and 59,527 were free. During this time the free population faced many of the same restrictions as the slave population: they could not walk on the streets after dark, travel between towns without a pass, or own weapons. There was also the danger of being captured and enslaved, whether one was free or not.

The United States Constitution, drafted in 1787 and ratified in 1788, provided fundamental political principles for the nation. Key among these principles were the belief that all people share a fundamental equality, that they possess certain unalienable rights, and that government derives its power from the people. But African Americans were not afforded the rights and privileges of the Constitution. At the time, it was generally believed by whites that people of African descent were racially inferior and incapable of being assimilated into society. It was also widely believed that they were not citizens of the new republic. Article I, section 2 of the Constitution specifies that all persons who are not free shall be counted as three-fifths a person for the sake of tax purposes, and article I, section 9 authorizes the continued importation of slaves until 1808.

The United States Constitution

In 1793 Eli Whitney invented the cotton gin, which separated cotton from cotton fiber; this led to a subsequent increase in the consumption of cotton and heightened the demand for slaves in the cotton-producing states. In 1800 there were more than 893,600 African slaves in the United States; by 1810 there were 1,191,300. Although the slave trade was technically discontinued in 1808, it is estimated that from that date until 1860 more than 250,000 slaves were illegally imported; furthermore, nothing prohibited slaves from being bartered, and the breeding of slaves for sale became a specialized business. Some of the largest slave-trading firms in the nation were located in Maryland, Virginia, and the District of Columbia. Such was the expansion of slavery that, between 1800 and 1859, the population of Mississippi grew from 3,489 slaves and 5,179 whites to 309,878 slaves and 295,718 whites.

Slavery in the New Nation

By the mid-eighteenth century, three-fourths of the cotton produced in the world came from the United States, and profits from cotton were so great that vast plantations were hacked from the wilderness, allowing armies of slaves to work the fields. By mid-century the states of Georgia, Alabama, Mississippi, and Louisiana annually produced 1,726,349 bales of cotton, forty-eight million pounds of rice, and 226,098,000 pounds of

Engraving depicting slaves cultivating cotton.

sugar. With the outbreak of the Civil War there were nearly four million slaves in the United States, and nearly three-fourths of them worked in cotton agriculture.

The Denmark Vesey Conspiracy

The mistreatment of slaves in the years after the Revolution led to an atmosphere of suspicion and terror. Masters lived in constant fear of uprisings, and much time was given over to surveillance. Although organized rebellions were rare, there were many instances of angry slaves burning dwellings and murdering their masters. Slave codes became increasingly strict, but no amount of regulation could dissipate the anger of the slaves, nor the guilt and unease that many slave owners experienced.

In 1800 an African American named Denmark Vesey purchased his freedom and from about 1817 planned a slave revolt in Charleston, South Carolina. The revolt was scheduled to begin on July 14, 1822. With the help of five other African Americans as many as nine thousand slaves were recruited before their plans were uncovered. As word of the revolt began

Fieldworkers returning from the fields.

to leak out, Vesey was forced to move the date to June 16; again word was leaked. The state militia was mustered, and an intense investigation of the plot was begun. One hundred and thirty-five slaves were arrested during the course of the investigation; ninety-seven were bound over for trial; forty-five were transported out of the country; and Vesey and thirty-four others were hanged. As news of the conspiracy spread, southern states further tightened their slave codes.

♦ **EXPANSION OF SLAVERY**

In the early seventeenth century the French began to settle in what comprises present-day Illinois, Indiana, Michigan, Ohio, and Wisconsin, and part of Minnesota. The British began to settle in the area during the mid-eighteenth century; and in July 1787 Congress passed the Northwest Ordinance, which established a government for the Northwest Territory and provided terms

Slavery in the Northwest Territory

under which states could be formed for entrance into the Union. The ordinance also contained controversial provisions: one prohibited slavery and involuntary servitude in the territory, and the other provided for the return of fugitive slaves to the states from which they had escaped. The European farmers who had brought slaves into the territory were angered by the clause prohibiting slavery, and Congress was petitioned for its repeal. The prohibition against slavery was practically circumvented when the Illinois and Indiana territories established a system of indentured servitude under which any person owning slaves could bring them into the region and place them under lifetime indenture. The restrictions placed on these servants were much like the slave codes of the southern colonies: indentured servants could not travel alone without a pass or attend public gatherings independently.

The Missouri Compromise

In April 1803 the United States paid $15 million for the Louisiana Territory, an area comprising the entire Mississippi drainage basin, which had been settled by the French in the late-seventeenth century. Many southerners hoped to extend slavery into the vast new territory, and it was widely expected that Missouri would be admitted to the Union as a slave state. A series of heated debates erupted over the extension of slavery in the region, and in 1819 the House of Representatives introduced legislation authorizing statehood for Missouri while prohibiting the further introduction of slavery into the new state. This drew angry protest from proslavery supporters. The controversy was further escalated by two events: Alabama was admitted to the Union as a slave state in 1819, making the total number of slave and free states equal, and Maine applied for statehood in 1820. In 1820–1821 the Missouri Compromise was reached, admitting Missouri to the Union as a slave state with a slave population of almost 10,000, and Maine as a free state, with the understanding that the future expansion of slavery would be prohibited above the latitude of 36° 33'N.

Texas and the Mexican-American War

The territory comprising Texas was part of the Louisiana Territory when the United States purchased it in 1803, but by 1819 it had become part of Mexico. Mexico provided land grants to American settlers (many of whom brought their slaves with them), and soon Americans outnumbered the Mexicans of the region. In 1836 Texas declared its independence from Mexico and requested annexation to the United States. The possibility of another slave state entering the Union stirred fresh debate. On March 1, 1845 President John Tyler signed the joint resolution of Congress to admit Texas as a slave state; the voters of Texas supported the action, and Texas became a slave state on December 29, 1845. In 1846 Mexican and American troops clashed in Texas, and the United States declared war on the Republic of Mexico. The war ended in 1848, with Mexico relinquishing its claims to Texas, and with the United States having acquired all of the region extending to the Pacific Ocean.

In 1846 David Wilmot, a Democrat from Pennsylvania, introduced an amendment to a bill appropriating $2 million for President James Polk to use in negotiating a territorial settlement with Mexico; the amendment stipulated that none of the newly acquired land would be open to slavery. Although the amendment received strong support from northern Democrats and was passed by the House of Representatives, the Senate adjourned without voting on it. During the next session of Congress a new bill providing $3 million for territorial settlement was introduced. Wilmot again proposed an amendment prohibiting the expansion of slavery into the newly acquired territory. The bill was passed by the House of Representatives, but the Senate drew up a new bill excluding the Wilmot proviso.

The Wilmot Proviso

Tensions between northern and southern politicians continued to mount over the issue of fugitive slaves. Article IV, Section 2 of the Constitution authorized the return of fugitive slaves and provided procedures for recovery, and in 1793 the Fugitive Slave Act was passed. In northern states that strongly opposed slavery, "personal liberty" laws were passed in order to undermine federal law; liberty laws placed the burden of proof on masters in cases concerning alleged fugitive slaves. Such a law was enacted in Pennsylvania in 1826, requiring state certification before alleged fugitives could be returned. When Edward Prigg, a professional slave catcher, attempted to capture a fugitive slave residing in the state, he was arrested on kidnapping charges for failing to acquire necessary certification. The Supreme Court ruled in *Prigg v. Pennsylvania* (1842) that the state's law could not interfere with federal action regarding fugitives and the right of slaveholders to recover property; it also found that states would not be obligated to enforce federal fugitive slave statutes. This led abolitionists to seize upon the idea of not enforcing federal statutes. Following the court's decision several northern states enacted even more radical personal liberty laws prohibiting the enforcement of the Fugitive Slave Act.

Fugitive Slave Laws

> ## CAUTION!!
> ## COLORED PEOPLE
> ### OF BOSTON, ONE & ALL,
> You are hereby respectfully CAUTIONED and advised, to avoid conversing with the
> ## Watchmen and Police Officers of Boston,
> For since the recent ORDER OF THE MAYOR & ALDERMEN, they are empowered to act as
> # KIDNAPPERS
> ### AND
> # Slave Catchers,
> And they have already been actually employed in KIDNAPPING, CATCHING, AND KEEPING SLAVES. Therefore, if you value your LIBERTY, and the *Welfare of the Fugitives* among you, *Shun* them in every possible manner, as so many *HOUNDS* on the track of the most unfortunate of your race.
> ## Keep a Sharp Look Out for KIDNAPPERS, and have TOP EYE open.
> *APRIL 24, 1851.*

Poster warning blacks of the ever-present danger of slave catchers.

ANTI-SLAVERY MOVEMENTS ✦ ✦ ✦ ✦ ✦ ✦ ✦ ✦ ✦ ✦ ✦ ✦ ✦ ✦ ✦ ✦ ✦

Quakers and Mennonites

The early opposition to slavery was generally based on religious beliefs; Christian ethics were seen as incompatible with slavery. Quakers (or the Society of Friends) and Mennonites were two of first groups to oppose the practice in the United States. Quakers and Mennonites settled mainly in Pennsylvania, though also in the South, and advocated simple living, modest dress, and nonviolence. In 1652 the Quakers passed a resolution against lifetime indenture, and in 1688 the Mennonites did the same. With the continued rise of slavery in the South, many Quakers protested and moved north into Indiana and Ohio.

In 1787 the Free African Society was organized in Philadelphia by two African Americans, the Reverends Richard Allen and Absalom Jones; Adams later founded the Bethel African Methodist Church, and Jones became the rector of a Protestant Episcopal Church. The society was an important model for political consciousness and economic organization for African Americans throughout the country. It provided economic and medical aid, advocated abolition, and maintained channels of communication with African Americans in the South. Like the many other African-American organizations that followed, the society was rooted in religious principles. Throughout the nineteenth century a number of mutual aid societies also sprung up in African-American communities of the eastern seaboard, providing loans, insurance, and various other economic and social services to their members and the larger community.

The Free African Society

In 1816 the American Colonization Society was organized in Washington, DC, with the objective of encouraging the repatriation of African Americans to Africa. While the idea of returning free African Americans was motivated in part by humanitarian intent, the society was rather moderate in its opposition to slavery. Support for the society came in part from those who feared the possibility of a large free African-American population in the United States.

The American Colonization Society

Congress issued a charter to the society for the transportation of freed slaves to the west coast of Africa, provided funds, and assisted in negotiations with African chiefs who ceded the land that comprised what became Liberia. While northerners contributed support and donations to the society, southern patrols threatened freedmen into emigrating. In 1822 the first settlers landed at the site on the western coast of Africa that was later named Monrovia after President James Monroe. In 1838 the Commonwealth of Liberia was formed and placed under the administration of a governor appointed by the society.

The earliest abolition societies were the Pennsylvania Society for Promoting the Abolition of Slavery, formed in Philadelphia in 1775, and the New York Manumission Society, formed in the city in 1785. Prior to the 1830s a num-

The Abolition Movement

A page from the American
Anti-Slavery Almanac, *1840*.

ber of anti-slavery societies arose in both the North and the South, and during the 1830s and 1840s numerous abolitionist organizations arose alongside the women's rights organizations as part of the general social reform
movement. The American Anti-Slavery Society was formed in Philadelphia
in 1833, and after attending one of its meetings, the Quaker abolitionist Lucretia Coffin Mott formed the Philadelphia Female Anti-Slavery Society with
the assistance of Elizabeth Cady Stanton. Mott and her husband, James, were
active in the underground railroad and various other anti-slavery activities,
and James served as a delegate to the World Anti-Slavery Convention.

A photograph of the
Pennsylvania Abolition Society.

The primary tool of the anti-slavery movement was the press. In 1827 the journalists Samuel Cornish and John Russwurmlaunched *Freedom's Journal*, the first African-American owned and edited newspaper; in 1831 William Lloyd Garrison published the first issue of the *Liberator*; and other anti-slavery papers followed, including *Anti-Slavery Record*, the *Emancipator*, *Human Rights*, and the *North Star*, launched by Frederick Douglass.

The first black newspaper in the South—The Colored American—was published in Augusta, Georgia, in 1865, and edited by J. T. Shutten.

While many of the anti-slavery organizations were dominated by whites, African-American leaders played an important role in the abolition movement. Some of the most notable leaders were Alexander Crummell, Frederick Douglass, Sarah Mapp Douglass, Charlotte Forten, Henry Highland Garnet, Sojourner Truth, and David Walker. Most of these leaders were committed to cooperative relations with whites and opposed separatist doctrines, while some of the more militant abolitionists (like Garnet and Walker) stressed the conditional necessity of violence in the struggle against slavery.

In the South the activities of the abolition movement only hardened the resolve of the slaveholding class to maintain the system of slavery. Depending on the circumstances, southern justification of slavery continued along several lines: it was an economic necessity, a means of converting African pagans to Christianity, and a means of controlling a supposedly inferior race.

The Underground Railroad

A vast network of individuals and groups developed throughout the country to help African Americans escape from slavery. Abolitionists provided "stations," food, shelter, and financial assistance, while experienced "conductors," who were often themselves runaway slaves, led thousands of "passengers" to freedom in the North, Canada, and the Caribbean. Most of the movement occurred at night, with passengers hiding in the barns and homes of sympathetic whites and African Americans during the day. Two of the most famous conductors were Josiah Henson and Harriet Tubman.

Nat Turner

In February 1831 Nat Turner, a slave in Southampton County, Virginia, began to plan a slave revolt, and on August 22 Turner and his co-conspirators killed Turner's master and family. Within twenty-four hours about sixty whites in the county had been killed. Turner was captured on October 30 and hanged on November 11. The incident contributed to the increasing paranoia of southern society.

The Free Labor and Free Soil Movements

Radical Democrats and members of the Whig party who opposed slavery united to form a new political party in Buffalo, New York, in 1848. The party adopted a platform supporting free labor and free soil in response to feelings among northerners that slavery restricted the freedom of northern workers to contract for work and should therefore be excluded from the developing regions of the West. Southerners wanted the freedom to expand westward and take their slaves with them. Senator John C. Calhoun of South Carolina and other southern delegates maintained that both Congress and the territorial legislatures lacked the authority to restrict the

Former slaves believed to have used the Underground Railroad to escape the South.

expansion of slavery into the territories. The control of northern states over the national government led these men to consider secession from the Union.

♦ ♦ ♦ ♦ ♦ ♦ ♦ ♦ ♦ ♦ ♦ ♦ ♦ ♦ ♦ ♦ ♦ ♦ ♦ **THE COMPROMISE OF 1850**

As the debate over the admission of new western states continued, southerners argued that the South should be given guarantees of equal positioning in the territories. In 1850 Senator Henry Clay proposed a compromise in which California would be admitted as a free state, the new territories of New Mexico and Utah would be organized, slavery would be abolished in the District of Columbia, more forceful fugitive slave legislation would be enacted, and the Texas war debt would be resolved. At the time the compromise was hailed by many as the solution to the debate over slavery.

Dred Scott v.
Sandford

The slavery debate presented supporters and opponents of the institution with two very important questions: how should fugitives from slavery be treated in jurisdictions where slavery was illegal, and should a slave brought into a free state by his master be viewed as free? The first question was partially addressed by Article IV, Section 2 of the Constitution and by the Fugitive Slave Acts of 1793 and 1850, but the second question had not yet been addressed. During the 1830s and 1840s a slave by the name of Dred Scott accompanied his master, a surgeon in the U.S. Army, on numerous trips to military posts around the country, including the free states of Illinois and the territory of Wisconsin. In 1846 Scott sued his master for his freedom, asserting that his sojourns in free jurisdictions made him free. After numerous delays, trials, and retrials, the case reached the Supreme Court in 1856. The court responded with nine separate opinions, and Chief Justice Roger Brook Taney delivered the deciding opinion. The ruling was both complex and controversial: the Missouri Compromise of 1820 was ruled unconstitutional on the grounds that Congress did not have authority to limit the expansion of slavery; slavery was found to be legal in the territories until the citizens voted for or against it; and Africans and their descendants were found to be ineligible for citizenship in the United States as the framers of the Constitution had not viewed Africans as citizens. Since African Americans were not viewed by the court as citizens, they could not file suit. Despite the finality of the court's decision, the issue of slavery remained unresolved.

John Brown and Harpers Ferry

On October 16, 1859, a white, visionary abolitionist named John Brown led a band of twenty-one men (five of whom were African Americans) in the seizure of the federal arsenal at Harpers Ferry. After holding the site for several hours, Brown and his followers were captured by federal troops under the command of Robert E. Lee. Southerners were outraged by Brown's actions, interpreting them as symptomatic of a willingness among northerners to attempt the forcible overthrow of slavery. In December 1859 Brown was hanged alongside Dangerfield Newby, a runaway slave; John A. Copeland of Carolina; Sheridan Leary, a harness maker and freedman; and Shields Gree, a sailor from South Carolina.

CIVIL WAR ✦

In 1860 Abraham Lincoln, a northern Republican, was elected president amid continuing polarization over the issue of slavery. Lincoln had voiced opposition to the expansion of slavery in the past, and with his election southerners became even more fearful of an ideological assault on states' rights and the abolition of slavery nationwide. In 1860 a delegation from South Carolina voted unanimously for the repeal of the state's 1788 ratification of the Constitution and the severing of all relations with the Union; Georgia, Florida, Alabama, Mississippi, Louisiana, and Texas soon followed. In February 1861 the seven states drew up a constitution and elected Jefferson Davis as president of the Confederate States of America. As northern leaders sought a means of preserving the nation, southern troops seized federal installations, post offices, and customs houses, and in April 1861 Confederate forces took one of the last Union holds in the South, Fort Sumter in Charleston Harbor, South Carolina. Lincoln was forced to retaliate.

African-American Soldiers in the Civil War

From the beginning of the war African Americans engaged in the fighting, although Lincoln at first refused to officially employ them in the Union army. By 1862 Lincoln concluded that the use of African-American soldiers was a necessity. An estimated 180,000 black soldiers served in the Union army and another 20,000 served in its navy. But not all of those

Abraham Lincoln

African Americans who participated in the war fought on the Union side; although there are no accurate records of how many fought for the South, the numbers grew as white southerners became more desperate.

Lincoln faced a dilemma in that if he issued an order of universal emancipation, as the abolitionists encouraged him to do, he risked alienating the border states that remained supportive of the Union: these were Delaware, Maryland, Kentucky, and Missouri. In a letter to Horace Greely, Lincoln stated:

If I could save the Union without freeing any slave, I would do it; if I could save it by freeing all the slaves, I would do it; and if I could save it by freeing some and leaving others alone, I would also do that. What I do about slavery and the colored race, I do because I believe it helps save the Union ....

During the summer of 1862 Lincoln began to feel that the emancipation of the slaves would be necessary to realizing victory over the South, and on January 1, 1863, he issued the Emancipation Proclamation, freeing slaves in those states that had seceded from the Union. Because the proclamation did not apply to the areas under occupation by Union forces, 800,000 slaves remained unaffected by its provisions. He dared not alienate the slave-owning states on the Union side, especially in light of the growing antipathy toward African Americans in many northern cities. In the Draft Riots of July 13–16, 1863, huge mobs of whites in New York City (angry over the provisions of the Conscription Act) attacked blacks and abolitionists, destroying property and viciously beating many to death.

The Civil War lasted from April 1861 to April 1865, and at the end more than 360,000 Union soldiers and 258,000 Confederate solders were dead. By the end of the war twenty-one African Americans had received the Medal of Honor, and indeterminate numbers of others had made sacrifices for the cause. On December 18, 1865, the Thirteenth Amendment of the Constitution was ratified, formally abolishing slavery in the United States.

Engraving depicting freed blacks in North Carolina.

◆ **RECONSTRUCTION**

On March 3, 1865, Congress enacted the first of several acts that set up and empowered the Bureau of Refugees, Freedmen and Abandoned Lands (or the Freedmen's Bureau). The organization provided former slaves with basic health and educational services, and administered land which had been abandoned during the war. In 1866 Congress passed the Civil Rights Act, in which a number of personal liberties were outlined, including the right to make contracts, sue or be sued, own and sell property, and receive the equal benefit of the law. The Reconstruction Act of March 2, 1867, outlined the terms under which the southern states might re-enter the Union; one of these terms required the drafting of a new state constitution with the guarantee of voting rights for all races. President Andrew Johnson vetoed this bill, but radical Republicans in Congress were able to muster the necessary two-thirds majority needed to override the veto.

Civil Rights and Reconstruction Acts

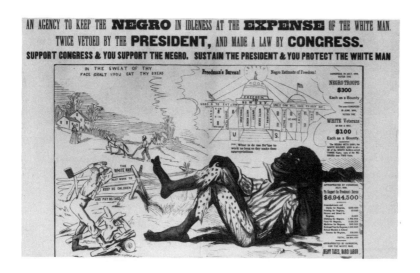

Poster mocking the Freedmen's Bureau.

◆ ◆ ◆ **AFRICAN-AMERICAN STATUS AFTER RECONSTRUCTION**

On July 23, 1868, the Fourteenth Amendment was ratified, providing definitions of national and state citizenship, effectively overriding the Supreme Court's decision in *Dred Scott v. Sandford*, and providing for equal privileges of citizenship and protection of the law. On March 30, 1870, the Fifteenth Amendment was ratified to ensure the right to vote.

The Fourteenth and Fifteenth Amendments

But the amendment proved unsuccessful in its aims, since many state and local governments created voting regulations that ensured African Americans would not vote: these included grandfather clauses, requiring that one's grandfather had voted; literacy tests; poll taxes; and "white primaries," which were held prior to general elections and permitted only whites to vote. In addition, southern states enacted many laws (known as black codes) that curbed the new rights of the freed slaves: South Carolina made it illegal for African Americans to possess firearms, and other states restricted their right to make and enforce contracts; to marry and intermarry; and even to assemble, "wander," or be "idle."

The Civil Rights Act of 1875

In 1875 Congress attempted to establish a semblance of racial equality by enacting a law that made it illegal to deprive another person of the "full and equal enjoyment of the accommodations, advantages, facilities, and privileges of inns, public conveyance, ... and other places of public amusement" on account of race. In a number of cases (known as the Civil Rights Cases) the Supreme Court ruled that the Fourteenth Amendment did not authorize Congress to legislate against discriminatory state action, while disregarding discrimination by private individuals, including the owners of hotels, theaters, and restaurants. This point led to an end of federal efforts to protect the civil rights of African Americans until the mid-twentieth century.

Plessy v. Ferguson

In *Hall v. DeCuir* (1878) the Supreme Court decided that states could not outlaw segregation on common carriers such as streetcars and railroads, and in 1896 the Court again faced the issue of segregation on public transportation in the case of *Plessy v. Ferguson*. The case concerned Homer Adolph Plessy, an African American who was arrested for refusing to ride in the "colored" railway coach while traveling by train from New Orleans to Covington, Louisiana. The law in Louisiana required that "equal but separate" accommodations for blacks and whites be maintained in public facilities, but Plessy challenged this. Justice Billings Brown delivered the majority opinion that separate but equal accommodations constituted a reasonable use of state police power and that the Fourteenth Amendment could not have been an effort to abolish social or racial distinctions or to force a co-mingling of the races. In his dissenting opinion, Justice John Marshall Harlen remarked:

> The judgement this day rendered will, in time, prove to be quite as pernicious as the decision made by this tribunal in the *Dred*

Scott case. The thin disguise of equal accommodation for passengers in railroad coaches will not mislead anyone nor atone for the wrong this day done.

The ruling paved the way for the doctrine of separate but equal in all walks of life, and not until the case of *Brown v. Board of Education of Topeka* (1954) would the constitutionality of segregation be seriously challenged.

◆ FIGURES OF THE PAST

Crispus Attucks (c. 1723–1770)

Revolutionary Patriot

A runaway slave who lived in Boston, he was the first of five men killed on March 5, 1770, when British troops fired on a crowd of colonial protesters in the Boston Massacre. The most widely accepted account of the incident is that of John Adams, who said at the subsequent trial of the British soldiers that Attucks undertook "to be the hero of the night; and to lead this army with banners, to form them in the first place in Dock Square, and march them up to King Street with their clubs." When the crowd reached the soldiers it was Attucks who "had hardiness enough to fall in upon them, and with one hand took hold of a bayonet, and with the other knocked the man down." At that point the panicked soldiers fired, and in the echoes of their volley, five men lay dying; the seeds of the Revolution were sown. Attucks is remembered as "the first to defy, the first to die."

Joseph Cinque (1811–1852)

Leader of the *Amistad* Mutiny

Purchased by Spaniards in Havana, Cuba, in 1839, he was placed aboard the *Amistad* bound for Puerto Principe. When the crew became exhausted from battling a storm, Cinque led the slaves in seizing the ship and killing all but two of the crew, who were kept alive to navigate a course back to Africa. The captive pilots headed north, against the slaves' knowledge, and when the ship was sighted off the coast of Long Island the slaves were taken to Connecticut and placed in prison. Abolitionists took up the cause of the men and enabled Cinque to raise funds for judicial appeals by speaking on their lecture circuit; his words were translated from Mendi, and he became known as an excellent speaker. In 1841 John Quincy Adams won the slaves' case, and they were released.

Frederick Douglass
(c. 1817–1875)

Abolitionist

Born in Talbot County, Maryland, he was sent to Baltimore as a house servant at the age of eight, where his mistress taught him to read and write. Upon the death of his master he was sent to the country to work as a field hand. During his time in the South he was severely flogged for his resistance to slavery. In his early teens he began to teach in a Sunday school that was later forcibly shut down by hostile whites. After an unsuccessful attempt to escape from slavery, he succeeded in making his way to New York disguised as a sailor in 1838. He found work as a day laborer in New Bedford, Massachusetts, and after an extemporaneous speech before the Massachusetts Anti-Slavery Society became one of its agents.

Douglass quickly became a nationally recognized figure among abolitionists. In 1845 he bravely published his *Narrative of the Life of Frederick Douglass*, which related his experiences as a slave, revealed his fugitive status, and further exposed him to the danger of reenslavement. In the same year he went to England and Ireland, where he remained until 1847, speaking on slavery and women's rights, and ultimately raising sufficient funds to purchase his freedom. Upon returning to the United States he founded the *North Star* journal. In the tense years before the Civil War he was forced to flee to Canada when the governor of Virginia swore out a warrant for his arrest.

Douglass returned to the United States before the beginning of the Civil War, and after meeting with President Abraham Lincoln he assisted in the formation of the 54th and 55th Negro regiments of Massachusetts. During Reconstruction he became deeply involved in the civil-rights movement, and in 1871 he was appointed to the territorial legislature of the District of Columbia. He served as one of the presidential electors-at-large for New York in 1872 and shortly thereafter became the secretary of the Santo Domingo Commission. After serving for a short time as the police commissioner of the District of Columbia, he was appointed marshall in 1871 and held the post until he was appointed the recorder of deeds in 1881. In 1890 his support of the presidential campaign of Benjamin Harrison won him his most important federal posts: he became minister resident and consul general to the Republic of Haiti and, later, the chargé d'affaires of Santo Domingo. In 1891 he resigned the position in protest of the unscrupulous business practices of American businessmen. Douglass died at home in Washington, DC.

The son of a black father and white mother, Haynes was deserted and brought up by Deacon David Rose of Granville, Massachusetts. He was a precocious child and began writing mature sermons while still a boy. His preparation for the ministry was interrupted by the American Revolution. On April 19, 1775, he fought in the first battle of the war at Lexington, Massachusetts; he then joined the regular forces and served with Ethan Allen's Green Mountain Boys at the capture of Fort Ticonderoga.

Lemuel Haynes (1753–1833)

Revolutionary Soldier, Minister

Born a slave in Charles County, Maryland, Henson grew up with the experience of his family being cruelly treated by his master. By the time he was eighteen he was supervising the master's farm. In 1825 he and his wife and children were moved to Kentucky, where conditions were greatly improved, and in 1828 he became a preacher in a Methodist Episcopal Church. Under the threat of being sold, he and his family escaped to Ohio in 1830, and in the following year entered Canada by way of Buffalo, New York. In Canada he learned to read and write from one of his sons, and he soon began preaching in Dresden, Ontario.

Josiah Henson (1789–1883)

Abolitionist

While in Canada he became active in the underground railroad, helping nearly two hundred slaves to escape to freedom. In 1842 he and several others attempted to start the British-American Manual Labor Institute, but the industrial school proved unsuccessful. Henson related his story to Harriet Beecher Stowe (the author of *Uncle Tom's Cabin*), and it has been disputed whether or not her story is based in part on aspects of his life. He traveled to England three times, where he met distinguished people, was honored for his abolitionist activities and personal escape from slavery, and was offered a number of positions which he turned down in order to return to Canada. He published his autobiography in 1849 and rewrote and reissued it in 1858 and 1879. Henson died in Ontario.

Born a slave, he risked his life behind enemy lines collecting information for the Continental Army. He furnished valuable information to the Marquis de Lafayette and enabled the French commander to check the troop advances of British General Cornwallis; this set the stage for General George Washington's victory at Yorktown in 1781 and for the end of the Revolutionary War. In recognition of his services, he was granted his freedom by the Virginia legislature in 1786, although it was not until 1819 that Virginia awarded him a pension of $40 a year and a grant of $100. He adopted the surname "Lafayette" in honor of his former commander, who visited him during a trip to the United States in 1824.

James Armistead Lafayette

Revolutionary Spy

**Toussaint
L'Ouverture
(1743–1803)**

Haitian Revolutionary

Born Francois Dominique Toussaint L'Ouverture, a slave on the island of Hispaniola (now Haiti and the Dominican Republic), he learned to read and write under a benevolent master. When he was fifty a violent revolt erupted on the island. White French planters, African slaves, and free mulattoes (some of whom owned slaves) clashed over issues of rights, land, and labor, as the forces of France, Britain, and Spain manipulated the conflict. At first the slaves and mulattoes shared the goals of the French revolution in opposition to the Royalist French planters, but with time a coalition of planters and mulattoes arose in opposition to the slaves.

Toussaint became the leader of the revolutionary slave forces, which by 1794 consisted of a disciplined group of four thousand mostly ex-slaves. He successfully waged various campaigns first against the French and then against the British, and was at the height of his power and influence when in 1796 General Rigaud (who led the mulatto forces) sought to re-impose slavery on the black islanders. He quickly achieved victory, captured Santo Domingo, and by 1801 had virtual control of the Spanish part of the island. In 1802 a French expeditionary force was sent to re-establish French control of the island. Toussaint was tricked, captured, and sent to France where he died on April 7, 1803, under inhumane conditions.

**Gabriel Prosser
(c. 1775–1800)**

Leader of Slave
Insurrection

The coachman of Thomas Prosser of Henrico County, Virginia, Gabriel Prosser planned a large, highly organized revolt to take place on the last night of August 1800 around Richmond, Virginia. There were about 32,000 slaves and only eight thousand whites in the area, and it was his intention to kill all of the whites except for the French, Quakers, elderly women, and children. The ultimate goal was that the remaining 300,000 slaves in the state would follow his lead and seize the entire state. The revolt was set to coincide with the harvest so that his followers would be spared any shortage of food, and it was decided that the conspirators would meet at the Old Brook Swamp outside of Richmond and marshal forces to attack the city.

The insurrection fell apart when a severe rainstorm made it impossible for many of the slaves to assemble and a pair of house slaves who did not wish their master killed revealed the plot. Panic swept through the city, martial law was declared, and those suspected of involvement were rounded up and hanged; when it became clear that the slave population would be decimated if all of those implicated were dealt with in like fashion, the courts began to mete out less severe sentences. Prosser was apprehended in the hold of a schooner that docked in Norfolk, Virginia, and was brought back in chains, interrogated by the governor (though he refused to divulge details of the conspiracy), and hanged.

Born in Southhampton, Virginia, his first name was simply "Sam." He worked as a farmhand, handyman, and stevedore, and moved with his master to Huntsville, Alabama, and later to St. Louis, Missouri. In 1831 his owner, Peter Blow, died, and he was bought by John Emerson, a surgeon in the U.S. Army. Sam accompanied his new master to Illinois (a free state) and Wisconsin (a territory). Sometime after 1836 he received permission to marry, and by 1848 he had changed his name to Dred Scott. At various times he attempted to buy his freedom or escape but was unsuccessful. In 1843 Emerson died and left his estate to his widow Irene Emerson, who also refused Scott his freedom. He then obtained the assistance of two attorneys who helped him to sue for his freedom in county court.

Scott lost this case, but the verdict was set aside, and in 1847 he won a second trial on the grounds that his slave status had been nullified upon entering into a free state. Scott received financial backing and legal representation through the sons of Peter Blow, Irene Emerson's brother John Sanford, and her second husband Dr. C.C. Chaffee, all of whom apparently saw the case as an important challenge to slavery. In 1857 the United States Supreme Court ruled against Scott, stating that slaves were not legally citizens of the United States and therefore had no standing in the courts. Shortly after the decision was handed down Mrs. Emerson freed Scott. The case led to the nullification of the Missouri Compromise of 1820, allowing the expansion of slavery into formerly free territories, and strengthening the abolition movement.

Born Isabella Baumfree in Ulster County, New York, she was freed by the New York State Emancipation Act of 1827 and lived in New York City for a time. After taking the name Sojourner Truth, which she felt God had given her, she assumed the "mission" of spreading "the Truth" across the country. She became famous as an itinerant preacher, drawing huge crowds with her oratory (and some said "mystical gifts") wherever she appeared. She became one of an active group of black women abolitionists, lectured before numerous abolitionist audiences, and was friends with such leading white abolitionists as James and Lucretia Mott and Harriet Beecher Stowe. With the outbreak of the Civil War she raised money to purchase gifts for the soldiers, distributing them herself in the camps. She also helped African Amer-

Dred Scott
(1795–1858)

Litigator

Sojourner Truth
(c. 1797–1883)

Abolitionist, Women's Rights Advocate

icans who had escaped to the North to find habitation and shelter. Age and ill health caused her to retire from the lecture circuit, and she spent her last days in a sanatorium in Battle Creek, Michigan.

Harriet Ross Tubman (1820–1913)

Underground Railroad Conductor and Rights Activist

Born about 1820 in Dorchester County, Maryland, Harriet Tubman lived the hard childhood of a slave: much work, little schooling, and severe punishment. In 1848 she escaped, leaving behind her husband John Tubman, who threatened to report her to their master. As a free woman, she began to devise practical ways of helping other slaves escape. Over the following ten years she made about twenty trips from the North into the South and rescued more than three hundred slaves. Her reputation spread rapidly, and she won the admiration of leading abolitionists (some of whom sheltered her passengers). Eventually a reward of $40,000 was posted for her capture.

Tubman met and aided John Brown in recruiting soldiers for his raid on Harpers Ferry—Brown referred to her as "General Tubman." One of her major disappointments was the failure of the raid, and she is said to have regarded Brown as the true emancipator of her people, not President Abraham Lincoln. In 1860 she began to canvass the nation, appearing at anti-slavery meetings and speaking on women's rights. Shortly before the outbreak of the Civil War she was forced to leave for Canada, but she returned to the United States and served the Union as a nurse, soldier, and spy; she was particularly valuable to the army as a scout because of the knowledge of the terrain she had gained as a conductor on the underground railroad.

Tubman's biography (from which she received the proceeds) was written by Sarah Bradford in 1868. Tubman's husband, John, died two years after the end of the war, and in 1869 she married the war veteran Nelson Davis. Despite receiving many honors and tributes (including a medal from Queen Victoria), she spent her last days in poverty, not receiving a pension until thirty years after the Civil War. With the $20 dollars a month that she finally received, she helped to found a home for the aged and needy, which was later renamed the Harriet Tubman Home. She died in Auburn, New York.

A slave in Southampton County, Virginia, Turner was an avid reader of the Bible who prayed, fasted, and experienced "voices," ultimately becoming a visionary mystic with a belief that God had given him the special destiny of conquering Southampton County. After recruiting a handful of conspirators, he struck at isolated homes in his immediate area, and within forty-eight hours the band of insurrectionists had reached sixty armed men. They killed fifty-five whites before deciding to attack the county seat in Jerusalem, but while en route they were overtaken by a posse and dispersed. Turner took refuge in the Dismal Swamp and remained there for six weeks before he was captured, brought to trial, and hanged along with sixteen other African Americans.

Nat Turner
(1800–1831)

Leader of Slave Insurrection

Sold by his master at an early age and later bought back because of epilepsy, he sailed with his master, Captain Vesey, to the Virgin Islands and Haiti for twenty years. He enjoyed a considerable degree of mobility in his home port of Charleston, South Carolina, and eventually purchased his freedom from his master for $600; he had won $1,500 in a lottery. He became a Methodist minister and used his church as a base to recruit supporters to take over Charleston. The revolt was planned for the second Sunday in July 1822.

Denmark Vesey
(1767–1822)

Leader of Slave Insurrection

Vesey's plans were betrayed when a slave alerted the white authorities of the city. Hundreds of African Americans were rounded up, though some of Vesey's collaborators most likely escaped to the Carolinas where they fought as maroons. After a twenty-two–day search, Vesey was apprehended and stood trial. During the trial he adeptly cross examined witnesses, but ultimately could not deny his intention to overthrow the city, and he was hanged along with several collaborators.

Born in Amabon, Africa, it has been claimed that he was sent to the United States to obtain an education and sold into slavery upon arriving in Baltimore. He succeeded in joining the Continental Army as a bodyguard to General Whipple of New Hampshire and served in many of General George Washington's campaigns. After enduring the hardship of the Long Island retreat, he crossed the Delaware with Washington on Christmas night, an event commemorated in the painting by Emanuel Gottlieb Leutze. Whipple is buried at North Cemetery in Portsmouth, New Hampshire.

Prince Whipple

Revolutionary Soldier

Civil Rights

Throughout the history of the United States, African Americans have strug-gled to obtain basic civil rights. It is a stuggle that has spanned several cen-turies—from the mutinies by Africans during the Atlantic crossing, to the insurrections organized by slaves in the New World, to the founding of such organizations as the Free African Society, to the abolition movement, and to the civil-rights marches and demonstrations of the twentieth century.

EARLY RIGHTS MOVEMENTS ♦ ♦ ♦ ♦ ♦ ♦ ♦ ♦ ♦ ♦ ♦ ♦ ♦ ♦ ♦ ♦ ♦ ♦

The Free African Society

As a result of segregation and discriminatory practices within the Methodist church, the Free African Society was organized in 1787 in Philadelphia by the Reverends Richard Allen and Absalom Jones. As the Philadelphia organization grew, other Free African societies formed in such places as Boston, New York, and Newport. Like many black movements to follow, the Free African Society provided spiritual guidance and religious instruction, while providing economic aid, burial assistance, and relief to widows and orphans. The society also helped to faciliate communications between free blacks throughout the country.

The Abolition Movement

The press and the pulpit served as important tools in the anti-slavery movement. In 1827 in New York, Samuel Cornish and John Russwurm founded *Freedom's Journal*, the first black owned and operated newspaper in the United States. *Freedom's Journal*, which ceased publication after

Frederick Douglass

only three years, was concerned not only with eradicating slavery but also with the growing discrimination and cruelty against free blacks in both the South and North.

In 1847 abolitionist Frederick Douglass published the first edition of *The North Star*, which eventually became one of most successful black newspapers in America prior to the outbreak of the Civil War. Douglass, an escaped slave from Maryland, became one of the best known black abolitionists in the country. He lectured extensively throughout the United States and England. In 1845 he published his autobiography, *Narrative of Frederick Douglass.*

Although the abolition movement was dominated by whites, numerous black leaders played a major role in the movement, including such figures as Henry Highland Garnet, Harriet Tubman, and Sojourner Truth.

CIVIL RIGHTS AT THE END OF THE
♦ **CIVIL WAR**

Following the war, Republicans, who controlled the United States Congress, took up the cause of the newly freed African Americans. Between 1865 and 1875, three amendments to the Constitution and a string of civil-rights and Reconstruction legislation was passed by Congress. The Thirteenth Amendment, ratified December 18, 1865, abolished slavery and involuntary servitude. The Fourteenth Amendment, ratified July 28, 1868, guaranteed citizenship and provided equal protection under the laws. Ratified March 30, 1870, the Fifteenth Amendment was designed to protect the right of all citizens to vote. In 1866, 1870, 1871, and 1875 Congress passed civil-rights legislation outlining and protecting basic rights, including the right to purchase and sell property and access to public accommodations. The Reconstruction acts, passed between 1867 and 1869, called for new state constitutional conventions in those states that had seceded from the Union prior to the Civil War.

Reconstruction eventually produced a wave of anti-African sentiment. White organizations, like the Ku Klux Klan, which were aimed at intimi-

In 1845, Macon B. Allen became the first African-American lawyer formally admitted to the bar after he passed the state bar examination in Worcester, Massachusetts. Twenty years later, John Rock became the first African-American lawyer admitted to practice before the United States Supreme Court.

dating blacks and preventing them from taking their place in society, sprang up throughout the North and the South. In 1871 Congress enacted the Ku Klux Klan Act as an effort to end intimidation and violence directed at blacks. The act failed, however, to exterminate the Klan and other terrorist organizations.

The civil-rights and Reconstruction legislation were difficult for many whites to accept and did little to change their attitudes. The last of the civil-rights acts, passed by Congress in 1875, prohibited discrimination in public accommodations. However, by the 1880s the debate as to the constitutionality of such legislation had reached the United States Supreme Court. Ruling in a group of five cases in 1883, which became known as the Civil Rights Cases, the United States Supreme Court concluded that the 1875 Civil Rights Act was unconstitutional on the grounds that the Fourteenth Amendment authorized Congress to legislate only against discriminatory state action, and not discrimination by private individuals. The Court's ruling brought about an end to federal efforts to protect the civil rights of African Americans until the mid-twentieth century.

Anti-lynching Efforts

By the late nineteenth and early twentieth century, lynching had become a weapon used by whites against blacks throughout the country. Between 1882 and 1990, approximately 1,750 African Americans were lynched in the United States. Victims, who included women, had been accused of a variety of "offenses" ranging from testifying in court against a white man to failing to use the word "mister" when addressing a white person. Ida B. Wells Barnett, a journalist and social activist, became one of the leading voices in the anti-lynching crusade by writing and lecturing throughout the United States against the practice of lynching.

Institutionalized Segregation

In 1896 the United States Supreme Court was faced with the issue of segregation on public transportation. At the time, as was the case in many parts of the South, a Louisiana state law was enacted requiring that "separate but equal" accommodations for blacks and whites be maintained in all public facilities. When Homer Adolph Plessy, a black man traveling by train from New Orleans to Covington, Louisiana, refused to ride in the "colored" railway coach, he was arrested.

Prior to the case of *Plessy v. Ferguson*, the Court had started to build a platform upon which the doctrine of separate but equal would be based. In

Ida B. Wells Barnett wrote and lectured throughout the United States against the practice of lynching.

1878, ruling in the case *Hall v. DeCuir*, the Court declared that states could not outlaw segregation on common carriers, such as streetcars and railroads. Segregation laws sprung up throughout the South.

With Justice Billings Brown delivering the majority opinion in the *Plessy* case, the Court declared that "separate but equal" accommodations constituted a reasonable use of state police power and that the Fourteenth Amendment of the Constitution could not be used to abolish social or racial distinctions or to force a co-mingling of the two races.

America's inability squarely to face the "race" question can trace its origins to the institution of African slavery. That blot on the national history still clouds the country's ability to discuss issues of race with candor.

A Colored drinking fountain in North Carolina.

The Supreme Court had effectively reduced the significance of the Fourteenth Amendment, which was designed to give blacks specific rights and protections. The *Plessy* ruling, which was termed the "separate but equal" doctrine, paved the way for the segregation of African Americans in all walks of life.

CIVIL RIGHTS IN THE TWENTIETH CENTURY ◆ ◆ ◆ ◆ ◆ ◆ ◆ ◆ ◆ ◆

Booker T. Washington and W.E.B. DuBois

During the late nineteenth and early twentieth centuries, two figures—Booker T. Washington and William Edward Burghardt DuBois—emerged as leaders in the struggle for black political and civil rights.

Washington, an educator and founder of the Tuskegee Normal and Industrial Institute, was a strong advocate of practical, utilitarian education and

Booker T. Washington

manual training as a means for developing African Americans. Tuskegee Normal and Industrial Institute, which was founded in 1881 and based on a program at Hampton Institute, provided vocational training and prepared its students to survive economically in a segregated society. In Washington's opinion, education was to provide African Americans with the means to become economically self-supporting. Speaking at the Cotton States International Exposition in Atlanta in 1895, Washington outlined his philosophy of self-help and cooperation between blacks and whites.

> To those of my race who depend on bettering their condition in a foreign land, or who underestimate the importance of cultivating friendly relations with the Southern white man, who is their next door neighbor, I would say: "Cast down your bucket where you are"—cast it down in making friends in every manly way of the people of all races by whom we are surrounded.

W.E.B. DuBois, a young historian and Harvard graduate, challenged Washington's passive policies in a series of stinging essays and speeches.

W.E.B. DuBois

DuBois advocated the uplifting of African Americans through an educated black elite, which he referred to as the "Talented Tenth," or roughly
a tenth of the African-American population. He beleived that these
African Americans must become proficient in education and culture,
which would eventually benefit all.

In 1905 DuBois, along with a group of other black intellectuals, formed
the Niagara Movement. The group drew up a platform which called for
full citizenship rights for blacks and public recognition of their contribu-

tions to America's stability and progress. The movement eventually evolved into what became known as the National Association for the Advancement of Colored People.

Civil Rights in the Mid- to Late-Twentieth Century

The civil-rights movement suffered many defeats in the first half of the twentieth century. Repeated efforts to obtain passage of federal anti-lynching bills failed. The all-white primary system, which effectively disenfranchised southern blacks, resisted numerous court challenges. The Depression worsened conditions on farms and in ghettos. On the positive side, the growing political power of blacks in northern cities and an increasing liberal trend in the Supreme Court portended the legal and legislative victories of the 1950s and 1960s.

Brown v. Board of Education of Topeka

A great deal of the civil-rights struggle throughout this period was carried on by the National Association for the Advancement of Colored People, which had begun chipping away at the roots of legalized segregation in a series of successful lawsuits. A major breakthrough for the NAACP came in 1954 when the United States Supreme Court ruled in *Brown v. Board of Education of Topeka* that discrimination in education was unconstitutional. This decision was as momentous as the Supreme Court's ruling in *Plessy v. Ferguson* in 1896, which legalized the doctrine of "separate but equal" treatment for blacks.

The *Brown* case involved the practice of denying black children equal access to state public schools due to state laws requiring or permitting racial segregation. The United States Supreme Court unanimously held that segregation deprived the children of equal protection under the Fourteenth Amendment to the United States Constitution, overturning the "separate but equal" doctrine established in *Plessy*.

A. Philip Randolph

In 1941 A. Philip Randolph, organizer of an employment bureau for untrained blacks and founder the Brotherhood of Sleeping Car Porters, came up with the idea of leading a protest march of blacks in Washington, DC to protest discrimination. On July 25, less than a week before the scheduled demonstration, President Franklin D. Roosevelt issued Executive Order No. 8802, which banned discrimination in the defense industry and led to the creation of the Fair Employment Practices Committee.

Bayard Rustin (left) and A. Philip Randolph at a news conference, 1963.

Civil Rights in the 1960s

The Civil Rights Act of 1964 prohibited discrimination in the use of public accommodations whose operations involve interstate commerce, and provided enforcement measures to ensure equal access to public facilities.

Rosa Parks was one of the major catalysts of the 1960s civil-rights movement. When on December 1, 1955, Parks refused to give up her seat on a Montgomery bus to a white man, as the law required, she was arrested and sent to jail. As a result of Parks's arrest, blacks throughout Montgomery refused to ride city buses. The Montgomery Bus Boycott led by Martin Luther King, Jr. was highly successful and ultimately led to the integration of all Montgomery city buses.

The eventual success of the Montgomery Bus Boycott encouraged a wave of massive demonstrations that swept across the South. In 1960 a group of students who were denied service at a Greensboro, North Carolina lunch counter started the "sit-in" movement. That same year, the Student Non-Violent Coordinating Committee was created and would include among its members Julian Bond, H. Rap Brown, Stokely Carmichael, and John Lewis.

The civil-rights movement of the 1960s galvinized blacks and sympathetic whites as nothing had ever done before, but was not without cost. Thousands of people were jailed because they defied Jim Crow laws. Others were murdered, and homes and churches were bombed. People lost their jobs and their homes because they supported the movement.

On August 28, 1963, nearly 250,000 blacks and whites marched in Washington, DC to awaken the nation's consciousness regarding civil rights and to encourage the passage of civil-rights legislation pending in

High-pressure hoses are turned on demonstrators in Birmingham, Alabama, 1963.

Congress. The march was a cooperative effort of several civil-rights organizations, including the Southern Christian Leadership Conference, the Congress of Racial Equality, the NAACP, the Negro American Labor Council, and the National Urban League. It was during this demonstration that Dr. Martin Luther King, Jr., in the shadow of the Lincoln Memorial, gave his "I Have a Dream" speech.

At its zenith, the civil-rights movement was the most important event taking place in America. Through demonstrations, sit-ins, marches, and soaring rhetoric, the movement aroused widespread public indignation, thus creating an atmosphere in which it was possible to make positive changes in American society.

Although the civil-rights movement of the 1950s and 1960s produced significant gains for African Americans, progress continues today. This progress is evident in the passage of the most recent civil-rights legislation. In June 1989, the United States Supreme Court delivered opinions

The Voting Rights Act of 1965 struck down requirements such as literacy and knowledge tests and poll-tax payments, and provided for federal registrars to register voters should state registrars refuse to do so.

Civil Rights Legislation in the 1990s

Police officers using police dogs to break up a demonstration in Birmingham, Alabama, 1963.

in several cases dealing with seniority systems and racial discrimination in employment. Ruling in the cases *Lorance v. AT&T Technologies Inc.*, *Martin v. Wilks*, *Patterson v. McLean Credit Union*, and *Wards Cove Packing Co. v. Antonio*, the Court appeared to reverse earlier civil-rights rulings.

Prior to the Court's ruling in *Wards Cove*, the burden of proof in job discrimination suits had been placed on employers, requiring businesses to prove that there was a legitimate business reason for alleged discrimina-

Nearly 250,000 gather in Washington, DC, August 1963.

tory practices. With the *Wards Cove* decision, the Court made it more difficult for groups to win such suits by requiring workers to prove that there was no clear business reason for an employer's use of practices that result in discrimination.

Civil-rights organizations were quick to protest the rulings; opponents of the ruling, including the NAACP Legal Defense and Educational Fund and the Leadership Conference on Civil Rights, argued that the Court had undermined the protection granted by federal civil rights and equal employment legislation.

On October 16 and 17, 1990, both houses of Congress approved a bill designed to reverse the Court's ruling. The proposed legislation not only reversed the Court's ruling in *Wards Cove*, but strengthened provisions of the 1964 Civil Rights Act. On October 22, President George Bush vetoed the bill, claiming that the bill's provisions would encourage employers to establish hiring quotas.

The Civil Rights Act of 1991 was designed to provide guidelines for the adjudication of cases arising under Title VII of the Civil Rights Act of 1964, to expand the scope of civil-rights legislation weakened by Supreme Court decisions, and to establish a means for studying and addressing the underrepresentation of women and minorities at management and decision-making levels in the workforce.

This was not the first time that Congress moved to reverse a Court action in the area of civil rights—in 1987 Congress passed the Civil Rights Restoration Act of 1988, which reversed the Court's ruling in *Grove City College v. Bell* (1984). In the *Grove City College* case, the United States Supreme Court ruled that not all programs and activities of an institution were covered by Title IX of the Education Amendments of 1972 (Public Law 89–10, 79 Stat. 27), which prohibits discrimination in educational programs receiving federal financial assistance.

After vetoing Congress's 1990 civil-rights legislation, the Bush administration joined both houses of Congress in working on alternative bills. On October 30, following months of negotiation, the Senate passed a bill designed to provide additional remedies to deter harassment and intentional discrimination in the workplace, provide guidelines for the adjudication of cases arising under Title VII of the Civil Rights Act of 1964, and expand the scope of civil-rights legislation weakened by Supreme Court decisions. The House of Representatives passed the bill on November 7, and on November 21, President George Bush signed the Civil Rights Act of 1991.

CIVIL RIGHTS ACTIVISTS ✦ ✦ ✦ ✦ ✦ ✦ ✦ ✦ ✦ ✦ ✦ ✦ ✦ ✦ ✦ ✦ ✦ ✦

Ralph D. Abernathy (1926–1990)

Former President, Southern Christian Leadership Conference

Born March 11, 1926, in Linden, Alabama, the Reverend Ralph David Abernathy was ordained a minister in 1948. He received his bachelor's degree from Alabama State College (now Alabama State University) in 1950 and his master's degree from Atlanta University in 1951.

The alliance between Abernathy and Martin Luther King, Jr., stretched back to the mid-1950s. While attending Atlanta University, Abernathy had the opportunity to hear King preach at Ebenezer Baptist Church. After obtaining his master's degree, Abernathy returned to Alabama to serve as a part-time minister at the Eastern Star Baptist Church in Demopolis. In 1951 Abernathy moved to First Baptist Church in Montgomery. Around this time King accepted a position at Montgomery's Dexter Avenue Baptist Church; Abernathy and King became close friends.

In 1955 Abernathy and King organized the Montgomery Improvement Association to coordinate a citywide bus boycott. The success of the boy-

Ralph D. Abernathy

cott led to the creation of the Southern Negro Leaders Conference; the organization's name was later changed to the Southern Leadership Conference and finally the Southern Christian Leadership Conference. In January 1957 King was elected the organization's first president.

From the time of King's death in 1968 until 1977, Abernathy served as president of the Southern Christian Leadership Conference. Abernathy continued as a leading figure in the movement until his resignation in 1977.

In 1977 Abernathy made an unsuccessful bid for a United States Congressional seat. In 1989 he published his autobiography, *And the Walls Came Tumbling Down*, which was criticized by some black leaders for Abernathy's inclusion of details regarding King's extramarital affairs. Abernathy died of cardiac arrest on April 17, 1990.

Clifford Alexander (1933–)

Former Associate Counsel to the President of the United States

Born in New York City, September 21, 1933, Clifford Alexander went to Harvard and earned a bachelor's degree cum laude in 1955, and attended Yale Law School afterward, earning his LL.B. in 1958. After attending these prestigious universities, he went on to become the assistant district attorney of New York County, working there from 1959 to 1961. Positions as the executive director of the Hamilton Grange Neighborhood Conservation district in Manhattanville from 1961 to 1962, and as executive program director of HARYOU from 1962 to 1963, followed. In 1963, he became a member of the National Security Council.

Alexander was hired by President Lyndon Johnson as his deputy special assistant in 1964, and quickly rose to become the president's deputy special counsel in 1967. He became chairman of the Equal Employment Opportunity Commission in 1967, where he was under constant pressure from Republican Senators like Everett Dirksen, who accused him of bullying reluctant employers into complying with federal guidelines for minority employment. He left that position in 1969.

In the years between 1969 and 1976, Alexander worked for several different law offices in private practice. He also became an overseer at Harvard University, where he negotiated with craft unions that were obliged to offer and implement concrete proposals for improving minority employment opportunities.

President Jimmy Carter appointed Alexander the secretary of the Department of the Army, the first African American to serve in that position. Alexander won the Outstanding Civilian Service Award from the Department of the Army in 1980, after he finished his 1977–80 appointment to that position. Since 1981, Alexander has been president of Alexander Associates, Inc., and served as a consultant to Major League Baseball, working to improve minority hiring practices.

In addition, Alexander has had his own television program, "Black on White," has been director of several Dreyfus money funds, served on the board of directors for the Mexican–American Legal Defense and Education Fund, and taught as a professor at Howard University.

Ella Josephine Baker (1903–1986)

Civil Rights Activist

Ella Baker was born in Norfolk, Virginia to Blake and Georgiana Ross Baker, both educated people who worked hard to educate their children. The family and community in which she grew up instilled in her a sense of sharing and community cooperation; neighbors shared food from their gardens and gave a helping hand when needed. Her family instilled in her a sense of racial pride and resistance to any form of oppression. Her grandfather, a minister and community leader, was an ardent proponent of civil rights and universal suffrage, and passed his beliefs on to her.

When she was fifteen, Baker was sent to the Shaw Boarding School in Raleigh. The Shaw school was both a high school and college, and she graduated with a bachelor's degree as valedictorian in 1927. After graduation, she moved to New York City. She quickly became involved in progressive politics and attended as many meetings and discussions as she could find. During the depression, she was outraged at the poverty she saw in the black areas of the city. Believing in the power of community and group action, in 1930 she became involved with the Young Negroes Cooperative League, a buying cooperative that bought food in bulk to distribute at low prices to members; in 1931, she became the national director of the League. When President Franklin Roosevelt's Works Progress Administration started, she became involved with their literacy program. Throughout these years she worked closely with other politically aware and motivated people, discussing and evolving a political philosophy of cooperation, equality, and justice.

In the 1940s, Baker began to work for the NAACP. Between 1940 and 1943, she was a field secretary, traveling all over the country setting up branch offices and teaching people to fight for their own rights; her traveling gave her the opportunity to develop a vast network of contacts in the south that she later relied on when working for the Student Non-Violent Coordinating Committee and Southern Christian Leadership Conference. In 1943, she became the director of branches for the NAACP. During the 1950s, she started fund-raising activities in New York for the civil-rights struggles in the South, and in 1958 moved to Atlanta to work with the SCLC.

Working for the Southern Christian Leadership Conference, Baker became disillusioned with the top-heavy, male-dominated organizational structure of the group. In 1960 she quit the SCLC and took a job with the Young Women's Christian Association instead. When students began leading sit-ins, she shifted her focus to the development of the Student Non-Violent Coordinating Committee. She acted as an unofficial adviser for the group, counseling them to set up their own student-run organization rather than be subsumed under the SCLC or the NAACP. She helped launch the Mississippi Freedom Democratic Party that challenged the all-white Democratic delegation at the 1964 presidential convention. She also acted as staff consultant for the interracial SCLC educational fund.

Baker returned to New York City in 1965 but kept working with national and international civil-rights organizations. Among her other activities, she raised money to send to the freedom fighters in Rhodesia and South Africa. She remained an active organizer and speaker as long as her health allowed.

Baker's belief in the power of communal action and reliance on the workers rather than the leaders had an enormous impact. She worked for all of the major civil-rights organizations at their time of greatest need. By the time the SCLC and the SNCC were formed, she had almost thirty years of civil-rights and community organizing experience to offer. She continually strove to keep the movement people oriented, and she succeeded in helping the SNCC remain a student group. Through her philosophy and actions, she motivated hundreds to act to help themselves and their neighbors as she had learned to do as a child.

Daisy Lee Gatson Bates (1920-)

Civil Rights Activist

After attending segregated schools where all of the new equipment and up-to-date texts were reserved for whites only, Daisy Bates spent much of her energy as an adult successfully integrating the schools of Little Rock, Arkansas.

Shortly after their marriage in 1941, Daisy and her husband Lucius Christopher Bates, a journalist, started to publish a newspaper, the Arkansas *State Press*. They made it a point in their paper to report incidents of police brutality and other racially motivated violence; their newspaper became known throughout the state for its campaign to improve the social and economic circumstances of African Americans. Because of their work, the city of Little Rock began to hire black police officers, and the number of racial incidents lessened.

In 1952, Daisy Bates became the Arkansas president of the NAACP; after the 1954 court decision in the *Brown v. Board of Education* case, she became very active in school desegregation. She began taking black children to white schools to be registered, and if the school refused to register the children, she would report it in her paper. In 1957, the superintendent of schools in Little Rock decided to try to integrate the schools and chose

Daisy Bates leaving Little Rock Police headquarters, 1957.

nine students, now called the Little Rock Nine, to be the first black children to attend Central High, a white school. Most white citizens of Little Rock objected. Bates organized the Little Rock Nine, accompanied them to Central High, and stood with them against the state troopers that Governor Orval Faubus had sent in to prevent the integration. For days she escorted the children to school, only to be turned away by an angry mob. On September 25, 1957, Daisy Bates entered Central High in Little Rock with the nine children, escorted by 1,000 paratroopers that President Dwight Eisenhower had sent in; the first steps toward integration were

Stokely Carmichael, one of the most influential leaders of the SNCC, popularized the phrase "black power."

successful. For the rest of their years at Central High, Bates kept track of the students and acted as their advocate when problems arose, frequently accompanying them and their parents to meetings with school officials.

In October of 1957, one month after she marched into Central High, Daisy Bates was arrested on charges of failing to provide membership information on the NAACP to city officials. The charges were later overturned. Two years later, the Arkansas *State Press* folded, but Bates kept active in the civil-rights fight, touring and speaking, and working with the Student Non-Violent Coordinating Committee to register voters. In 1985, the *State Press* began to publish again, and it has continued to serve the needs of the African-American community in Little Rock.

If there was one individual during the 1960s who stood at the forefront of the Black Power movement, it was Stokely Carmichael. He soared to fame as popularizer of the dynamic phrase "black power" and as one of the most powerful and influential leaders of the Student Non-Violent Coordinating Committee.

Stokely Carmichael (Kwame Toure) (1941–)

Political Activist, Student Non-Violent Coordinating Committee Former President

He was born in Trinidad and moved to the United States with his family when he was eleven. As a teenager, Carmichael was jolted by ghetto life in which "black" and "impotent" seemed to be synonymous terms. He was not reassured later when he was admitted to the Bronx High School of Science, encountered white liberals, and felt he had been adopted by them as a mascot. Although he was offered good scholarships to white universities, Carmichael opted to attend Howard University. During his first year there, 1960, he joined the Congress of Racial Equality in its efforts to integrate public accommodations in the South. After graduation in 1964, he rejected scholarship opportunities for graduate school and went south to join the SNCC. As one of their finest organizers, he worked ceaselessly registering and educating voters in the South. In 1966, he was elected chairman of the SNCC, but as the group's youngest chair he espoused views that were considered too radical by some members.

Carmichael's cry for "black power" thrilled many disenfranchised young African Americans but troubled others, who thought it sounded too violent. He was labeled as potentially violent by the media and the legal authorities. Disagreement with SNCC members arose over the issues of self-defense versus non-violence, and the participation of whites in black grass-roots organizations. In 1967, he resigned as chairman, and was later expelled from the SNCC.

Carmichael spent much of 1968 traveling around the world, speaking to many organizations, including some in communist countries. His travels included Ghana, where he joined the Pan-African movement. After returning to the United States, he went to work for the Black Panther party. In this country, however, he was subject to almost constant harassment from the FBI because of his connection with the Panthers, and because he had visited communist countries while traveling. In 1969, he resigned from the Black Panthers and moved to Guinea, where he had been offered political asylum.

In Guinea, Carmichael turned his efforts to supporting Pan-Africanism; he has organized many local chapters through the world of the All African Peoples Revolutionary Party. In 1978, to honor the two men who most influenced his Pan-African philosophical education, SeKou Toure and Kwame Nkrumah, he changed his name to Kwame Toure. Toure continues to live in Guinea and travel throughout the world, working toward a united African people.

Angela Davis
(1944–)

Political Activist

Angela Davis was born in Alabama to middle-class parents who stressed both academic excellence and political awareness and activism. He mother, Sallye E. Davis, had been politically active since her college days, and Angela participated in demonstrations with her mother from the time she was in elementary school. To insure her a better education than she could receive in the segregated schools of the South, her parents sent her to Elizabeth Irwin High School, a private progressive school in New York. The school had many radical teachers and students, and Angela soon joined a Marxist study group there.

After graduation, Davis continued to seek high-quality education. She majored in French at Brandeis College, studying at the Sorbonne in Paris her junior year. She then pursued graduate studies in philosophy at the Goethe University in Frankfurt, and in 1967 she returned to the United States to study with the well-known philosopher Herbert Marcuse at the University of California at San Diego. When she was almost done with her degree, she took a teaching job at the University of California at Los Angeles.

In 1969 Davis joined the Communist Party; the regents of UCLA tried to fire her, but she fought them in court. The following year she became involved with the Black Panther Party. Guns she had bought for self defense were used by a member of the Black Panthers in a courtroom shooting. Believing she was involved, the FBI sought her arrest, so she went underground to avoid them. She was put on the FBI's most-wanted list, and later arrested. In 1972 she was acquitted of all charges, but was not hired back by the university. California Governor Ronald Reagan and the Regents of the University decreed that she would never teach in California again.

Angela Davis

Since her trial, Davis has served as co-chair of the National Alliance against Racism and Political Repression, a legal group providing defense of minority prisoners. A writer and philosopher, she has written several books, including *If They Come in the Morning* (1971), *Women, Race and Class* (1983), *Angela Davis: An Autobiography* (1988), and *Women, Culture and Politics* (1989). She continues to write and lecture and remains politically active.

William Edward Burghardt DuBois

(1868–1963)

Civil Rights Activist, NAACP Founding Member

An outstanding critic, editor, scholar, author, and civil-rights leader, W.E.B. DuBois is certainly among the most influential blacks of the twentieth century.

Born in Great Barrington, Massachusetts on February 23, 1868, DuBois received a bachelor's degree from Fisk University and went on to win a second bachelor's, as well as a Ph.D., from Harvard. He was for a time professor of Latin and Greek at Wilberforce and the University of Pennsylvania, and also served as a professor of economics and history at Atlanta University.

One of the founders of the National Association for the Advancement of Colored People in 1909, DuBois served as that organization's director of publications and editor of *Crisis* magazine until 1934. In 1944 he returned from Atlanta University to become head of the NAACP's special research department, a post he held until 1948. DuBois emigrated to Africa in 1961 and became editor in chief of the *Encyclopedia Africana,* an enormous publishing venture that had been planned by Kwame Nkrumah, since then deposed as president of Ghana. DuBois died in Ghana in 1963 at the age of ninety-five.

His numerous books include *The Suppression of the Slave Trade* (1896), *The Philadelphia Negro* (1899), *The Souls of Black Folk* (1903), *John Brown* (1909), *Quest of the Silver Fleece* (1911), *The Negro* (1915), *Darkwater* (1920), *The Gift of Black Folk* (1924), *Dark Princess* (1928), *Black Folk: Then and Now* (1939), *Dusk of Dawn* (1940), *Color and Democracy* (1945), *The World and Africa* (1947), *In Battle for Peace* (1952), and a trilogy, *Black Flame* (1957-1961).

It is this enormous literary output on such a wide variety of themes that offers the most convincing testimony to DuBois's lifetime position that it was vital for blacks to cultivate their own aesthetic and cultural values even as they made valuable strides toward social emancipation. In this he was opposed by Booker T. Washington, who felt that black people should concentrate on developing technical and mechanical skills before all else.

DuBois was one of the first male civil-rights leaders to recognize the problems of gender discrimination. He was among the first men to understand the unique problems of black women, and to value their contributions. He supported the women's suffrage movement and strove to integrate this mostly white struggle. He encouraged many black female writers, artists, poets, and novelists, featuring their works in *Crisis* and sometimes providing personal financial assistance to them. Several of his novels feature women as prominently as men, an unusual approach for any author of his day. DuBois spent his life working not just for the equality of all men, but for the equality of all people.

Medgar Evers, field secretary for the NAACP, was one of the first martyrs of the civil-rights movement. On June 13, 1963, he drove home from a meeting, stepped out of his car, and was shot in the back.

Medgar Evers (1925–1963)

Civil Rights Activist

Evers was born in 1925 in Decatur, Mississippi to James and Jessie Evers. After a short stint in the army, he enrolled in Alcorn A&M College, graduating in 1952. His first job out of college was traveling around rural Mississippi selling insurance. He soon grew enraged at the despicable conditions of poor black families in his state, and joined the NAACP. In 1954, he was appointed Mississippi's first field secretary.

Evers was outspoken, and his demands were radical for his rigidly segregated state. He fought for the enforcement of the 1954 court decision of *Brown v. Board of Education of Topeka*, which outlawed school segregation; he fought for the right to vote, and he advocated boycotting merchants who discriminated. He worked unceasingly despite the threats of violence that his speeches engendered. He gave much of himself to this struggle, and in 1963, he gave his life.

Immediately after his death, the shotgun that was used to kill him was found in bushes nearby, with the owner's fingerprints still fresh. Byron de la Beckwith, a vocal member of a local white-supremacist group, was arrested. Despite the evidence against him, which included an earlier statement that he wanted to kill Evers, two trials with all-white juries ended in deadlock decisions, and Beckwith walked free.

Twenty years later, in 1989, information surfaced that suggested the jury in both trials had been tampered with. The assistant District Attorney, with the help of Evers's widow, began putting together a new case. In 1990, Beckwith was arrested one more time; toward the end of 1993, the case was still pending.

Evers's death changed the tenor of the civil-rights struggle. Anger replaced fear in the South, as hundreds of demonstrators marched in protest. His death prompted President John Kennedy to ask Congress for a comprehensive civil-rights bill, which President Lyndon Johnson signed into law the following year. Evers's death, as his life, contributed much to the struggle for equality.

Fannie Lou Hamer
(1917–1977)

Civil Rights Activist

As a poor sharecropper, she had only an elementary education, yet Fannie Lou Hamer was one of the most eloquent speakers for the civil-rights movement in the South. She worked for political, social, and economic equality for herself and all African Americans; she fought to integrate the national Democratic Party, and she became one of the party's first black delegates to a presidential convention.

Hamer, the youngest of twenty siblings born to Jim and Ella Townsend in Montgomery County, Mississippi, began picking cotton when she was six; she attended school until she had to drop out in the sixth grade to work full time. She worked first as a share cropper, and then as a time keeper on the same plantation in Mississippi for almost forty years. In 1962, because she tried to exercise her right to vote, she lost her job and, frightened by threats of violent reprisals, was forced to move away from her home and her family. Angered into action, she went to work for the Student Non-Violent Coordinating Committee, helping many blacks register to vote.

Because the Democratic party refused to send blacks as delegates to the national presidential convention, in 1964 Hamer and others formed the Mississippi Freedom Democratic Party to send black delegates to the convention. They challenged the Democratic delegates from Mississippi for their seats at the convention, arguing that the all-white delegation could not adequately represent their state, which had a large black population. Hamer's own speech on their behalf frightened the incumbent President Lyndon Johnson so much so that he tried to block the televised coverage of her. The MFDP lost its bid that year, but their actions did result in a pledge from the national party not to seat delegations excluding blacks in the 1968 convention. In 1968, Fannie Lou Hamer was among the first black delegates to the Democratic National Convention.

For the next decade, Hamer remained active in the struggle for civil and economic rights. In 1969, she founded the Freedom Farms Corporation to help needy families raise food and livestock. They also provided basic social services, scholarships and grants for education, and helped fund minority business opportunities. She became a sought-after speaker, and in the 1970s, even as her health was failing from cancer, she still toured the country speaking about civil rights for all.

From 1949 to 1971, William H. Hastie served as a United States Court of Appeals Judge of the Third Circuit, the first African-American man to hold a federal appeals judicial position.

Hastie was born in Knoxville, Tennessee, November 17, 1904. He was the son of William Henry and Roberta Child Hastie. He received his A.B. from Amherst College in 1925, an LL.B. from Harvard University in 1930, and an S.J.D. from the same institution in 1933. He received honorary LL.D.s from many institutions, including Rutgers University, Howard University, and Temple University. In 1943 he married Beryl Lockhart, and the couple had three children.

Hastie was admitted to the bar in 1930 and was in private practice from 1930 to 1933. In 1933, he became assistant solicitor of the Department of the Interior, where he served until 1937. That year he became a judge of the District Court of the Virgin Islands, leaving in 1939 to become dean of the Howard University School of Law. In 1942, he became the first civilian aide to the secretary of war. He was governor of the Virgin Islands between 1946 and 1949, before his subsequent position as United States Circuit Court of Appeals judge.

Hastie died April 14, 1976, in Philadelphia, Pennsylvania.

William H. Hastie (1904–1976)

First Black U.S. Court of Appeals Judge, Third Circuit

Leon Higginbotham, Jr. was appointed on October 13, 1977 by President Jimmy Carter to the United States Circuit Judge's position. Just prior to this appointment, he had served on the Federal Trade Commission—the first black and the youngest person ever to hold the post of commissioner.

Born in Trenton, New Jersey, on February 25, 1928, Higginbotham began as an engineering student at Purdue University, but later went to Antioch College to study liberal arts. He received his LL.B. in 1952 from Yale School of Law. This was quite a step for a man who started out as a shoe store porter.

A. Leon Higginbotham, Jr. (1928–)

Professor of Law, Former U.S. Court of Appeals Judge

After graduation, Higginbotham became an assistant district attorney in Philadelphia and later moved into private practice. He was sought out by Pennsylvania Governor David Lawrence to become a member of the Pennsylvania Human Rights Commission. Elected president of the Philadelphia chapter of NAACP, Higginbotham later earned the honor of "One of the 10 Outstanding Young Men in America" by the United States Junior Chamber of Commerce. He was made district judge in 1964, where he served until his appointment to the United States Circuit Court in 1977. Higginbotham was also a lecturer at Harvard Law School and an adjunct professor at the University of Pennsylvania.

Higginbotham is well known for his prolific writing. He has authored more than one hundred articles as well as an acclaimed book, *In the Matter of Color: Race and the American Legal Process; The Colonial Period*. He has also been praised for his unusual competency in logic and language. In his esteemed career, he has won over forty honorary degrees.

Anita Hill (1956–)

Professor of Law

Born on July 30, 1956, in Morris, Oklahoma, Anita Hill was a relatively unknown law professor at the University of Oklahoma when her name became a household word virtually overnight. It was during the Senate confirmation hearings in October 1991 for United States Supreme Court Justice Clarence Thomas that Hill became famous. She came forward with sexual harassment charges against Judge Thomas that shocked the nation, and many watched as she poured out painful details of Thomas's alleged sexual harassment, purportedly committed when both had worked for the Equal Employment Opportunities Commission. Hill claimed that Thomas repeatedly pressured her to date him, told her plots of pornographic movies, and bragged about his sexual exploits. When asked why she didn't quit her job or report Thomas when the incidents occurred during the early 1980s, Hill answered that she feared she wouldn't be able to get another job.

Following the hearings, Hill continued to be hounded by the press. Her experience with the hearings had changed her life, as well as her career direction. She had been a professor of commercial law. She decided to take a year-long sabbatical in order to look at the possibility of founding an institute with the purpose of researching racism and sexism. Hill also made many speeches around the country about her experience.

Controversy didn't escape her on campus, either. Several lawmakers made news when they asked that Hill be fired. Nonetheless, her dean and other members of the faculty support her. Funding is underway to create a University of Oklahoma professorship to study discrimination in the workplace. Most likely, Hill will be placed in that position.

Jesse Louis Jackson was born October 8, 1941, in Greenville, South Carolina. In 1959 Jackson left South Carolina to attend the University of Illinois. He became dissatisfied with his treatment on campus, however, and decided to transfer to North Carolina Agricultural and Technical College. After receiving his B.A. in sociology he went on to attend the Chicago Theological Seminary. He was ordained a Baptist minister in 1968.

Jesse Jackson (1941–)

President, People United to Save Humanity

Jackson joined the Southern Christian Leadership Conference in 1965. In 1966 Jackson became involved with the SCLC's Operation Breadbasket, and from 1967 to 1971 he served as the program's executive director. Jackson resigned from the SCLC in 1971 to found his own organization, Operation PUSH (People United to Save Humanity). Through PUSH Jackson continued to pursue the economic objectives of Operation Breadbasket and expanded into areas of social and political development.

From that point on, Jackson was on his way to becoming the most visible and sought-after civil-rights leader in the country. His magnetic personality came across as appealing on television, and while he described himself as "a country preacher," his command of issues and his ability to reach the heart of matters marked him as an individual of intellectual depth. Of all the civil-rights leaders, Jackson was the one who could relate best to the young. He was possessed with a gift of being able to summon out the best in them, in a phrase that became his trademark, "I am somebody."

Out of this came Jackson's program, PUSH-EXCEL, which sought to motivate young school children to do better academically. In 1981 *Newsweek* magazine credited Jackson with building a struggling community-improvement organization into a nationwide campaign to revive pride, discipline, and the work ethic in inner-city schools. With funding from the Carter administration, the PUSH-EXCEL program was placed in five other cities.

The Jesse Jackson of the 1980s is best remembered for his two runs for the Democratic nomination for President of the United States. In 1983, many, but not all, black political leaders endorsed the idea of a black presidential candidate to create a "people's" platform, increase voter registration, and establish a power base from which there could be greater input into the political process. His 1984 campaign was launched under the aegis of the National Rainbow Coalition, Inc., an umbrella organization of minority groups. Black support was divided, however, between Jackson and former Vice President Walter Mondale. During this campaign, Jackson attracted considerable media coverage with controversial remarks and actions, demonstrating a lack of familiarity with national politics.

Jackson's 1988 campaign demonstrated enormous personal and political growth; his candidacy was no longer a symbolic gesture but was a real and compelling demonstration of his effectiveness as a candidate. By the time the Democratic convention rolled around, media pundits were seriously discussing the likelihood of Jackson's nomination as the Democratic presidential candidate, and "what to do about Jesse" became the focus of the entire Democratic leadership. At the end of the primary campaign, Jackson had finished a strong second to Massachusetts Governor Michael Dukakis and changed forever the notion that a black president in America was inconceivable. Jackson took his defeat in stride and continued to campaign for the Democratic ticket until the November election.

Since the 1988 election Jackson has worked less publicly, but no less energetically. In 1989 he moved with his Rainbow Coalition from Chicago to Washington, DC; he believed that the coalition could be more effective working in the nation's capital. Still fighting hard for social change, his concerns include child care, health care, housing, discrimination, and a newer issue, statehood for the District of Columbia. While he has concentrated his efforts on national issues, he keeps active in foreign affairs as well. He has traveled throughout world to meet with leaders of other nations and has used his fame and influence to help Americans in trouble abroad. In 1991, he traveled to Iraq and convinced Saddam Hussein to begin releasing Americans held hostage after Hussein's invasion of Kuwait.

Although many expected him to run for president again in 1992, Jackson decided against it, saying that he was too tired, and the strain on his family too severe. He did not, however, rule out 1996.

Coretta Scott King

(1927-)

Civil Rights Activist

As the wife of civil-rights leader Martin Luther King, Jr., Coretta Scott King was ready to continue his work and perpetuate his ideals after his 1968 assassination. While her primary role in the early years of marriage was to raise her four children, she became increasingly involved in the

Coretta Scott King (left), Dr. Martin Luther King, Jr., and Floyd McKissick attend a rally in Chicago, 1966.

struggle for civil rights through her husband's activities. After his death, she quickly became a dynamic activist and peace crusader.

Born one of three children on April 27, 1927, King is a native of Heilberger, Alabama. During the Depression she was forced to contribute to the family income by hoeing and picking cotton, but she resolved early to overcome adversity, seek treatment as an equal, and struggle to achieve a sound education. After graduating from the private Lincoln High School in 1945, she entered Antioch College in Yellow Springs, Ohio, on a scholarship, majoring in education and music. A teaching career appealed to her, but she became badly disillusioned when she was not allowed to do her practice teaching in the public schools of the town. No black had ever taught there, and she was not destined to be the first to break the tradition.

Musical training in voice and piano absorbed much of her time, with the result that, upon graduation, she decided to continue her studies at the New England Conservatory of Music in Boston, attending on a modest fellowship that covered tuition but made part-time work a necessity. Her meeting with Martin Luther King thrust her into a whirlwind romance, and also presented her with the opportunity to marry an exceptional young minister whose intense convictions and concern for humanity brought her a measure of rare self-realization early in life. Sensing his incredible dynamism, she suffered no regrets at the prospect of relinquishing her own possible career.

Completing her studies in 1954, King moved back south with her husband, who became pastor of Drexel Avenue Baptist Church in Montgomery, Alabama. Within a year, Martin Luther King had led the Montgomery bus boycott and given birth to a new era of civil-rights agitation. Two years later, he was the head of the Southern Christian Leadership Conference (SCLC).

Over the years Coretta Scott King became gradually more involved in her husband's work. She would occasionally perform at his lectures, raising her voice in song as he did in speech. She became involved in separate activities as well. In 1962, she served as a Woman's Strike for Peace delegate to the seventeen-nation Disarmament Conference in Geneva, Switzerland. In the mid 1960s, she sang in the multi-arts Freedom Concerts that raised money for the SCLC. As demands on Martin became too much, she began to fill the speaking engagements he could not. After his assassination, she filled many of the commitments his death left empty, but soon became sought-after in her own right.

Her speech on Solidarity Day, June 19, 1968, is often identified as a prime example of her emergence from the shadow of her husband's memory. In it, she called upon American women to "unite and form a solid block of women power" to fight the three great evils of racism, poverty, and war. Much of her subsequent activity revolved around building plans for the creation of a Martin Luther King, Jr. Memorial in Atlanta, which she began to work on in 1969, and it was established under the care of the National Park Service in 1980. She also published a book of reminiscences, *My Life with Martin Luther King, Jr.*

Today, King remains an eloquent and respected spokesperson on behalf of black causes and nonviolent philosophy. As its president, she devotes most of her time to the Martin Luther King, Jr. Center for Non-Violent Social Change in Atlanta, which has grown into a well-respected institution visited by persons from across the world. King has also championed the cause against apartheid in South Africa. In 1985, she and two of her children were arrested for demonstrating outside the South African embassy in Washington, DC. In 1986, she visited South Africa for eight days, meeting with business and anti-apartheid leaders.

Martin Luther King, Jr. (1929–1968)

Civil Rights Activist

Any number of historic moments in the civil-rights struggle have been used to identify Martin Luther King, Jr.—prime mover of the Montgomery bus boycott (1956), keynote speaker at the March on Washington (1963), youngest Nobel Peace Prize laureate (1964). But in retrospect, single events are less important than the fact that King, with his policy of nonviolent protest, was the dominant force in the civil-rights movement during its decade of greatest achievement, from 1957 to 1968.

King was born Michael Luther King in Atlanta on January 15, 1929—one of the three children of Martin Luther King, Sr., pastor of Ebenezer Baptist Church, and Alberta (Williams) King, a former schoolteacher. (He did not receive the name of "Martin" until he was about six years of age.)

After attending grammar and high schools locally, King enrolled in Morehouse College (also in Atlanta) in 1944. At this time he was not inclined to enter the ministry, but while there he came under the influence of Dr. Benjamin Mays, a scholar whose manner and bearing convinced him that a religious career could have its intellectual satisfactions as well. After receiving his B.A. in 1948, King attended Crozer Theological Seminary in Chester, Pennsylvania, winning the Plafker Award as the outstanding student of the graduating class, and the J. Lewis Crozer Fellowship as well. King completed the course work for his doctorate in 1953, and was granted the degree two years later upon completion of his dissertation.

Married by then, King returned south, accepting the pastorate of the Dexter Avenue Baptist Church in Montgomery, Alabama. It was here that he made his first mark on the civil-rights movement, by mobilizing the black community during a 382-day boycott of the city's bus lines. Working through the Montgomery Improvement Association, King overcame arrest and other violent harassment, including the bombing of his home. Ulti-

Martin Luther King, Jr. joins other civil-rights leaders at a rally in Selma, Alabama, 1965.

mately, the U.S. Supreme Court declared the Alabama laws requiring bus segregation unconstitutional, with the result that blacks were allowed to ride Montgomery buses on equal footing with whites.

A national hero and a civil-rights figure of growing importance, King summoned together a number of black leaders in 1957 and laid the groundwork for the organization now known as the Southern Christian Leadership Conference (SCLC). Elected its president, he soon sought to assist other communities in the organization of protest campaigns against discrimination, and in voter-registration activities as well.

After completing his first book and making a trip to India, King returned to the United States in 1960 to become co-pastor, with his father, of Ebenezer Baptist Church. Three years later, in 1963, King's nonviolent tactics were put to their most severe test in Birmingham, Alabama during a mass protest for fair hiring practices, the establishment of a biracial committee, and the desegregation of department-store facilities. Police brutality used against the marchers dramatized the plight of blacks to the nation at large with enormous impact. King was arrested, but his voice was not silenced as he issued his classic "Letter from a Birmingham Jail" to refute his critics.

Later that year King was a principal speaker at the historic March on Washington, where he delivered one of the most passionate addresses of his career. At the beginning of the following year *Time* magazine designated him as its Man of the Year for 1963. A few months later he was named recipient of the 1964 Nobel Peace Prize.

Upon his return from Oslo, where he had gone to accept the award, King entered a new battle, this time in Selma, Alabama, where he led a voter-registration campaign that culminated in the Selma-to-Montgomery Freedom March. King next brought his crusade to Chicago where he launched a slum-rehabilitation and open-housing program.

In the North, however, King soon discovered that young and angry blacks cared little for his pulpit oratory and even less for his solemn pleas for peaceful protest. Their disenchantment was clearly one of the factors influencing his decision to rally behind a new cause and stake out a fresh battleground: the war in Vietnam. Although his aim was to fuse a new coalition of dissent based on equal support for the peace crusade and the civil-rights movement, King antagonized many civil-rights leaders by declaring the United States to be "the greatest purveyor of violence in the world."

The rift was immediate. The NAACP saw King's shift of emphasis as "a serious tactical mistake"; the Urban League warned that the "limited resources" of the civil-rights movement would be spread too thin; Bayard Rustin claimed black support of the peace movement would be negligible; Ralph Bunche felt King was undertaking an impossible mission in trying to bring the campaign for peace in step with the goals of the civil-rights movement.

From the vantage point of history, King's timing could only be regarded as superb. In announcing his opposition to the war, and in characterizing it as a "tragic adventure" which was playing "havoc with the destiny of the entire world," King again forced the white middle class to concede that no movement could dramatically affect the course of government in the United States unless it involved deliberate and restrained aggressiveness, persistent dissent, and even militant confrontation. These were precisely the ingredients of the civil-rights struggle in the South in the early 1960s.

As students, professors, intellectuals, clergymen, and reformers of every stripe rushed into the movement (in a sense forcing fiery black militants like Stokely Carmichael and Floyd McKissick to surrender their control over antiwar polemics), King turned his attention to the domestic issue that, in his view, was directly related to the Vietnam struggle: the War on Poverty.

Martin Luther King, Jr. addressing a crowd of protestors.

At one point, he called for a guaranteed family income, threatened national boycotts, and spoke of disrupting entire cities by nonviolent "camp-ins." With this in mind, he began to draw up plans for a massive march of the poor on Washington, DC itself, envisioning a popular demonstration of unsurpassed intensity and magnitude designed to force Congress and the political parties to recognize and deal with the unseen and ignored masses of desperate and downtrodden Americans.

King's decision to interrupt these plans to lend his support to the Memphis sanitation men's strike was based in part on his desire to discourage violence, as well as to focus national attention on the plight of the poor, unorganized workers of the city. The men were bargaining for little else beyond basic union representation and long-overdue salary considerations. Though he was unable to eliminate the violence that had resulted in the summoning and subsequent departure of the National Guard, King stayed on in Memphis and was in the process of planning for a march, which he vowed to carry out in defiance of a federal court injunction if necessary.

On the night of April 3, 1968, he told a church congregation: "Well I don't know what will happen now ... But it really doesn't matter...." (At other times, musing over the possibility that he might be killed, King had assured his colleagues that he had "the advantage over most people" because he had "conquered the fear of death.")

Death came for King on the balcony of the black-owned Lorraine Motel just off Beale Street on the evening of April 4. While King was standing outside with Jesse Jackson and Ralph Abernathy, a shot rang out. King fell over, struck in the neck by a rifle bullet that left him moribund. At 7:05 P.M. he was pronounced dead at St. Joseph's Hospital.

King's death caused a wave of violence in major cities across the country. King's legacy, however, has lasted much longer than the memories of those post-assassination riots. In 1969 his widow, Coretta Scott King, organized the Martin Luther King, Jr. Center for Non-Violent Social Change. Today it stands next to his beloved Ebenezer Baptist Church in Atlanta, and with the surrounding buildings it is a national historic landmark under the administration of the National Park Service. King's birthday, January 15, is a national holiday, celebrated each year with educational programs, artistic displays, and concerts throughout the United States. The Lorraine Motel where he was shot is now the National Civil Rights Museum.

Outside of Ebenezer Baptist Church in Atlanta, while King's body was lying in state.

Thurgood Marshall's long and illustrious career was capped by his 1967 nomination to the highest court in the land—the United States Supreme Court—where he became the first African American to hold the coveted position of Supreme Court Justice. At fifty-nine, the son of a sleeping-car porter and the great-grandson of a slave became a sign of progress for many. He was viewed with the utmost respect for all of his years on the bench, retiring June 27, 1991. Marshall died at the age of eighty-four in 1993. He was laid in state in the Great Hall of the Supreme Court of the United States on the same bier where Abraham Lincoln once rested. Over 20,000 mourners paid their last respects to Justice Marshall.

Born in Baltimore, Maryland on July 2, 1908, Marshall earned a B.A. from Lincoln University, hoping to become a dentist. He changed his mind, however, and instead went to Howard University's law school, graduating in 1933 at the top of his class. He immediately went into private practice in Baltimore, where he remained for five years.

Thurgood Marshall (1908–1993)

First African-American U.S. Supreme Court Associate Justice, Former NAACP Legal Counsel

In 1936, he entered into what was going to be a long and illustrious career with the NAACP, starting as an assistant special counsel and eventually becoming director–counsel of the Legal Defense and Educational fund, a position he left in 1961. In 1938, as a national special counsel, he handled all cases involving the constitutional rights of African Americans. Then, in 1950, he was named director–counsel of the organization's eleven-year-old Legal Defense and Education Fund. In 1954, as part of an imposing team of lawyers, he played a key role in the now-historic Supreme Court decision on school desegregation, *Brown v. Board of Education*, which over-ruled the "separate but equal" doctrine in public education. He also figured prominently in such important cases as *Sweatt v. Painter* (requiring the admission of a qualified black student to the law school of Texas University) and *Smith v. Allwright* (establishing the right of Texas blacks to vote in Democratic primaries). Of the thirty-two cases that he argued before the Supreme Court, Marshall won twenty-nine.

Marshall was also known for his lifelong support of rights for women. Constance Baker Motley commented that Marshall hired her for an NAACP counsel position when virtually every other employer had turned her down. He also encouraged her when he argued cases before the Supreme Court, and made certain he pointed out other African-American women role models.

In 1961 Marshall became a federal circuit judge for the second circuit. In 1946 he was awarded the prestigious Springarn Medal for his many achievements. He had over twenty honorary degrees to his credit, including LL.D. honors from the University of Liberia in 1960, the University of Michigan in 1964, and the University of Otago in Dunedin, New Zealand, in 1968. Marshall was also the representative for the White House Conference on Youth and Children, and a member of the National Bar Association. He was once sent by President John F. Kennedy to be a personal representative to the independence ceremonies of Sierra Leone.

Constance Baker Motley (1921–)

First African-American Female Federal Judge

Born September 14, 1921, in New Haven, Connecticut, Constance Baker Motley became the first African-American woman to become a federal judge. The child of West Indian parents was appointed in 1966 by President Johnson to the United States District Court for Southern New York. The appointment marked the high point of her long career in politics and civic affairs.

While still a law student at Columbia University, Motley began working with the NAACP Legal Defense and Educational Fund, beginning an association that was to make her famous as a defender of civil rights. In 1946 she was awarded her LL.B. and began to work full time with the NAACP, eventually becoming an associate counsel. During her twenty-year career with the organization, Motley had argued nine successful NAACP cases before the United States Supreme Court, and had participated in almost every important civil-rights case that had passed through the courts since 1954—from Autherine Lucy in Alabama to James Meredith in Mississippi.

In 1964 Motley decided to make a run for the New York State Senate, and was successful. She became the first African-American woman to hold that position. After only a year in the Senate, Motley ran for the position of Manhattan borough president, emerging the victor by the unanimous final vote of the city council. She thus became the first woman to serve as a city borough president, and, therefore, also the first woman on the Board of Estimate.

Motley was appointed to the United States District Court in 1966. In 1982 she was named chief judge of the federal district court that covers Manhattan, the Bronx, and six counties north of New York City. In 1986 she was named senior judge, the position she currently holds.

Rosa Parks has been called the spark that lit the fire, and the mother of the movement. Her courage to defy custom and law to uphold her personal rights and dignity inspired the African Americans in Montgomery, Alabama to fight for their rights by staging one of the longest boycotts in history.

Rosa Louise McCauley Parks (1913–)

Civil Rights Activist

Born Rosa Louise McCauley, she was raised by her mother and grandparents in Tuskegee and Montgomery, Alabama. After attending segregated schools, she went to the all-black Alabama State College. In 1932 she married Raymond Parks, a barber. Both of them worked for the local NAACP chapter, and Rosa became local NAACP secretary in the 1950s.

On December 1, 1955, as she was riding home from work, she was ordered by the bus driver to give up her seat so that a white man might sit. She refused. She was arrested and fined $14. Her case was the last straw for the blacks of Montgomery, as tired of being underclass citizens as Parks was. A city-wide boycott was organized to force the city to desegregate public transportation. A young, little-known minister by the name of Martin Luther King, Jr. became involved and lectured the nation on the injustice of it all. Blacks, and a few whites, organized peacefully together to transport boycotters to and from work, and they continued, despite opposition from the city and state governments, for 382 days.

When the boycott ended on December 21, 1956, both Parks and King were national heroes, and the Supreme Court had ruled that segregation on city buses was unconstitutional. The mass movement of nonviolent social change that was started lasted more than a decade, culminating in the Civil Rights Act of 1964 and the Voter's Rights Act of 1965.

Because of the harassment Rosa Parks and her family received during and after the boycott, they moved to Detroit, Michigan in 1957. She began working with Congressman John Conyers and continued to be involved in the civil-rights struggle. She marched on Washington in 1963, and into Montgomery in 1965. Even as her life has quieted down, she has received tributes for her dedication and inspiration; in 1980, she received the Martin Luther King, Jr. Nonviolent Peace Prize. As she headed toward retirement from John Conyers's office in 1988, she became involved in other activities, like the Rosa and Raymond Parks Institute of Self Development in Detroit, founded in 1987.

Al Sharpton
(1954–)

Social Activist

Sharpton was born in 1954 in Brooklyn, New York. He went to public schools, graduated from Tilden High School, and briefly attended Brooklyn College.

Al Sharpton (center) leads a demonstration in New York City, 1992.

At the early age of four Sharpton began delivering sermons, and at the age of thirteen he was ordained a Pentecostal minister. During and after high school Sharpton preached in neighborhood churches and went on national religious tours, often with prominent entertainers.

Sharpton was soon befriended by a number of well-known and influential African Americans, including Congressman Adam Clayton Powell, Jr., Jesse Jackson, and singer James Brown. In 1969 Jackson appointed Sharpton youth director of Operation Breadbasket.

Around this time James Brown made Sharpton one of his bodyguards, and soon he was doing promotions for the singer. In 1983 Sharpton married singer Kathy Jordan and soon became involved with fight promoter Don King.

Even though Sharpton was promoting boxers and entertainers, he had long before put himself in the public spotlight in the role of social activist. In 1971 he founded the National Youth Movement (later called the United African Movement) ostensibly to combat drug use. The movement, however, soon became known as a vehicle for Sharpton to draw attention to himself.

Sharpton made himself part of the publicity surrounding the Bernard Goetz murder trial (1984), the Howard Beach racial killing (1986), the Twana Brawley debacle (1987), and the Yusef Hawkins-Bensonhurst killing (1989). In 1988 Sharpton was accused of being an FBI informant and passing on information about Don King, reputed organized-crime figures, and various African-American leaders. In 1989 and 1990 he was acquitted on charges of income tax evasion and embezzling National Youth Movement funds. In 1991 Sharpton was briefly hospitalized after being stabbed by a man wielding a pocket knife.

While being shunned by many middle-class African-Americans, Sharpton draws support from the ranks of the youth and the disenfranchised. Does Sharpton embrace social causes in order to promote himself, or does he employ outrageous tactics to better fight for racial justice? That has been a difficult question to answer, and the answer goes to the heart of the man.

Leon Howard Sullivan (1922–)

Civil Rights Activist

Sullivan was born October 16, 1922 in Charlestown, West Virginia. After being ordained a Baptist minister at the age of seventeen, Sullivan earned a B.A. from West Virginia State College (1943) and an M.A. from Columbia University (1947). Sullivan also attended the Union Theological Seminary (1945) and earned a D.D. from Virginia Union University.

From 1950 to 1988 Sullivan was the pastor of the Zion Baptist Church in Philadelphia, where he entered into a lifelong crusade to provide better and expanding job opportunities for African Americans. Upon retiring from the church he was made pastor emeritus.

Sullivan fought racist hiring practices by protest and economic boycott. He provided job training through the Opportunities Industrialization Center. Opening in 1964 with money from a Ford Foundation grant, the Center offered training in electronics, cooking, power-sewing, and drafting. Sullivan also founded Zion Investment Associates, which makes available seed money for new African-American business ventures. Sullivan has also been associated with Progress Aerospace Inc., General Motors, and Mellon Bank, and he is a co-founder of Self-Help.

Clarence Thomas (1948–)

U.S. Supreme Court Associate Justice

Thomas was born June 23, 1948, in Pin Point, Georgia. His parents were poor, and when he was young his father left the family. At the age of seven, Thomas's house burned down and his mother could no longer hold the family together. With his brother, Thomas went to live with his maternal grandparents in Savannah. While his grandfather had little education, he was determined that Thomas would go to school and make something of himself. Thomas's early atmosphere was one of strict discipline. He attended various all-black and mixed-race Catholic schools, and he intended to enter the priesthood but left when he encountered a racist seminarian.

Thomas transferred to Holy Cross College and earned his B.A. He was accepted into Yale Law School in 1971, after Yale had adopted an affirmative action program. Thomas was never certain whether he was admitted for his credentials or because of his race. This is perhaps one of the reasons he has remained staunchly against affirmative action. He earned his J.D. in 1974.

After graduating, he became an assistant attorney general for the state of Missouri, working there from 1974 to 1977, then worked briefly at Monsanto Company in St. Louis as an attorney, specializing in pesticide, fungicide, and rodenticide law. He also worked as a legal assistant for Senator John C. Danforth.

From 1981 to 1982 he was an assistant secretary for civil rights with the Department of Education, then moved on to chair for the Equal Employment Opportunity Commission, a position he held until 1990. His tenure there was controversial, as he was not allied with either liberals or civil-rights leaders, and he didn't feel comfortable with the white conservative hierarchy. It has been debated whether the status of African-Americans was helped or hurt by the policies he set at the EEOC.

After Robert H. Bork resigned his Circuit Court position because he had been rejected for a place on the United States Supreme Court, Thomas was appointed to the post. He served there until he was made a justice on the Supreme Court in 1991. Since then Thomas has filled his role as a conservative presence on the bench. He has voted with Justice Scalia, the court's most notorious conservative, in fifty-six of ninety cases.

In 1992, Thomas was one of ten people to receive the Horatio Alger Award.

An honor student and Phi Beta Kappa at Harvard, Trotter founded the militant newspaper *Boston Guardian* in 1901 for the purpose of "propaganda against discrimination."

William Monroe Trotter (1872–1934)

Civil Rights Activist

In 1905 Trotter joined W.E.B. DuBois in founding the Niagara Movement but refused to move with him into the NAACP because he felt it would be too moderate. Instead, Trotter formed the National Equal Rights League. In 1919 Trotter appeared at the Paris Peace Conference in an unsuccessful effort to have it outlaw racial discrimination. The State Department had denied him a passport to attend, but he had reached Paris nonetheless by having himself hired as a cook on a ship.

Because of Trotter's strident unwillingness to work with established groups, the civil-rights movement has been slow to recognize his contributions. But many of his methods were later adopted in the 1950s, notably his use of nonviolent protest. In 1903 Trotter deliberately disrupted a meeting in Boston at which Booker T. Washington was preaching the support of segregation; Trotter's purpose was to be arrested to gain publicity for his militant position. Trotter also led demonstrations against plays and films that glorified the Ku Klux Klan.

Booker Taliaferro Washington (1856–1915)

Political Activist, Educator

Booker T. Washington was born a slave in Hale's Ford, Virginia, reportedly in April 1856. After emancipation, his family was so poverty stricken that he worked in salt furnaces and coal mines from age nine. Always an intelligent and curious child, he yearned for an education and was frustrated when he could not receive good schooling locally. When he was sixteen his parents allowed him to quit work to go to school. They had no money to help him, so he walked 200 miles to attend the Hampton Institute in Virginia and paid his tuition and board there by working as the janitor.

Dedicating himself to the idea that education would raise his people to equality in this country, Washington became a teacher. He taught first in his home town and then at the Hampton Institute, and in 1881 he founded the Tuskegee Normal and Industrial Institute in Tuskegee, Alabama. As head of the Institute, Washington traveled the country unceasingly to raise funds from blacks and whites both; soon he became a well-known speaker.

In 1895 he was asked to speak at the opening of the Cotton States Exposition, an unprecedented honor for a black man. His speech explained his major thesis, that blacks could secure their constitutional rights through their own economic and moral advancement rather than through legal and political changes. Although his conciliatory stand angered some blacks who feared it would encourage the foes of equal rights, whites approved of his views. Thus his major achievement was to win over diverse elements among southern whites, without whose support the programs he envisioned and brought into being would have been impossible.

In addition to Tuskegee Institute, which still educates many today, Washington instituted a variety of programs for rural extension work and helped to establish the National Negro Business League. Shortly after the election of President William McKinley in 1896, a movement was set in motion that Washington be named to a cabinet post, but he withdrew his name from consideration, preferring to work outside the political arena.

*B*lack Nationalism

Black nationalism, in its classic nineteenth-century form, consisted of efforts by African-American groups and individuals to create a sovereign nation-state. The quest for a national homeland expressed a perceived need to demonstrate the capacity of black people for self-government. In its more inclusive form, black nationalism has been indistinguishable from such movements as African Civilizationism, Pan-Negro Nationalism, and Pan-Africanism. Sometimes it has advocated a "back-to-Africa movement," but often it has simply implied moral support for decolonizing Africa and advancing the material and spiritual interests of African peoples everywhere.

THE IDEOLOGY OF BLACK NATIONALISM ✦ ✦ ✦ ✦ ✦ ✦ ✦ ✦ ✦ ✦ ✦ ✦

The back-to-Africa movement went through several phases of rise and decline, from its resurgence in the 1850s to its apex in the Garvey movement and its denouement thereafter. The major proponents of classical black nationalism invariably placed religious historicism and theology at the center of their ideological conceptions or utopian visions. While their goals were political and economic, they usually included a cultural agenda as well—though the cultural concerns of nineteenth-century nationalists were often Eurocentric and are not to be confused with the Negritude movement or the cultural nationalism of the late-twentieth century. Black nationalism met the psychological need for a response to the slavery, colonialism, and racism imposed by Europeans and white Americans. In the minds of its adherents, it was the only sensible reaction to the almost universal military, technological, and economic domination of blacks by whites.

Documents expressing the ideology of black nationalism began to appear during the late-eighteenth century. As Elie Kedourie has argued, nationalism, the idea that peoples are naturally divided into nations, is European in its origins. The American and French revolutions, and conceptions of the nation-state arising with them, came to dominate political thought not only in the North Atlantic but also among African and Asian peoples. The 1804 slave revolt and seizure of the state in Haiti, as W.E.B. DuBois and Eugene Genovese have argued, was both a cause and an effect of rising conceptions of nationalism and manifest destiny in the United States. It was also an inspiration to black nationalism among both the slaves and the free African Americans of the black population in the United States. Literary documents of black nationalism in England and the United States coincided with the revolutions in France and Haiti. Immanuel Geiss has referred to these expressions, typified by *The Interesting Narrative of the Life of Olaudah Equiano or Gustavus Vassa, the African, Written by Himself* (1787), as "proto-Pan-Africanism." (For a time, Vassa believed that the African condition could be improved by repatriating Afro-Europeans in Africa. Although he eventually abandoned that plan, he remained committed to the destruction of African slavery through the agencies of Christian missionary activity and free trade.)

♦ ♦ ♦ ♦ ♦ ♦ ♦ ♦ BLACK NATIONALISM IN THE UNITED STATES

Early black nationalism in the United States is associated with the activities of two enterprising capitalists in the maritime industries, Paul Cuffe, a New Bedford sea captain, and James Forten, a Philadelphia sailmaker. These two figures combined a bourgeois economic nationalism with a Christian thrust, and hoped to develop Christianity, commerce, and civilization in Africa while providing a homeland for African Americans. Their repatriationist activities were brought to a halt in 1817, when Henry Clay, Andrew Jackson, and other white Americans formed the American Society for Colonizing the Free People of Color in the United States, usually called the American Colonization Society. The American Colonization Society had other prominent slave holders among its leadership, and expressly denied any sympathy for abolition; large numbers of blacks reacted by demonstrating a marked hostility to the society and its aims. Cuffe died shortly after the society's founding, and Forten felt constrained to silence, although he continued to believe that black Americans would "never become a people until they come out from amongst the white people." Those who continued to support repatriation, or who migrated under the auspices of the American Colonization Society, became the objects of extreme vituperation.

The Early Years

Black nationalism, though it began as an effort to create a sovereign nation-state for African Americans, has come to mean support for decolonizing Africa and for advancing the interests of African peoples everywhere.

Black nationalism and repatriationism were not always the same thing, however, and hostility to the American Colonization Society did not always lead to the abandonment of nationalist rhetoric. Maria Stewart referred to herself as an African, but was hostile to the colonization movement. She insisted on her rights as an American, but at the same time denounced the United States with strident jeremiadic rhetoric. Stewart clearly viewed black America as a captive nation, existing in a type of Babylonian captivity, and conceived of African Americans as a people with a national destiny without advocating political separatism or the desire to form a nation-state. In a similar vein, David Walker denounced colonization and emigration with the religious fervor of an Old Testament prophet. Curiously, he insisted on the separate mission and destiny of African Americans as colored citizens of the world, while simultaneously maintaining that black and white Americans could be "a united and happy people."

Black nationalist motivations have been attributed to the major slave conspiracies of Gabriel Prosser and Denmark Vesey, who were inspired by the Haitian revolt, and both seem to have had as their goal the creation of a

Martin R. Delany founded the African Civilization Society in 1858.

black nation with ties to the Caribbean. For the most part, however, evidence of black nationalism in the United States is found among the free black population of the North. It was in the so-called Free African Societies, which sprang up in the black communities of New York, Boston, and Philadelphia, that a conception of black historical identity and destiny was strongest. During the 1830s and 1840s, black nationalist thinking was associated with religious leadership such as that provided by the bishop of the African Methodist Episcopal Church, Richard Allen, who believed in a special God-given mission for black Americans as a people but steadfastly opposed the American Colonization Society. Peter Williams, leader of the Afro-American Group of the Episcopal Church in New York, took a more tolerant view of colonization. He eulogized Paul Cuffe and remained friendly with John Russwurm, even after the latter emigrated to Liberia and was burned in effigy by anti-colonization activists.

The flourishing of black nationalism occurred during the 1850s and 1860s. To some degree, the movement owed its rebirth to the passage of the Fugitive Slave Act (1850) and the *Dred Scott v. Sandford* decision (1858). Emigration sentiment, which had been quiescent since the death of Cuffe, experienced a resurgence marked by the calling of several colonization conventions. The leaders of the movement were Henry Highland Garnet and Martin R. Delany, who founded the African Civilization Society in 1858. Edward Wilmot Blyden, the principal nineteenth-century Pan-African theorist, migrated to Liberia in 1850. Alexander Crummell emigrated to Liberia under the auspices of the Domestic and Foreign Missionary Society of the Protestant Episcopal Church in 1853, but eventually became involved with the American Colonization Society. During the early years of the Civil War, *The Weekly Anglo-African* became the principal journal of the emigration movement.

Emigrationism died out during the peak years of Reconstruction that followed the Civil War, as the black American population strove to take advantage of opportunities presented by emancipation. From 1876 to 1914 a number of back-to-Africa movements were organized. Most prominent among these were the movements under the leadership of the Rev. Henry McNeal Turner, an AME Bishop, the Rev. Orishatukeh Faduma, a Yoruba man from Barbados, and Chief Alfred C. Sam, a Twi speaker from the Gold Coast. Some scholars have detected black nationalist elements in the Kansas exodus of the 1870s and the Oklahoma movement that established all-black towns during the 1890s. Fadumah had been a missionary in Oklahoma, which proved an important recruiting ground for Alfred C. Sam.

The Twentieth Century

Marcus Garvey's revitalization of the emigration movement came at an opportune moment. He arrived in the United States in 1916, shortly after Alfred C. Sam's voyage to the Gold Coast and a few months after the death of Bishop Turner. His Universal Negro Improvement Association was, according to some speculations, the largest mass movement ever to occur among black Americans. Although Garvey was less successful as a repatriationist than some of his predecessors, he enjoyed tremendous success as a journalist and community organizer. His reputation became a source of great inspiration to many black leaders, and it spread among the masses of people in Africa and the Americas.

Cultural nationalism, the celebration of the contributions of black people to world history, appealed even to those who opposed political nationalism or the establishment of an African nation-state.

Cultural nationalism, the exaltation of the "African personality" and the celebration of the contributions of black people to world history, made its appearance in the mid-nineteenth century. Cultural nationalist rhetoric occasionally has been adopted even by persons who have strongly opposed political nationalism. Frederick Douglass shared with Edward Wilmot Blyden an admiration for the ancient Egyptians, whom he believed to be of exactly the same racial type as African Americans. Toward the end of the century, younger scholars, such as W.E.B. DuBois, were to make much of Egypt, Ethiopia, and Meroe as black contributors to world civilization. Writers such as William H. Ferris and John E. Bruce, who, like DuBois, were protégés of Alexander Crummell, sought to vindicate the black race and to popularize the notion that black peoples of the upper Nile were the progenitors of civilization. The height of the vindicationist school was reached in the writings of Joel Augustus Rogers, sometime contributor to Marcus Garvey's paper, the *Negro World*.

During the 1930s, new versions of cultural nationalism began to focus on the importance of West Africa, in addition to that of ancient Egypt. This development was partially due to the Negritude movement among Francophone intellectuals, but also due to the "Jazz Age" interest in Africa among white artists and social scientists. The researches of Leo Frobenius, the German scholar, kindled the interest of DuBois, Aime Cesaire, and Leopold Senghor in the cultures of "tribal" Africa. The growing interest of European artists such as Picasso and Modigliani in primitivism and African cultural expression led black Americans to a revaluation of their folk heritage and its African roots. The new-found respectability of jazz after its acceptance in continental Europe was another factor in the rise of black cultural nationalism. The ideology of scientific relativism in the writings of Franz Boas and Melville Herskovits, which stressed cultural relativism and a respect for "primitive" cultures, also helped to make an interest in sub-Saharan Africa fashionable.

Elijah Muhammad led the Nation of Islam, for which Malcolm X became a popular spokesperson until the two split over ideological differences.

After the deportation of Marcus Garvey in 1925, black nationalism went into decline, as John Henrik Clarke and other scholars have noted. The search for a black nationality was kept alive by such religious groups as the Black Jews of Harlem, the Moorish Science Temple, and the Nation of Islam, which was under the leadership of the Honorable Elijah Muhammad. The rise of Malcolm X, a follower of Elijah Muhammad, did much to popularize black nationalism with young radical intellectuals during the early 1960s. After his split with Elijah Muhammad, Malcolm X seemed to abandon traditional black nationalist separatism as well, embracing socialism and, at the same time, his white Muslim brethren. Black nationalist attitudes persisted in some radical groups during the late 1960s, but seldom showed any relationship to or awareness of the black nationalist traditions of the nineteenth century. In recent years, cultural black nationalists such as Molefi K. Asante have shown a renewed interest in black nationalist intellectual history, especially as it relates to figures like Edward Wilmot Blyden and Marcus Garvey.

BLACK NATIONALIST AND PAN-AFRICAN THEORISTS ✦ ✦ ✦ ✦ ✦

Edward Wilmot Blyden (1832-1912)

Repatriationist

Although he was not an American, Edward Blyden had a great influence on American Pan-African philosophy. As a scholar he wrote at great length about blacks in Africa and America, and about Christianity and Islam. He also held many different political and diplomatic offices in Liberia, where he tried to put his beliefs into action.

Blyden was born in St. Thomas in the West Indies. When he was twelve, a white pastor undertook his education, encouraging him to become a minister. When he was eighteen he went to America but was unable to find a seminary that would accept a black student. Instead, under the sponsorship of the New York Colonization Society, Blyden went to Liberia to study at the new Alexander High School in Monrovia. Seven years later, he was the principal of the school.

Throughout his adult life, Blyden had two concurrent careers. As a writer and editor he constantly defended his race, championed the achievements of other blacks, attacked slavery, and advocated the repatriation of blacks in Africa. As a teacher, he held many prominent posts, including professor of classics and president of Liberia College. At the same time, Blyden was also a politician and diplomat in Liberia, holding many different offices. He was secretary of state from 1864 to 1866, minister of the interior from 1880 to 1882, minister to Britain from 1877 to 1878 and again in 1892, and minister plenipotentiary to London and Paris in 1905.

Blyden traveled to America eight times. In 1861, he was commissioned by the Liberian government to interest Americans in a Liberian education. He returned again the following year to recruit African-American emigrants to Africa. His last visit in 1895 was in hopes of furthering racial accommodation in the South to prevent American racial problems from traveling to Africa with new emigrants.

Because of his own religious training, Blyden was interested in Islam as a religion for Africans. Between 1901 and 1906, he was director of education in Sierra Leone. He studied both Christianity and Islam extensively and summed up his views in an influential book, *Christianity, Islam and the Negro Race*. After his death in 1912, his funeral was attended by large numbers of both Christians and Moslems.

Crummell was born in New York City on March 3, 1819. He was descended from African royalty, as his paternal grandfather was the son of a West African ruler. Crummell began his schooling at the Mulberry Street School in New York City. In 1831 he began attending high school, but in 1835 transferred to a school founded by abolitionists in Canaan, New Hampshire. The school, however, was destroyed by a mob of angry townspeople, and Crummell began attending the Oneida Institute in Whitesboro, New York, where he stayed for three years. He later studied in Boston and was ordained into the Episcopal Church in 1844. In 1847 he went to England and studied at Queens College, Cambridge, from 1851 to 1853, where he earned an A.B. degree.

Alexander Crummell (1819–1898)

Repatriationist, Minister

Crummell then spent twenty years in Liberia and Sierra Leone, where he served a professor of mental and moral science at the College of Liberia. In 1873 he returned to St. Mary's Mission in Washington, DC, and soon founded St. Luke's Protestant Episcopal Church, where he spent his last twenty-two years. In 1897 he was instrumental in the founding of the American Negro Academy.

Crummell published many collections of his essays and sermons, including *Future of Africa* (1862), *Greatness of Christ* (1882), and *Africa and America* (1892). Crummell died September 10, 1898 at Point Pleasant, New York.

Paul Cuffe
(1759–1817)

Repatriationist,
Entrepreneur

Cuffe was born January 17, 1759 on Cuttyhunk Island near New Bedford, Massachusetts. He was the son of Cuffe Slocum, a freed slave, and Ruth Moses, a Wampanoag Indian.

By the time Cuffe was sixteen he was earning a living as a sailor on a whaling vessel. After making numerous voyages he was captured by the British but later released. He studied arithmetic and navigation but soon returned to the sea. In 1795 he had his own ship, *Ranger,* and in eleven years he had become a landholder and owner of numerous other sailing vessels.

Besides being a merchant seaman Cuffe was also a civil-rights activist. He discarded his father's slave surname and took his father's Christian first name in its place. He filed suffrage complaints in the Massachusetts court and, although unsuccessful, his court actions laid the groundwork for later civil-rights legislation.

Cuffe was also a believer in free blacks voluntarily returning to Africa. In 1811 aboard his ship *Traveller* he sailed to Sierra Leone where he founded the Friendly Society, which helped blacks return to Africa. In 1815 he sailed with thirty-eight colonists for Africa. It was to be his last voyage, however, for he died September 9, 1817.

Martin Robins
Delany
(1812–1885)

Repatriationist

Born in Charles Town, West Virginia, editor, author, physician, abolitionist, and black nationalist Martin Delany received his first education from a book peddler who also served as an itinerant teacher. Since blacks in the South were forbidden to learn to read, when others found out he could read, the family was forced to flee north to Pennsylvania so that their children could continue to study. At the age of nineteen Delany left home to seek further education. He studied with a young divinity student and a white doctor for a time.

As an adult, he became involved in anti-slavery reform and the literacy movement. He began to publish *The Mystery*, a weekly newspaper devoted to news of the anti-slavery movement. When it folded after only a year of publication, Delany became co-editor of the *North Star*, a newspaper started by Frederick Douglass.

In 1848 Delany quit the *North Star* to pursue his medical studies. After being rejected on account of his race from several prominent Pennsylvania medical schools, he was able to attend the Harvard Medical School for a year before he was expelled from there because of his race. While he did not receive his degree, he did learn enough to practice medicine the rest of his life. In the 1850s, he became something of a local legend when he saved many lives during a fierce cholera epidemic in Pittsburgh.

The years following medical school were a grave disappointment to Delany, for blacks in America continued to be treated inhumanely no matter how hard he worked against slavery. He became an ardent black nationalist and recommended emigration to establish an independent colony for African Americans in South America or Africa. He wrote prolifically on the subject, held several national conventions, and set out on an exploratory expedition to Africa.

After the Emancipation Proclamation of 1863, Delany met with President Abraham Lincoln to discuss the establishment of black regiments in the army. Lincoln commissioned him as the first black major in the United States Army.

After the Civil War, Delany continued to work with reconstructionists trying to get fair treatment for newly freed slaves, still advocating emigration. He continued to pursue his scholarship, and in 1879 published his *Principal of Ethnology: The Origin of Races and Color*, in which he discussed the role of black people in the world's civilization. He died in 1885, before he was able to actually move to Africa himself.

Louis Farrakhan (1933–)

Nation of Islam National Minister

Born in New York City, Louis Farrakhan (then known as Louis Eugene Walcott) was an outstanding student at Boston English High School and then attended Winston-Salem Teacher's College. Farrakhan was an excellent musician; he played the violin and was a calypso singer. It was as a singer that he earned his livelihood prior to converting to Elijah Muhammad's Nation of Islam in the 1950s. He quickly worked his way up to a leadership position, becoming the minister of the Boston mosque. He loudly denounced Malcolm X after the latter split with Elijah Muhammad in 1963. He soon assumed leadership of the Harlem mosque, which Malcolm had previously led. After Elijah Muhammad's death in 1975, he briefly supported Muhammad's son and designated successor, Warith Muhammad, as leader of the Nation of Islam. Shortly after Warith Muhammad began accepting whites as members within the Nation of

Louis Farrakhan became a leader in the Nation of Islam during the 1950s and 1960s, replacing Malcolm X as minister of the Harlem mosque, then in the 1970s established a rival organization with about 10,000 members.

Islam, now renamed the World Community of Al-Islam in the West, Farrakhan split from him and established a rival organization with about 10,000 members.

Farrakhan's vigorous support for Jesse Jackson's presidential candidacy in 1984 quickly became an issue after Farrakhan made several controversial statements, most notably calling Judaism a "gutter religion." Overshadowed in the controversy was the involvement of Nation of Islam leaders in American electoral politics for the first time. Previously, Black Muslims had generally followed Elijah Muhammad's counsel not to vote or to take part in political campaigns.

James Forten
(1766–1842)
Entrepreneur

Forten was born of free African-American parents in Philadelphia in 1766. He studied at a Quaker school but quit at the age of fifteen to serve as a powder boy aboard the privateer *Royal Louis* during the American Revolution. He was captured by the British and held prisoner for seven months. He eventually spent a year in England where he was introduced to abolitionist philosophy.

Upon returning to America he was apprenticed to a sailmaker, and by 1786 he was foreman and in 1798 became owner of the company. The business prospered and in 1832 employed forty white and African-American workers.

By the 1830s Forten had become active in the abolitionist movement and was a strong opponent of African colonization. He became a noted pamphleteer, a nineteenth-century form of social activism, and was an early fund-raiser for William Lloyd Garrison's *The Liberator*.

Forten was president and founder of the American Moral Reform Society and was active in the American Anti-Slavery Society. He was a vigorous opponent of northern implementation of the 1793 Fugitive Slave Act. Forten died in Philadelphia in 1842.

Marcus Garvey (1887–1940)

Pan-African Theorist

Born in St. Ann's Bay, Jamaica, Garvey was the youngest of eleven children. Garvey moved to Kingston at the age of fourteen, found work in a printshop, and became acquainted with the abysmal living conditions of the laboring class. He quickly involved himself in social reform, participating in the first Printers' Union strike in Jamaica in 1907 and in setting up the newspaper *The Watchman*. Leaving the island to earn money to finance his projects, he visited Central and South America, amassing evidence that black people everywhere were victims of discrimination.

Garvey returned to Jamaica in 1911 and began to lay the groundwork of the Universal Negro Improvement Association, to which he devoted his life. Undaunted by lack of enthusiasm for his plans, Garvey left for England in 1912 in search of additional financial backing. While there, he met a Sudanese-Egyptian journalist, Duse Mohammed Ali. While working for Ali's publication *African Times and Oriental Review*, Garvey began to study the history of Africa—particularly the exploitation of black peoples by colonial powers—and he read Booker T. Washington's *Up From Slavery*, which advocated black self-help.

In 1914 Garvey organized the Universal Negro Improvement Association and its coordinating body, the African Communities League. In 1920 the

Marcus Garvey's Universal Negro Improvement Association organized perhaps the largest mass movement ever to occur among black Americans by the early twentieth century.

organization held its first convention in New York. The convention opened with a parade down Harlem's Lenox Avenue. That evening, before a crowd of 25,000, Garvey outlined his plan to built an African nation-state. In New York City his ideas attracted popular support, and thousands enrolled in the UNIA. He began publishing the newspaper *The Negro World* and toured the United States preaching black nationalism. In a matter of months, he had founded over thirty UNIA branches and launched some ambitious business ventures, notably the Black Star Shipping Line.

In the years following the organization's first convention, the UNIA began to decline in popularity. With the Black Star Line in serious financial difficulties, Garvey promoted two new business organizations—the African Communities League and the Negro Factories Corporation. He also tried to salvage his colonization scheme by sending a delegation to appeal to the League of Nations for transfer to the UNIA of the African colonies taken from Germany during World War I.

Financial betrayal by trusted aides and a host of legal entanglements (based on charges that he had used the U.S. mails to defraud prospective investors) eventually led to Garvey's imprisonment in Atlanta Federal Penitentiary for a five-year term. In 1927 his half-served sentence was commuted, and he was deported to Jamaica by order of President Calvin Coolidge.

Garvey then turned his energies to Jamaican politics, campaigning on a platform of self-government, minimum wage laws, and land and judicial reform. He was soundly defeated at the polls, however, because most of his followers did not have the necessary voting qualifications.

In 1935 Garvey left for England where, in near obscurity, he died five years later in a cottage in West Kensington.

Malcolm X (El-Hajj Malik El-Shabazz) (1925-1965)

Black Nationalist

Born Malcolm Little in Omaha, Nebraska on May 19, 1925, Malcolm was the son of a Baptist minister who was an avid supporter of Marcus Garvey's United Negro Improvement Association. While living in Omaha, the family was often harassed—at one point the family's house was set afire. In 1929 the family moved to Lansing, Michigan. While in Michigan, Malcolm's father was killed—his body severed in two by a streetcar and his

Malcolm X, one of the most fiery and controversial blacks of the twentieth century, is shown here being interviewed during a Black Muslim demonstration in 1963.

head smashed. In his autobiography, written with Alex Haley, Malcolm asserted that his father may have been killed by members of the Ku Klux Klan. His mother, stricken by the death of her husband and the demands of providing for the family, was committed to a mental institution.

Leaving school after the eighth grade, Malcolm made his way to New York, working for a time as a waiter at Smalls Paradise in Harlem. Malcolm began selling and using drugs, turned to burglary, and, in 1946, was sentenced to a ten-year prison term on burglary charges.

While in prison Malcolm became acquainted with the Black Muslim sect, headed by Elijah Muhammad, and was quickly converted. Following his parole in 1952, he soon became an outspoken defender of Muslim doctrines, accepting the basic argument that evil was an inherent characteristic of the "white man's Christian world."

Unlike Muhammad, Malcolm sought publicity, making provocative and inflammatory statements to predominantly white civic groups and college campus audiences. Branding white people "devils," he spoke bitterly of a philosophy of vengeance and "an eye for an eye." When, in 1963, he characterized the Kennedy assassination as a case of "chickens coming home to roost," he was suspended from the Black Muslim movement by Elijah Muhammad.

Disillusioned with Elijah Muhammad's teachings, Malcolm formed his own organizations, the Organization of Afro-American Unity and the Muslim Mosque Inc. In 1964 he made a pilgrimage to Islam's holy city, Mecca, and adopted the name El-Hajj Malik El-Shabazz. He also adopted views that were not popular with other black nationalists, including the idea that not all whites were evil and that blacks could make gains by working through established channels.

As a result of his new views, Malcolm became the victim of death threats. On February 14, 1965, his home was firebombed; his wife and children escaped unharmed. A week later, Malcolm was shot and killed at the Audubon Ballroom in Harlem, while preparing to speak. Three of the men arrested were later identified as members of the Nation of Islam.

Malcolm X had a profound influence on both blacks and whites. Many blacks responded to a feeling that he was a man of the people, experienced in the ways of the street rather than the pulpit or the college campus, which traditionally had provided the preponderance of black leaders. Many young whites responded to Malcolm's blunt, colorful language and unwillingness to retreat in the face of hostility.

The memory and image of Malcolm X has changed as much after his death as his own philosophies changed during his life. At first thought to be a violent fanatic, he is now understood as an advocate of self-help, self-defense, and education; as a philosopher and pedagogue, he succeeded in integrating history, religion, and mythology to establish a framework for his ultimate belief in world brotherhood and human justice. Faith, in his view, was a prelude to action; ideas were feckless without policy. At least three books published since his death effectively present his most enduring thoughts. In 1992 a monumental film by Spike Lee based on Malcolm's autobiography renewed interest and understanding in the meaning of the life and death of Malcolm X.

Elijah Muhammad was born Elijah Poole in Sandersville, Georgia. His father, a Baptist preacher, had been a slave.

As a boy, Elijah worked at various jobs involving manual labor. At the age of twenty-six, he moved with his wife and two children (he was to have eight children in all) to Detroit. There in 1930, Poole met Fard Muhammad, also known as W.D. Fard, who had founded the Lost-Found Nation of Islam. Poole soon became Fard's chief assistant and in 1932 went to Chicago, where he established the Nation of Islam's Temple, Number Two, which soon became the largest. In 1934, he returned to Detroit. When Fard disappeared in that year, political and theological rivals accused Poole of foul play. He returned to Chicago where he organized his own movement, in which Fard was deified as Allah, and Elijah (Poole) Muhammad became known as Allah's Messenger. This movement soon became known as the Black Muslims.

During World War II, Elijah Muhammad expressed support for Japan, on the basis of its being a nonwhite country, and was jailed for sedition. The time Muhammad served in prison was probably significant in his later, successful attempts to convert large numbers of black prison inmates, including Malcolm X, to the Nation of Islam. During the 1950s and 1960s, the Nation grew under Muhammad's leadership. Internal differences between Muhammad and Malcolm X, followed by the break between the two men and Malcolm's assassination, for which three Black Muslim gunmen were convicted, provided a great deal of unfavorable media coverage, but this did not slow the growth of the movement. In the late 1960s and early 1970s, Elijah Muhammad moderated the Nation's criticism of whites without compromising its message of black integrity. When Muhammad died in 1975, the Nation was an important religious, political, and economic force among America's blacks, especially in the country's major cities.

Elijah Muhammad (1897–1975)

Nation of Islam Spiritual Leader

Elijah Muhammad, a follower of Nation of Islam founder Fard Muhammad, eventually became leader of the Nation and was instrumental in its dramatic growth during the mid-twentieth century.

Elijah Muhammad was not original in his rejection of Christianity as the religion of the oppressor. Noble Drew Ali and the Black Jews had arrived at this conclusion well before him. But Muhammad was the most successful salesman for this brand of African-American religion. Thus he was able to build the first strong, black religious group in the United States that appealed primarily to the unemployed and underemployed city dweller, and ultimately to some in the black middle class. In addition, his message on the virtues of being black was explicit and uncompromising, and he sought with at least a little success to bolster the economic independence of African Americans by establishing schools and businesses under the auspices of the Nation of Islam.

Henry McNeal
Turner
(1834–1915)

Repatriationist, Minister

Henry McNeal Turner was born near Abbeville, South Carolina, of free parents. He was ordained a minister in the African Methodist Episcopal Church in 1853 and bishop in 1880. In 1863 Turner became the first African-American Army chaplain. He was also president of Morris Brown College for twelve years.

Turner was a leading advocate of repatriation. In 1876 he was elected vice president of the American Colonization Society. He made several trips to Africa and lectured throughout world.

By Wilson
Jeremiah Moses

Turner was convinced that blacks had no future in America. Instead, he felt that God had brought blacks to the New World as a means of spreading Christianity and preparing them to redeem Africa. Turner edited and published several papers, including *Voice of Missions* and *Voice of the People*, in which he advocated black colonization of Africa.

National Organizations

In a dispute between the National Association for the Advancement of Colored People and the state of Alabama, Justice Harlan of the United States Supreme Court pointed out the significance of association membership, claiming that it is through associations that individuals have sought "to make more effective the expression of their own views." Associations are among the largest and most influential forces in the United States and have played an important part in the economic, social, and educational development of African Americans; organizations have been crucial in developing and disseminating information, ensuring representation for private interests, and promoting social and policy objectives.

A BRIEF HISTORY ♦

**Early Black
Organizations**

Due to restrictive ordinances and limited tolerance by whites, prior to the eighteenth century only the most informal and limited assembling of blacks was permitted. Most often meeting as religious assemblies, African Americans were forced to gather secretly, in small numbers. Thus the very first black organizations to exist in the United States cannot definitively be identified.

The Free African Society, organized in Philadelphia in 1787, has been generally accepted as the first African-American organization in the United States. Founded by Methodist ministers Richard Allen and Absalom Jones, the Free African Society served as an important source of political consciousness and welfare for blacks throughout the country, combining economic and medical aid for poor blacks with support of abolition and sub-rosa communication with blacks in the South.

The first African-American organization, called the Free African Society, was founded by Richard Allen and Absalom Jones in 1787 to offer economic and medical aid for poor blacks, and to support abolition.

The abolitionist movement of the nineteenth century produced numerous organizations concerned with issues of importance to African Americans, including the American Colonization Society (founded in 1816), the New England Anti-Slavery Society (founded in 1832), and the American Anti-Slavery Society (founded in 1833). Although most of these organizations were dominated by whites, black leaders, including Paul Cuffe and Frederick Douglass, played an active role in the movement and in anti-slavery organizations of the time.

During the late nineteenth and early twentieth centuries a great many black organizations came into existence; the thrust of most of these groups was toward education, betterment, and religious training. In 1895 the National Medical Association was founded to further the interests of black physicians, pharmacists, and nurses; Mary McLeod Bethune organized the National Association of Colored Women in 1896; and in 1900 the National Negro Business League was formed to promote commercial development.

**The Niagara
Movement**

The Niagara Movement of 1905 marked a turning point in African-American history. This new organization, founded by a group of black intellectuals and headed by W.E.B. DuBois, a professor at Atlanta University, met

W.E.B. DuBois led the Niagara Movement, which preceded the National Association for the Advancement of Colored People.

July 11–13, 1905 in Buffalo, New York. The organization represented a formal renunciation of Booker T. Washington's program of manual and industrial training for the black as a means of gaining economic security, and conciliation as a means of gaining social equality.

The Niagara Movement, however, suffered from weak finances and a policy that restricted membership to black intellectuals. In 1909 the Niagara Movement was succeeded by a new organization—one that would later become the National Association for the Advancement of Colored People.

National Association for the Advancement of Colored People

The new organization was largely the brainchild of three people: William English Walling, a white Southerner who feared that racists would soon carry "the race war to the North"; Mary White Ovington, a wealthy young white woman who had attended the 1905 meeting of the Niagara group as a reporter for the *New York Evening Post* and had experience with conditions in the black ghettos of New York City; and Dr. Henry Moskowitz, a New York social worker. The trio proposed that a conference be called "for the discussion of present evils, the voicing of protests, and the renewal of the struggle for civil and political liberty." The three-day conference, held May 30 through June 1, was followed by four meetings, the results of which were an increase in membership and the selection of an official name—the National Negro Committee. In 1910 the organization adopted its present name and was incorporated in New York state; by 1914 the association had established some fifty branches throughout the country.

Over the years, the organization has attempted to better the condition of African Americans through litigation, legislation, and education; *Crisis* magazine, edited by W.E.B. DuBois, became its chief vehicle for the dissemination of information. Perhaps its most significant victory was won in 1954 when the historic *Brown v. Board of Education of Topeka* case threw out the "separate but equal" doctrine established by the Supreme Court in *Plessy v. Ferguson* in 1896, and eliminated segregation in public education.

NAACP Legal Defense and Educational Fund

Established in 1939 by the National Association for the Advancement of Colored People, the NAACP Legal Defense and Educational Fund maintained its own board, program, staff, office, and budget for some twenty years. It has served in the forefront of legal assaults against discrimination and segregation and has an outstanding record of victories. In addition to its litigation, the Legal Defense Fund provides scholarships and training for young lawyers, advises lawyers on legal trends and decisions, and monitors federal programs.

Originally for tax purposes, the NAACP Legal Defense Fund had been maintained as a separate arm of the NAACP, until it officially was divorced from its parent organization in 1959. Following the separation of the organizations, a dispute over identity and the use of the parent organization's name erupted. The National Association for the Advancement of Colored People sued the NAACP Legal Defense Fund for name infringement. After several months of legal wrangling, however, a federal court ruled that the LDF could keep NAACP in its name, since the NAACP was its parent organization.

During the early part of the twentieth century several organizations concerned with the plight of urban blacks emerged. In 1906, at the urging of William H. Baldwin, president of the Long Island Railroad, a group of blacks and whites met to study the employment needs of African Americans. This group, known as the Committee for the Improvement of the Industrial Conditions Among Negroes in New York, studied the racial aspects of the labor market (particularly the attitudes and policies of employers and unions) and sought to find openings for qualified African Americans.

At the same time, the League for the Protection of Colored Women was established to provide similar services for black women in New York and Philadelphia arriving from various parts of the South. These women, who often had no friends or relatives in the North, often fell prey to unscrupulous employment agencies that led them into low-wage jobs.

A third organization, the Committee on Urban Conditions Among Negroes, appeared in 1910. It was organized by Ruth Standish Baldwin, widow of the former Long Island Railroad president, and Dr. George Edmond Haynes, one of only three trained black social workers in the country and the first black person to receive a doctorate from Columbia University. Haynes was named as the first executive secretary of the new agency. A year later the organization merged with the Committee for the Improvement of Industrial Conditions Among Negroes in New York and the National League for the Protection of Colored Women to form the National League on Urban Conditions Among Negroes. That name was later shortened to the now-familiar National Urban League.

Urban Problems

According to a theory called the Black Organizational Autonomy (BOA) Model, viable black communities possess community-based organizations with five basic components: economic autonomy; internally developed and controlled data sources; programs to develop and promote black female leadership; programs that emphasize black history and culture; and socially inclusive leadership.

Black women looking for work in northern cities often fell prey to unscrupulous employment practices and low-wage jobs.

From the outset, the organization focused on the social and economic needs of blacks, seeking training, improved housing, health, recreation, and job assistance for blacks. The organizational model that the League had established in New York City attracted attention, and soon affiliates were formed in various cities across the country.

A major goal of the National Urban League and its affiliates was to broaden economic opportunities for African Americans. It was not until the 1960s when Whitney M. Young, Jr. became its new leader that the League began to emerge as a force in the civil-rights struggle.

Leadership Conference on Civil Rights

The Leadership Conference on Civil Rights was organized in 1950 by A. Philip Randolph, Roy Wilkins, and Arnold Aronson to implement the historic report of President Harry S Truman's Committee on Civil Rights, "To Secure These Rights." Beginning with only thirty organizations, the conference has grown in numbers, scope, and effectiveness, and has been responsible for coordinating the campaigns that have resulted in the passage of the civil-rights legislation of the 1950s and 1960s, including the Civil Rights Acts of 1957, 1960, and 1964, the Voting Rights Act of 1965, and the Fair Housing Act of 1968.

The Leadership Conference on Civil Rights currently consists of approximately 157 national organizations representing minorities, women, major religious groups, the handicapped, the aged, labor, and minority businesses and professions. These organizations speak for a substantial portion of the population and together constitute one of the most broad-based coalitions in the nation.

Southern Christian Leadership Conference

Following the arrest of Rosa Parks, who had refused to give up her seat on a public bus, the Reverends Martin Luther King, Jr. and Ralph Abernathy organized the Montgomery Improvement Association in 1955 to coordinate a citywide bus boycott. The success of the boycott led to the creation of a new organization.

This new organization, consisting mainly of black ministers, met at the Ebenezer Baptist Church in January 1957 and elected King as its first president. Initially called the Southern Negro Leaders Conference, and later the Southern Leadership Conference, the Southern Christian Leader-

A. Philip Randolph, founder of the Brotherhood of Sleeping Car Porters, helped organize the Leadership Conference on Civil Rights in 1950.

ship Conference grew to become one of the most influential and effective of all the civil-rights organizations.

Although public and private associations of all kinds have traditionally flourished in this country, it has not always been an easy road for organizations for blacks and other minorities. The freedom of association—the freedom to assemble and immunity from state scrutiny—like the First

Organizations and the Court

Amendment freedoms of speech and press, has from time to time been questioned and challenged.

Since the founding of the NAACP and similar organizations, state and local governments have attempted to prevent the operation of such groups. During the late 1950s the state of Alabama set out to ban the NAACP from conducting activities with the state, claiming that the association had failed to comply with statutes governing corporations operating within the state. The dispute, *NAACP v. Alabama*, was finally resolved by the United States Supreme Court in 1958 in favor of the association. However, the association has met with other interferences; some of the most notable disputes include *Bates v. Little Rock* (1960), *Louisiana ex rel. Gremillion v. NAACP* (1961), and *Gibson v. Florida Legislative Investigating Committee* (1963).

Congress of Racial Equality

The Congress of Racial Equality (CORE), an interracial organization designed to confront racism and discrimination, was founded in 1942 by James Farmer as the result of a campaign protesting discrimination at a Chicago restaurant. From Chicago, the organization spread to other cities and other causes, organizing sit-ins and Freedom Rides throughout the South.

By the mid-1960s CORE had changed directions, and Farmer turned leadership of the organization over to Floyd McKissick, a North Carolina lawyer. With McKissick as national director, the organization moved toward an all-black membership and staff. (In 1967 CORE, at its convention, eliminated the word "multiracial" from its constitution). McKissick left the organization in 1968 and was replaced by the present national director, Roy Innis, former chairman of the Harlem chapter.

Student Non-Violent Coordinating Committee

In 1960 a group of black college students founded the Student Non-Violent Coordinating Committee (SNCC) to coordinate the activities of students engaged in direct action protest. SNCC achieved enormous results in the desegregation of public facilities and earned respect from the country for its determination to act peacefully, no matter how violent or demeaning the provocation.

By 1964, however, the organization's leader, Stokely Carmichael, had become convinced that the American system could not be turned around

Floyd McKissick speaks at a demonstration, 1967.

without the threat of wholesale violence. In 1967 Carmichael left the organization to join the more militant Black Panther Party. H. Rap Brown, the former SNCC minister of justice, took over leadership, renaming the organization the Student National Coordinating Committee and promoting violent retaliation when situations so demanded. The organization gradually declined in membership and is now essentially defunct.

Stokely Carmichael, head of the Student Non-Violent Coordinating Committee, at a rally at the University of California in 1966.

Black Panther Party

From its founding by Huey P. Newton and Bobby Seale in 1966, the Black Panther Party departed from the platform and tactics of other civil-rights organizations. It rejected the institutional structure that, in its view, made American society corrupt; it rejected established channels of authority that oppressed the black community; and it rejected middle-class values, which it felt contributed to indifference toward—and contempt for—the disinherited black urban youth.

The party imposed strict discipline on its members, denouncing the use of intoxicants, drugs, and artificial stimulants "while doing party work." The intellectual fare of every party member was the ten-point program (supplemented by daily reading of political developments), which every member was obliged to know and understand, presumably even to commit to memory.

By 1970, however, most of the organization's leadership was either jailed, in exile, or dead—Newton was jailed in 1968 on manslaughter changes; Seale had been jailed on charges stemming from the 1968 Chicago convention riot; minister of information Eldridge Cleaver fled in 1969 to Algeria to avoid a prison sentence; in 1970 Mark Clark and Fred Hampton were killed during a police raid.

Community Support

In 1967 the National Urban Coalition was founded to improve the quality of life for the disadvantaged in urban areas through the combined efforts of business, labor, government, and community leaders. Another organization, the National Black United Fund, which provides financial and

Bobby Seale (left) and Huey Newton, founders of the Black Panther Party.

technical support to projects serving the critical needs of black communities nationwide, was founded in 1972.

The Reverend Jesse Jackson, in 1971, organized Operation PUSH (People United to Save Humanity). The organization has pursued its economic objectives through its Operation Breadbasket program. It also has worked to motivate young people through its PUSH-EXCEL program, which is designed to instill pride and build confidence in young people. Jackson left Operation PUSH to organize another group, the National Rainbow Coalition, Inc., in 1984.

During the nineteenth and early part of the twentieth century, a number of individuals and organizations arose to unite Africans throughout the world. Most notable was Marcus Garvey, black nationalist and advocate of repatriation of blacks to Africa, who founded the Universal Negro Improvement Association in 1914. Garvey's organization, whose goals were to instill pride, gain economic and political power for blacks in the United

Responses to Africa and the Caribbean

TransAfrica founder Randall Robinson meets with African National Congress President Nelson Mandela, 1991.

States, establish an independent black colony in Africa, and promote unity between Africans throughout the world, attracted millions world-wide. On February 19, 1918, under the leadership of W.E.B. DuBois, the first Pan-African Congress was held in Paris. The meeting was attended by blacks from around the world and focused on the problems facing Africans worldwide.

More recently, new organizations have formed to address the concerns of Africans around the world. Founded in 1977 by Randall Robinson,

TransAfrica has worked to influence American foreign policy regarding political and human rights in Africa and the Caribbean by informing the public of violations of social, political, and civil rights. Responding to the continued policy of apartheid in South Africa, TransAfrica has supported sanctions against South Africa and has organized demonstrations in front of the South African embassy in Washington, DC. During one such demonstration, Robinson and numerous others were arrested. Other organizations have also taken a stand on policies affecting Africans around the world. In 1986 leaders representing major black organizations united to press for passage of the more stringent legislation regarding sanctions against South Africa.

♦ ♦ ♦ ♦ ♦ ♦ ♦ ♦ ♦ ♦ ♦ ♦ ♦ ♦ ♦ ♦ ♦ ♦ **ORGANIZATION LEADERS**

H. Rap Brown (Jamil Abdullah Al-Amin) (1943–)

Student National Coordinating Committee Chairman

In 1967 H. Rap Brown took over leadership of the Student Non-Violent Coordinating Committee, renaming the organization the Student National Coordinating Committee. Since the late 1960s the organization has gradually declined in membership and is now essentially defunct.

In 1968 Brown was charged with inciting a riot in Cambridge, Maryland and was convicted in New Orleans on a federal charge of carrying a gun between states. In 1969 Brown published the book *Die Nigger Die*. Brown disappeared in 1970, after being slated for trial in Maryland, and in 1972 he was shot, arrested, and eventually convicted for a bar holdup in New York City.

While in prison, Brown converted to the Islamic faith and took the name Jamil Abdullah Al-Amin. On his release, he founded a community grocery store in Atlanta. He is currently leader of the Community Mosque in Atlanta.

Benjamin Franklin Chavis, Jr. (1948–)

NAACP Executive Director

Benjamin Chavis was born January 22, 1948 in Oxford, North Carolina. He received a B.A. from the University of North Carolina in 1969. Chavis went on to earn an M.A. from the Duke University Divinity School and a Ph.D. in theology from Howard University in Washington, DC.

Benjamin Chavis succeeded Benjamin Hooks as executive director of the National Association for the Advancement of Colored People.

He came to national attention in 1971, when as a civil-rights organizer for the United Church of Christ he was indicted along with nine other people for the fire-bombing of a grocery store in Wilmington, Delaware during a period of racial unrest. In the controversial trial that followed, all of the "Wilmington 10" were found guilty. Chavis was sentenced to a prison term of twenty-nine to thirty-four years. Chavis was granted parole and in 1980 his conviction was reversed amidst conflicting testimony by various witnesses.

Prior to becoming active in the civil-rights movement, Chavis taught chemistry at the high school level. He also worked as an AFSCME labor organizer (1969), a civil-rights organizer for the Southern Christian Leadership Council (1967–1969), and a minister for the United Church of Christ as well as the director of their Commission for Racial Justice in Washington, DC (1972). In 1985 he was appointed executive director of the Commission for Racial Justice. Chavis has also served as co-chairman of the National Alliance Against Racism and Political Repression (1977) and as co-chairman of the Organizing Committee for Economic and Social Justice.

In 1977 Chavis wrote *Let My People Go: Psalms From Prison*. That year he also received the George Collins Service Award from the Congressional Black Caucus, the William L. Patterson award given by the Patterson Foundation, and the Shalom award presented by the Eden Theological Seminary. Chavis has since become active in the South African civil-rights struggle and continues his position with the United Church of Christ.

On April 9, 1993, the NAACP board elected Chavis to succeed retiring executive director Benjamin Hooks.

Born in Los Angeles, California, Ramona Hoage Edelin received her B.A. (magna cum laude) from Fisk University, her M.A. from the University of East Anglia, in Norwich, England, and her Ph.D. from Boston University. She has been a lecturer at the University of Maryland and a visiting professor at Brandeis University; she has also served as chair of Afro-American studies at Emerson College.

Ramona Hoage Edelin (1945–)

National Urban Coalition President and Chief Executive

In 1977 Edelin joined the National Urban Coalition as an executive assistant to the president. The National Urban Coalition, an organization to improve the quality of life for the disadvantaged in urban areas, has been active in advocating initiatives designed to encourage and promote youth leadership. Between 1979 and 1982 she moved from director of operations to vice president of operations, then to senior vice president of program and policy, during which time she directed programs in housing, health, education, and advocacy. In 1982 Edelin became the organization's chief executive.

Marian Wright Edelman (1939–)

Children's Defense Fund President

A native of Bennettsville, South Carolina, Marian Wright Edelman received her undergraduate degree from Spelman College and her law degree from Yale. In 1963 she joined the NAACP Legal Defense and Education Fund as staff attorney. A year later she organized the Jackson, Mississippi branch of the NAACP Legal Defense and Educational Fund, serving as its director until 1968. That year she founded the Washington Research Project of the Southern Center for Public Policy, which later developed into the Children's Defense Fund.

Wright has served as director of the Harvard University Center for Law and Education, chairman of the Spelman College board of trustees, a member of the Yale University Corporation and the National Commission on Children, and on the boards of the Center on Budget and Policy Priorities, the US Committee for UNICEF, and the Joint Center for Political and Economic Studies.

Edelman's Children's Defense Fund is devoted to teen pregnancy prevention, an important consideration for blacks since African-American girls in their mid-teens are almost three times more likely than white girls to give birth, almost five times more likely to have a second baby, and seven times more likely to have a third baby.

As Children's Defense Fund president, Edelman has become the nation's most effective lobbyist on behalf of children. Even while social spending was being cut, she managed to score some victories. In 1986, nine federal programs known as "the Children's Initiative" received a $500 million increase in their $36 billion budget for families and children's health care, nutrition, and early education.

The most visible focus of CDF is its teen pregnancy prevention program. Through Edelman's efforts, Medicaid coverage for expectant mothers and children was boosted in 1984. In 1985, Edelman began holding an annual Pregnancy Prevention Conference, bringing thousands of religious leaders, social and health workers, and community organizations to Washington to discuss ways of dealing with the problem.

In her 1987 book, *Families in Peril: An Agenda for Social Change*, Edelman wrote, "As adults, we are responsible for meeting the needs of children. It is our moral obligation. We brought about their births and their lives, and they cannot fend for themselves." Her other books include *Children Out of School in America*, *School Suspensions: Are They Helping Children?*, *Portrait of Inequality: Black and White Children in America*, *Families in Peril: An Agenda for Social Change*, and *The Measure of Our Success: A Letter to My Children*.

James Farmer, founder and director of CORE, inspects picket lines in Bogalusa, Louisiana, in 1965.

Born in Marshall, Texas on January 12, 1920, Farmer attended public schools throughout the South. He earned his B.S. in chemistry from Wiley College in 1938 and his B.D. from Howard University in 1941. Active in the Christian Youth Movement, and once vice-chairman of the National Council of Methodist Youth and the Christian Youth Council of America, Farmer refused ordination when confronted with the realization that he would have to practice in a segregated ministry.

In 1941 Farmer accepted a post as race relations secretary for the Fellowship of Reconciliation. The following year he and a group of University of Chicago students organized the Congress of Racial Equality (CORE), the first protest organization in the United States to utilize the techniques of nonviolence and passive resistance advocated by the Indian nationalist Mohandas Karamchand Gandhi.

In June 1943 CORE staged the first successful sit-in demonstration at a restaurant in the Chicago Loop. The organization soon supplemented this maneuver with what came to be known as the standing-line, which in-

James Farmer (1920–)

Congress of Racial Equality Founder and Former National Director

volved the persistent waiting in line by CORE members at places of public accommodation where blacks had been denied admission.

In 1961 CORE introduced the Freedom Ride into the vocabulary and methodology of civil-rights protest, dispatching bus riders throughout the South to test the desegregation of terminal facilities. Attacked in Alabama and later arrested in Mississippi, the Freedom Riders eventually succeeded in securing the court-ordered desegregation of bus terminals, with the United States Supreme Court decision of 1960 that outlawed segregated interstate transportation.

Farmer left the organization in 1966. In 1969, President Richard Nixon appointed Farmer to the post of assistant secretary of Health, Education and Welfare. The appointment created a furor in some black circles, where it was felt that it was inappropriate for a former civil-rights leader to serve in such an administration; in other circles, the appointment was praised by those who thought it necessary for African Americans to be represented in all areas. However, Farmer found that there was little of substance in the position and resigned.

Farmer began to give lectures, and for a while headed a think tank at Howard University. In 1976 he broke all ties with CORE, criticizing its leader, Roy Innis, for such things as attempting to recruit black Vietnam veterans as mercenaries in Angola's civil war. Disturbed by the course the organization had taken, Farmer and a score of former CORE members attempted to create a new racially mixed civil-rights organization in 1980. Farmer, along with Floyd McKissick, attempted to meet with Innis to reach an agreement on the future of the organization, but nothing developed.

Farmer has written several books, including *Freedom When?* and *Lay Bare the Heart*.

Prince Hall
(1735?–1807)

Founder of Black Freemasonry in the United States

Prince Hall is believed to have been born in Bridge Town, Barbados and to have migrated to the United States in 1765; other records claim that during the late 1740s he had been a slave to William Hall of Boston, Massachusetts, and freed by Hall on April 9, 1770.

In March 1775 Hall and fifteen other blacks were initiated into a lodge of British army Freemasons stationed in Boston. The group of black masons was issued a permit to meet at a lodge on March 17, 1775, and on July 3, 1775, they organized the African Lodge No. 1, with Hall as master of the lodge. The lodge received official recognition from England as a regular Lodge of Free and Accepted Masons in 1784 and was designated the African Lodge 459.

Hall, in addition to leading the organization of Black Freemasonry, was active as an abolitionist. In January 1777, he was the prime force behind a black petition sent to the Massachusetts state legislature requesting the abolition of slavery in the state. Another important petition, drawn up under his leadership in 1788, called for an end to the kidnapping and sale of free blacks into slavery. He also actively lobbied for the organization of schools for black children in Boston. Prince Hall died on December 4, 1807 in Boston.

A native of Richmond, Virginia, Dorothy Height holds a master's degree from New York University and has studied at the New York School of Social Work. In the fall of 1952, she served as a visiting professor at the Delhi School of Social Work in New Delhi, India. Six years later, she was appointed to the Social Welfare Board of New York by Governor Averell Harriman, and was reappointed by Governor Nelson Rockefeller in 1961. Since 1957 she has been president of the National Council of Negro Women, an organization founded by Mary McLeod Bethune in 1935.

Before becoming the fourth president of the National Council of Negro Women, Height had served on the organization's board of directors. She has also served as associate director for leadership training services for the Young Women's Christian Association, as a member of the Defense Advisory Committee on Women in the Services, as president of Delta Sigma Theta sorority, as vice president of the National Council of Women, and as president of Women in Community Services, Inc.

Dorothy I. Height (1912–)

National Council of Negro Women President

Hooks was born in Memphis, Tennessee and attended LeMoyne College and Howard University. He received his J.D. from DePaul University College of Law in 1948. During World War II he served in the 92nd Infantry Division in Italy.

From 1949 to 1965, and again from 1968 to 1972, Hooks worked as a lawyer in Memphis. In 1966 Hooks became the first black judge to serve

Benjamin L. Hooks (1925–)

NAACP Former Executive Director

Benjamin Hooks gives his final keynote speech as executive director of the NAACP in 1992.

in the Shelby County (Tennessee) criminal court. As an ordained minister, he preached at Middle Baptist Church in Memphis and the Greater New Mount Moriah Baptist Church in Detroit. As a prominent local businessman, he was the co-founder and vice president of the Mutual Federal Savings and Loan Association in Memphis.

On January 10, 1977, Hooks was unanimously elected executive director of the NAACP by its board of directors, succeeding the retiring Roy Wilkins.

Under his progressive leadership, the association took an aggressive posture on United States policy toward African nations. Among his many battles on Capitol Hill, Hooks led the historical prayer vigil in Washington, DC in 1979 against the Mott anti-busing amendment, which was eventually defeated in Congress; led in the fight for passage of the District of Columbia Home Rule bill; and was instrumental in gathering important Senate and House votes on the Humphrey–Hawkins Full Employment Bill.

At the NAACP's national convention in 1986, Hooks was awarded the association's highest honor, the Spingarn Medal. In February 1992 Hooks announced his retirement.

Roy Innis (1934–)

Congress of Racial
Equality National
Chairman

Born June 6, 1934 in St. Croix, Virgin Islands, Roy Emile Alfredo Innis has lived in the United States since the age of twelve. He attended Stuyvesant High School in New York City and majored in chemistry at City College of New York.

In 1963 Innis joined the Congress of Racial Equality (CORE). In 1965 Innis was elected chairman of the Harlem branch and went on to become associate national director three years later. In 1968 Innis became national director of the organization. Innis founded the Harlem Commonwealth Council, an agency designed to promote the development of black-owned businesses and economic institutions in Harlem. He also took a plunge into journalism, serving with William Haddad as co-editor of the *Manhattan Tribune*, a weekly that featured news from Harlem and the upper West Side.

Innis's leadership of CORE has been marked with controversy. Numerous members have left the organization, charging that Innis has run it as a one-man show. CORE was also the target of a three-year investigation by the New York State attorney general's office into allegations that it had misused charitable contributions. (An agreement was reached in 1981 that did not require CORE to admit to any wrongdoing in its handling of funds, but stipulated that Innis would have to contribute $35,000 to the organization over the next three years.) Innis was challenged by a group of former CORE members, headed by James Farmer, the founder and former chairman of organization; the effort was unsuccessful and Innis continued as head of the organization.

Roy Innis, national director of CORE, at a press conference in 1976.

While remaining president of the largely inactive CORE, Innis has sought to build a political base in Brooklyn. He has run for public office twice, most recently as a Republican candidate in the 1986 elections for Brooklyn's twelfth congressional district, but he has lost both times. In 1981 Innis became national chairman of the organization.

Born in Trout, Louisiana on December 16, 1934, John Edward Jacob grew up in Houston, Texas. He received his bachelor's and master's degrees in social work from Howard University. During the early 1960s Jacob worked for the Baltimore Department of Public Welfare, first as a caseworker, then later as a child welfare supervisor. In 1965 he joined the Washington Urban League as director of education and youth incentives.

During his early career with the organization he held a number of increasingly important positions, serving as director of its Northern Virginia Branch in 1966, associate director for administration of the affiliate in 1967, and acting executive director from 1968 until 1970. He also spent several months as director of community organization training in the Eastern Regional Office of the NUL.

Jacob left the Washington Urban League in 1970 to serve as executive director for the San Diego Urban League, a post he held until his return to the Washington Urban League in 1975. In 1982 Jacob replaced Vernon E. Jordan, Jr. as the organization's president.

John E. Jacob

(1934–)

National Urban League President

Vernon Eulion Jordan, Jr. was born in Atlanta in 1935. After graduating from DePauw University in 1957 and from Howard Law School in 1960, he returned to Georgia.

From 1962 to 1964 Jordan served as field secretary for the Georgia branch of the NAACP. Between 1964 and 1968 Jordan served as director of the Voter Education Project of the Southern Regional Council and led its successful drives that registered nearly two million blacks in the South. In 1970 Jordan moved to New York to become executive director of the United Negro College Fund, helping to raise record sums for its member colleges, until he was tapped by the Urban League to become the successor to the late Whitney Young.

Taking over as National Urban League executive director in January 1972, Jordan moved the organization into new arenas, including voter registration in northern and western cities, while continuing to strengthen the League's traditional social service programs. An outspoken advocate of the cause of the black and the poor, Jordan has taken strong stands in favor of busing, an income maintenance system that ends poverty, scatter-site

Vernon E. Jordan, Jr. (1935–)

National Urban League Former President

housing, and a federally financed and administered national health system. Maintaining that the "issues have changed" since the 1960s, Jordan has called for "equal access and employment up to and including top policy-making jobs."

The nation was stunned on May 29, 1980 when Jordan, who had just delivered an address to the Fort Wayne Urban League, was shot by a sniper as he returned to his motel; Jordan was confined to the hospital, first in Fort Wayne, Indiana, and later in New York City, for ninety days.

On September 9, 1981, Jordan announced his retirement after ten years as head of the National Urban League. During Jordan's tenure, the League increased its number of affiliates from 99 to 118, its staff from 2,100 to 4,200, and its overall budget from $40 million annually to $150 million. Most recently Jordan was selected to serve on President Bill Clinton's transition team.

Joseph E. Lowery
(1924–)

Southern Christian
Leadership Conference
President

The Reverend Joseph E. Lowery was born in Huntsville, Alabama. He holds a doctor of divinity degree, among others, and has attended numerous educational institutions, including Clark College, the Chicago Ecumenical Institute, Garrett Theological Seminary, Payne College and Theological Seminary, and Morehouse University. Reverend Lowery's ministry began in 1952 at the Warren Street Church in Birmingham, where he served until 1961. From there he moved on to become pastor of St. Paul Church from 1964 to 1968.

Since 1986, Lowery has served as pastor of the Cascade United Methodist Church in Atlanta, Georgia.

Lowery was one of the co-founders of the Southern Negro Leaders Conference (which later became the Southern Christian Leadership Conference); the Reverend Martin Luther King, Jr. served as the organization's first president, with Lowery serving as vice-president.

In 1977, Lowery succeeded the Reverend Ralph David Abernathy as president of the SCLC. Under his leadership, the SCLC has broadened its activities to include the reinstitution of its Operation Breadbasket to encourage businesses that earn substantial profits in the black community to reinvest equitably and employ blacks in equitable numbers; involvement in the plight of Haitian refugees jailed by the American government; and a march from Selma to Washington, DC in connection with the renewal of the Voting Rights Act of 1982.

Born in Asheville, North Carolina on March 9, 1922, Floyd Bixler McKissick did his undergraduate work at Morehouse and North Carolina colleges. Intending to become a lawyer, McKissick applied to the University of North Carolina at Chapel Hill Law School. Since the school was not integrated at that time, he was denied admission. With the help of NAACP lawyer Thurgood Marshall, McKissick sued the university and became the first African American to earn an LL.B. degree there.

Floyd B. McKissick (1922–1991)

Congress of Racial Equality Former National Director

While still in school, McKissick had become an active member of the Congress of Racial Equality (CORE). When McKissick replaced James Farmer as head of CORE on January 3, 1966, he quickly made a name for himself. Under McKissick's direction the organization moved more firmly into the Black Power movement, refusing to support Martin Luther King's call for massive nonviolent civil disobedience in northern cities, and concentrating instead on programs to increase the political power and improve the economic position of African Americans. In 1967 the organization moved to eliminate the word "multiracial" from its constitution.

McKissick resigned as national director of CORE in 1968. After leaving CORE, he launched a plan to establish a new community, Soul City, in Warren County, North Carolina. McKissick saw Soul City as a community with sufficient industry to support a population of fifty thousand. For his venture, he received a $14 million bond issue guarantee from the Department of Housing and Urban Development and a loan of $500,000 from the First Pennsylvania Bank.

Soul City, however, ran into difficulties, and despite the best efforts of McKissick, the project never developed as planned. In June 1980 the Soul City Corporation and the federal government reached an agreement that would allow the government to assume control of the project. Under the agreement, the company retained eighty-eight acres of the project, including the site of a mobile home park and a 60,000-square-foot building that had served as the project's headquarters.

McKissick died on April 28, 1991 of lung cancer and was buried at Soul City.

Huey P. Newton
(1942–1989)

Black Panther
Party Co-Founder

The youngest of seven children, Huey Newton was born in Monroe, Louisiana on February 17, 1942. He attended Oakland City College, where he founded the Afro-American Society, and later studied at San Francisco Law School. In 1966 Newton joined forces with Bobby Seale and established the Black Panther Party for Self-Defense.

Newton and his partner almost immediately became targets of sharp police resentment and uneasiness. The hostility came to a climax in 1967, when Newton allegedly killed an Oakland police officer. His eight-week trial was a *cause célèbre* in which more than 2,500 demonstrators surrounded the courthouse chanting Panther slogans and demanding his release. Newton was convicted of voluntary manslaughter and sent to the California Men's Colony. His conviction was later overturned by the California Court of Appeals.

By the 1970s the Black Panther Party became a potent political force in California. Co-leader Bobby Seale made an almost-successful bid for the mayorship of Oakland in 1973. In 1977, the Panthers helped to elect the city's first black mayor, Lionel Wilson. Meanwhile, Newton continued to have problems with the law. He was charged with shooting a prostitute, but after two hung juries, the charges were dropped. He was retried and convicted for the 1967 death of the police officer; however, the conviction was reversed.

In 1980, he earned his Ph.D. in philosophy from the University of California; his doctoral thesis was "War Against the Panthers: Study of Repression in America." However, this achievement was followed by further problems. He was charged with embezzling state and federal funds from an educational and nutritional program he headed in 1985, and in 1987 he was convicted of illegal possession of guns. In 1989, he was fatally shot by a small-time drug dealer.

Asa Philip
Randolph
(1889–1979)

Brotherhood of Sleeping
Car Porters and A. Philip
Randolph Institute
Founder

Asa Philip Randolph was born in Crescent City, Florida on April 15, 1889. He attended Cookman Institute in Jacksonville, Florida, before moving to New York City.

In New York Randolph worked as a porter, railroad waiter, and elevator operator. While attending the College of the City of New York, he was exposed to the socialist movement, and in 1917 he organized *The Messenger*, a socialist newspaper. In 1925 Randolph founded the Brotherhood of Sleeping Car Porters to help black railway car attendants working for the

A. Philip Randolph Institute,

Cincinnati, Ohio.

Pullman Palace Car Company. In 1935, after a ten-year struggle, Randolph and the union negotiated a contract with Pullman.

Randolph served as a member of New York City's Commission on Race and as president of the National Negro Congress. In 1941 he organized a march on Washington, DC to bring attention to discrimination in employment. In 1942 Randolph was appointed to the New York Housing Authority and in 1955 he was appointed to the AFL-CIO executive council.

In 1960 Randolph organized the Negro American Labor Council. He was also one of the organizers of the 1963 March on Washington. In 1964 he founded the A. Philip Randolph Institute in New York City to eradicate discrimination and to defend human and civil rights.

Randall S. Robinson (1942?–)

TransAfrica Founder and Director

Randall Robinson, brother to the late news anchor Max Robinson, was born in Richmond, Virginia, and is a graduate of Virginia Union University and Harvard Law School. In 1977 Robinson founded TransAfrica to lobby Congress and the White House on foreign policy matters involving Africa and the Caribbean. Since its creation, the organization has grown from two to over fifteen thousand members.

In 1984 and 1985, in protest of the policy of apartheid in South Africa, TransAfrica organized demonstrations in front of the South African embassy in Washington, DC; Robinson and other protesters, including singer Stevie Wonder, were arrested. In addition to its opposition to apartheid, the organization has been active in the Free South Africa Movement and advocates the cessation of aid to countries with human-rights problems. In 1981 TransAfrica Forum, an educational and research arm of TransAfrica, was organized to collect and disseminate information on foreign policy affecting Africa and the Caribbean and to encourage public participation in policy debates.

Bayard Rustin
(1910–1987)

A. Philip Randolph
Institute Former
Executive Director

Bayard Rustin was born in West Chester, Pennsylvania. While in school, he was an honor student and a star athlete, experiencing his first act of public discrimination when he was refused restaurant service in Pennsylvania while on tour with the football team. He attended Wilberforce University, Cheyney State Normal School (now Cheyney State College), and the City College of New York.

Rustin was active in various peace organizations, efforts to restrict nuclear armaments, and movements toward African independence. Between 1936 and 1941, Rustin worked as an organizer of the Young Communist League. In 1941 he joined the Fellowship of Reconciliation, a nonviolent antiwar group, and later served as its director of race relations. In 1942 Rustin, along with James Farmer, became active in the Chicago Committee of Racial Equality, out of which the Congress of Racial Equality (CORE) grew.

Rustin was one of the founding members of the Southern Christian Leadership Conference (SCLC). In 1963 he was named chief logistics expert and organizational coordinator of the March on Washington. From 1964 to 1979, Rustin served as executive director of the A. Philip Randolph Institute in New York City. In 1975 he founded the Organization for Black Americans to Support Israel.

Throughout the 1960s Rustin was hard pressed to maintain support for the nonviolent philosophy to which he had dedicated his life. Nonviolence, he argued, was not outdated; it was a necessary and inexorable plan called for by the blacks' condition in the United States. Guerrilla warfare and armed insurrection, Rustin explained, required friendly border sanctuaries, a steady source of arms and equipment, and the support of the majority of a country's inhabitants. Rustin continued to be active in the civil-rights movement until his death in August 1987 at the age of seventy-seven.

Born Robert George Seale in Dallas, Texas, Bobby Seale, along with Huey P. Newton and Bobby Hutton, founded the Black Panther Party for Self-Defense. His family, poverty-stricken, moved from Dallas to Port Arthur, Texas, before settling in Oakland, California.

Seale joined the United States Air Force and trained as a sheet-metal mechanic after leaving high school, but was discharged for disobeying an officer. Returning home, he found sporadic work as a sheet-metal mechanic. In 1959 Seale enrolled at Merritt College to study engineering drafting. While attending Merritt, Seale joined the Afro-American Association, a campus organization that stressed black separatism and self-improvement. It was through this organization that Seale met Panther co-founder Huey Newton.

Seale and Newton soon became disenchanted with the association. In 1966 they formed the Black Panther Party for Self-Defense. One of their objectives was to form armed patrols to protect citizens from what they considered racist police abuse.

In March of 1971, Seale was charged with kidnapping and killing Panther Alex Rackley, a suspected police informant. A mistrial was declared, however, and the charges dismissed. Seale began to steer the Panthers away from the group's revolutionary agenda and toward one of creating community-action programs. In 1974 Seale left the party to form the Advocates Scene to help the underprivileged form grass-root political coalitions.

More recently Seale has served as a community liaison for Temple University's African-American Studies department. He has lectured throughout the country and has written several books, including *Seize the Time: The Story of the Black Panther Party* (1970), *A Lonely Rage: The Autobiography of Bobby Seale* (1978), and *Barbeque'n with Bobby Seale* (1987).

Born in St. Louis, Missouri on August 30, 1901, Wilkins was reared in St. Paul, Minnesota. He attended the University of Minnesota, where he majored in sociology and minored in journalism. He served as night editor of the *Minnesota Daily* (the school paper) and edited a black weekly, the St. Paul *Appeal*. After receiving his B.A. in 1923, he joined the staff of the Kansas City *Call*, a leading black weekly.

Bobby Seale

(1936–)

Black Panther
Party Co-founder

Roy Wilkins

(1901–1981)

NAACP Former
Executive Director

In 1931 Wilkins left the *Call* to serve under Walter White as assistant executive secretary of the NAACP. In 1934 he succeed W.E.B. DuBois as editor of *Crisis* magazine. Wilkins was named acting executive secretary of the NAACP in 1949, when White took a year's leave of absence from the organization. Wilkins assumed the position of executive secretary of the NAACP in 1955. He quickly established himself as one of the most articulate spokesmen in the civil-rights movement. He testified before innumerable Congressional hearings, conferred with United States presidents, and wrote extensively.

For several years, Wilkins served as chairman of the Leadership Conference on Civil Rights, an organization of more than 100 national civic, labor, fraternal, and religious organizations. He was a trustee of the Eleanor Roosevelt Foundation, the Kennedy Memorial Library Foundation, and the Estes Kefauver Memorial Foundation. He was also a member of the Board of Directors of the international organization Peace with Freedom and many other institutions.

Whitney M. Young, Jr. (1922-1971)

National Urban League
Former Executive
Director

Whitney Moore Young, Jr. was born in Lincoln Ridge, Kentucky. He received his B.A. from Kentucky State College in 1941, then went on to attend the Massachusetts Institute of Technology. In 1947 he earned an M.A. in social work from the University of Minnesota.

In 1947 Young was made director of industrial relations and vocational guidance for the St. Paul, Minnesota Urban League. In 1950 he moved on to become executive secretary of the St. Paul chapter. Between 1954 and 1961 Young served as dean of the Atlanta University School of Social Work. He also served as a visiting scholar at Harvard University under a Rockefeller Foundation grant.

In 1961 the National Urban League's board of directors elected Young as president of the organization. Young instituted new programs like the National Skills Bank, the Broadcast Skills Bank, the Secretarial Training Project, and an on-the-job training program with the United States Department of Labor. Between 1961 and 1971, the organization grew from sixty-three to ninety-eight affiliates.

In addition to his work with the National Urban League, Young served as president of the National Association of Social Workers and the National

Conference on Social Welfare, and on the boards and advisory committees of the Rockefeller Foundation, Urban Coalition, and Urban Institute, and on seven presidential commissions. In 1969 Young was selected by President Johnson to receive the Medal of Freedom, the nation's highest civilian award. Young authored two books, *To Be Equal* (1964) and *Beyond Racism: Building an Open Society* (1969), and coauthored *A Second Look* (1958).

Young died in 1971 while attending a conference in Africa.

*P*olitics

Throughout the past several decades, African Americans have been selected for political offices in ever-increasing numbers. One of the most significant recent political developments was the election of the first black woman, Carol Moseley Braun, to the United States Senate in 1992. Braun, a native of Chicago, Illinois, shocked political observers by scoring a stunning upset over incumbent Senator Alan Dixon in the Democratic primary on March 17, 1992. In the November 1992 election, she easily defeated her Republican challenger, Richard Williamson, by a wide margin. Among Braun's many assets is her eclectic base of political supporters, which includes African Americans, feminists, Jews, trade unionists, and working people. Braun is a strong supporter of abortion rights, environmental protection, educational and health-care reform, and job creation. Braun, whose term in the Senate expires in 1998, is only the fifth African American to serve in the Senate and only the second since Reconstruction. Her election to the United States Senate is an important victory for African Americans and women alike.

RECENT POLITICAL HISTORY ♦

The 1992 national elections increased the number of African American representatives in Congress. Thirty-nine African Americans occupy seats in the current 103rd Congress, compared with only twenty-five African-American representatives in the 102nd Congress. African Americans elected to their first Congressional term in November 1992 include Earl Hilliard (Alabama); Walter Tucker (California); Alcee Hastings (Florida); Sanford Bishop (Georgia); Bobby Rush (Illinois); Mel Reynolds (Illinois); Cleo Fields (Louisiana); Albert Wynn (Maryland); Jim Clyburn (South Carolina); Eddie B. Johnson (Texas); and Bobby Scott (Virginia). Four of the new Congressional representatives are women: Corinne Brown (Florida); Carrie Meek (Florida); Cynthia McKinney (Georgia); and Eva Clayton (North Carolina). Many of the gains in representation can be attributed to an increasing acceptance of African Americans as viable political candidates. Also, the process of redistricting has benefited minority political candidates. Redistricting occurs every ten years and involves the

Carol Moseley Braun, the first black woman elected to the United States Senate.

reapportionment of all 435 seats in the United States House of Representatives according to population shifts among the fifty states.

On November 3, 1992, Americans elected a new president, Bill Clinton. President Clinton's cabinet includes seven African Americans. Ron Brown, former Democratic National Committee chairman, was chosen as Secretary of Commerce and is the first African American to hold this post. Also, Clinton chose Jesse Brown to serve as head of the Veterans Affairs Department. Brown, a former director of the Disabled Veterans of America, is the first African American veteran affairs secretary. On December 24, 1992, the position of Secretary of Agriculture was awarded to Michael Espy. Espy, a Congressman from Mississippi, was elected in 1986 and was the first African American from Mississippi to serve in Congress since Reconstruction. Another African American, Lee P. Brown, was selected as head of the Office of National Drug Control Policy. Brown is a former police commissioner from New York City. He is faced with the difficult challenge of balancing the desire for tough penalties for drug offenders with the urgent need for drug rehabilitation and anti-drug education. Hazel R. O'Leary, one of two African-American women selected for cabinet positions, was chosen as Secretary of Energy. O'Leary, who served as an energy regulator during the Ford and Carter administrations, brings a wealth of experience to her new position. The position of surgeon general was awarded to Dr. Joycelyn Elders. Elders is a talented physician known for her innovative research on diabetes. She is also a controversial figure who has clashed with conservatives regarding her views concerning abortion rights and her support of contraception in school health clinics. Also, Clifton R. Wharton, an economist and business executive, was chosen as deputy secretary of state.

In the past, much of the occupational improvement within the African-American community stemmed from greater employment opportunities in federal government for the black middle class. During the 1990s concern arose that the prevailing emphasis on major cuts in federal programs would reverse some of the gains of the black middle class.

◆ ◆ ◆ ◆ ◆ ◆ ◆ AFRICAN-AMERICAN GOVERNMENT OFFICIALS

Bradley was born December 29, 1917 in Calvert, Texas. In 1924 he moved with his family to Los Angeles. Bradley graduated from Polytechnic High School in 1937 and attended the University of California at Los Angeles on an athletic scholarship. He excelled at track before quitting college in 1940 and joining the Los Angeles Police Department.

Thomas Bradley (1917–)

Former Mayor of Los Angeles

While a member of the police force, Bradley worked as a detective, as a community relations officer, and in the department's juvenile division. In

Thomas Bradley was mayor of Los Angeles for two decades.

the early 1950s Bradley began studying law at two Los Angeles colleges, Loyola University and later Southwestern University, where he earned an LL.B. in 1956. Bradley stayed with the LAPD until 1961 when he entered private law practice.

In 1963 Bradley became the first African American elected to the Los Angeles City Council, and was re-elected in 1967 and 1971. In a hotly contested 1973 election Bradley became mayor of Los Angeles, winning 56% of the vote.

Bradley has served as president of the National League of Cities and the Southern California Association of Governments. He belongs to the Urban League of Los Angeles and is a founding member of the NAACP's Black Achievers Committee. On the national level he has served on President Gerald Ford's National Committee on Productivity and Work Quality and on the National Energy Advisory Council.

Bradley retired as mayor of Los Angeles in 1993.

Carol Moseley Braun was born in Chicago on August 16, 1947. She received her B.A. from the University of Illinois in 1969 and her J.D. from the University of Chicago Law School in 1972. While attending law school Braun worked as a legal intern and an associate attorney for a number of private law firms.

After graduating from law school Braun was an assistant U.S. attorney for the northern district of Illinois from 1973 until 1977. In 1979 she was elected an Illinois state representative from the 25th district, where she became known as an ardent supporter of civil-rights legislation. After a bid for the lieutenant governorship was thwarted Braun was elected Cook County recorder of deeds in 1986. In 1992 Braun became the nation's first African-American woman elected to the United States Senate.

Carol Moseley Braun (1947–)

United States Senator

Barthelemy was born in New Orleans on March 17, 1942. He attended Epiphany Apostolic Junior College from 1960 to 1963 and received a B.A. from the St. Joseph Seminary in 1967. Two years later he earned a master's degree in social work from Tulane University.

After graduation Barthelemy worked in administrative and professional positions in numerous organizations, including Total Community Action, the Adult Basic Education Program, the Parent-Child Development Center, Family Health Inc., and the Urban League of New Orleans.

From 1972 to 1974 Barthelemy was the director of the Welfare Department of the City of New Orleans. In 1974 he was elected to the Louisiana State Senate. In 1978 he left the state legislature after winning a seat on the New Orleans City Council, where he stayed until his election as mayor in 1986.

Barthelemy has taught at Xavier University as an associate professor of sociology, and at Tulane University and the University of New Orleans. He has been the vice-chairman for voter registration for the Democratic National Party, second vice-president for the National League of Cities, and president of the Louisiana Conference of Mayors.

Sidney John Barthelemy (1942–)

Mayor of New Orleans

New Orleans Mayor Sidney Barthelemy campaigns for reelection in 1990.

Mary Frances Berry

(1938–)

Former Assistant Cabinet Member, Civil Rights Commissioner

Mary Frances Berry was born in 1938. She received her bachelor's degree from Howard University in 1961 and her master's degree in 1962. In 1966 she received a Ph.D. from the University of Michigan and her J.D. from its law school in 1970. Berry worked for several years as a professor of history and law at universities throughout the United States. She was appointed Assistant Secretary of Education at the United States Department of Health, Education, and Welfare by President Jimmy Carter in 1977, and became commissioner and vice chairman of the United States Commission on Civil Rights in 1980. She was removed from the Civil

Rights Commission by President Ronald Reagan in 1983 but was reinstated in a compromise with Congress.

She is currently a Geraldine R. Segal professor of American Social Thought at the University of Pennsylvania.

Throughout his successful career and personal and political adversity, Julian Bond has been labeled everything from a national hero to a national traitor. He has faced violent segregationists and his own political failures and scandals. In spite of everything, he has kept his head above water and has remained an influential voice in politics, education, and the media.

**Julian Bond
(1940-)**

Civil Rights Activist,
Politician

Bond was born on January 14, 1940. His father, an eminent scholar and president of Lincoln University in Pennsylvania, wanted Julian to follow his footsteps into the world of academics. Although Julian attended fine private schools, he showed little desire for educational pursuits. In 1960, Bond attended Morehouse College in Atlanta, where he was a mediocre student. While at Morehouse, however, Bond developed an interest in civil-rights activism. He and several other students formed the Atlanta Committee on Appeal for Human Rights (COAHR). Along with other members, Bond participated in several sit-ins at segregated lunch counters in downtown Atlanta. The activities of Bond and his cohorts attracted the attention of Martin Luther King, Jr. and the Southern Christian Leadership Conference (SCLC). King invited Bond and other COAHR members to Shaw University in North Carolina to help devise new civil-rights strategies. At this conference, the Student Non-Violent Coordinating Committee (SNCC) was created. The SNCC eventually absorbed COAHR and Bond accepted a position as the SNCC director of communications. By 1966, Bond had grown tired of the SNCC and decided to embark on a new career in politics.

In 1966, Bond campaigned for a seat in the Georgia House of Representatives. He won the election and prepared to take his seat in the Georgia legislature. However, Bond was soon embroiled in a bitter controversy when he publicly announced that he opposed U.S. involvement in Vietnam and supported students who burned their draft cards to protest against the Vietnam War. These statements outraged many conservative members of the Georgia House of Representatives and, on January 10, 1966, they voted to prevent Bond's admission to the legislature. Bond sought legal recourse to overturn this vote and the case eventually went to the U.S. Supreme Court. On December 5, 1966, the Court ruled that the Georgia vote was a violation of Bond's First Amendment right of free speech and ordered that he be admitted to the legislature. The members of the Georgia House of Representatives reluctantly allowed Bond to take his seat, but treated him as an outcast.

Bond's battle with the Georgia House of Representatives was not his last experience as the center of controversy. In 1968, Bond and several other members of the Georgia Democratic Party Forum protested Governor Lester Maddox's decision to send only six African-American delegates out of 107 to the Democratic National Convention. Bond and his supporters arrived at the convention and set up a rival delegation. After several bitter arguments with Georgia's official delegation, Bond's delegation had captured nearly half of Georgia's delegate votes. Bond's actions made him a national hero to many African Americans. He became the Democratic Party's first black candidate for the U.S. vice presidency, a position he declined.

Throughout the 1970s, Bond was no longer in the national spotlight. In 1974, he became president of the Atlanta branch of the NAACP and served until 1989. Also, Bond was elected to the Georgia Senate in 1975 and remained a member until 1987. In 1976, he refused a cabinet position in the Carter administration. Although Bond continued to express his political views as a writer and lecturer, his popularity plummeted dramatically.

The 1980s proved to be difficult for Bond on both a professional and personal level. Bond ran for a seat in the U.S. Congress in 1986, but lost the election. In 1989, he divorced his wife after twenty-eight years of marriage. Shortly thereafter, he became embroiled in a paternity suit. He initially denied the allegations, but admitted in May 1990 to fathering the child and was ordered to pay child support. Bond remarried in March 1990.

Today, Julian Bond is retired from political life. He remains extremely active, however. He has served as a visiting professor at Drexel University, Harvard University, the University of Virginia, and American University. He is a popular lecturer and writer and is often called upon to comment on political and social issues. Bond has hosted a popular television program, *America's Black Forum*, and narrated the highly acclaimed public television series *Eyes on the Prize*.

During his two terms in the United States Senate, Edward W. Brooke, the first black to be elected to that body since 1881, defied conventional political wisdom. In Massachusetts, a state that was overwhelmingly Democratic and in which blacks constituted only 3% of the population, he was one of its most popular political figures and a Republican.

He first achieved statewide office in 1962 when he defeated Elliot Richardson to become Attorney General. He established an outstanding record in that post and in 1966 was elected to the Senate over former Massachusetts governor Endicott Peabody.

Born into a middle-class Washington, DC environment, Brooke attended public schools locally and went on to graduate from Howard. Inducted into an all-black infantry unit during World War II, Brooke rose to the rank of captain and was ultimately given a Bronze Star for his work in intelligence.

Moving to Massachusetts after the war, Brooke attended the Boston University Law School, compiling an outstanding academic record and editing the *Law Review* in the process. After law school, he established himself as an attorney and also served as chairman of the Boston Finance Commission.

Brooke was later nominated for the attorney general's office, encountering stiff opposition within his own party. He eventually won both the Republican primary and the general election against his Democratic opponent.

Upon entering the national political scene, Brooke espoused the notion that the Great Society could not become a reality until it was preceded by the "Responsible Society." He called this a society in which "it's more profitable to work than not to work. You don't help a man by constantly giving him more handouts."

When first elected, Brooke strongly supported United States participation in the Vietnam War, though most black leaders were increasingly opposing it. However, in 1971, Brooke supported the McGovern-Hatfield Amendment, which called for withdrawal of the United States from Vietnam.

Matters of race rather than foreign affairs were to become Brooke's area of expertise. Reluctant and subdued, Brooke proceeded carefully at first,

Edward W. Brooke (1919–)

Former United States Senator

waiting to be consulted by President Richard Nixon and loyally accepting the latter's apparent indifference to his views. As pressure mounted from the established civil-rights groups and impatient black militants, however, he decided to attack the Nixon policies. Brooke was roused into a more active role by the administration's vacillating school desegregation guidelines; its "firing" of Health, Education, and Welfare official Leon Panetta; and the nominations to the Supreme Court of judicial conservatives Clement Haynsworth and G. Harrold Carswell.

In 1972 Brooke was reelected to the Senate overwhelmingly, even though Massachusetts was the only state not carried by his party in the presidential election. While Brooke seconded the nomination of President Nixon at the 1972 Republican Convention, he became increasingly critical of the Nixon administration. He also began to appear publicly at meetings of the Congressional Black Caucus, a group he had tended to avoid in the past. Brooke was considered a member of the moderate-to-liberal wing of the Republican Party.

In 1978, Brooke's bid for a third term in the Senate was defeated by Democrat Paul Tsongas, and he returned to his private law practice.

Ronald H. Brown (1941–)

Cabinet Member

Born in Washington, DC on August 1, 1941, Brown was raised in Harlem and attended White Plains High School and Rhodes and Walden Preparatory Schools in New York. He graduated from Middlebury College in Middlebury, Vermont with a B.A. in political science in 1962. Upon graduating he enlisted in the army and achieved the rank of captain while serving in West Germany and Korea. Brown then graduated from New York City's St. Johns University Law School in 1970.

While attending law school Brown began working for the National Urban League's job training center in the Bronx, New York in 1968. He continued with them until 1979, working as general counsel, Washington spokesperson, deputy executive director, and vice president of Washington operations. In 1980 he resigned to become chief counsel of the United States Senate judiciary committee and in 1981 general counsel and staff coordinator for Senator Edward Kennedy. In that year he also became a partner in the Washington law firm of Patton, Boggs & Blow. In 1989 Brown was appointed Chairman of the Democratic National Committee and was thus the first African American to head a major American political party. In 1993 Brown was appointed Commerce Secretary by President Bill Clinton.

Blanche Kelso Bruce was born a slave in Farmville, Prince Edward County, Virginia on March 1, 1841. He received his early formal education in Missouri, where his parents had moved while he was still quite young, and later studied at Oberlin College in Ohio. In 1868, Bruce settled in Floreyville, Mississippi. He worked as a planter and eventually built up a considerable fortune in property.

In 1870, Bruce entered politics and was elected sergeant-at-arms of the Mississippi Senate. A year later he was named assessor of taxes in Bolivar County. In 1872 he served as sheriff of that county and as a member of the Board of Levee Commissioners of Mississippi.

Bruce was nominated for the United States Senate from Mississippi in February 1874. Upon his election he became the first black person to serve a full term in the United States Senate. Bruce became an outspoken defender of the rights of minority groups, including the Chinese and Indians. He also investigated alleged bank and election frauds and worked for the improvement of navigation on the Mississippi in the hope of increasing interstate and foreign commerce. Bruce also supported legislation aimed at eliminating reprisals against those who had opposed Negro emancipation.

After Bruce completed his term in the Senate, he was named Register of the United States Treasury Department by President James A. Garfield. Bruce held this position until 1885. In 1889, President Benjamin Harrison appointed him recorder of deeds for the District of Columbia. Bruce served as recorder of deeds until 1893, when he became a trustee for the District of Columbia public schools. In 1897, President William McKinley reappointed him to his former post as register of the treasurer. Bruce died on March 17, 1898.

Blanche K. Bruce (1841–1898)

Former United States Senator

The first black American to win the Nobel Peace Prize, Ralph Bunche was an internationally acclaimed statesman whose record of achievement places him among the most significant American diplomats of the twentieth century. Bunche received the coveted award in 1950 for his role in effecting a ceasefire in the Arab-Israeli dispute that threatened to engulf the entire Middle East in armed conflict.

Born in Detroit, Michigan on August 7, 1904, Bunche graduated from UCLA in 1927 summa cum laude and with Phi Beta Kappa honors. A year

Ralph J. Bunche (1904–1971)

United Nations Undersecretary for Special Political Affairs

later he received his M.A. in government from Harvard. Soon thereafter he was named head of the Department of Political Science at Howard University, remaining there until 1932, when he was able to resume work toward his doctorate from Harvard. He later studied at Northwestern University, the London School of Economics, and Capetown University.

Before World War II broke out in 1939, Bunche did field work with the Swedish sociologist Gunnar Myrdal, author of the widely acclaimed *An American Dilemma*. During the war, he served initially as Senior Social Analyst for the Office of the Coordinator of Information in African and Far Eastern Affairs, and was then reassigned to the African section of the Office of Strategic Services. In 1942, he helped draw up the territories and trusteeship sections ultimately earmarked for inclusion in the United Nations charter.

The single event that brought the name of Ralph Bunche into the international spotlight occurred soon after his appointment in 1948 as chief assistant to Count Folke Bernadotte, the U.N. mediator in the Palestine crisis. With the latter's assassination, Bunche was faced with the great challenge of somehow continuing ceasefire talks between Egypt and Israel. After six weeks of intensive negotiations, Bunche worked out the now-famous "Four Armistice Agreements," which brokered an immediate cessation of the hostilities between the two combatants. Once the actual ceasefire was signed, Bunche received numerous congratulatory letters and telegrams from many heads of state and was given a hero's welcome upon his return to the United States.

Bunche served as undersecretary of Special Political Affairs from 1957 to 1967. By 1968, Bunche had attained the rank of undersecretary general, the highest position ever held by an American at the United Nations.

Bunche retired in October 1971 and died on December 9, 1971.

Yvonne Brathwaite Burke (1932–)

Former United States Representative

Attorney and former California State Assemblywoman Yvonne Brathwaite Burke became the first black woman from California to be elected to the House of Representatives in November 1972.

Prior to her governmental career, Burke was a practicing attorney, during which time she served as a Deputy Corporation Commissioner, a hearing officer for the Los Angeles Police Commissioner, and an attorney for the McCone Commission, which investigated the Watts riots.

Congresswoman Burke served in the state Assembly for six years prior to her election to Congress. During her final two years there, she was chair of the Committee on Urban Development and Housing and a member of the Health, Finance, and Insurance committees.

As a state legislator, Burke was responsible for the enactment of bills providing for needy children, relocation of tenants and owners of homes taken by governmental action, and one that required major medical insurance programs to grant immediate coverage to newborn infants of the insured.

Burke's congressional district, created in 1971 by the California legislature, contains low- and middle-income black and integrated neighborhoods, plus some white suburban tracts and beach communities, including Venice, which is noted for its "counterculture" scene. About 50% of the district's population is black, with another 10% of Hispanic and Asian origin. In 1972, the district gave 64% of its vote to Burke.

During Burke's first term in Congress, she proved to be an ardent spokesperson for the downtrodden. She became a member of the Committee on Appropriations in December 1974 and used her position on this committee to advocate an increase in funding for senior citizen services and community nutrition and food programs. Although her proposal for increased spending was defeated by the House of Representatives, Burke's efforts earned the respect of the African-American community. In January 1977, Burke worked diligently for the passage of the Displaced Homemakers Act, which proposed the creation of counseling programs and job training centers for women entering the work force for the first time.

In 1978, Burke resigned to run for attorney general in California. She lost that race but, in 1979, she was appointed to the Los Angeles County Board of Supervisors. She resigned from the board in December 1980 and returned to her private law practice. Although she no longer holds public office, Burke remains a prominent figure in California politics. She has also taken on a number of civic responsibilities, including serving as a member of the University of California Board of Regents.

Shirley Chisholm

(1924–)

Former United States
Representative

Chisholm was born November 30, 1924 in New York City. She graduated cum laude from Brooklyn College in 1946 with a B.A. in sociology and with an M.A. in elementary education from Columbia University in 1952. She had an early career in child care and pre-school education culminating in her directorship of the Hamilton-Madison Child Care Center in New York. Leaving that position in 1959, she served until 1964 as a consultant to the Day Care Division of New York City's Bureau of Child Welfare.

In 1964 she was elected New York State Assemblywoman representing the 55th district in New York City. In 1968 she was elected to the United States House of Representatives and represented the twelfth district until her retirement in 1982. Throughout her political career Chisholm has been a staunch democrat in her elected positions, as a delegate to the Democratic National Mid-Term Conference in 1974, and as a Democratic National Committeewoman.

After retiring from politics Chisholm taught political science at Mount Holyoke College and in 1985 she was a visiting scholar at Spelman College. In 1984 Chisholm co-founded the National Political Congress of Black Women. She has also written two books, *Unbossed & Unbought* (1970) and *The Good Fight* (1973).

William Clay

(1931–)

United States
Representative

William Clay, the first black man to represent the state of Missouri in the United States Congress, was born in 1931 in the lower end of what is now St. Louis's first district. Clay was educated locally and later took a degree in political science at St. Louis University, where he was one of four blacks in a class of 1,100. After serving in the Army until 1955, Clay became active in a host of civil-rights organizations, including the NAACP Youth Council and CORE. During this time he worked as a cardiographic aide, bus driver, and insurance agent, but his heart had already surrendered to politics, at least judging from the number of demonstrations and picket lines he had joined.

In 1959, and again in 1963, Clay was elected alderman of the predominantly black twenty-sixth ward. During his first term, he served nearly four months of a nine-month jail sentence for demonstrations at a local bank. Meanwhile, the number of white-collar jobs held by blacks in St. Louis banks began a steady ascent from a low of sixteen to a high of 700. In 1964, Clay stepped down from his alderman's post to run for ward committeeman, winning handily and being reelected in 1968.

Clay's election platform in 1969 included a number of progressive, even radical, ideas. He advocated that all penal institutions make provisions for the creation of facilities in which married prisoners could set up house with their spouses for the duration of their sentences. He branded most testing procedures and diploma requirements, as well as references to arrest records and periods of unemployment, unnecessary obstacles complicating the path of a prospective employee. In his view, a demonstrated willingness to work and an acceptance of responsibility should be the criteria determining one's selection for a job.

Clay's last job before his election to Congress was as race relations coordinator for Steamfitters Union Local 562. Subjected to considerable criticism from other St. Louis blacks who labeled the union racist, Clay pointed out that dramatic changes in the hiring practices of the union since he had joined it in 1966 were responsible for the employment of thirty black steamfitters in St. Louis—thirty more than the union had previously put to work. Still, Clay conceded that the high-paying job had led him to reduce his active involvement with the civil-rights struggle to some degree.

As a member of the United States House of Representatives, Clay has proven himself a capable legislator. He has sponsored many pieces of legislation, including the Hatch Act Reform Bill, the City Earnings Tax Bill, and the IRS Reform Bill. Clay has served as chairman of the Subcommittee on Postal Operations and Civil Service, the House Education and Labor Committee, and the House Administration Committee.

Cardiss Collins (1931–)

United States Representataive

Collins was born Cardiss Robertson on September 24, 1931 in St. Louis, Missouri, and by the time she was ten years old her family had moved to Detroit. After graduating from Detroit's Commerce High School, Collins moved to Chicago, where she worked as a secretary for the state's Department of Revenue. She began studying accounting at Northwestern University and was promoted first to accountant, then auditor.

In 1973 Collins was elected United States Representative from Illinois's seventh district. She was elected to fill the seat vacated by her husband, George Collins, who was killed in an airplane crash. She soon became the first African American and the first woman to hold the position of Democratic whip-at-large. Collins has served on congressional subcommittees dealing with consumer protection, national security, hazardous materials, and narcotic abuse and control. She has been a proponent of civil-rights, pro-busing, and anti-apartheid legislation.

John Conyers

(1929–)

United States
Representative

Conyers was born in Detroit on May 16, 1929 and graduated from North-western High School in 1947. In 1950 he enlisted in the United States Army as a private and served in Korea before being honorably discharged as a second lieutenant in 1957. He then attended Wayne State University in Detroit, and after studying in a dual program he received a B.A. in 1957 and a law degree in 1958.

Conyers served as a legislative assistant to Congressman John Dingell, Jr. from 1958 to 1961 and was a senior partner in the law firm of Conyers, Bell & Townsend from 1959 to 1961. In that year he took a referee position with the Michigan Workman's Compensation Department and stayed until 1963. In 1964 he won election as a democrat to the United States House of Representatives. Conyers had long been active in the Democratic Party, belonging to the Young Democrats and the University Democrats and serving as a precinct delegate to the Democratic Party.

After his election Conyers was assigned to the powerful House Judiciary Committee. From that position he worked for legislation dealing with civil rights, medicare, immigration reform, and truth-in-packaging laws. He was an early opponent of United States involvement in Vietnam and an early proponent of the Voting Rights Act of 1965.

Conyers has been vice-chairman of the National Board of Americans for Democratic Action and the American Civil Liberties Union. He is on the executive board of the Detroit Chapter of the NAACP and belongs to the Wolverine Bar Association.

Ronald V. Dellums

(1935–)

United States
Representative

Dellums was born in Oakland, California on November 24, 1935. After attending McClymonds and Oakland Technical High Schools, Dellums joined the United States Marine Corps in 1954 and was discharged after two years of service. He returned to school, receiving an associate of arts degree from Oakland City College (1958), a bachelor's degree from San Francisco State College (1960), and a master's degree in social work from the University of California at Berkeley (1962).

After graduation Dellums was involved in numerous social work positions from 1962 to 1970. He was a psychiatric social worker with the Berkeley

Department of Mental Hygiene, program director of the Bayview Community Center, director of the Hunters Point Youth Opportunity Center, consultant to the Bay Area Social Planning Council, and program director for the San Francisco Economic Opportunity Council. From 1968 to 1970 Dellums lectured at San Francisco State College and the University of California's School of Social Work. He also served as a consultant to Social Dynamics, Inc.

Dellums was elected to the Berkeley City Council in 1967 and served until his election as a Democrat to the United States House of Representatives in 1971. As a representative he chaired the House Committee on the District of Columbia and served on the House Armed Services Subcommittee on Military Facilities and Installations as well as the Subcommittee on Military Research and Development. He has been the chairman of the Defense Policy Panel and in 1983 authored *Defense Sense: The Search for a Rational Military Policy*.

Oscar De Priest was the first black to win a seat in the United States House of Representatives in the twentieth century, and the first to be elected from a northern state.

Oscar Stanton De Priest (1871–1951)

Former United States Representative

Born in Florence, Alabama, De Priest moved to Kansas with his family at the age of six. His formal education there consisted of business and bookkeeping classes, which he completed before running away to Dayton, Ohio with two white friends. By 1889, he had reached Chicago and become a painter and master decorator.

In Chicago, De Priest amassed a fortune in real estate and the stock market and in 1904 entered politics successfully when he was elected Cook County Commissioner. In 1908, he was appointed an alternate delegate to the Republican National Convention and in 1915 became Chicago's first black alderman. He served on the Chicago City Council from 1915 to 1917 and became Third Ward Committeeman in 1924.

In 1928, De Priest became the Republican nominee for the Congressional seat vacated by fellow Republican Martin Madden. De Priest won the November election over his Democratic rival and an independent candidate to become the first black from outside the South to be elected to Congress.

Following his election to Congress, De Priest became the unofficial spokesman for the eleven million blacks in the United States during the 1920s and 1930s. He proposed that states that discriminated against black Americans should receive fewer Congressional seats. Also, he proposed that a monthly pension be given to ex-slaves over the age of seventy-five. During the early 1930s, with the United States mired in the Depression, De Priest was faced with a difficult dilemma. Although he empathized with the plight of poor black and white Americans, he did not support the emergency federal relief programs proposed by President Franklin Roosevelt. Rather, De Priest and his fellow Republicans believed that aid programs should be created and implemented by individual states or local communities. De Priest's stance on the issue of federal relief programs dismayed many of his constituents. In 1934, he was defeated by Arthur Mitchell, the first black Democrat elected to serve in Congress.

De Priest remained active in public life, serving from 1943 to 1947 as alderman of the Third Ward in Chicago. His final withdrawal from politics came about after a sharp dispute with his own party. De Priest returned to his real estate business, and he died in 1951.

David Dinkins
(1927–)

Former Mayor of New York

In September 1989, David Dinkins surprised political observers by defeating incumbent mayor Edward I. Koch in New York's Democratic mayoral primary. In the November election of that year, he defeated Rudolph Giuliani, a popular district attorney. Dinkins's victory marked the first time an African American was elected as mayor of New York City. During his time in this office, Mayor Dinkins faced the difficult task of leading a racially polarized and financially troubled city. Evaluations of Dinkins's tenure in office are somewhat mixed. Many supporters have cited Dinkins's calm, professional demeanor as having a soothing effect upon New York's festering racial problems. Others have chided Dinkins for not responding forcefully enough to the many fiscal and social challenges facing the city.

David Dinkins was born in Trenton, New Jersey in 1927. His parents separated when he was quite young and he moved to Harlem with his mother and sister. He returned to Trenton to attend high school. He was a fine student and well liked by his peers. Following a stint in the Marines during World War II, he attended Howard University in Washington, DC and graduated with a bachelor of science degree in 1950. In 1953, Dinkins enrolled at Brooklyn Law School and graduated in 1956. He became an attorney and, eventually, a partner in the law firm of Dyett, Alexander, Dinkins, Patterson, Michael, Dinkins & Jones.

Dinkins's first foray into the world of politics occurred in 1965 when he won an election to the New York State Assembly. He served until 1967 but did not seek reelection after his district was redrawn. In 1972, Dinkins was appointed president of elections for the City of New York and served for one year. Two years later, in 1975, he was appointed city clerk and served until 1985. Dinkins ran for the office of Manhattan borough president in 1977 and 1981. He lost both elections by a wide margin. Dinkins ran again in 1985 and was elected. As Manhattan borough president, Dinkins was viewed as a mediator who tried to address a myriad of community concerns such as school decentralization, AIDS treatment and prevention services, and pedestrian safety.

As the 1993 mayoral election approached, Dinkins was facing a steady stream of criticism that he had hired incompetent workers to top municipal posts, that he acted reactively rather than proactively, and that, while displaying a talent for pacifying, he lacked the consistently strong leadership and stalwart vision that the city's multifaceted problems demand. In November 1993, Dinkins lost the election to the opponent he had triumphed over in the 1989 campaign, Republican Rudolph Giuliani.

Julian C. Dixon (1934–)

United States Representative

Dixon was born August 8, 1934 in Washington, DC. He served in the U.S. Army from 1957 to 1960, and later received a B.S. in political science from California State University and in 1967 an LL.B. from Southwestern University Law School.

In 1972 Dixon was elected on the democratic ticket to the California State Assembly. Staying in that position until 1978, Dixon wrote legislation dealing with criminal justice, education, and fair employment. In 1978 he was elected to the United States House of Representatives.

Sharon Pratt Dixon (1944–)

Mayor of Washington, DC

Dixon was born Sharon Pratt in Washington, DC on January 30, 1944. She graduated from Howard University with a B.A. in political science in 1965 and a J.D. from their law school in 1968. She edited the Howard University Law School Journal in 1967.

From 1970 through 1971 Dixon was the house counsel for the Joint Center for Political Studies in Washington, DC. Between 1971 and 1976 she was an associate in the law firm of Pratt & Queen. During this time she

also taught at Antioch Law School. In 1976 Dixon began a fourteen-year association with the Potomac Electric Power Company. While there she held increasingly responsible positions, including associate general counsel, director of consumer affairs, and vice-president of public policy.

In 1990 Dixon left the private sector to win the office of mayor of Washington, DC. In doing so she became the first African-American woman to be mayor of a major American city.

Dixon has long been active in the Democratic Party. In 1976 and 1977 she was general counsel to the Washington, DC Democratic Committee. Between 1985 and 1989 she was treasurer of the Democratic Party. She has also served as a national committeewoman on the Washington, DC Democratic State Committee.

While in law school she married Arrington Dixon, from whom she was divorced in 1982. In 1991 Dixon married James Kelly III.

Michael Espy
(1953–)

Cabinet Member,
Former Congressman

Espy was born November 30, 1953. He received a B.A. from Howard University in 1975 and a J.D. from the Santa Clara School of Law in 1978.

After graduation Espy practiced law in Yazoo City, Mississippi and managed Central Mississippi Legal Services. From 1980 until 1984 he was director of Public Lands and Elections, which is a division of the Mississippi State Secretary's Office. In 1984 Espy left the directorship to become the Chief of the Consumer Protection Division of the State Attorney General's Office. Espy was then elected to the United States House of Representatives, and in 1993 Espy was appointed Secretary of Agriculture by President Bill Clinton.

Walter E. Fauntroy
(1933–)

Delegate to the
United States House of
Representatives

Delegate Walter E. Fauntroy, pastor of New Bethel Baptist Church in Washington, DC, represents the District of Columbia. A Yale Divinity School alumnus, he was chairman of the Caucus task force for the 1972 Democratic National Committee and of the platform committee of the National Black Political Convention. Fauntroy was Washington, DC coordinator for the March on Washington for Jobs and Freedom in 1963, coordinator for the Selma-to-Montgomery march in 1965, and national coordinator for the Poor People's Campaign in 1969. He is also a chairman of the board of directors of the Southern Christian Leadership Conference. Fauntroy was the chief architect of legislation in 1973 that permitted the District of Columbia to elect its own mayor and city council and engineered the passage by both the House and Senate of a constitutional amendment calling for full Congressional representation for District of Columbia residents in the United States Congress. He has strong support from the city's overwhelmingly black population, especially the large population of black civil servants.

Since his election to Congress, he has continued to build a record of achievement by playing key roles in the mobilization of black political power from the National Black Political Convention in 1972 to the presidential elections of 1972 and 1976. He is a member of the House Select Committee on Narcotics Abuse and Control and co-sponsored the 1988 $2.7 billion anti-drug bill. On Thanksgiving Eve in 1984, Fauntroy and two prominent national leaders launched the Free South Africa Movement (FSAM) with their arrest at the South African embassy. He serves as co-chair of the steering committee of the FSAM.

In the 95th Congress Fauntroy was a member of the House Select Committee on Assassinations and chairman of its Subcommittee on the Assassination of Martin Luther King, Jr. He is a ranking member of the House Banking, Finance, and Urban Affairs Committee and chairman of its Subcommittee on Government Affairs and Budget. He is also the first ranking member of the House District Committee.

**Gary A. Franks
(1953–)**

United States
Representative

Franks was born February 9, 1953 in Waterbury, Connecticut. He received a B.A. from Yale University in 1975.

Before being elected to the United States House of Representatives, Franks was active in local politics and business. He was president of GAF Realty in Waterbury and was also on the Board of Aldermen, vice-chairman of the Zoning Board, a member of the Environmental Control Commission, director of the Naugatuck, Connecticut chapter of the American Red Cross, president of the Greater Waterbury Chamber of Commerce, and a member of the Waterbury Foundation.

In 1991 he was elected to the United States House of Representatives, where he is currently the only African-American Republican.

W. Wilson Goode
(1938-)

Former Mayor of
Philadelphia

Goode was born August 19, 1938 in Seaboard, North Carolina. He received a B.A. from Morgan State University and a master's degree in public administration from the University of Pennsylvania's Wharton School in 1968.

Between 1966 and 1978 Goode held a wide variety of positions, including probation officer, building maintenance supervisor, insurance claims adjuster, and president of the Philadelphia Council for Community Advancement. From 1978 until 1980 Goode was chairman of the Pennsylvania Public Utilities Commission, and from 1980 until 1982 he was managing director of the City of Philadelphia. In 1984 Goode was elected first African-American mayor of Philadelphia and held office until 1991.

Goode's term as mayor was marred by a violent and deadly confrontation between the city of Philadelphia and members of MOVE, a radical "back-to-nature" cult.

Goode also served in the U.S. Army from 1960 to 1962. He left the service with a commendation medal for meritorious service and the rank of captain with the military police.

Patricia Roberts
Harris (1924–1985)

Former Ambassador,
Former Cabinet Member

As U.S. ambassador to Luxembourg, Patricia Harris was the first black woman to hold this diplomatic rank. Until President Ronald Reagan took office in 1980, Harris served as secretary of the Department of Health and Human Services and also as secretary of Housing and Urban Development under President Jimmy Carter.

Born in Mattoon, Illinois, Harris attended elementary school in Chicago and received her undergraduate degree from Howard University in 1945. While at Howard, Harris also served as vice-chairman of a student branch of the NAACP and was involved in early nonviolent demonstrations against racial discrimination. After completing post-graduate work at the University of Chicago and at American University, she earned her doctorate in jurisprudence from George Washington University Law School in 1960.

An attorney and professor before she entered politics, Harris was appointed co-chair of the National Women's Committee on Civil Rights by President John F. Kennedy and was later named to the Commission on the Status of Puerto Rico. In 1965, Harris was chosen by President Lyndon Johnson to become U.S. ambassador to Luxembourg, the first black woman ever to be named an American envoy.

In 1977, Harris was chosen by President Jimmy Carter to serve as secretary of Housing and Urban Development. She was also selected as secretary of the Department of Health and Human Services in 1979. Harris remained in these positions until the inauguration of President Ronald Reagan in 1981.

Harris ran an unsuccessful campaign for mayor of Washington, DC in 1982. She became a law professor at George Washington University in 1983 and remained there until her death from cancer in 1985.

Jackson was born on March 23, 1938 in Dallas, Texas. At the age of fourteen he was admitted to Morehouse College as a Ford Foundation Early Admissions Scholar. He graduated with a B.A. in 1956 with a concentration in history and political science. After graduation he worked for the Ohio State Bureau of Unemployment Compensation and as a sales manager for P.F. Collier, Inc.

Maynard Jackson (1938–)

Mayor of Atlanta

In 1964 Jackson received a J.D. from the North Carolina Central University law school and then worked as a lawyer for the National Labor Relations Board. In 1968 and 1969 Jackson was the managing attorney and director of community relations for the Emory Neighborhood Law Office in Atlanta, and from 1970 to 1973 he was a senior partner in the law firm of Jackson, Patterson & Parks.

Jackson had been active in Democratic politics, and from 1970 to 1974 he was the vice-mayor of Atlanta. In 1974 he was elected mayor, a position he held until 1982. He worked as a bond lawyer before being re-elected mayor in 1989.

On the federal level Jackson has served as vice-chairman of the White House Committee on Balanced Growth & Economic Development and the White House Committee on the Windfall Profits Tax. Jackson is also the founding chairman of the Atlanta Economic Development Corporation and the chairman of the Atlanta Urban Residential Finance Authority.

Barbara Jordan speaks to United Auto Workers Union members at the group's 29th Constitutional Convention in 1989.

**Barbara Jordan
(1936–)**

Former United States
Representative

Jordan was born on February 21, 1936 in Houston, Texas. She attended Phillis Wheatley High School, where she graduated a member of the honor society in 1952. In 1956 Jordan received a B.A. from Texas Southern University in history and political science. She went on to Boston University, where she earned a J.D. in 1959.

After teaching at Tuskegee Institute for a year, Jordan returned to Houston, where she practiced law and was appointed administrative assistant to a Harris County judge. In 1966 Jordan was elected to the Texas Senate. She was the first African-American to serve as president pro tem of that body and to chair the important Labor and Management Relations Committee. In 1972 Jordan was elected to the U.S. House of Representatives, where she stayed until 1978. During her terms in both the Texas Senate and the U.S. House, Jordan was known as a champion of civil rights, minorities, and the poor.

From 1979 to 1982 she was a professor at the Lyndon Baines Johnson School of Public Affairs at the Austin campus of the University of Texas. In 1982 she was made holder of the Lyndon Baines Johnson Centennial Chair of National Policy.

Jordan has co-authored two books, *Barbara Jordan: A Self-Portrait* (1979), and *The Great Society: A Twenty Year Critique* (1986). She has served on the Democratic Caucus Steering and Policy Committee, and in 1976 and 1992 she was the keynote speaker at the Democratic National Convention.

John Mercer Langston was born in Virginia in 1829. Upon the death of his father, Ralph Quarles, an estate owner, young Langston was emancipated and sent to Ohio, where he was given over to the care of a friend of his father. Langston spent his childhood there, attending private school in Cincinnati before graduating from Oberlin College in 1849. Four years later, after getting his degree from the theological department of Oberlin, he studied law and was admitted to the Ohio bar in 1854.

John Mercer Langston (1829–1897)

Former United States Representative

Langston began his practice in Brownhelm, Ohio. He was chosen in 1855 to serve as clerk of this township by the Liberty Party. During the Civil War, he was a recruiting agent for Negro servicemen, helping to organize such famed regiments as the 54th and 55th Massachusetts, and the 5th Ohio.

In 1867, Langston served as inspector general of the Freedmen's Bureau, and he served as dean and vice president of Howard University from 1868 to 1875. In 1877 he was named minister resident to Haiti and chargé d'affaires to Santo Domingo, remaining in diplomatic service until 1885.

Soon after his return to the United States and to his law practice, he was named president of the Virginia Normal and Collegiate Institute. In 1888 he was elected to Congress from Virginia, but he was not seated for two years until vote-counting irregularities had been investigated. He was defeated in his bid for a second term. In 1894 Langston wrote an autobiography, *From the Virginia Plantation to the National Capital.* Eleven years earlier, he had published a volume of his speeches, *Freedom and Citizenship.*

Langston died in 1897.

George Thomas "Mickey" Leland (1944–1989)

Former United States Representative

Leland was born November 27, 1944 in Lubbock, Texas. He graduated from Texas Southern University in 1970 with a B.S. in pharmacy and taught clinical pharmacy there for a short time.

Leland had been active in the civil-rights movement during his student years, and in an effort to affect social change he ran for and was elected to the Texas state legislature in 1973. In 1978 he was elected to the United States House of Representatives, filling Barbara Jordan's vacated seat.

Leland was devoted to easing the hunger of starving persons in the United States and in other countries, especially African countries. To this end he chaired the House Select Committee on World Hunger and visited underprivileged areas throughout Africa. In 1989, while Leland was traveling to a United Nations refugee camp in Ethiopia, the plane he was on crashed near Gambela, Ethiopia, killing all on board.

John Robert Lewis (1940–)

United States Representative

Lewis was born in Troy, Alabama on February 21, 1940. He received a B.S. in 1961 from the American Baptist Theological Seminary and in 1967 he earned another B.A. from Fisk University.

Before entering politics Lewis was associated with numerous social activist organizations, including the Student Non-Violent Coordinating Committee; he served as associate director of the Field Foundation, project director of the Southern Regional Council, and executive director of the Voter Education Project Inc. In 1982 Lewis was elected Atlanta City Councilman-at-large, and in 1986 voters sent him to the U.S. House of Representatives as a Democrat.

Lewis is a recipient of the Martin Luther King, Jr. Non-Violent Peace Prize.

President Bill Clinton meets with Kweisi Mfume and Senator Carol Moseley Braun in 1993.

Kweisi Mfume
(1948–)

United States Representative

Mfume was born Fizzell Gray in Baltimore on October 24, 1948. He received a B.S. from Morgan State University in 1976 and an M.A. from Johns Hopkins University in 1984.

In 1978 Mfume was elected to the Baltimore City Council, where he became especially interested in health issues. In 1987 he was elected to the U.S. House of Representatives as a Democrat. He had previously been a member of the Maryland Democratic State Central Committee and a delegate to the Democratic National Convention in 1980, 1984, and 1988.

Mfume is vice-chairman of the Congressional Black Caucus and a member of the narcotics abuse and control subcommittee.

Arthur W. Mitchell
(1883–1968)

Former United States Representative

Born to slave parents in 1883 in Chambers County, Alabama, Mitchell was educated at Tuskegee Institute and at Columbia and Harvard universities. By 1929, he had founded Armstrong Agricultural School in West Butler, Alabama, and become a wealthy landowner and a lawyer with a thriving practice in Washington, DC. When he left the nation's capital that year, it was with the avowed purpose of entering politics and becoming a representative from Illinois.

Mitchell won Democratic approval only after Harry Baker (who had defeated him in the primary) died suddenly, leaving the nomination vacant.

Aided by the overwhelming national sentiment for the Democratic party during this period, he unseated Oscar De Priest by the slender margin of three thousand votes.

Mitchell's most significant victory on behalf of civil rights came not in the legislative chamber, but in the courts. In 1937, Mitchell brought suit against the Chicago and Rock Island Railroad after having been forced to leave his first class accommodations en route to Hot Springs, Arkansas, and sit in a "Jim Crow" car. He argued his own case before the Supreme Court in 1941, and won a decision that declared "Jim Crow" practices illegal.

Mitchell used his influence in Congress to improve the lot of African Americans. He proposed that states that discriminated against black Americans should receive fewer Congressional seats and advocated strong sanctions against states that practiced lynching. Also, he worked for the elimination of poll taxes to make it easier for black persons to vote. Following the end of World War II, Mitchell held that because blacks fought bravely for the United States, they should be able to vote for their government representatives.

In 1942, Mitchell retired from Congress and continued to pursue his civil-rights agenda as a private citizen. He also lectured occasionally and pursued farming on his estate near Petersburg, Virginia, where he died in 1968 at the age of 85.

Eleanor Holmes Norton (1938–)

Delegate to the
United States House of
Representatives

Norton was born Eleanor Holmes on April 8, 1938 in Washington, DC. She attended Antioch College in Ohio but transferred to Yale University and received an M.A. in American Studies in 1963 and a J.D. from Yale's law school in 1964.

After graduating from law school Norton clerked for a federal judge in Philadelphia before joining the American Civil Liberties Union in 1965 as a litigator specializing in free-speech issues. She stayed with the ACLU until 1970, reaching the position of assistant legal director and successfully arguing a first amendment case before the United States Supreme Court. In 1970 she became chairwoman of the New York City Commission on Human Rights, a post she held until 1977 when she headed the Equal Employment Opportunity Commission. In 1981 she was a senior fellow at the Urban Institute, and in 1982 she accepted the position of

Professor of Law at Georgetown University. Norton had previously taught black history at Pratt Institute in Brooklyn, New York, and law at New York City University Law School.

In 1990 Norton was elected congressional delegate to the United States House of Representatives for the District of Columbia, a non-voting position.

Hazel O'Leary (1937–)

Cabinet Member

O'Leary was born Hazel Reid on May 17, 1937 in Newport News, Virginia. She received a B.A. from Fisk College in 1959 and a J.D. from Rutgers University School of Law in 1966.

O'Leary was a utilities regulator under Presidents Ford and Carter and an executive vice-president of the Northern States Power Co., where she functioned as a Washington lobbyist. O'Leary has been a proponent of energy conservation and alternate energy sources. She is a certified financial planner and a member of the New Jersey and Washington bars, and has been vice-president and general counsel of O'Leary Associates in Washington, DC.

In January of 1993 O'Leary was confirmed as President Bill Clinton's Secretary of Energy.

Clarence McClane Pendleton, Jr. (1930–1988)

Former Civil Rights Commissioner

Pendleton was born in Louisville, Kentucky on November 10, 1930. Raised in Washington, DC, he attended Dunbar High School and received a B.S. from Howard University in 1954. Pendleton served three years in the U.S. Army, where he was assigned to a medical unit. After his discharge in 1957 Pendleton returned to Howard University, where he received a master's degree in 1961 and coached swimming, football, rowing, and baseball.

In 1968 Pendleton became the recreation coordinator of the Baltimore Model Cities Program and in 1970 the director of the Urban Affairs Department of the National Recreation and Parks Association. Pendleton soon began attracting national attention, and in 1972 he headed San Diego's Model Cities Program and in 1975 became the director of the San Diego Urban League.

By 1980 there had been a change in Pendleton's political philosophy. He began to feel that African Americans' reliance on government programs were trapping them in a cycle of dependence and welfare handouts. Pendleton believed that it was in the best interest of African Americans to build strong ties with an expanding private sector and eschew the more traditional ties with liberal bureaucrats and liberal philosophies.

To this end he supported the election of Ronald Reagan to the presidency, and in 1981 Pendleton was appointed chairman of the Civil Rights Commission by President Reagan. Pendleton was the first African American to hold this post.

Pendleton's chairmanship was controversial mostly because of his opposition to affirmative action and forced busing as a means of desegregating schools. Pendleton retained a more liberal philosophy on other matters, however, by supporting the Equal Rights Amendment and the Voting Rights Act.

Pendleton died unexpectedly of an apparent heart attack on June 5, 1988 in San Diego.

Pinckney Stewart Pinchback
(1837–1921)

Former Lieutenant Governor

Pinchback was born in Macon, Georgia on May 10, 1837. Although his mother had been a slave, by the time Pinchback was born she had been emancipated by Pinchback's father. Moving to Ohio with his mother, Pinchback attended high school in Cincinnati in 1847, but in 1848 he began working on riverboats, first as a cabin boy and then as a steward.

At the outbreak of the Civil War Pinchback went to Louisiana and in 1862 he enlisted in the Union Army. He soon began recruiting soldiers for an African-American troop variously known as the Louisiana Native Guards and the Corps d'Afrique. Racial problems soon arose with the military hierarchy and Pinchback resigned his commission in protest.

After the war Pinchback became active in Louisiana politics. He organized a Republican Club in 1867 and in 1868 was a delegate to a state constitutional convention. In that year he was also elected to the state senate and in 1871 he became president pro-tem of that body. He soon became lieutenant governor of Louisiana through the line of succession. For five weeks in late 1872 and early 1873 Pinchback was governor of Louisiana while the elected official underwent impeachment proceedings. In 1872 and 1873 Pinchback was elected to the U.S. Senate and the U.S. House of Representatives. He was refused seating both times when the elections were contested and ruled in favor of his Democratic opponent. He did, however, receive what would have been his salary as an elected official.

In 1877 Pinchback switched his allegiance to the Democratic Party and in 1882 was appointed surveyor of customs for New Orleans. In 1887 he began attending law school at Straight University in New Orleans and was later admitted to the bar. In 1890 Pinchback moved to Washington, DC, where he died December 21, 1921.

Born in 1908 to Mattie Fletcher and Adam Clayton Powell, Sr., Powell was raised in New York City, attended high school there, and then went to Colgate University, where he earned a bachelor's degree in 1930. In 1931 Powell graduated from Columbia University with a master's degree in religious education.

The young Powell launched his career as a crusader for reform during the Depression. He forced several large corporations to drop their unofficial bans on employing blacks and directed a kitchen and relief operation which fed, clothed, and provided fuel for thousands of Harlem's needy and destitute. He was instrumental in persuading officials of Harlem Hos-

Adam Clayton Powell, Jr. (1908–1972)

Former United States Representative

Adam Clayton Powell giving a speech to civil-rights demonstrators in 1963.

pital to integrate their medical and nursing staffs, helped many blacks find employment along Harlem's "main stem," 125th Street, and campaigned against the city's bus lines, which were discriminating against black drivers and mechanics.

When Powell Sr. retired from Abyssinian Baptist Church in 1936, his son, who had already served as manager and assistant pastor there, was named his successor.

In 1939, Powell served as chairman of the Coordinating Committee on Employment, which organized a picket line before the executive offices of the World's Fair in the Empire State Building and eventually succeeded in getting employment at the fair for hundreds of blacks.

Powell won a seat on the New York City Council in 1941 with the third highest number of votes ever cast for a candidate in municipal elections. In 1942 he turned to journalism for a second time (he had already been on the staff of the New York *Evening Post* in 1934), and published and edited the weekly *People's Voice,* which he called "the largest Negro tabloid in the world." He became a member of the New York State Office of Price Administration in 1942 and served until 1944.

In 1944, Powell was elected to Congress and represented a constituency of three hundred thousand, 89% of whom were black. Identified at once as "Mr. Civil Rights," he encountered a host of discriminatory procedures upon his arrival in the nation's capital. He could not rent a room or attend a movie in downtown Washington. Within Congress itself, he was not allowed to use such communal facilities as dining rooms, steam baths, showers, and barber shops. Powell met these rebuffs head-on by making use of all such facilities and insisting that his entire staff follow his lead.

As a freshman legislator, Powell engaged in fiery debates with segregationists, fought for the abolition of discriminatory practices at United States military installations, and sought—through the controversial Powell Amendment—to deny federal funds to any project where discrimination existed. This amendment eventually became part of the Flanagan School Lunch Bill, making Powell the first black Congressman since Reconstruction to have legislation passed by both houses.

Powell also sponsored legislation advocating federal aid to education, a minimum-wage scale, and greater benefits for the chronically unemployed.

He also drew attention to certain discriminatory practices on Capitol Hill and worked toward their elimination. It was Powell who first demanded that a black journalist be allowed to sit in the Senate and House press galleries, introduced the first Jim Crow transportation legislation, and introduced the first bill to prohibit segregation in the Armed Forces. At one point in his career, the *Congressional Record* reported that the House Committee on Education and Labor had processed more important legislation than any other major committee. In 1960, Powell, as senior member of this committee, became its chairman. He had a hand in the development and passage of such significant legislation as the Minimum Wage Bill of 1961, the Manpower Development and Training Act, the Anti-Poverty Bill, the Juvenile Delinquency Act, the Vocational Educational Act, and the National Defense Education Act. In all, the Powell committee helped pass forty-eight laws involving a total outlay of fourteen billion dollars.

The flamboyant congressman, however, was accused of putting an excessive number of friends on the congressional payroll, of a high rate of absenteeism from congressional votes, and of excessive zeal for the "playboy's" life.

In 1967, the controversies and irregularities surrounding him led to censure in the House and a vote to exclude him from his seat in the 90th Congress. The House based its decision on the allegation that he had misused public funds and was in contempt of the New York courts due to a lengthy and involved defamation case that had resulted in a trial for civil and criminal contempt. Despite his exclusion, Powell was readmitted to the 91st Congress in 1968. In mid-1969, the Supreme Court ruled that the House had violated the Constitution by excluding him from membership, but left open the questions of his loss of twenty-two years' seniority and the chairmanship of the Education and Labor Committee. Also unresolved were the $25,000 fine levied against him and the matter of back pay.

However, rather than return to Congress, Powell spent most of his time on the West Indian island of Bimini, where process servers could not reach him. But photographers did, and the ensuing photos of Powell vacationing on his boat while crucial votes were taken in Congress began to affect Powell in his home district. In 1970, he lost the Democratic Congressional primary to Charles Rangel by 150 votes. Powell retired from public office and worked as a minister at the Abyssinian Baptist Church. On April 4, 1972, Powell died in Miami.

Joseph H. Rainey
(1832–1887)

Former United
States Representative

Joseph H. Rainey, the first black member of the House of Representatives, was born in 1832 in Georgetown, South Carolina. Rainey's father purchased his family's freedom and moved them to Charleston in 1846. During the Civil War, Rainey was drafted to work on Confederate fortifications in Charleston harbor and serve passengers on a Confederate ship. However, Rainey escaped with his wife to the West Indies and remained there until the end of the Civil War in 1865.

Rainey and his wife returned to South Carolina in 1866. In 1868, Rainey was elected as a delegate to the state constitutional convention, and he was elected to the state senate in 1870. A year later, he was elected to the U.S. House of Representatives.

As a member of Congress, Rainey presented some ten petitions for a civil-rights bill which would have guaranteed blacks full constitutional rights and equal access to public accommodations. On one occasion, Rainey dramatized the latter issue by refusing to leave the dining room of a hotel in Suffolk, Virginia. He was forcibly ejected from the premises. Rainey was a staunch supporter of legislation that prevented racial discrimination in schools, on public transportation, and in the composition of juries. He supported legislation that protected the civil rights of the Chinese minority in California, and advocated the use of federal troops to protect black voters from intimidation by the Ku Klux Klan. Rainey was reelected in 1872 and, during a debate on Indian rights in 1874, became the first black representative to preside over a session of Congress. Rainey gained reelection to Congress in 1874 and 1876.

Rainey retired from Congress in 1879. He was appointed as a special agent for the United States Treasury Department in Washington, DC. He served until 1881, after which he worked for a banking and brokerage firm. Unfortunately, the firm failed and Rainey took a job at a wood and coal factory. In 1886 he returned to Georgetown, where he died in 1887.

Charles Rangel
(1930–)

United States
Representative

Harlem-born Charles Rangel vaulted into the national spotlight in 1970 when he defeated Adam Clayton Powell, Jr. for the Democratic nomination in New York's 18th Congressional District. Rangel's upset victory stirred hopes among black leaders that a grassroots political movement that was generated from within Harlem, rather than stemming from beyond the community, might result in the grooming of an energetic, capable, and untainted successor to the volatile and unpredictable Powell.

Born June 11, 1930, Rangel attended Harlem elementary and secondary schools before volunteering to serve in the U.S. Army during the Korean war. While stationed in Korea with the 2nd Infantry, he saw heavy combat and received the Purple Heart and the Bronze Star Medal for Valor, as well as United States and Korean Presidential citations. Discharged honorably as a staff sergeant, Rangel returned to finish high school and to study at New York University's School of Commerce, from which he graduated in 1957. The recipient of a scholarship, Rangel then attended St. John's Law School, graduating in 1960.

After being admitted to the bar, Rangel earned a key appointment as assistant United States attorney in the Southern District of New York in 1961. For the next five years, he acquired legal experience as legal counsel to the New York City Housing and Redevelopment Board, as legal assistant to Judge James L. Watson, as associate counsel to the speaker of the New York State Assembly, and as general counsel to the National Advisory Commission on Selective Service. In 1966, Rangel was chosen to represent the 72nd District, Central Harlem, in the State Assembly. Since then, he has served as a member of, and secretary to, the New York State Commission on Revision of the Penal Law and Criminal Code.

In 1972, Rangel easily defeated Livingston Wingate in the Democratic congressional primary and went on to an overwhelming victory in November. In 1974, he was elected chairman of the Congressional Black Caucus.

In his first term, he was appointed to the Select Committee on Crime and was influential in passing the 1971 amendment to the drug laws that authorized the President to cut off all military and economic aid to any country that refused to cooperate with the United States in stopping the international traffic in drugs. In 1976, he was appointed to the Select Committee on Narcotics Abuse and Control. Rangel is regarded as one of the leading congressional experts on the subject.

Rangel served as chairman of the Congressional Black Caucus in 1974–1975 and was a member of the Judiciary Committee when it voted to impeach President Nixon. In 1975, he moved to the Ways and Means Committee, becoming the first black to serve on this committee. Two years later, his colleagues in the New York congressional delegation voted him the majority whip for New York State.

Rangel is a ranking member of the Ways and Means Committee and chairs the Select Revenue Measures Subcommittee. He is also chairman of the Select Committee on Narcotics Abuse and Control and deputy whip for the House Democratic Leadership.

Hiram Rhodes Revels (1827–1901)

Former United States Senator

Hiram Rhodes Revels, a native of North Carolina, was the first black to serve in the United States Senate. Revels was elected from his adopted state of Mississippi, and served for approximately one year.

Born in 1827, Revels was educated in Indiana and attended Knox College in Illinois. Ordained a minister in the African Methodist Church, he worked among black settlers in Kansas, Maryland, Illinois, Indiana, Tennessee, Kentucky, and Missouri before settling in Baltimore in 1860. There he served as a church pastor and school principal.

During the Civil War, Revels helped organize a pair of Negro regiments in Maryland, and in 1863 he went to St. Louis to establish a freedmen school and to carry on his work as a recruiter. For a year he served as chaplain of a Mississippi regiment before becoming provost marshal of Vicksburg.

Revels settled in Natchez, Mississippi in 1866 and was appointed alderman by the Union military governor of the state. In 1870, Revels was elected to the United States Senate to replace Jefferson Davis, the former president of the Confederacy. Revels's appointment caused a storm of protest from white Southerners. Nonetheless, Revels was allowed to take his seat in the Senate.

As a United States Senator, Revels quickly won the respect of many of his constituents for his alert grasp of important state issues and for his courageous support of legislation that would have restored voting and office-holding privileges to disenfranchised Southerners. He believed that the best way for blacks to gain their rightful place in American society was not through violent means, but by obtaining an education and leading an exemplary life of courage and moral fortitude. He spoke out against the segregation of Washington, DC's public school system and defended the rights of black men who were denied work at the Washington Navy Yard because of their race.

Revels left the Senate in 1871 after serving one full term. He was named president of Alcorn University near Lorman, Mississippi. He left Alcorn in

1873 to serve as Mississippi's secretary of state on an interim basis. He returned to Alcorn in 1876 and became editor of the *South-Western Christian Advocate,* a religious journal. He retired from Alcorn University in 1882.

Revels lived in Holly Springs, Mississippi during his later years and taught theology at Shaw University. He died on January 16, 1901.

The first black woman to be named an official representative to the United Nations, Edith Sampson served in this body from 1950 until 1953, first as an appointee of President Harry S Truman and later during a portion of the Eisenhower administration.

A native of Pittsburgh, Sampson acquired a bachelor of laws degree from the John Marshall Law School in Chicago in 1925, and two years later she joined the Illinois bar and became the first woman to receive a master of laws from Loyola University.

One of Sampson's cases took her all the way to the Supreme Court in 1934. During the 1930s, she maintained her own private practice, specializing particularly in domestic relations and criminal law.

After her U.N. appointment, Sampson traveled around the world, often as a lecturer under State Department auspices. She was elected associate judge of the Municipal Court of Chicago in 1962, becoming the first black woman ever to sit as a circuit court judge. She gained acclaim for her superior mediating powers, her heartfelt sincerity, and her humanistic approach to rendering judgments. In 1978, she retired from Cook County Circuit Court.

Sampson died on October 7, 1979 at Northwestern Hospital in Chicago, Illinois.

Kurt L. Schmoke was inaugurated as the first black mayor of Baltimore on December 8, 1987. Schmoke grew up and attended public school in Baltimore. He graduated with honors from Baltimore City College high school, and in 1967 won the award as the top scholar-athlete in the city. Schmoke went on to receive his bachelor's degree from Yale University in

Edith Sampson
(1901-1979)

Former Alternate
Delegate to the
United Nations

Kurt L. Schmoke
(1949-)

Mayor of Baltimore

1971, studied at Oxford University as a Rhodes scholar, and in 1978 earned his law degree from Harvard University.

After graduating from Harvard, Schmoke began his law practice with the prestigious Baltimore firm of Piper & Marbury, and shortly thereafter was appointed by President Carter as a member of the White House Domestic Policy staff.

Schmoke returned to Baltimore as an assistant U.S. attorney, where he prosecuted narcotics and white-collar crime cases, among others. He then returned to private practice and immersed himself in assorted civic activities.

In November 1982, Schmoke was elected state's attorney for Baltimore, which is the chief prosecuting office of the city. As state's attorney, he created a full-time narcotics unit to prosecute all drug cases, and underscored the criminal nature of domestic violence and child abuse by setting up separate units to handle those cases. Also, Schmoke hired a community liaison officer to make sure that his office was being responsive to neighborhood questions and concerns.

In his inaugural address, Mayor Schmoke set the tone and future direction for his administration by saying he wanted Baltimore to reduce its large high school dropout and teenage pregnancy rates and combat illiteracy. He has overseen the passage of the largest-ever increase in the city's education budget, and in partnership with Baltimore businesses and community-based organizations, Schmoke developed the Commonwealth Agreement and the College Bound Foundation to guarantee opportunities for jobs or for college to qualifying high school graduates. Also since taking office, Schmoke has begun major initiatives in housing, economic development, and public safety, and he has proposed educational programs to prepare Baltimore's citizens for high-tech jobs.

Robert Smalls

(1839–1915)

Former United
States Representative

Robert Smalls of South Carolina served a longer period in Congress than any other black Reconstruction congressman. Born a slave in Beaufort, South Carolina in 1839, Smalls received a limited education before moving to Charleston with the family of his owner. While in Charleston, Smalls worked at a number of odd jobs and eventually became adept at piloting boats along the Georgia and South Carolina coasts.

At the outbreak of the Civil War, Smalls was forced to become a crew member on the Confederate ship *Planter,* a transport steamer. On the morning of May 13, 1862, Smalls smuggled his wife and three children on board, assumed command of the vessel, and sailed it into the hands of the Union squadron blockading Charleston harbor. Single-handedly, he was thus responsible for the freedom of his own family and for that of the twelve black crewmen. His daring exploit led President Abraham Lincoln to name him a pilot in the Union Navy. He was also awarded a large sum of money for what constituted the delivery of war booty. In December 1863, during the siege of Charleston, Smalls again took command of the *Planter* and sailed it to safety—a feat for which he was promoted to captain, the only black to hold such a rank during the Civil War.

After the war, Smalls was elected to the South Carolina House of Representatives, serving there from 1868 to 1870. In 1870, Smalls became a member of South Carolina's State Senate and served there until 1874. Smalls campaigned for a congressional seat in 1874 against an independent candidate and won the election. He took his seat in Congress on March 4, 1875.

During his tenure in Congress, Smalls consistently supported a wide variety of progressive legislation, including a bill to provide equal accommodations for blacks in interstate travel and an amendment designed to safeguard the rights of children born of interracial marriages. He also sought to protect the rights of black Americans serving in the armed forces.

Smalls won reelection in 1876, an election that was bitterly contested by Smalls's Democratic challenger, George Tillman. Tillman tried unsuccessfully to have Smalls's election to Congress overturned. However, Tillman's supporters were undeterred. In 1877, Smalls was accused of taking a $5,000 bribe while serving as a senator. Although Smalls was exonerated by Governor William D. Simpson, his popularity plummeted. Smalls lost his reelection bid in 1878.

Although Smalls was defeated, he did not fade from the political scene. In 1880, Smalls ran again for Congress. He lost the election but maintained that the results were invalid due to vote-counting irregularities. Smalls's charges were substantiated and he was allowed to take his seat in Congress in July 1882. Two months later, another congressional election was held and Smalls lost his seat to fellow Republican Edward W. M. Mackey. However, Mackey died in January 1884 and Smalls was allowed to serve the remainder of Mackey's term. In 1886, Smalls's career in Congress was ended when he lost an election to Democratic challenger William Elliott.

Although Smalls was no longer a congressman, he remained involved in political activities. From 1889 to 1913, Smalls served as collector of the port of Beaufort. He died on February 22, 1915.

Louis Stokes

(1925–)

United States
Representative

Stokes was born in Cleveland, Ohio on February 23, 1925. He served in the U.S. Army from 1943 until 1946, then attended Case Western Reserve University from 1946 to 1948. In 1953 he received a J.D. from Cleveland Marshall Law School. After fourteen years in private practice with the law firm of Stokes, Character, Terry & Perry he was elected as a Democrat to the U.S. House of Representatives in 1969.

As Ohio's first African-American representative, Stokes has served on a number of committees, including the House Assassination Committee, which investigated the deaths of Martin Luther King, Jr. and President John F. Kennedy. In 1972 and 1973 Stokes chaired the Congressional Black Caucus and in 1972, 1976, and 1980 he was a delegate to the Democratic National Convention.

Louis W. Sullivan

(1933–)

Former Cabinet Member

On March 1, 1989 Dr. Louis W. Sullivan was confirmed as Secretary of Health and Human Services by the Senate by a vote of 98 to 1, becoming the first African American appointed to a cabinet position in the Bush administration.

Instrumental in the development of the Morehouse School of Medicine as a separate entity from Morehouse College, Sullivan served as professor of biology and medicine and as founder, dean, and director of the medical education program at Morehouse College. In 1981, he was nominated as Morehouse School of Medicine's first dean and president.

Sullivan graduated from Morehouse College magna cum laude with a bachelor's degree in 1954, and went on to medical school at Boston University, graduating cum laude in 1958. He completed his internship at New York Hospital Cornell Medical Center, and his medical and general pathology residencies at Cornell Medical Center and Massachusetts General Hospital.

He then fulfilled two fellowships and served in a variety of positions with Harvard Medical School, Boston City Hospital, New Jersey College of Medicine, Boston University Medical Center, the Boston Sickle Cell Center, and other institutions.

Described as a "distinguished and dedicated individual who makes things happen," Sullivan has led an academic and professional life of excellence. He has been involved in numerous educational, medical, scientific, professional, and civic organizations, has held advisory, consulting, research, and academic positions, and has received many professional and public service awards. Sullivan's research and activities focus on hematology and he has authored and co-authored more than 60 publications on this and other subjects. He is also the founding president of the Association of Minority Health Professions.

In 1989 Sullivan was nominated by President George Bush for the position of Secretary of Health and Human Services, where he was responsible for ensuring the safety of food, drugs, and medical research and for promoting health education. His term expired in January 1993.

Harold Washington (1922–1987)

Former Mayor of Chicago

Washington was born in Chicago on April 15, 1922. After serving with the Army Air Corps in the Pacific theater during World War II, he received a B.A. from Roosevelt University in 1949. Washington then received a J.D. from Northwestern University Law School in 1952.

After graduation Washington worked as an assistant city prosecutor in Chicago, and while establishing a private law practice he was an arbitrator with the Illinois Industrial Commission from 1960 to 1964.

Running on the Democratic ticket, Washington was elected to the Illinois State House of Representatives (1965–1976) and the Illinois State Senate (1977–1980). While a legislator he helped establish the Illinois Fair Employment Practices Commission and the naming of Martin Luther King, Jr.'s birthday as a state holiday. Washington was also concerned with consumer protection legislation and the Illinois Legislative Black Caucus. In 1980 Washington was elected to the U.S. House of Representatives and in 1983, after a tightly contested primary and subsequent election, Washington became Chicago's first African-American mayor.

Although Washington's mayoralty was marred by political infighting, he did manage to institute reforms such as increased city hiring of minorities, deficit reduction, the appointment of an African-American police commissioner, and reduction of patronage influence. Washington died while in office on November 25, 1987.

Maxine Waters
(1938–)

United States
Representative

Waters was born in St. Louis on August 15, 1938. After graduating from high school she moved to Los Angeles, where she worked at a garment factory and for a telephone company. She eventually attended college and received a B.A. in sociology from California State University. She became interested in politics after teaching in a Head Start program and serving as a delegate to the Democratic National Convention in 1972. She later attended the convention four more times in the same capacity.

In 1976 Waters was elected to the California State Assembly, and in 1990 she was elected to the U.S. House of Representatives. She is a vociferous spokesperson for the poor and minorities, fighting for legislation to promote aid to poor and minority neighborhoods in American cities and to combat apartheid in South Africa.

Robert Weaver
(1907–)

Former Cabinet Member

Robert Weaver became the first black appointed to a presidential cabinet when Lyndon B. Johnson named him to head the newly created Department of Housing and Urban Development (HUD) on January 13, 1966. Previously, Weaver had served as head of the Housing and Home Finance Agency (HHFA) from 1961 to 1966.

Robert Weaver was born on December 29, 1907 in Washington, DC, where he attended Dunbar High School and worked during his teens as an electrician. Encountering discrimination when he attempted to join a union, he decided instead to concentrate on economics, and eventually received his Ph.D. in that field from Harvard University. Weaver's grandfather, Dr. Robert Tanner Freeman, was the first black American to earn a doctorate in dentistry at Harvard.

During the 1940s and 1950s, Weaver concentrated his energies on the field of education. He had already been a professor of economics at the Agricultural and Technical College of North Carolina in Greensboro from 1931 to 1932. In 1947, he became a lecturer at Northwestern University and then became a visiting professor at Teachers College, Columbia University, and at the New York University School of Education. During this period, he was also a professor of economics at the New School for Social Research.

From 1949 to 1955 he was director of the Opportunity Fellowships Program of the John Hay Whitney Foundation. Weaver also served as a member of the National Selection Committee for Fulbright Fellowships, chairman of the Fellowship Committee of the Julius Rosenwald Fund, and a consultant to the Ford Foundation.

In 1955 Weaver was named Deputy State Rent Commissioner by New York's Governor Averell Harriman. By the end of the year, he had become State Rent Commissioner and the first black to hold state cabinet rank in New York. From 1960 to 1961, he served as vice chairman of the New York City Housing and Redevelopment Board, a three-person body that supervised New York's urban renewal and middle-income housing programs.

Weaver headed the Department of Housing and Urban Development until 1968. From 1969 to 1970, he served as president of Baruch College. Weaver accepted a teaching position at the Department of Urban Affairs at Hunter College in New York in 1971 and retired seven years later.

Lawrence Douglas Wilder (1931–)

Former Governor of Virginia

Wilder was born on January 17, 1931 in Richmond, Virginia. He graduated from Virginia Union University in 1951 with a B.S. in chemistry. After graduation he was drafted into the U.S. Army and assigned to a combat infantry unit in Korea. During the Korean War he was awarded a Bronze Star for bravery and valor in combat. After being discharged from the army in 1953 Wilder worked as a chemist in the Virginia State Medical Examiner's Office. In 1959 Wilder graduated with a J.D. from Howard University Law School.

Wilder practiced law in Richmond until he became the first African American elected to the Virginia State Senate since Reconstruction. While there Wilder chaired the important Privileges and Elections committee and worked on legislation supporting fair housing, union rights for public employees, and minority hiring, and he voted against capital punishment (a position he has since rescinded). In 1985 Wilder was elected lieutenant

L. Douglas Wilder announces his candidacy for the Democratic presidential nomination in 1991.

governor, and in 1989 he became Virginia's first African-American governor, winning the election by a razor-thin one-third of one percent of the vote; he served one term as governor, stepping down in 1993.

Andrew Young
(1932–)

Former U.N. Ambassador, Former Mayor of Atlanta

Andrew Young came into national prominence nearly three decades ago and has become a figure of international prominence and stature. Soft-spoken yet eloquent, Young is widely admired for his incisive thinking and his willingness to express his opinion.

Young was born in New Orleans in 1932, and received a bachelor of science degree from Howard University and a bachelor of divinity degree from Hartford Theological Seminary in 1955. He was ordained a minister in the United Church of Christ and then served in churches in Alabama and Georgia before joining the National Council of Churches in 1957. The turning point of his life came in 1961 when he joined Martin Luther King, Jr., and became a trusted aide and close confidante. He did much of the negotiating for the Southern Christian Leadership Conference and was respected for his calmness and rationality. He became executive vice president of SCLC in 1967 and remained with King until the latter's murder in 1968. During his years with SCLC, Young also developed several programs, including antiwar protests, voter registration projects and other major civil-rights drives.

In 1970 Young, a Democrat, lost a bid for the United States House of Representatives to Republican Fletcher Thompson. In the aftermath of the election, Young was appointed chair of the Community Relations Committee. Although the CRC was an advisory group with no enforcement powers, Young took an activist role, pressing the city government on issues from sanitation and open housing to mass transit, consumer affairs, and Atlanta's drug problem. Young's leadership in the CRC led to a higher public profile and answered critics' charges that he was inexperienced in government.

Young launched another bid for the United States Congress in 1972. The campaign was difficult for Young since blacks comprised only 44% of the voters in Young's congressional district, and his Republican opponent, Rodney Cook, was considered a more appealing candidate than Fletcher Thompson had been in 1970. However, Young captured 23% of the white vote and 54% of the total vote to win by a margin of 8,000 votes. Young was the first black representative to be elected from Georgia since Jefferson Long in 1870.

Thereafter, Young was reelected with ease every two years. He was one of the most vocal supporters of his fellow Georgian Jimmy Carter's campaign for the presidency in 1976. Following President Carter's inauguration, Young left Congress in 1977 to become America's ambassador to the United Nations.

His tenure there was marked by controversy as well as solid achievement. The controversy resulted from his outspoken manner, which sometimes ruffled diplomatic feathers. His solid achievements were represented primarily in the tremendous improvement he fostered in relations between America and the Third World.

Young's career as a diplomat came to an end in 1979 when he met secretly with a representative of the Palestine Liberation Organization to discuss an upcoming vote in the United Nations. America had a policy that none of its representatives would meet with the PLO as long as it refused to recognize the right of Israel to exist as a state. When the news of Young's meeting leaked out, an uproar ensued. Young had originally told the State Department that the meeting was by chance, but later he admitted that it had been planned.

Though the meeting had secured a vote in the United Nations that the United States wanted, the pressure mounted and Young tendered his resignation, which President Carter accepted. The incident badly strained black–Jewish relations because of the feeling within the black community that Jewish leaders were instrumental in Young's removal, a charge that they vehemently denied.

Young became a private citizen, but not for long. When Maynard Jackson was prevented by law from running for his third term of office as mayor of Atlanta in 1981, Young entered the race. Once again, it was not easy. He faced a black candidate and a strong white candidate and was forced into a runoff. Race entered the campaign when the outgoing mayor, himself a black, charged blacks who supported the white candidate, state legislator Sidney Marcus, with "selling out" the civil-rights movement.

Jackson's remarks were widely criticized, and it was feared that they would create a backlash against Young. However, Young ended up with 55% of the total vote. He took office at a time when Atlanta was going through several economic and social problems. Its population was shrinking, the tax base stagnating, almost a quarter of the city's residents were below the poverty line, and the city was still shaken by the recent murders of twenty-eight black youths and the disappearance of another—even though a man had been convicted of several of the murders.

Some critics doubted Young's ability to deal with Atlanta's problems. He was seen as antibusiness and a weak administrator. However, by 1984, the city had become so successful at attracting new businesses that it was experiencing a major growth spurt. In addition, the crime rate dropped sharply, and racial harmony seemed an established fact. Young was re-elected decisively in 1985.

Limited by law to two terms as mayor, Young ran unsuccessfully for governor of Georgia in 1990. He remains active as president of Young Ideas, a consulting firm he founded. Young is also chair of the Atlanta Committee for the Olympic Games, an organization responsible for preparing Atlanta to host the 1996 Summer Olympics.

In 1989, Coleman Young won his fifth term as mayor of Detroit, Michigan. The vote was considered remarkable because even with the heavy unemployment in Detroit, a shortage of cash, and a high crime rate, the voters returned Young to office. In 1993, however, Young decided not to seek re-election for the following term, pledging his support to candidate Sharon McPhail, who ultimately lost the 1993 mayoral race to Dennis Archer.

Part of Young's support stemmed from a sense of revitalization that he breathed into Detroit and the confidence of the voters who believed that though things were rough, the mayor would persevere. A Democrat, and one of the first big-city mayors to support Jimmy Carter's presidential campaign in 1976, Young had a very close relationship with the Carter administration. This relationship proved helpful in securing funds for Detroit.

Young was born in Tuscaloosa, Alabama in 1918. His family moved to Detroit's east side in 1926 after the Ku Klux Klan ransacked a neighborhood in Huntsville where his father was learning to be a tailor. In Detroit, Young attended Catholic Central and then Eastern High School, graduating from the latter with honors. He had to reject a scholarship to the University of Michigan when the Eastern High School Alumni Association, in contrast to policies they followed with poor white students, declined to assist him with costs other than tuition.

Young entered an electrician's apprentice school at Ford Motor Company. He finished first in the program but was passed over for the only available electrician job in favor of a white candidate. He went to work on the assembly line, and soon engaged in underground union activities. One day, a man Young describes as a "company goon" tried to attack him. Young hit him on the head with a steel bar and was fired.

During World War II, he became a navigator in the Army Air Force and was commissioned a second lieutenant. Stationed at Freeman Field, Indiana, he demonstrated against the exclusion of blacks from segregated officers' clubs and was arrested along with 100 other black airmen, among them the late Thurgood Marshall and Percy Sutton, former president of New York's borough of Manhattan. Young spent three days in jail. Shortly thereafter, the clubs were opened to black officers.

After the war, Young returned to his union-organizing activities and in 1947 was named director of organization for the Wayne County AFL-CIO. How-

Coleman A. Young (1918–)

Former Mayor of Detroit

ever, the union fired him in 1948 when he supported Henry Wallace, candidate of the Progressive Party, in the Presidential election. The union regarded Wallace as an agent of the Communist Party and supported Harry Truman.

Young managed a dry cleaning plant for a few years and, in 1951, founded and directed the National Negro Labor Council. According to Young, the Council was ahead of its time and successfully prevailed on Sears Roebuck & Co. and the San Francisco Transit System to hire blacks. However, the Council also aroused the interest of the House Un-American Activities Committee, which was then holding hearings around the country at which alleged Communists were required to produce names of people allegedly associated with the Party. Young, who denies he was ever a Communist, refused to name anyone. He emerged from the battle with his self-respect intact, but his Labor Council was placed on the Attorney General's subversive list. In 1956, the Labor Council was disbanded. Charges that Young was a Communist were later used against him, unsuccessfully, during his first mayoral campaign.

After working at a variety of jobs, Young won a seat on the Michigan Constitutional Convention in 1961. In 1962, he lost a race for state representative but became director of campaign organization for the Democratic gubernatorial candidate in Wayne County (Detroit). He sold life insurance until 1964 when, with union support, he was elected to the state senate. In the senate, he was a leader of the civil-rights forces fighting for low-income housing for people dislocated by urban renewal and for an end to discrimination in the hiring practices of the Detroit Police Force.

By
David G. Oblender

Young declared his candidacy for mayor of Detroit in 1973 and mounted a vigorous campaign for the office. He won the office after a racially divisive campaign. Among his early successes in office were the integration of the Detroit Police Department and the promotion of black officers into administrative positions.

*E*ntrepreneurship

African Americans have a long and rich history of entrepreneurship in America; blacks have been in business since before the Civil War and continue their entrepreneurial tradition today. Segments of the African-American population have exhibited the same entrepreneurial spirit as segments of other ethnic groups who have migrated to this country. Very often, however, the history of black entrepreneurship has been either overlooked or misconstrued.

PRE–CIVIL WAR ENTREPRENEURSHIP ✦ ✦ ✦ ✦ ✦ ✦ ✦ ✦ ✦ ✦ ✦ ✦ ✦ ✦

As the United States began to take shape, a number of people of African origin were successful in their attempt to carve out an economic stake for themselves. Anthony Johnson, who accumulated substantial property in Jamestown, Virginia, is believed to be the first person of African descent to have become an entrepreneur in America. Jean Baptist DuSable, a wholesaler and merchant who established the first settlement in Chicago in the early 1770s, was another pre–Civil War era entrepreneur.

Prior to the Civil War, however, slavery defined the existence of most African Americans. Thus, two categories of business persons were able to develop and sustain business enterprises. The first group was composed of free African Americans, numbering approximately sixty thousand, who could accumulate the capital to generate business activity. They developed enterprises in almost every area of the business community, including merchandising, real estate, manufacturing, construction, transportation, and extractive industries.

Since African Americans in the South were denied the right to assemble, it was illegal for black civic, business, or benevolent organizations to convene. Black enterprise, therefore, grew more quickly in the North.

The second group consisted of slaves who—as a result of thrift, ingenuity, industry, and/or the liberal paternalism of their masters—were able to engage in business activity. Although the constraints of slavery were such that even highly skilled slaves could not become entrepreneurs in the true sense of the word, slaves did, during their limited free time, sell their labor and create products to sell.

The fact that African-American entrepreneurship existed at all during the era of slavery is testimony to an entrepreneurial spirit and the determination of a people to achieve economic freedom even under the harshest conditions.

If it was all but impossible for slaves to engage in private enterprise, it was also hazardous for "free" blacks to do so, since they were effectively only half free. Free blacks lived under a constant fear of being labeled as "runaway" slaves and being sold into slavery. In addition, in areas where free blacks lived, laws were passed to restrict their movement and thus their economic freedom. This was one intention, for example, of the laws that Virginia, Maryland, and North Carolina had passed by 1835 forbidding free blacks to carry arms without a license. The right of assembly was also denied blacks throughout the South—leaving it illegal for black civic, business, or benevolent organizations to convene. In addition to reflecting white slaveowners' fears of an African-American uprising, such legal restriction had the purpose and effect of making it difficult for free blacks to earn a living.

The southern economic exploitation of blacks, however, indirectly had a positive impact on black entrepreneurship: the development of business enterprise by African Americans in the North. In 1838, for example, the *Register of Trades of Colored People* in the city of Philadelphia listed eight bakers, twenty-five blacksmiths, three brass founders, fifteen cabinet makers and carpenters, five confectioners, two caulkers, two chair bottomers, fifteen tailoring enterprises, thirty-one tanners, five weavers, and six wheelwrights.

The Philadelphia business register also listed businesses run by African-American women. Among these were eighty-one dressmakers and tailors, four dyers and scourers, two fullers, and two glass and paper makers. The ninety-eight hairdressers registered, comprising the largest trade group, operated some of the most lucrative enterprises.

Another profitable business controlled by African Americans in Philadelphia during the 1820s and 1830s was sailmaking. Nineteen sailmakers were recorded in the business register of 1838. James Forster, who lived between 1766 and 1841, ran a major manufacturing firm that made sails; in 1829, Forster employed forty workers, black and white.

Historically, black-owned firms have been concentrated in a narrow range of service businesses, including small restaurants, cleaning establishments, funeral parlors, shoe shops, hair salons, automobile dealers, and gas stations.

Although several individuals succeeded in the manufacturing trades, the business enterprise that brought prosperity to the largest number of African Americans in Philadelphia was catering. Robert Boyle, a black waiter, is believed to have developed the idea of contracting to provide and serve formal dinners in domestic entertaining. Catering quickly spread across the developing country, but it was in Philadelphia, the city of its birth, that catering was king.

Significantly, most of the businesses discussed thus far involved the craft or service trades. These were small enterprises that required only a modest capital investment and allowed African Americans to develop a niche without threatening larger white-owned businesses.

POST–CIVIL WAR ENTREPRENEURSHIP ✦ ✦ ✦ ✦ ✦ ✦ ✦ ✦ ✦ ✦ ✦ ✦ ✦

The promise of freedom and political enfranchisement held out by Lincoln's Emancipation Proclamation of 1862 was soon undermined by racist judicial rulings. In 1878, in *Hall v. DeCuir*, the United States Supreme Court ruled that a state could not prohibit segregation on a common carrier. In 1896, with the *Plessy v. Ferguson* ruling, "separate but equal" became the law of the land. Following these decisions, a pattern of rigid segregation of the races was established that remained the norm until the advent of the civil-rights movement in the 1960s.

Nevertheless, even within the context of disenfranchisement and segregation, Booker T. Washington saw the possibility of securing African-American economic stability through business development. In 1900, Washington spearheaded the development of the National Negro Business League to encourage black enterprise. During the organization's first meeting, the delegates concluded that:

Booker T. Washington, who believed that African-American economic stability could be achieved through business development, helped found the National Negro Business League to encourage black enterprise.

Through her development of the "hot" comb and other hair-care products, Madame C. J. Walker became America's first self-made black female millionaire.

a useless class is a menace and a danger to any community, and ... when an individual produces what the world wants, whether it is a product of the hand, heart, or head, the world does not long stop to inquire what is the color of the skin of the producer.... If every member of the race should strive to make himself the most indispensable man in his community, and to be successful in business, however humble that business might be, he would contribute much toward soothing the pathway of his own and future generations. (John Sibly Butler, 1991, *Entrepreneurship and Self-Help Among Black Americans*, New York: State University of New York Press, pp. 67–68.)

During the early 1900s, although services continued to be the cornerstone of the black business community, blacks found it easier to raise capital and ventured into more entrepreneurial endeavors.

In 1905, for example, Madame C. J. Walker developed a hair care system that gave dry hair a soft texture; millions of women, both black and white, became customers for Madame Walker's products. Before her death in 1919, Madame Walker had more than 2,000 agents marketing her ever-expanding line of products, which made her America's first self-made black female millionaire.

Durham, North Carolina: A Special Case

Turn-of-the-century Durham, North Carolina represented a special case of enterprise and economic resilience. In publications of the time, Durham was referred to as "The Wall Street of Negro America." By the late 1940s, more than 150 businesses owned by African Americans flourished in Durham. Among these businesses were traditional service providers, such as cafes, movie houses, barber shops, boarding houses, pressing shops, grocery stores, and funeral parlors. What distinguished Durham, however, was the presence of large black businesses, including the extremely successful North Carolina Mutual Life Insurance Company.

Among the many black businesses in Durham early in the century were the Banker's Fire Insurance Company, the Mutual Building and Loan Association, the Union Insurance and Realty Company, the Durham Realty and Insurance Company, the People's Building and Loan Association, the Royal Knights Savings and Loan Association, T. P. Parham and Associates, and the Mortgage Company of Durham.

Although Durham was a success, external economic pressure and racial hostility made it impossible for blacks, on a large scale, to develop stores that could compete in the larger economy. As a result of Jim Crow laws and segregation, most black-owned businesses were forced to limit their market to their own community. A partial exception was the Durham textile mill, at the time the only hosiery mill in the world owned and operated by African Americans. It operated eighteen knitting machines and did business in the open market; their salesmen, who traveled mostly in North Carolina, Indiana, Georgia, South Carolina, and Alabama, were white. This manufacturing firm was exceptional in the sense that it was perhaps the first large-scale black-owned enterprise to hire whites.

African-American businesses were so stable and looked so promising for the future that, in 1924, Durham was chosen as the location for the headquarters of the National Negro Finance Corporation, which was capitalized at $1 million. The organization was started to provide working capital to individuals, firms, and corporations in all parts of the country. Durham, from the turn of the century until the 1950s, remained unrivaled as the black business capital of America.

Present-Day Durham

Today, 150 or so black entrepreneurs and professionals are still held together by the Durham Business and Professional Chain, an organization founded fifty-two years ago. It would be difficult, however, to replicate the entrepreneurial excitement that existed in Durham between 1900 and

1950. Indeed, scholars have noted that grass-roots entrepreneurship tends to develop quickly by groups who newly enter the economy of a country, as did African Americans after the abolition of slavery. However, from generation to generation, there is typically a decrease in the number or rate of entrepreneurs. In the case of African Americans, a full-blown civil-rights movement was required to create another surge in the entrepreneurial spirit.

♦ ♦ ♦ ♦ ♦ ♦ ♦ ♦ ♦ ♦ POST–CIVIL RIGHTS ERA ENTREPRENEURSHIP

The civil-rights movement prompted the development of legislation and a number of government agencies to ensure the social, political, and economic rights of African Americans. Perhaps the greatest boost to black entrepreneurship came in 1967 with the establishment of the Small Business Administration (SBA) Section 8 (a) program. Under that section of the Small Business Act Amendments, the SBA is authorized to enter into contract with federal agencies on behalf of small and disadvantaged businesses. Entry into the program is contingent upon SBA approval of the business plan prepared by prospective firms. The total dollar value of contracts processed through Section 8 (a) has grown from $8.9 million in 1969 to $2.7 billion in 1985. Through the program, many small and black-owned businesses have been able to stabilize and grow.

Another product of the civil-rights movement has been the 1977 Public Works Employment Act. Supplementing the SBA 8 (a) program, the Pub-

Freedom National Bank, Harlem's first black commerical bank, was founded in 1965.

The most recent Bureau of the Census survey, from 1987, indicates that African Americans are starting business enterprises at a greater rate than Americans in general. The number of black-owned businesses grew by 37.6 percent between 1982 and 1987, which is greater than the 26.2 percent increase for the general population.

lic Works Act requires that all general contractors bidding for public works projects allocate at least 10 percent of their contracts to minority sub-contractors.

During the early 1980s, the SBA Section 8 (a) program was criticized because less than 5 percent of the firms have achieved open-market competitiveness, which implies that the program is in effect assisting the marginal entrepreneur, as opposed to the promising self-employed minority businessperson.

The fundamental concept of set-aside minority assistance programs was called into question during the height of the Reagan–Bush era. In 1989, the landmark United States Supreme Court ruling in *City of Richmond v. Croson* struck down as unconstitutional under the Fourteenth Amendment a city ordinance of Richmond, Virginia, requiring that 30 percent of each public-construction contract be set aside for minority businesses. The Supreme Court did make a distinction between local/state and federally enacted business development programs, holding that the United States Congress has far more authority than the states in formulating remedial legislation.

The *Croson* decision has had a devastating impact on minority businesses. In Richmond, during the month of July 1987, when a lower court first ruled against the city's set-aside program, 40 percent of the city's total construction dollars were allocated for products and services provided by minority-owned construction firms. Immediately following the court's decision, the minority businesses' share of contracts fell to 15 percent, dropping to less than 3 percent by the end of 1988. In Tampa, Florida the number of contracts awarded to black-owned companies decreased 99 percent, and contracts with Latino-owned firms fell 50 percent, after *Croson*. Such dramatic decreases in contracts awarded to minority businesses occurred throughout the country. More than thirty-three states and political subdivisions have taken steps to dismantle their racial/ethnic set-aside programs; more than seventy jurisdictions are conducting studies and/or holding hearings to review and evaluate their programs in light of *Croson*.

Growth Industries

Historically, African-American businesses have been restricted to the narrow range of service enterprises. They have tended to establish businesses that require relatively limited capital and technical expertise, such as personal services and small-scale retailing. These firms have had to rely heavily on the African-American community as their market for goods and services. Recent business initiation trends, however, indicate increasing diversity among black businesses. An examination of the nation's largest black-owned corporations reveals considerable diversity.

The location of corporate headquarters in urban areas has provided increased business opportunity for black business service enterprises. Large cities have become areas where administrative and service functions are the dominant economic activities. The growth in corporate and government administration in central-city business districts has created a need for complementary advertising, accounting, computer, legal, temporary secretarial, and maintenance business services. Employment in such business firms owned by African Americans grew by 224 percent between 1972 and 1987; the number of firms increased nearly five times, and gross receipts grew by 700 percent.

◆ ◆ ◆ ◆ ◆ ◆ ◆ ◆ BUSINESS EXECUTIVES AND ENTREPRENEURS

Wally Amos

(1937–)

Entrepreneur

Born Wallace Amos, Jr. in Tallahassee, Florida in 1937, he achieved success as the first African-American talent agent for the William Morris Agency. Starting there as a mail clerk, he quickly worked his way up to executive vice president. While there he "discovered" the singing duo Paul Simon and Art Garfunkel for the agency and has been the agent for such well-known acts and entertainers as the Supremes, the Temptations, Marvin Gaye, Dionne Warwick, and Patti Labelle.

In 1975 Amos founded Famous Amos Chocolate Chip Cookies. Based on his Aunt Della's recipe, the cookies became a nationwide success as they spread across the country from his original store on Sunset Boulevard in Los Angeles. By 1980 Amos was selling five million dollars' worth of cookies each year, and his operation had expanded to include a large production facility in Nutley, New Jersey. Amos's success and expansion was enhanced by the backing of such well-known entertainers as Bill Cosby and Helen Reddy. In 1985 Amos became vice chairman of the company.

Amos had previously spent four years in the United States Air Force, where he served as a cook and radio technician. He has donated personal items to the Business Americana Collection at the Smithsonian's Collec-

Wally Amos was the first African-American talent agent for the William Morris Agency, and later founded the Famous Amos Chocolate Chip Cookies company.

tion of Advertising History and has received the Excellence Award from President Ronald Reagan. Amos's company is presently headquartered in San Francisco, California.

Dave Bing (1943–)
Business Executive,
Former Professional
Basketball Player

Bing was born November 29, 1943 in Washington, DC, where he played basketball at Springarn High School. He was named to play on a national All-Star team and was voted most valuable player on the tour. Bing attended Syracuse University on a basketball scholarship, graduating in 1966 with a

B.A. in economics. He was the second overall pick in the 1966 National Basketball Association draft and was chosen by the Detroit Pistons.

During his first season he was the league's top rookie, and the league's high scorer his second year. In the 1974–1975 season Bing played for the Washington, DC Bullets, and in the 1977–1978 season he was with the Boston Celtics. Bing was voted the league's most valuable player in 1976 and played in seven NBA All-Star games. The Professional Basketball Writer's Association of America gave him their Citizenship Award in 1977. In 1989 he was elected to the Naismith Memorial Basketball Hall of Fame.

After being associated with management programs at the National Bank of Detroit, Chrysler Corporation, and Paragon Steel, Bing formed Bing Steel Inc. in Detroit, a steel supplier to the automobile industry.

George E. Johnson (1927–)

Business Executive

Johnson was born in Richton, Mississippi on June 16, 1927. He attended Wendell Phillips High School in Chicago and then went to work as a production chemist for a firm that produced cosmetic products for African Americans. While there he developed a hair straightener for men and began marketing it himself in 1954. By 1957 he had formed Johnson Products and was selling products under the Ultra-Sheen label. The company prospered, and by 1971 its stock was being traded on the American Stock Exchange. Johnson Products was the first African-American–owned company to trade on a major stock exchange. In June 1993 Joan B. Johnson, chair and CEO of Johnson Products, announced the sale of the company.

Johnson has served as a director of the Independence Bank of Chicago, the United States Postal Service, and the Commonwealth Edison Company. Johnson is also responsible for the George E. Johnson Foundation, which funds charitable and educational programs for African Americans.

Johnson has received the Abraham Lincoln Center's Humanitarian Service Award (1972), *Ebony* magazine's Black Achievement Award (1978), and the public service award presented by the Harvard Club of Chicago. He has also been awarded the Horatio Alger Award (1980) and the Babson Medal (1983), along with honorary degrees from many institutions of learning, including Chicago State University, Fisk University, and the Tuskegee Institute.

Reginald F. Lewis
(1942–1993)

Business Executive

Lewis was born December 7, 1942 in Baltimore, Maryland. He received an A.B. from Virginia State College in 1965 and a law degree from Harvard Law School in 1968. He first worked with the firm of Paul, Weiss, Rifkind, Wharton & Garrison until 1970. He was a partner in Murphy, Thorpe & Lewis, the first African-American law firm on Wall Street until 1973. Between 1973 and 1989 Lewis was in private practice as a corporate lawyer. In 1989 he became president and CEO of TLC Beatrice International Holdings Inc. With TLC's leveraged acquisition of the Beatrice International Food Company Lewis became the head of the largest African-American–owned business in the United States. TLC Beatrice had revenues of $1.54 billion in 1992.

Lewis was a member of the American and National Bar Associations and the National Conference of Black Lawyers. He was on the board of directors of the New York City Off-Track Betting Corporation, the Central Park Conservance, the NAACP Legal Defense Fund, and WNET–Channel 13, the public television station in New York. He was the recipient of the Distinguished Service Award presented by the American Association of MES-BIC and the Black Enterprise Achievement Award for the Professions.

Lewis died January 19, 1993 in New York.

James B. Llewellyn
(1927–)

Business Executive

Llewellyn was born July 16, 1927 in New York City and earned a B.S. from City College of New York. He attended Columbia University's Graduate School of Business and New York University's School of Public Administration before receiving a degree from New York Law School.

Before attending law school Llewellyn was the proprietor of a retail liquor store. While attending law school he was a student assistant in the District Attorney's Office for New York County from 1958 to 1960. After graduating he practiced law as part of Evans, Berger & Llewellyn. Between 1964 and 1969 he worked in a variety of professional positions for various governmental agencies including the Housing Division of the Housing and Re-Development Board, the Small Business Development Corporation, and the Small Business Administration.

In 1969, as part of a syndicate buyout, Llewellyn became president of Fedco Food Stores of New York. By 1975 the company had grown from eleven to fourteen stores and had annual revenues of $30 million and 450 employees.

Llewellyn has served on the boards of the City College of New York and its Graduate Center, American Can Company, American Capital Management Research, and Freedom National Bank. He has belonged to the Harlem Lawyers Association, the New York Interracial Council for Business Opportunity, and the New York Urban Coalition and its Venture Capital Corporation.

Llewellyn has honorary doctorates from Wagner College, City University of New York, and Atlanta University. During the 1940s He spent four years in the United States Army Corps of Engineers. He is currently CEO of Queen City Broadcasting, Inc.

Parks was born September 20, 1916 in Atlanta, Georgia. He received a B.S. from Ohio State University and did graduate work there in marketing.

Henry G. Parks (1916–)

Entrepreneur, Business Executive

After graduating Parks worked at the Resident War Production Training Center in Wilberforce, Ohio, where he was associated with Mary McLeod Bethune. In 1939 he was a national sales representative for the Pabst Brewing Company. In addition, he has been involved in other enterprises such as theatrical bookings in New York City; a failed attempt at marketing a beverage with Joe Louis, the former heavyweight boxing champion (now deceased); real estate; drug store operations; and cement block production, mostly in Baltimore, Maryland.

Parks ultimately bought into Crayton's Southern Sausage Company of Cleveland, Ohio. After becoming familiar with the meat packing industry he sold his interest in the company for a profit. In 1951 he started H.G. Parks Inc., a sausage packer and distributor, with the aid of a group of investors. By 1971 the company reported annual revenues of $10.4 million dollars and distributed its products to more than twelve thousand East Coast stores.

Parks has also been vice president of the Chamber of Commerce of Metropolitan Baltimore, served on the board of directors of Magnavox, held a seat on the Baltimore City Council, and has an interest in Tuesday Publications.

Naomi R. Sims
(1949–)

Business Executive, Model

Sims was born March 30, 1949 in Oxford, Mississippi. She attended New York University (where she studied psychology) and the Fashion Institute of Technology, both on scholarships.

Sims was a fashion model with the Ford Agency in New York from 1970 to 1973. She was the first African-American woman to be a high fashion model and the first to appear in a television commercial. She also appeared on the cover of *Life* magazine.

In 1970 Sims began to lecture and write fashion and beauty articles on a free-lance basis. In 1973 she co-developed a new fiber for her line of wigs and founded the Naomi Sims Collection, which by 1977 reported annual revenues of $4 million. Sims has also written a number of books, including *All About Health and Beauty for the Black Woman* (1975), *How to Be a Top Model* (1979), *All About Hair Care for the Black Woman* (1982), and *All About Success for the Black Woman*.

In 1969 and 1970 Sims was voted Model of the Year by International Mannequins and won the *Ladies' Home Journal* Women of Achievement Award. For her work with underprivileged children in Bedford-Stuyvesant she also won an award from the New York City Board of Education. In 1977 Sims was voted into the Modeling Hall of Fame by International Mannequins and made the International Best Dressed List, 1971–73 and 1976–77. Sims has also received recognition for her fund-raising efforts for sickle cell anemia and cancer research. She belongs to the NAACP and works closely with drug rehabilitation programs.

She is currently affiliated with Naomi Sims Beauty Products Limited in New York City.

Percy E. Sutton
(1920–)

Business Executive, Attorney

Sutton was born November 24, 1920 in San Antonio, Texas. He graduated from the Phillis Wheatley High School and attended a number of colleges, including Prairie View College, Tuskegee Institute, and the Hampton Institute. His education was interrupted by World War II when he enlisted in the United States Army Air Corps. He was promoted to captain and served as a combat intelligence officer in the Italian and Mediterranean theaters. He was decorated with Combat Stars for his service.

After his discharge, Sutton attended law school on the G.I. Bill, first at Columbia University in New York, and then Brooklyn Law School where he received an LL.B. in 1950. During the Korean conflict Sutton re-enlisted in the USAF and served as an intelligence officer and a trial judge advocate.

Returning to civilian life, he opened a law office in Harlem with his brother and another attorney. In 1964 he was elected to the New York State Assembly, where he served until 1966. In 1966 he was appointed and later elected to the office of president of the borough of Manhattan, a post he held until 1977. Sutton then founded the Inner-City Broadcasting Corporation, from which he is now retired.

Sutton has been a civil-rights advocate both as an attorney and a politician. He was a national director of the Urban League and president of the New York branch of the NAACP, and he was voted Assemblyman of the Year by the Intercollegiate Legislative Assembly in 1966. Sutton has also served as a director of the Museum of the City of New York and the American Museum of Natural History.

Madame C. J. Walker (1867–1919)

Entrepreneur

Walker was born Sarah Breedlove near Delta, Louisiana in 1867. She was orphaned as a child, raised by a sister in Vicksburg, Mississippi, married at the age of fourteen, and widowed in 1887 at the age of twenty.

Walker moved with her daughter to St. Louis, where she earned a living by taking in laundry and sewing. By 1905 she had become interested in hair care products for African-American women and had begun working on a hot comb and her "Wonderful Hair Grower." In 1906 she moved to Denver and, with $1.50 in her pocket, started a hair preparations company. She soon married C. J. Walker, a newspaper journalist who taught her the fundamentals of advertising and mail-order promotion. In 1908 she moved with her daughter to Pittsburgh, where she founded a beauty school that trained cosmetologists in the use of her products.

In 1910, with a more central location in mind, she moved to Indianapolis, Indiana, where she established a laboratory and factory and developed a nationwide network of 5,000 sales agents, mostly African-American women.

Her business prospered and Walker became very wealthy. She had a townhouse in Harlem and a custom-built mansion on the Hudson River near Irvington, New York. She died in New York on May 25, 1919.

Walker was a strong believer in self-reliance and education. She was proud of her accomplishments, especially of providing employment for thousands of African-Americans who might otherwise have had less meaningful jobs. Walker was also a genius at marketing, promotion, and mail-order sales. Beneficiaries of her estate included Mary McLeod Bethune's school in Daytona, Florida and other African-American schools, the NAACP, and the Frederick Douglass home restoration project in Florida.

Maggie Lena Walker

(1867–1934)

Banker

Walker was born on or around July 15, 1867 in Richmond, Virginia. She was the daughter of Elizabeth Draper, a former slave, and Eccles Cuthbert, a New York journalist of Irish extraction.

Walker attended Richmond public schools, and after graduating in 1883 she taught in the Richmond schools for three years before marrying building contractor Armstead Walker in 1886.

While she had been in school, Walker joined the Grand United Order of Saint Luke, a mutual aid society that served as an insurance underwriter for African Americans. Walker became active in the organization and held a number of lesser positions before becoming the Right Worthy Grand Secretary in 1899. She soon changed the name of the organization to the Independent Order of Saint Luke and moved its headquarters to Richmond.

In 1903 she became the head of the Saint Luke Penny Bank and the first woman in the United States to hold such a position. Although legally separate, the bank had a close financial association with the Independent Order of Saint Luke. The bank later became the Saint Luke Bank and Trust Company and finally the Consolidated Bank and Trust Company.

By 1924, under Walker's guidance, the Order had a membership of one hundred thousand, a new headquarters building, more than two hundred employees, and its own newspaper, the *Saint Luke Herald*.

Walker was active in many other organizations, including the National Association of Colored Women, the Virginia Federation of Colored Women's Clubs, and the federation's Industrial School for Colored Girls. In 1912 she founded the Richmond Council of Colored Women and was a founding member of the Negro Organization Society, a blanket association for African-American clubs and organizations.

She was a board member of the NAACP from 1923 to 1934 and the recipient of an honorary degree from Virginia Union University. In 1927 she received the Harmon Award for Distinguished Achievement. Walker died December 15, 1934.

By Michael D. Woodard

*E*ducation

Since the first arrival of Africans in America, the African-American community has worked to sustain a system for educating its youth. In addition to the efforts of individuals, churches and charitable organizations have also played an important role in the creation of educational institutions for blacks in the United States.

THE ORIGINS OF BLACK EDUCATIONAL INSTITUTIONS ♦ ♦ ♦ ♦

Early Christian Missionary Endeavors

Early attempts to educate blacks in America can be traced back to efforts by Christian churches. Although the primary goal of these missionaries was to convert Africans to Christianity, the process often involved general education.

French Catholics in Louisiana were probably the earliest group to begin providing instruction to black laborers in the early 1600s. The French code noir, a system of laws, made it incumbent upon masters to educate slaves.

Pennsylvania Quakers, who opposed the institution of slavery, organized monthly educational meetings for blacks during the early 1700s. One such Quaker, Anthony Benezet, in 1750 established an evening school in his home, which remained successful until 1760. In 1774 Quakers in Philadelphia joined together to open a school for blacks.

An engraving depicting an early black schoolroom.

The Society for the Propagation of the Gospel in Foreign Parts, organized by the Church of England in 1701 for the purpose of converting African slaves to Christianity, was another organization that provided educational opportunities to blacks. In 1751 the society sent Joseph Ottolenghi to convert and educate blacks in Georgia. Ottolenghi "promised to spare no pains to improve the young children."

African Free Schools in New York and Philadelphia

Like the church, the anti-slavery movement played an important part in the creation of schools. In 1787 the Manumission Society founded the New York African Free School; by 1820 more than 500 black children were enrolled. Support increased as other African Free Schools were established in New York, until 1834 when the New York Common Council took over control of the schools.

In 1804 African Episcopalians in Philadelphia organized a school for black children. In 1848 a black industrial training school opened in Philadelphia at the House of Industry. Other Philadelphia schools founded during the nineteenth century included the Corn Street Unclassified School, the Holmesburg Unclassified School, and the Home for Colored Children. By the mid-1860s there were 1,031 pupils in the black public schools of Philadelphia, 748 in the charity schools, 211 in the benevolent schools, and 331 in private schools.

Freedmen's Organizations and Agencies

At the close of the Civil War hundreds of thousands of free blacks were left without homes and adequate resources. As a means for providing temporary assistance to the newly freed slaves, numerous organizations were formed.

The New England Freedmen's Aid Society, organized in Boston on February 7, 1862, was founded to promote education among free African Americans. Supporters of the organization included Edward Everett Hale, Samuel Cabot, Charles Bernard, William Lloyd Garrison, and William Cullen Bryant. In New York a similar organization was founded, the National Freedmen's Relief Association, on February 20, 1862. This was followed by the Port Royal Relief Committee, later known as the Pennsylvania Freedmen's Relief Association, founded in Philadelphia on March 3, 1862. In 1863 several of these organizations merged to form the United States Commission for the Relief of the National Freedmen, which, in 1865, became the American Freedmen's Aid Union.

A freedmen's school in Beaufort, South Carolina, around 1862.

During the 1860s Congress passed several Freedmen's Bureau Acts, creating and financing an agency designed to provide temporary assistance to newly freed slaves. Under the acts, the bureau's chief functions were to provide food, clothing, and medical supplies. Working in conjunction with various benevolent organizations, bureau Commissioner General Oliver Otis Howard established and maintained schools, as well as provisions for teachers. By 1870 the bureau operated over 2,600 schools in the South with 3,300 teachers educating 150,000 students; almost 4,000 schools were in operation prior to the abolition of the agency.

Independent Schools in the Late-Nineteenth Century

The education of African Americans has been largely a function of independent schools, private institutions founded to meet the educational and employment needs of African Americans.

One of the earliest surviving black independent schools, Tuskegee Normal and Industrial Institute (now Tuskegee Institute), was established in 1881 by an act of the Alabama general assembly. Booker T. Washington,

Booker T. Washington organized the Tuskegee Normal and Industrial Institute, now known as the Tuskegee Institute.

the school's organizer and first principal, established at the school a curriculum to provide black students with the means to become economically self-supporting.

Similarly, other independent schools developed around the country. In a lecture room at the Christ Presbyterian Church, Lucy Laney in 1883 opened what became the Haines Normal and Industrial Institute in Savannah, Georgia. In 1901 Nannie Helen Burroughs founded the National

Training School for Women and Girls in Washington, DC. By the end of the first year the school had enrolled thirty-one students; twenty-five years later more than 2,000 women had trained at the school. In Sedalia, North Carolina in 1901, Charlotte Hawkins Brown founded the Palmer Memorial Institute.

With only $1.50 and five students, in 1904 Mary McLeod Bethune founded Daytona Normal and Industrial Institute for Girls in Daytona Beach, Florida. Nineteen years later, the institute merged with the Cookman Institute of Jacksonville, Florida, founded in 1872 by D.S.B. Darnell. Some 2,000 students currently study at what is now known as Bethune-Cookman College.

Early Black Institutions of Higher Education

One of the oldest of the historically black institutions of higher education, named for the English abolitionist William Wilberforce, Wilberforce College (now Wilberforce University) was founded in 1856 by the African Methodist Episcopal Church. The school awarded its first degree in 1857. The oldest institution in operation today, Cheyney State in Pennsylvania, was founded in 1837.

Between 1865 and 1871 several predominantly black institutions of higher learning were founded, including Atlanta University (now Clark-Atlanta University), Shaw University, Virginia Union University, Fisk University, Lincoln Institute (now Lincoln University), Talladega College, Augusta Institute (now Morehouse College), Biddle University (now Johnson

Students at Tuskegee Institute, 1902.

C. Smith University), Howard University, Scotia Seminary (now Barber-Scotia College), Tougaloo College, Alcorn College (now Alcorn State University), and Benedict College. Religious organizations were instrumental in the founding and support of these early black institutions. Atlanta, Fisk, Talladega, and Tougaloo were founded by the American Missionary Association; Benedict, Shaw, and Virginia Union were founded and supported by the American Baptist Home Mission Society.

Alcorn College, founded in 1871, was the first black land grant college. This was made possible under the Morrill Act of 1862, which provided federal land grant funds for higher education. In 1890 Congress passed the second Morrill Act, also known as the Land Grant Act of 1890. The second act stipulated that no federal aid could be provided for the creation or maintenance of any white agricultural and mechanical school unless that state also provided for a similar school for blacks. As a result, a system of separate black land-grant institutions developed, which became the basis of black higher education in the South.

By 1900 there were some thirty-four black institutions in the United States for higher education and more than 2,000 blacks with earned degrees, according to John Hope Franklin in his 1988 publication *From Slavery to Freedom, A History of Negro Americans.*

In 1870, Richard Greener became the first African American to receive a degree from Harvard. Active as a teacher and editor, Greener was admitted to the South Carolina bar in 1876 and became dean of Howard University Law School in 1879.

Early Promoters of African-American Studies

One of the forerunners in the field of black studies, theologian and educator Reverend Alexander Crummell, along with a group of black intellectuals, founded the American Negro Academy in Washington, DC, in 1897. The purpose of the organization was to foster scholarship and promote literature, science, and art among African Americans. The organization's members hoped that through the academy, an educated black elite would be born to shape and direct society. Crummell first conceived the idea of an American Negro Academy while he was a student at Cambridge University in England. The organization's founding members included Paul Laurence Dunbar, William Sanders Scarborough, and W.E.B. DuBois, among other noted educators. Following Crummell's death in 1908, DuBois was elected president of the academy.

In September 1915 Carter G. Woodson, a Harvard Ph.D. graduate, organized the Association for the Study of Negro Life and History (now the Association for the Study of Afro-American Life and History). The association's primary purpose was to promote research, encourage the study of

African-American history, and publish material on black history. In 1916 the association began publishing the *Journal of Negro History*, for which Woodson served as editor until his death in 1950.

Other early scholars of African-American studies include sociologist E. Franklin Frazier (1894–1963), historian George Washington Williams (1849–1991), John Edward Bruce (1856–1924) and Arthur Schomburg, founders of the Negro Society for Historical Research in 1911, and Alain Locke, founder of the Associates in Negro Folk Education in 1934.

The End of Segregation in Public Education

In the years that followed the United States Supreme Court's 1896 ruling in the case *Plessy v. Ferguson*, segregation in public education became general practice. Prior to the Court's decision in *Brown v. Board of Education of Topeka*, black children were often subjected to inferior educational facilities. By the 1930s, however, a string of school desegregation cases reached the Court.

When Lloyd Lionel Gaines, an African American, was refused admission to the law school of the State University of Missouri, he applied to state courts for an order to compel admission on the grounds that refusal constituted a denial of his rights under the Fourteenth Amendment of the U.S. Constitution. At that time, the state of Missouri maintained a practice of providing funds for blacks to attend graduate and professional schools outside of the state, rather than provide facilities itself. The university defended its action by maintaining that Lincoln University, a predominantly black institution, would eventually establish its own law school, which Gaines could then attend. Until then the state would allow him to exercise the option of pursuing his studies outside the state on a scholarship. Ruling in the case *Missouri ex rel. Gaines v. Canada* in 1938, the Supreme Court ruled that states were required to provide equal educational facilities for blacks within its borders.

The first black woman lawyer, Charlotte E. Roy, received her degree from Howard University School of Law in Washington, DC, in 1872.

Taking an even greater step, in 1950 the United States Supreme Court ruled that a separate law school for blacks provided by the state of Texas violated the equal protection clause of the Fourteenth Amendment, when Herman Marion Sweat was refused admission to the law school of the University of Texas on the grounds that substantially equivalent facilities were already available in another Texas school open to blacks only. Ruling in the case *Sweat v. Painter*, the Court ruled that the petitioner be admitted to the University of Texas Law School, since "in terms of number of the

Daisy Bates with four black students, who will attend formerly all-white high schools in Little Rock, Arkansas, 1959.

faculty, variety of courses and opportunity for specialization, size of the student body, scope of the library, availability of law review and similar activities, the University of Texas Law School is superior."

In 1952, five different cases, all dealing with segregation in public schools but with different facts and from different places, reached the Supreme Court. Four of the cases, *Brown v. Board of Education of Topeka* (out of Kansas), *Briggs v. Elliott* (out of South Carolina), *Davis v. Prince Edward County School Board* (out of Virginia), and *Gebhart v. Belton* (out of Delaware) were considered together; the fifth case, *Bolling v. Sharpe*, coming out of the District of Columbia, was considered separately since the district is not a state.

After hearing initial arguments, the Court found itself unable to reach an agreement. In 1953, the Court heard reargument. Thurgood Marshall, legal consul for the NAACP Legal Defense and Education Fund, presented arguments on behalf of the black students. On May 17, 1954, the Court unanimously ruled that segregation in all public education deprived minority children of equal protection under the Fourteenth Amendment. (In the *Bolling* case, the Court determined that segregation violated provisions of the Fifth Amendment, since the Fourteenth Amendment is expressly directed to the states.)

Predominantly black colleges and universities continue to account for the majority of black graduates. This is especially true in the areas of science, mathematics, and engineering. In 1964, more than 51 percent of all

Black Colleges in the 20th Century

Students being bused in Woodville, Mississippi.

blacks in college were still enrolled in the historically black colleges and universities. By 1970 the proportion was 28 percent, and by fall of 1978, 16.5 percent. As recently as 1977, 38 percent of all blacks receiving baccalaureate degrees earned them at black institutions. In 1980, 190,989 African Americans were enrolled at historically black institutions. By 1988 the total black enrollment at these institutions reached 217,462.

Independent Schools in the Late-20th Century

For years independent schools have been founded in order to exert greater control, ensure quality in education, and to meet the needs of African-American children.

In 1932, in order to promote religious growth in the Muslim community, the Nation of Islam founded the University of Islam, an elementary and secondary school to educate black Muslim children in Detroit. Clara Muhammad, wife of Elijah Muhammad, served as the school's first instructor. In 1934 a second school was opened in Chicago; by 1965 schools were operating in Atlanta and Washington, DC. The current sys-

Marva Collins with her class at the Westside Preparatory School, Chicago.

tem of black Muslim schools, named for Clara Muhammad, is an outgrowth of the earlier University of Islam. As of 1992 there were thirty-eight Sister Clara Muhammad schools in the United States.

Gertrude Wilks and other black community leaders in East Palo Alto, California in 1966 organized the Nairobi Day School, a Saturday school. In 1969 the school became a full-time school, then closed in 1984.

Also founded as a Saturday school program in 1972, the New Concept Development Center in Chicago set out to create an educational institution that promoted self-respect, cooperation, and an awareness of African-American history and culture. In 1975 public school teacher and nurse Marva Collins founded the Westside Preparatory School in Chicago.

Recently the educational and social needs of urban youth, particularly African-American males, have been given increased attention. Studies show that nearly forty percent of adult black males are functionally illiterate, and that the number of African-American males incarcerated far outnumbers the number of black males in college. Addressing these issues, large urban school systems, including Baltimore, Detroit, and Milwaukee, have attempted to create programs that focus on the needs of African-American males.

Although progress has been made in the quality of education for black children, inadequacies remain in the provision of resources for the educa-

Although African-American students have shown improved performance on achievement tests, gaps between black students and white still exist, and inadequacies remain in the provision of resources for the education of blacks.

tion of blacks. In recent years, efforts at creating alternative schools designed to meet the needs of African-American children and to reflect the culture and social experiences of blacks have received increased attention. In 1991 the Institute for Independent Education, an organization providing technical assistance to independent neighborhood schools, reported an estimated 300 such schools serving children of color in the United States.

TOWARD AFRICAN-CENTERED EDUCATION ♦ ♦ ♦ ♦ ♦ ♦ ♦ ♦ ♦ ♦ ♦

The African-centered thrust in education has sparked national enthusiasm, debates, and attacks. Whereas many people of African descent see this as a dream come true, others see African-centrism as an attack on American fundamentalism.

American fundamentalism can be defined as a Eurocentric world view, based on the myth of white supremacy. In other words, the fundamental principles of education in America are rooted in the theory that whites are superior and that all people of color are inferior. This myth of white supremacy laid the foundation for manifest destiny and eminent domain, thereby giving justification for the annihilation of the Native Americans, and enslavement of Africans.

Attacks on African-Centered Education

The attacks on African-centered education in recent years have been concerted and consistent. Most evident have been the many books, national magazines, and newspaper articles, charging African-centerism with the "dis-uniting" and "fraying" of American society. Arthur Schlesinger, the author of *The Dis-Uniting of America*, and Diane Ravitch, author of *The Troubled Crusade*, have been the lead gladiators in the fight against African-centered education. Schlesinger has charged that African-centered education is un-American and promotes the teaching of inaccuracy and distorted history; Diane Ravitch has argued that African-centrism is "particularism that is spreading like wildfire through the educational system, promoted by organizations and individuals with a political and professional interest in strengthening ethic power bases." Schlesinger, Ravitch, and other defenders of the Eurocentric world view have worked to discredit African scholars such as Dr. Leonard Jeffries, Dr. Molefe Asante, Dr. Asa Hillard, and Dr. John Henrik-Clark. All of this is designed to convince both blacks and whites that African-centrism is nothing more than an Africanized curriculum.

However, one point that Schlesinger makes about African-centrism is true—the point that African-centrism in "un-American." He states that European ideas and culture formed the American republic and that the United States is an extension of European civilization. African-centrism, on the other hand, provides a world view that is contrary to European ideas and culture—a culture that has oppressed Africans and other people of color.

In an article that appeared in the *Wall Street Journal* on April 23, 1990, Schlesinger argues that Native Americans and person of African descent must be able to assimilate in the same way that Russians, Jews, French, Germans, and the Irish immigrants have. However, European immigrants have not been oppressed, exploited, and enslaved because of their color. Native Americans and Africans, on the other hand, have been and continue to be oppressed and exploited. Therefore, it is clear that assimilation of people of color never has been and never will be a reality in America.

The Foundations of African-Centered Education

African-centrism is not just historical facts and figures centered around time and space. African-centrism is based on the principles of truth, justice, balance, and order. African-centrism presents to black students their own cultural life experiences. The classroom is transformed into a holistic learning environment, in which the student is the center. Although African-centrism benefits all students, the overall thrust of African-centered education is the recentering of children of African descent.

Many African children do not graduate, they simply drop out. They become statistics at juvenile centers, group homes, foster care, adoption agencies, prison yards, and grave yards. They are often referred to by such code names as "at risk" and "inner city youth." They are at risk because they have been targeted for failure.

This Eurocentric definition of education, according to many, must change as we move toward the twenty-first century. Educating children must be based on the principles of self-determination, in which African Americans define, defend, and develop what is in their best interest. African-centered

Principal Clifford Watson with students of the Malcolm X Academy in Detroit, Michigan.

education will instill in youth a sense of self-confidence, pride, and responsibility.

As we move toward an African-centered education, African children will no longer see the contributions of their people as a footnote of history, but rather as the center and origin of history—African-centrism will stand and be celebrated as one of the most progressive educational philosophies in the twenty-first century.

ADMINISTRATORS, EDUCATORS, AND SCHOLARS ♦ ♦ ♦ ♦ ♦ ♦ ♦

Molefi Kete Asante

(1942-)

Scholar

Asante was born Arthur Lee Smith, Jr. on August 14, 1942 in Valdosta, Georgia. His name was legally changed in 1975. He graduated cum laude with a B.A. from Oklahoma Christian College in 1964, received an M.A. from Pepperdine University in 1965, and a Ph.D. from UCLA in 1968.

Asante has taught speech and communications at many universities in the United States. Beginning in 1966 he was an instructor at California State Polytechnic University at Pomona and California State University at Northridge. In 1968 he accepted an assistant professorship at Purdue University in Lafayette, Indiana, where he remained until 1969 when he began teaching at UCLA, advancing from assistant to associate professor of speech. While at UCLA he also served as the director of the Center for Afro-American Studies. In 1973 he accepted the position of professor of communications at the State University of New York. He soon became department chairman, a position he held until 1979 when he became a visiting professor at Howard University in Washington, DC. In 1981 and 1982 he was a Fulbright Professor at the Zimbabwe Institute of Mass Communications. Since 1980 he has been a professor at Temple University in Philadelphia in the school's Department of Pan African Studies.

Asante is a prolific author with more than twenty-four books dealing with both communication theory and the African-American experience. He has published books under both his former and his current name. Some of his recent titles are *Afrocentricity: The Theory of Social Change* (1980), *African Culture: The Rhythms of Unity* (1985), and *The Historical and Cultural Atlas of African-Americans* (1991).

Asante is also a founding editor of the *Journal of Black Studies* and has been a member of the advisory board of the *Black Law Journal* and *Race Relations Abstract*.

Born on July 10, 1875 in Mayesville, South Carolina, Mary McLeod received a sporadic education in local schools. She eventually received a scholarship and studied for seven years at the Scotia Seminary in Concord, North Carolina. In 1893 she went on to study at the Moody Bible Institute in Chicago in lieu of a missionary position in Africa. In 1895 she began teaching at the Haines Institute in Augusta, Georgia. Between 1900 and 1904 she taught in Sumter, Georgia and Palatka, Florida.

Mary McLeod Bethune (1875–1955)

Educator, Bethune-Cookman College Founder

In 1904 she founded her own school in Daytona Beach, Florida—the Daytona Educational and Industrial School for Negro Girls. John D. Rockefeller became an early admirer and supporter of the school after hearing a performance by its choir. Bethune went on to found the Tomoka Missions and in 1911 the McLeod Hospital. In 1922 her school merged with the Cookman Institute to become Bethune-Cookman College.

Bethune's work received national attention, and she served on two conferences under President Herbert Hoover. In 1936 President Franklin Roosevelt appointed her director of the Division of Negro Affairs of the National Youth Administration. During World War II she served as special assistant to the Secretary of War, responsible for selecting Negro WAC officer candidates.

Bethune also served on the executive board of the National Urban League and was a vice president of the NAACP. She received the Spingarn Award in 1935, the Frances A. Drexel Award in 1936, and the Thomas Jefferson Medal in 1942. Bethune was also instrumental in the founding of the National Council of Negro Women. She retired from public life in 1950 on her seventy-fifth birthday and died five years later on May 18, 1955.

Much of Bethune's philosophy involved ennobling labor and empowering African Americans to achieve economic independence. Although a tireless fighter for equality, she eschewed rhetorical militancy in favor of a doctrine of universal love.

Nannie Helen
Burroughs
(1879–1961)

Educator

Known as a brilliant orator, Burroughs was a lifelong booster of women's education and a tireless civic organizer. In 1901 the National Training School for Women and Girls opened in Washington, DC, with Burroughs as president; by the end of the first school year the school had enrolled thirty-one students. In 1934 the name was changed to the National Trades and Professional School for Women. In 1964 the school was again renamed the Nannie Helen Burroughs School, with a new elementary school curriculum.

Burroughs was active in the antilynching campaign and a life member of the Association for the Study of Negro Life and History. She helped organize the Women's Industrial Club of Louisville and was responsible for organizing Washington, DC's first black self-help program.

Fanny Coppin
(1873–1913)

Educator

Fanny Coppin was born in slavery but rose to prominence in the field of education. After her aunt purchased her freedom, Coppin went on to become the second African-American woman to receive a degree from Oberlin College.

Coppin was appointed principal of the women's department of the Institute for Colored Youth, a high school established by Quakers in 1837, and later principal of the entire school. In 1894 Coppin founded the Women's Exchange and Girls' Home. She served as president of the local Women's Mite Missionary Society and the Women's Home and Foreign Missionary Society, and as a vice president of the National Association of Colored Women.

Coppin, an active member of the African Methodist Episcopal Church, served as president of the AME Home Missionary Society and accompanied her husband, Levi J. Coppin, on a missionary venture to South Africa.

Before her death Coppin began writing an autobiography, *Reminiscences of School Life, and Hints on Teaching*.

Joe Clark (1939–)

Educator

Best known as the feisty, dedicated, baseball-bat-wielding school principal portrayed in the film *Lean on Me*, Clark has served as an exemplar of school discipline and boasts a distinguished record of achievements and laurels. A fourteen-year member of the New Jersey Board of Education and an elementary and secondary school principal since 1979, he has been honored by the White House, the NAACP, his alma mater Seton Hall University, and various newspapers and magazines.

Born in Rochelle, Georgia, Clark served in the United States Army Reserve from 1958 to 1966. He received a B.A. from New Jersey's William Paterson College in 1960 and his master's degree from Seton Hall in 1974. Between the degrees he served on the Board of Education and from 1976 to 1979 he was a coordinator of language arts. He then began his career as school principal, and only a few years after he began, the accolades came pouring in. Clark received the NAACP Community Service Award and was named New Jerseyan of the Year by the Newark *Star Ledger* in 1983; the next year *New Jersey Monthly* named him an outstanding educator. In 1985 Clark appeared in Washington, DC to receive honors at a presidential conference on academic and disciplinary excellence, and he also took awards from Seton Hall and Farleigh Dickinson University. The National School Safety Center gave Clark the Principal of Leadership Award in 1986 and the National Black Policemen's Association bestowed their humanitarian award upon him in 1988.

Johnnetta Betsch Cole (1936–)

Spelman College President

A distinguished scholar, Johnnetta Cole has served on the faculties of Washington State University, University of Massachusetts, Hunter College, and Spelman College, the historically black women's institution in Atlanta where she is president. Born in Jacksonville, Florida, Cole attended Oberlin College, which awarded her a B.A. in 1957; she went on to earn her master's degree and doctorate at Northwestern.

Cole held her first teaching post at Washington State, where she taught anthropology and served as director of black studies; the university dubbed her Outstanding Faculty Member of the Year for 1969–70. She has served as a visiting professor of anthropology at several of the institutions named above. As an anthropologist, she has done field work in Liberia, Cuba, and in the African-American community. A prolific writer, she has published in many mainstream periodicals as well as scholarly journals, and since 1979 she has been a contributor and advising editor to *The Black Scholar*. She headed the Association of Black Anthropologists in 1980 and has been a fellow of the American Anthropological Association since 1970, as well as a board member of the Center for Cuban Studies since 1971.

Marva Collins (1936–)

Educator

Schoolteacher Marva Delores Nettles Collins's dedication and ingenuity moved the producers of television's "60 Minutes" to broadcast a feature about her and even inspired a made-for-TV film.

The Monroeville, Alabama native received a bachelor's degree from Clark College in 1957, after which she attended Northwestern University; her teaching career began at the Monroe County Training School in her hometown in 1958. She taught at Delano Elementary School from 1960 to 1975 and has been a fixture at Chicago's Westside Preparatory School ever since.

Collins served as director of the Right to Read Foundation in 1978, and has been a member of the President's Commission on White House Fellowships since 1981. A variety of organizations have honored her, including the NAACP, the Reading Reform Foundation, the Fred Hampton Foundation, and the American Institute for Public Service. Among the institutions that have given her honorary degrees are Washington University, Amherst, Dartmouth, Chicago State University, Howard University, and Central State University.

The free-born Sarah Mapp Douglass was an outspoken antislavery activist and accomplished educator. She attended the Ladies Institute of the Pennsylvania Medical University. In the 1820s she organized a school for black children in Philadelphia.

Douglass was an active member of the Philadelphia Female Anti-Slavery Society, which also provided support to Douglass's school. She also served as vice chairman of the Freedmen's Aid Society and was a member of the New York Anti-Slavery Women.

In 1853 Douglass was appointed head of the girls' department at the Institute of Colored Youth (forerunner of Cheney State College), where she remained until her retirement in 1877. Douglass died in Philadelphia on September 8, 1882.

Sarah Mapp
Douglass
(1806–1882)

Educator

Franklin's long and distinguished career has included the publication of numerous books of history and biography, numerous awards and honorary degrees, and a position of great stature in the scholarly community.

Franklin was born in Rentiesville, Oklahoma. He received his bachelor's degree from Fisk University in 1935 and then began graduate work at Harvard, which awarded him a master's in 1936 and a Ph.D. in 1941. He taught history at Fisk and St. Augustine's College while working on his doctorate, later moving on to North Carolina College at Durham, Howard University, Brooklyn College (where he chaired the history department), Cambridge University, the University of Chicago, and Duke University.

Among his many publications are such books as *From Slavery to Freedom*, *A History of Negro Americans*, *Militant South*, *Reconstruction After the Civil War*, *The Emancipation Proclamation*, *A Southern Odyssey*, and *Race and History: Selected Essays*. Twice a Guggenheim Fellow, Franklin received honors from the Fellowship of Southern Writers, Encyclopedia Britannica, and many other organizations, was made professor emeritus of history at Duke University, and earned the Publications Prize of the American Studies Association established in his name in 1986.

John Hope Franklin
(1915–)

Scholar

William H. Gray III
(1941–)

United Negro College
Fund President

Born to a minister and a high school teacher in Baton Rouge, Louisiana, William H. Gray III began his professional life as an assistant pastor at Union Baptist Church in New Jersey. He earned a bachelor's degree from Franklin and Marshall College in 1963, serving during his senior year as an intern for Pennsylvania congressman Robert C. Nix. He received a master of divinity degree from Drew Theological School in 1966 and a master of theology degree from Princeton Theological Seminary in 1970. In between he attended the University of Pennsylvania, Temple University, and Oxford University. He then served as pastor of Union Baptist.

In 1976 Gray moved into politics, challenging Nix for his congressional seat. He lost the first time, but returned to unseat Nix in 1979. He became a vocal and influential member of the House, challenging the administration of Ronald Reagan on such issues as social spending and U.S. support for the government of South Africa. He served on the House Budget Committee, becoming chair in 1985; he there earned the admiration and respect of even his most implacable political foes. Gray left the House of Representatives in 1991 to head the United Negro College Fund.

Franklin G. Jenifer
(1939–)

Howard University
President

A distinguished scholar, Franklin Jenifer was trained as a biologist and taught in the biology departments of such institutions as Livingston College at Rutgers University, where he chaired the biology department from 1974 to 1977. He obtained his doctorate from the University of Maryland, but it was to his alma mater, Howard University—where he received his bachelor's and master's degrees—that he returned to take up his most visible position: university president. He became Howard's president in 1990 after a series of assignments ranging from vice chancellor of the New Jersey Department of Higher Education to chancellor of the Massachusetts Board of Regents.

A native of Washington, DC, Jenifer is chairman of the AAAS National Council for Science & Technology Education and a board member of the American Council on Education and the Council for Aid to Education. He holds honorary doctorates from Babson College, Boston College, Mount Holyoke College, the University of Medicine and Dentistry of New Jersey, and Wheelock College.

Charles Spurgeon Johnson was born in Bristol, Virginia. He earned a B.A. from Virginia Union University and a Ph.D. from the University of Chicago.

Johnson occupied a number of diverse positions, from editor to administrator. He served as the assistant executive secretary of the Chicago Commission on Race Relations and as research director of the National Urban League, where he founded the organization's journal, *Opportunity*.

In 1928 Johnson was made chairman of Fisk University's department of social sciences, and while there he established the Fisk Institute of Race Relations. In 1933 he was appointed director of Swarthmore College's Institute of Race Relations. In 1946 Johnson was appointed president of Fisk University—the first black to hold the position.

Johnson wrote several books, including *The Negro in American Civilization* (1930), *The Economic Status of the Negro* (1933), *The Negro College Graduate* (1936), and *Educational and Cultural Crisis* (1951).

Charles Spurgeon Johnson (1893–1956)

Scholar, Former Fisk University President

Born on September 3, 1886 in Philadelphia, Locke graduated Phi Beta Kappa with a B.A. from Harvard University in 1907. He was then awarded a Rhodes Scholarship for two years' study at Oxford University in England and did further graduate study at the University of Berlin. Upon returning to the United States, Locke took an assistant professorship in English and philosophy at Howard University in Washington, DC. He received his Ph.D. from Harvard in 1918 and the same year was made chairman of the philosophy department at Howard, where he stayed until his retirement in 1953.

In 1934 Locke founded the Associates in Negro Folk Education. In 1942 he was named to the Honor Role of Race Relations. A prolific author, Locke's first book was entitled *Race Contacts and Inter-Racial Relations* (1916). His best known works include *The New Negro: An Interpretation* (1925), a book that introduced America to the Harlem Renaissance, and *The Negro in Art: A Pictorial Record of the Negro Artist and of the Negro Theme in Art* (1940). Locke died in New York City on June 9, 1954.

Alain Locke (1886–1954)

Scholar

Benjamin Mays and others meet with President John F. Kennedy.

Benjamin E. Mays (1894–1984)

Former Morehouse College President

In addition to occupying the president's office at Morehouse, Benjamin Mays wrote, taught mathematics, worked for the Office of Education, served as chairman of the Atlanta Board of Education, preached in a Baptist church, acted as an advisor to the Southern Christian Leadership Council, and was a church historian.

Born in Epworth, South Carolina, Mays attended Bates College and later received his master's degree and Ph.D. from the University of Chicago. He served as a pastor at Georgia's Shiloh Baptist Church from 1921 to 1924, and later taught at Morehouse College and South Carolina's State College at Orangeburg. After a stint at the Tampa Urban League, he worked for the YMCA as National Student Secretary and then directed a study of black churches for the Institute of Social and Religious Research. From 1934 to 1940 he acted as dean of Howard University's School of Religion, before taking up the presidency of Morehouse from 1940 to 1967. He served in several other distinguished posts, including the Atlanta Board of Education chairmanship and positions at HEW and the Ford Foundation. Mays earned forty-three honorary degrees and the Dorie Miller Medal of Honor, among others.

Jesse Edward Moorland (1863–1940)

Archivist, Clergyman

Moorland was born on September 10, 1863 in Coldwater, Ohio. Following the untimely death of his parents, Moorland was reared by his grandparents. His early education consisted of sporadic attendance at a small rural schoolhouse and being read to by his grandfather. Moorland eventually attended Normal University in Ada, Ohio, married, and taught school in Urbana, Ohio. He went on to Howard University in Washington and graduated with a degree in theology in 1891.

Moorland was ordained a congregational minister and between 1891 and 1896 he served at churches in South Boston, Virginia; Nashville, Tennessee; and Cleveland, Ohio. In 1891 he also became active in the YMCA, an association he maintained for much of his life.

In 1909 Moorland's well-known essay "Demand and the Supply of Increased Efficiency in the Negro Ministry" was published by the American Negro Academy. In it Moorland called for a more pragmatic ministry, both in terms of the education of its members and its approach to dealing with social issues.

By 1910 Moorland had become quite active in the YMCA and was appointed secretary of the Colored Men's Department. In this position Moorland raised millions of dollars for the YMCA's construction and building fund.

Having reached the mandatory retirement age in 1923, Moorland resigned from the YMCA and began devoting his time and considerable energy to other pursuits. Moorland was active with the Association for the Study of Negro Life and History, the National Health Circle for Colored People, and the Frederick Douglass Home Association.

From 1907 on, Moorland served as a trustee of Howard University. In 1914 he donated his private library of African-American history to the university. Out of this gift grew the Moorland Foundation, which was renamed the Moorland-Spingarn Collection and later the Moorland-Spingarn Research Center. This collection of documents on black history and culture was the first African-American research collection in a major American university. Moorland died in New York on April 30, 1940.

Frederick Douglass Patterson was born in Washington, DC. He received a D.V.M. degree in 1923 and an M.S. in 1927 from Iowa State University. In 1932 he received a Ph.D. from Cornell University.

Patterson joined the faculty of Tuskegee Institute in 1928, first as an instructor of veterinary science, later as director of the school of agriculture,

Frederick D. Patterson (1901–1988)

United Negro College Fund Founder

and finally as president. He also chaired the R. R. Moton Memorial Institute and served as director of education for the Phelps-Stokes Fund.

In 1944 Patterson organized the United Negro College Fund, a cooperative fund-raising organization, to provide financial assistance to predominantly black colleges and universities.

Benjamin F. Payton (1932-)

Tuskegee University President

Born in Orangeburg, South Carolina, Benjamin Franklin Payton took a bachelor's degree with honors from South Carolina State College in 1955. Earning a Danforth Graduate Fellowship, he proceeded to distinguish himself with a B.D. from Howard University, a master's from Columbia, and, in 1963, a Ph.D. from Yale. He then took a position as assistant professor at Howard University before working for the National Council of Churches as the Commission on Religion and Race's executive director of social justice, a position he retained even as he took over the presidency of Benedict College in 1967. He left Benedict in 1972 for a position at the Ford Foundation, where he remained until he became Tuskegee's president in 1981.

Payton holds honorary degrees from Eastern Michigan University, Morris Brown, Benedict, and Morgan State. A recipient of the Napoleon Hill Foundation Gold Medal Award and the Benjamin E. Mays Award, he served as educational advisor to Vice President George Bush on Bush's seven-nation tour of Africa in 1982. Payton has also served as a member of myriad organizations, including the National Association for Equal Opportunity in High Education, the Alabama Industrial Relations Council, the National Association of Independent Colleges and Universities, and the Executive Board of the National Consortium for Educational Access.

Arthur A. Schomburg (1874–1938)

Archivist, American Negro Academy President

Born in Puerto Rico as Arturo Schomburg, he led a richly varied public life. He worked as a law clerk and was a businessman, journalist, editor, lecturer, New York Public Library curator, and teacher of Spanish.

In 1911 Schomburg co-founded the Negro Society for Historical Research. He was also a lecturer for the United Negro Improvement Association. Schomburg was a member of the New York Puerto Rico Revolutionary Party and served as secretary of the Cuban Revolutionary Party. In 1922 he headed the American Negro Academy, an organization founded by Alexander Crummell in 1879 to promote black art, literature, and science.

Schomburg collected thousands of works on black culture during his life-time. In 1926 Schomburg's personal collection was purchased by the Carnegie Corporation and given to the New York Public Library. In 1973 the collection became known as the Schomburg Collection of Negro Literature and History, and the name was later changed to the Schomburg Center for Research in Black Culture.

Steele was born January 1, 1946 in Chicago but grew up in Phoenix, Illinois, a blue-collar suburb of Chicago. He attended high school in Harvey, Illinois, where he was student council president his senior year prior to graduating in 1964. Steel then attended Coe College in Cedar Rapids, Iowa, where he was active in SCOPE—an organization associated with Martin Luther King, Jr.'s Southern Christian Leadership Council. He graduated in 1968, and in 1971 received an M.S. in sociology from Southern Illinois University. He went on to receive a Ph.D. in English literature from the University of Utah in 1974. While at Southern Illinois University he taught African-American literature to impoverished children in East St. Louis. Steele is currently a professor of English literature at San Jose State University.

Shelby Steele (1946–)

Scholar

In 1990 Steele published *The Content of Our Character: A New Vision of Race in America*, which won the National Book Critics Circle Award. In this controversial book Steele argued that African-American self-doubt and its exploitation by the white and black liberal establishment is as great a cause of problems for African Americans as more traditional forms of racism. Steele has also written articles on this theme for such respected publications as *Harper's*, *New Republic*, *American Scholar*, and *Commentary*.

Because of his beliefs Steele has been identified as part of an emerging black neo-conservative movement, but in an interview with *Time* magazine published August 12, 1991, he categorized himself as a classical liberal focusing on the freedom and sacredness of the individual.

Clifton R. Wharton was the first African American to head the largest university system in the United States—the State University of New York. He also helmed Michigan State University and served as chairman and CEO of the Teachers Insurance and Annuity Association and College Retirement Equities Fund.

Clifton R. Wharton, Jr. (1926–)

Former University President

A native Bostonian, Wharton took a bachelor's degree cum laude from Harvard in 1947. He received a master's degree at Johns Hopkins the following year, as the first African American admitted into the university's School for Advanced International Studies. In 1956 he took a second M.A. from the University of Chicago, which awarded him a Ph.D. in 1958. Between master's degrees he worked as a research associate for the University of Chicago. He then proceeded to the Agricultural Development Council, Inc., where he worked for twelve years. He also held a post as visiting professor at the University of Malaya and served as director and eventually vice president of the American Universities Research Program. Wharton took over the presidency of Michigan State in 1970 and stayed there for eight years; he moved on to the SUNY system from 1978 to 1987. He then worked for the Teachers Insurance and Annuity Association and has since become the first African American to chair the Rockefeller Foundation.

**Carter G. Woodson
(1875–1950)**

Scholar

Carter Godwin Woodson was born December 9, 1875, in New Canton, Virginia. He received a B.Litt. degree from Berea College in 1903, a B.A. and an M.A. in 1907 and 1908 from the University of Chicago, and a Ph.D. from Harvard University in 1912.

Known as the "Father of Modern Black History," Woodson was a passionate exponent of African-American economic self-sufficiency. In 1915 Woodson founded the Association for the Study of Negro Life and History (now the Association for the Study of Afro-American Life and History). One year later, the organization began publishing the *Journal of Negro History*. In 1920 he founded Associated Publishers, Inc., and in 1921 he founded the *Negro History Bulletin*. In 1926 Woodson launched Negro History Week (now Black History Month) to promote the study of African-American history.

A historian, author, editor, and teacher, Woodson served as dean of the Howard University School of Liberal Arts and the West Virginia Institute, and he was a Spingarn Medalist. His works include *The Education of the Negro Prior to 1861* (1915), *A Century of Negro Migration* (1918), *The Negro in Our History* (1922), and *The Miseducation of the Negro* (1933).

**Ivan Van Sertima
(1935–)**

Scholar

Born in British Guyana, anthropologist, linguist, and literary critic Ivan Van Sertima is currently professor of African studies at Rutgers University.

In 1977 Van Sertima published *They Came Before Columbus: The African Presence in Ancient America*. Drawing from various disciplines, Van Ser-

Known as the "Father of Modern Black History," Carter G. Woodson launched Negro History Week in 1926, which has since been expanded to Black History Month.

tima presents evidence of pre-Columbian contact with the New World by Africans.

In 1979 Van Sertima founded *The Journal of African Civilizations*, which presents a revisionist approach to world history. He is also the author of *Caribbean Writers*, a collection of essays.

By Kenneth Estell and Kwame Kenyatta

*R*eligion

The first Africans who arrived on North American shores (an event tradi-tionally dated to 1619) brought their own religious world views with them. While a minority had been Muslims or Christians prior to their kidnapping by slave traders, most adhered to their native African religions. There were hundreds of these religions, but, in general, the Africans believed that the world had been created by a high god who removed himself from direct in-tervention in worldly affairs after the act of creation.

THE ORIGINS AND HISTORY OF BLACK RELIGIOUS TRADITIONS

The Beginnings of African-American Religion

In Africa, worshipers directed their prayers to intermediary spirits, chief among whom were their ancestors, or the "living dead." If proper offering was made to an ancestor, the individual would be blessed with great prosperity, but if the ancestor was slighted, misfortune would result. In addition, the Yorubas worshiped a variety of nature spirits (or orishas). These spirits often possessed their devotees, who then became mediums of their gods. This kind of spirit-possession is a prominent feature of some modern African-American religions such as santería, which recently has spread in large urban areas, including Miami and New York. Also a part of the African world view, especially among the Bakongo, was the practice of magic, variously known in the New World as obeah, vaudou (voodoo), or conjure. This magic, designed to help friends (myalism) or to hurt enemies (obeah), at one time was widely practiced by Africans throughout the Western Hemisphere.

The type of African spirituality that took root in North America merged elements from many African cultures. Since slave masters intentionally mixed Africans from many tribal backgrounds, no "pure" African religion preserving one tradition emerged. Nevertheless, the longstanding scholarly controversy about the extent to which African traditions have been retained in African-based religions is gradually being resolved in favor of those who see extensive survivals. In addition to singing, church music, and preaching style—aspects where an African influence has generally been conceded—scholars have made persuasive arguments for African survivals in family structure, funeral practices, church organization, and many other areas.

Christian Missionary Efforts

The first sustained effort to convert African Americans to Christianity was made by the Anglican Society for the Propagation of the Gospel in Foreign Parts, which sent missionaries to North America in 1701. These missionaries had little success among the Africans; many mocked those who imitated the whites too closely, and thus resisted the missionaries. In addition, white slave masters often resented losing slaves' time to church services and feared that slaves would lay a claim to freedom through conversion. The numerous colonial laws, starting with Virginia in 1669, that proclaimed that conversion failed to entitle slaves to freedom did not comfort some slave masters, who suspected that Christianity would undermine slave discipline—indeed, some remained unconvinced of the advisability of missionary efforts until emancipation occurred. On the other hand, some slave masters believed the Christianization of Africans to be justification for enslaving them.

The first African-American missionary minister to work with Native Americans was John Morront of New York in 1785.

Subsequent efforts to convert African Americans to Christianity were more successful. In his seven missionary tours throughout North America between 1742 and 1770, the spellbinding orator George Whitefield effected the conversions of large numbers of both black and white Americans. The ministry of Methodist circuit riders, such as Francis Asbury, was also well received by African Americans at the end of the eighteenth century. Baptist and Methodist churches were the most successful in attracting black members. Since these churches did not require their ministers be well educated, doors were opened for aspiring African-American ministers, many of whom lived in states where teaching African Americans to read and write was forbidden by law. Furthermore, the Baptists and Methodists were not as hostile to the emotionalism of black preachers and congregations as were more staid denominations such as the Episcopalians. Finally, the anti-slavery stance of notable Methodist and Baptist leaders, such as John Wesley, Francis Asbury, and John Leland, and the greater degree of equality nurtured within many Baptist and Methodist congregations, were attractive to African Americans.

Probably the first organizing effort by African Americans to bear fruit in an independent black congregation was the Silver Bluff Baptist Church in South Carolina, which came into existence between 1773 and 1775.

Early Black Congregations

First African Baptist Church, Savannah, Georgia.

David George, an African American, and seven other men and women formed its organizing nucleus. George Liele, one of George's associates, often preached at the Silver Bluff Church before emigrating to Jamaica in 1782. Andrew Bryan, one of Liele's converts, founded the First African Baptist Church in Savannah, Georgia, in 1788.

Bryan's life well represented the complex predicament faced by African-American religious leaders in the antebellum South. In the early years of his ministry, Bryan was whipped and twice imprisoned by whites who feared him. But he bought his freedom, prospered, and eventually came to own much property, including eight black slaves; his death in 1812 was mourned by blacks and whites alike. While many black churches continued to be served by white ministers until 1865, black pastors, licensed ministers, and exhorters ministering to black Baptist and Methodist congregations were not at all unusual at this time, either in the South or the North.

Discrimination in White Churches

While white preachers urged black Americans to convert and many predominantly white congregations welcomed them into membership, racial prejudice was never absent from the religious scene. Although the level of discrimination varied from region to region and from congregation to congregation, some factors were relatively constant.

One such factor was the relative paucity of ordained African-American clergy. To take the Methodists as an example, some African-American ministers were ordained as deacons within the Methodist Episcopal Church prior to 1820, but none in the four decades thereafter. No African-American Methodist minister was ordained by the Methodist Episcopal Church to the higher office of elder or consecrated as a bishop prior to the Civil War, unless he was willing to emigrate to Liberia.

Resistance to discrimination took many forms. In the North, Peter Spencer in Wilmington, Delaware, Richard Allen in Philadelphia, and James Varick in New York, led their black followers out of white Methodist churches and set up independent black congregations. In Allen's case, his departure was preceded by a dramatic confrontation over segregated seating in Philadelphia's white Methodist church. Each of these men then used his congregation as the nucleus of a new black Methodist denomination—Spencer formed the African Union Church in 1807, Allen the African Methodist Episcopal Church (AME) in 1816, and

Varick a denomination eventually called the African Methodist Episcopal Zion Church (AME Zion) in 1821.

Meanwhile, in Charleston, South Carolina, a more explosive situation was taking shape. Morris Brown, a black Methodist minister from Charleston who had helped Richard Allen organize the African Methodist Episcopal Church, organized an independent black Methodist church in his home city. The authorities harassed Brown's church and sometimes arrested its leaders. Nevertheless, within a year, more than three-quarters of Charleston's black Methodists had united with him. The oppression of African Americans in Charleston was so severe that many members of Brown's congregation, including prominent lay leaders, joined the insurrection planned by Denmark Vesey to take over the Charleston armory and, eventually, the whole environs of Charleston. The conspirators, apprehended before they could carry out their plans, testified that Brown had not known of their scheme, and the minister was allowed to move to Philadelphia, where Richard Allen made him the second bishop of the African Methodist Episcopal Church.

A few African Americans became acquiescent as a result of Christianity. One such example was Pierre Toussaint, a black Haitian slave who fled in 1787 to New York with his white owners, the Berards, just prior to the Haitian Revolution. In 1811, Mrs. Berard manumitted Toussaint on her death bed. Over the next forty years, Toussaint became a notable philanthropist, contributing funds to the building of St. Patrick's Cathedral. However, when the cathedral opened, Toussaint did not protest when a white usher refused to seat him for services. Some American Catholics recently revived the controversy over Toussaint by campaigning for his canonization. Many black Catholics have strongly objected, seeing Toussaint as passive and servile and thus a poor candidate for sainthood.

The mid-nineteenth century saw increased anti-slavery activity among many black church leaders and members. Some gave qualified support to the gradual emancipation program sponsored by the American Colonization Society, which sought to encourage free African Americans to emigrate from the United States to Africa to Westernize and Christianize the Africans. Virginia Baptist pastor Lott Cary and Maryland Methodist minister Daniel Coker were the two most prominent African-American religious leaders to emigrate to Africa in the 1820s. By the 1850s, there were enough black Methodists in Liberia for the Methodist Episcopal Church to consecrate a black bishop, Francis Burns, to serve the Liberian

Discriminatory practices within the religious landscape took many forms. Many denominations tried to reserve the administration of sacraments as the exclusive province of white clergy; segregated seating in churches was pervasive in both the North and the South; and church discipline was often unevenly applied. Such racial discrimination in the churches, of course, was only a small part of the much larger political and moral controversy over slavery.

Responses to the Slavery Question

Northern African-American religious leaders, who could afford to be more open and forthright in their political stance than those in the South, included Presbyterian minister Henry Highland Garnet, AME bishop Daniel Payne, and AME Zion bishop Christopher Rush.

churches. While some black Americans were migrating to Africa, others migrated to the West Indies—Episcopalian Bishop James T. Holly, for example, settled in Haiti to undertake missionary work.

Because of the extreme repression in the slave states, southern blacks were unable to express openly their views on political issues. They were, however, often able to make their views clear; for example, a white minister who dwelled too long on the Biblical text that servants should obey their masters was apt to find his African-American listeners deserting him. In addition, black Christians often held secret meetings in "brush arbors" (rude structures made of pine boughs) or in the middle of the woods. There they could sing spirituals and pray openly for the quick advent of freedom. Slave revolts provided a violent outbreak of dissent much feared by whites. The 1831 revolt of Nat Turner, a Baptist preacher, in Northampton County, Virginia, was suppressed only after tremendous bloodshed had been visited upon both blacks and whites. Frightened whites in the South intensified their surveillance of black churches in the aftermath of the Turner revolt. Even conservative black preachers such as Presbyterian John Chavis in North Carolina and the Baptist "Uncle Jack" in Virginia were prohibited from preaching.

Northern African-American leaders could afford to be more open and forthright in their political stance. Most rejected outright the views of the American Colonization Society in favor of the immediate abolition of slavery. Presbyterian minister Henry Highland Garnet was a prominent abolitionist, urging African-American slaves in 1843 to "let your motto be RESISTANCE! RESISTANCE! RESISTANCE!" African Methodist Episcopal bishop Daniel Payne and African Methodist Episcopal Zion bishop Christopher Rush, both emigrants from the Carolinas to the North, were outspoken abolitionists who, after the mid-1840s, became the most prominent leaders in their respective churches. Frederick Douglass was one of the few leading black abolitionists who did not pursue a ministerial career, and even he had briefly served as an African Methodist Episcopal Zion preacher in New Bedford, Massachusetts. Black clergy were extraordinarily active in recruiting black men to join the Union armies during the Civil War, after the Emancipation Proclamation opened up the possibility of military service to them. During the Civil War nearly a dozen black ministers, including the African Methodist Episcopal Church's Henry McNeal Turner, served as chaplains to black army regiments.

A baptism service on the Potomac River.

The contributions of black women ministers were also vital. Women sometimes served as traveling evangelists, especially within the black denominations. While Sojourner Truth's oratory has become appropriately famous, Maria Stewart, Jarena Lee, Zilpha Elaw, and other early nineteenth-century women also spoke eloquently and, in Lee's and Elaw's cases, traveled widely and labored diligently. None of these women was ordained, but Elizabeth (whose last name is unknown), a former slave from Maryland whose ministry began in 1796, spoke for many female preachers when she was accused of preaching without a license: "If the Lord has ordained me, I need nothing better." Rebecca Cox Jackson left the African Methodist Episcopal Church in the 1830s when she felt that men denied her the chance to exercise her ministry, and she eventually became head eldress of a predominantly black Shaker community in Philadelphia.

During the postbellum years, some black women sought and obtained formal ordination from their denominations. Sarah Ann Hughes, a successful North Carolina evangelist and pastor, was ordained by Bishop Henry McNeal Turner in 1885, but complaints from male pastors caused her ordination to be revoked two years later. Two women were ordained by African Methodist Episcopal Zion bishops not long thereafter—Mary J. Small in 1895 as a deacon and 1898 as an elder, and Julia A. J. Foote in 1894 and 1900. Many women exercised their ministry through para-ecclesiastical structures, such as women's temperance and missionary societies, while others, such as Anna Cooper and the African Methodist Episcopal Church's Frances Jackson Coppin, became renowned educators.

Black Female Religious Leadership

BLACK CHURCHES DURING RECONSTRUCTION ✦ ✦ ✦ ✦ ✦ ✦ ✦ ✦ ✦

Black Churches and the Government

Black church membership grew explosively after the Civil War, especially in the South, where the black clergy played a prominent part in the Reconstruction governments. African Methodist Episcopal minister Hiram Revels became the first African American to serve as a United States Senator when the Mississippi legislature sent him to Washington, DC, in 1870. Revels, however, was only the ground breaker; many black ministers went on to serve in the Congress or in their state governments. African-American participation in Reconstruction politics was effective in large part because ministers in the AME and AME Zion Churches, and many black Baptist ministers, carefully and patiently educated their congregation members on every civic and political issue (although one newly established black denomination, the Colored Methodist Episcopal Church, largely stayed away from politics during Reconstruction).

Even though African Americans were largely expelled from southern state governments after the end of political Reconstruction in the 1870s, many black ministers and laity continued to play an active political role on such issues as temperance, often campaigning on behalf of prohibition referenda. The southern white campaign of terror, lynching, and disfranchisement steadily reduced black political power and participation, however, until the onset of mid-twentieth century civil-rights movements.

Responses to Segregation

As the system of racial segregation imposed in the 1880s and 1890s took hold, black ministers coordinated a manifold response. First, they forthrightly challenged new segregation laws, engaging in civil disobedience and boycotts. For example, when the city of Nashville, Tennessee segregated its street cars in 1906, influential Baptist minister R. H. Boyd led a black boycott of the streetcars, even operating his own streetcar line for a time. No defeat was ever seen as final.

Second, black ministers helped to nurture a separate set of black institutions to serve African Americans who were excluded from white establishments. The Congregationalists, Baptists, and Northern Methodists established schools in the South for African Americans during Reconstruction, but the African Methodist Episcopal, African Methodist Episcopal Zion, and Christian Methodist Episcopal bishops forged ahead with establishment of their own network of schools. The black denominations also

Pentecostalism, which burst on the American scene in 1906, has become a major religious force within the black community.

built up their publishing houses, and the books and periodicals that they published were vital to the black community. Virtually every institution with ties to African-American communities received some support from black churches.

Third, some black ministers believed that the civil-rights retreats of the late-nineteenth century should spur African Americans to leave the United States for a destination where their full civil rights would be respected. A "Back to Africa" movement grew to enable African Americans to find a home where they could run governments, banks, and businesses without interference from whites. Thus, Bishop Turner helped to organize a steamship line to carry black Americans back to Africa, and two shiploads of black emigrants sailed to Liberia in 1895 and 1896 as a result of his efforts. Some black church leaders, such as Christian Methodist Episcopal Bishop Lucius Holsey and AME Bishop Richard Cain, held views similar to those advocated by Turner, but many more church leaders opposed Turner's emigrationism vigorously. Simultaneously, African American missionary work continued to occupy the attention of African

Americans at the end of the nineteenth century. Under the guidance of Bishops Payne and Turner, for example, the African Methodist Episcopal Church had a vigorous missionary presence in Sierra Leone, Liberia, and South Africa.

BLACK CHURCHES IN THE TWENTIETH CENTURY ✦ ✦ ✦ ✦ ✦ ✦ ✦

In the past one hundred years, black religious life has become characterized by a far greater degree of diversity and pluralism. At the same time, traditional African-American concerns, including the continuing quest for freedom and justice, have been not only maintained but strengthened.

Pentecostalism

Pentecostalism, which burst on the American scene in 1906, has become a major religious force within the black community. The Church of God in Christ, a Pentecostal denomination, has become the second largest black denomination in the United States. Meanwhile, the charismatic or Neo-Pentecostal movement has revitalized many congregations within mainline black denominations. The black nationalism of Bishop Turner came to full flower in the work of such men as Marcus Garvey (and his chaplain general, George A. McGuire), Elijah Muhammad, and Malcolm X. There has been a spectacular rise of storefront churches, some of which were led by flamboyant showmen such as Father Divine and "Sweet Daddy" Grace. Each of these trends has been significantly aided by the black migrations from the South to the North, which greatly strengthened northern black communities.

The Social Gospel Movement

Many black ministers became advocates of a "Social Gospel." One of the most famous was Reverend Ransom of the African Methodist Episcopal Church, who came into prominence between 1901 and 1904 as pastor of an Institutional Church in Chicago. ("Institutional churches" provided a whole panoply of social services to needy members and neighbors, in addition to regular worship.) Social Gospellers highlighted the reality of collective, societal sin such as the starvation of children and the denial of human rights, and maintained that Christian repentance of these sins must be followed by concrete actions to rectify injustice and to assist the poor. The Reverend Dr. Martin Luther King, Jr., was profoundly influenced by this Social Gospel movement.

It is worth recalling that many black religious leaders in the 1960s thought that King's brand of social activism was too radical. One of King's most determined critics during the 1960s was the theologically conservative president of the National Baptist Convention of the U.S.A., Inc., Joseph H. Jackson. The attempt by King's ministerial allies to unseat Jackson as president of the Convention in 1960 and 1961 led to a schism, with King and his supporters forming a new denomination, the Progressive National Baptist Convention. King came under further criticism when, in 1967 and 1968, he made it clear that his advocacy of pacifism extended to opposition to American military involvement in Vietnam.

The Black Theology Movement

The "Black Theology" movement, which grew rapidly after King's assassination, attempted to fashion a critique of the prevalent Christian theology out of the materials that King and Malcolm X provided. One such theologian, Albert Cleage, pastor of the Shrine of the Black Madonna in Detroit, argued that Jesus is a black messiah and that his congregation should follow the teachings of Jehovah, a black god. "Almost everything you have heard about Christianity is essentially a lie," he stated. Cleage was representative of black theologians in arguing that black liberation should be seen as situated at the core of the Christian gospels. In the 1980s, black women such as Jacquellyn Grant, Delores Williams, and Katie Cannon have formulated "womanist" theologies that seek to combat the triple oppression of race, class, and gender suffered by most black women.

Current Trends

African-American churches remain strong, healthy institutions in the 1990s. Some denominations are growing substantially, and none is declining precipitously. While secularization has diminished its influence somewhat, the black church is still the central institution in the black community. Many black churches are vigorously confronting such problems as drug abuse and homelessness that are visible symptoms of the increasing desperation of the black underclass.

The largest denomination among the black churches remains the National Baptist Convention of the U.S.A., Inc. Its current president, veteran civil-rights activist Theodore J. Jemison, was first elected in 1982. Under Jemison's leadership, the denomination in 1989 completed a $10 million world-headquarters building in Nashville, Tennessee. More recently, Jemison has come under criticism for his role in attempting to forestall Mike Tyson's 1992 trial (and eventual conviction) on rape charges. The Convention continues to extend its strong support to Jemison who, under

Members of the Ministers Coalition for Peace pray for an end to civil unrest in Los Angeles.

current church rules, will not be able to succeed himself when his term expires in 1994.

Black churches continue to address a wide variety of social problems affecting the African-American community. Perhaps most urgently, many churches have strong anti-drug programs. The First AME Church of Los Angeles sponsors a "Lock In" program, which on weekends presents anti-drug messages to youth. Similarly, many congregations have undertaken vigorous action against "crack" houses. Parochial schools, feeding centers, and housing for senior citizens are also part of the black church's outreach to the black community. Many black ministers have noted, however, the growing division of the African-American community along social-class lines and have exhorted middle-class black Americans to give more generously to programs that aid the poor. James Cone, a leading black theologian, has stated that black churches need to devote less time and attention to institutional survival and more to finding ways to deal with such pressing issues as poverty, gang violence, and AIDS.

Black churches address a wide variety of social problems affecting the African-American community, including drug issues, education, housing concerns, gang violence, teen pregnancy and parenting, and poverty.

Toward this end, black churches participate in a wide variety of ecumenical projects among themselves and often with white denominations. The Congress of National Black Churches, a consortium of six black churches, continues to sponsor a variety of projects to improve the economic and social situation of the African-American community. Partners in Ecumenism, a project of the National Council of Churches, has challenged white denominations to be more responsive to black concerns. At a grassroots level, African-American churches are successfully joining forces to combat problems that are too large for any congregation to address alone. In Marks, Mississippi, for example, the Quitman County Development Organization has sponsored a Black Church Community and Economic Development Project, which has helped church leaders develop programs on teen pregnancy and parenting.

The spirit of cooperation has inspired individual denominations to explore merging or establishing close working relationships with other denominations with similar backgrounds and traditions. Three black Methodist churches, the African Methodist Episcopal Zion, Christian Methodist Episcopal, and United American Methodist Episcopal churches, have been planning a merger that they hope to consummate in the near future. In the spring of 1991, bishops of the AME, AME Zion, Christian Methodist Episcopal, and United Methodist churches requested that their denominations approve a study commission to explore an even

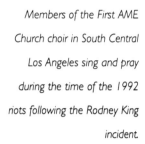

Members of the First AME Church choir in South Central Los Angeles sing and pray during the time of the 1992 riots following the Rodney King incident.

broader reunion of churches. The Progressive National Baptists have recently entered into a formal dialogue with the Southern Baptist Alliance, an organization of more than 72,000 mostly white Baptists who recently have distanced themselves from the Southern Baptist Convention.

Black churches also have found themselves compelled to address issues related to the multi-ethnic tensions of the 1990s. Leading black pastors in Los Angeles have deplored both the violence of police revealed in the Rodney King incident and the violence of inner city rioters, while advocating urgent attention to the problems of inner-city residents. For example, James Lawson of the Holman United Methodist Church stated that those who burned buildings during the 1992 Los Angeles riots were "responding to a society of violence, not simply a society of racism," and he issued "a call to repent." In Queens, New York, a black Baptist congregation in 1991 warmly welcomed the opportunity to perform an ordination service for a Korean-American minister, Chong S. Lee.

In a few recent cases, furthermore, tensions have surfaced between black pastors and predominantly white congregations. For example, after Joan Salmon Campbell resigned in 1992 as pastor of the Old Pine Presbyterian Church in Philadelphia, black ministers protested to the Philadelphia Presbyters that the differences over preaching style and theology that led to her resignation had been caused by alleged racist attitudes in her former congregation.

While many black Methodist and Baptist denominations are showing only limited membership growth, other black denominations are showing marked membership increases. Foremost among these are the Pentecostalist churches, whose lively worship and extensive social ministries are attracting members from all classes within the black community. The largest of these denominations, the Church of God in Christ, is now estimated to have over three million members. Charismatic congregations (also known as neo-Pentecostalist) within mainline black churches such as the African Methodist Episcopal Church are also thriving, and for similar reasons.

Many black religious groups continue to grow significantly in terms of membership, including the Pentecostalist churches, Roman Catholicism, and Islam.

Other groups that have made substantial membership gains among African Americans include Roman Catholicism and Islam. While estimates differ, apparently more than 1.5 million African Americans now belong to the Roman Catholic Church, which has worked hard in recent years to be sensitive to their needs. In many inner cities, it has maintained churches and schools in predominantly African-American neighborhoods, although closings, mostly for financial reasons, are increasing in such dioceses as Detroit. Moreover, the Roman Catholic Church has been receptive to some liturgical variation, allowing gospel choirs and African vestments for priests in black churches. Nevertheless, Roman Catholics confront some serious problems in serving black parishioners. Fewer than 300 of the 54,000 priests in the United States are black, meaning that some black congregations must be served by white priests. In 1989, George A. Stallings, Jr., a priest in Washington, DC, broke away from Catholicism, arguing that the Catholic Church was still racist and did not do enough for its African-American members.

Mainstream Islam, despite raising its own complexities, has also made large gains in the United States. Of the six million Muslims in this country, one million are believed to be black. Most African-American Muslims do not distinguish between people of different races and worship cordially side by side with recent Muslim immigrants from Asia and Africa. Louis Farrakhan's Nation of Islam, however, which retains Elijah Muhammad's black separatist teachings, continues to maintain a devoted following. Because of its very conservative stance on gender issues, Islam has proven to be more popular among black men than among black women.

The cause of gender equality continues to progress slowly in black churches. While two predominantly white denominations, the United Methodist and Protestant Episcopal churches, have elevated black women to the episcopacy in the past decade, none of the largest historically black denominations have done so. Nevertheless, women in some black churches are achieving ever-more-prestigious ministerial assignments. Vashti McKenzie, a former model, disc jockey, and radio program director, has recently been appointed pastor of the Payne Memorial AME Church, an "old-line" church in Baltimore. Her innovative ministry, she says, is designed to "provide a message of hope for a hurting community." There are presently more than 600 female pastors in the African Methodist Episcopal Church.

Preaching the gospel in a faithful but relevant fashion remains the most important objective of black churches. In a recent survey, twenty-two percent of black clergy considered the most important problem of the black church to be "lack of evangelism in fulfilling its religious role." That was more than twice the figure for any other problem identified. Ministerial training and financial support is another area needing improvement in many black churches. There is no danger, however, that the black churches will lose sight of their many vital functions, within both the black community and American society as a whole. It is safe to predict that the black churches will continue to sustain and develop their important and prophetic witness.

Black Jews   Several different groups in the past century have been known as Black Jews. Included among these are the Commandment Keepers, founded in Harlem in 1919 by a Nigerian-born man known as "Rabbi Matthew"; the Church of God and Saints in Christ, founded in 1896 in Lawrence, Kansas, by William Crowdy; and the Church of God founded in Philadelphia by Prophet F. S. Cherry. In terms of doctrine, these groups share little more than a dislike of Christianity and an affection for the Old Testament. Some black Jews claim descent from the Falasha Jews of Ethiopia, who now reside in Israel. However, few black Jews are recognized as such by orthodox rabbis. The Church of God and Saints of Christ is probably the largest of these groups, with more than 200 churches and a membership of 38,000.

Members of this religion regard Ethiopian Emperor Haile Selassie, who died in 1975, as God. Marcus Garvey, a Jamaican-born nationalist who advocated a back-to-Africa movement in the United States in the early 1920s, is also a central figure in the faith. Reggae musician Bob Marley, a Rastafarian, helped to increase the religion's popularity in the United States.

Rastafarians

Today, Rastas differ on specific dogma, but they basically believe that they are descended from black Hebrews exiled in Babylon and therefore are true Israelites. They also believe that Haile Selassie (whose name before ascending the throne was Lij Ras Tafari Makonnen) is the direct descendent of Solomon and Sheba, and that God is black.

Most white men, they believe, have been worshipping a dead god and have attempted to teach the blacks to do likewise. They hold that the Bible was distorted by King James and that the black race sinned and was punished by God with slavery. They view Ethiopia as Zion and the Western world as Babylon, and believe that one day they will return to Zion. They preach love, peace, and reconciliation between races but warn that Armageddon is imminent.

Rastas don't vote, tend to be vegetarians, abhor alcohol, and wear their hair in long, uncombed plaits called dreadlocks. The hair is never cut, since it is part of the spirit, nor is it ever combed.

There are an estimated 50,000 Rastas in Britain and almost a million in the United States, approximately 80,000 of whom live in New York City, mainly in Brooklyn, where there is a high concentration of West Indians and Haitians.

♦ **RELIGIOUS LEADERS**

Noble Drew Ali, whose birth name was Timothy Drew, was born in North Carolina. He is principally important for his role in establishing the first North American religious movement combining black nationalist and Muslim themes with rejection of Christianity as the religion of whites. In 1913, he established the first Moorish Science Temple in Newark, New Jersey. He taught that black Americans were "Asiatics" who had originally

Noble Drew Ali

(1886–1929)

Moorish Science
Temple Founder

lived in Morocco before enslavement. Every people, including black Americans, needed land for themselves, he proclaimed, and North America, which he termed an "extension" of the African continent, was the proper home for black Americans. The holy book for the Moorish Science Temple was a "Holy Koran" which was "divinely prepared by the Noble Prophet Drew Ali." (This book should not be confused with the Q'uran of Islam.) Every member of the Temple carried a card stating that "we honor all the Divine Prophets, Jesus, Mohammed, Buddha and Confucius" and that "I AM A CITIZEN OF THE U.S.A."

In the 1920s, the Moorish Science Temple expanded to Pittsburgh, Detroit, and Chicago. Noble Drew Ali also started several small businesses, which he and his followers ran. Drew Ali was stabbed to death in his Chicago offices in apparent strife over the leadership of the Temple. The Moorish Science Temple survived Drew Ali's death, but the Nation of Islam was able to attract some of its followers.

Richard Allen (1760–1831)

African Methodist Episcopal Church Founder

Born a slave in Philadelphia, Allen converted to Christianity in 1777 and soon thereafter bought his freedom. He traveled widely through the Middle Atlantic States as an exporter. Francis Asbury, the first bishop of the Methodist Episcopal Church, asked Allen to join him as a traveling companion, stipulating that Allen would not be allowed to fraternize with slaves and would sometimes have to sleep in his carriage. Allen refused to accept such an offer, instead settling down in Philadelphia, where he helped to found the Free African Society, an African-American society for religious fellowship and mutual aid. One day in the early 1790s, Allen was worshipping in Philadelphia's St. George's Methodist Church when he was pulled off his knees during prayer by white deacons who insisted that Allen was sitting outside the area reserved for African Americans. Allen left, establishing his own church for Philadelphia's African Americans in a converted blacksmith shop in 1794. White Methodists tried to exert their control over his church in various ways, and Allen resisted successfully. In 1816, after the Pennsylvania Supreme Court settled a suit over this church in Allen's favor, Allen called for a conference of black Methodists. The African Methodist Episcopal Church was founded at this conference, and Allen was consecrated as its first bishop. Allen remained both religiously and politically active in his later years, and he was especially active in opposing schemes to colonize free African Americans in Africa.

Born in Canton, Mississippi, Thea Bowman, daughter of a medical doctor, joined the Roman Catholic Church at age twelve because of the Catholic education she had received. Three years later, she joined the Franciscan Sisters of Perpetual Adoration. She was extensively educated, earning a Ph.D. in literature and linguistics.

Bowman was a distinguished teacher who taught elementary and high school as well as college. She helped to found the Institute of Black Catholic Studies at Xavier University and was a distinguished scholar known for her writings on Thomas More. But it is probably for the spiritual inspiration that she provided in numerous lectures, workshops, and concerts that she is best remembered. She said that she brought to her church "myself, my black self, all that I am, all that I have, all that I hope to become, my history, my culture, my experience, my African-American song and dance and gesture and movement and teaching and preaching and healing."

**Thea Bowman
(1938–1990)**

Roman Catholic Nun

Born in Orange Springs, Virginia, Nannie Helen Burroughs became one of the most significant Baptist lay leaders of the twentieth century. She addressed the National Baptist Convention in Virginia in 1900 on the subject, "How the Sisters Are Hindered from Helping," and from that time until her death more than sixty years later she exercised pivotal leadership. She was elected corresponding secretary for the Woman's Convention and auxiliary to the National Baptist Convention, U.S.A., Inc., and in 1948 she became president of the Women's Convention. She founded the National Training School for Women and Girls, emphasizing industrial arts and proficiency in African-American history, in Washington, DC. She edited such periodicals as the *Christian Banner* and was the author of such books as the *Roll Call of Bible Women*.

**Nannie Helen
Burroughs
(1883–1961)**

Baptist Lay
Leader, Educator

Born in Fordyce, Arkansas, James Cone received a B.A. from Philander Smith College, a B.D. from Garrett Evangelical Seminary, and an M.A. and Ph.D. from Northwestern University. After teaching at Philander Smith and Adrian Colleges, Cone moved to Union Theological Seminary in 1969. He is currently the Charles A. Briggs Professor of Systematic Theology. Cone is the author of numerous books, including *Black Theology and Black Power* (1969); *The Spirituals and the Blues* (1972); *For My People: Black Theology and the Black Church* (1984); and most recently, *Martin & Malcolm & America: A Dream or a Nightmare* (1991). Perhaps more than any other black theologian, Cone has provided a systematic exposition of

**James Cone
(1938–)**

Theologian

the argument that since God, according to the Bible, is on the side of the poor and oppressed, God is siding with the black liberation struggle in the American context. He has made this argument using a diverse set of sources, including the writings of modern European theologians such as Karl Barth, and the writings and speeches of Malcolm X and Martin Luther King, Jr. Cone has worked painstakingly in the past two decades to build ties between black, feminist, and third-world liberation theologians.

Father Divine
(1877–1965)

Peach Mission Founder

Mystery shrouds the early identity and real name of Father Divine. There is reason to believe he was born George Baker in 1877 on Hutchinson's Island in Georgia. In 1907 he became a disciple of Sam Morris, a Pennsylvania black man who called himself Father Jehovia. Two years later he switched over to John Hickerson's "Lift Ever, Die Never" group before returning to Georgia, where he began his own campaign to promote himself as a "divine messenger."

Threatened by local authorities (he was once booked as "John Doe, alias God"), Father Divine left Georgia in 1914 and later settled in New York City, where he worked as an "employment agent" for the few followers still loyal to him. Calling his meeting place "Heaven," he soon attracted a larger following and moved to Sayville, Long Island, in 1919. It was at this time that Father Divine began to provide shelter and food to the poor and homeless. Spiritually, Father Divine fostered what amounted to a massive cooperative agency, based on the communal spirit of the Last Supper. His movement practiced complete racial equality. Services included songs and impromptu sermons and were conducted without Scripture readings and the use of clergy.

Once he was sentenced to six months in jail as a public nuisance. Four days after his trial, the judge in his case died of a heart attack, whereupon Father Divine was quoted as having said: "I hated to do it." The ensuing publicity enhanced his popularity.

The Divine movement, a non-ritualistic cult whose followers worshipped their leader as God incarnate on earth, grew rapidly in the 1930s and 1940s, with "Father" speaking out across the country and publicizing his views in the *New Day*, a weekly magazine published by his organization. He set up "Peace Mission Kingdom" throughout the United States and the world. In 1946, he married his "Sweet Angel," a twenty-one-year-old Canadian stenographer known thereafter as Mother Divine.

Father Divine died peacefully at Woodmont, an estate he had acquired in the Philadelphia suburbs, and his wife pledged to continue the work of the movement.

Elijah Fisher exemplifies the great charismatic black preachers of the nineteenth and early twentieth centuries who, with very little formal education, built large religious institutions, counseled racial pride, and expounded the cause of blacks as a people.

Fisher was born in La Grange, Georgia, the youngest of eight boys in a family of seventeen children. His father was an unordained preacher of a Baptist congregation that met in a white church. Fisher worked in a Baptist parsonage as a boy slave, and he was taught to read by a former house slave and a white missionary. In his teens, he worked in mines in Alabama and then as a butler, all the while studying theology on his own time. Though he lost a leg in an accident, Fisher in his early twenties became pastor of several small country churches and then, in 1889, of the Mount Olive Baptist Church in Atlanta. In that year, when past the age of thirty, he enrolled in the Atlanta Baptist Seminary, passed his examinations, and went to preach in Nashville and then Chicago, where he led the Olive Baptist Church from 1902 until his death.

Throughout his life, Fisher continued his studies, preached from coast to coast, and involved the churches in youth work, food programs for poor people, and black-run businesses. An active member of the Republican Party, Fisher strongly criticized blacks who advised their brethren to rely solely on the good will of whites and publicly criticized Booker T. Washington for not speaking out against lynching.

Elijah John Fisher (1858–1915)

Baptist Minister

Born in the Cape Verde Islands, "Sweet Daddy" Grace probably opened his first church in New Bedford, Massachusetts, in 1921, but his first success occurred five years later when he opened a church in Charlotte. Grace's church, the United House of Prayer for All People, had an ecstatic worship style, where speaking in tongues was encouraged. Grace claimed great powers, including the power of faith healing, and he stated that "Grace has given God a vacation, and since God is on His vacation don't worry Him.... If you sin against God, Grace can save you, but if you sin against Grace, God cannot save you." Even the numerous products that he sold, such as "Daddy Grace" coffee, tea, soaps, and hand creams, were

"Sweet Daddy" Grace (1881–1960)

United House of Prayer for All People Founder

reputed to have healing powers. By the time of his death, the church had 375 branches and about 25,000 members nationwide.

Barbara C. Harris

(1930–)

Episcopalian Bishop

Born in Philadelphia, Barbara Harris, a former public relations executive, was ordained a deacon in the Protestant Episcopal Church in 1979 and a priest one year later. She served as the priest-in-charge of an Episcopalian Church in Norristown, Pennsylvania, the interim pastor of a church in Philadelphia, and the executive director of the publishing company associated with the Episcopal Church. In February of 1989 she was consecrated as suffragan (or assistant) bishop for the diocese of Massachusetts. She thus became the first woman bishop in the history of the Episcopal Church. She received considerable support despite the concerns of some that her views were too liberal. Her supporters said that despite the lack of a college degree or seminary training, she would broaden the outreach of her church.

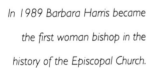

In 1989 Barbara Harris became the first woman bishop in the history of the Episcopal Church.

James Augustine Healy was the first black Catholic bishop in the United States. For twenty-five years he presided over a diocese covering the states of Maine and New Hampshire.

A native of Macon, Georgia, Healy received his education in the North, first at Franklin Park Quaker School in Burlington, New York, and later at Holy Cross in Worcester, Massachusetts. Healy graduated from the latter with first honors. Healy continued his studies abroad and was ordained in Paris at Notre Dame Cathedral in 1854. He then returned to the United States.

Pastor of a predominantly Irish congregation that was at first reluctant to accept him, Healy performed his priestly duties with devotion and eventually won the respect and admiration of his parishioners—particularly after performing his office during a typhoid epidemic.

Thereafter, he was made an assistant to Bishop John Fitzpatrick of Boston, who appointed him chancellor and entrusted him with a wide variety of additional responsibilities. In 1875, he was named Bishop of Portland, Maine, and in this capacity he founded sixty parishes, as well as eighteen schools.

Healy's brother, Patrick Francis Healy, was a Jesuit priest who served as president of Georgetown University from 1873 to 1882.

James Augustine Healy (1830–1900)

Catholic Bishop

Born in Rudyard, Mississippi, Jackson received a B.A. from Jackson College, an M.A. from Creighton University, and a B.D. from Rochester Colgate School of Divinity. After pastoring churches in Mississippi, Jackson accepted a call to pastor the historic Olivet Baptist Church in 1941. From 1953 to 1982, Joseph H. Jackson was the president of the National Baptist Convention, U.S.A., Inc., the third largest Protestant denomination in the United States. His role in the civil-rights movement was a fairly conservative one. He was supportive of the efforts of Martin Luther King, Jr. during the Montgomery bus boycott of 1955 but criticized the massive non-violent civil-disobedience campaigns of the early 1960s. Jackson's main emphasis was on the need for African Americans to build a viable economic base. His favorite slogan was "From Protest to Production." He was supportive of Baptist missions in Africa and attempted to finance them by developing farmland in Liberia.

Joseph H. Jackson (1904–1990)

National Baptist Convention, U.S.A., Inc., Former President

Joseph H. Jackson was president for nearly thirty years of the National Baptist Convention, U.S.A., the third largest Protestant denomination in the United States and the largest of the predominantly black churches.

Leontine T.C. Kelly

(1920–)

Methodist Bishop

Leontine T.C. Kelly, the first black woman bishop in any large American denomination, was born in Washington, DC. She received an M.Div. degree from Union Theological Seminary in Richmond, Virginia, in 1969. She served as a schoolteacher, pastor of Virginia churches, and a staff member of the Virginia Conference of Churches before being elected a bishop in the United Methodist Church in 1984. She currently presides over the California–Nevada conference of that denomination. She is married to James David Kelly and has four children.

A great religious leader and educator whose life spanned more than a century, Isaac Lane was born a slave in Jackson, Tennessee. Self-educated, in 1856 he was granted a license to exhort, a category assigned to blacks who were forbidden to preach, in the Methodist Episcopal Church South.

Lane was ordained a minister in 1865 and in 1873 was made a bishop of the Colored Methodist Episcopal Church (now known as the Christian Methodist Episcopal Church) at a salary so low he had to raise cotton to supplement his income and support his family—which included eleven children. His missionary work was instrumental in establishing the CME Church in Louisiana and Texas. In the 1880s, he established Lane College in Jackson with $9,000 he raised himself.

Isaac Lane (1834–1937)

Colored Methodist Episcopal Bishop

Born in Cape May, New Jersey, Jarena Lee worked as a servant for a family who lived near Philadelphia. She had a conversion experience in 1804 but was unable to find a church with which to unite until she heard Richard Allen, founder of the African Methodist Episcopal Church, preach in Philadelphia. She experienced a call to preach about 1808, and sought permission twice from Richard Allen to exercise her call. On her first attempt in 1809, Allen refused her request, but eight years later he granted it and licensed her as a preacher. Subsequently she traveled widely throughout the North and Midwest, and many of her listeners, especially women, were moved by her eloquent preaching. After Allen's death in 1831, male African Methodist Episcopal preachers in Philadelphia attempted to deny her permission to preach from their pulpits, but she continued her ministry despite such opposition. In 1848, she attempted to form a connection of female African Methodist Episcopal preachers for mutual support, but her organization soon fell apart. Many black women, especially within the African Methodist Episcopal Church, have seen Jarena Lee as a courageous foremother and a model for church activism.

Jarena Lee (1783–?)

Methodist Church Pioneer

Born a slave in Virginia, George Liele was sold while very young into Georgia. He experienced a Christian conversion after hearing a sermon by Matthew Moore, a white preacher, in 1773. Liele began conducting worship services on nearby plantations, and, with Moore's sponsorship, he soon became the first ordained black Baptist preacher in America. Liele's slave master, Henry Sharp, granted him his freedom before Sharp was killed in the American Revolution. Liele preached at the Silver Bluff Baptist Church in Silver Bluff, South Carolina, probably the first independent black congregation formed in North America, and at a location out-

George Liele (c. 1750–1820)

Baptist Minister

side Savannah. One of his notable converts was Andrew Bryan, who founded the First African Baptist Church in Savannah. Some whites attempted to re-enslave Liele, but a British officer in Savannah ensured that he would maintain his freedom. Liele migrated to Jamaica in 1784, and he started a school and preached to a small Baptist congregation in Kingston. Liele was married to a woman he converted in Savannah, and his four American-born children accompanied him to Jamaica.

Eugene A. Marino

(1934–)

First African-American Roman Catholic Archbishop

Born May 29, 1934, in Biloxi, Mississippi, Marino received his training at Epiphany Apostolic College, St. Joseph Seminary, Fordham University, and Catholic University. He was ordained to the priesthood in 1962. In 1963 he was made director of St. Joseph.

In 1971 he was made vicar general of the Josephites and was consecrated a bishop in 1974. Marino became the first black Roman Catholic archbishop in the United States in 1988, when he was made archbishop of the Atlanta Archdiocese. Marino retired in 1990.

Charles H. Mason

(1866–1961)

Church of God in Christ Founder

Born to former slaves on a farm outside Memphis, Tennessee, Charles Mason was converted at the age of fourteen and he joined a Missionary Baptist Church. Mason obtained a preaching license from the Missionary Baptists in 1893, and, in the same year, he claimed to have the experience of entire sanctification, thus aligning himself with the Holiness Movement. He had little formal education beyond a brief period of study at the Arkansas Bible College. In 1895, the Baptists expelled him because of his beliefs on sanctification. Mason then held holiness revivals in Mississippi with the help of Charles Price Jones, a prolific writer of hymns and gospel songs, and others. In Lexington, Mississippi, his meetings were held in an abandoned cotton gin house. Despite an armed attack, probably by hostile African Americans, he achieved much success and many new converts with his revival preaching. In 1897, Mason and Jones founded a new Holiness Church and called it the Church of God in Christ; they worked together harmoniously over the next decade.

In 1907, Mason attended the Azusa Street Revival, conducted by William Seymour in Los Angeles, and he received the gift of speaking in tongues. He believed that the ability to speak in tongues was a necessary precondition for baptism of the spirit. He and Jones disagreed on this point and parted company, and Mason re-formed the Church of God in Christ along the lines of his new spiritual insights. Over the next four decades, Mason, as bishop, general overseer, and "chief apostle," shepherded his denomination through a period of tremendous growth. He traveled extensively, preaching at revivals throughout the United States and the world. He was imprisoned for making pacifist statements during World War I. He died in 1961.

Born a slave in Kentucky, Miles was manumitted by his owner in her will. He joined the Methodist Episcopal Church South and soon perceived a call to preach. In 1859 he was ordained a deacon. Uncertain about church affiliation after the war, he investigated the possibility of joining the African Methodist Episcopal Zion Church, but soon thought better of it. Thus he remained a preacher in the Methodist Episcopal Church South until its African-American members, those who had decided not to join the African Methodist Episcopal or African Methodist Episcopal Zion Churches, were allowed to form a separate denomination, the Colored Methodist Episcopal Church. At the first General Conference of the Colored Methodist Episcopal Church in 1870, Miles was elected one of the denomination's first two bishops. He was an active advocate of black colleges, especially those affiliated with the CME Church, such as Lane College in Jackson, Tennessee, and Paine Seminary in Atlanta, Georgia.

William Henry Miles (1828–1892)

Christian Methodist
Episcopal Bishop

Payne is a towering figure in the history of African-American religion and probably the greatest educator in the history of the African Methodist Episcopal Church. Born to free parents in Charleston, South Carolina, Payne received an excellent education and opened a school for black Charlestonians in 1829. An act of the South Carolina legislature forced him to close the school six years later. Payne traveled north and studied at the Lutheran Theological Seminary in Gettysburg, Pennsylvania. He delivered forceful anti-slavery speeches and, in 1841, switched his affiliation to the African Methodist Episcopal Church. He was ordained one year later and was elected a bishop in 1852.

Daniel Alexander Payne (1811–1893)

African Methodist
Episcopal Bishop,
Educator

Payne visited President Abraham Lincoln in the White House in 1862 and was a persistent advocate for emancipation and the freed people. In 1863, Payne bought Wilberforce University from the Methodist Episcopal Church. That university was the flagship school for the African Methodist Episcopal Church, and as its president and chief booster, Payne was the dominant presence there for the next thirty years. After the Civil War, Payne plunged himself deeply into oversight of the missionary work to the southern and western states and eventually to Africa. He was one of the first African Americans to visit Charleston after its liberation by the Union Army in 1865. He initially was a strong supporter of black ministerial involvement in Reconstruction governments in the South, but Payne (widely known to have an impeccable character) changed his mind after exposures of southerners' corruption and misdeeds soured him on political participation. In 1882, he refused a conductor's order to move to a segregated smoking car, and after the conductor evicted him from the train, protest meetings were held in many American cities. During his last five years of life he published two important books, *Recollections of Seventy Years* (1888) and his well-researched *History of the African Methodist Episcopal Church* (1891).

Harold Robert Perry (1916-)

Roman Catholic Bishop

Harold Robert Perry was consecrated a Bishop of New Orleans on January 6, 1966—and thus became the first Catholic bishop in the United States in the twentieth century.

One of six children, Perry was born the son of a rice-mill worker and a domestic cook in Lake Charles, Louisiana. He entered the Divine Word Seminary in Mississippi at the age of thirteen, was ordained a priest in 1944, and spent the next fourteen years in parish work. In 1958, he was appointed rector of the seminary.

Louisiana has the largest concentration of black Catholics in the South, some 200,000 in all. As of 1989, Perry was one of thirteen African-American bishops serving Catholic parishes around the nation.

Adam Clayton Powell, Sr. (1865–1953)

Baptist Minister

Adam Clayton Powell, Sr., father of the late Harlem congressman named after him, was largely responsible for building the Abyssinian Baptist Church into one of the most celebrated black congregations in the world.

Born in the backwoods of Virginia in 1865, Powell attended school locally and, between sessions, worked in the coal mines of West Virginia. After deciding to enter the ministry, he began his studies at Wayland Academy (now Virginia Union University), working his way through as a janitor and waiter. He later attended the Yale University School of Divinity and served as pastor of the Immanuel Baptist Church in New Haven.

Powell became pastor of Abyssinian in 1908 when it had a membership of only 1,600 and indebtedness of over $100,000. By 1921, the church had not been made solvent but was able to move into a $350,000 Gothic structure at its present location on 138th Street in Harlem.

During the Depression, Powell opened soup kitchens for Harlem residents and served thousands of meals. Later he and his son campaigned vigorously to expand job opportunities and city services in Harlem. Powell retired from Abyssinian in 1937.

Born in Elizabeth City, North Carolina, to a free mother, Price was educated in the school established for freed people, and later at Shaw and Lincoln Universities, graduating from the latter in 1879. At age twenty-one, he was licensed to preach in the African Methodist Episcopal Zion Church, and he received the ordination of elder six years later. Price was renowned for the eloquence of his public addresses. It was Price who was the most responsible for the African Methodist Episcopal Zion Church's success in establishing a church college—Livingstone College in North Carolina—after ministers in that denomination had failed in several previous attempts. As president of Livingstone College, he quickly gave his school a solid grounding both academically and financially. For example, he raised $10,000 for his school during a lecture tour of England. He was an active participant in politics, campaigned for civil rights and prohibition, and assumed such offices as chairman of the Citizens' Equal Rights Association of Washington, DC. He died a tragically early death from kidney failure.

Joseph Charles Price (1854–1893)

African Methodist Episcopal Zion Minister, Educator

Born in Centerville, Louisiana, to parents who had been slaves, Seymour taught himself to read and write. In 1900, Seymour encountered the prominent promoter of Holiness doctrine, Martin Knapp, and studied under him. He suffered a bout of smallpox that left him blind in one eye. He was ordained as an evangelist by the "Evening Light Saints," a group that eventually became known by the title Church of God, based in Anderson, Indiana. Moving to Houston, he sat immediately outside the door of white evangelist Charles Parham's segregated classroom while Parham lectured on Christian doctrine and, especially, on the importance of speaking in tongues.

William Joseph Seymour (1870–1922)

Pentecostal Minister

In 1906, Seymour moved to Los Angeles to pastor a small black Holiness church, but his congregation, which opposed Seymour's contention that speaking in tongues was an important part of Christian experience, dismissed him after one week. Seymour continued to hold religious meetings, attracting an interracial audience. A widely publicized outburst of speaking in tongues brought him an ever-larger audience, so he moved his "Apostolic Faith Gospel Mission" to a former AME Church building on Azusa Street. The extremely successful meetings that he held before ecstatic, interracial throngs of listeners over the next three years have been universally acknowledged as the beginnings of modern Pentecostalism in the United States and around the world. Seymour was greatly saddened when the racial unity displayed in the early stages of Pentecostalism began to break apart under the pressures exerted by racial discrimination in the nation at large. He held services at the Azusa Street mission until his death in 1922.

Amanda Berry Smith (1837–1915)

Holiness Evangelist, Missionary

Born in Long Green, Maryland, Smith was manumitted during her childhood after her father paid for her freedom. She had a emotional conversion experience in 1856. She began attending religious meetings faithfully, and while she resisted identification with any single denomination, her religious practice was most strongly influenced by Quakers and Methodists. Attendance at the religious meetings of white evangelists Phoebe Palmer and John Inskip introduced her to Holiness doctrine, and she experienced entire sanctification in 1868. Her husband died the following year, and Smith soon became a full-time traveling evangelist. She never sought to breach the barriers against women's ordination erected by male preachers, stating that the calling she had received directly from God was justification enough for her ministry.

From 1878 to 1890 Smith worked as a missionary in England, Ireland, Scotland, India, and Liberia. A Methodist bishop who heard her preach in India stated that he "had never known anyone who could draw and hold so large an audience as Mrs. Smith." On her return to the United States in 1890, she preached widely and wrote her autobiography in 1893, an extremely detailed work now regarded as a classic. Her last twenty years were devoted to the construction and management of the Amanda Smith Orphan's Home for Colored Children in Illinois.

Bishop of the African Methodist Episcopal Zion Church from 1952 to 1972 and board chairman of the National Association for the Advancement of Colored People from 1961 until his death in 1974, Bishop Spottswood embodied the religious faith and intellectual incisiveness that has produced so many effective black religious activists.

Spottswood was born in Boston and attended Albright College, Gordon Divinity School, and then received a doctor of divinity from Yale University. As a religious leader, Spottswood was president of the Ohio Council of Churches and served on the boards of numerous interfaith conferences as well as heading the African Methodist Episcopal Zion Church. His activity with the NAACP started in 1919, when he joined the organization. He was appointed to the national board in 1955. In 1971, he became the center of a political storm when he chastised the Nixon administration for its policies toward blacks and refused, under strong pressure from the administration, to retract his comments.

Stephen Gill Spottswood (1897–1974)

African Methodist Episcopal Bishop

Born in New Bern, North Carolina, Stallings received his bachelor of arts degree from St. Pius X Seminary in 1970. He received his bachelor of science degree in theology from the University of St. Thomas Aquinas in 1973 and his master of arts degree in pastoral theology the following year. In 1974 Stallings was ordained and in 1976 was named pastor of St. Teresa of Avila, located in one of Washington, DC's poor black neighborhoods. In 1975 he was granted a licentiate in sacred theology by the University of St. Thomas Aquinas.

While pastor at St. Teresa, Stallings stressed that the contributions of Africans and African Americans to Christianity should be recognized and that the needs of blacks must be addressed by the church. In an effort to confront what he considered the church's racial insensitivity, he made use of what is known as the Rite of Zaire, incorporated jazz and gospel music to the Mass, and added readings by celebrated African-American writers to the liturgy. Stallings received much criticism and in 1988 was removed from St. Teresa and named head of evangelism for Washington, DC.

In 1989 Stallings, still convinced that the church was not meeting the cultural, spiritual, and social needs of African-American Catholics, announced that he would leave the diocese to found a new congregation, the Imani Temple African-American Catholic Congregation. In 1991,

George Augustus Stallings, Jr. (1948–)

Imani Temple African-American Catholic Congregation Founder and Bishop

Stallings ordained former Roman Catholic nun Rose Vernell a priest. The congregation's membership is currently estimated at 3,500 members.

Leon Howard Sullivan (1922–)

Baptist Minister

Born in Charleston, South Carolina, Sullivan was ordained to the ministry at age nineteen. He was educated at the Union Theological Seminary in New York, and served as pastor of the Zion Baptist Church in Philadelphia from 1950 to 1988.

Much of his efforts during his ministry were directed toward improving employment prospects of African Americans. During the 1950s, he organized a selective patronage campaign, boycotting Philadelphia-area businesses that employed too few black employees. Sullivan's campaign experienced some success, but businesses requested black workers with technical skills that few possessed. Accordingly, Sullivan founded the Opportunities Industrialization Center in 1964 to impart employment skills to inner-city youths. By 1980, the O.I.C. operated programs in 160 cities. He was also a major force in many other economic development initiatives, such as the Philadelphia Community Investment Cooperative. His acceptance within the American business community is well symbolized by his long-time membership on the boards of General Motors and Philadelphia's Girard Bank.

Sullivan is also renowned for his leadership in addressing international issues as they affect the African-American community, and in particular for his intensive involvement in political and economic reform in South Africa. In the mid-1970s he devised his "Sullivan Principles," which successfully encouraged American-owned companies to hire more black South African workers and to treat them equitably in relation to promotions and working conditions. Sullivan, however, parted company with President Ronald Reagan's "constructive engagement" policy toward South Africa, endorsing instead a policy of South African divestment in 1987.

Gardner C. Taylor (1918–)

Baptist Minister

Reverend Taylor is widely regarded as the dean of the nation's black preachers. He received a B.A. from Leland College in 1937 and a B.D. from the Oberlin Graduate School of Theology in 1940.

Taylor has long been a community activist. He demonstrated for civil rights and suffered arrest for civil disobedience with Martin Luther King, Jr. in the 1960s, and introduced Nelson Mandela to a New York audience in 1990. He is a trusted counselor to New York Mayor David Dinkins. Taylor served on the New York City Board of Education. He is the past president of the New York Council of Churches and the past vice president of the Urban League in New York, City. After forty-two years as pastor of the Concord Baptist Church in Brooklyn, Taylor resigned his post in 1990.

Born in Daytona Beach, Florida, Thurman studied at Morehouse College, Rochester Theological Center, and Haverford College. Thurman, named by *Life* magazine as one of the twelve great preachers of the twentieth century, served as a pastor to a Baptist church in Ohio and, from 1944 to 1953, an interracial and interdenominational Fellowship Church he founded in San Francisco. He also served as dean of the chapel at Howard University from 1932 to 1944, and at Boston University from 1953 until his retirement. Thurman was one of the leading theologians of his time, writing *The Negro Spiritual Speaks of Life and Death* and his opposition to segregation and support of the civil-rights movement in *This Luminous Darkness*. Altogether, he wrote nineteen books, including an autobiography published in 1979.

Howard Thurman (1899–1981)

Theologian, Educator

Born in Newberry Courthouse, South Carolina, to free parents, Turner was educated when South Carolina lawyers employing him as a janitor tutored him in many subjects. Turner joined the Methodist Episcopal Church South in 1848, and was licensed to preach in 1853. He toured the South as an itinerant evangelist for the next five years, reaching as far west as New Orleans, where an African Methodist Episcopal minister made a strong impression on him. In 1858, Turner traveled north, and switched his affiliation to the AME Church. For the next five years, he pastored churches in Baltimore and Washington, DC.

Henry McNeal Turner (1834–1915)

African Methodist Episcopal Bishop

In 1863, Turner was appointed chaplain of the First United States Colored Troops. He was present at more than a dozen battles, including the Battle of Petersburg. After the war, Turner moved to Georgia to take part in the great task of organizing the AME Church and the Republican Party in the post-emancipation South. In 1868, he was elected as a State Representative to the Georgia legislature. He made an eloquent speech protesting his expulsion from that body later that year, after the legislature voted that African Americans were ineligible to serve. Turner was reinstated in the legislature in 1870, but was defeated for re-election in a closely fought contest.

Turner was elected a bishop of the AME Church in 1880. He remained active in politics, supporting prohibition and opposing disfranchisement of the African American. In 1883, when the Supreme Court voided the Civil Rights Act, Turner advocated that African Americans return to Africa where their human rights would be respected. The bishop made four missionary trips to Africa in the 1890s. Protesting against the idolatry of whiteness in contemporary American theology and proclaiming that "God is a Negro," Turner is appropriately seen as a forerunner of modern-day black theology. He died in Windsor, Ontario.

James Varick
(c.1750–1827)

African Methodist
Episcopal Zion Bishop

By
Stephen W. Angell

Born near Newburgh, New York, to a slave mother, Varick was a leader in the movement among African-American Methodists in New York to set up a separate congregation. This was accomplished with the formation of the Zion Church in 1796. Varick was ordained a deacon by Bishop Francis Asbury ten years later. Varick sought to obtain full ordination (as elder) for himself and other African-American ministers, and would have preferred to have received such an ordination within the Methodist Episcopal Church, but this did not prove possible. He did not favor joining Richard Allen's African Methodist Episcopal Church, especially since Allen had been attempting to set up a New York congregation seen by Varick as in competition with the Zion Church. Eventually, Varick participated in setting up the African Methodist Episcopal Zion Church, and he was elected the first superintendent or bishop. He was also deeply involved in issues relating to freedom and human rights, preaching against the slave trade in 1808 and subscribing to the first newspaper in the country owned by African Americans, *Freedom's Journal*.

*L*iterature

African-American literature in the United States reached an artistic pinnacle in the period between the two world wars with the Harlem Renaissance. Since then the fate of African-American writing has reached a level of high visibility; the themes have varied from highly charged and political to private and introspective. The Black Aesthetic Movement of the 1960s and 1970s brought acclaim and prominence to many African-American writers and fostered the growth of many black studies departments at universities around the country. In the 1980s and 1990s, African-American writers were working in every genre—from scriptwriting to poetry—and the names of African-American writers consistently were found on best-seller lists around the country.

BEFORE THE HARLEM RENAISSANCE ◆ ◆ ◆ ◆ ◆ ◆ ◆ ◆ ◆ ◆ ◆ ◆ ◆ ◆

Perhaps the greatest satisfaction for black writers before the 1920s, or the Harlem Renaissance, was to have the freedom to write; in fact, knowing how to read and write was a tremendous accomplishment for many post-Reconstruction African Americans.

For Frederick Douglass, to write stirring diatribes against slavery powerful enough to shake the consciousness of a nation was more a political than an artistic accomplishment. Likewise, when Jupiter Hammon, George Moses Horton, and Frances Harper prosaically wrote about the evils of slavery and racism, their verse seemed somewhat stilted; they followed the molds of Methodism, neoclassicism, and the Bible, traditions ill suited to their subject matter. However admirable their writing was, they never quite found a vehicle that fit their revolutionary thoughts.

The first novel written and published by a black American is a work by William Wells Brown, entitled Clotel. *The novel was published in 1853.*

As the bonds of slavery were loosened, black writers clamored to be heard, but the range of their work was limited. Since slavery and plantations were practically the only subjects in their repertoire, early African-American works were often locked into these themes. In addition, being a black writer before 1920 was certainly a unique profession, almost an oddity. Many writers were essentially unknown during their lives. Still others, like Phillis Wheatley and Horton, gained a certain amount of acclaim. In fact, a number of blacks, including Paul Laurence Dunbar and Charles W. Chestnutt, became truly appreciated as writers.

White society, however, still controlled much of publishing in America; African-American work was often filtered and distorted through this lens. As a result, much of the post-Reconstruction era work by African-Americans was an attempt to prove that blacks could fit into middle-American society. In fact, much of the literature of this era was an attempt by blacks to appear happy with their assigned lot. Yet some writers—Dunbar and Chestnutt, for example—tried to break the chains of this imposed expression by presenting a view of black life as it really was, not as society wanted it to be.

Although the accomplishments of writers of this era were remarkable, existing conditions seemed to keep African-American letters from truly flourishing. What these authors most notably did was to pave the way for the Harlem Renaissance and to provoke authors to think about and develop a truly African-American culture.

◆ ◆ ◆ ◆ ◆ ◆ ◆ ◆ ◆ ◆ ◆ ◆ ◆ ◆ ◆ ◆ ◆ ◆ THE HARLEM RENAISSANCE

Resistant to the easy categorization of a timeline, the Harlem Renaissance began roughly around World War I and extended into the early 1930s. It began mostly as a movement of African-American artists and writers into Harlem from practically every state in the country. At the same time, another hub of artistic activity was forming in Washington, DC. In fact, Harlem artists often journeyed to Washington for a break and a new perspective.

As African-American journals such as *Crisis* and *Opportunity* began to appear, it became much easier for black writers to publish in a style that

Jessie Fauset, Langston Hughes, and Zora Neale Hurston.

The conscious agenda of the mostly young, African-American artists of the Harlem Renaissance was to define and celebrate black art and culture and to change the preconceived and erroneous notions most Americans had of black life.

suited their tastes. Also, African-American writers were finding that some white patrons in the publishing fields were, in fact, interested in promoting their work. Bohemianism was flourishing, and many of the Harlem Renaissance artists fit this label. Being called "New Negroes," they sought to chisel out a unique, African-centered culture for blacks, and to improve race relations while maintaining a distinct cultural identity.

Important writers of this era include Langston Hughes, Countee Cullen, Claude McKay, Nella Larsen, and Zora Neale Hurston. These younger writers were encouraged by the older, established writers, critics, and editors, including W.E.B. DuBois, with his journal *Crisis*, and Charles S. Johnson, editor of *Opportunity*, a sponsor of many literary contests. In fact, Langston Hughes actually believed that the Renaissance came about directly because of the nurturing of older writers, including Jessie Fauset and Alain Locke.

The Harlem Renaissance was marked by a shift away from the moralizing work, which had been characteristic of much post-Reconstruction writing that decried racism. Even though much of this writing was excellently written and eloquently executed, people like DuBois and Locke realized that it was doing very little to change the consciousness of the country. For this reason, they decided instead to challenge these new writers to produce works that came directly out of personal experience—to communicate the ills of the racist world with art rather than essay. In this way, readers were not struck so bluntly with the grim realities presented by African-American writers. These issues could be experienced through the lives of characters and in verse, and the message delivered more subtly and effectively.

AFTER THE HARLEM RENAISSANCE ♦ ♦ ♦ ♦ ♦ ♦ ♦ ♦ ♦ ♦ ♦ ♦ ♦

As the economic Depression deepened, the Harlem Renaissance slowly faded. Richard Wright's publication in 1940 of *Native Son* marked a new era in African-American literature. The years from 1940 to 1955 served as a transition period for black letters; they bridged the wildly creative period of the Renaissance with the more intense creativity and political activity that was to define the work produced during the civil-rights movement.

Richard Wright, whose classic novel Native Son *was published in 1940, believed artistic works must aim directly to end racism.*

With the publication of his classic novel, Wright maintained that the era of the Harlem Renaissance—with its motto of "art for art's sake"—must die and be replaced instead with works directly intended to end racism. He believed that blacks were an essential part of American society—a belief that was one of the foundations for the ideology of the civil-rights movement.

During this time, other black writers, notably poets, were taking a different road in their quest to be heard. Poets such as Gwendolyn Brooks,

Gwendolyn Brooks was awarded the Pulitzer Prize for her volume of poetry, Annie Allen, in 1950. She was the first African-American woman to win the award.

Melvin B. Tolson, and Robert Hayden were using classical and mythical themes in their works. Indeed, Brooks won a Pulitzer Prize in 1950 for her book *Annie Allen*. These poets used a blend of extreme eclecticism with realistic, African-American issues. The blend seemed to work, as their writing was met with acceptance in the university community and beyond.

Ralph Ellison's *Invisible Man*, arguably one of the best novels published in America during this century, and James Baldwin's *Go Tell It on the Mountain*, were two other books that brought serious African-American issues to mainstream culture. In addition, many African-American works were gaining acceptance with the literary establishment and being taught in English classes around the country.

THE BLACK AESTHETIC MOVEMENT ♦ ♦ ♦ ♦ ♦ ♦ ♦ ♦ ♦ ♦ ♦ ♦ ♦

The Black Aesthetic Movement, or the Black Arts Movement, has been the first major African-American artistic movement since the Harlem Renaissance. Beginning in the early 1960s and lasting through the mid-1970s, this movement was brought on not by white patrons (as the Renaissance had been in part), but by the anger of Richard Wright, Ralph Ellison, and other notable African-American writers.

For the most part, Black Aesthetics were supportive of separatist politics and a black nationalist ideology. Rebelling against the mainstream society by being essentially anti-white, anti-American, and anti-middle class, these artists moved from the Renaissance view of art for art's sake into a philosophy of art for politics' sake.

This artistic movement was closely paralleled by the civil-rights marches and the call for independence being experienced in the African-American community. As phrases like "Black is beautiful" were popularized, African-American writers of the Aesthetic Movement consciously set out to define what it meant to be a black writer in a white culture. While writers of the Harlem Renaissance seemed to stumble upon their identity within, writers of the Aesthetic Movement were serious about defining themselves and their era before being defined by others.

The Black Aesthetic Movement attempted to produce works of art that would be meaningful to the black masses. Toward this end, popular black music of the day, including John Coltrane's jazz and James Brown's rhythm and blues, as well as street talk, were some of the inspirational forces for their art. In fact, much of the language used in these works was

Imamu Amiri Baraka was as well known for his poetry as for his political activism.

vulgar and shocking—this was often a conscious attempt to show the vitality and power of black activists. These writers tended to be revolutionaries rather than diplomats—Malcolm X was more of an idol than Martin Luther King, Jr. In addition, they believed that artists had more of a responsibility than just art: artists also had to be political activists in order to achieve nationalist goals.

Leading writers in this movement include Imamu Amiri Baraka (also known as Leroi Jones), whose poetry was as well known as his political prowess; Haki R. Madhubuti (Don L. Lee), a poet and essayist who was overwhelmingly popular, selling over 100,000 copies of his books without a national distributor. Ishmael Reed, on the other hand, an early organizer of the Black Aesthetic Movement, later dissented with some of the movement's doctrines; he became inspired more and more by the black magic and spiritual practices of the West Indies (in what he called the "HooDoo Aesthetic").

Sonia Sanchez was another leading voice of the movement. She managed to combine feminism with her commitment to nurturing children and men in the fight for black nationalism. She joined up with the Nation of Islam from 1972 to 1975, and through her association with the Black Aesthetic Movement managed to instill stronger support for that religion.

THE POST-AESTHETIC MOVEMENT ✦ ✦ ✦ ✦ ✦ ✦ ✦ ✦ ✦ ✦ ✦ ✦ ✦ ✦ ✦ ✦

Many women, however, wrote in response to the Black Aesthetic Movement, protesting the role they felt women were forced to play in the male-oriented black nationalist movement. Zora Neale Hurston's work was resurrected and used for inspiration and impetus in their work. These women were also supported by the women's liberation movement, allowing their works to reach a wider audience. In this way, the somewhat female-repressive politics of the Black Aesthetic Movement provoked women writers to express their own unique voice. Alice Walker, Gayl Jones, Toni Morrison, Terry McMillan, and Gloria Naylor are examples of successful women authors who have become prominent figures in the publishing world. In fact, during the 1980s, black women writers were at the leading edge of publishing—in quality as well as quantity of work—and in 1993 Morrison's talent was recognized worldwide when she was bestowed the Nobel Prize for literature.

Since the Black Aesthetic Movement, African-American writing has become more legitimized in America, and black studies departments have emerged in many universities around the country. Variety was the key to African-American writing after 1950, and barriers went down in various genres. For example, Octavia Butler and Samuel Delany broke into the world of science fiction. Donald Goines wrote detective fiction that rivaled that of his contemporaries. Novels of both folk history and the urban ex-

Gloria Naylor, who won the American Book Award for first fiction for The Women of Brewster Place, *is one of several successful contemporary black female writers.*

perience were equally well received, and many artists found that they could straddle more than one genre—Alice Walker and Gayl Jones being good examples—and delve into the worlds of fiction, poetry, essay, and children's books.

Alex Haley's *Roots* was perhaps one of the greatest African-American writing coups of the post-1950s era. With his book, as well as the highly popular television mini-series that followed, many blacks became interested in their African ancestors. Other books explored the history of blacks in other areas, namely the American West, the South, and the North.

Writers after the 1960s seem to have changed the tone a bit—no longer was there as much emphasis on the disparity between black and white in America. In the words of Toni Morrison, John Edgar Wideman, and Kristin Hunter, the themes of self-reflection and healing were evident. African Americans were portrayed looking into their own inner worlds for answers, rather than letting themselves be defined by the outer world.

AFRICAN-AMERICAN NOVELISTS, POETS, AND PLAYWRIGHTS ♦

Raymond Andrews

(1934–)

Novelist

Born in Madison, Georgia, Raymond Andrews left his sharecropper farm home at fifteen to live, work, and attend high school at night in Atlanta. After graduation, he served in the United States Air Force and attended Michigan State University before moving to New York City, where he worked in a variety of jobs: airline reservations clerk, hamburger cook, photo librarian, proofreader, inventory taker, mail room clerk, messenger, air courier dispatcher, and bookkeeper. During his spare time, Andrews perfected his literary skills.

His first novel, *Appalachee Red* (1978), set in the black neighborhood of a northern Georgia town called Appalachee, was widely acclaimed. In the view of the reviewer for the *St. Louis Globe Democrat,* it marked the literary debut of a significant modern American novelist of the stature of Richard Wright or James Baldwin. The following year Raymond Andrews was the first recipient of the annual James Baldwin Prize presented by Dial Press at a ceremony attended by Baldwin.

Andrews's second work, *Rosiebelle Lee Wildcat Tennessee: A Novel* (1980), chronicled the forty-year reign in Appalachee, beginning in 1906, of the spiritual and temporal leader of the black community there. Like his previous novel, it was illustrated by his brother Benny Andrews.

His third novel, *Baby Sweets* (1984), was also published by Dial Press and illustrated by Benny. Baby Sweets is the name given to the brothel opened by the eccentric son of Appalachee's leading citizen to provide black prostitutes to the white population. This novel examines how such intermingling of the races affects an entire community.

Maya Angelou (1928-)

Novelist, Poet

Born Marguerite Johnson, Angelou spent her formative years shuttling between St. Louis, Missouri, a tiny, totally segregated town in Arkansas, and San Francisco, where she realized her ambition of becoming that city's first black streetcar conductor.

During the 1950s, she studied dancing with Pearl Primus in New York, later appearing as a nightclub singer in New York and San Francisco. She worked as an editor for *The Arab Observer,* an English-language weekly published in Cairo; lived in Accra, Ghana, where under the black nationalist regime of Kwame Nkrumah she taught music and drama; and studied cinematography in Sweden. She became a national celebrity in 1970 with the publication of *I Know Why the Caged Bird Sings*, the first volume of her autobiography, which detailed her encounters with southern racism and a pre-pubescent rape by her mother's lover.

In 1971, she produced *Just Give Me a Cool Drink of Water 'fore I Die: The Poetry of Maya Angelou*; in 1975, *Oh Pray My Wings Are Gonna Fit Me Well*; in 1979, *And Still I Rise*; and in 1983, *Shaker Why Don't You Sing?* In 1977, she was nominated for an Emmy award for her portrayal of Nyo Boto in the television adaptation of the best-selling novel *Roots*.

Three more volumes of her autobiography have been published: *Gather Together in My Name* (1974); *Singin' and Swingin' and Gettin' Merry Like Christmas* (1976); and *The Heart of a Woman* (1981). In 1986, *All God's Children Need Traveling Shoes* was published. Angelou's other works include *Mrs. Flowers: A Moment of Friendship*, *Now Sheba Sings the Song*, and *Wouldn't Take Nothing for My Journey Now*.

On January 20, 1993, Angelou read her poem "On the Pulse of Morning" during the inauguration of President Bill Clinton.

James Baldwin (1924–1987)

Novelist, Essayist, Playwright

Born in New York City, Baldwin turned to writing after an early career as a boy preacher in Harlem's storefront churches. He attended Frederick Douglass Junior High School in Harlem and later graduated from DeWitt Clinton High School, where he was editor of the school magazine. Three years later, he won a Eugene Saxton Fellowship, which enabled him to

write full-time. After leaving the United States, Baldwin resided in France and in Turkey.

Baldwin's first novel, *Go Tell It on the Mountain*, was published in 1953 to critical acclaim. Two years later, his first collection of essays, *Notes of a Native Son*, again won favorable acclaim. This was followed in 1956 by the publication of his second novel, *Giovanni's Room*. His second collection of essays, *Nobody Knows My Name*, brought him into the literary spotlight and established him as a major voice in American literature.

In 1962, *Another Country*, Baldwin's third novel, was a critical and commercial success. A year later, he wrote *The Fire Next Time*, an immediate best-seller regarded as one of the most brilliant essays written in the history of the black protest.

Since then, two of Baldwin's plays, *Blues for Mister Charlie* and *The Amen Corner*, have been produced on the New York stage, where they achieved modest success.

His novel *Tell Me How Long the Train's Been Gone* was published in 1968. Baldwin himself regards it as his first "grown-up novel," but it has generated little enthusiasm among critics.

Much to the distress of his public, Baldwin then entered an extended fallow period, and the question of whether he had stopped writing was widely debated. After a silence of several years, he published the 1974 novel *If Beale Street Could Talk*. In this work, the problems besetting a ghetto family, in which the younger generation is striving to build a life for itself, are portrayed with great sensitivity and humor. Baldwin's skill as a novelist is evident as he sets and solves the difficult problem of conveying his own sophisticated analyses through the mind of his protagonist, a young woman. To many critics, however, the novel lacks the undeniable relevance and fiery power of Baldwin's early polemical essays.

Baldwin's other works include *Going to Meet the Man* (short stories); *No Name in the Street*; *One Day When I Was Lost*, a scenario based on Alex Haley's *The Autobiography of Malcolm X*; *A Rap on Race* with Margaret Mead; and *A Dialogue* with Nikki Giovanni. He was one of the rare authors who worked well alone or in collaboration. Other books by Baldwin are *Noth-*

ing Personal (1964), with photographs by Richard Avedon; *The Devil Finds Work* (1976), about the movies; his lengthy sixth novel *Just Above My Head* (1979); and *Little Man, Little Man: A Story of Childhood* (1977), a book for children. He wrote sixteen books and co-authored three others. Six books have been written about Baldwin's life and writings, including a reference guide and bibliography.

Just Above My Head, published in 1979, deals with the intertwined lives from childhood to adulthood of a gospel singer, his brother, and a young girl who is a child preacher. The next year Baldwin's publisher announced *Remember This House,* described as his "memoirs, history and biography of the civil rights movement" interwoven with the biographies of three assassinated leaders: Martin Luther King, Jr., Malcolm X, and Medgar Evers. Meanwhile, in his lectures Baldwin remained pessimistic about the future of race relations.

His last three books were *The Evidence of Things Not Seen* (1985), about the killing of 28 black youths in Atlanta, Georgia in the early 1980s; *The Price of the Ticket: Collected Non-fiction, 1948–1985* (1985), and *Harlem Quartet.*

Baldwin spent most of the remainder of his life in France. In 1986, the French government made him a commander of the Legion of Honor, France's highest civilian award. He died at his home in France on November 30, 1987, at the age of sixty-three.

Imamu Amiri Baraka (Leroi Jones) (1934–)

Poet, Playwright, Essayist

Baraka was born in Newark in 1934. He attended Rutgers University in Newark, New Jersey, and Howard University in Washington, DC. In 1958 he founded *Yugen* magazine and Totem Press. From 1961 to 1964 Baraka worked as an instructor at New York's New School for Social Research. In 1964 he founded the Black Arts Repertory Theater. He has since taught at the State University of New York at Stony Brook, the University of Buffalo, Columbia University, George Washington University, and San Francisco University, and has served as director of the community theater Spirit House in Newark.

In 1961 Baraka published his first book of poetry, *Preface to a Twenty Volume Suicide Note.* His second book, *The Dead Lecturer,* was published in 1964. However, he did not achieve fame until the publication of his play *Dutchman* in 1964, which received the Obie Award for the best off-Broadway play of the season. The shocking honesty of Baraka's treatment of racial conflict in this and later plays became the hallmark of his work.

During the late 1960s Baraka became a leading black power spokesman in Newark. He became head of the Temple of Kawaida, which Baraka describes as an "African religious institution—to increase black consciousness." The Temple and Baraka soon became a focal point of black political activism in the racially polarized city. In 1972 Baraka achieved prominence as a black leader as chairman of the National Black Political Convention

In 1966 Baraka's play *The Slave* won second prize in the drama category at the First World Festival of Dramatic Arts in Dakar, Senegal. Baraka's other published plays include *The Toilet* (1964); *The Baptism* (1966); *The System of Dante's Hell* (1965); *Four Black Revolutionary Plays* (1969); *J-E-L-L-O* (1970); and *The Motion of History and Other Plays* (1978).

He has edited, with Larry Neal, *Black Fire: An Anthology of Afro-American Writing* (1968) and *Afrikan Congress: A Documentary of the First Modern Pan-African Congress* (1972). His works of fiction include *The System of Dante's Hell* (novel, 1965) and *Tales* (short stories, 1967). Baraka has also published *Black Music* (1967), *Blues People: Negro Music in White America* (1963), *Home: Social Essays* (1966), *In Our Terribleness: Some Elements and Meanings in Black Style* with Billy Abernathy (1969), *Raise Race Rays Raze: Essays Since 1965* (1971), *It's Nation Time, Kawaida Studies: The New Nationalism, A Black Value System,* and *Strategy and Tactics of a Pan Afrikan Nationalist Party.*

Arna Bontemps
(1902–1973)

Poet, Novelist

Arna Bontemps was one of the most productive black writers of the twentieth century. Born in Alexandria, Louisiana and raised in California, Bontemps received his B.A. from Pacific Union College in Angwin in 1923. The next year, his poetry first appeared in *Crisis* magazine, the NAACP periodical edited by W.E.B. DuBois. Two years later, *Golgotha Is a Mountain* won the Alexander Pushkin Award, and in 1927, *Nocturne at Bethesda* achieved first honors in the *Crisis* poetry contest. *Personals*, Bontemps's collected poems, was published in 1963.

In the late 1920s Bontemps decided to try his hand at prose, and over the next decade produced such novels as *God Sends Sunday* (1931); *Black Thunder* (1936); and *Drums at Dusk* (1939).

His books for young people include *We Have Tomorrow* (1945) and *Story of the Negro* (1948). Likewise of literary merit are such children's books as *Sad-Faced Boy* (1937) and *Slappy Hooper* (1946). He edited *American Negro Poetry* and two anthologies, with Langston Hughes among others.

In 1968 he completed the editing of a volume of children's poetry. Other publications were *One Hundred Years of Negro Freedom* (1961); *Anyplace But Here* (published in 1966 in collaboration with Jack Convoy); *Black Thunder* (1968 reprint); *Great Slave Narratives* (1969); *The Harlem Renaissance Remembered: Essays* (1972, 1984); and *The Old South*.

Gwendolyn Brooks is one of many blacks to win a Pulitzer Prize. Brooks received this prestigious award in 1950 for *Annie Allen*, a volume of her poetry that had been published a year earlier.

Gwendolyn Brooks (1917–)

Poet

Brooks was born in Topeka, Kansas, moved to Chicago at an early age, and was educated there, graduating from Wilson Junior College in 1936.

In 1945 she completed a book of poems, *A Street in Bronzeville*, and was selected by *Mademoiselle* as one of the year's ten most outstanding American women. She was made a fellow of the American Academy of Arts and Letters in 1946, and received Guggenheim Fellowships for 1946 and 1947.

In 1949 she won the Eunice Tietjen Prize for Poetry in the annual competition sponsored by *Poetry* magazine. She was also poet laureate of the state of Illinois.

Her other books include a collection of children's poems, *Bronzeville Boys and Girls* (1956); a novel, *Maud Martha* (1953); and two books of poetry, *The Bean Eaters* (1960) and *Selected Poems* (1963). She has also written *In the Mecca*; *Riot*; *The World of Gwendolyn Brooks*; *Report from Part One: The Autobiography of Gwendolyn Brooks*; *Family Pictures*; *Beckonings*; *Aloneness*; *Primer for Blacks*; and *To Disembark*. She has edited *A Broadside Treasury* and *Jump Bad: A New Chicago Anthology*.

Claude Brown
(1937-)

Novelist

Claude Brown's claim to literary fame rests largely on his best-selling autobiography *Manchild in the Promised Land*, which was published in 1965 when its author was twenty-eight.

The book is the story of Brown's life in Harlem and, as such, is a highly realistic documentary of life in the ghetto. It tells of Brown's escapades with the Harlem Buccaneers, a "bopping gang," and of his later involvement with the Forty Thieves, an elite stealing division of this same gang.

After attending the Wiltwyck School for emotionally disturbed and deprived boys, Brown returned to New York, was later sent to Warwick Reform School three times, and eventually made his way downtown to a small loft apartment near Greenwich Village. Changing his style of life, Brown finished high school and went on to graduate from Howard University in 1965.

Brown began work on his book in 1963, submitting a manuscript of some 1,500 pages that was eventually cut and reworked into the finished product over a two-year period. Brown completed law school in the late 1960s and is now practicing in California. In 1976, he published *The Children of Ham*, about a group of young blacks living as a family in a condemned Harlem tenement, begging, stealing, and doing whatever is necessary to survive.

William Wells
Brown (1815-1884)

Novelist, Playwright

Williams Wells Brown was the first American black to publish a novel, the first to publish a drama, and the first to publish a travel book.

Born a slave in Lexington, Kentucky and taken to St. Louis as a young boy, Brown worked for a time in the offices of the *St. Louis Times,* and then took a job on a riverboat in service on the Mississippi. In 1834 Brown fled to Canada, taking his name from a friendly Quaker whom he met there. While working as a steward on Lake Erie ships, he educated himself and became well known as a public speaker. In 1849, he went to England and Paris to attend the Peace Congress, remaining abroad for five years.

His first published work, *The Narrative of William H. Brown*, went into three editions within eight months. A year later, a collection of his poems was published, *The Anti-Slavery Harp*, and in 1852 his travel book *Three Years in Europe* appeared in London.

Brown's *Clotel, or the President's Daughter*, a melodramatic novel about miscegenation, was first published in London in 1853. As the first novel by an American black—which subsequently went through two revisions—its historical importance transcends its aesthetic shortcomings.

Brown's other books include the first black drama *The Escape, or a Leap for Freedom* (1858); *The Black Man: His Antecedents, His Genius, and His Achievements* (1863); *The Negro in the American Rebellion: His Heroism and Fidelity* (1867); and *The Rising Son* (1874).

Ed Bullins was born in Philadelphia and grew up in Los Angeles. Bullins is a writer of drama and one of the founders of the Black Arts/West in the Fillmore District of San Francisco. He patterned this experiment after the Black Arts Repertory Theater School in Harlem, which was founded and directed by Imamu Baraka. In 1977, when *Daddy*, the sixth play in his "Twentieth-Century Cycle," opened at the New Federal Theatre in New York's Henry Street Settlement, Bullins in an interview with the *New York Times* foresaw black theatrical producers taking plays to cities with large black populations and spreading out from there—unless something happened to ruin the economy. A leader of the black theater movement and creator of more than fifty plays, he has yet to have a play produced on Broadway.

Ed Bullins (1935–)

Playwright, Essayist, Poet

Bullins's main themes are the violence and tragedy of drug abuse and the oppressive life-style of the ghetto. He presents his material in a realistic and naturalistic style. Between 1965 and 1968 he wrote *The Rally*; *How Do You Do*; *Goin' a Buffalo*; *Clara's Old Man*; *The Electronic Nigger*; and *In the Wine Time*. He has also produced *The Fabulous Miss Marie*.

He has been a creative member of Black Arts Alliance, working with Baraka in producing films on the West Coast.

Bullins has been connected with the New Lafayette Theater in Harlem, where he was a resident playwright. His books include *Five Plays: New Plays from the Black Theatre*, which he edited; *The Reluctant Rapist*; *The New Lafayette Theatre Presents*; *The Theme Is Blackness*; *Four Dynamite Plays*; *The Duplex*; *The Hungered One: Early Writings*; and *How Do You Do: A Nonsense Drama*.

Octavia E. Butler

(1947–)

Novelist

Born in Pasadena, California, Octavia Butler is a graduate of Pasadena City College. She has attended science fiction workshops and is a member of Science Fiction Writers of America. Her writing has focused on the impact of race and gender on future society.

In 1985 Butler won three of science fiction's highest honors for her novella *Bloodchild*: the Nebula Award, the Hugo Award, and the Locus Award. Her other works include *Patternmaster*; *Mind of My Soul*; *Survivor*; *Kindred*; *Wild Seed*; *Clay's Ark*; *Dawn*; and *Xenogenesis*.

Charles Waddell

Chesnutt

(1858–1932)

Novelist

Born in Cleveland, Ohio, in 1858, Chesnutt moved to North Carolina with his family at the age of eight. Largely self-educated, he was admitted to the Ohio bar in 1887, the same year in which his first story, "The Go-phered Grapevine," was published in the *Atlantic Monthly*. This was followed in 1899 by two collections of his stories, *The Conjure Woman* and *The Wife of His Youth*.

His first novel, *The House Behind the Cedars* (1900), dealt with a young girl's attempt to "pass" for white. A year later, *The Marrow of Tradition* examined the violence of the post-Reconstruction period. His final novel, *The Colonel's Dream*, was published in 1905 and typified Chesnutt's basically ingratiating approach to his art, which writers of the Harlem School were later to reject. Chesnutt also wrote a biography, *Frederick Douglass* (1899).

Alice Childress

(1920–)

Playwright, Novelist

Born in Charleston, South Carolina, Childress studied acting at the American Negro Theatre and attended Radcliffe Institute from 1966 to 1968 through a Harvard University appointment as a scholar-writer. Her plays are *Florence* (one-act play); *Gold Through the Trees*; *Just a Little Simple* (based on Langston Hughes's *Simple Speaks His Mind*); *Trouble in Mind*; *Wedding Band*; *Wine in the Wilderness*; and *When the Rattlesnake Sounds: A Play about Harriet Tubman*. Childress also edited *Black Scenes* (1971), excerpts from plays in the Zenith series for children. Her other books include *Like One of the Family: Conversations from a Domestic's Life* (1956); *A Hero Ain't Nothing but a Sandwich* (novel, 1973); *A Short Walk* (1979); *Rainbow Jordan* (1981); and *Many Closets* (1987). Childress's play *Trouble in Mind* won the Obie Award in 1956 as the best original off-Broadway production. Her book *Rainbow Jordan* for young people was published in 1982. She wrote, in the 1980s, a play based on the life of the black woman comedian Jackie "Moms" Mabley, which was produced in New York City.

Countee Cullen's own selections of his best work have been collected in a volume published as On These I Stand.

Born Countee Porter on May 30, 1903 in Baltimore, he was orphaned at an early age and adopted by the Reverend Frederick Cullen, pastor of New York's Salem Methodist Church. At New York University, Cullen won Phi Beta Kappa honors and was awarded the Witter Bynner Poetry Prize. In 1925, while still a student at New York University, Cullen completed *Color*, a volume of poetry that received the Harmon Foundation's first gold medal for literature two years later.

Countee Cullen

(1903–1946)

Poet

In 1926 he earned his M.A. at Harvard and a year later finished both *The Ballad of the Brown Girl* and *Copper Sun*. This was followed in 1929 by *The Black Christ*, written during a two-year sojourn in France on a Guggenheim fellowship. In 1927, he edited *Caroling Dusk: An Anthology of Verse by Negro Poets*. The book was reprinted in 1972.

Upon his return to New York City, Cullen began a teaching career in the public school system. During this period, he also produced a novel, *One Way to Heaven* (1932); *The Medea and Other Poems* (1935); *The Lost Zoo* (1940); and *My Lives and How I Lost Them* (1942, 1971).

In 1947, a year after his death, Cullen's own selections of his best work were collected in a volume published under the title *On These I Stand*.

Samuel R. Delany

(1942–)

Novelist

Born in Harlem, and a published writer at the age of nineteen, Delany has been a prolific writer of science fiction novelettes and novels. His first book was *The Jewels of Aptor* (1962), followed by *Captives of the Flame* (1963); *The Towers of Toron* (1964); *City of a Thousand Suns* (1965); *The Ballad of Beta-2* (1965); *Babel-17* (1966); *Empire Star* (1966); *The Einstein Intersection* (1967); *Out of the Dead City* (1968); and *Nova* (1968). *Babel-17* and *The Einstein Intersection* both won Nebula Awards from the Science Fiction Writers of America, as have his short stories "Aye, and Gomorrah" and "Time Considered as a Helix of Semi-Precious Stones," which also won a Hugo Award at the World Science Fiction Convention at Heidelberg. Delany co-edited the speculative fiction quarterly *Quark, Nos. 1, 2, 3, 4* with his former wife, National Book Award–winning poet Marilyn Hacker. He also wrote, directed, and edited the half-hour film *The Orchid*. In 1975, Delany was Visiting Butler Chair Professor of English at the State University of New York at Buffalo.

His other books include *Distant Stars* (1981); *Stars in My Pocket Like Grains of Sand* (1984); *The Splendor and Misery of Bodies of Cities* (1985); *Flight from Neveryona* (1985); *Neveryona* (1986); and *The Bridge of Lost Desire* (1988). His non-fiction works include *The Jewel-Hinged Jaw*; *The American Shore*; *Starboard Wine*; *The Straits of Messina*; and *The Motion of Light in Water*, an autobiography.

Dove was born on August 28, 1952 in Akron, Ohio. She received a B.A. from Miami University in Oxford, Ohio in 1973 and a master of fine arts from the University of Iowa in 1977. Dove also attended the University of Tubingen in Germany in 1974 and 1975.

Dove began her teaching career at Arizona State University in 1981 as an assistant professor. By 1984 she was an associate professor and by 1987 a full professor. In 1989 she joined the University of Virginia's English department, where she continues to teach creative writing.

Dove is a renowned poet, having won the 1987 Pulitzer Prize for poetry for a collection titled *Thomas & Beulah*. Her themes are universal, encompassing much of the human condition and occasionally commenting on racial issues. She has also published *Yellow House on the Corner* (1980), *Museum* (1983), *Grace Notes* (1989), and a collection of short stories, *Fifth Sunday* (1985).

Besides the Pulitzer Prize, Dove has received many honors, including a Presidential scholarship (1970), two Fulbright scholarships (1974, 1975), two literary grants from the National Endowment for the Humanities (1978, 1989), two Guggenheim fellowships (1983, 1984), the General Electric Foundation Award for Younger Poets (1987), the Ohio Governor's Award (1988), two Andrew W. Mellon fellowships (1988, 1989), a fellowship at the Center for Advanced Studies at the University of Virginia (1989–1992), and the Walt Whitman Award (1990). In 1993 she was named United States Poet Laureate.

Rita Dove

(1952–)

Poet, Educator

The first black poet to gain a national reputation in the United States, Paul Laurence Dunbar was also the first to use black dialect within the formal structure of his work.

Born of former slaves in Dayton, Ohio, Dunbar went to work as an elevator operator after graduating from high school. His first book of poetry, *Oak and Ivy*, was privately printed in 1893 and was followed by *Majors and Minors*, which appeared two years later. Neither book was an immediate sensation, but there were enough favorable reviews in such magazines as *Harper's* to encourage Dunbar in the pursuit of a full-fledged literary career. In 1896, Dunbar completed *Lyrics of a Lowly Life*, the single work upon which his subsequent reputation was irrevocably established.

Paul Laurence

Dunbar

(1872–1906)

Poet

Before his untimely death in 1906, Dunbar had become the dominant presence in the world of American Negro poetry. His later works included *Lyrics of Sunshine and Shadow* (1905), *Li'l Gal* (1904), *Howdy, Honey, Howdy* (1905), *A Plantation Portrait* (1905), *Joggin'erlong* (1906), and *Complete Poems,* published posthumously in 1913. This last work contains not only the dialect poems that were his trademark, but many poems in conventional English as well. The book has enjoyed such enormous popularity that it has, to this day, never gone out of print. He also published four novels, including *The Sport of Gods, The Love of Landry,* and *The Uncalled,* and four volumes of short stories.

Ralph Ellison

(1914–)

Novelist, Essayist

Ralph Ellison's critical and artistic reputation rests largely on a single masterpiece, his first and only novel, *Invisible Man.* Acclaimed by virtually all who have read it, the novel was given the National Book Award for fiction in 1952. It had been years in the making, and its success heralded the emergence of a major writing talent.

Ellison was born in Oklahoma City, Oklahoma and came to New York City in the late 1930s, after having studied music at Tuskegee Institute for three years. At first interested in sculpture, he turned to writing after coming under the influence of T.S. Eliot's poetry, and as a direct consequence of his friendship with Richard Wright.

In 1955, the American Academy of Arts and Letters awarded Ellison the Prix de Rome, which enabled him to live and write in Italy for a time. Since then, he has lectured at New York University and at Bennington College, and has been writer in residence at Rutgers University.

His second published work was *Shadow and Act,* a book of essays that appeared in 1964. Excerpts from his second novel have been published in several literary journals, and three books of essays have been written about the author and his novel.

He has retired as Albert Schweitzer Professor of Humanities at New York University (1970–1980), and in 1974 was awarded an honorary doctor of letters degree by Harvard University.

The thirtieth anniversary edition of *Invisible Man,* with a new introduction by Ellison, was published in 1982.

Ralph Ellison's novel
Invisible Man *is considered*
a masterpiece of modern
literature.

Elected to the National Institute of Arts and Letters and the American Academy of Arts and Letters, Ellison was the subject of a *New Yorker* magazine profile in 1976. He received the Medal of Freedom from President Richard M. Nixon in 1969, and an honorary doctor of letters degree from Wesleyan University in June 1980 "for his insight into the role of the artist in American culture."

His third book, *Going to the Territory* (1986), was hailed as highly literate essay writing, although some reviewers disagreed with some of his opinions. Ellison's writings are represented in many literary anthologies and collections, and chapters about his work exist in scores of books.

Mari Evans

(1923–)

Poet

Born in Toledo, Ohio, Evans studied at the University of Toledo. In 1963, her poetry was published in *Phylon, Negro Digest,* and *Dialog.* Two years later she was awarded a John Hay Whitney fellowship.

One of her better-known works is *The Alarm Clock,* which deals with the rude awakening of the black American to the white establishment. It captures and summarizes the scene of the 1960s in the United States.

Her books include *I Am a Black Woman; Where Is All the Music?; Black Women Writers (1950-1980): A Critical Evaluation* (1984), edited by Evans and covering fifteen black women poets, novelists, and playwrights; *Nightstar: Poems From 1973-1978* (1982); *I Look at Me; Singing Black; The Day They Made Benani;* and *Jim Flying High.*

Charles Fuller

(1939–)

Playwright

Fuller became "stagestruck" in his high-school days when he went to the Old Walnut Street Theater in his native Philadelphia and saw a Yiddish play starring Molly Picon and Menasha Skulnik. He didn't understand a word of it, "but it was live theater, and I felt myself responding to it."

In 1959, Fuller entered the Army and served in Japan and South Korea, after which he attended Villanova University and La Salle College. While Fuller was working as a housing inspector in Philadelphia, the McCarter Theater in Princeton, New Jersey produced his first play. The theme was intermarriage, and its creator is quick now to tag it "one of the world's worst interracial plays." During this time, however, he met members of The Negro Ensemble Company, and in 1974 he wrote his first play for them, *In the Deepest Part of Sleep.* For NEC's tenth anniversary Fuller wrote *The Brownsville Raid* about the black soldiers who were dishonorably discharged on President Teddy Roosevelt's orders in 1906 after a shootout in Brownsville, Texas. The play was a hit, and Fuller followed it a few seasons later with *Zooman and the Sign,* a melodrama that won two Obie awards.

A Soldiers Play, which won a Pulitzer Prize in 1982, was his fourth play for The Negro Ensemble Company. This drama, dealing with a murder and set in a backwater New Orleans Army camp in 1944, opened NEC's fifteenth anniversary season in 1981 with a long run and was hailed by the *New York Times* as "tough, taut and fully realized." *A Soldier's Play* became *A Soldier's Story* when it was produced as a film in 1984 by Columbia Pictures. Fuller wrote the screenplay and black actor Howard E. Rollins, Jr. was the film's star.

The recipient of a Guggenheim fellowship, a Rockefeller fellowship, and the National Endowment for the Arts and CAPS fellowship in playwriting, Fuller describes himself as a playwright who happens to be black, rather than a black playwright.

Ernest J. Gaines (1933–)
Novelist, Short Story Writer

Gaines was born on a plantation in Louisiana. He moved to California in 1949, where he did his undergraduate study at San Francisco State College. In 1959, he received the Wallace Stegner fellowship in creative writing. The following year he was awarded the Joseph Henry Jackson Literary Award.

His first novel to be published was *Catherine Carmier* (1964). Other novels by Gaines are *Of Love and Dust* (1967); *Barren Summer* (completed in 1963 but never published); *The Autobiography of Miss Jane Pittman* (1971); *A Warm Day in November* (for young people); and *In My Father's House* (1978). The 1974 television production of *The Autobiography of Miss Jane Pittman* with Cicely Tyson boosted his reputation. Another work by Gaines, the novel *A Gathering of Old Men*, published in 1983, has been made into a movie.

Nikki Giovanni (1943–)
Poet

Nikki Giovanni was born in Knoxville, Tennessee, and she studied at Fisk University and at the University of Pennsylvania. Her first book of poetry, *Black Feeling, Black Talk*, published in the mid-1960s, was followed by *Black Judgment* in 1968. These two were combined as *Black Feeling, Black Talk, Black Judgment* in 1970.

By 1974, her poems were to be found in many black literature anthologies, and she had also become a media personality through her TV appearances, where she read her poetry. Many of her poems were put to soul or gospel music accompaniment. One such recording is *Truth Is on Its Way*.

Giovanni is a prolific author, having written *Recreation*; *Spin a Soft Black Song*; *Night Comes Softly: Anthology of Black Female Voices*; *My House*; *Gem-*

ini: An Extended Autobiographical Statement; Ego Tripping and Other Poems for Young People; A Dialogue (with James Baldwin); and *A Poetic Equation: Conversations Between Nikki Giovanni and Margaret Walker.* Her other works include *The Women and the Men: Poems* (1975); *Cotton Candy on a Rainy Day* (1978); *Vacation Time* (1980), a collection of poems for children that was dedicated to her son, Tommy; *Those Who Ride the Night Winds* (1984); and *Sacred Cows ... and Other Edibles* (1988).

Alex Haley
(1921–1992)

Journalist, Novelist

The author of the widely acclaimed novel *Roots* was born in Ithaca, New York and reared in Henning, Tennessee. The oldest of three sons of a college professor father and a mother who taught grade school, Haley graduated from high school at fifteen and attended college for two years before enlisting in the United States Coast Guard as a messboy in 1939.

A voracious reader, he began writing short stories while working at sea, but it took eight years before small magazines began accepting some of his stories. By 1952, the Coast Guard had created a new rating for Haley, chief journalist, and he began handling United States Coast Guard public relations. In 1959, after twenty years of military service, he retired from the Coast Guard and launched a new career as a free-lance writer. He eventually became an assignment writer for *Reader's Digest* and moved on to *Playboy,* where he initiated the "Playboy Interviews" feature.

One of the personalities Haley interviewed was Malcolm X—an interview that inspired Haley's first book, *The Autobiography of Malcolm X* (1965). Translated into eight languages, the book has sold over six million copies.

Pursuing the few slender clues of oral family history told him by his maternal grandmother in Tennessee, Haley spent the next twelve years traveling three continents tracking his maternal family back to a Mandingo youth named Kunta Kinte, who was kidnapped into slavery from the small village of Juffure, in The Gambia, West Africa. During this period, he lectured extensively in the United States and in Great Britain on his discoveries about his family in Africa, and he wrote many magazine articles on his research in the 1960s and the 1970s. For his work he received several honorary doctor of letters degrees.

The book *Roots,* excerpted in *Reader's Digest* in 1974 and heralded for several years, was finally published in the fall of 1976 with wide publicity and reviews. In January 1977, ABC-TV produced a twelve-hour series based on the book, which set records for the number of viewers. With cover stories, book reviews, and interviews with Haley in scores of magazines and newspapers, the book became the number-one national best-seller, sold in the millions, and was published as a paperback in 1977. *Roots* became a phenomenon. It was serialized in the *New York Post* and the *Long Island Press*. Instructional packages, lesson plans based on *Roots*, and other books about *Roots* for schools were published along with records and tapes by Haley.

Haley's book stimulated interest in Africa and in black genealogy. The United States Senate passed a resolution paying tribute to Haley and comparing *Roots* to *Uncle Tom's Cabin*, written by Harriet Beecher Stowe in the 1850s. Among the book's awards are the National Book Award for 1976 and a special Pulitzer Prize the same year for making an important contribution to the literature of slavery. *Roots* was not without its critics, however. A 1977 lawsuit brought by Margaret Walker charged that *Roots* plagiarized her novel *Jubilee*. Another author, Harold Courlander, also filed a suit charging that *Roots* plagiarized his novel *The African*. Courlander received a settlement after several passages in *Roots* were found to be almost verbatim from *The African*. Haley claimed that researchers helping him had given him this material without citing the source.

Haley received the NAACP's Spingarn Medal in 1977. Four thousand deans and department heads of colleges and universities throughout the country in a survey conducted by *Scholastic Magazine* selected Haley as America's foremost achiever in the literature category. (Martin Luther King, Jr. was selected in the religious category.) The ABC-TV network presented another series, *Roots: The Next Generation*, in February 1979 (also written by Haley). *Roots* had sold almost five million copies by December 1978 and had been reprinted in twenty-three languages.

In 1988, Haley conducted a promotional tour for a novella called *A Different Kind of Christmas* about slave escapes in the 1850s. He also promoted a drama, *Roots: The Gift*, a two-hour television program shown in December 1988. This story revolved around two principal characters from *Roots* who are involved in a slave break for freedom on Christmas Eve.

Haley died February 10, 1992, of a heart attack.

Jupiter Hammon

(1720?–1800?)

Poet

Hammon was the first black poet to have his work published in America. *An Evening Thought, Salvation by Christ, with Penitential Cries* appeared in 1761, when Hammon was a slave belonging to a Mr. Lloyd of Long Island, New York.

Due to his fondness for preaching, the major portion of Hammon's poetry is religious in tone, and is usually dismissed by critics as being of little aesthetic value because of its pious platitudes, faulty syntax, and forced rhymes. Hammon's best-known work is a prose piece, *An Address to the Negroes of the State of New York,* delivered before the African Society of New York City on September 24, 1786. This speech was published the following year and went into three editions.

Lorraine Hansberry

(1930–1965)

Playwright

Born in Chicago, Hansberry studied art at Chicago's Art Institute, the University of Wisconsin, and, finally, in Guadalajara, Mexico.

Hansberry wrote the award-winning play *A Raisin in the Sun* while living in New York's Greenwich Village, having conceived the play after reacting distastefully to what she called "a whole body of material about Negroes. Cardboard characters. Cute dialect bits. Or hip-swinging musicals from exotic scores." The play opened on Broadway on March 11, 1959, at a time when it was generally held that all plays dealing with blacks were "death" at the box office. Produced, directed, and performed by blacks, it was later made into a successful movie starring Sidney Poitier. It was then adapted into *Raisin,* a musical that won a Tony Award in 1974.

Her second Broadway play, *The Sign in Sidney Brustein's Window,* dealt with "the western intellectual poised in hesitation before the flames of involvement." Shortly after its Broadway opening, Hansberry succumbed to cancer on January 12, 1965 in New York City.

Her books include *To Be Young, Gifted and Black*; *The Movement: Documentary of a Struggle for Equality*; and *Les Blancs: The Collected Last Plays of Lorraine Hansberry.*

Robert E. Hayden

(1913–1980)

Poet

Robert E. Hayden, a graduate of Detroit City College (now called Wayne State University), who was chief researcher on African-American history and folklore for the Federal Writers Project in 1936, later accomplished advanced work in English, play production, and creative writing at the

University of Michigan. While there, he won the Jule and Avery Hopwood Prize for poetry twice. Hayden also completed radio scripts and a finished version of a play about the Underground Railroad, *Go Down Moses*.

His first book of poems, *Heart-Shape in the Dust*, was published in 1940 shortly before he assumed the music and drama critic function for the *Michigan Chronicle*. He taught at Fisk University from 1946 to the early 1970s and later at the University of Michigan. His works include *The Lion and the Archer* (with Myron O'Higgins); *A Ballad of Remembrance*; *Selected Poems*; *Words in the Mourning Time*; and *The Night-Blooming Cereus*. He edited *Kaleidoscope: Poems by American Negro Poets* and *Afro American Literature: An Introduction* (with David J. Burrows and Frederick R. Lapsides). His other books include *Figure of Time*; *Angle of Ascent: New and Selected Poems*; and *American Journal* (poems). In 1975, the Academy of American Poets elected him its Fellow of the Year, and in 1976 he was awarded the Grand Prize for Poetry at the First World Festival of Negro Arts in Dakar, Senegal. From 1976 to 1978 he served as Consultant in Poetry at the Library of Congress. He was a professor of English at the University of Michigan at the time of his death on February 25, 1980.

Chester Himes (1909–1984)

Novelist

Born in Jefferson City, Missouri, Himes was educated at Ohio State University and later lived in France and in Spain.

In 1945 he completed his first novel, *If He Hollers Let Him Go*, the story of a black working in a defense plant. His second book, *The Lonely Crusade* (1947), was set in similar surroundings.

His other books include *The Third Generation*, *Cotton Comes to Harlem*, *Pinktoes*, *The Quality of Hurt: The Autobiography of Chester Himes*, and *Black on Black: Baby Sister and Selected Writings*.

Following a stroke, which confined him to a wheelchair, he and his wife lived in Alicante, Spain. In 1977 they returned to New York for the publication of the concluding volume of his autobiography, *My Life of Absurdity*.

Himes died in Spain in November 1984, at the age of seventy-five. He was a prolific author of almost twenty books, and several of his popular novels are being reprinted posthumously in hardcover and paperback editions.

George Moses Horton

(1797–1883?)

Poet

George Moses Horton was the first black professional man of letters in America and one of the first professional writers of any race in the South. Horton was the first black southerner to have a volume of poetry published.

Horton was born into slavery in North Carolina. While growing up on a farm, and between chores, Horton was able to cultivate a love of learning. With the aid of his mother and her Wesley hymnal, Horton learned to read. While working as a janitor at the University of North Carolina, Horton wrote light verse for some students in exchange for spending money.

Some of his early poems were printed in the newspapers of Raleigh and Boston. When Horton published his first book of poems in 1829, he called it *The Hope of Liberty* in the belief that profits from its sales would be sufficient to pay for his freedom. His hopes did not materialize, however, with the result that he remained a slave until the coming of Emancipation. This book was reprinted in 1837 under the title *Poems by a Slave*.

In 1865 he published *Naked Genius*, a poem containing many bitter lines about his former condition that contrast sharply with the conformist verse of earlier black poets. Richard Walser's *The Black Poet* was written about Horton and published in 1967.

Langston Hughes

(1902–1967)

Poet, Novelist, Playwright

Born in Joplin, Missouri, Hughes moved to Cleveland at the age of fourteen, graduated from Central High School, and spent a year in Mexico before studying at Columbia University. After roaming the world as a seaman and writing some poetry as well, Hughes returned to the United States, winning the Witter Bynner Prize for undergraduate poetry while attending Lincoln University. In 1930 he received the Harmon Award, and in 1935, with the help of a Guggenheim fellowship, he traveled to Russia and Spain.

The long and distinguished list of Hughes's prose works includes *Not Without Laughter* (1930), a novel; *The Big Sea* (1940); and *I Wonder as I Wander* (1956), his autobiography. To this must be added such collections of poetry as *The Weary Blues* (1926); *The Dream Keeper* (1932); *Shakespeare in Harlem* (1942); *Fields of Wonder* (1947); *One Way Ticket* (1947); and *Selected Poems* (1959).

Hughes was also an accomplished song lyricist, librettist, and newspaper columnist. Through his newspaper columns, he created Jesse B. Simple, a Harlem character who saw life on the musical stage in *Simply Heavenly*. There are also several volumes of the Simple columns.

Throughout the 1960s, Hughes edited several anthologies in an attempt to popularize black authors and their works. Some of these are *An African Treasury* (1960); *Poems from Black Africa* (1963); *New Negro Poets: U.S.A.* (1964); and *The Best Short Stories by Negro Writers* (1967). Published posthumously were *The Panther and the Lash: Poems of Our Times* (1969) and *Good Morning Revolution: Uncollected Writings of Social Protest*. Hughes wrote many plays, including *Emperor of Haiti* and *Five Plays by Langston Hughes*. *Mulatto* was produced on Broadway in the 1930s. He also wrote gospel-song plays such as *Tambourines to Glory; Black Nativity;* and *Jericho—Jim Crow*.

Zora Neale Hurston (1903–1960)

Novelist, Folklorist

After traveling north as a maid with a Gilbert and Sullivan company, Hurston acquired her education at Morgan State, Howard, and Columbia universities. While at Howard, under Alain Locke's influence, she became a figure in the Harlem Renaissance, publishing short stories in *Opportunity* and serving with Langston Hughes and Wallace Thurman on the editorial board of the magazine *Fire*.

In 1934, *Jonah's Gourd Vine* was published after her return to Florida. Her important novel *Their Eyes Were Watching God* appeared three years later. *Moses, Man of the Mountain* (1939) was followed in 1948 by *Seraph on the Suwanee*. Her other three works are two books of folklore, *Mules and Men* (1935) and *Tell My Horse* (1938), and *Dust Tracks on a Road* (1942), her autobiography, which was reprinted in 1985 with a new introduction and with several altered or expunged chapters restored.

Toward the end of her life, Hurston was a drama instructor at the North Carolina College for Negroes in Durham. She died in obscurity and poverty on January 28, 1960. Since then, six of her works have been reprinted with new introductions.

Georgia Douglas Johnson

(1886–1966)

Poet

As one of the first modern black female poets to gain recognition, Georgia Douglas Johnson, whose collections of verse were published between 1918 and 1930, is an important link in the chain of American black female lyric poets. Johnson's life spanned most of the literary movements of this century, and her Washington, DC home was the popular gathering place of early Harlem Renaissance writers.

Johnson was born in Atlanta, Georgia, on September 10, 1886. She was educated in the public schools of the city and at Atlanta University, and she went on to attend Howard University in Washington, DC, and Oberlin Conservatory of Music in Ohio.

Initially, she was interested in musical composition, but gradually she turned toward lyric poetry. After teaching school in Alabama, she moved to Washington, DC with her husband, who had been appointed Recorder of Deeds by President William Howard Taft. While in the nation's capital, she too engaged in government work while completing such books as *The Heart of a Woman* (1918); *Bronze* (1922); *An Autumn Love Cycle* (1928); and *Share My World*, published in 1962.

Johnson was a prolific writer: more than two hundred of her poems were published in her four literary works, and other poems and several dramas have appeared in journals and books primarily edited by blacks.

James Weldon Johnson

(1871–1938)

Poet, Lyricist, Civil Rights Leader

Like W.E.B. DuBois, black intellectual James Weldon Johnson played a vital role in the civil-rights movement of the twentieth century—as poet, teacher, critic, diplomat, and NAACP official. Johnson is perhaps most often remembered as the lyricist for *Lift Every Voice and Sing*, the poem that is often referred to as the black national anthem.

Born in 1871 in Jacksonville, Florida, Johnson was educated at Atlanta and Columbia Universities. His career included service as a school principal, a lawyer, and a diplomat (United States Consul at Puerto Cabello, Venezuela, and later, in Nicaragua). From 1916 to 1930, he was a key policy maker of the NAACP, eventually serving as the organization's executive secretary.

In his early days, Johnson's fame rested largely on his lyrics for popular songs, but in 1917 he completed his first book of poetry, *Fifty Years and*

Other Poems. Five years later he followed this with *The Book of American Negro Poetry*, and in 1927 he established his literary reputation with *God's Trombones*, a collection of seven folk sermons in verse. Over the years, this work has been performed countless times on stage and television.

In 1930, Johnson finished *St. Peter Relates an Incident of the Resurrection*, and three years later, his lengthy autobiography *Along This Way*.

Johnson died in 1938 following an automobile accident in Maine.

Gayl Jones (1949–)

Novelist, Poet, Short Story Writer

Born in Lexington, Kentucky, Jones received a bachelor's degree in English from Connecticut College in 1971 and a master's degree in creative writing from Brown University in 1973. Jones's work includes two novels, *Corregidora* (1975) and *Eva's Man* (1976), short stories, and several collections of poetry, including *Song for Anninho* (1981), *The Hermit Woman* (1983), and *Xarque and Other Poems* (1985).

June Jordan (1936–)

Poet, Novelist

Born in Harlem of parents from Jamaica, in the West Indies, June Jordan attended Barnard College and the University of Chicago. She has been married and has a son. She has taught African-American literature, English, and writing at several colleges and universities, and was co-founder and co-director of The Voice of the Children, Inc., a creative workshop. Her poems have been published in many magazines, newspapers, and anthologies. She received a Rockefeller grant in creative writing for 1969. Her books for children and young people include *Fannie Lou Hamer* (1972); *His Own Where* (1971), her first novel nominated for the National Book Award; *Who Look at Me* (1969); *Dry Victories* (1972); *New Room, New Life* (1974); and *The Voice of the Children: Writings by Black and Puerto Rican Young People* (1970, 1974), edited by Jordan and Terri Bush. Her books for adults include *Soulscript* (1970), edited by Jordan; *Some Changes* (1971); *New Days: Poems of Exile and Return* (1973); *Things That I Do in the Dark: Selected Poems* (1976); and *Passion: New Poems, 1977–1980* (1980).

Nella Larsen (1891–1964)

Novelist

Nella Larsen was born in Chicago, Illinois of a Danish mother and a West Indian father. She attended Fisk University in Nashville, Tennessee, and the University of Copenhagen in Denmark. Larsen's two novels are *Quicksand* (1928), for which she received a bronze medal from the Harmon Foundation, and *Passing* (1929).

Audre Lorde

(1934–1993)

Poet

Audre Lorde was born in New York City, educated at Hunter College with a master's in library science from Columbia University; was poet in residence at Tougaloo College; and taught at Lehman College in the Bronx and John Jay College, CCNY. She received a National Endowment for the Arts grant for poetry and a Cultural Council Foundation grant, also for poetry.

Her books of poetry include *Cables to Rage* (1970); *The First Cities* (1968); *From a Land Where Other People Live* (1973); *Coal* (1968); *The New York Head Shop and Museum* (1974); *Between Ourselves* (1976); *The Black Unicorn* (1978); *Chosen Poems—Old and New* (1982); *Zami: A New Spelling of My Name* (1982); *Sister/Outsider: Essays and Speeches* (1984); *Lesbian Poetry: An Anthology* (1982); and *Woman Poet—The East* (1984). Lorde's poetry has been published in many anthologies, magazines, and lesbian books and periodicals.

Claude McKay

(1890–1948)

Poet

Born the son of a farmer in Jamaica (then British West Indies), McKay began writing early in life. Two books of his poems, *Songs of Jamaica* and *Constab Ballads*, were published just after he turned twenty. In both, he made extensive use of Jamaican dialect.

In 1913, McKay came to America to study agriculture at Tuskegee Institute and at Kansas State University, but his interest in poetry prompted him to move to New York City, where he published his work in small literary magazines.

McKay then made a trip abroad, visiting England. While there, he completed a collection of lyrics entitled *Spring in New Hampshire*. When he returned to the United States, he became associate editor of *The Liberator* under Max Eastman. In 1922 he completed *Harlem Shadows*, a landmark work of the Harlem Renaissance period.

McKay then turned to the writing of such novels as *Home to Harlem* (1928), *Banjo* (1929), and four other books, including an autobiography and a study of Harlem. *The Passion of Claude McKay: Selected Prose and Poetry 1912–1948* edited by Wayne Cooper, was published in 1973. McKay traveled extensively abroad before returning to the United States, where he died. His final work, *Selected Poems,* was published posthumously in 1953.

During World War II, when Winston Churchill addressed a joint session of the United States Congress in an effort to enlist American aid in the battle against Nazism, the climax of his oration was his reading of the famous poem "*If We Must Die*," originally written by McKay to assail lynchings and mob violence in the South. McKay's *Trial by Lynching* (1967), edited and translated stories, and his *The Negroes in America* (1979), edited and translated from the Russian language, have also been published. Many of his books or works have been reprinted since his death: *Home to Harlem; Banana Bottom; Banjo; A Long Way from Home* (1970); *Harlem: Negro Metropolis* (1972); and *Selected Poems of Claude McKay* (1971). *Songs of Jamaica* and *Constab Ballads* have been bound together as *The Dialect Poems of Claude McKay*. Also, Wayne F. Cooper's *Claude McKay: Rebel Sojourner in the Harlem Renaissance* (1987) is an important book detailing McKay's life and work.

McMillan was born and raised in Port Huron, Michigan. She attended Los Angeles City College, but later transferred to Berkeley and then to Columbia University to study film. She later enrolled in a writing workshop at the Harlem Writers Guild and was accepted at the MacDowell Colony in 1983.

**Terry McMillan
(1951–)**

Novelist

McMillan's novels include *Mama* (1987), *Disappearing Acts* (1989), and *Waiting to Exhale* (1992). Her novel *Waiting to Exhale* remained on the best-seller list for several months, proving that there is a demand for African-American literature. She has also edited an anthology of contemporary African-American fiction, *Breaking Ice* (1992).

James McPherson, born in Savannah, Georgia, received his B.A. in 1965 from Morris Brown College in Atlanta, a law degree from Harvard University in 1968, and an M.F.A. from the University of Iowa in 1969. He has taught writing at several universities, presently at the University of Iowa, and is a contributing editor of *Atlantic Monthly*. His short stories have appeared in several magazines. *Hue and Cry*, a collection of short stories published in 1969, was highly praised by Ralph Ellison. A Guggenheim Fellow in 1972–1973, McPherson published a second book of short stories, *Elbow Room*, in 1977 and was given the Pulitzer Prize for fiction in 1978. He taught fiction writing for several years at the University of Virginia in Charlottesville. McPherson was one of the three black writers who in 1981, with Elma Lewis, were awarded five-year grants by the McArthur Foundation of Chicago for exceptional talent.

**James Alan
McPherson
(1943–)**

Short Story Writer

Loften Mitchell

(1919–)

Playwright

Raised in the Harlem of 1920s, Loften Mitchell first began to write as a child, creating scripts for backyard shows he and his brother put on. After completing junior high school, he decided to enroll at New York Textile High because he had been promised a job on the school newspaper there. But Mitchell soon realized that he needed the training of an academic high school, and with the help of one of his teachers, he transferred to DeWitt Clinton.

Graduating with honors, Mitchell found a job as an elevator operator and a delivery boy to support himself while he studied play writing at night at the City College of New York. He eventually met a professor from Talladega College in Alabama who helped him win a scholarship to study there. He graduated with honors in 1943, having won an award for the best play written by a student.

After two years of service in the Navy, Mitchell enrolled as a graduate student at Columbia University in New York. A year later, he accepted a job with the Department of Welfare as a social investigator and continued to go to school at night. During this time, he wrote one of his first successful plays, *Blood in the Night*, and in 1957 he wrote *A Land Beyond the River*, which had a long run at an off-Broadway theater and was published as a book.

The following year Mitchell won a Guggenheim award, which enabled him to return to Columbia and write for a year. Since then, he has written a new play, *Star of the Morning*, the story of black entertainter Bert Williams.

In 1967 Mitchell published a study African-American theater entitled *Black Drama*. His other books include *Tell Pharaoh*, a play; *The Stubborn Old Lady Who Resisted Change* (1973), a novel; and *Voices of the Black Theatre* (1976). Mitchell also wrote the books for the Broadway musicals *Ballads for Bimshire* (1963); *Bubbling Brown Sugar* (1975); *Cartoons for a Lunch Hour* (1978); *A Gypsy Girl* (1982); and *Miss Ethel Waters* (1983).

Toni Morrison

(1931–)

Novelist, Editor

Born Chloe Anthony Wofford in Lorain, Ohio, Morrison received a B.A. from Howard University in 1953 and an M.A. from Cornell in 1955. After working as an instructor in English and the humanities at Texas Southern University and Howard University, Morrison eventually became a senior

Toni Morrison, author of such works as Song of Solomon, Beloved, *and* Jazz, *received the 1993 Nobel Prize in recognition of her contribution to literature.*

editor at Random House in New York City. She has been responsible for the publication of many books by blacks at Random House: Middleton Harris's *The Black Book*, which she edited, and books by Toni Cade Bambara and others. In 1971–1972, she was also an associate professor at the State University of New York at Purchase. From 1984 to 1989, Morrison served as Albert Schweitzer Professor of the Humanities at the State University of New York at Albany, after twenty years as a senior editor for Random House. Formerly married, she has two sons.

Morrison's first novel, *The Bluest Eye*, was published in 1969. Her second novel, *Sula*, was published in 1974 and won a 1975 Ohioana Book Award. Morrison's third novel, *Song of Solomon* (1977), was critically acclaimed and received the 1977 National Book Critics Circle Award and the 1978 American Academy and Institute of Arts and Letters Award. Her fourth novel, *Tar Baby* (1981), also received positive reviews. She was elected to the American Institute of Arts and Letters in 1981 and gave the keynote address at the American Writers' Congress in New York City in the fall of that year. She has also written the story for the musical *Storyville*, which is about jazz music originating in the brothels of New Orleans; the story for the musical *New Orleans*, a New York Public Theater workshop production; and also a screenplay of her novel *Tar Baby*.

Morrison's fifth novel, *Beloved*, was published in 1987. A historical novel, it received rave reviews. In 1988 *Beloved* won both the Pulitzer Prize for fiction and the Robert F. Kennedy Award. *Beloved* was a finalist for the 1988 National Book Critics Circle Award and was one of the three contenders for the Ritz Hemingway prize in Paris, from which no winner emerged. This novel by Morrison was also a finalist for the National Book Award for 1987. Her most recent works include a collection of essays and *Jazz*, a novel. In 1993 Morrison was awarded the Nobel Prize for literature.

Gloria Naylor
(1950–)

Novelist

Gloria Naylor was born in New York City, where she currently lives. She received a B.A. in English from Brooklyn College in 1981 and a M.A. in Afro-American studies from Yale University in 1983. She has taught writing and literature at George Washington University, New York University, Brandeis University, Cornell University, and Boston University. In 1983 she won the American Book Award for first fiction for her novel *The Women of Brewster Place*, produced in 1988 for television. Her second novel was *Linden Hills*, published in 1985. Her third novel, *Mama Day* (1988), was written with the aid of a grant from the National Endowment for the Arts. In 1988, Naylor was awarded a Guggenheim fellowship. In 1993 Naylor published a new novel, *Bailey's Cafe*.

Ann Petry (1908–)

Novelist,
Short Story Writer

Ann Petry was born in Old Saybrook, Connecticut, where her father was a druggist. After graduating from the College of Pharmacy at the University of Connecticut, she went to New York, where she found employment as a social worker and newspaper reporter, studying creative writing at night.

Her early short stories appeared in *Crisis* and *Pylon*. In 1946, after having received a Houghton Mifflin fellowship, she completed and published her first novel, *The Street*. This was followed by *Country Place* (1947); *The Narrows* (1953); and *Miss Mural and Other Stories* (1971). Her works for children and young people include *The Drugstore Cat*; *Harriet Tubman*; *Tituba of Salem Village*; and *Legends of the Saints*. Many of her earlier novels are being reprinted.

Born in Chattanooga, Tennessee, Reed grew up in Buffalo, New York. His first volume of poetry published in the United States, *Conjure* (1972), was nominated for the National Book Award, as was his third novel, *Mumbo Jumbo* (1972). He has also published *Chattanooga*, a second volume of poetry, and four other novels: *The Free-lance Pallbearers*; *Yellow Back Radio Broke Down*; *The Last Days of Louisiana Red*; and *Flight to Canada*.

Reed edited the breakthrough anthology *19 Necromancers from Now* and *Yardbird Lives*. His poetry has appeared in numerous anthologies and magazines, including *The Poetry of the Negro*, *The New Black Poetry*, *The Norton Anthology*, *Cricket*, and *Scholastic* magazine. *His Shrovetide in Old New Orleans* (1978) is a collection of essays.

Reed published two novels in the 1980s, *The Terrible Twos* (1982), a political satire; and *Reckless Eyeballing* (1986), a farce in which the sinister Flower Phantom punishes feminists for defaming black manhood. Both novels were reissued in paperback in 1988 by Atheneum Publishers. Reed's two books of essays, editorials, and book reviews for this period are *God Made Alaska for the Indians: Selected Essays* (1983) and *Writin' Is Fightin': Thirty-Seven Years of Boxing on Paper* (1988). Reed's novel *The Terrible Threes* was published in 1989.

Ishmael Reed (1938–)

Novelist, Poet

Sonia Sanchez was born in Birmingham, Alabama. She studied at New York University and Hunter College in New York City. She is married to Etheridge Knight, a black writer of poetry and fiction. She has taught at San Francisco State College and is now teaching in the Black Studies Department of Temple University in Philadelphia. Her plays are published in the special black drama issue of *The Drama Review* (Summer 1968) and in *New Plays from the Black Theatre* (1969), edited by Ed Bullins. Books written or edited by her include six volumes of poetry: *Homecoming* (1969); *We a BaddDDD People* (1970); *It Is a New Day* (1971); *A Blues Book for Blue Black Magical Women* (1973); *Love Poems* (1975); and *I've Been a Woman* (1978). Sanchez has edited two anthologies: *Three Hundred and Sixty De-*

Sonia Sanchez (1934–)

Poet, Playwright

grees of Blackness Comin at You: An Anthology of the Sonia Sanchez Writers Workshop at Countee Cullen Library in Harlem (1971); and *We Be Word Sorcerers: Twenty-five Stories by Black Americans* (1973). She has also written *A Sound Investment* (1979), a collection of short stories; and *homegirls and handgrenades* (1984).

Ntozake Shange
(1948–)

Playwright, Poet, Novelist

Born in Trenton, New Jersey, Ntozake Shange graduated from Barnard College and received her master's degree from the University of Southern California. She studied African-American dance and gave many poetry readings in California. Shange taught at Sonoma Mills College in California from 1972 to 1975. Her play *For Colored Girls Who Have Considered Suicide When the Rainbow Is Enuf*, a choreopoem, was first produced in California after her dance-drama *Sassafrass* was presented in 1976. *For Colored Girls* was later produced in New York City, where it had a long run before going on to other cities. Other works by Shange that have been produced on the stage are *Spell #7*; *A Photograph: Lovers in Motion* (1979); and *Boogie Woogie Landscapes* (1979). *For Colored Girls* has been published twice as a book, and Shange's book *Three Pieces* (1981) contains *Spell #7*, *A Photograph: Lovers in Motion*, and *Boogie Woogie Landscapes*. Her other books include *Sassafrass, Cypress & Indigo* (1982), *A Daughter's Geography* (1983), and *From Okra to Greens* (1984). Earlier she published *Nappy Edges* (1978), a book of poetry. Her novel *Betsey Brown* was published in 1985. *See No Evil: Prefaces & Accounts, 1976–1983* was published in 1984. A version of *Betsey Brown* for the stage, with music by the jazz trumpeter and composer Baikida Carroll, opened the American Music Theater Festival in Philadelphia March 25, 1989.

Lucy Terry
(1730–1821)

Poet

Lucy Terry is generally considered to be the first black poet in America. In a ballad that she called "Bars Fight," she recreated an Indian massacre that occurred in Deerfield, Massachusetts in 1746 during King George's War; "Bars Fight" has been hailed by some historians as the most authentic account of the massacre.

A semi-literate slave in the household of Ensign Ebenezer Wells, she won her freedom and was married to a freed man named Prince. The Prince house served as a center for young people who gathered to listen to their hostess's storytelling. Lucy Terry was a strong woman who argued eloquently for her family's rights in several cases.

Jean Toomer's *Cane,* published in 1923, has been called one of the three best novels ever written by an American black—the others being Richard Wright's *Native Son* and Ralph Ellison's *Invisible Man.* According to Columbia University critic Robert Bone, "*Cane* is by far the most impressive product of the Negro Renaissance."

A mixture of poems and sketches, *Cane* was written during that period in which most black writers were reacting against earlier "polite" forms by creating works marked by literary realism. Toomer even went beyond this realm to the threshold of symbol and myth, using a "mystical" approach that is much more akin to the current mood than it was to the prevailing spirit of his own day. *Cane* sold only 500 copies on publication, and it was still little known until its recent reprint with new introductions. Much has been written about Toomer and *Cane* in recent years, including a *Cane* casebook.

Born in Washington, DC in 1894, Toomer was educated in law at the University of Wisconsin and City College of New York before he turned to writing. The transcendental nature of his writings is said to have stemmed in part from his early study under Gurdjieff, the Russian mystic.

Toomer also published quite a bit of poetry. Darwin T. Turner edited *The Wayward and the Seeking: A Collection of Writings by Jean Toomer* (1980), a book of his poetry, short stories, dramas, and autobiography. Other books about Toomer and his writings are Therman O'Daniel's *Jean Toomer: A Critical Evaluation* (1985), which includes more than forty essays of the most thorough, up-to-date scholarship on Toomer; Robert B. Jones and Margery Toomer Latimer's *The Collected Poems of Jean Toomer* (1988); and Nellie Y. McKay's *Jean Toomer, Artist: A Study of His Literary Life and Work, 1894–1936* (1984, 1987).

**Jean Toomer
(1894–1967)**

Novelist, Poet

Gustavus Vassa was born in 1745, in Benin, in southern Nigeria. At the age of eleven, he was kidnapped and shipped to the New World as a slave. His masters included a Virginia plantation owner, a British officer, and a Philadelphia merchant from whom he eventually purchased his freedom. Vassa then settled in England, where he worked diligently for the elimination of slavery. He even went so far as to present a petition to Parliament calling for its abolition.

His autobiography, *The Interesting Narrative of the Life of Oloudah Equiano, or Gustavus Vassa,* was published in London in 1789 and went through

**Gustavus Vassa
(Oloudah Equiano)
(c. 1745–c. 1801)**

Narrative writer

five editions in the next five years. It is regarded as a highly informative account of the evils of slavery as it affected both master and slave. Vassa died around 1801.

Alice Walker
(1944–)
Poet, Novelist

Alice Walker was born in Eatonton, Georgia and has lived in Mississippi, New York City, and San Francisco, California. She was educated at Spelman College in Atlanta, Georgia, and at Sarah Lawrence College in Bronxville, New York.

Alice Walker, a poet and fiction writer, wrote such works as The Color Purple, *which won the Pulitzer Prize for fiction in 1982;* In Love & Trouble: Stories of Black Women; Revolutionary Petunias and Other Poems; *and* Possessing the Secret of Joy.

Her short stories and poems have been published in *Freedomways,*
Essence, and other magazines and anthologies. She has been writer in residence and teacher at Jackson State College and Tougaloo College in Mississippi and is a prolific writer. Her first book was poetry entitled *Once,*
published in 1968. Her second book, published in 1970, was a novel, *The*
Third Life of Grange Copeland. A second book of poetry, *Revolutionary Petu-*
nias and Other Poems, was published in 1973. She also wrote *In Love and*
Trouble: Stories of Black Women (1973); *Langston Hughes, American Poet*
(1974), for children; *Meridian* (1976), a novel; *Good Night, Willie Lee, I'll*
See You in the Morning (1979), poetry; and *You Can't Keep a Good Woman*
Down (1981), short stories.

Her book *In Love & Trouble: Stories of Black Women* (1973) won the American Academy and Institute of Arts and Letters' Rosenthal Award. *Revolu-*
tionary Petunias and Other Poems was nominated for the National Book
Award and received the Lillian Smith Award. She has received the Merrill
fellowship for writing, a National Endowment for the Arts grant, a Radcliffe Institute fellowship, and other honors.

In 1983 Walker's third novel, *The Color Purple* (1982), won the American
Book Award in the hardcover category and also the Pulitzer Prize. The
book was reviewed negatively by black men and some women reviewers
for its degrading depiction of black men. *The Color Purple* became a best
seller in hardcover and paperback. It was released in 1985 as a widely acclaimed film.

Walker's other books include *In Search of Our Mothers' Gardens: Womanist*
Prose (1983); *Horses Make the Landscape Look More Beautiful* (1984), a
book of poems; *To Hell With Dying* (1988), a book for children; *Living by*
the Word: Selected Writings, 1973–1987 (1988), a book of essays; *The Tem-*
ple of My Familiar (1989), which was both panned and praised by critics;
and *Possessing the Secret of Joy* (1992). Walker also edited *A Zora Neale*
Hurston Reader, published in 1980.

Margaret Walker was born on July 7, 1915 in Birmingham, Alabama, and
received her early education in Alabama, Louisiana, and Mississippi. She
earned her B.A. from Northwestern University and her M.A. from the
University of Iowa in 1940.

In 1942 Walker published *For My People* and two years later was awarded
a Rosenwald fellowship for creative writing. She has taught English and

Margaret Abigail
Walker (Margaret
Walker Alexander)
(1915–)

Poet, Novelist

literature at Livingston College in North Carolina, at West Virginia State College, and at Jackson State College in Mississippi. Her novel *Jubilee* appeared in 1965, and *For My People* was reprinted in 1969. Her other works are *Prophets for a New Day; How I Wrote Jubilee; October Journey*, and *A Poetic Equation: Conversations Between Nikki Giovanni and Margaret Walker*. June 17, 1976, was proclaimed Margaret Walker Alexander Day by the mayor of her native Birmingham.

Walker's other works include *Richard Wright: Daemonic Genius* (1988). Also, a second edition of *A Poetic Equation: Conversations between Nikki Giovanni and Margaret Walker* was published in 1983.

Phillis Wheatley (1753–1784)

Poet

Born in Senegal, Phillis Wheatley was brought to the United States as a slave and received her name from Mrs. Susannah Wheatley, the wife of the Boston tailor who had bought Phillis.

Wheatley received her early education in the household of her master. Her interest in writing stemmed from her reading of the Bible and the classics under the guidance of the Wheatleys' daughter, Mary.

In 1770, her first poem was printed under the title "A Poem by Phillis, A Negro Girl, on the Death of Reverend George Whitefield." Her book *Poems on Various Subjects: Religious and Moral* was published in London in 1773. After a trip to England for health reasons she later returned to the United States, and was married. She published the poem "Liberty and Peace" in 1784, shortly before her death. Most of the old books of her poems, letters, and memories about her life were reprinted in the late 1960s and early 1970s. Two books about her are Julian D. Mason, Jr.'s *The Poems of Phillis Wheatley* (1966) and William H. Robinson's *Phillis Wheatley, A Biography* (1981). Robinson also compiled and published *Phillis Wheatley: A Bio-Bibliography* (1981).

Although George Washington was among her admirers (she had once sent him a tributary poem, which he graciously acknowledged), her poetry is considered important today largely because of its historical role in the growth of American Negro literature. Wheatley's poetry reflects Anglo-Saxon models, rather than her African heritage. It is nevertheless a typical example of the verse manufactured in a territory—the British colonies—not yet divorced from its maternal origins.

The first of Wilson's plays was *Ma Rainey's Black Bottom.* First produced at the Yale Repertory Theater and directed by Lloyd Richards, then brought to New York, the play was named the New York Drama Critics Circle's best new play in 1985. Wilson's next play, *Fences,* describing the 1930s, 1940s, and 1950s, was the best new play in 1987 for the New York Drama Critics Circle, after first being produced at the Yale Repertory Theater. Wilson's third play produced in New York, *Joe Turner's Come and Gone,* also started at the Yale Repertory Theater and was named the best new play in 1988 by the New York Drama Critics Circle. *Joe Turner's Come and Gone* is about 1911 and the earlier period of black migration from the South, sharecropping, and being dispossessed—about a search for cultural roots and identity in a dark and distant past from the psychic burden of years of slavery.

In 1986 Wilson was one of ten writers to win the Whiting Writer's Awards of ten tax-free checks for $25,000 each. The awards were established in 1985 by the Whiting Foundation to reward "exceptionally promising, emerging talent." In 1988, Yale University gave Wilson an honorary degree.

Wilson's *Joe Turner* opened in Boston before coming to New York. It was produced in 1987 by the Seattle Repertory Theater. *Fences* was also produced in San Francisco in 1987, and it received a Pulitzer Prize and a Tony award. In 1990, Wilson's *The Piano Lesson* was awarded a Pulitzer Prize.

August Wilson (1945–)

Playwright

Born on a plantation near Natchez, Mississippi, Wright drew on his personal experience to dramatize racial injustice and its brutalizing effects. In 1938, under the auspices of the WPA Illinois Writers Project, Wright published *Uncle Tom's Children,* a collection of four novellas based on his Mississippi boyhood memories. The book won an award for the best work of fiction by a WPA writer, and Wright received a Guggenheim fellowship.

Two years later, *Native Son,* a novel of Chicago's Negro ghetto, further enhanced Wright's reputation. A Book-of-the-Month Club choice, it was later a successful Broadway production under Orson Welles's direction and was filmed in South America with Wright himself in the role of Bigger Thomas. He published *Twelve Million Black Voices* in 1941.

In 1945, Wright's largely autobiographical *Black Boy* was selected by the Book-of-the-Month Club and went on to become a second best-seller.

Richard Wright (1908–1960)

Novelist

Wright later moved to Paris, where he continued to write fiction and non-fiction, including *The Outsider* (1953); *Black Power* (1954); *Savage Holiday* (1954, 1965); *The Color Curtain* (1956); *White Man Listen* (1957); *The Long Dream* (1958); *Lawd Today* (1963); *Eight Men* (1961); and *American Hunger* (1977), a continuation of Wright's autobiographical work *Black Boy.*

By Nancy Rampson

Wright died of a heart attack on November 28, 1960. More than a dozen books have been written about Richard Wright, two casebooks on *Native Son,* a children's book, and a critical pamphlet in a writers' series.

Media

Religious publishers were the first in the media industry to represent African-American interests. Although the first black-owned publishing enterprise, AME Book Concern, eventually folded more than a century after its founding in 1817, the AME Zion Book Concern (formed in 1841) continues to be active today. In the commercial book industry, the oldest continually operating black publisher is Third World Press, founded in 1967 by Haki Madhubuti, and other currently successful publishers are Black Classic Press, Africa World Press, and Just Us Books, which produces children's books. A decade after the AME Book Concern was established, Samuel Cornish and John B. Russwurm founded the first black newspaper, Freedom's Journal, which was followed twenty years later by Frederick Douglass's North Star. A host of successful journals arose in the twentieth century, including the NAACP's Crisis in 1910; Negro Digest and Ebony (which has become the most successful African-American magazine) in the 1940s; Jet in 1950; Black Enterprise and Essence in 1970; and Black Family and American Visions in the 1980s.

African-American representation in the broadcast industry began in 1929 when black radio pioneer Jack Cooper began hosting a new radio program, "The All-Negro Hour," on a white-owned Chicago station. A boom period occurred between 1946 and 1955, when the number of black-oriented stations jumped from twenty-four to six hundred, and in 1962 the country saw its first black network TV reporter, Mal Goode, at ABC-TV. The 1960s also brought the beginning of Ed Bradley's career (who now co-hosts "60 Minutes"), and that of the late Max Robinson—who was once fired from a UHF station after he broke its rules by showing his face on camera. Fourteen years later Robinson became the first black regular co-anchor for ABC-TV. Today, the nation's most visible journalists include "MacNeil-Lehrer NewsHour" correspondent Charlayne Hunter-Gault, and veteran journalist Bernard Shaw, who in January 1991 was one of three Cable News Network reporters who covered the first night of bombing on Baghdad during Operation Desert Storm. In 1980 an African-American cable network, Black Entertainment Television, made its debut.

BOOK PUBLISHERS ✦

Since black book publishing began in the United States in 1817, three types of publishers have emerged in this sector of the American book publishing industry: religious publishers; institutional publishers; and trade book publishers.

Religious Publishers

Religious publishing enterprises were established by black religious denominations in order to publish books and other literature to assist clergy and laity in recording denominational history and to provide religious instruction. Some black religious publishers also published books on secular subjects, which were generally related to celebrating some aspect of black culture or documenting black history.

Prior to the Civil War, two black religious publishing enterprises existed. The African Methodist Episcopal Church organized the AME Book Concern in Philadelphia in 1817—the first black-owned book publishing enterprise in the United States. Publishing its first book in that same year, *The Book of Discipline,* the AME Book Concern published a host of classic religious and secular books until its operations were suspended in 1952 by the General Conference of the African Methodist Episcopal Church. In 1841 the African Methodist Episcopal Zion Church formed the AME Zion Book Concern in New York City. This firm, which only published religious works, was moved to its present location in Charlotte, North Carolina, in 1894, where it continues to be an active book publisher.

In Jackson, Tennessee, the Colored Methodist Episcopal Church (CME), presently known as the Christian Methodist Episcopal Church, started the CME Publishing House in 1870. The CME Publishing House, which only publishes books on religious subjects, is currently located in Memphis, Tennessee.

Another book publishing enterprise owned by black Methodists is the AME Sunday School Union and Publishing House, which was established in Bloomington, Illinois, in 1882, but moved to Nashville, Tennessee, in 1886. Publishing secular and religious books, the AME Sunday School Union and Publishing House remains today as the oldest publishing unit owned by the AME Church.

One of the most successful black religious publishers to come into existence during the nineteenth century was the National Baptist Publishing Board. Under the leadership of Dr. Richard Henry Boyd and the auspices of the National Baptist Convention, USA, the National Baptist Publishing Board was organized in Nashville in 1896. By 1913, this well-managed firm, publishing religious and secular books, grew to become one of the largest black-owned businesses in the United States. In 1915, however, a dispute arose between the National Baptist Convention, USA and Boyd over the ownership of the National Baptist Publishing Board. In a court suit, the Tennessee Supreme Court decided in favor of Boyd; today the National Publishing Board, owned by the Boyd family, is a thriving religious publishing enterprise.

In 1907 the Church of God in Christ established the Church of God in Christ Publishing House in Memphis. Restricting its publications to religious books and pamphlets, this publisher continues today to meet the ever-expanding need for religious literature for one of the fastest-growing black religious denominations in the United States.

Faced with the loss of the National Baptist Publishing Board, the National Baptist Convention, USA, Inc. established in 1916 the Sunday School

Religious book publishers were African Americans' first representatives in the media, and many companies that were founded in the nineteenth century continue to thrive today. The oldest of these is the AME Zion Book Concern, founded in 1841.

Publishing Board in Nashville. Over the years, this firm has developed into one of the largest black-owned publishing enterprises in the United States, publishing religious and secular books and pamphlets.

Like the Sunday School Publishing Board of the National Baptist Convention, USA, Inc., Muhammad's Temple No. 2 Publications Department, which was founded in 1956 by the Nation of Islam, published religious as well as secular books. Between 1956 and 1974, several books were issued by this firm. However, since 1974, Muhammad's Temple No. 2 Publications Department has become inactive.

Institutional Publishers

During the last decades of the nineteenth century and the early decades of the twentieth century, educational, cultural, social, and political institutions were established to meet the specific needs of black Americans. Many of these institutions developed publishing programs, which included book publishing.

Colleges and Universities

Hampton Institute became the first black educational institution to publish books when the Hampton Institute Press was established in 1871. An active publisher until 1940, the Hampton Institute Press published travel books, poetry, textbooks, songbooks, conference proceedings, and the *Southern Workman,* one of the leading national African-American periodicals published between 1871 and its demise in 1939.

In 1896 the Atlanta University Press entered the book publishing market with the release of the *Atlanta University Publication Series,* which were monographs reporting on the findings of studies conducted by the university's department of sociology under the direction of W.E.B. DuBois. These works represented some of the earliest studies in urban sociology conducted in the South. The Atlanta University Press remained in operation until 1936.

Industrial Work of Tuskegee Graduates and Former Students During the Year 1910, compiled by Monroe N. Work in 1911, was the first book released by the Tuskegee Institute Press. With the publication of this book and other works by the press, Booker T. Washington sought to publicize the success of Tuskegee's program to white philanthropists in the North. The

Tuskegee Institute Press, which was active until 1958, published several other important works, including John Kenny's *The Negroes in Medicine* (1912) and *Lynching by States, 1882–1958* (1958), by Jessie Parkhurst Guzman.

In 1910 another book publishing enterprise was launched on the campus of Tuskegee Institute—the Negro Yearbook Publishing Company. A partnership consisting of Robert E. Park, the famed white sociologist, Emmett J. Scott, secretary to Booker T. Washington, and Monroe N. Work, a sociology professor, this firm published the first edition of *The Negro Yearbook* in 1912. The most comprehensive reference book to appear to date on African Americans, *The Negro Yearbook* was highly regarded as the definitive work on statistics and facts on blacks worldwide. However, the Negro Yearbook Publishing Company fell into financial trouble in 1929 and was taken over by Tuskegee Institute, which financed its operation until 1952. Between 1912 and 1952, *The Negro Yearbook* remained a classic model for most general reference works on blacks.

John W. Work's *The Negro and His Song* (1915) was the first book issued under the Fisk University Press imprint. During the 1930s and 1940s, when Charles Spurgeon Johnson chaired the university's department of sociology, several important studies were published by Fisk University Press, including E. Franklin Frazier's *The Free Negro Family* (1932); *The Economic Status of the Negro,* by Charles Spurgeon Johnson (1933); and *People versus Property,* by Herman Long and Charles Spurgeon Johnson (1947). The last publication released by the Fisk University Press was *Build a Future: Addresses Marking the Inauguration of Charles Spurgeon Johnson* (1949).

Although the board of trustees of Howard University approved the establishment of a university press on February 17, 1919, no university press was organized at the university until 1974. Nonetheless, between 1919 and 1974, several books bearing the Howard University Press imprint were published, including *The Founding of the School of Medicine of Howard University, 1868–1873,* by Walter Dyson (1929), and *The Housing of Negroes in Washington, DC: A Study in Human Ecology,* by William H. Jones (1929). On April 8, 1974, the Howard University Press was officially organized as a separate administrative unit within the university with a staff of twelve professionals experienced in book publishing. The Howard University Press's inaugural list of thirteen books included such titles as *A Poetic Equation: Conversations Between Nikki Giovanni and Margaret Walker*

The Negro Yearbook, first published in 1912 by Tuskegee Institute's Negro Yearbook Publishing Company, was at the time the most comprehensive reference book on blacks worldwide. Published for four decades, it was considered the classic model for such works.

(1974) and *Saw the House in Half: A Novel,* by Oliver Jackman (1974). The Howard University Press continues to flourish as one of the most viable university presses in the country.

Cultural and Professional Organizations and Institutions

Black cultural and professional organizations and institutions have also developed publishing programs that include book publishing. The books published by these organizations have documented areas of black history and depicted various aspects of African-American culture.

The Bronze Booklets, edited by Alain Locke during the 1930s for the Associates of Negro Folk Education, included such titles as A World View of Race, *by Ralph J. Bunche (1936);* The Negro and Economic Reconstruction, *by T. Arnold Hill (1937); and* Negro Poetry and Drama, *by Sterling Brown (1937).*

Founded in 1897 by the Reverend Alexander Crummell, nineteenth-century black scholar, clergyman, and missionary, the American Negro Academy quickly organized a publishing program that embraced book publishing. The Academy, whose membership included many of the foremost black intellectuals of the day, released twenty-one occasional papers as pamphlets and monographs. The American Negro Academy went out of existence in 1928.

The Association for the Study of Negro Life and History (now the Association for the Study of Afro-American History and Literature) began its book publishing program in 1918. By 1940, the association had published twenty-eight books. After that year, the book publishing activities of the association declined until 1950, when its founder, Carter G. Woodson, died and provided in his will for the transfer of the Associated Publishers, Inc. to the association.

The Associates of Negro Folk Education was organized in Washington, DC, by Howard University philosophy professor Alain Locke under a grant from the American Adult Education Association. From 1935 to 1940 the organization published a series of seven books written by black scholars on various aspects of black American life, known as the Bronze Booklets.

Civil Rights, Social Welfare, and Political Organizations

In 1913, five years after its founding, the National Association for the Advancement of Colored People launched its book publishing program with the publication of three books: *A Child's Story of Dunbar,* by Julia L. Henderson (1919); *Norris Wright Cuney,* by Maude Cuney Hare (1913); and *Hazel,* by Mary White Ovington (1913). In 1914 George Williamson Crawford's *Prince Hall and His Followers* appeared, and in 1919 *Thirty Years of Lynching in the United States, 1889–1918* was released. After 1919 few books were published by the NAACP, with the organization limiting its publishing to *Crisis* magazine, pamphlets, and its annual reports.

In contrast, the National Urban League has been an active book publisher. The League first embarked on book publishing in 1927 when it published *Ebony and Topaz,* an anthology of Harlem Renaissance writers, poets, and artists, which was edited by Charles Spurgeon Johnson. Through the years numerous sociological and economic studies on the plight of black Americans have been published by the Urban League, including *Negro Membership in Labor Unions* (1930), *Race, Fear and Housing in a Typical American Community* (1946), and *Power of the Ballot: A Handbook for Black Political Participation* (1973). In addition to these monograph studies, the organization began publishing *The State of Black America* in 1976.

Although the publishing program of the Universal Negro Improvement Association and African Communities League focused on the publication of its newspaper, the *Negro World,* this political organization also published books. Two volumes of *The Philosophy and Opinions of Marcus Garvey,* compiled and edited by Amy Jacques-Garvey, were published under the imprint of the Press of the Universal Negro Improvement Association.

Commercial Publishers

Until the 1960s, most black commercial publishers that engaged in book publishing enterprises were short-lived. In 1967, however, Haki Madhubuti founded Third World Press in Chicago. Third World Press is now the oldest continually operating black commercial book publisher in the United States.

Over the years, black publishers have come to find that a sizable black readership exists; since 1970 several major black publishers have emerged. In 1978 Black Classic Press was founded by librarian Paul Coates to publish obscure but significant works by and about people of African descent. In 1978 Dempsey Travis founded Urban Research Press. Open Hand Publishing, Inc. was founded in 1981 by Anna Johnson.

In 1983 Kassahun Checole founded Africa World Press to publish material on the economic, political, and social development of Africa. Checole, a former African studies instructor at Rutgers University, found it difficult to attain books needed for his courses. Now Africa World Press publishes nearly sixty titles a year, and its sister company, Red Sea Press, is now one of the largest distributors of material by and about Africans.

In 1967 Haki Madhubuti founded Third World Press, now the oldest continually operating black commercial book publisher in the United States.

Just Us Books, Inc., founded by writer Wade Hudson and graphic artists Cheryl Willis Hudson, publishes books and educational materials for children that focus on the African-American experience. The idea to start the children's book publisher first came to Cheryl in 1976, when she was unable to find black images to decorate her daughter's nursery. Just Us Books published its first book in 1988—an alphabet book featuring African-American children posed to create the letters. The company currently has sales of over $800,000.

◆ ◆ ◆ ◆ ◆ ◆ ◆ ◆ ◆ ◆ NEWSPAPER AND MAGAZINE PUBLISHERS

The black press in the United States is heir to a great, largely unheralded tradition. It began with the first black newspaper, *Freedom's Journal,* edited and published by Samuel Cornish and John B. Russwurm, on March 16, 1827. *The North Star,* the newspaper of abolitionist Frederick Douglass, was first published on December 3, 1847.

Newspapers

By the 1880s, African Americans' ability to establish a substantial cultural environment in many cities of the North led to the creation of a new wave of publications, including the *Washington Bee,* the *Indianapolis World,* the *Philadelphia Tribune,* the *Cleveland Gazette,* the *Baltimore Afro-American,* and the *New York Age.* By 1900, daily papers appeared in Norfolk, Kansas City, and Washington, DC.

Among the famous black newspaper editors were William Monroe Trotter, editor of the *Boston Guardian,* a self-styled "radical" paper that showed no sympathy for the conciliatory stance of Booker T. Washington; Robert S. Abbott, whose *Chicago Defender* pioneered the use of headlines; and T. Thomas Fortune of the *New York Age,* who championed free public schools in an age when many opposed the idea.

In 1940 there were over two hundred black newspapers, mostly weeklies with local readerships, and about 120 black magazines in the country.

Headquarters for the Baltimore Afro-American, *founded in 1892.*

The *Pittsburgh Courier,* a weekly, had the largest circulation, about 140,000 per issue.

The National Negro Newspaper Publishers Association

The National Negro Newspaper Publishers Association was founded in 1940 to represent black newspaper publishers. The organization scheduled workshops and trips abroad to acquaint editors and reporters with important news centers and news sources. One result was a trend to more progressive and interpretive reporting. In 1956 the association changed its name to the National Newspaper Publishers Association. Today it represents 148 publishers.

The Amsterdam News

Founded in 1909 by James H. Anderson, the *Amsterdam News* has become one of the best-known black newspapers in the nation. It was first published on December 4, 1909 in Anderson's home on 132 W. 65th Street in New York City. At that time one of only fifty black "news sheets" in the country, the *Amsterdam News* had a staff of ten, consisted of six printed pages, and sold for two cents a copy. Since then, the paper has been printed at several Harlem addresses.

In 1935 the paper was sold to two black physicians, Clilan B. Powell and P.M.H. Savory. In 1971 the paper was again sold to a group of investors, headed by Clarence B. Jones and Percy E. Sutton.

Black Newspapers in the 1990s

A number of newspapers that began publishing in the 1960s, 1970s, and 1980s have gone out of business, mainly due to their inability to attract local or national advertising and because of general economic decline. Today there are a reported 214 black newspapers in the United States. Of these, the papers with the largest paid circulations include New York's *Black American,* the *Hartford Inquirer,* and the *Atlanta Voice.*

Magazines

As early as the 1830s, black magazines were being published in the United States. However, it was not until the 1900s that the first truly successful magazines appeared. In 1910 the National Association for the Advancement of Colored People began publishing *Crisis.* In November 1942 John H. Johnson launched the *Negro Digest,* and in 1945 he published the first issue of *Ebony.* The idea for the new magazine came from two *Digest* writers, and the magazine's name was designated by Johnson's wife, Enice

John Johnson with daughter,
Linda Johnson.

Johnson. Its first print run of 25,000 copies sold out immediately. The success of *Ebony* led to the demise of the *Negro Digest,* and in 1951 the magazine ceased publication. However, *Ebony,* which has remained a success, has a circulation rate of almost two million.

In 1950 Johnson launched the magazine *Tan,* and in 1951 *Jet* magazine. Like *Ebony, Jet* was an instant success, selling over 300,000 copies in its first year. *Tan,* a woman's magazine, was later converted into a show business and personality monthly called *Black Stars.*

Since the founding of *Ebony,* several new and specialized black magazines have appeared. In 1967 *Black American Literature Review,* a journal presenting essays, interviews, poems, and book reviews, was founded. Also in 1967 Project Magazines, Inc. began publishing *Black Careers.* In 1969 the Black World Foundation published the first edition of the *Black Scholar.*

In 1993 a reported sixty-one black magazines were being published in the United States. Ebony was by far the best seller with circulation rates of more than one million; Jet trailed with 968,545, and Essence followed with 850,116.

In 1970 Earl G. Graves founded Black Enterprise, which promoted an active, socially responsive black middle class and quickly became known as the authority on African Americans in business.

Earl G. Graves, a young businessman, in 1970 embarked on a concept to publish a monthly digest of news, commentary, and informative articles for blacks interested in business enterprise. Within a few short years his magazine, *Black Enterprise,* was accepted as the authority on African Americans in business and as an important advocate for an active, socially responsive black middle class. Today *Black Enterprise* has a subscription rate of over 251,000. A second magazine directed at black women founded in 1970, *Essence,* has steadily gained in its circulation since its inception. Featuring health and beauty, fashion, and contemporary living sections, *Essence* is considered one of the top women's magazines. Since 1981 Susan Taylor has been the magazine's editor in chief.

In 1980 *Black Family,* a magazine promoting positive life-styles for African Americans, was founded. In 1986 *American Visions: The Magazine of Afro-American Culture,* the official magazine of the African American Museums Association, was first published.

♦ **BROADCASTING**

There were black journalists before there was a broadcast industry, but in the Jim Crow America of the 1920s, there had to be black-oriented radio before there could be black broadcast journalists. That mission fell to a vaudevillian jack-of-all-trades from Cincinnati, Jack L. Cooper (1888–1970).

While early radio shows featured black singing groups, they featured no blacks talking. To Cooper, this "was like taxation without representation," and so on Sunday, November 3, 1929, at 5 P.M., Chicago's white-owned WSBC premiered "The All-Negro Hour," starring Cooper and friends. Born was the concept of black radio, and Cooper went on to become the nation's first black radio station executive, the first black newscaster, the first black sportscaster, and the first to use radio as a service medium.

Radio

"The All-Negro Hour" was like a vaudeville revue on the air, featuring music, comedy, and serials. Although it ended its run in 1935, Cooper continued with WSBC, pioneering the black-radio format by producing several black-oriented shows. Crucial to that format was local news and public affairs of interest to African Americans.

The first example of public service programming aired December 9, 1938, when Cooper launched the "Search for Missing Persons" show. Aimed at reuniting people who had lost contact with friends and relatives through migration and over time, it reportedly had reunited 20,000 people by 1950. According to *Ebony* magazine, Cooper also remodeled a van into a mobile unit to relay "on-the-spot news events directly to four radio stations in the Chicago and suburban area," including news flashes from the *Pittsburgh Courier* and interviews of famous personalities who came to town, such as boxer Joe Louis. Cooper also did play-by-play sportscasts of black baseball games from the van.

In addition to radio broadcasting, Jack Cooper played second base for a semi-pro baseball team, fought 160 amateur boxing bouts, managed theaters, and performed as a singer, a buck-and-wing dancer, and an end man in a minstrel show. He had also worked as a journalist for a number of black newspapers, including the Chicago Defender, *where he was assistant theatrical editor.*

"Listen Chicago," a news discussion show that ran from 1946 to 1952, provided African Americans with their first opportunity to use radio as a public forum. Following Cooper's lead, between 1946 and 1955 the number of black-oriented stations jumped from twenty-four to six hundred. News was a part of the explosion. "We have learned to do newscasts that answer the question, 'How is this news going to affect me as a Negro?',", Leonard Walk of WHOD Pittsburgh said in 1954. "We have learned that church and social news deserves a unique place of importance in our daily Negro programming." Yet by and large these broadcasters were not trained journalists. Black stations did not begin to broadcast news as we know it today until the 1960s.

In 1972 the Mutual Black Network was formed for news and sports syndication, under the auspices of the Mutual Broadcasting Network. By the end of the 1970s, the Mutual Black Network had just over one hundred affiliates and 6.2 million listeners. The Sheridan Broadcasting Corporation, a black-owned broadcasting chain based in Pittsburgh, purchased the Mutual Black Network in the late 1970s, renaming it the Sheridan Broadcasting Network. A second African-American radio network, the National Black Network, was formed in 1973. Among its regular features was commentary by journalist Roy Wood, which he named "One Black Man's Opinion." In January 1992 the American Urban Radio Network was formed, and the National Black Network has since gone out of business.

The networks were a mixed blessing. They provided their affiliates with broadcast-quality programs produced from an African-American perspective. But this relatively inexpensive access to news, sports, and public affairs features discouraged the local stations that subscribed from producing their own shows. News and public affairs staffs at the black-oriented stations remained minimal. There were some notable exceptions. New York's WLIB-AM had a black format that included a highly acclaimed news and public affairs department. A series of shows produced by the station on disadvantaged youth in the city won two Peabody Awards in 1970. After the station was purchased in 1972 by African-American civic leader Percy Sutton, the station became "Your Total Black News and Information Station," offering more news and public affairs programming than any other black-formatted radio outlet in the country.

In Washington, DC, *The Washington Post* donated its commercial FM radio license to Howard University in 1971. The new station, WHUR-FM, inaugurated "The Daily Drum," a full hour-long evening newscast that featured special coverage of the local black community, as well as news from Africa and the diaspora.

Television   Until the late 1960s, most serious black journalists were in print journalism—chiefly the black press—not in broadcasting. An exception was Li-

In 1962 Mal Goode became the first African-American network TV reporter, at ABC-TV.

onel Monagas, who died at age seventy on April 5, 1992, and who worked in the early 1950s as a director of CBS-TV network programs such as "Person to Person" and "Face the Nation." He had started out as a traffic typist with the CBS affiliate in Washington, DC.

In 1956 Monagas became the first black professional at public station Channel 35 in Philadelphia, later known as WHYY-TV. He produced several children's programs there, including a ten-part series on "The History of the Negro," narrated by Ossie Davis.

Mal Goode became the first African-American network TV reporter in 1962, at ABC-TV. Baseball great Jackie Robinson had complained to James Hagerty, the former press secretary to President Dwight Eisenhower, who was hired as an ABC vice president to set up a competitive news department. Robinson told Hagerty that the only two Negroes he had seen at ABC were "a lady with a white uniform in the lobby dusting and a Negro doorman. [Hagerty's] face got red, and he said we intend to do something about that," Goode said. Goode was a reporter at *The Pittsburgh Courier* at the time, but in 1949 Pittsburgh's KQV-Radio had given the newspaper two fifteen-minute slots to fill on Tuesday and Wednesday nights. Goode read the news on the program. According to Goode, ABC chose him for the job after spending half a year interviewing thirty-eight black male candidates. One reason he was chosen, he said, was because he was considered dark enough so blacks would know he was black, but light enough so that whites wouldn't feel threatened. Goode went on to work for ABC for eleven years. He was its United Nations correspondent, and he covered the Cuban missile crisis, the aftermath of Martin Luther King, Jr.'s assassination, and the Poor People's March on Washington.

In his memoir Black Is the Color of My TV Tube, *Emmy-winner Gil Noble recalls auditioning for jobs at major radio stations. He would intone in the ultimate radio voice—"a [Walter] Cronkite delivery that outdid the original"—only to get the familiar brush-off: "Thanks very much. You're fine, but we already have a Negro on staff."*

Jobs like Goode's were hard to come by. In his memoir *Black Is the Color of My TV Tube*, Emmy-winner Gil Noble of New York's WABC-TV describes his time at WLIB-AM radio during this era. "We would sit in the newsroom and fantasize about earning $300 a week, but few of our number worked at that level. Pat Connell, a former disc jockey at Newark's WNJR, known as 'Pat the Cat,' was anchoring the CBS morning newscast. Mal Goode was reporting for ABC-TV news, as well as for the local station WABC. NBC didn't have any blacks at that time, as far as I can recall, and in the mid-'60s, WNEW-TV had none, nor did WPIX-TV or WOR-TV have any."

A few blacks, however, were allowed on the white-controlled airwaves. William C. Matney, Jr., who had been managing editor of the *Michigan Chronicle,* a black community paper, and a reporter for the *Detroit News,* in 1963 became a TV and radio reporter for WMAQ-TV, the NBC-owned station in Chicago. He joined NBC-TV news in 1966. Veteran Norma Quarles, now at CNN, was hired as a trainee at NBC News in 1966, moving a year later to the NBC station in Cleveland as a reporter and anchor. Lem Tucker, who died in March 1991, joined NBC News as a copy boy in 1965 and moved up to assistant bureau chief in Vietnam.

In 1967, a self-described "teacher moonlighting as a jazz disc jockey" who also called play-by-play for basketball games and read the news, applied

Ed Bradley, co-host of CBS-TV's most successful news show, "60 Minutes," on location in Cambodia.

for a job at soon-to-be all-news WCBS radio in New York. Ed Bradley, who would later co-host CBS-TV's most successful news show, "60 Minutes," impressed a news director by refusing to write some copy and record it because, he explained, "You won't learn enough about me that way." Instead, he borrowed a tape recorder, went out on the street, did an update of a story about an anti-poverty program, and got the job. But in Portsmouth, Virginia, an audacious twenty-five–year–old newscaster named Max Robinson was fired from a UHF station after he broke the rules by showing his face on camera. It was 1964, and only the word

"News" was to appear on the screen. White viewers were enraged to see that one of "those" people was allowed to work in the studio. According to his news director, James Snyder, in 1971 Robinson became the first black anchor in a major market, at WTOP-TV in Washington, DC. Seven years later, at ABC-TV, Robinson became the network's first black regular co-anchor.

It took the riots of the 1960s and a stern warning from a federal commission for the broadcast industry to undertake any concentrated hiring of African Americans. When American cities began to burn, blacks held about 3.6 percent of TV news jobs. White news directors had to scramble to find black journalists to cover the story. In 1968, the National Advisory Commission on Civil Disorders, known as the Kerner Commission, concluded that "the world that television and newspapers offer to their black audience is almost totally white, in both appearance and attitude." "Within a year," wrote Noble, "many of us found ourselves working downtown at major radio and TV stations."

In June 1969 the Federal Communications Commission adopted rules prohibiting discrimination in broadcast industry employment and required stations to file annual reports showing the racial makeup of their workforce by job category. Black public-affairs shows were aired, such as Noble's "Like It Is," public broadcasting's "Black Journal" hosted by Tony Brown, and Philadelphia's "Black Perspectives on the News," in nearly every city with a substantial black population. Still, by the time Mal Goode retired in 1973, there were only seven black reporters at the three networks.

By the 1990s, African Americans were breaking into broadcast management and ownership, although the numbers were still small. TV general managers included Charlotte Moore English of KSHB-TV Kansas City; Marcellus Alexander of WJZ-TV in Baltimore; Eugene Lothery of WCAU-TV in Philadelphia; Clarence McKee, CEO and chairman of WTVT-TV in Tampa, Florida; and Dorothy Brunson, owner of a small UHF station, WGTW-TV, in Philadelphia.

Ronald Townsend, president of the Gannett Television Group, comprising ten stations, chaired the National Association of Broadcasters' TV board. Jonathan Rodgers became president of the CBS Television Stations Division in August 1990, making him network television's highest-rank-

NBC "Today Show" host Bryant Gumbel interviews former President Richard Nixon, 1990.

ing African-American news executive. Bryant Gumbel, co-host of the NBC-TV "Today" show, CBS News correspondent Ed Bradley, and talk-show host Oprah Winfrey became three of the most highly paid and recognized faces on television, and Bradley among the most respected. ABC-TV's Carole Simpson became a substitute and weekend network TV anchor. African Americans were anchoring local newscasts in markets around the country.

Still, African Americans, while 12 percent of the population in the 1990 census, represented only 9.8 percent of the television news workforce and 5 percent of the radio workforce. They were 4 percent of the news directors at commercial TV stations and about 5 percent at commercial radio stations. Those heading news operations included Gary Wordlaw at WJLA-TV Washington, DC, and Will Wright at WWOR-TV New York. And, according to an annual survey by the Center for Media and Public Affairs, most of the news on nightly network television shows continued to be presented by white males. Blacks accounted for only 5 percent of all field reports and anchor stories combined, its 1991 survey found. The most visible African American correspondent was George Strait, ABC-TV health reporter, who tied for fifty-seventh in the number of stories filed. Simpson was in sixth place, based on the number of brief news reports read.

Public Television

For most of its short history, public television, begun in the early 1950s, failed to realize the hopes of many African Americans. Tony Brown's "Black Journal," later "Tony Brown's Journal," was well received by black viewers as the only national black public affairs series on television. It was constantly threatened with cancellation, however, after conservatives complained about its anti-administration attitude. The show was rescued after it secured underwriting from Pepsi Cola.

PBS's most acclaimed piece of African-American journalism was "Eyes on the Prize," a history of the civil-rights movement produced by Henry Hampton, which aired in 1987 with a sequel in 1990. Its most controversial was a one-hour film on black homosexual men, "Tongues Untied," by filmmaker Marlon Riggs in 1991.

In 1975, the only black FCC commissioner, Benjamin Hooks, joined the critics, accusing public broadcasters of "arrogance" and of concentrating their efforts on the cultured, white cosmopolitans. A United States House of Representatives subcommittee held hearings on the matter. A 1975 review of public broadcasting stations' top three job categories (officials, managers, and professionals) showed that 59 percent (or 108) of the 184 public radio licensees and 33 percent (52) of the 160 public television licensees had no minority staff at these levels.

In the early 1990s, the highest-ranking African Americans in public television were Jennifer Lawson, who joined PBS in November 1989 as its first executive vice president for national programming and promotion services; Donald L. Marbury, director of the Television Program Fund of the Corporation for Public Broadcasting; and George L. Miles, Jr., executive vice president and chief operating officer of WNET-TV New York. Lawson was responsible for obtaining and commissioning the programs that PBS provides to its member stations, as well as the promotion of those programs. Marbury was charged with managing the $45 million television program fund, which provides funding support for major series in public television, such as "Frontline."

The most visible African-American journalist on public television has been "MacNeil-Lehrer News Hour" correspondent Charlayne Hunter-Gault, a former *New York Times* reporter noted for her in-depth reporting. Other black journalists with the show include Kwame Holman, Washington correspondent, and producer Jackie Farmer.

Tony Brown hosts the only national black public affairs series on television, "Tony Brown's Journal."

In 1980, Howard University launched WHMM-TV, becoming the first licensee of a public TV station on a black campus and the only black-owned public television station in the nation. On August 31, 1991, San Francisco's Minority Television Project went on the air with KMTP-TV, which became the nation's second black-owned public television station. One of the principals was Adam Clayton Powell III, son of the late Harlem congressman.

Public Radio

Before 1967, only two black educational outlets existed in the country; by 1990 there were forty black public radio stations. Many of them were community radio stations, owned and operated by nonprofit foundations, controlled by a local board of directors, and relying on listener donations. Others were on college campuses. One of the most successful was WPFW-FM, a 50,000-watt outlet controlled by African Americans, launched in 1977 by the Pacifica Foundation.

Stations such as WCLK-FM at Clark College in Atlanta, WBVA-FM in Harrodsburg, Kentucky, and WVAS-FM at Alabama State University in Montgomery, tailored news and public affairs programming to their local, African-American audiences. WVAS was used as a broadcast journalism lab by students majoring in the field. On National Public Radio, African-American journalists Phyllis Crockett, Vertamae Grosvenor, Cheryl Duvall, and Brenda Wilson have won awards for reports on South Africa and issues involving African Americans.

Cable Television

The 1980s saw the explosion of cable television and the decline of the television networks. Black Entertainment Television, founded by former congressional aide Robert L. Johnson, made its debut in 1980 and established a news division by the end of the decade. That division produced a weekly news show, "BET News" and "Lead Story," a talk show featuring black pundits.

The biggest development in cable journalism, however, was the spectacular growth of Ted Turner's Cable News Network, which went on line in June 1980. By the 1991 Persian Gulf War, CNN had established itself as the station to watch in a crisis. Transmitted across the globe, it became a medium for world leaders to communicate among one another.

Veteran journalist Bernard Shaw, principal Washington anchor, was one of three CNN reporters who captivated the world's audiences with their continuous coverage of the first night of bombing on Baghdad during Operation Desert Storm on January 16, 1991. Other African Americans at CNN include Jay Suber, vice president and executive producer of news features, CNN Newsroom; Graylian Young, Southeast bureau chief; CNN anchors Andrea Arceneaux, Leon Harris and Joe Oliver; Cassandra Henderson, anchor for the CNN Newsroom, Lyn Vaughn and Gordon Graham, Headline News anchors; sports anchor Fred Hickman; and correspondent Norma Quarles.

Robert Johnson founded the successful Black Entertainment Television (BET) cable network in 1980.

♦ ♦ ♦ ♦ ♦ ♦ EDITORS, JOURNALISTS, AND MEDIA EXECUTIVES

A native of St. Simon Island, Georgia, Abbott studied at Beach Institute in Savannah, and later completed his undergraduate work at Claflin College in Orangeburg, South Carolina. Migrating to Chicago, he attended Kent Law School and took a job in a printing house until he completed his law studies in 1899.

Robert S. Abbott (1870–1940)

Chicago Defender Founder

Abbott returned to Chicago and published the first edition of the Defender on May 5, 1905, which he initially sold on a door-to-door basis. Abbott died in 1940, whereupon the Defender was handed over to his nephew, John H. Sengstacke, who introduced a daily edition of the paper in 1956.

Ida B. Wells

Barnett

(1864–1931)

Editor, Anti-lynching Crusader

Ida B. Wells was born in Mississippi and educated at Rusk University. She served as editor of the black newspaper the Memphis Free Speech, and in 1892 became part owner. Through the paper she engaged in a vigorous campaign against the practice of lynching. On May 27, 1882, the paper's offices were destroyed by a mob.

In 1895 she married Chicago Conservator editor Ferdinand Lee Barnett. That same year Barnett published her first pamphlet against lynching, *A Red Record*. Over the years Barnett wrote numerous other pamphlets and articles and conducted speaking tours throughout the United States and Europe.

Ed Bradley

(1941–)

Television News Correspondent

A native of Philadelphia, Pennsylvania, Edward R. Bradley received a B.S. in education from Cheyney State College in Cheyney, Pennsylvania. From 1963 to 1967 Bradley worked as a disc jockey and news reporter for WDAS radio in Philadelphia. From there he moved on to WCBS radio in New York. He joined CBS as a stringer in the Paris bureau in 1971. Within a few months he was transferred to the Saigon bureau, where he remained until he was assigned to the Washington bureau in June 1974.

Until 1981 Bradley served as anchor for the "CBS Sunday Night News" and as principal correspondent for "CBS Reports." In 1981 he replaced Dan Rather as a correspondent for the weekly news program "60 Minutes." In 1992 Bradley was made host of the CBS news program "Street Stories."

Bradley has won seven Emmy Awards for broadcast journalism, two Alfred I. duPont–Columbia University Awards for broadcast journalism, a George Foster Peabody Broadcasting Award, a George Polk Award, and an NCAA Anniversary Award.

William Anthony Brown, born in Charleston, West Virginia, is probably best known as the producer and host of the longest-running minority affairs program in history, "Tony Brown's Journal."

He received his bachelor of arts degree in 1959 and his master's degree in social work in 1961 from Wayne State University in Detroit. Brown took a job with the *Detroit Courier* as drama critic. It was during this time that he began to be active in the civil-rights movement, helping to organize the 1963 "March to Freedom" with Martin Luther King, Jr. in Detroit. After leaving the paper, where he had worked up to the position of city editor, Brown landed a job with the local PBS station, WTVS, where he became involved in television programming and production. At WTVS he produced the station's first series aimed at a black audience, "C.P.T." (Colored People's Time). He joined the New York staff of the PBS program "Black Journal" in 1970 as the show's executive producer and host—in 1977 the show's name was changed to "Tony Brown's Journal" and can still be seen on PBS.

In 1971 Brown founded and became the first dean of Howard University's School of Communications. He continued in that post until 1974.

Brown has been an advocate of community and self-help programs. In 1980 he organized a "Black College Day," designed to emphasize the importance of historically black colleges and universities. In 1985 Brown organized the Council for the Economic Development of Black Americans and launched the "Buy Freedom" campaign (now known as the "Buy Freedom Network"), which encourages black consumers nationwide to patronize black-owned businesses.

Brown has written, produced, and directed a film, *The White Girl,* has appeared as a commentator for National Public Radio, and writes a syndicated newspaper column. He is a member of the National Association of Black Television and Film Producers, the National Association of Black Media Producers, the National Communications Council, and the National Black United Fund. Brown is the recipient of a Black Emmy Award and the NAACP Image Award. He is currently president of Tony Brown Productions in New York City.

Tony Brown

(1933–)

Commentator,
Columnist, Producer

Edward J. Castleberry

(1928–)

Broadcast Journalist

Born July 28, 1928 in Birmingham, Alabama, Castleberry spent two years at Miles College in that city. His career has been in radio broadcasting at many stations in the United States. He started as a disc jockey at WEDR and WJLD in Birmingham, Alabama (1950–1955), and has worked in the various capacities of disc jockey, program director, and newsman at WMBM in Miami, Florida (1955–1958), WCIN in Cincinnati, Ohio (1958–1961), WABQ in Cleveland, Ohio (1961–1964), WVKD in Columbus, Ohio (1964–1967), WHAT in Philadelphia, Pennsylvania (1967–1968), and WEBB in Baltimore, Maryland. He then became an anchor and entertainment editor at the Mutual and National black networks.

Castleberry has been twice named Newsman of the Year in 1980 and received the Outstanding Citizen award from the Alabama House of Representatives in 1983. In 1985 he was honored by the Smithsonian Institution in Washington, DC. Castleberry was awarded the World War II Victory Medal for his service in the United States Navy from 1945 to 1947.

Spencer Christian

(1947–)

Television Weatherperson

Born in Richmond, Virginia, Spencer Christian received his B.A. in English from Hampton University. Upon graduation he worked as a teacher in New York.

In 1971 Christian went to work for WWBT-TV in Richmond as a news reporter; from 1972 to 1975 he served as the station's weatherperson. In 1975 he moved to WBAL-TV in Baltimore and to New York's WABC-TV in 1977. Christian joined the "Good Morning America" team on ABC in 1986, where he is currently weatherperson and co-host. He has recently published *Spencer Christian's Weather Book*, with Tom Biracree.

Xerona Clayton

(1930–)

Broadcast Executive

Clayton was born Xerona Brewster on August 30, 1930 in Muskogee, Oklahoma. She received a B.S. from Tennessee State University in 1952. She also attended the Ru-Jac School of Modeling in Chicago.

Clayton was the first African-American woman to have her own television show in the South when she became hostess of the "Xerona Clayton Show" at WAGA-TV in Atlanta. She has also been a newspaper columnist for the *Atlanta Voice*, taught public school in Chicago and Los Angeles, and has dabbled in photography and fashion modeling.

Clayton has also been active in the civil-rights movement. Her first husband, now deceased, was the public relations director for Martin Luther King, Jr. Clayton came to the attention of Atlanta officials, who appointed her as community-relations director of the Model Cities Program. She has also raised funds for sickle cell anemia research and the Martin Luther King, Jr. Birthplace Memorial Restoration Committee.

In 1968 Clayton won the Outstanding Leadership award given by the National Association of Market Developers and a year later the Bronze Woman of the Year in Human Relations award given by Phi Delta Kappa sorority. She is also the recipient of the Georgia Associated Press award for Superior Television Programming (1969–1971).

Clayton is the founder of the Atlanta chapter of Media Women and a member of the National Academy of Television Arts and Sciences. She has co-starred in a major motion picture, *House on Skull Mountain.* Clayton has remarried and is currently the corporate vice president for urban affairs at the Turner Broadcasting System in Atlanta, Georgia.

T. Thomas Fortune (1856–1928)

New York Age Founder

T. Thomas Fortune was one of the most prominent black journalists involved in the flourishing black press of the post–Civil War era.

Born in Florida, the son of a Reconstruction politician, Fortune was particularly productive before his thirtieth year, completing such works as *Black and White: Land, Labor and Politics in the South* and *The Negro in Politics* while in his twenties.

Fortune attended Howard University for two years, leaving to marry Carrie Smiley of Jacksonville, Florida. The couple went to New York in 1878, with Fortune taking a job as a printer for the *New York Sun.* In time, Fortune caught the attention of *Sun* editor Charles A. Dana, who eventually promoted him to the editorial staff of the paper.

Fortune also edited the *Globe,* a black daily, and was later chief editorial writer for the *Negro World.* In 1900 Fortune joined Booker T. Washington in helping to organize the successful National Negro Business League. His later activity with Washington gained him more notoriety than his earlier writing, although the latter is clearly more vital in affording him an important niche in the history of black protest.

In 1883 Fortune founded the *New York Age,* the paper with which he sought to "champion the cause" of his race. In time, the *Age* became the leading black journal of opinion in the United States. One of Fortune's early crusades was against the practice of separate schools for the races in the New York educational system.

Fortune was later responsible for coining the term "Afro-American" as a substitute for Negro in New York newspapers. He also set up the Afro-American Council, an organization that he regarded as the precursor of the Niagara Movement. In 1907 Fortune sold the *Age,* although he remained active in journalism as an editorial writer for several black newspapers.

Mal Goode
(1908–)

Television News Correspondent

Malvin Russell Goode had been with the *Pittsburgh Courier* fourteen years when in 1962 he joined ABC to cover the United Nations. His first test was the Cuban missile crisis that arose just two months later, during which Goode distinguished himself with incisive TV and radio reports during the long hours of UN debate.

Goode was born in White Plains, Virginia; educated in the public schools of Homestead, Pennsylvania; and graduated from the University of Pittsburgh. He was employed for twelve years as a laborer in the steel mills while in high school and college and for five years after graduation. In 1936, he was appointed to a post in Juvenile Court and became boys work director of the Centre Avenue YMCA, where he led the fight to eliminate discrimination in Pittsburgh branches of the YMCA.

Goode served with the Pittsburgh Housing Authority for six years and in 1948 joined the *Pittsburgh Courier.* The following year he started a career in radio with station KQV, doing a fifteen-minute news show two nights each week. In 1950, he started a five-minute daily news program on WHOD.

Goode was named news director at WHOD in 1952. He and his sister, the late Mary Dee, had the only brother–sister team in radio for six years. He was the first black to hold membership in the National Association of Radio and TV News Directors.

For two months in 1963 he joined with three colleagues to conduct courses in journalism for 104 African students in seminars at Lagos, Nigeria; Addis Ababa, Ethiopia; and Dar es Salaam, Tanzania.

In the 1970s, Earl Graves emerged as one of America's leading publishers and exponents of black entrepreneurship. Within a few short years his magazine, *Black Enterprise,* was accepted as the authority on African Americans in business and as an important advocate for an active, socially responsive black middle class.

Born in Brooklyn, Graves graduated from Morgan State College. In 1965 he was hired to a position on the staff of Robert Kennedy, then senator from New York. In 1968 he organized Earl Graves Associates, a firm that serves as a consultant on urban affairs and black economic development, and publishes *Black Enterprise.*

Graves also has interests in radio as president of EGG Dallas Broadcasting, Inc., which operates KNOK-AM and KNOK-FM in Fort Worth, Texas.

**Earl G. Graves
(1935–)**

Publisher and
Media Executive

In January 1981 Bryant Gumbel was named co-anchor (with Jane Pauley) of the "Today" show on NBC. Prior to that time, Gumbel had made regular sports reports on "Today," although his primary responsibilities were with NBC Sports as host of pre-game programming during coverage of the National Football League, Major League Baseball, and other sports broadcasts.

He began his broadcasting career in October 1972 when he was named a weekend sportscaster for KNBC, the NBC station in Los Angeles. Within a year, he became weekday sportscaster and was appointed the station's sports director in 1976. He remained in that post until July 1980.

Before embarking on his career in television, Gumbel was a sports writer. After submitting his first piece to *Black Sports* magazine in 1971, he was given additional free-lance assignments and was soon hired as a staff writer. Within eight months he was elevated to editor in chief.

A native of New Orleans, Gumbel grew up in Chicago. He received a liberal arts degree from Bates College in Lewiston, Maine in 1970.

**Bryant Gumbel
(1948–)**

Television Anchor

Ragan A. Henry

(1934-)

Broadcast and
Newspaper Executive

Ragan A. Henry is president of Broadcast Enterprises National, Inc. and former publisher of the *National Leader,* a black national newspaper launched in May 1982, both headquartered in Philadelphia. Henry is also president of radio stations in several states and is a partner in the Philadelphia law firm of Wolf, Black, Schorr & Solis-Cohen.

Henry was born in Sadiesville, Kentucky on February 2, 1934. He received his A.B. from Harvard College in 1956 and his LL.B. from Harvard Law School in 1961. He also attended Temple University Graduate School in 1963. Prior to joining his current law firm, he had been a partner in the Philadelphia firm of Goodis, Greenfield, Henry & Edelstein from 1964 to 1977.

Henry has been a visiting professor at Syracuse University's S.I. Newhouse School of Communications since 1979 and was a lecturer at LaSalle College from 1971 to 1973. He serves on the boards of directors of numerous firms and associations.

Cheryl Willis

Hudson

(1948-)

Wade Hudson

(1948-)

Publishing Executives

Cheryl Willis Hudson, publisher, and Wade Hudson, president and chief executive officer, founded Just Us Books, Inc. in 1988 to publish children's books and learning material that focus on the African-American experience.

A native of Portsmouth, Virginia, Cheryl Willis Hudson graduated (cum laude) from Oberlin College, and has studied at Northeastern University and Parsons School of Design. Prior to founding Just Us Books, she worked as an art editor and designer for several publishers, including Houghton Mifflin, MacMillan Publishing, and Arete Publishing.

Wade Hudson, a native of Mansfield, Louisiana, attended Southern University and has worked with numerous civil-rights organizations, including CORE, the Southern Christian Leadership Conference, and the Society for Opportunity, Unity and Leadership, which he co-founded. He has worked as a public relations specialist for Essex County and Kean colleges in New Jersey.

Eugene D. Jackson is president of Unity Broadcasting Network in New York City, parent company of the National Black Network, and of four radio stations of which Jackson is also president—WDAS-AM and -FM in Philadelphia and KATZ-AM and WZEN-FM in St. Louis.

Jackson was born in Wauhomis, Oklahoma on September 5, 1943. He received a B.S. from the University of Missouri at Rolla in 1967 and an M.S. from Columbia University in 1971.

Jackson serves on the boards of directors of the National Association of Broadcasters, the Council of Concerned Black Executives, Freedom National Bank, and TransAfrica. He was a member of the Council on Foreign Relations in 1978 and on the board of governors of the International Radio and TV Society from 1974 to 1976.

From 1969 to 1971, Jackson directed major industry programs for the Interracial Council for Business Opportunity in New York City. He was a production and project engineer for the Black Economic Union in New York City from 1968 to 1969 and an industrial engineer for Colgate-Palmolive from 1967 to 1968.

Eugene D. Jackson
(1943–)

Broadcast Executive

One of America's foremost business executives, John H. Johnson sits at the head of the most prosperous and powerful black publishing company in the United States. Beginning with *Negro Digest* in 1942, and following with *Ebony* in 1945, Johnson built a chain of journalistic successes that now also includes *Jet, Ebony Jr.*, and *EM: Ebony Man.*

Johnson was born in Arkansas City, Arkansas, and at age six lost his father, a mill worker, and was raised by his mother and stepfather. His segregated schooling was obtained locally until the family moved to Chicago. Johnson attended DuSable High School in Chicago, excelling academically and in extracurricular activities, writing for the yearbook and school paper.

After Johnson graduated, an insurance executive heard a speech he delivered and was so impressed that he offered Johnson a partial scholarship at the University of Chicago. After two years, however, Johnson quit classes. He entered the Northwestern School of Commerce in 1938, studying for an additional two years before joining the Supreme Liberty Life Insurance

John H. Johnson
(1918–)

Publisher, Media Executive

Company. While running the company's house organ, it occurred to Johnson that a digest of weekly or monthly gathered news items of special interest and importance to the black community might achieve a wide black readership. The idea resulted in the creation of *Negro Digest,* a periodical containing both news reprints and feature articles. Of the latter, perhaps the most beneficial to circulation was Eleanor Roosevelt's contribution, "If I Were a Negro."

Buoyed by success, Johnson decided to approach the market with yet another offering, a pictorial magazine patterned after *Life.* The first issue of *Ebony* sold out its press run of 25,000 copies and soon became a permanent staple in the world of journalism as large companies began to advertise regularly in it.

In addition to serving as president and publisher of Johnson Publishing Company, Inc., Johnson is chairman and chief executive officer of Supreme Life Insurance Company, chairman of WJPC-AM in Chicago, and president of Fashion Fair Cosmetics. He has served on the boards of directors of the Greyhound Corporation, Verex Corporation, Marina Bank, Supreme Life Insurance Company, and Zenith Radio Corporation. Johnson also serves as a trustee for the Art Institute of Chicago and United Negro College Fund; on the advisory council of the Harvard Graduate School of Business; as a director for the Chamber of Commerce of the United States; and on the advertising council of Junior Achievement and Chicago USO. He has received honorary doctoral degrees from numerous colleges and universities, and many honors and awards from civil and professional organizations.

Robert L. Johnson

(1946–)

Cable Television
Executive

Robert Johnson worked for the Washington, DC Urban League, the Corporation for Public Broadcasting, and as a press secretary, before joining the National Cable Television Association in 1976. While serving as vice president of government relations for the association, Johnson came up with the idea of creating a cable channel aimed at black viewers. In 1989 he took out a $15,000 personal loan to start Black Entertainment Television (BET).

In addition to running BET, Johnson functions as the publisher of the magazines *Emerge* and *YSB: Young Sisters and Brothers* and operates a radio network. He serves as a board member of the Cable Television Advertising Bureau and has been awarded the Pioneer award by the Capitol Press

Club (1984) and the Business of the Year award by the Washington, DC Chamber of Commerce.

Born in Philadelphia, Jones graduated from Columbia University and Boston University Law School and then practiced as an attorney, specializing in civil-rights and copyright cases for a New York City law firm. During this period, he was counsel for Martin Luther King, Jr. and the Southern Christian Leadership Conference. In 1968 and again in 1972, he served as a delegate from New York State to the Democratic Convention. Jones was also an observer at Attica prison during the uprising there in 1971.

Clarence B. Jones (1931–)

Publishing Executive

In 1971, Jones, as head of Inner City Broadcasting, led a group of investors in the purchase of the New York *Amsterdam News,* the nation's largest black newspaper. Inner City Broadcasting also owned radio station WLIB and has full ownership of WBLS-FM.

Born Don L. Lee in Little Rock, Arkansas, Madhubuti has studied at Wilson Junior College, Roosevelt University, and the University of Illinois, and received a master of fine arts degree from the University of Iowa. His published works include *Think Black; Black Pride; For Black People (and Negroes Too); Don't Cry, Scream; Enemies: The Clash of Races; Killing Memory: Seeking Ancestors;* and *Black Men: Obsolete, Single, Dangerous?* He has taught and served as writer in residence at numerous universities, including Chicago State University, Cornell, Howard, Morgan State, and the University of Illinois.

Haki R. Madhubuti (1942–)

Publisher, Poet, Writer

Madhubuti was one of the founding members of the Organization of Black American Culture Writers Workshop, and has served as vice chairperson of the African Liberation Day Support Committee and on the executive council of the Congress of African People.

Currently Madhubuti is director of the Institute of Positive Education in Chicago, publisher and editor of Third World Press, president of the African-American Publishers, Booksellers, and Writers Association, and the operator of a chain of bookstores.

Third World Press, founded by Madhubuti in 1967, has published numerous titles by African-American writers, including Frances Cress-Welsing's *The Isis Papers: The Keys to the Colors* and Chancellor Williams's *The Destruction of Black Civilization.*

John Henry Murphy

(1840–1922)

Publisher

John Henry Murphy was born a slave in Baltimore, Maryland. He became superintendent of Bethel African Methodist Episcopal Church and founded the Sunday school newspaper, the *Sunday School Helper.* In 1892 he purchased the *Baltimore Afro-American* for $200. By 1922 the *Afro-American* had reached a circulation of 14,000, becoming the largest black newspaper in the Northeast.

At first, Murphy set the paper's type himself, having acquired this skill during his forties. Throughout, he insisted that his paper maintain political and editorial independence. Murphy died April 5, 1922. The paper grew and is now under the helm of Murphy's great-nephew, John H. Murphy III.

Norma Quarles

(1936–)

Television News
Correspondent

Born in New York City, Norma Quarles is an alumna of Hunter College and City College of New York. She first worked as a buyer for a New York specialty shop before moving to Chicago, where she became a licensed real estate broker.

In 1965 she began her broadcast career in Chicago at WSDM-Radio, working as a news reporter and disk jockey. She later returned to New York, where she joined NBC in 1966 for a one-year training program. After three years with WKYC-TV in Cleveland, she was transferred to WNBC-TV. In 1978 Quarles moved to NBC News as a correspondent based in Chicago. She had been producing and reporting the "Urban Journal" series for WMAQ-TV for a year at that time. Before joining WMAQ, Quarles was an award-winning reporter for WNBC-TV in New York, where she also anchored the early local news broadcasts during the "Today" show. In 1988 Quarles left NBC, after twenty-one years, to join Cable News Network's New York bureau.

Quarles is a member of the National Academy of Television Arts and Sciences and Sigma Delta Chi, and a board member of the Governor's National Academy of Television Arts and Sciences.

Dudley Randall was born in Washington, DC on January 14, 1914 and was living in Detroit by the time he was nine years old. An early harbinger of Randall's poetic talent was the appearance of one of his poems in the *Detroit Free Press* at the early age of thirteen. After serving in the United States Army Signal Corps from 1942 to 1946, Randall worked in the foundry at Ford Motor Company and as a postal carrier and clerk while attending Wayne State University in Detroit. He received his B.A. in 1949 and an M.A. in library science from the University of Michigan in 1951. He has also done graduate work at the University of Ghana.

Randall worked in progressively responsible librarian positions at Lincoln University in Jefferson City, Missouri (1951–1954), Morgan State College in Baltimore, Maryland (1954–1956), and the Wayne County Federated Library System in Michigan (1956–1969). From 1969 to 1975 he was a reference librarian and poet in residence at the University of Detroit. In 1969 he also served as a visiting lecturer at the University of Michigan.

Randall's love of poetry led to his founding of the *Broadside Press,* and in 1980 he founded the Broadside Poets Theater and the Broadside Poetry Workshop.

Randall has been active in many Detroit cultural organizations and institutions, including the Detroit Council for the Arts and the International Afro-American Museum in Detroit. In 1981 Randall received the Creative Artist award in literature from the Michigan Council for the Arts, and in 1986 he was named the first poet laureate of Detroit.

Dudley Randall

(1914–)

Publisher, Poet, Librarian

Born in Okolona, Mississippi, on October 12, 1935, Raspberry received his B.S. in history from Indiana Central College in 1958. While a student there, he worked at the *Indianapolis Recorder* as a reporter, photographer, and editorial writer. In 1960 Raspberry was drafted by the army and served as a Public Information Officer until his discharge in 1962. He began working for the *Washington Post* as a teletypist but soon worked his way up to reporter, assistant city editor, and finally columnist in 1966. He continues writing today as a nationally syndicated columnist.

Raspberry has also appeared as a television panelist and commentator and in 1965 was named Journalist of the Year by the Capital Press Club for his coverage of the Los Angeles Watts riot. He is generally regarded as an independent thinker beholden to no particular orthodoxy. His 1991 book

William J. Raspberry

(1935–)

Commentator, Journalist

Looking Backward at Us, like much of his other writings, deals with the African-American experience and social conditions and race relations in the United States.

Raspberry has taught journalism at Howard University and the University of Maryland School of Journalism. He is also a member of the Poynter Institute for Media Studies board of advisors and the Pulitzer Prize Board.

**Max Robinson
(1939–1988)**

Television News
Correspondent

Born in Richmond, Virginia, Max Robinson attended Oberlin College, Virginia Union University, and Indiana University. He began his career as a newsreader at WTOV-TV in Portsmouth, Virginia. In 1965 he worked as a studio floor director at WTOP-TV (now WUSA) in Washington, DC, before moving on to WRC-TV to work as a news reporter, and to WTOP-TV, where he worked as anchor.

In 1978 Robinson joined ABC's "World News Tonight," becoming the first black network anchor. Almost immediately, Robinson took it upon himself to fight racism at whatever cost necessary. ABC management became frustrated with Robinson and moved him to the post of weekend anchor. In 1983 Robinson left ABC for WMAQ-TV in Chicago, where he remained until 1985.

Robinson died of complications from acquired immune deficiency syndrome (AIDS) on December 20, 1988, in Washington, DC. He was the recipient of three Emmy awards, the Capital Press Club Journalist of the Year Award, the Ohio State Award, and an award from the National Education Association. He taught at Federal City College, in Washington, DC, and the College of William and Mary, in Williamsburg, Virginia.

**Carl Thomas
Rowan (1925–)**

Commentator, Journalist

Carl Rowan was born August 11, 1925, in Ravenscroft, Tennessee. He attended Tennessee A&I (now Tennessee State University) in Nashville and Washburn University in Topeka, Kansas. He received his bachelor of arts degree from Oberlin College in 1947; in 1948 he received a master of arts degree from the University of Minnesota.

In 1948 he was hired as a copywriter, later advancing to staff writer, by the *Minneapolis Tribune,* where he worked until 1961. In 1961 he was hired by the United States Department of State as deputy assistant secretary for public affairs. After three years with the Department of State, Rowan was appointed United States ambassador to Finland by President Lyndon Johnson in 1963, and in 1964 he was appointed director of the United States Information Agency, which operates overseas educational and cultural programs, including the worldwide radio service "Voice of America." In 1965 Rowan resigned from the USIA.

He has authored several books, including *South of Freedom, Wait Till Next Year, Between Us Blacks,* and a memoir entitled *Breaking Barriers.* He is a syndicated columnist whose work appears in numerous newspapers across the country.

Rowan has served as a political commentator for the Post-Newsweek Broadcasting Company, and he has been a frequent panelist on the NBC program "Meet the Press" and the syndicated programs "Agronsky & Co." and "Inside Washington."

Born in Port Antonio, Jamaica, Russwurm graduated from Bowdoin College in Brunswick, Maine, in 1826. From Brunswick, Russwurm moved to New York, where on March 16, 1827 he and Samuel E. Cornish published the first edition of *Freedom's Journal*—the nation's first African-American newspaper.

John B. Russwurm (1799–1851)

Freedom's Journal Co-Founder

In 1829 Russwurm decided to immigrate to Monrovia, Liberia, where he published the *Liberia Herald* from 1830 to 1850. Cornish, who had left the paper in late 1827, resumed his role as editor in 1830, publishing the paper under the name *Rights of All.*

Russwurm went on to serve as superintendent of education in Monrovia, and later as governor of a settlement. Russwurm died June 9, 1851.

A nephew of the great publisher Robert Abbott, John Sengstacke was born in Savannah, Georgia. He received a B.A. from Hampton Institute in 1933. Upon graduation, he went to work with Robert Abbott, attended school to learn printing, and wrote editorials and articles for three Abbott papers. In 1934, he became vice president and general manager of the company.

John Herman Henry Sengstacke (1912–)

Publishing Executive

During World War II, Sengstacke was an advisor to the United States Office of War Information through a period of severe tension between the government and black press. He also presided over the Chicago rationing board.

In 1940, after the death of his uncle, Sengstacke became president of the Robert S. Abbott Publishing Company. In 1905, his uncle had founded the weekly *Defender.* In 1956, Sengstacke founded the *Daily Defender,* one of only three black dailies in the country. In 1940 he founded the Negro Newspaper Publishers Association, now known as the National Newspaper Publishers Association, and served six terms as president. Today he is president of Tri-State Defender, Inc., Florida Courier Publishing Company, New Pittsburgh Courier Publishing Company, and Amalgamated Publishers, Inc.; chairman of the Michigan Chronicle Publishing Company and Sengstacke Enterprises, Inc.; and treasurer of Chicago Defender Charities, Inc.

Sengstacke has served in leadership positions with many professional, educational, and civic organizations, received a number of presidential appointments, and is the recipient of several academic awards. He has been trustee of Bethune-Cookman College, chairman of the board of Provident Hospital and Training School Association, member of the board of directors of the American Society of Newspaper Editors, on the advisory board of the Boy Scouts of America, and a principal in Chicago United.

Bernard Shaw
(1940–)
Television News Anchor

Bernard Shaw has been Washington anchor for the Cable News Network (CNN) since the network went on the air June 1, 1980. Shaw has often reported first-hand on major international news stories. He was present when the Chinese government's tanks rolled into Tiananmen Square in May 1989, crushing the student-led pro-democracy movement. In January of 1991, Shaw, along with two other colleagues from CNN, were stranded in Baghdad when allied bombing attacks launched Operation Desert Storm. From their hotel room, Shaw and the others provided first-hand accounts of the bombing raid on the city.

Shaw's first job as a television journalist came in 1971 with CBS News at the network's Washington bureau. He conducted an exclusive interview with Attorney General John Mitchell at the height of the Watergate scandal. Shaw left CBS in 1977 to join ABC News as Miami bureau chief and Latin American correspondent. Shaw was one of the first reporters to file from location on the Jonestown massacre story in Guyana, and he and his team provided the only aerial photos of the mass suicide–murder site. ABC sent Shaw to Iran to report on the 1979 hostage crisis in at the American Embassy in Teheran. He then returned to Washington as ABC's senior Capitol Hill correspondent.

Prior to joining CBS News, Shaw was a reporter for Group W, Westinghouse Broadcasting Company, based first in Chicago and then in Washington (1966–1971). Shaw served as Group W's White House correspondent in 1968, the last year of the Johnson Administration. His other assignments included local and national urban affairs, the struggles of Mexican Americans and Puerto Ricans, and the plight of the American Indians in Billings, Montana. In 1968, he reported on the aftermath of the assassination of Martin Luther King, Jr., in Memphis, and on his funeral in Atlanta.

Carole Simpson, a native of Chicago, graduated from the University of Michigan with a bachelor of arts degree in journalism and did graduate work in journalism at the University of Iowa. She first entered broadcasting in 1965 as a reporter for a local radio station, WCFL, in Morris, Illinois. In 1968 she moved to radio station WBBM in Chicago, and in 1970 she went to work as a reporter for the Chicago television station WMAQ.

**Carole Simpson
(1940–)**

Television News Anchor

Simpson made her first network appearance as a substitute anchor for NBC "Nightly News" and as anchor on NBC's "Newsbreak" on weekends. In 1982 Simpson joined ABC in Washington as a general assignment correspondent. She is currently an ABC News correspondent and weekend anchor.

Simpson has served as president of the Radio and Television Correspondents Association, as chairperson of the ABC Women's Advisory Board, and as a member of the board of directors of the Washington Chapter of the Society of Professional Journalists, and she is a member of Theta Sigma Phi. She has been awarded the Media Journalism award, the Milestone Award in Broadcast Journalism from the National Commission of Working Women, and the Silver Bell award from the Ad Council.

Barbara Smith has co-authored and co-edited numerous books, including *Yours in Struggle, Three Feminist Perspectives on Anti-Semitism and Racism, Home Girls: A Black Feminist Anthology, But Some of Us Are Brave,* and *Black Women's Studies.* Smith, together with Myrna Bain, Cherrie Moraga, Mariana Romo-Carmona, operate Kitchen Table: Women of Color Press, the

**Barbara Smith
(1946–)**

Publisher, Editor, Writer

first publisher in the United States committed to publishing and distributing the work of third-world women and women of color.

Pierre Montea Sutton (1947-)

Broadcast Executive

Pierre Sutton is president of Inner City Broadcasting Corporation in New York City and president of its radio stations in New York and California. He is the son of Percy E. Sutton, chairman of the board of Inner City Broadcasting and former borough president of Manhattan.

Sutton was born in New York City on February 1, 1947. He received a B.A. from the University of Toledo in 1968 and attended New York University in 1972.

He began his career in 1971 as vice president of Inner City Research and Analysis Corporation, was executive editor of the New York Courier newspaper in 1971 and 1972, served as public affairs director for WLIB-Radio from 1972 to 1975, was vice president of Inner City Broadcasting from 1975 to 1977, and became president in 1977. He has served as a board member of the Minority Investment Fund, first vice president of the National Association of Black Owned Broadcasters, chairman of the Harlem Boy Scouts, member of the board and executive committee of the New York City Marathon, trustee of the Alvin Ailey Dance Foundation, board member of the Better Business Bureau of Harlem, and member of the board of the Hayden Planetarium.

Susan Taylor (1946-)

Editor

Since 1981, Susan Taylor has been editor in chief of *Essence,* a magazine established in 1970 for black women.

A former actress, cosmetologist, and founder of her own cosmetics company, Nequai Cosmetics, Taylor began her relationship with *Essence* magazine as a free-lance writer. In 1971 she became the magazine's beauty editor, and from 1971 to 1980 she served as fashion and beauty editor. Taylor, now as editor in chief, is also executive coordinator of Essence Communications.

Lem Tucker (1938-1991)

Correspondent

A native of Saginaw, Michigan, Lemuel Tucker was a graduate of Central Michigan University. Tucker worked as a Washington bureau correspondent for CBS news from 1977 until 1988. Prior to that he was with ABC News as New York City correspondent. From 1965 through 1972, Tucker was with NBC News, where he served for some of that time as assistant bureau chief in Vietnam. He was awarded an Emmy for his reporting on hunger in the United States, a series of seven reports broadcast during 1968 and 1969. He died in March of 1991 in Washington, DC.

By Donald Franklin Joyce and Richard Prince

*P*erforming Arts

For more than two hundred years, African-American performers have appeared on the American stage, often in the face of prejudice and bigotry. Showcasing their talents, they have made unique contributions to American performance art. The artistic heritage of today's African-American actors, dancers, and comedians can be traced back to the last decades of the eighteenth century.

THE ORIGINS OF AFRICAN-AMERICAN PERFORMING ARTS ♦ ♦ ♦

The Earliest Plays

The first performances by African-American actors on the American stage were in plays written by white playwrights who portrayed blacks as buffoons or intellectually inept characters. In 1769, for example, Lewis Hallam's comedy *The Padlock* was staged with a West Indian slave character named Mongo, who was a clown to be played by a black. Other white-authored plays from the period that depicted blacks in demoralizing roles were *Robinson Crusoe, Harlequin* (1792), and *The Triumph of Love* (1795) by John Randolph, which included the native black character named Sambo. Thus, the earliest appearances of blacks on the American stage were as characters void of intellectual and moral sensibilities.

The African Grove Theatre

New York City's free African-American community founded the first African-American theater in 1821—the African Grove Theatre, located at Mercer and Bleecker streets "in the rear of the one-mile stone on Broadway." A group of amateur African-American actors organized by Henry Brown presented *Richard III* at the theater on October 1, 1821. The African Grove Theatre subsequently produced *Othello, Hamlet,* and such lighter works as *Tom and Jerry* and *The Poor Soldier, Obi.*

One of the principal actors at the African Grove Theatre was James Hewlet, a West Indian–born black who distinguished himself in roles in *Othello* and *Richard III.* Hewlet later toured England and billed himself as "The New York and London Colored Comedian." Ira Aldridge, who later distinguished himself as one of the great Shakespearean tragic actors, was also a member of the permanent group that performed at the African Grove Theatre. Aldridge was cast in comic and singing roles as well as in Shakespearean tragedies.

It was at the African Grove Theatre that the first play written and produced by an African American was performed on the American stage. The play was Henry Brown's *The Drama of King Shotaway*, which was presented in June of 1823.

Because of disturbances created by whites in the audience, the local police raided the African Grove Theatre on several occasions. The theater evidently was wrecked by police and hoodlums during one of these raids, which forced its closing in late 1823. The theater's black actors, who were determined to preserve their company, continued for several years to present plays at different rented locations throughout New York City.

♦ **MINSTRELSY**

Talented slaves were among the earliest black entertainers in colonial and antebellum America. On plantations throughout the South, slave performers—using clappers, jawbones, and blacksmith rasps—danced, sang, and told jokes for the entertainment of their fellow slaves as well as their masters, who often showcased their talents at local gatherings. Some masters hired out talented slaves to perform in traveling troupes.

During the late 1820s and early 1830s, white entertainers, observing the artistry of black performers, began to imitate blacks in their routines. Blackening their faces with cork, these white entertainers performed jigs, songs, and jokes with topical allusions to blacks in their lyrics. Thus, the art of minstrelsy as theatrical material was born.

White minstrel troupes in blackface became very popular on the American stage in the 1830s. Among some of the more famous white minstrel performers were Thomas Dartmouth Rice, "Daddy Rice," the original "Jim Crow," Edwin Forrest and Dan Emmett, and the Christy Minstrels.

Some traveling white minstrel troupes used African-American performers to enhance the authenticity of their productions. One such troupe was the Ethiopian Minstrels, whose star performer was William Henry Lane, an African-American dancer who used the stage name "Master Juba." Lane was one of the greatest dancers of his generation. Throughout the United States and England, "Master Juba" was enthusiastically praised by audiences and critics alike. One anonymous English critic, quoted by dance historian Marian Hannah Winter in Paul Magriel's *Chronicles of the American Dance,* wrote the following critique of one of Lane's performances:

> Juba exceeded anything ever witnessed in Europe. The style as well as the execution is unlike anything seen in this country. The manner in which he beats time with feet, and the extraordinary command he possesses over them, can only be believed by those who have been present at the exhibition.

Black minstrel troupes began to appear in the 1850s, but it was not until after the Civil War that they became established on the American stage. Although black minstrels inherited the negative stereotypes of blacks that white minstrels had established, the African-American performer won a permanent place on the American stage, providing a training ground for the many black dancers, comedians, singers, and composers to come. Notable among these stage personalities were dancer–comedians Billy Kersands, Bert Williams, Bob Height, Dewey "Pigmeat" Martin, and Ernest Hogan; singers like Gertrude "Ma" Rainey and Bessie Smith; and composers James Bland and William Christopher Handy. To a great extent, black minstrelsy created a national appreciation for the talent of black stage entertainers, drawing audiences to black shows and other forms of black entertainment for generations to come.

RECLAIMING THE BLACK IMAGE: 1890 TO 1920 ♦ ♦ ♦ ♦ ♦ ♦ ♦ ♦

Between 1898 and 1911, thirteen all-black musicals opened on Broadway, showcasing the talents of black musicians, lyricists, directors, producers, and writers.

By the 1890s, black producers, writers, and stage performers sought to reform the demeaning images of blacks that were prevalent on the American stage. *The Creole Show*, cast by black producer Sam Jack in 1891, was the first all-black musical to depart from minstrelsy. Featuring an all-black chorus line, *The Creole Show* premiered in Boston in 1891 and later played at the Chicago World's Fair for the entire season. In 1895 black producer John W. Ishaw presented *The Octoroon*, another all-black musical that moved away from the minstrel tradition. *Oriental America*, which Ishaw also produced, broke further from minstrel conventions by not closing with the traditional walkaround, but with an operatic medley.

Trip to Coontown, written and directed by Bob Cole in 1898, completely broke away from the minstrel tradition. The plot of this all-black musical was presented completely through music and dance. The first musical produced, written, and performed by African Americans on Broadway, it ushered in a new era for blacks on the American stage.

The highly popular *Clorinda: The Origin of the Cakewalk*, with music by composer Will Marion Cook and lyrics by poet Paul Laurence Dunbar, opened in 1898 at the Casino Roof Garden and featured comedian–singer Ernest Hogan. The comic–dance duo of Bert Williams and George Walker premiered their first Broadway musical, *The Policy Players*, in l899. This

Bert Williams and George Walker.

success was followed by Williams and Walker's *Sons of Ham*, which played on Broadway for two seasons beginning in September 1900. Their *In Dahomey*, premiered on Broadway in 1903 and, after a long run, toured successfully in England. *The Southerners*, with music by Will Marion Cook, opened on Broadway in 1904 with an interracial cast starring Abbie Mitchell. The Williams and Walker team returned to Broadway in 1906 with a new musical, *Abyssinia*, which consistently played to a full house.

In the same year the versatile Ernest Hogan appeared on Broadway in *Rufus Rastus*, and in 1902 Hogan starred in *Oyster Man*, which enjoyed a successful run on Broadway. Bob Cole, J. Rosamond Johnson, and James Weldon Johnson wrote and performed in *The Shoo-Fly Regiment*, another musical that opened on Broadway in 1902. Williams and Walker appeared in their last Broadway production together, *Bandanna Land*, in 1908. George Walker fell into ill health after the show closed, and died in 1911. Bert Williams went on to appear in *Mr. Lord of Koal* on Broadway in 1909, and later was the star comedian performer in the *Ziegfeld Follies*. The last black musical to open on Broadway before the 1920s was *His Honor the Barber* in 1911, with S. H. Dudley in the lead.

Black actors on the dramatic stage, like the performers in all-black musicals, were attempting to shed the demeaning image of the African American projected by most white-produced minstrelsy and drama. The presentation of three plays—*The Rider of Dreams, Granny Maumee,* and *Simon the Cyrenian*—by white playwright Ridgely Torrence at the Garden Theatre in Madison Square Garden on April 5, 1917, was an exceptional and highly successful effort to objectively portray the African American on the dramatic stage.

AFRICAN-AMERICAN PERFORMERS FROM 1920 TO 1960 ♦ ♦ ♦ ♦

Black Musicals

On May 23, 1921, *Shuffle Along* opened on Broadway, signaling the return of black musicals to "The Great White Way" and the arrival of the Harlem Renaissance on the American stage. Featuring the talented singer–dancer Florence Mills, *Shuffle Along* was written by Noble Sissle, Eubie Blake, Flournoy Miller, and Aubrey Lyles. Florence Mills quickly became a sought-after performer, appearing in *The Plantation Revue* (which opened on Broadway on July 17, 1922) and touring England. In 1926, Mills returned to Harlem and played the lead in *Black Birds* at the Alhambra Theatre for a six-week run. Subsequently, Mills performed in Paris for six months.

Noble Sissle and Eubie Blake returned to Broadway on September 24, 1924, with their new musical *Chocolate Dandies*. Two years later Flournoy Miller and Aubrey Lyles opened on Broadway in *Runnin' Wild,* which introduced the Charleston to the country. Bill "Bojangles" Robinson, starring in *Blackbirds of 1928,* dazzled Broadway audiences with his exciting tap-dancing style. Several other black musicals opened on Broadway during the 1920s, including *Rang Tang* (1927), *Keep Shuffling* (1928), and *Hot Chocolates* (1929).

Porgy and Bess, opening on Broadway in 1935, became the major all-black musical production of the 1930s. With music by George Gershwin, this adaptation of the novel and play by DuBose and Dorothy Heyward was an immediate success as a folk opera. Todd Duncan was cast as Porgy, with Ann Brown as Bess, and comedian–dancer John Bubbles as the character Sportin' Life.

Bill "Bojangles" Robinson performing with Shirley Temple in the movie "The Little Colonel," 1935.

In the 1940s, black musicals were scarce on Broadway. *Cabin in the Sky,* starring Ethel Waters, Dooley Wilson, Todd Duncan, Rex Ingram, J. Rosamond Johnson, and Katherine Dunham and her dancers, ran for 165 performances after it opened on October 25, 1940. *Carmen Jones,* perhaps the most successful all-black musical of the decade, opened in 1943 with Luther Saxon, Napoleon Reed, Carlotta Franzel, and Cozy Cove; it had a run of 231 performances and was taken on tour. In 1946 *St. Louis Woman,* featuring Rex Ingram, Pearl Bailey, Juanita Hall, and June Hawkins, played a short run to mixed reviews.

The Dramatic Theater

During the Harlem Renaissance years, the African-American dramatic actor remained less active than the black performer in musicals, and the image of the African American projected by white playwrights was generally inadequate. The 1967 book *Black Drama: The Story of the American Negro in the Theatre* recounts, for example, that when Charles Gilpin starred in Eugene O'Neill's *Emperor Jones* at the Provincetown Theatre in 1920, critic Loften Mitchell stated:

> This play, while offering one of the most magnificent roles for a Negro in the American theatre, is the first in a long line to deal with the Negro on this level. O'Neill obviously saw in the Negro rich subject matter, but he was either incapable or unwilling to deal directly with the matter.

Nonetheless, African-American actors and actresses had to accept the roles in which they were cast by white playwrights. In 1924, the O'Neill play *All God's Chillun' Got Wings* opened at the Provincetown Theatre, with Paul Robeson and Mary Blair, to mixed reviews because of its interracial theme. Rose McClendon starred in Paul Green's Pulitzer Prize–winning *In Abraham's Bosom* in 1926, and was ably supported by Abbie Mitchell and Jules Bledsoe. Marc Connelly's *Green Pastures* opened on Broadway on February 26, 1930; with Richard B. Harrison playing "De Lawd" it ran for 557 performances and was taken on an extensive road tour.

Three plays by Langston Hughes that did treat African Americans objectively were produced successfully on Broadway in the 1930s. *Mulatto,* which opened in 1935 and starred Rose McClendon and Morris McKenney, had the longest Broadway run of any play written by an African American in the history of the American theater, with 373 consecutive performances. It was followed by *Little Ham* (1935) and *Troubled Island* (1936).

The Federal Theater Project

In the mid-1930s the Works Progress Administration (WPA) sponsored one of the greatest organized efforts to assist and encourage American actors, especially African-American actors. The Federal Theater Project employed a total of 851 black actors to work in sixteen segregated units of the project in Chicago, New York, and other cities from 1935 until 1939, when Congress ended the project. While the project was in operation, black actors appeared in seventy-five plays, including classics, vaudeville contemporary comedy, children's shows, circuses, and "living newspaper" performances. Notable among the black actors who worked in the project, and later became stars on Broadway and in the film, were Butterfly McQueen, Canada Lee, Rex Ingram, Katherine Dunham, Edna Thomas, Thomas Anderson, and Arthur Dooley Wilson.

In the wake of the Federal Theater Project, The American Negro Theater was established in Harlem by Abram Hill, Austin Briggs-Hall, Frederick O'Neal, and Hattie King-Reeves. Its objective was to authentically portray black life and give black actors and playwrights a forum for their talents. Some of their productions eventually made it to Broadway. In 1944, the theater produced *Anna Lucasta* in the basement of the 135th Street Library in Harlem. It was successful enough to move to Broadway, and featured Hilda Simms, Frederick O'Neal, Alice Childress, Alvin Childress, Earle Hyman, and Herbert Henry. Abram Hill's *Walk Hard* opened in Harlem in 1946 and became a Broadway production with Maxwell Glanville in the lead. The American Negro Theater provided a training ground for many black actors who later became stars on Broadway and in Hollywood, including Ruby Dee, Ossie Davis, Harry Belafonte, and Sidney Poitier.

Dramatic Theater in the 1950s

The rise of television in the 1950s generally had an adverse affect on the American theater. Employment for all actors fell sharply, but especially for black actors. Ethel Waters did, however, open on Broadway in 1950 as the lead in *Member of the Wedding*, which was well received. Louis Peterson's *Take a Giant Step* opened on Broadway in September 1953 to critical praise; in the cast were Frederick O'Neal, Helen Martin, Maxwell Glanville, Pauline Myers, Estelle Evans, and Louis Gossett, Jr.

One of the most successful all-black plays to appear on Broadway opened in March 1959: Lorraine Hansberry's *Raisin in the Sun*, which won the New York Drama Critics Circle Award. Its cast included Sidney Poitier, Ruby Dee, Diana Sands, Claudia McNeil, Louis Gossett, Jr., Ivan Dixon, Lonnie Elder, III, and Douglas Turner Ward. *Raisin in the Sun* indicated the future of blacks in the American theater.

Black Dance

Black dance, like other forms of black entertainment, had its beginnings in Africa and on the plantations of early America, where slaves performed to entertain themselves and their masters. White minstrels in blackface incorporated many of these black dance inventions into their shows, while black minstrel dancers, such as "Master Juba" (William Henry Lane), thrilled audiences with their artistry.

By the early 1930s, black pioneers of modern dance— including Hemsley Winfield, Asadata Dafore, Katherine Dunham, and Pearl Primus— were appearing on the dance stage.

Many performers in the early black musicals that appeared on Broadway from 1898 and 1910 were expert show dancers, such as George Walker and Bert Williams. Similarly, in the all-black musicals of the 1920s, performers like Florence Mills and Bill "Bojangles" Robinson captivated audiences with their show dancing. The musical *Runnin' Wild* (1926) was responsible for creating the Charleston dance craze of the "Roaring Twenties."

Hemsley Winfield presented what was billed as "The First Negro Concert in America" in Manhattan's Chanin Building on April 31, 1931. Two suites on African themes were performed, along with solos by Edna Guy and Winfield himself. In 1933, Winfield became the first black to dance for the Metropolitan Opera, performing the role of the Witch Doctor in *Emperor Jones.*

Austin "Asadata Dafore" Horton, a native of Sierra Leone, electrified audiences in New York with his 1934 production of *Kykunkor.* Dance historian Lynne Fauley Emery concludes in *Black Dance from 1619 to Today* that *Kykunkor* "was the first performance by black dancers on the concert stage which was entirely successful. It revealed the potential of ethnic material to black dancers, and herein lay Dafore's value as a great influence on black concert dance."

Katherine Dunham had her first lead dance role in Ruth Page's West Indian ballet *La Guiablesse* in 1933. In 1936, Dunham received a master's degree in anthropology from the University of Chicago; her thesis studied *The Dances of Haiti,* the result of her on-site study of native dances in the West Indies. For the next thirty years, Dunham and her dance company toured the United States and Europe, dazzling audiences with her choreography. During the 1963–64 season, Dunham choreographed the Metropolitan Opera's production of *Aida,* becoming the first black American to do so.

Pearl Primus, like Katherine Dunham, was trained in anthropology. Her research in primitive African dance inspired her first composition performed as a professional dancer, *African Ceremonial,* which she presented on February 14, 1943. On October 4, 1944, Primus made her Broadway debut at the Belasco Theater in New York. Her performance included dances of West Indian, African, and African-American origin; the concert was widely acclaimed and launched her career as a dancer. Primus has

Katherine Dunham, a pioneer of modern dance, 1992.

traveled to Africa many times to research African dances; in 1959 she was named director of Liberia's Performing Arts Center. She later opened the Primus–Borde School of Primal Dance with her husband, dancer Percival Borde, and is currently involved in the Pearl Primus Dance Language Institute in New Rochelle, New York.

By late 1950s, several black dancers and dance companies were distinguishing themselves on the concert stage. Janet Collins was the "première danseuse" of the Metropolitan Opera Ballet from 1951 until 1954. Arthur Mitchell made his debut as a principal dancer with the New York City Ballet in 1955. Alvin Ailey established his company in 1958. And Geoffrey Holder, who made his Broadway debut in 1954 in *House of Flowers*, became a leading choreographer.

The Black Comedian

The earliest black comedians in America, like other early black entertainers, were slaves who in their free time entertained themselves and their masters. In the early minstrel shows, white comedians in blackface created comic

The Apollo Theater, a legendary venue for black entertainment.

caricatures of blacks, whom they referred to as "coons." When African Americans began appearing in minstrel shows shortly after the Civil War, they found themselves burdened with the "coon" comic caricatures created by white performers. The dance–comedy team of Bert Williams and George Walker were the most famous of the early black comedians, appearing in numerous all-black musicals between 1899 and 1909.

In the all-black musicals of the 1920s, a new comic movement emerged: the comedy of style, which emphasized such antics as rolling the eyes or shaking the hips. The venom and bite of black folk humor was replaced by a comedy of style that was more acceptable to the white audiences of these all-black musicals.

Real black folk humor, however, did survive and thrive in black night-clubs and black theaters such as the Apollo in Harlem and the Regal in Chicago in the 1930s, 1940s, and 1950s. In these settings, known as the "Chitterling Circuit," such black comedians as Tim Moore, Dusty Fletcher, Butterbeans and Susie, Stepin Fetchit, Jackie "Moms" Mabley, Redd Foxx, and Slappy White performed without restrictions.

◆ ◆ ◆ ◆ ◆ ◆ ◆ AFRICAN-AMERICAN PERFORMERS AFTER 1960

As the civil-rights movement challenged the national conscience in the 1960s, every facet of African-American life changed, including black performing arts. More plays about African Americans by both black and white playwrights were produced, providing increased employment for black actors. On the dance stage, more opportunities were opened to blacks as composers, choreographers, and dancers. And many black comedians, by invitation, moved from the "Chitterling Circuit" to posh white-clientele nightclubs and, in some instance, to theaters.

Three events in the 1960s signaled trends that would affect African-American dramatic actors for the next thirty years: the production of Jean Genet's play, *The Blacks*; the staging of the Leroi Jones (Imamu Amiri Baraka) play, *The Dutchman*; and the founding of the Negro Ensemble Company.

The Dramatic Theater

On May 4, 1961, *The Blacks*, by French playwright/author Jean Genet, opened off Broadway at the St. Mark's Theater. A play about African Americans written for white audiences, *The Blacks* provided employment for a host of black actors, including Roscoe Lee Browne, James Earl Jones, Louis Gossett, Jr., Helen Martin, Cicely Tyson, Godfrey Cambridge, Raymond St. Jacques, Maya Angelou, Charles Gordone, and many others who appeared in its road tours. Subsequently, black dramatic actors appeared on and off Broadway in several major plays by white playwrights. Notable among them were *In White America* by Judith Rutherford Marechal (1968), with

Gloria Foster and Moses Gunn; *The Great White Hope* by William Sackler (1968), starring James Earl Jones; and *So Nice, They Named It Twice* by Neil Harris (1975), featuring Bill Jay and Veronica Redd.

On May 23, 1961, when the Leroi Jones (Imamu Amiri Baraka) play *Dutchman* opened at the Cherry Lane Theatre, the black revolutionary play was introduced to theater audiences. Black actors were provided with the opportunity to perform in roles that not only affirmed blackness, but portrayed black political militancy. Several black revolutionary plays subsequently afforded opportunities for black actors, including James Baldwin's *Blues for Mr. Charlie* (1964), with Al Freeman, Jr., and Diana Sands; and *The Toilet/The Slave* (1964) by Leroi Jones, starring James Spruill, Walter Jones, Nan Martin, and Al Freeman, Jr. In 1991, black revolutionary plays such as *General Hag's Skeezag* continued to provide important roles for black actors.

The Negro Ensemble has staged more than one hundred productions, including the work of forty black playwrights, and has provided work for countless aspiring and seasoned black actors.

Perhaps most beneficial to black actors was the founding of the Negro Ensemble Company in New York in 1967. This theatrical production company, initially financed by a three-year grant of $1.2 million from the Ford Foundation, was the brainchild of playwright/actor Douglas Turner Ward. Housed originally at the St. Mark's Theater and currently at Theater Four, the Negro Ensemble is headed by actor Robert Hooks as executive director, Gerald Krone as administrative director, and Douglas Turner Ward as artistic director. The Negro Ensemble's objective is to develop African-American managers, playwrights, actors, and technicians.

The Negro Ensemble has staged more than one hundred productions, including the work of forty black playwrights, and provided work for countless aspiring and seasoned black actors. Several plays produced by the Negro Ensemble have eventually gone to Broadway, including Douglas Turner Ward's *The River Niger* (1973), which won a Tony award and an Obie award, and Charles Fuller's Pulitzer Prize–winning *The Soldier's Play* (1981). A plethora of outstanding black actors and actresses have appeared in Ensemble productions, including Marshall Williams, Denise Nichols, Esther Rolle, Roxie Roker, Adolph Ceasar, Denzel Washington, Moses Gunn, and Barbara Montgomery.

Several black playwrights had plays successfully produced on Broadway independently of the Negro Ensemble Company. Ntozake Shange's widely acclaimed *For Colored Girls Who Have Considered Suicide/When the Rainbow*

James Earl Jones performing in the play Fences, *1987.*

Is Enuf (1972) had a cast of seven black actresses. August Wilson's *Fences*, which opened on March 26, 1987, and featured James Earl Jones, won the 1987 Pulitzer Prize for drama. Wilson's *Two Trains Running*, which opened April 13, 1992, and starred Roscoe Lee Browne and Laurence Fishburne, received the New York Drama Critic's Award for 1992.

One of the most active periods for African-American performers in musical theater occurred between 1961 and the mid-1980s. Many of the black musicals produced during these years, both on and off Broadway, enjoyed substantial runs and extended road tours.

Black Musicals

Langston Hughes's musical *Black Nativity* opened on Broadway on December 11, 1961. Directed by Vinette Carroll, the cast was headed by gospel singers Marion Williams and the Stars of Faith, and also featured Alex Bradford, Clive Thompson, Cleo Quitman, and Carl Ford. Although it ran for only fifty-seven performances on Broadway, it went on to tour extensively throughout the United States and abroad.

In 1964, Sammy Davis, Jr. dazzled Broadway in Clifford Odets's *Golden Boy*. Davis was supported by a brilliant cast that included Robert Guillaume, Louis Gossett, Jr., Lola Falana, and Billy Daniels. *Golden Boy* ran for 586 performances.

Leslie Uggams and Robert Hooks appeared in *Hallelujah Baby*, which opened in New York's Martin Beck Theater on April 26, 1967. *Hallelujah*

Ossie Davis, with co-star Ruby Dee, in the play Purlie Victorious, *1961.*

Baby, a musical look at five decades of black history, received a Tony award and ran for 293 performances.

Purlie, based on Ossie Davis's 1961 play *Purlie Victorious,* opened on May 9, 1970, with Melba Moore and Robert Guillaume in lead roles. *Purlie* received good reviews and enjoyed a run of 688 performances.

Micki Grant's *Don't Bother Me, I Can't Cope,* starring Micki Grant and Alex Bradford, opened on April 19, 1972 to rave reviews. For this musical, which ran for 1,065 performances, Micki Grant received a Drama Desk award and an Obie award.

Virginia Capers, Joe Morton, and Helen Martin opened *Raisin,* based on Lorraine Hansberry's play *Raisin in the Sun,* on October 13, 1973. *Raisin* received the Tony award for the best musical in 1974 and had a run of 847 performances.

Despite initially poor reviews, *The Wiz,* a black musical version of *The Wizard of Oz,* became a highly successful show. Opening on Broadway on January 5, 1975, *The Wiz* featured an array of talented performers, including Stephanie Mills, Hinton Battle, Ted Ross, Andre DeShields, Dee Dee Bridgewater, and Mabel King. *The Wiz* swept the Tony award ceremonies in 1975 and became the longest-running black musical in the history of Broadway, with 1,672 performances.

Ain't Misbehavin', another popular black musical of the 1970s, opened on May 8, 1978. Based on a cavalcade of songs composed by Thomas "Fats" Waller, *Ain't Misbehavin'* starred Nell Carter, Andre DeShields, Armelia McQueen, Ken Page, and Charlene Woodard. It played to Broadway audiences for 1,604 performances, and Nell Carter received a Tony award as "best featured actress."

Two spectacular black musicals premiered on Broadway in the 1980s. *Dream Girls,* which opened at the Imperial Theater on December 20, 1981, captivated Broadway audiences with a cast that included Jennifer Holiday, Cleavant Derricks, Loretta Devine, and Cheryl Alexander. *Dream Girls* ran for 1,522 performances on Broadway and had an extensive road tour. Jennifer Holiday won a Tony award for her role as Effie Melody White. On April 27, 1986, Debbie Allen opened in the lead role of *Sweet Charity.* Reviews were favorable, and the musical enjoyed a run of 386 performances, establishing Debbie Allen as a musical theater actress.

A few new all-black musicals have opened in the early 1990s, including *Five Guys Name Moe,* a tribute to musician Louis Jordan, with Clarke Peters and Charles Augin; and *Jelly's Last Jam,* featuring Gregory Hines.

Black Dance

Since the early 1960s, two of the leading dance companies in the United States, the Alvin Ailey American Dance Theater and the Dance Theater of Harlem, have been headed by black males and composed largely of black dancers.

The Alvin Ailey American Dance Theater

The Alvin Ailey American Dance Theater, since its founding in 1958, has performed before more people throughout the world than any other American dance company. With a touring circuit that has included forty-eight states and forty-five countries on all continents, the Alvin Ailey American Dance Theater has been seen by more than fifteen million people. Today, the Alvin Ailey organization consists of three components: the Alvin Ailey American Dance Theater, the Alvin Ailey Repertory Ensemble, and the Alvin Ailey American Dance Center.

Between 1958 and 1988, the Alvin Ailey Dance Theater performed 150 works by forty-five choreographers, most of whom were black. Notable among these black choreographers have been Tally Beatty, Donald McKayle, Louis Johnson, Eleo Romare, Billy Wilson, George Faison, Pearl Primus, Judith Jamison, Katherine Dunham, Ulysses Dove, Milton Myers, Kelvin Rotardier, and Gary DeLoatch. More than 250 dancers, again mostly black, have performed with the dance theater. Among its star performers have been Judith Jamison, Clive Thompson, Dudley Wilson, Donna Wood, Gary DeLoatch, George Faison, and Sara Yaraborough. A prolific choreographer, Alvin Ailey has created numerous works for his dance theater and other dance companies, including *Revelations* (1958); *Reflections in D,* with music by Duke Ellington (1962); *Quintet* (1968); *Cry* (1971); *Memoria* (1974); and *Three Black Kings* (1976). Alvin Ailey choreographed *Carmen* for the Metropolitan Opera in 1973 and *Precipice* for the Paris Opera in 1983.

Alvin Ailey's American Dance Theater has performed before more than fifteen million people—a greater number than any other American dance company.

The Alvin Ailey Repertory Ensemble was established in 1974 as a training and performing company. Many of its graduates advance to the dance theater or perform with other dance companies. In 1988, the AARE had more than one hundred members.

The Alvin Ailey American Dance Center is the official school of the Ailey organization. It attracts students from across the United States and abroad and offers a certificate in dance. The center's curriculum includes training in ballet, the Dunham Technique, jazz, and modern dance.

The Dance Theater of Harlem

In 1969, Arthur Mitchell, who had established himself as one of the leading ballet dancers in the United States, and Karel Shook, a white ballet teacher, founded the Dance Theater of Harlem. The Dance Theater of Harlem made its formal debut in 1971 at the Guggenheim Museum in

Judith Jamison, a dancer in the Alvin Ailey Dance Theater, performing with Lazaro Carreno and Mia Llorente in 1977.

New York City. Three of Mitchell's works were premiered at this concert: *Rhythmetron, Tones,* and *Fête Noire.*

Today, the dance theater's repertory is wide ranging. It includes works in the Balanchine tradition such as *Serenade,* as well as black-inspired works like *Dougla.* Among the most spectacular works performed by the theater are *Firebird, Giselle, Scheherazade,* and *Swan Lake.* Dancers Lowell Smith, Virginia Johnson, Shelia Rohan, and Troy Game have had long associa-

Arthur Mitchell formed the Dance Theater of Harlem, a ballet company, with Karel Shook in 1969.

tions with the theater, and many of the theater's graduates have gone on to perform with other dance companies in the United States and Europe. The Dance Theater of Harlem's school currently has about 1,000 students.

Other Black Dancers

Between 1960 and 1990, several other black dancers have led distinguished careers in concert dance and show dancing. Among them have been Eleo Pomare, Debbie Allen, Rod Rogers, Fred Benjamin, Pepsi Bethel, Eleanor Hampton, Charles Moore, Garth Fagan, Carmen de Lavallade, and Mary Hinkson. Foremost among black choreographers have been Geoffrey Holder, Louis Johnson, and Donald McKayle. Prominent among the black dancers who are reviving the tap-dance tradition are Chuck Green, Buster Brown, Honi Coles, Hinton Battle, Maurice and Gregory Hines, Lavaughn Robinson, and Nita Feldman.

The Black Comedian

Black comedians enjoyed great exposure during the 1960s. No longer confined to the "Chitterling Circuit," comedians such as Jackie "Moms" Mabley, Redd Foxx, and Slappy White began to perform to audiences in

Gregory Hines (right), dancing with his brother Maurice, 1982.

exclusive white clubs as well as to audiences within the black community. They used black folk humor to comment on politics, civil rights, work, sex, and a variety of other subjects. Jackie "Moms" Mabley made two popular recordings: *Moms Mabley at the UN* and *Moms Mabley at the Geneva Conference*. In January 1972, Redd Foxx premiered on television as Fred Sanford in "Sanford and Son," which remains one of the most popular syndicated shows.

Several younger black comedians came into prominence in the early 1960s. Dick Gregory used black folk humor to make political commentary. Bill Cosby specialized in amusing chronicles about boyhood in America. Godfrey Cambridge, although successful, did not rely on black folk humor. During the late 1960s and the early 1970s, Flip Wilson, who parodied historical and social experience by creating black characters who lived in a black world, became extremely popular on television. His cast of characters, which included "Freddy the Playboy," "Sammy the White House Janitor," and "Geraldine," were the epitome of black folk humor as commentary on an array of issues.

Bill Cosby, shown holding an Emmy award in 1992, came to prominence in the early 1960s, recounting droll stories about boyhood in America.

Another pivotal black comedian who began his career in the 1960s was Richard Pryor. His well-timed, risqué, sharp folk humor quickly won him a large group of faithful fans. Pryor, who has recorded extensively, also starred in several successful films, including *Lady Sings the Blues, Car Wash,* and *Stir Crazy.*

During the 1980s and 1990s, numerous black comedians have become successful in the various entertainment media. Eddie Murphy made his first appearance on the television show "Saturday Night Live" on Novem-

Eddie Murphy first appeared on "Saturday Night Live" in 1980, then went on to a successful Hollywood career.

ber 15, 1980. From television, Murphy went on to Hollywood, making his movie debut in the film *48 Hours* in 1982. Starring roles followed in such films as *Beverly Hills Cop,* which was the highest-grossing comedy film in history, and *Coming to America.* Murphy has established his own company, Eddie Murphy Productions, to create and produce television and film projects. Arsenio Hall came to prominence in 1987 as a successful interim guest host on the now defunct "The Late Show," which won him a lucrative movie contract with Paramount Pictures. In 1988, Hall was featured with Eddie Murphy in the film *Coming to America.* Arsenio Hall now hosts his own highly successful late-night talk show.

AFRICAN-AMERICAN PERFORMING ARTISTS ♦ ♦ ♦ ♦ ♦ ♦ ♦ ♦ ♦

Alvin Ailey

(1931–1991)

Dancer, Choreographer

Alvin Ailey, founder of the Alvin Ailey American Dance Theatre, won international fame as both dancer and choreographer. Ailey studied dancing after graduating from high school, where he was a star athlete. After briefly attending college, Ailey joined the stage crew of the Lester Horton Theater in Los Angeles, for which Ailey eventually performed as a dancer. In 1953, after Horton's death, Ailey became the company choreographer. In 1954, Ailey performed on Broadway as the lead dancer in *House of Flowers.*

Ailey formed his own dance group in 1958 and began giving four performances annually. In 1962, the Ailey troupe made an official State Department tour of Australia, receiving accolades throughout the country. One critic called Ailey's work "the most stark and devastating theatre ever presented in Australia."

After numerous appearances as a featured dancer with Harry Belafonte and others, Ailey performed in a straight dramatic role with Claudia McNeil in Broadway's *Tiger, Tiger Burning Bright.* Other Broadway appearances included *Ding Dong Bell, Dark of the Moon,* and *African Holiday.* Ailey also choreographed or staged several operas, including Barber's *Anthony and Cleopatra* (1966), Bernstein's *Mass* (1971), and Bizet's *Carmen.* In addition, Ailey created works for various international ballet stars and companies.

In 1965, Ailey took his group on one of the most successful European tours ever made by an American dance company. In London, it was held over for six weeks to accommodate the demand for tickets, and in Hamburg it received an unprecedented sixty-one curtain calls. A German critic called this performance "a triumph of sweeping, violent beauty, a furious spectacle. The stage vibrates. One has never seen anything like it." In 1970, Ailey's company became the first American modern dance group to tour the Soviet Union.

During the mid-seventies Ailey, among his other professional commitments, devoted much time to creating special jazz dance sequences for America's Bicentennial celebration. Among numerous honors, including several honorary degrees, Ailey was awarded the NAACP's Spingarn Medal in 1976.

Ira Aldridge

(c. 1807–1867)

Actor

Ira Aldridge was one of the leading Shakespearean actors of the nineteenth century. Although he was denied the opportunity to perform before the American public in his prime, the fame that he won abroad established him as one of the prominent figures of international theater.

Aldridge's origins are obscure. Some accounts give his birthplace as Africa; others name Bel-Air, Maryland; still others list New York City. The year of his birth is also uncertain; reported dates range from 1804 to 1807. It seems clear that he attended the African Free School in New York until he was about sixteen years old, at which time he left home.

Aldridge's early dramatic training centered around the African Grove Theatre in New York in 1821. His first role was in *Pizarro,* and he subsequently played a variety of small roles in classical productions before accepting employment as a steward on a ship bound for England.

After studying briefly at the University of Glasgow in Scotland, Aldridge went to London in 1825 and appeared in the melodrama *Surinam, or a Slave's Revenge.* In 1833, he appeared in London's Theatre Royal in the title role of *Othello,* earning wide acclaim. For the next three decades, he toured the continent with great success, often appearing before European royalty.

Aldridge died in Lodz, Poland, on August 7, 1867. He is honored by a commemorative tablet in the New Memorial Theatre in Stratford-upon-Avon, England.

Debbie Allen

(1950–)

Actress, Singer,
Dancer, Director

A cum laude graduate of Howard University, the Houston-born Debbie Allen began her career on the Broadway stage in the chorus line of the hit musical *Purlie* (1972). She then portrayed Beneatha in the Tony and Grammy award–winning musical *Raisin* (1973). Other early stage roles were in the national touring company of *Guys and Dolls* and the drama *Anna Lucasta,* performed for the New Federal Theatre at the Henry Street Settlement in New York.

Allen was subsequently selected to star in an NBC pilot, "3 Girls 3," and then appeared on other television hits such as "Good Times" and "The Love Boat." At this time, her talent as a choreographer recognized, she worked on such television projects as "Midnight Special" as well as two films, *The Fish That Saved Pittsburgh* (1979) and *Under Fire* (1981).

The year 1982 was pivotal for Allen. She appeared in the film *Ragtime* and the television series "Fame," as well as the Joseph Papp television special "Alice at the Palace." Allen also starred in a dance performance for the Academy Awards ceremonies.

Allen's career continued with roles in the television special *Ben Vereen: His Roots* and the miniseries "Roots: The Next Generation" (1979). She also appeared on stage again in *Ain't Misbehavin* (1979) and a revival of *West Side Story* (1980), which earned her a Tony award nomination and a Drama Desk award.

As each season passed on "Fame," Allen became more involved as choreographer and was soon regularly directing episodes of the series. In 1988 she was selected by the producers to become director of the television sitcom "A Different World." In another acknowledgment of her stature as a performer and creative talent, she starred in her own television special during the 1988–89 season.

Eddie "Rochester"

Anderson

(1906–1977)

Comedian

For many years, Eddie Anderson was the only black performing regularly on a network radio show. As the character Rochester on the Jack Benny program, he became one of the best-known black American entertainers.

Anderson was born in Oakland, California in 1906, the son of "Big Ed" Anderson, a minstrel performer, and Ella Mae, a tightwire walker. During the 1920s and early 1930s, Anderson traveled throughout the Middle and Far West singing, dancing, and performing as a clown in small clubs. On Easter Sunday, 1937, he was featured on Jack Benny's radio show, in what was supposed to be a single appearance; Anderson was such a hit that he quickly became a regular on the program.

Anderson is best known for his work with Benny (in television as well as on radio), but he also appeared in a number of movies, including *What Price Hollywood?* (1932), *Cabin in the Sky* (1943), and *It's a Mad, Mad, Mad, Mad World* (1963).

Anderson died on February 28, 1977, at the age of seventy-one.

Born March 29, 1918 in Newport News, Virginia, Pearl Bailey moved to Philadelphia with her family in 1933. She sang at small clubs in Scranton, Pennsylvania and in Washington, DC, before becoming the vocalist for the band of Cootie Williams and later for Count Basie. In the early 1940s, Bailey had her first successful New York engagements at the Village Vanguard and the Blue Angel. During World War II, she toured with the USO. Bailey made her New York stage debut in 1946 in *St. Louis Woman*, for which she won a Donaldson Award as the year's most promising new performer. She also appeared in the films *Variety Girl* (1947) and *Isn't It Romantic?* (1948).

Pearl Bailey (1918–1990)

Singer, Actress

During the 1950s Bailey appeared in the movies *Carmen Jones, That Certain Feeling,* and *Porgy and Bess,* and on Broadway in *House of Flowers.* In the 1950s and 1960s, she worked as a recording artist, nightclub headliner, and television performer. In 1967, she received a special Tony award for her starring role on Broadway in *Hello, Dolly.* In 1969, she published an autobiography, *The Raw Pearl.* Her other books include *Talking to Myself* (1971), *Pearl's Kitchen* (1973), *Duey Tale* (1975), and *Hurry Up, America, and Spit* (1976).

In 1975, Bailey was named a special adviser to the United States Mission to the United Nations. In 1976, she appeared in the film *Norman, Is That You?* with Redd Foxx, and on stage in Washington, DC in *Something to Do,* a musical saluting the American worker. She also received an award in 1976 from the Screen Actors Guild for outstanding achievement in fostering the finest ideals of the acting profession. Georgetown University made her an honorary doctor of human letters in 1977.

In January 1980, Bailey gave a one-night concert at Radio City Music Hall in New York. In 1981 she performed as the voice of the cartoon character "Owl" in the Disney movie *The Fox and the Hound.*

Bailey married the jazz drummer Louis Bellson in 1952. She died August 17, 1990, in Philadelphia.

Josephine Baker (1906–1975)

Dancer, Singer

Born in St. Louis on June 3, 1906, Josephine Baker received little formal education; she left school at the age of eight to supplement the family income by working as a kitchen helper and baby-sitter. While still in elementary school, she took a part-time job as a chorus girl. At seventeen, she performed as a chorus girl in Noble Sissle's musical comedy *Shuffle Along,* which played in Radio City Music Hall in 1923. Her next show was *Chocolate Dandies,* followed by a major dancing part in *La Revue Nègre,* an American production that introduced *le jazz hot* to Paris in 1925.

In Paris, Baker left the show to create her most sensational role, that of the "Dark Star" of the Folies Bergère. In her act, she appeared topless on a mirror, clad only in a protective waist shield of rubber bananas. The spectacular dance made her an overnight star and a public figure with a loyal following. In true "star" tradition, she catered to her fans by adopting such flamboyant eccentricities as walking pet leopards down the Champs Elysées.

In 1930, after completing a world tour, Baker made her debut as a singing and dancing comedienne at the Casino de Paris. Critics called her a "complete artist, the perfect master of her tools." In time, she ventured into films, starring alongside French idol Jean Gabin in *Zouzou* (1934), and into light opera, performing in *La Créole* (1934), an operetta about a Jamaican girl.

During World War II, Baker served first as a Red Cross volunteer and later did underground intelligence work through an Italian Embassy attaché. After the war, the French government decorated her with the Legion of Honor. She returned to the entertainment world, regularly starring at the Folies Bergère, appearing on French television, and going on another extended international tour. In 1951, during the course of a successful American tour, Baker made headlines by speaking out against discrimination and refusing to perform in segregated venues.

Josephine Baker, shown here in 1951, was an international sensation as a dancer and also did underground intelligence work through an Italian Embassy attaché during World War II, for which the French government decorated her with the Legion of Honor.

Beginning in 1954, Baker earned another reputation—not as a lavish and provocative entertainer, but as a progressive humanitarian. She used her fortune to begin adopting and tutoring a group of orphaned babies of all races, retiring from the stage in 1956 to devote all her time to her "rainbow family." Within three years, however, her "experiment in brotherhood" had taken such a toll on her finances that she was forced to return to the stage, starring in *Paris, Mes Amours,* a musical based in part on her own fabled career.

Baker privately, and without voicing discouragement, survived numerous financial crises. Illness hardly managed to dampen her indomitable spirit. Through her long life, she retained her most noteworthy stage attributes—an intimate, subdued voice, coupled with an infectiously energetic and vivacious manner.

Baker died in Paris on April 12, 1975, after opening a gala to celebrate her fiftieth year in show business.

Harry Belafonte
(1927-)

Singer, Actor

Born in New York City, Harry Belafonte moved to the West Indies at the age of eight. At thirteen, Belafonte returned to New York, where he attended high school. Belafonte joined the Navy in 1944; after his discharge, while working as a janitor in New York, he became interested in drama. He studied acting at Stanley Kubrick's Dramatic Workshop and with Erwin Piscator at the New School for Social Research, where his classmates included Marlon Brando and Walter Matthau. A successful singing engagement at the Royal Roost, a New York jazz club, led to other engagements around the country. But Belafonte, dissatisfied with the music he was performing, returned to New York, opened a restaurant in Greenwich Village, and studied folk singing. His first appearances as a folk singer in the 1950s "helped give folk music a period of mass appeal," according to John S. Wilson in a 1981 *New York Times* article. During his performances at the Palace Theater in New York, Belafonte had audiences calypsoing in the aisles.

Belafonte produced the first integrated musical shows on television, which won him two Emmy awards and resulted in his being fired by the sponsor. The famous incident in which white British singer Petula Clark touched his arm while singing a song caused a national furor in pre–civil rights America. When Martin Luther King, Jr. marched on Montgomery, Alabama, and Washington, DC, Harry Belafonte joined him and brought along a large contingent of performers. Touring in the stage musical *Three for Tonight,* in which he had appeared on Broadway in 1955, Belafonte was forced to flee in the middle of a performance in Spartanburg, South Carolina and be rushed to the airport in the mayor's car. Word had come that the Ku Klux Klan was marching on the theater.

Belafonte also appeared on Broadway in John Murray Anderson's *Almanac* (1953), and his movies include *Carmen Jones* (1954), *Island in the Sun* (1957), *The World, the Flesh, and the Devil* (1958), *Odds against Tomorrow* (1959), *The Angel Levine* (1969), *Buck and the Preacher* (1972), and *Uptown Saturday Night* (1974).

During the 1980s Belafonte appeared in his first dramatic role on television in the NBC presentation of "Grambling's White Tiger," and in 1981 Columbia Records released his first album in seven years, *Loving You Is Where I Belong,* consisting mostly of ballads. He has received numerous awards and honors, including the 1982 Martin Luther King, Jr. Nonviolent Peace Prize and three honorary doctorates.

Eubie Blake was born in Baltimore on February 7, 1883. The son of former slaves, Blake was the last of ten children and the only one to survive beyond two months. His mother worked as a laundress, his father as a stevedore.

James Hubert "Eubie" Blake (1883–1983)

Musician, Composer

At the age of six Blake started taking piano lessons. He studied under the renowned teacher Margaret Marshall and subsequently was taught musical composition by Llewelyn Wilson, who at one time conducted an all-black symphony orchestra sponsored by the city of Baltimore. At the age of seventeen, Blake was playing for a Baltimore night club.

In 1915 Blake joined Noble Sissle. That year, Blake and Sissle sold their first song, "It's All Your Fault," to Sophie Tucker, and her introduction of the song started them on their way. Blake and Sissle moved to New York and, together with Flournoy Miller and Aubrey Lyles, created one of the pioneer black shows, *Shuffle Along,* in 1921; the show was produced again on Broadway in 1952. *Chocolate Dandies* and *Elsie* followed in 1924.

During the early 1930s, Blake collaborated with Andy Razaf and wrote the musical score for Lew Leslie's *Blackbirds.* Out of this association came the hit *Memories of You.* During World War II, Blake was appointed musical conductor for the United Services Organizations (USO) Hospital Unit. In 1946 he announced his retirement and enrolled in New York University.

For many years, Blake's most requested song was "Charleston Rag," which he composed in 1899 and which was written down by someone else because Blake could not then read music. Among his most famous songs were "How Ya' Gonna Keep 'Em Down on the Farm," "Love Will Find a Way," and "You're Lucky to Me." Some of his other works include "I'm Just Wild About Harry," "Serenade Blues," "It's All Your Fault," and "Floradora Girls," with lyrics by Sissle.

Though known as the master of ragtime, Blake loved best the music of the classical masters. In the intimacy of his Brooklyn studio, Blake rarely played the music for which the world reveres him. In 1978, Blake's life and career were celebrated in the Broadway musical *Eubie!* Several thousand people attended concerts at the Shubert Theatre and St. Peter's Lutheran Church celebrating Blake's 100th birthday on February 8, 1983. Blake also received honorary doctorates from numerous colleges and universities. He died on February 12, 1983.

John Bubbles (1902–1986)

Dancer, Singer

John Bubbles, inventor of rhythm tap dancing, was born John William Sublett in 1902 in Louisville, Kentucky. At the age of seven, he teamed with a fellow bowling-alley pinboy, Ford "Buck" Washington, to form what became one of the top vaudeville acts in show business. Throughout the 1920s and 1930s, Buck and Bubbles played the top theaters in the country at fees of up to $1,750 a week. The two appeared in several films, including *Cabin in the Sky* (1943). Bubbles captured additional fame as "Sportin' Life" in the 1935 version of *Porgy and Bess.* After Buck's death in 1955, Bubbles virtually disappeared from show business until 1964, when he teamed up with Anna Maria Alberghetti in a successful nightclub act.

In 1979, at the age of seventy-seven and partially crippled from an earlier stroke, Bubbles recreated his characterization of "Sportin' Life" for a one-night show entitled *Black Broadway* at New York's Lincoln Center. The show was repeated in 1980 for a limited engagement at the Town Hall in New York. In the fall of 1980, Bubbles received a lifetime achievement award from the American Guild of Variety Artists and a certificate of appreciation from the city of New York.

Bubbles died on May 19, 1986, at the age of eighty-four.

Anita Bush was involved with the theater from early childhood. Her father was the tailor for the Bijou, a large neighborhood theater in Brooklyn, and Anita used to carry the costumes to the theater for him, which gave her a backstage view of performers and productions. Her singing and acting career took off in her early twenties, when she was in the chorus of the Williams and Walker Company. With Williams and Walker, she performed in such Broadway hits as *Abyssinia* and *In Dahomey*, which also had a successful European tour. When the group split up in 1909, she went on to form the Anita Bush Stock Company, which included her own show of chorus girls and such greats as Charles Gilpin and Dooley Wilson, with whom she also founded the Lafayette Players.

Bush died on February 16, 1974.

Anita Bush (1883–1974)

Actress, Singer

Born in New York, Godfrey Cambridge's parents had emigrated from British Guiana. He attended grammar school in Nova Scotia while living with his grandparents. After finishing his schooling in New York at Flushing High School and Hofstra College, he went on to study acting.

Cambridge made his Broadway debut in *Nature's Way* (1956), and was featured in *Purlie Victorious* both on stage in 1961, and later on screen. He also appeared off Broadway in *Lost in the Stars* (1958), *Take a Giant Step*, and *The Detective Story* (1960). Cambridge won the Obie award for the 1960–1961 season's most distinguished off-Broadway performance for his role in *The Blacks*. In 1965, he starred in a stock version of *A Funny Thing Happened on the Way to the Forum*.

As a comedian, Cambridge appeared on "The Tonight Show" and many other variety hours. His material, drawn from the contemporary racial situation, was often presented in the style associated with the contemporary wave of black comedians. One of Cambridge's most memorable roles was as the star of a seriocomic Hollywood film, *The Watermelon Man* (1970), in which the comedian played a white man who changes color overnight. Cambridge has also performed dramatic roles on many television series.

During the mid-seventies Cambridge remained in semi-retirement, making few public appearances. Cambridge died at the age of forty-three in California on November 29, 1976. His death occurred on a Warner Brothers set, where he was playing the role of Ugandan dictator Idi Amin for the television film "Victory at Entebbe."

Godfrey Cambridge (1933–1976)

Actor, Comedian

Diahann Carroll
(1935-)

Actress, Singer

Diahann Carroll was born in the Bronx, the daughter of a subway conductor and a nurse. As a child, she was a member of the Abyssinian Baptist Church choir; at the age of ten, Carroll won a Metropolitan Opera scholarship. Singing lessons held little appeal for her, however, so she continued her schooling at the High School of Music and Art. As a concession to her parents, Carroll enrolled at New York University, where she was to be a sociology student, but stage fever led her to an appearance on a television talent show, which netted her $1,000. A subsequent appearance at the Latin Quarter club launched her professional career.

In 1954, Carroll appeared in *House of Flowers*, winning favorable press notices. In that year, she also appeared in a film version of *Carmen Jones*, in the role of Myrt.

Movie and television appearances kept Carroll busy until 1958, the year she was slated to appear as an Asian in Richard Rodgers' *Flower Drum Song*. The part did not materialize. Three years later, Rodgers cast her in *No Strings* as a high-fashion model, a role for which she earned a Tony award in 1962.

In the late 1960s, Carroll was cast as lead in the television series "Julia," in which she played a nurse and war widow. She also appeared in the films *Porgy and Bess* (1959); *Goodbye Again* (1961); *Paris Blues* (1961); *Claudine,* with James Earl Jones (1974); *Sister, Sister* (1982); and *The Five Heartbeats* (1991). She has been featured in the television series "Dynasty" and "A Different World" and has written an autobiography.

Bill Cosby (1937-)

Actor, Comedian

Bill Cosby is one of the most successful performers and businessmen in the United States.

A native of Philadelphia, Cosby dropped out of high school to become a medic in the Navy, obtaining his diploma while in the service. On becoming a civilian, he entered Temple University, where he played football and worked evenings as a bartender.

While doing this work, Cosby began to entertain the customers with his comedy routines and, encouraged by his success, left Temple in 1962 to pursue a career in show business. He began by playing small clubs around Philadelphia and in New York's Greenwich Village. Within two years, he

Bill Cosby, with cast members of "The Cosby Show," 1987.

was playing the top nightclubs around the country and making television appearances with Johnny Carson (also acting as guest host), Jack Paar, and Andy Williams. Cosby became the first black to star in a prime time television series. "I Spy" ran from 1965 to 1968 and won Cosby three Emmy awards.

In the 1970s Cosby appeared regularly in nightclubs in Las Vegas, Tahoe, and Reno, and did commercials for such sponsors as Jell-O, Del Monte, and Ford. From 1969 until 1972 he had his own television series, *The Bill Cosby Show.* During the early 1970s he developed and contributed vocals to the Saturday morning children's show "Fat Albert and the Cosby Kids." He appeared in such films as *Uptown Saturday Night* (1974), *Let's Do It Again* (1975), *A Piece of the Action* (1977), and the award-winning television movie "To All My Friends on Shore."

In 1975 Random House published his book *Bill Cosby's Personal Guide to Tennis; or, Don't Lower the Lob, Raise the Net.* For several years, he was involved in educational television with the Children's Television Workshop.

He also earned a master's degree and a doctorate in education from the University of Massachusetts.

He was star and creator of the consistently top-rated "The Cosby Show" from 1985 to 1992, author of two best-selling books, *Fatherhood* (1986) and *Time Flies* (1987), and a performer at the top venues in Las Vegas, where he earned $500,000 a week. He also won top fees as a commercial spokesperson for Jell-O, Kodak, and Coca Cola. He has recorded more than twenty-seven albums and has received five Grammy awards. Cosby is currently interested in hosting a new version of the old Groucho Marx game show, "You Bet Your Life."

Cosby and his wife, Camille, live in rural New England with their five children. The Cosbys made headlines when they donated $20 million to Spelman College in Atlanta.

Rupert Crosse

(1928–1973)

Actor

Born in Nevis, British West Indies, Rupert Crosse moved to Harlem at an early age. Crosse returned to Nevis at the age of seven, after the death of his father. Reared by his grandparents and strongly influenced by his grandfather, a schoolmaster, Crosse received a solid education before returning to New York, where he attended Benjamin Franklin High School. Crosse also later worked at odd jobs before interrupting high school to spend two years in military service in Germany and Japan. Once out of the service, Crosse finished high school and entered Bloomfield College and Seminary in New Jersey. Though he intended to become a minister, it seemed obvious from the jobs he had held—machinist, construction worker, and recreation counselor—that his career plans were not yet definite.

Crosse subsequently enrolled at the Daykarhanora School, studying acting and appearing in the Equity Library Theatre off-Broadway production *Climate of Eden*. He then transferred to John Cassavetes's workshop, where he helped to create *Shadows* (1961), winner of a Venice Film Festival award. Crosse's first Hollywood role was in a Cassavetes movie, *Too Late Blues* (1962). His most important film role was as Ned McCaslin in the screen adaptation of William Faulkner's Pulitzer Prize–winning novel, *The Reivers* (1969). Crosse was nominated for an Academy award as best supporting actor for this outstanding performance. His other film credits include *The Wild Seed* and *Ride in the Whirlwind*.

Crosse's stage credits are also numerous, including appearances in *Sweet Bird of Youth*, *The Blood Knot*, and *Hatful of Rain*. Television viewers saw

Crosse in "Dr. Kildare," "I Spy," and "The Man from U.N.C.L.E.," as well as several other series.

Rupert Crosse died of cancer on March 5, 1973, at his sister's home in Nevis.

Dorothy Dandridge (1922–1965)

Actress

Dorothy Dandridge was born on November 9, 1922, in Cleveland, Ohio; her mother was the actress Ruby Dandridge. As children, Dorothy and her sister, Vivian, performed as "The Wonder Kids," touring the United States. In 1934, they were joined by a third performer, Etta Jones, and the trio became the Dandridge Sisters. The Dandridge Sisters were a popular act, performing at the Cotton Club in Harlem and in the motion picture *A Day at the Races* (1937). By the 1940s, Dorothy Dandridge had struck out on her own, appearing in the "soundies" (musical shorts) *Easy Street; Yes, Indeed; Cow Cow Boogie; Jungle Jig; Paper Doll;* and *Sing for My Supper.*

Dandridge married Harold Nicholas (of the famed Nicholas Brothers dance team) in 1942, and had a daughter, Harolyn, in 1943. Harolyn was diagnosed as having a severe developmental disability, and was sent to an institution; shortly thereafter, Dandridge divorced Nicholas. She carried on a fairly successful career as a nightclub singer during the 1940s and 1950s. Her greatest triumph, however, came as a film actress, particularly in the all-black musical *Carmen Jones* (1954), for which she received an Oscar nomination for best actress, becoming the first African-American woman to receive this nomination. Another important role was in *Island in the Sun* (1957), where she was paired romantically with a white man, John Justin—a breakthrough in desegregating the screen. In 1959, Dandridge played Bess opposite Sidney Poitier's Porgy in the movie version of *Porgy and Bess.* Ultimately, she appeared in over twenty-five films.

Dandridge married the white Las Vegas restaurateur Jack Dennison in 1959, but three years later divorced him and declared personal bankruptcy. She died of an overdose of a prescription antidepressant on September 8, 1965.

Ossie Davis (1917–)

Actor

Ossie Davis grew up in Waycross, Georgia, and attended Howard University in Washington, DC, where Dr. Alain Locke suggested he pursue an acting career in New York. After completing service in the Army, Davis landed his first role in 1946 in the play *Jeb,* where he met Ruby Dee, whom he married two years later.

After appearing in the movie *No Way Out* (1950), Davis won Broadway roles in *No Time for Sergeants, Raisin in the Sun,* and *Jamaica.* In 1961, he and Dee starred in *Purlie Victorious,* which Davis himself had written. Two years later, they repeated their roles in the movie version, *Gone Are the Days.*

Davis's other movie credits from this period include *The Cardinal* (1963), *Shock Treatment* (1964), *The Hill* (1965), *A Man Called Adam* (1966), and *The Scalphunter* (1968).

Davis then directed such films as *Cotton Comes to Harlem* (1970) and *Black Girl* (1972). His play *Escape to Freedom: A Play about Young Frederick Douglass* had its debut at Town Hall in New York and later was published by Viking Junior Books. Davis has also been involved with television scripts and educational programming. "The Ruby Dee/Ossie Davis Story Hour" was produced for television in 1974. The arts education television series "With Ossie and Ruby" appeared in 1981. Davis and Ruby Dee also founded the Institute of New Cinema Artists and the Recording Industry Training Program.

Davis's continued movie appearances include roles in *Let's Do It Again* (1975), *Hot Stuff* (1979), and *Nothing Personal* (1979). Recent film credits include *Harry and Son* (1984) and Spike Lee's *School Daze* (1988) and *Do the Right Thing* (1989). In addition, Davis has appeared on such television series as "The Defenders," "The Nurses," "East Side, West Side," and "Evening Shade."

Sammy Davis, Jr.
(1925–1990)

Actor, Comedian, Dancer, Singer

Sammy Davis, Jr. was often called "the world's greatest entertainer," a title that attested to his remarkable versatility as singer, dancer, actor, mimic, and musician.

Davis was born in New York City on December 8, 1925. Four years later he began appearing in vaudeville shows with his father and uncle in the Will Mastin Trio. In 1931, Davis made his movie debut with Ethel Waters in *Rufus Jones for President;* this was followed by an appearance in *Season's Greetings.*

Throughout the 1930s, the Will Mastin Trio continued to play vaudeville, burlesque, and cabarets. In 1943 Davis entered the Army and served for

two years by writing, directing, and producing camp shows. After his discharge, he rejoined the trio, which in 1946 cracked the major club circuit with a successful Hollywood engagement.

Davis recorded a string of hits ("Hey There," "Mr. Wonderful," "Too Close for Comfort") during his steady rise to the top of show business. In November of 1954 he lost an eye in an automobile accident, which fortunately did not interfere with his career. He scored a hit in his first Broadway show, *Mr. Wonderful* (1956), and later repeated this success in *Golden Boy* (1964).

In 1959, Davis played Sportin' Life in the movie version of *Porgy and Bess*. Other Davis movies from this period include *Oceans 11* (1960) and *Robin and the Seven Hoods* (1964). His 1966 autobiography *Yes, I Can* became a best seller, and he starred in his own network television series.

In 1968, the NAACP awarded Davis its Spingarn Medal, and in subsequent years Davis continued to appear in films, television, and nightclubs. In 1972 he was involved in a controversy over his support of Richard Nixon, which was publicized by a famous photograph of Nixon hugging Davis at the 1972 Republican Convention. In 1974, Davis renounced his support of Nixon and Nixon's programs. In the same year, his television commercials for Japan's Suntory Whiskey won the grand prize at the Cannes Film Festival, and the National Academy of TV Arts and Sciences honored him for his unique contributions to television.

In 1975, Davis became host of an evening talk and entertainment show. In 1980, he marked his fiftieth anniversary as an entertainer, and the Friars Club honored him with its Annual Life Achievement Award. In 1989, he appeared in the film *Tap* with Gregory Hines and Harold Nicholas.

Davis married three times. His first marriage was in 1959 to singer Loray White. He married his second wife, actress Mai Britt, in 1961; she is the mother of his three children. In 1970, he married dancer Altovise Gore.

Ruby Dee was born in Cleveland but grew up in Harlem, attending Hunter College in New York. In 1942 she appeared in *South Pacific* with Canada Lee. Five years later, she met Ossie Davis while they were both playing in *Jeb*. They were married two years later.

Ruby Dee (1923–)

Actress

Ruby Dee's movies roles from this period include parts in *No Way Out* (1950), *Edge of the City* (1957), *Raisin in the Sun* (1961), Genet's *The Balcony* (1963), and *Purlie Victorious* (1963), written by Davis. Since 1960, she has appeared often on network television.

In 1965 Ruby Dee became the first black actress to appear in major roles at the American Shakespeare Festival in Stratford, Connecticut. She subsequently appeared in movies, including *The Incident* (1967), *Uptight* (1968), *Buck and the Preacher* (1972), *Black Girl* (1972; directed by Davis), and *Countdown at Kusini* (1976). Her musical satire *Take It from the Top,* in which she appeared with her husband in a showcase run at the Henry Street Settlement Theatre in New York, premiered in 1979.

As a team, Ruby Dee and Ossie Davis have recorded several talking story albums for Caedmon. In 1974, they produced "The Ruby Dee/Ossie Davis Story Hour," which was sponsored by Kraft Foods and carried by more than sixty stations of the National Black Network. Together they founded the Institute of New Cinema Artists to train young people for jobs in films and television, and then the Recording Industry Training Program to develop jobs in the music industry for disadvantaged youths. In 1981, Alcoa funded a television series for the Public Broadcasting System titled "With Ossie and Ruby," which used guests to provide an anthology of the arts. Recent film credits include *Cat People* (1982) and, with Ossie Davis, Spike Lee's *Do the Right Thing* (1989).

Katherine Dunham
(1910-)

Choreographer, Dancer

Katherine Dunham has for many years been one of the leading exponents of primitive dance in the world of modern choreography.

Born in Joliet, Illinois on June 22, 1910, Dunham attended Joliet Township Junior College and the University of Chicago, where she majored in anthropology. With funding from a Rosenwald fellowship, she was able to conduct anthropological studies in the Caribbean and Brazil. She later attended Northwestern University, where she earned her Ph.D., MacMurray College, where she received an L.H.D in 1972, and Atlanta University, where she received a Ph.D.L. in 1977.

In the 1930s she founded the Dunham Dance Company, whose repertory drew on techniques Dunham learned while studying in the Caribbean. She has used her training in anthropology and her study of primitive rituals from tropical cultures to create unique dance forms that blend primitive qualities with sophisticated Broadway stage settings. In 1940, she appeared in the musical *Cabin in the Sky,* which she had choreographed with George Balanchine. She later toured the United States with her dance group; after World War II, she played to enthusiastic audiences in Europe.

Among Dunham's choreographic pieces are *Le Jazz Hot* (1938), *Bhahiana* (1939), *Plantation Dances* (1940), *Haitian Suite (II)* (1941), *Tropical Revue* (1943), *Havana 1910/1919* (1944), *Carib Song* (1945), *Bal Negre* (1946), *Rhumba Trio* (1947), *Macumba* (1948), *Adeus Terras* (1949), *Spirituals* (1951), *Afrique du Nord* (1953), *Jazz Finale* (1955), *Ti 'Cocomaque* (1957), and *Anabacoa* (1963). Under the pseudonym Kaye Dunn, Dunham has written several articles and books on primitive dance. She has been referred to as "the mother of Afro-American dance." Dunham has founded schools of dance in Chicago, New York, Haiti, Stockholm, and Paris. She has also lectured at colleges and universities across the country.

On January 15, 1979, at Carnegie Hall in New York, Dunham received the 1979 Albert Schweitzer Music Award, and selections from her dance repertory from 1938 to 1975 were staged.

Stepin Fetchit (1902–1985)

Actor

Stepin Fetchit's place in movie history is a controversial one. Praised by some critics as an actor who opened doors for other African Americans in Hollywood, he has been berated by others for catering to racist stereotypes and doing little to raise the status of black actors. His characters—lazy, inarticulate, slow-witted, and always in the service of whites—have become so uncomfortable to watch that his scenes are sometimes cut when films in which he appeared are shown on television. Even at the height of his career, civil-rights groups protested his roles, which they considered demeaning caricatures.

Born Lincoln Theodore Monroe Andrew Perry in Key West, Florida in 1902, Stepin Fetchit's early career was in the Royal American Shows plantation revues. He and his partner, Ed Lee, took the names "Step 'n' Fetchit: Two Dancing Fools from Dixie." When the duo broke up, Fetchit appropriated "Stepin Fetchit" for himself.

Fetchit appeared in numerous motion pictures in the 1920s and 1930s, including *In Old Kentucky* (1927), *Salute* (1929), *Hearts in Dixie* (1929),

Show Boat (1929), *Swing High* (1930), *Stand Up and Cheer* (1934), *David Harum* (1934), *One More Spring* (1936), and *Zenobia* (1939). Fetchit earned a great deal of income from these films, and he spent it wildly. His extravagant lifestyle ended when he filed for bankruptcy in the 1930s.

Fetchit made sporadic appearances in films later in his life, among them *Miracle in Harlem* (1949), *Bend of the River* (1952), *Amazing Grace* (1974), and *Won Ton Ton, the Dog Who Saved Hollywood* (1976).

Redd Foxx

(1922–1991)

Actor, Comedian

Redd Foxx's most famous role was Fred Sanford, the junkman on the popular NBC series "Sanford and Son," which began in 1972. It was the second most popular role on television (after Archie Bunker in "All in the Family"). As a result, Foxx became one of the highest paid actors in show business. In 1976, it was reported that he was earning $25,000 per half-hour episode, plus 25 percent of the producer's net profit.

Sanford is actually Foxx's family name. He was born John Elroy Sanford in St. Louis, and both his father and his brother were named Fred. As a boy, he concocted a washtub band with two friends and played for tips on street corners, earning as much as $60 a night. At fourteen, Foxx and the band moved to Chicago; the group broke up during World War II.

Foxx then moved to New York, where he worked as a rack pusher in the garment district as he sought work in night clubs and on the black vaudeville circuit. While in New York, he played pool with a hustler named Malcolm Little, who later changed his name to Malcolm X.

In the early 1950s, Foxx tried to find work in Hollywood. He had a brief stint with *The Dinah Washington Show,* but mostly survived by performing a vaudeville act and working as a sign painter. His comedy act was adult entertainment, which limited his bookings.

Foxx's first real success came in 1955, when he began to record party records. He ultimately made more than fifty records, which sold over twenty million copies. His television career was launched in the 1960s with guest appearances on "The Today Show," "The Tonight Show," and other variety programs. He also began to appear in Las Vegas nightclubs.

Throughout the long run of "Sanford and Son," Foxx disputed with his producers over money. Originally, he was not receiving a percentage of the show's profits, which led him to sit out several episodes; a breach of contract suit filed by the producers resulted. There were racial undertones to these disputes, with Foxx referring to himself as a "tuxedo slave" and pointing to white stars who owned a percentage of their shows. Eventually, Foxx broke with the show and with NBC.

Foxx then signed a multimillion-dollar, multiyear contract with ABC, which resulted in a disastrous comedy variety hour that he quit on the air in October 1977. The ABC situation comedy "My Buddy," which he wrote, starred in, and produced, followed. In 1978, however, ABC filed a breach of contract suit. In 1979, Foxx was back at NBC planning a sequel to "Sanford and Son." He also made a deal with CBS, which in 1981 was suing him for a second time, allegedly to recover advances not paid back.

In 1976, Foxx performed in the MGM movie *Norman, Is That You?* He continued his appearances in nightclubs in Las Vegas and New York. In 1979, the book *Redd Foxx, B.S.* was published, comprised of chapters written by his friends.

In 1973, Foxx received the Entertainer of the Year award from the NAACP. In 1974, he was named police chief of Taft, Oklahoma, an all-black village of 600 people. He also ran a Los Angeles nightclub to showcase aspiring young comedians, both black and white. In addition, Foxx did numerous prison shows, probably more than any other famous entertainer, which he paid for out of his own pocket.

Al Freeman, Jr. (1934–)

Actor

Al Freeman, Jr. has won recognition for his many roles in the theater and motion pictures. His title role in the television film "My Sweet Charlie" (1970) earned him an Emmy award nomination.

Albert Cornelius Freeman, Jr. was born in San Antonio, Texas, son of the pianist Al Freeman, Sr., and Lottie Coleman Freeman. After attending schools in San Antonio and then Ohio, Freeman moved to the West Coast to study law at Los Angeles City College. Following a tour of duty with the Army in Germany, Freeman returned to college and changed his major to theater arts after being encouraged by fellow students to audition for a campus production.

Freeman did radio shows and appeared in small theater productions in the Los Angeles area before performing in his first Broadway play, *The*

Long Dream, in 1960. Other Broadway credits include *Kicks and Company* (1961), *Tiger, Tiger Burning Bright* (1962), *Blues for Mr. Charley* (1964), *Conversations at Midnight* (1964), *The Dozens* (1969), *Look to the Lilies* (1970), and *Medea* (1973).

Off Broadway, Freeman worked in *The Living Premise* (1963), *Trumpets of the Lord* (1963), *The Slave* (1964), and *Great MacDaddy* (1974). He also appeared in *Troilus and Cressida* (1965) and *Measure for Measure* (1966) for the New York Shakespeare Festival. He has also done more than a dozen feature films, including *Dutchman* (1967), *Finian's Rainbow* (1968), *The Detective* (1968), *The Lost Man* (1969), and *Castle Keep* (1969).

Freeman has appeared in such television series as "The Defenders," "The FBI," and "Naked City," and was featured as Lieutenant Ed Hall in ABC's daytime drama "One Life to Live." He also appeared on television in Norman Lear's "Hot[e]l Baltimore" (1975).

Morgan Freeman

(1937–)

Actor

Born in Memphis, Tennessee on June 1, 1937, Morgan Freeman grew up in Greenwood, Mississippi. He joined the U.S. Air Force in 1955, but left a few years later to pursue an acting career in Hollywood, taking classes at Los Angeles City College. He moved to New York City in the 1960s.

Freeman's first important role was in the short-running off-Broadway play *The Nigger-Lovers* in 1967. Soon thereafter, he appeared in the all-black version of the musical *Hello, Dolly!*

Americans who grew up in the 1970s remember Freeman fondly as a regular on the public television program "The Electric Company," in which he appeared from 1971–76; his most notable character was the hip Easy Reader. More theater roles followed in productions of *The Mighty Gents* (1978), *Othello* (1982), *The Gospel at Colonus* (1983), and *The Taming of the Shrew* (1990).

In 1987, Freeman was cast in the Broadway play *Driving Miss Daisy*. He won an Obie award for his portrayal of Hoke, the chauffeur for a wealthy white woman in the American South. Freeman recreated his Broadway role for the 1989 movie version of the play, receiving an Academy award nomination for best actor. In the same year, Freedman appeared in the highly successful movie *Glory,* about an all-black Union regiment in the Civil War.

Charles Gilpin was born in Virginia in 1878. After a brief period in school, he took up work as a printer's devil. In 1890, he began to travel intermittently with vaudeville troupes, a practice he continued for two decades, working as a printer, elevator operator, prizefight trainer, and porter during long interludes of theatrical unemployment.

From 1911 to 1914, Gilpin toured with a group called the Pan-American Octette. In 1914 he had a bit part in a New York production, *Old Ann's Boy*. Two years later he founded the Lafayette Theatre Company, one of the earliest black stock companies in New York.

After Eugene O'Neill saw Gilpin in *Abraham Lincoln,* he chose him to play the lead in *Emperor Jones,* the role in which he starred from 1920 to 1924. In 1921, Gilpin was awarded the NAACP Spingarn Award for his theatrical accomplishment.

Gilpin lost his voice in 1926 and was forced to earn his living once again as an elevator operator. He died in 1930.

Charles Gilpin (1878–1930)

Actor

A native of San Francisco, Danny Glover attended San Francisco State University and trained at the Black Actors Workshop of the American Conservatory Theatre.

Glover went on to appear in many stage productions, including *Island, Macbeth, Sizwe Banzi Is Dead,* and New York productions of *Suicide in B Flat, The Blood Knot,* and *Master Harold ... and the Boys,* which won him a Theatre World Award.

Glover's film credits include *Escape from Alcatraz* (1979), *Chu Chu and the Philly Flash* (1984), *Iceman* (1984), *Witness* (1985), *Places in the Heart* (1985), *The Color Purple* (1985), *Lethal Weapon* (1987) and its sequels, and *Bat 21* (1988).

On television, Glover appeared in the hit series "Hill Street Blues," the miniseries "Chiefs," "Lonesome Dove," and other projects, including "Many Mansions," "Face of Rage," "A Place at the Table," "Mandela," and "A Raisin in the Sun."

Danny Glover (1947–)

Actor

Whoopi Goldberg (1949–)

Actress, Comedienne

Born Caryn E. Johnson in Manhattan's Chelsea district on November 13, 1949, Whoopi Goldberg began performing at the age of eight at the children's program at Hudson Guild and Helen Rubenstein Children's Theatre. After trying her hand at theater, improvisation, and chorus parts on Broadway, she moved to San Diego in 1974 and appeared in repertory productions of *Mother Courage* and *Getting Out.*

Goldberg joined the Black St. Hawkeyes Theatre in Berkeley as a partner with David Schein, then went solo to create *The Spook Show,* performing in San Francisco and later touring the United States and Europe.

In 1983 Goldberg's work caught the attention of Mike Nichols, who created and directed her Broadway show a year later. She made her film debut in *The Color Purple* (1985), winning an NAACP Image award as well as a Golden Globe award.

Goldberg's other film credits include *Jumpin' Jack Flash, Burglar, Fatal Beauty, The Telephone, Homer and Eddie, Clara's Heart, Beverly Hills Brats, Ghost* (for which she won an Academy award as best supporting actress), *Sister Act, The Player,* and *Made in America.*

On television, she starred in "Whoopi Goldberg on Broadway," "Carol, Carl, Whoopi and Robin," and "Funny, You Don't Look 200," and hosted "Comedy Tonight." She received an Emmy nomination in 1985 for her guest appearance on "Moonlighting," has had a recurring role on "Star Trek: The Next Generation," and was a founding member of the Comic Relief benefit shows.

Louis Gossett, Jr. (1936–)

Actor

Born in Brooklyn on May 27, 1936, Louis Gossett began acting at the age of seventeen when a leg injury prevented him from pursuing his first love—basketball. In 1953, he won out over 445 contenders for the role of a black youngster in *Take a Giant Step,* for which he received a Donaldson Award as best newcomer of the year.

While performing in *The Desk Set* in 1958, Gossett was drafted by the professional basketball team the New York Knicks, but decided to remain in theater. Ultimately, he appeared in more than sixty stage productions, including such plays as *Lost in the Stars, A Raisin in the Sun, The Blacks,* and *Murderous Angels.*

On television, Gossett played character roles in such series as "The Nurses," "The Defenders," and "East Side, West Side." In 1977, he won an Emmy for his performance in the acclaimed mini-series "Roots." He also starred in such films as *Skin Game* (1971), *The Deep* (1977), *Officer and a Gentleman* (1983), *Iron Eagle* (1986), and *Iron Eagle II* (1988).

In 1989, Gossett starred in his own television series, "Gideon Oliver."

A Cleveland native, Arsenio Hall started his professional career as a standup comic, making the rounds of clubs and honing his presentation. Soon he was appearing on television specials as well as touring with noted musical performers.

Arsenio Hall (1960–)

Actor, Comedian, Talk Show Host

Hall was selected as a guest host of Fox Television's "Joan Rivers Show" when Rivers left, and soon won over both studio and television audiences. When this show concluded, he went on to star with Eddie Murphy in the movie *Coming To America* in 1988.

Paramount then hired Arsenio Hall to be the host of his own show. Within weeks after the show's premiere in 1989, Hall had again built a solid audience following, particularly with young viewers, and provided the most substantial competition that established evening talk shows had ever faced.

Arsenio Hall, on the set of his popular talk show "The Arsenio Hall Show," 1990.

Juanita Hall
(1902–1968)

Singer

Born on November 6, 1902 in Keyport, New Jersey, Hall studied at the Juilliard School of Music after singing in Catholic Church choirs as a child. Hall devoted her life to music as a singer in choirs and in stage and movie productions.

Her first major stage appearance was in Ziegfield's *Showboat* in 1927. Her lengthy stage career culminated in her role as "Bloody Mary" in Rodgers and Hammerstein's *South Pacific* in 1949. Hall went on to appear in *Flower Drum Song* and the movie version of both shows. She served as a soloist and assistant director of the Hall Johnson Choir (1931–1936), conducted the Works Progress Administration chorus in New York City (1936–1941), and organized the Juanita Hall Choir in 1942.

Hall performed at the Palladium in London and was a guest on the Ed Sullivan and Perry Como television shows. She was the recipient of the Donaldson, Antoinette Perry (Tony), and Bill Bojangles awards. Hall died February 28, 1968 in Bay Shore, New York.

Richard B.
Harrison
(1864–1935)

Actor

Richard B. Harrison was one of the few actors to gain national prominence on the basis of one role, his characterization of "De Lawd" in *Green Pastures.*

Harrison was born in Canada in 1864, and moved to Detroit as a young boy. There he worked as a waiter, porter, and handyman, saving whatever money he could to attend the theatrical offerings playing in town. After studying drama in Detroit, he made his professional debut in Canada in a program of readings and recitations.

For three decades, Harrison entertained black audiences with one-man performances of *Macbeth, Julius Caesar,* and *Damon and Pythias,* as well as with poems by Shakespeare, Poe, Kipling, and Paul Laurence Dunbar. In 1929, while serving on the faculty of North Carolina A&T as drama instructor, he was chosen for the part in *Green Pastures.*

When he died in 1935, Harrison had performed as "De Lawd" 1,656 times. His work earned him the 1930 Spingarn Medal and numerous honorary degrees.

After a distinguished career as a tap dancer, Gregory Hines made an unusual transition to dramatic actor.

Born in New York City, Hines began dancing with his brother Maurice under the instruction of tap dancer Henry LeTang. When Gregory was five, the brothers began performing professionally as the Hines Kids. Appearing in nightclubs and theaters around the country, they were able to benefit from contact with dance legends such as "Honi" Coles, Sandman Sims, the Nicholas Brothers, and Teddy Hale.

As teenagers, the two performed as the Hines Brothers. When Gregory reached age eighteen, the two were joined by their father, Maurice Sr., on drums, and the trio became known as Hines, Hines and Dad. They performed internationally and appeared on "The Tonight Show." Eventually, Gregory tired of the touring and settled in California, where he formed the jazz-rock band Severance.

Gregory Hines subsequently moved back to New York and landed a role in *The Minstrel Show* (1978). He later appeared in such Broadway musicals as *Eubie!* (1978), *Sophisticated Ladies* (1981), and *Comin' Uptown* (1990), as well as feature films, including *The Cotton Club* (1985), *White Nights* (1985), *Running Scared* (1985), and *Off Limits* (1988). Hines starred in the 1989 Tri-Star film *Tap* with Sammy Davis, Jr., not only acting and dancing, but singing as well.

On television, Hines appeared in the series "Amazing Stories" and the special "Motown Returns to the Apollo," which earned him an Emmy nomination. When not appearing in films or television, he toured internationally with a solo club act. *Gregory Hines*, his first solo album, was released by CBS/Epic in 1988. The album was produced by Luther Vandross, who teamed with Gregory for a single, *There's Nothing Better Than Love*, which reached number one on the R&B charts in 1987.

Hines has received numerous awards, including the Dance Educators award and the Theater World award. Hines has been nominated for several Tony awards, and in 1992 received the award for best actor in a musical for his role in *Jelly's Last Jam*.

Gregory Hines (1946–)

Actor, Dancer

Geoffrey Holder
(1930–)

Actor, Dancer,
Choreographer, Costume
Designer, Director

Geoffrey Holder has succeeded as an artist in many areas. Holder was born on August 1, 1930, in Port-of-Spain, Trinidad. At an early age, he left school to become the costume designer for his brother's dance troupe, which he took over in 1948. Holder led the dancers, singers, and steel band musicians through a series of successful small revues to the Caribbean Festival in Puerto Rico, where they represented Trinidad and Tobago. His appearances with his troupe in the mid-1950s were so popular that he is credited with launching the calypso vogue.

Early in his career, Holder appeared in New York as a featured dancer in *House of Flowers* (1954). He later performed with the Metropolitan Opera and as a guest star on many television shows. Film credits include the James Bond adventure *Live and Let Die* (1973) and *Dr. Doolittle* (1967), the children's classic starring Rex Harrison.

Holder received two Tony awards in 1976, as director and costume designer for the Broadway show *The Wiz*, the all-black adaptation of *The Wizard of Oz*. In 1978, he directed and choreographed the successful Broadway musical *Timbuktu*. In 1982 Holder appeared in the film *Annie* based on the hit Broadway musical, playing Punjab, a character from the original comic strip.

Holder received a Guggenheim fellowship to pursue his painting, and his impressionist paintings have been shown in galleries such as the Corcoran in Washington, DC. Holder also has written two books. *Black Gods, Green Islands* is a retelling of West Indian legends; his *Caribbean Cookbook* is a collection of recipes that Holder also illustrated.

Holder is married to the ballet dancer Carmen de Lavallade.

Lena Horne
(1917–)

Actress, Singer

Lena Horne has been called the most beautiful woman in the world, and her beauty has been no small factor in the continued success of her stage, screen, and nightclub career.

Horne was born on June 30, 1917, in Brooklyn, New York. She joined the chorus line at the Cotton Club in 1933, and then left to tour as a dancer with Noble Sissle's orchestra. She was given a leading role in *Blackbirds of 1939*, but the show folded quickly, whereupon she left to join Charlie Barnett's band as a singer. She made her first records (including the popular

"Haunted Town") with Barnett. In the early 1940s she also worked at New York's Cafe Society Downtown.

Horne then went to Hollywood, where she became the first black woman to sign a term contract with a film studio. Her films included *Panama Hattie* (1942), *Cabin in the Sky* (1943), *Stormy Weather* (1943), and *Meet Me in Las Vegas* (1956). In 1957 she took a break from her film and nightclub schedule to star in her first Broadway musical, *Jamaica*. Her popular recordings included "Stormy Weather," "Blues in the Night," "The Lady Is a Tramp," and "Mad about the Boy."

Throughout the 1960s and 1970s, Horne appeared in nightclubs and concerts. Her greatest recent success has been on Broadway. On May 12, 1981 she opened a one-woman show called *Lena Horne: The Lady and Her Music* to critical and box-office success. Although it opened too late to qualify for the Tony award nominations, the show was awarded a special Tony at the June ceremonies. In December of that year, she received New York City's highest cultural award, the Handel Medallion.

Horne was married for 23 years to Lennie Hayton, a white composer, arranger, and conductor who died April 24, 1971. She had been married previously to Louis Jones. A generous and gracious woman, Horne has quietly devoted much time to humane causes.

Eddie Hunter got his start while working as an elevator operator in a building frequented by the great tenor Enrico Caruso. Hunter had been writing vaudeville comedy parts on the side, and Caruso encouraged and helped him. In 1923, Hunter's show *How Come?*, a musical revue, reached Broadway.

Eddie Hunter

(1888–1974)

Comedian

Hunter performed in his own persona in the majority of the shows he wrote. *Going to the Races*, produced at the Lafayette Theatre in Harlem, had Hunter and his partner live on stage, interacting with a movie of themselves playing on the screen. Hunter considered this show one of his best. As one of the principal performers in *Blackbirds*, he toured Europe during the late 1920s. His show *Good Gracious* also toured Europe.

Depicting himself as "the fighting comedian," Hunter developed a reputation for speaking out against racial discrimination in the performing arts.

He frequently told the story about Phoenix, Arizona, where the male members of the show were forced to sleep in the theater where they were performing; accommodations for blacks simply did not exist at the time. Hunter characterized his European reception as being relatively free of prejudice, and felt that he only received the respect and recognition due to him when abroad.

By 1923, Hunter had a full recording contract with Victor Records. His recordings included "It's Human Nature to Complain," "I Got," and "My Wife Mamie." Shortly thereafter, he suspended his singing career to begin traveling with a new show he had developed. But when "talking" movies came into being, vaudeville fell out of favor. Eddie Hunter thus retired from show business and entered the real estate business in the 1930s.

He died in 1974, at the age of eighty-six.

Earle Hyman (1926–)

Actor

Earle Hyman was born in Rocky Mount, North Carolina on October 11, 1926. He began his acting career with the American Negro Theatre in New York City.

In 1963, Hyman made his foreign-language acting debut in Eugene O'Neill's *Emperor Jones* in Oslo, Norway, becoming the first American to perform a title role in a Scandinavian language. Hyman had originally become acquainted with Norway during a European trip made in 1957. He

Earle Hyman, performing with Frances Sternhagen in Driving Miss Daisy.

had planned to spend only two weeks in the Scandinavian country, but found himself so enchanted with Norway that he all but forgot the rest of Europe. When Hyman returned to New York, he resolved at once to learn Norwegian, and for practice, began to study the role of Othello (which he was performing for the Great Lakes Shakespeare Festival of 1962) in that language. By sheer coincidence, the director of *Den Nationale Scene* of Bergen, Norway, invited him to play Othello there in the spring of the following year, a performance that marked Hyman's first success in the Norwegian theater.

In 1965 Hyman returned to Norway to play *Emperor Jones* for a different theater company, and received high critical acclaim for his portrayal; Hyman remained in Norway intermittently for six years. Hyman has been the subject of several Norwegian radio broadcasts and television interviews, and he still spends six months each year in Scandinavia playing "Othello" and other classic roles. A bronze bust of the actor as Othello has been erected in the Norwegian theater where Hyman performed, and he has also been presented with an honorary membership in the Norwegian Society of Artists, the third foreigner and first American to be so honored.

Hyman's many Broadway and off-Broadway credits include *No Time for Sergeants* (1955), *St. Joan* (with Diana Sands at Lincoln Center; 1956), *Mister Johnson* (1956), *Waiting for Godot* (1957), Lorraine Hansberry's *Les Blancs* (1970), Edward Albee's *Lady from Dubuque,* and the black version of Eugene O'Neill's *Long Day's Journey into Night* (at the Public Theatre; 1981). Among other film and television work, Hyman has appeared on the daytime drama "Love of Life" and on "The Cosby Show."

Rex Ingram (1895–1969)

Actor

A major movie and radio personality during the 1930s and 1940s, Rex Ingram was born in 1895 aboard the *Robert E. Lee,* a Mississippi riverboat on which his father was a stoker.

Ingram attended military schools, where he displayed an interest in acting. After working briefly as a cook for the Union Pacific Railroad and as head of his own small window-washing business, Ingram gravitated to Hollywood, where in 1919 he appeared in the original Tarzan film. Roles in such classics as *Lord Jim, Beau Geste* (1926), *King Kong* (1933), *The Green Pastures* (1936), and *Huckleberry Finn* (1939) followed. During the late 1920s and early 1930s, Ingram also appeared prominently in theater in San Francisco. During the late 1930s he starred in daytime radio soap operas and in Works Progress Administration theater projects.

Ingram continued with a distinguished career on the New York stage, and in film and television. In 1957, he played Pozzo in *Waiting for Godot*. Later film credits include *Elmer Gantry* (1960), *Your Cheating Heart* (1964), *Hurry Sundown* (1967), and *Journey to Shiloh* (1968).

**Judith Jamison
(1944–)**

Choreographer

Born in Philadelphia, Judith Jamison started to study dance at the age of six. She was discovered in her early twenties by the choreographer Agnes De Mille, who admired her spontaneous style.

From 1965 to 1980, Jamison was a principal dancer for Alvin Ailey's American Dance Theater, performing a wide gamut of black roles that Ailey choreographed for her. She has made guest appearances with many other dance companies, including the American Ballet Theatre, and with such opera companies as the Vienna State Opera and the Munich State Opera. In the 1980s, Jamison scored a great success on Broadway in *Sophisticated Ladies,* a musical featuring the music of Duke Ellington. In 1988 she formed the Jamison Project, of which she is currently director.

**James Earl Jones
(1931–)**

Actor

Jones (whose father Robert Earl Jones was featured in the movie *One Potato, Two Potato*) was born in Tate County, Mississippi, and raised by his grandparents on a farm near Jackson, Michigan. He turned to acting after a brief period as a premedical student at the University of Michigan (from which he graduated cum laude in 1953) and upon completion of military service with the Army's Cold Weather Mountain Training Command in Colorado.

After moving to New York, Jones studied at the American Theatre Wing, making his off-Broadway debut in 1957 in *Wedding in Japan*. Since then, he has appeared in numerous plays, on and off Broadway, including *Sunrise at Campobello* (1958), *The Cool World* (1960), *The Blacks* (1961), *The Blood Knot* (1964), and *Anyone, Anyone*.

Jones's career as an actor progressed slowly until he portrayed Jack Jefferson in the Broadway smash hit *The Great White Hope*. The play was based on the life of Jack Johnson, the first black heavyweight champion. For this performance, Jones received the 1969 Tony award for the best dramatic actor in a Broadway play, and a Drama Desk award for one of the best performances of the 1968–1969 New York season.

By the 1970s, Jones was appearing in roles traditionally performed by white actors, including the title role in *King Lear* and an award-winning performance as Lenny in Steinbeck's *Of Mice and Men.*

In 1978, Jones appeared in the highly controversial *Paul Robeson,* a one-man show on Broadway. Many leading blacks advocated a boycott of the show because they felt it did not measure up to the man himself. Many critics, however, gave the show high praise.

In 1980, Jones starred in Athol Fugard's *A Lesson from Aloes,* a top contender for a Tony award that year. He also appeared in the Yale Repertory Theater Production of *Hedda Gabler.* In the spring of 1982, he co-starred with Christopher Plummer on Broadway in *Othello,* a production acclaimed as among the best ever done. In 1987 Jones received a Tony award for his performance in August Wilson's Pulitzer Prize–winning play *Fences.*

Jones's early film credits include *Dr. Strangelove* (1964) and *River Niger* (1976). He was the screen voice of Darth Vader in *Star Wars* (1977) and its sequel *The Empire Strikes Back* (1980). Jones has also appeared in the horror movie *Red Tide,* the adventure film *Conan the Barbarian* (1982), *Matewan* (1987), and *Field of Dreams* (1989).

Among numerous television appearances, Jones portrayed author Alex Haley in "Roots: The Next Generation" (1979) and has narrated documentaries for the Public Broadcasting System.

In 1976, Jones was elected to the Board of Governors of the Academy of Motion Picture Arts and Sciences. In 1979, New York City presented him with the Mayor's Award of Honor for Arts and Culture. He received an honorary doctorate of humane letters from the University of Michigan in 1971 and the New York Man of the Year Award in 1976. In 1985, he was inducted into the Theater Hall of Fame.

Canada Lee
(1907–1951)

Actor

Canada Lee was born Leonard Corneliou Canagata in Manhattan on May 3, 1907. After studying violin as a young boy, he ran off to Saratoga to become a jockey. Failing in this, he returned to New York and began a boxing career. In 1926, after winning ninety out of one hundred fights, including the national amateur lightweight title, he turned professional. Over the next few years, he won 175 out of some 200 fights against such top opponents as Jack Britton and Vince Dundee. In 1933, a detached retina brought an end to his ring career. He had acquired the name Canada Lee when a ring announcer could not pronounce his real name.

In 1934 Lee successfully auditioned at the Harlem YMCA for his first acting role, which was in a Works Progress Administration production of *Brother Moses*. In 1941, Orson Welles, who had met Lee in the Federal Theatre's all-black production of *Macbeth,* chose him to play Bigger Thomas in the stage version of Richard Wright's famed novel, *Native Son*.

In 1944, Lee served as narrator of a radio series called "New World Comin'," the first such series devoted to racial issues. That same year, he also appeared in Alfred Hitchcock's film *Lifeboat,* and in the Broadway play *Anna Lucasta*.

Spike Lee
(1957–)

Filmmaker

Lee was born March 20, 1957 in Atlanta, Georgia. His family moved briefly to Chicago before settling in New York in 1959. Lee received a B.A. in mass communication in 1979 from Morehouse College. After a summer internship at Columbia Pictures in Burbank, California, Lee enrolled in New York University's prestigious Institute of Film and Television. He received an M.A. in filmmaking in 1983. While at New York University he wrote and directed *Joe's Bed-Sty Barbershop: We Cut Heads,* for which he won the 1982 Student Academy award given by the Academy of Motion Picture Arts and Sciences. The movie was later shown on public television's Independent Focus Series.

Notable films by Lee include *She's Gotta Have It* (1986), *School Daze* (1988), *Do The Right Thing* (1989), *Mo' Better Blues* (1990), *Jungle Fever* (1991), and *Malcolm X* (1992). *She's Gotta Have It* won the L.A. Film Critics New Generation award and the Prix de Jeunesse at the Cannes Film Festival.

Lee has also written two books: *Spike Lee's Gotta Have It: Inside Guerilla Filmmaking* (1987) and *Uplift the Race* (1988). He has established a fellow-

Spike Lee, in a scene from the movie She's Gotta Have It, *1986.*

ship for minority filmmakers at New York University and is a trustee of Morehouse College. Lee's production company, Forty Acres and a Mule Filmworks, is located in Brooklyn, New York.

Jackie "Moms" Mabley (1897–1975)

Comedienne

Mabley was born Loretta Mary Aiken in North Carolina, and entered show business as a teenager when the team of Buck and Bubbles gave her a bit part in a vaudeville skit called "Rich Aunt from Utah."

With the help of comedienne Bonnie Bell Drew, Mabley developed a monologue and was soon being booked on the black vaudeville circuit. Influenced by such acts as Butterbeans and Susie, she developed her own comic character, a world-weary old woman in a funny hat and droopy stockings, delivering her gags with a mixture of sassy folk wisdom and sly insights.

Her first big success came in 1923 at Connie's Inn in New York. Engagements at the Cotton Club in Harlem and at Club Harlem in Atlantic City followed.

Moms Mabley was noticed by white audiences in the early 1960s. Her record album *Moms Mabley at the U.N.* became a commercial success, and was followed by *Moms Mabley at the Geneva Conference.* In 1962 she made her Carnegie Hall debut on a program with Cannonball Adderley and Nancy Wilson. Her subsequent Broadway, film, television, and record successes made her the favorite of a new generation.

Moms Mabley died on May 23, 1975 at the age of seventy-eight in the White Plains, New York hospital.

Hattie McDaniel

(1898-1952)

Actress

Hattie McDaniel was born on June 10, 1898 in Wichita, Kansas, and moved to Denver, Colorado as a child. After a period of singing for Denver radio as an amateur, she entered vaudeville professionally, and by 1924 was a headliner on the Pantages circuit.

By 1931 McDaniel had made her way to Hollywood. After a slow start, during which she supported herself as a maid and washer woman, she gradually began to acquire more movie roles. Her early film credits included *Judge Priest* (1934), *The Little Colonel* (1935), *Showboat* (1936), *Saratoga* (1937), and *Nothing Sacred.* Her portrayal of a "mammy" figure in *Gone with the Wind,* a role for which she received an Oscar award in 1940 as best supporting actress, is still regarded as a definitive interpretation. McDaniel was the first African American to receive an Oscar.

McDaniel subsequently appeared in films such as *The Great Lie* (1941), *In This Our Life* (1942), *Johnny Come Lately* (1943), *Since You Went Away* (1944), *Margie* (1946), *Never Say Goodbye* (1946), *Song of the South* (1946), *Mr. Blandings Builds His Dream House* (1948), *Family Honeymoon* (1948), and *The Big Wheel* (1949).

In addition to her movie roles, McDaniel enjoyed success in radio during the 1930s as Hi-Hat Hattie, and during the 1940s in the title role of the very successful "Beulah" series.

McDaniel died on October 26, 1952.

Butterfly McQueen's portrayal of Prissy in *Gone With the Wind* (1939) rivals Hattie McDaniel's Oscar-winning role as the "mammy," and is certainly as popular with audiences as Vivien Leigh's Scarlett O'Hara or Clark Gable's Rhett Butler.

Born Thelma McQueen on January 8, 1911 in Tampa, Florida, McQueen began her career in the 1930s performing as a radio actress in "The Goldbergs," "The Danny Kaye Show," "The Jack Benny Show," and "The Beulah Show." She also appeared on stage in *Brown Sugar* (1937), *Brother Rat* (1937), and *What a Life* (1938).

After her role in *Gone with the Wind* in 1939, McQueen was cast in other motion pictures such as *I Dood It* (1943), *Cabin in the Sky* (1943), *Mildred Pierce* (1945), and *Duel in the Sun* (1947). She appeared as Oriole on the television series "Beulah" from 1950 to 1952.

Given her outspokenness against racism and discrimination and her refusal to play stereotyped servant roles, McQueen's appearances after this period were sporadic. In 1968, she won accolades for her performance in the off-Broadway play *Curley McDimple*. She was cast in the television program "The Seven Wishes of Joanna Peabody" in 1978, and the film *Mosquito Coast* in 1986. McQueen received a B.A. in Spanish from New York City College in 1975.

Butterfly McQueen (1911–)

Actress

Micheaux was born in 1884 at Metropolis, Illinois. Little is known about his early years, other than his leaving home at age seventeen and his brief work as a pullman porter. In 1904 he began homesteading in Gregory County, South Dakota.

Micheaux was a farmer who loved to read and had a flair for writing. In 1913 he wrote, published, and promoted *The Conquest: Story of a Negro Pioneer*. This novel was followed by *Forged Note: Romance of the Darker Races* in 1915 and *The Homesteader* in 1917. Much of his writing was melodramatic and probably autobiographical.

In 1918 the Lincoln Picture Company, an independent African-American film producer, tried to buy the film rights to *The Homesteader*. When Micheaux insisted that he direct the planned movie, the deal fell through.

Oscar Deveraux Micheaux (1884–1951)

Filmmaker, Author

Micheaux went to New York where he formed the Oscar Micheaux Corporation. Between 1919 and 1937 Micheaux made about thirty films, including *Body and Soul,* a 1924 movie in which Paul Robeson made his first cinematic appearance.

Although Micheaux was an excellent self-promoter of his books and films, his company went into bankruptcy in 1928. By 1931, however, Micheaux was back in the film business, producing and directing *The Exile* (1931) and *Veiled Aristocrats* (1932). Between 1941 and 1943 he wrote four more books, *Wind from Nowhere, Case of Mrs. Wingate, Masquerade,* and *Story of Dorothy Stansfield.* In 1948 he made his last film, *The Betrayal.* While none of Micheaux's films achieved critical acclaim, they were quite popular with African-American audiences and attracted a limited white following. While his characters broke with the black stereotypes of the day, the themes of his movies ignored racial injustice and the day-to-day problems of African Americans.

Micheaux was known as a hard worker and a natty dresser who consumed neither alcohol nor tobacco. Although he made a great deal of money, all of it was squandered away. Micheaux died penniless in Charlotte, North Carolina. Conflicting dates are given for his death: March 26, 1951 and April 1, 1951.

Florence Mills

(1895–1927)

Singer, Dancer

Florence Mills was born in Washington, DC on January 25, 1895. She made her debut there at the age of five in *Sons of Ham.* In 1903 the family moved to Harlem, and in 1910 she joined her sisters in an act called the Mills Trio. She later appeared with a group called the Panama Four, which included Ada "Bricktop" Smith.

In 1921 Mills appeared in *Shuffle Along,* a prototype for African-American musicals, and her success led to a long engagement at the Plantation, a New York night spot. After a successful appearance in London, she returned to the United States in 1924 to star in *From Dixie to Broadway,* in which she performed her trademark song, "I'm Just a Little Blackbird Lookin' for a Bluebird." Later, her own *Blackbirds* revue was a great success in London and Paris.

Mills returned to the United States in 1927. Exhausted by her work abroad, she entered the hospital on October 25 for a routine appendectomy, and died suddenly a few days later.

Most celebrated as a concert artist, Abbie Mitchell also performed on the stage and in light musical comedy. At the age of thirteen she came to New York City from Baltimore, joining Will Marion Cook's Clorindy Company, and later achieving her first real success with the Williams and Walker Company.

By 1923, having performed in almost every European country, Mitchell returned home to give the first of her many vocal concerts in the United States. Mitchell also performed with many opera companies and acted in several plays, including *Coquette* (with Helen Hayes; 1927), *Stevedore* (1934) and Langston Hughes's *Mulatto* (1937). She also headed the voice department at Tuskegee Institute for three years.

Mitchell died in 1960 after a long illness.

Abbie Mitchell (1884–1960)

Singer, Actress

Mitchell was born in Harlem on March 27, 1934, and attended New York's famed High School of the Performing Arts. Mitchell was the first African-American male to receive the high school's dance award in 1951.

Upon graduation in 1952, Mitchell enrolled on a scholarship in the School of American Ballet, run by the eminent choreographer George Balanchine, who also directed the New York City Ballet. In 1955 Mitchell was invited by Balanchine to join the New York City Ballet. Before long he was a principal dancer in the company, performing in such works as *Agon* and *A Midsummer Night's Dream*.

Mitchell left the New York City Ballet in 1969 to establish the Dance Theater of Harlem, which he founded to give young African Americans an opportunity to get out of the ghetto through the arts. Mitchell and the studio have received numerous awards and citations, including the Changers Award given by *Mademoiselle* magazine in 1970 and the Capezio Dance Award in 1971. Surviving a financial crisis in 1990, the school and company are now back on their feet, though treading carefully due to the precarious state of the arts in the United States.

Arthur Mitchell (1934–)

Dancer, Choreographer

Eddie Murphy was born on April 3, 1961 in the Bushwick section of Brooklyn, the son of a New York City policeman and an amateur comedian. As a youngster he performed imitations of cartoon characters and, as he grew older, began preparing comic routines with impressions of Elvis Presley, Jackie Wilson, Al Green, and the Beatles.

Eddie Murphy (1961–)

Actor, Comedian

Murphy attended Roosevelt Junior-Senior High School on Long Island and hosted a talent show at the Roosevelt Youth Center before beginning to call local talent agents to secure bookings at Long Island nightclubs. He was a little-known stand-up comedian when he made his first appearance on the late-night television show "Saturday Night Live" in 1980. He made a memorable impression, and within three years was hailed as a major new star based on his work in the hit films *48 Hours* (1982) and *Trading Places* (1983).

After his success with the first two Paramount films, Murphy starred in *Beverly Hills Cop* (1985) and its sequel *Beverly Hills Cop II* (1987), which were two of the major box office hits of the decade. The concert film *Raw* followed, as well as an effort at light-hearted fantasy, *The Golden Child*. Murphy's more recent film appearances include *Coming to America, Harlem Nights, Boomerang,* and *The Distinguished Gentleman*.

Clarence Muse
(1889–1979)

Actor, Director

Perhaps best known for his film acting, Clarence Muse was also successful as a director, playwright, and actor on the stage.

Muse was born in Baltimore, though his parents came from Virginia and North Carolina, and his grandfather from Martinique. After studying law at Dickinson University in Pennsylvania, Muse sang as part of a hotel quartet in Palm Beach, Florida. A subsequent job with a stock company took him on tour through the South with his wife and son. Coming to New York, he barely scraped together a living, mostly performing as a vaudevillian.

After several plays with the now-famous Lincoln Theatre group and the Lafayette Players in Harlem, and a Broadway stint in *Dr. Jekyll and Mr. Hyde,* where having white roles played by blacks in white-face created quite a controversy, Muse had established himself as an actor and singer.

Muse's first movie role was in *Hearts in Dixie* (1929), produced at the William Fox Studio, in which Muse played a ninety-year-old man. Later, he returned to the stage for the role of a butler in the show that was to be called *Under the Virgin Moon.* After Muse wrote the theme song, the title was changed to his *When It's Sleepy Time Down South.* Both the song and the show were hits.

When the Federal Theatre Project in Los Angeles presented Hall Johnson's *Run Little Chillun,* Muse directed the show. After its successful two-year run, Muse made the screen adaption *Way Down South* (1939).

During Muse's career, he appeared in 219 films, and was at one time one of the highest paid black actors, often portraying faithful servant "Uncle Tom" characters. His movie credits include *Huckleberry Finn* (1931), *Cabin in the Cotton* (1932), *Count of Monte Cristo* (1934), *So Red the Rose* (1935), *Showboat* (1936), *The Toy Wife* (1938), *The Flame of New Orleans* (1941), *Tales of Manhattan* (1942), *Heaven Can Wait* (1943), *Night and Day* (1946), *An Act of Murder* (1948), *Porgy and Bess* (1959), *Buck and the Preacher* (1971), and *Car Wash* (1976). His last film was *Black Stallion* in 1979. He also appeared over the years in concerts and on radio.

Muse died October 13, 1979, the day before his ninetieth birthday. He had lived in Perris, California, on his Muse-a-While Ranch.

Fayard Nicholas (1917–)

Harold Nicholas (1924–)

Dancers

The Nicholas Brothers were one of the great tap dance teams of the first half of the twentieth century, whose acrobatics and precision were admired by the likes of Fred Astaire and George Balanchine, and whose appearances in motion pictures provide a record of their astounding abilities.

Fayard Nicholas was born in 1917; Harold in 1924. Their professional debut came on the radio program "The Horn and Hardart Kiddie Hour" in 1931. The following year they became a featured act at Harlem's Cotton Club. They made their first Broadway appearance in the *Ziegfeld Follies* of 1936; this was followed by *Babes in Arms* in 1937.

The Nicholas Brothers' film debut was in *Pie Pie Blackbird* in 1932, and they appeared in several other movies in the 1930s and 1940s, including *Sun Valley Serenade* (1941) and *Stormy Weather* (1943). The latter is particularly memorable for the sequence in which they are featured.

Harold Nicholas married actress Dorothy Dandridge in 1942, but the couple later divorced. The two brothers continue to be active in the world of dance: Harold co-starred with Gregory Hines in the movie *Tap* in 1989, and Fayard won a Tony award for best choreographer for the Broadway musical *Black and Blue* in the same year. In 1992, the Nicholas Brothers were honored by the Kennedy Center.

**Frederick O'Neal
(1905–)**

Actor

Frederick O'Neal is the first black to hold the position of president of Actor's Equity, a fitting tribute to his long years of service to the American theater as both actor and teacher.

O'Neal was born August 27, 1905 in Brookville, Mississippi. After his father's death in 1919, he moved with his family to St. Louis, finishing high school there and appearing in several Urban League dramatic productions.

In 1927, with the help of some friends in St. Louis, O'Neal founded the Ira Aldridge Players, the second African-American acting troupe in America. For the next ten years, he played in thirty of its productions. In 1937 he came to New York, and three years later helped found the American Negro Theater. Today, its alumni include such established stars as Sidney Poitier, Earle Hyman, Harry Belafonte, Ruby Dee, Ossie Davis, and Hilda Simms.

O'Neal himself starred in *Anna Lucasta* (1944), for which he won the Clarence Derwent Award and the Drama Critics award for the best supporting performance by an actor on Broadway. He was later featured in *Take a Giant Step, The Winner,* and several other stage productions. His films include *Pinky* (1949) and *The Man with the Golden Arm* (1956). He has also appeared on several television dramatic and comedy shows.

In 1964, O'Neal became the first black president of Actor's Equity. After devoting himself full time to Actor's Equity, O'Neal was in 1970 elected international president of the Associated Actors and Artists of America, the parent union of all show-business performers' unions. He became president and chairman of the board of the Schomburg Center for Research in Black Culture to raise money to conserve and preserve materials in the center, to solicit material, and toward construction of a new building. He has been a member of the New York State Council on the Arts, president of the Catholic Interracial Council, chairman of the AFL-CIO Civil Rights Committee, and vice president of the A. Philip Randolph Institute. In 1980 he received the National Urban Coalition's Distinguished Trade Unionist award, and in 1990 he received a special tribute from the Black Filmmakers Hall of Fame.

**Sidney Poitier
(1927–)**

Actor

Sidney Poitier was born on February 20, 1927 in Miami, Florida, but moved to the Bahamas with his family at a very early age. At age fifteen he returned to Miami; he later rode freight trains to New York City, where he found employment as a dishwasher. After Pearl Harbor, he enlisted in the Army and served on active duty for four years.

Back in New York, Poitier auditioned for the American Negro Theater but was turned down by director Frederick O'Neal. After working diligently to improve his diction, Poitier was accepted in the theater group, receiving acting lessons in exchange for doing backstage chores.

In 1950 Poitier made his Hollywood debut in *No Way Out,* followed by successful appearances in *Cry the Beloved Country* (1952), *Red Ball Express* (1952), *Go, Man, Go* (1954), *Blackboard Jungle* (1956), *Goodbye, My Lady* (1956), *Edge of the City* (1957), *Band of Angels* (1957), *Something of Value* (1957), and *Porgy and Bess* (1959), among others. Poitier starred on Broadway in 1959 in Lorraine Hansberry's award-winning *Raisin in the Sun,* and repeated this success in the movie version of the play in 1961.

In 1965 Poitier became the first black to win an Oscar for a starring role, receiving this award for his performance in *Lilies of the Field.* Seven years earlier, Poitier had been the first black actor nominated for the award for his portrayal of an escaped convict in *The Defiant Ones.*

Subsequent notable film appearances include performances in *To Sir with Love* (1967), *Heat of the Night* (1967), *Guess Who's Coming to Dinner* (1968; with Spencer Tracy and Katharine Hepburn), *Buck and the Preacher* and *A Warm December* (1972 and 1973; both of which he also directed), *Uptown Saturday Night* (1974), and *A Piece of the Action* (1977). After years of inactivity, Poitier performed in two additional films, *Little Nikita* and *Shoot To Kill,* both released in 1988. His directing ventures include *Stir Crazy* (with Richard Pryor and Gene Wilder; 1980), *Hanky Panky* (with Gilda Radner; 1982), and the musical *Fast Forward* (1985).

Poitier spent two years writing his memoirs, *This Life,* published by Knopf in 1980. In 1981, Citadel Press published *The Films of Sidney Poitier,* by Alvin H. Marill.

Pearl Primus's anthropological approach to dance makes her one of the most purposeful figures in that medium: for her, dance is education, not merely entertainment. Her aim is to show audiences and dancers alike the African roots of dance.

Pearl Primus
(1919–)

Dancer, Choreographer

Primus was born in Trinidad on November 29, 1919. Originally intending to pursue a career in medicine, she received a bachelor of arts degree in pre-medical sciences and biology from Hunter College, with graduate work in medical education and psychology. But 1940s America did not welcome blacks or women in medicine, and after seeking employment in vain, Primus sought assistance from the government's National Youth Administration. She was put into a youth administration dance group, and by 1941 was accepted into New York City's New Dance Group. Her professional debut was at the Young Men's Hebrew Association in New York City on February 14, 1943. In April of that year, she began appearing at Café Society Downtown, the famed New York City nightclub, but left after ten months for an appearance on Broadway at the Belasco Theater. By this time she had her own dance company, Pearl Primus, Percival Borde & Company. She toured Africa and the southern United States, and incorporated what she learned into her choreography.

Primus is best known for the dances *African Ceremonial* and *Strange Fruit,* which were incorporated into her *Solos for Performance at the Café Society* (c. 1944), and *Hard Times Blues* (1945).

Richard Pryor

(1940–)

Comedian, Actor

Comedian Richard Pryor has had great success as a stand-up comedian, writer, actor, and recording star. He has often used elements of his unconventional upbringing and adult life as material in his comedy routines.

Born Richard Franklin Lennox Thomas Pryor III on December 1, 1940, he was raised by his grandmother in the Peoria, Illinois brothel she ran. His mother worked there as a prostitute. His parents married when he was three years old, but the union did not last. His grandmother was a strict disciplinarian and young Richard was often beaten.

In school Pryor was often in trouble with the authorities; he was expelled from high school for striking a teacher. In 1958 he joined the Army and spent two years in Germany. He returned to Peoria after his military service and during the early 1960s began his work as a stand-up comic on a local circuit. He moved to New York City's Greenwich Village in 1963, where he honed his stand-up routine. A 1964 appearance on "The Ed Sullivan Show" led to his first movie role in *The Busy Body* (1966), followed by bit parts in *The Green Berets* and *Wild in the Streets.* During this time Pryor continued to play to live audiences.

In 1972 Pryor played Piano Man in *Lady Sings the Blues* and earned an Academy award nomination for his performance. Throughout the 1970s,

Pryor continued his work as a stand-up comic and also contributed his writing talents to television's "The Flip Wilson Show" and "Sanford and Son," Mel Brooks's film *Blazing Saddles,* and Lily Tomlin's television special, "Lily," for which he won an Emmy award. He won two of his five Grammy awards for his comedy albums *That Nigger's Crazy* (1974) and *Bicentennial Nigger* (1976).

Pryor wrote and starred in *Bingo Long and the Traveling All Stars and Motor Kings* in 1976 and received raves for his work in *Silver Streak,* also in 1976. In 1979 the comedian's film *Richard Pryor Live in Concert* brought his stand-up act to millions.

In 1978 Pryor suffered a major heart attack, and in 1980, while freebasing cocaine, he set himself ablaze and suffered severe injuries. He addresses these incidents in his second concert movie, *Live on Sunset Strip* (1982). In 1985 Pryor co-wrote, directed, and starred in *Jo Jo Dancer, Your Life Is Calling,* a semi-autobiographical tale of a comedian who relives his life immediately following a near fatal accident. Pryor's later films include *The Toy, Some Kind of Hero, Brewster's Millions, Critical Condition, Stir Crazy, Bustin' Loose, Moving,* and *See No Evil, Hear No Evil.* In 1989 Pryor co-starred with Eddie Murphy in *Harlem Nights.*

Pryor has been in failing health in recent years. He was diagnosed with multiple sclerosis in 1986 and has had triple bypass heart surgery. He is reportedly often wheelchair bound and lives a reclusive life in his Bel Air, California home.

Phylicia Rashad (1948-)

Actress

Known to millions as Claire Huxtable, "America's Favorite Mom" from "The Cosby Show," Phylicia Rashad has led a distinguished acting career on television and the stage. She was born on June 19, 1948, in Houston, Texas, and until 1985 was known as Phylicia Ayers-Allen. Her sister is the famous Debbie Allen; both sisters received early instruction in music, acting, and dance. Phylicia graduated magna cum laude from Howard University in 1970 with a B.F.A. in theater.

Early in her career, Rashad played the character Courtney Wright in the soap opera "One Life to Live." Her big break came with "The Cosby Show," in which she and Bill Cosby presided over the Huxtable family for seven years, from 1985 to 1992. Rashad has also appeared in Broadway and off-Broadway productions of *The Cherry Orchard, The Wiz, Zora, Dreamgirls, A Raisin in the Sun,* and *Into the Woods.*

Rashad has received two honorary doctorates, one from Providence College in Rhode Island and one from Barber-Scotia College in North Carolina. She and her husband Ahmad Rashad, a sportscaster for NBC, live in Westchester County, New York.

Bill "Bojangles" Robinson (1878–1949)

Dancer

Bill Robinson was born on May 25, 1878 in Richmond, Virginia. Having been orphaned early, he was raised by his grandmother, a former slave. By the time he was eight, he was earning his own way by dancing in the street for pennies and working as a stable boy.

In 1887, Robinson toured the South in a show called *The South Before the War.* The following year, he moved to Washington, DC, where he again worked as a stable boy. By 1896 he had teamed up with George Cooper. This act was successful on the Keith circuit until the slump of 1907 caused it to fold. Robinson returned to Richmond and worked as a waiter until a year later when he was taken up by a theatrical manager and became a cabaret and vaudeville headliner.

In 1927 Robinson starred on Broadway in *Blackbirds,* and in 1932 he had top billing in *Harlem's Heaven,* the first all-black motion picture with sound. Later, he scored a Hollywood success by teaching his famous stair dance to Shirley Temple in *The Little Colonel* (1936). Robinson made fourteen movies, including *The Littlest Rebel* (1935), *In Old Kentucky* (1936), *Rebecca of Sunnybrook Farm* (1938), *Stormy Weather* (1943), and *One Mile from Heaven* (1938).

Throughout his long career on stage and in movies, Robinson was known as the "King of Tap Dancers." Robinson died on November 25, 1949.

Richard Roundtree (1942–)

Actor

Richard Roundtree is best known as John Shaft, the tough, renegade detective from the movie *Shaft* (1971). Born in New Rochelle, New York, on July 9, 1942, Roundtree graduated from New Rochelle High School and attended Southern Illinois University on a football scholarship. After brief stints as a suit salesman and a model, he began a stage career with the Negro Ensemble Company. With *Shaft* (1971) and its sequels, *Shaft's Big*

Score (1972) and *Shaft in Africa* (1973), Roundtree reached the peak of his career and became a pop icon.

Roundtree subsequently appeared in the films *Embassy* (1972), *Charley One Eye* (1973), *Earthquake* (1974), *Diamonds* (1975), and *Man Friday* (1976). He appeared in the television miniseries "Roots" (1977) and continues to be cast in various television programs and motion pictures.

The 6'5" red-haired Sinbad has delighted audiences with his comedy, which combines street parlance—noticeably free of obscenities—with tales of American life. Born David Adkins on November 10, 1956 in Benton Harbor, Michigan, Sinbad aspired to be a basketball star, winning a basketball scholarship to the University of Denver. A serious knee injury caused him to give up basketball, and he left college in 1978. Shortly thereafter, he renamed himself Sinbad, after the heroic character in *The Arabian Nights,* to boost his spirits. He spent three and a half years in the U.S. Air Force, reportedly hating every minute until his 1983 discharge.

Sinbad (1956–)

Comedian, Actor

By that time, Sinbad had decided to try his hand at stand-up comedy. A series of low-paying engagements throughout the United States followed, and his break came when he appeared on the television talent contest "Star Search" seven times in the mid-1980s. He later worked as a warm-up comedian for "The Cosby Show," and in 1989 was cast as dorm director Walter Oakes on "A Different World"—a role that was broadened in 1991 when Oakes became a counselor. In 1993, Sinbad starred in his own situation comedy about a single foster parent.

Singleton was born in Los Angeles in 1968. After graduating from high school in 1986 he enrolled in the University of Southern California's prestigious Film Writing Program, which is part of their School of Cinema–Television. While there he formed an African-American Film Association and did a six month director's internship for the "Arsenio Hall Show." He twice won the school's Jack Nicholson Award for best feature-length screenplays. Before graduating in 1990, he signed with the well-known Creative Artists Agency.

John Singleton (1968–)

Filmmaker

Singleton was soon approached by Columbia Pictures to sell the film rights to *Boyz N the Hood,* his original screenplay and college thesis. Singleton agreed, but only if he could be the movie's director. The movie was released in July of 1991 to mixed critical reviews. Although its first showings were marred by movie-house violence, the film garnered Singleton an Academy award nomination for best director. He became the youngest director and the first African American to be so honored.

Since *Boyz N the Hood* Singleton has done a short cable television film for Michael Jackson entitled *Remember the Time*. His second film, *Poetic Justice*, was released in the summer of 1993.

Noble Sissle
(1889–1975)

Lyricist, Singer

Noble Sissle was born in Indianapolis, Indiana. He reaped his early successes teamed up with the great musician/composer Eubie Blake. Sissle wrote the lyrics and sang them in performance; Blake composed and played the music. Together the two created such songs as "I'm Just Wild about Harry," "It's All Your Fault," "Serenade Blues," and "Love Will Find a Way."

The 1921 *Shuffle Along,* the first black musical with a love theme, made Sissle and Blake famous. Joining forces with the writing and comedy team of Flournoy Miller and Aubrey Lyles, Sissle and Blake wrote the words and music to more than a dozen songs for the show. *Shuffle Along* became a huge success in the United States and Europe, where it had a prolonged tour. As with most black performers in the early 1900s, Sissle and his troupe had to travel as far as twenty or thirty miles out of their way to find a place to eat and sleep, since blacks were not welcome in the white hotels of the towns where they played.

Other Sissle and Blake shows included *Chocolate Dandies* (1924) and *Keep Shufflin* (1928). Noble Sissle died December 17, 1975 at his home in Tampa, Florida.

Wesley Snipes
(1962–)

Actor

Born in Orlando, Florida, Wesley Snipes spent his childhood in the Bronx, New York. At the age of twelve, he appeared in his first off-Broadway production, a minor role in the play *The Me Nobody Knows*. His interest in dance led him to enroll in New York's High School for the Performing Arts. Before he completed the curriculum, however, his mother sent him back to Orlando to finish school, where he continued to study drama.

Upon high school graduation, Snipes was awarded a scholarship to study theater at the State University of New York at Purchase. Snipes subsequently appeared in Broadway and off-Broadway productions, including Wole Soyinka's *Death and the King's Horsemen,* Emily Mann's *Execution of Justice,* and John Pielmeier's *The Boys of Winter.* He has also appeared in Michael Jackson's video "Bad" and in the HBO production *Vietnam War Story,* for which he received cable television's best actor award.

Snipes's film appearances include roles in *Wildcats* (1986), *Streets of Gold* (1986), *Major League* (1989), and *King of New York* (1990). In 1990 Snipes appeared in Spike Lee's *Mo' Better Blues,* with Denzel Washington. This was followed by a role in Mario Van Peebles's *New Jack City* (1991) and in Spike Lee's *Jungle Fever* (1991). His most recent films include *White Men Can't Jump, Passenger 57, Rising Sun,* and *Demolition Man.*

Familiar to generations of Americans, Billie "Buckwheat" Thomas, better known simply as "Buckwheat," was one of the principal characters in the "Our Gang" film shorts of the 1930s and 1940s. Buckwheat succeeded the character Farina, and like Farina, his gender was ambiguous: he was in most respects a boy, but wore dress-like gingham smocks, and in some episodes sported pigtails.

Billie "Buckwheat" Thomas (1931–1980)

Actor

Billie Thomas was born in 1931 and joined the "Our Gang" cast in 1934, appearing in ninety-three episodes, the last in 1944. The film historian David Bogle described the character of Buckwheat as "a quiet, odd-ball type, the perfect little dum-dum tag-along." The comedian Eddie Murphy's parodies of Buckwheat in the 1980s were enormously popular; Buckwheat's generally unintelligible speech, blank expression, and untidy hair provided a wealth of material for Murphy's routine.

Billie Thomas pursued little acting after the "Our Gang" series ended. He died in 1980 at the age of 49.

During the early 1970s, Cicely Tyson emerged as America's leading black dramatic star. She achieved this through two sterling performances—as Rebecca, the wife of a southern sharecropper in the film *Sounder,* and as the lead in a television special, "The Autobiography of Miss Jane Pittman," the story of an ex-slave who, past her hundredth year, challenges racist

Cicely Tyson (1933–)

Actress

authority by deliberately drinking from a "white only" water fountain as a white deputy sheriff looks on.

Cicely Tyson was born in New York City and raised by a religious, strict mother, who associated movies with sin and forbade Cicely to go to movie theaters. Blessed with poise and natural grace, Tyson became a model and appeared on the cover of America's two foremost fashion magazines, *Vogue* and *Harper's Bazaar,* in 1956. Interested in acting, she began to study drama, and in 1959 she appeared on a CBS culture series, "Camera Three," with what is believed to be the first natural African hair style worn on television.

Tyson won a role in an off-Broadway production of Jean Genet's *The Blacks* (1961), for which she received the 1962 Vernon Rice Award. She then played a lead part in the CBS series "East Side, West Side." Tyson subsequently moved into film parts, appearing in *The Comedians* (1967) and *The Heart Is a Lonely Hunter* (1968). Critical acclaim led to her role as Rebecca in *Sounder* (1972), for which she was nominated for an Academy award and named best actress by the National Society of Film Critics. She won an Emmy television acting trophy for "Jane Pittman" (1974).

Tyson's other film appearances include *The Blue Bird* (1976) and *The River Niger* (1976). On television, she has appeared in "Roots" (1977), "King" (1978), and "Wilma" (1978). She portrayed Harriet Tubman in "A Woman Called Moses," and Chicago schoolteacher Marva Collins in a made-for-television movie in 1981. Recent television appearances include "Cry Freedom" (1987) and "The Women of Brewster Place" (1989).

In 1979, Marymount College presented Tyson with an honorary doctorate of fine arts. Tyson owns a house on Malibu Beach in California. In November of 1981 she married jazz trumpeter Miles Davis, but the couple divorced before Davis's death.

Leslie Uggams

(1943–)

Singer, Actress

Born in the Washington Heights section of New York City on May 25, 1943, Leslie Uggams enjoyed a comfortable childhood. She made her singing debut at the age of six, performing with the choir of St. James Presbyterian Church in New York, and followed shortly thereafter with her acting debut in the television series "Beulah." Uggams developed her poise and stage presence early in life, attending the Professional Children's School, where she was chosen student body president in her senior year.

Uggams subsequently won $25,000 on the popular television quiz show "Name That Tune," which renewed her interest in a singing career. In 1961 Uggams became a regular on "The Mitch Miller Show," a variety show featuring old favorites. She was at the time the only black performer appearing regularly on network television.

Throughout the 1960s, Uggams appeared in numerous nightclubs and had several supperclub and television engagements. Her big break came when she was signed as a replacement for Lena Horne in *Hallelujah Baby*, a show that presented a musical chronicle of the civil-rights movement. Uggams won instant stardom and received a Tony award for her performance.

In 1977, Uggams appeared as Kizzy in the television adaption of Alex Haley's novel *Roots*. In May 1982, she performed in a new Broadway show, *Blues in the Night*, at the Rialto Theater in New York City. She has also appeared on television in "Backstairs at the White House," a miniseries, and "The Book of Lists"; in the film *Skyjacked*; and in the musicals *Jerry's Girls*, *The Great Gershwin*, and *Anything Goes*.

Ben Augustus Vereen (1946–)

Dancer, Actor

Ben Vereen was born October 10, 1946, in the Bedford-Stuyvesant section of Brooklyn, New York and attended the High School of Performing Arts in Manhattan. His dancing ability had been discovered almost accidentally after he had been sent to dance school by his mother. Vereen has since been called America's premier song-and-dance man.

Ben Vereen made his stage debut in 1965 in *The Prodigal Son*. He went on to appear in *Sweet Charity* (1966), *Golden Boy* (1968), *Hair* (1968), and *No Place to Be Somebody* (1970). Vereen is best known for his Broadway role in *Pippin* (1972), for which he won a Tony award. He was also nominated for a Tony for his co-starring role in *Jesus Christ Superstar* (1971). His film appearances include roles in *Funny Lady* (1975), *All That Jazz* (1979), and *The Zoo Gang*.

Vereen has starred in the ABC comedy series "Tenspeed and Brown Shoe" and is known for his television specials; the highly acclaimed "Ben Vereen—His Roots" (1978) won seven Emmy awards. He also portrayed Louis "Satchmo" Armstrong and received wide acclaim for his role of Chicken George in television's adaption of Alex Haley's *Roots* (1977) and for his performance in *Jubilee*.

Denzel Washington
(1954–)

Actor

Born in December 1954 in Mt. Vernon, New York, Denzel Washington attended an upstate private high school, the Oakland Academy, and then entered Fordham University as a pre-med major. Washington did not originally intend to become an actor, but when he auditioned for the lead role in a student production of Eugene O'Neill's *The Emperor Jones*, he won the part over theater majors. His performance in that play, and later in a production of *Othello,* led his drama instructor to encourage Washington to pursue an acting career.

Washington's first major role was in the off-Broadway drama *A Soldier's Story;* Washington recreated his role when the play was adapted into a motion picture in 1984. He played Dr. Phillip Chandler on the television series "St. Elsewhere" and appeared in a string of films, including *Carbon Copy* (1980), *Cry Freedom* (in which he portrayed South African activist Steven Biko; 1987), *The Mighty Quinn* (1989), *Glory* (which won him an Academy award for best supporting actor; 1989), *Mo' Better Blues* (1990), *Mississippi Masala* (1992), and *Malcolm X* (1992).

Washington is married to actress Pauletta Pearson.

Ethel Waters
(1900–1977)

Actress, Singer

The distinguished career of Ethel Waters spanned half a century and made its mark in virtually every entertainment medium—stage, screen, television, and recordings.

Ethel Waters was born on October 31, 1900, and spent most of her childhood in Chester, Pennsylvania. By the age of seventeen, she was singing professionally at the Lincoln Theatre in Baltimore. During this early phase of her career, she became the first woman to perform W. C. Handy's "St. Louis Blues" on stage.

After several years in nightclubs and vaudeville, Waters made her Broadway debut in the 1927 review *Africana.* In 1930 she appeared in *Blackbirds,* and in 1931 and 1932 she starred in *Rhapsody in Black.* The following year she was featured with Clifton Webb and Marilyn Miller in Irving Berlin's *As Thousands Cheer.* In 1935 she co-starred with Bea Lillie in *At Home Abroad,* and three years later she played the lead in *Mamba's Daughters.*

In 1940, Waters appeared in the stage version of *Cabin in the Sky,* a triumph that she repeated in the 1943 movie version. Her other film ap-

Denzel Washington as Malcolm X in Spike Lee's film Malcolm X.

pearances include *Rufus Jones for President* (1931), *Tales of Manhattan* (1941), *Cairo* (1942), *Stage Door Canteen* (1943), and *Pinky* (1949).

Her autobiography, *His Eye Is on the Sparrow*, was a 1951 Book-of-the-Month Club selection. The title is taken from a song that she sang in her 1950 stage success, *Member of the Wedding*.

Keenan Ivory Wayans (1958-)

Comedian

Keenan Ivory Wayans was born in New York City in 1958. He began his career as a stand-up comic at the Improv Clubs in New York City and Los Angeles. After appearances on such television series as "Benson," "Cheers," "Chips," and in the movies *Star 80* (1983) and *Hollywood Shuffle* (1987), Wayans struck fame with *I'm Gonna Git You, Sucka* (1989)—a hilarious sendup of 1970s "blaxploitation" films—which he wrote and produced. His greatest success has been the hit television series "In Living Color," a lively and irreverent show in which celebrities are often outrageously parodied. "In Living Color" won an Emmy award in 1990.

Wayans is the oldest of a family of ten; three of his siblings—Damon, Shawn, and Kim—are regulars on "In Living Color."

Bert Williams (1876-1922)

Comedian, Dancer

The legendary Bert Williams is considered by many to be the greatest black vaudeville performer in the history of the American stage.

Born in 1876 in the Bahamas, Williams moved to New York with his family and then on to California, where he graduated from high school. After studying civil engineering for a time, he decided to try his hand at show business.

In 1895 Williams teamed with George Walker to form a successful vaudeville team. Five years later, they opened in New York in *The Sons of Ham* and were acclaimed for the characterizations that became their stock-in-trade—Walker as a dandy, and Williams in blackface, complete with outlandish costumes and black dialect. The show ran for two years.

In 1902 their show *In Dahomey* was so popular that they took it to England, where it met with equal success. The partners continued to produce such shows as *The Policy Players, Bandanna Land,* and *Abyssinia* until Walker's death in 1909.

Thereafter, Williams worked as a featured single in the *Ziegfeld Follies,* touring America for ten years in several versions of the show. His most famous songs were "Woodman, Spare That Tree"; "O, Death, Where Is Thy Sting"; and "Nobody," his own composition and trademark.

Williams died of pneumonia on March 4, 1922.

A screen, television, and stage actor with impressive credits, Billy Dee Williams has starred in some of the most commercially popular films ever released.

Born William December Williams in Harlem on April 6, 1937, Williams was a withdrawn, overweight youngster who initially planned to become a fashion illustrator. While he was studying on scholarship at the School of Fine Arts in the National Academy of Design, a CBS casting director helped him secure bit parts in several television shows, including "Lamp Unto My Feet" and "Look Up and Live."

Williams then began to study acting under Sidney Poitier and Paul Mann at the Actors Workshop in Harlem. He made his film debut in *The Last Angry Man* (1959), then appeared on stage in *The Cool World* (1960), *A Taste of Honey* (1960), and *The Blacks* (1962). He later appeared briefly on Broadway in *Hallelujah Baby* (1967) and in several off-Broadway shows, including *Ceremonies in Dark Old Men* (1970).

Williams's next major role was in the acclaimed television movie "Brian's Song" (1970), a performance for which he received an Emmy nomination. Motown's Berry Gordy then signed Williams to a seven-year contract, after which he starred in *Lady Sings the Blues* (1972) and *Mahogany* (1976) with Diana Ross. His last movie for Gordy was *The Bingo Long Traveling All-Stars and Motor King* (1976).

In the early 1980s Williams appeared in two of George Lucas's *Star Wars* adventures, *The Empire Strikes Back* and *Return of the Jedi*. He has appeared in numerous television movies, including "Scott Joplin," "Christmas Lilies of the Field," and the miniseries "Chiefs." When he was cast opposite Diahann Carroll in the prime time drama "Dynasty," his reputation as a romantic lead was secured. At the end of the decade, he starred in action films such as *Oceans of Fire* and *Number One With a Bullet*.

Flip Wilson reached the pinnacle of the entertainment world with a series of original routines and ethnic characters rivaled only by those of Bill Cosby. Wilson's hilarious monologues, seen on a number of network television shows, made him the most visible black comedian of the early 1970s.

Born Clerow Wilson on December 8, 1933, Wilson was the tenth in a family of twenty-four children, eighteen of whom survived. The family

Billy Dee Williams (1937–)

Actor

Flip Wilson (1933–)

Comedian, Actor

was destitute, and Wilson was a troublesome child during his youth in Jersey City; he ran away from reform school several times and was ultimately raised in foster homes.

Wilson's comic talents first surfaced while he was serving in the Air Force. Sent overseas to the Pacific, Wilson entertained his buddies with preposterous routines. Back in civilian life, he worked as a bellhop and part-time showman. Opportunity struck in 1959 when a Miami businessman sponsored him for one year at $50 a week, thus enabling Wilson to concentrate on the evolution of his routine. For the next five years or so, Wilson appeared regularly at the Apollo Theatre in Harlem. In 1965 he began a series of nationwide appearances on "The Tonight Show." Long-term contracts and several hit records followed in quick sequence, and Wilson became firmly established as one of the truly innovative talents in the comedy profession.

With "The Flip Wilson Show" in the early 1970s, Wilson became the first black to have a weekly prime-time television show under his own name. He became famous for his original character creations, such as "Geraldine." On January 31, 1972 he appeared on the cover of *Time* magazine. In 1976, he made his dramatic debut on television in the ABC series "The Six Million Dollar Man."

During the early 1980s, Wilson appeared in numerous nightclubs and television specials. He has also made comedy albums, including *The Devil Made Me Buy This Dress*, for which he received a Grammy award.

Paul Winfield

(1941-)

Actor

Born in Los Angeles on May 22, 1941, Paul Winfield grew up in a poor family. Excelling in school, he attended a number of colleges—the University of Portland, Stanford University, Los Angeles City College, and the University of California at Los Angeles—but left UCLA before graduation to pursue his acting career.

Winfield appeared on television shows in the late 1960s and early 1970s—most notably as one of Diahann Carroll's boyfriends in the series "Julia." His great success in that period was in the film *Sounder* (1972), in which he played a sharecropper father in the nineteenth-century American South. For this role, he received an Academy award nomination for best actor.

Winfield subsequently appeared in the motion pictures *Gordon's War* (1973), *Conrack* (1974), *Huckleberry Finn* (1974), and *A Hero Ain't Nothing but a Sandwich* (1978). He received accolades for his portrayal of Martin Luther King, Jr. in the NBC movie "King" (1978), for which he received an Emmy nomination. His second Emmy nomination came with his role in the television miniseries "Roots: The Next Generation" (1979).

In the 1980s, Winfield kept busy with appearances on television in "The Charmings," "The Women of Brewster Place," "Wiseguy," and "227"; on film in *Star Trek II: The Wrath of Khan* (1982), *Damnation Alley* (1983), and *The Terminator* (1984); and on the stage in *A Midsummer Night's Dream, Othello,* and *The Seagull.* In 1990 he played the sarcastic Judge Larren Lyttle in the movie *Presumed Innocent,* and in 1992 appeared on Broadway in the cast of *A Few Good Men.*

Winfield has won several major awards, including an NAACP Image award and election to the Black Filmmakers Hall of Fame.

Oprah Winfrey's rise to fame is a tale at once moving and inspiring. She was born on January 29, 1954, in Kosciusko, Mississippi. Her name was supposed to have been "Orpah," after a biblical figure in the book of Ruth; accounts vary as to the origin of the misspelling.

Oprah Winfrey (1954–)

Talk Show Host, Actress, Broadcasting Executive

Winfrey was a precocious child who asked her kindergarten teacher to advance her to the first grade; Winfrey also skipped the second grade. Her parents, who were not married, separated when she was very young and sent her to live with her grandparents. At the age of six, Winfrey moved to Milwaukee to live with her mother. From the time she was nine she was abused sexually by male family members and acquaintances; these events, which she did not discuss publicly until the 1980s, have had a profound effect on her life.

When she was fourteen Winfrey went to live with her father in Nashville, Tennessee, and it was there that her life was put back on track. Her father insisted on hard work and discipline as a means of self-improvement, and Winfrey complied, winning a college scholarship that allowed her to attend Tennessee State University. In 1971 she began working part time as a radio announcer for WVOL in Nashville. Two years later, after receiving a B.A. from Tennessee State, she became a reporter at WTVF-TV in

Nashville. From 1976 to 1983 she lived in Baltimore, working for the ABC affiliate WJZ-TV, progressing from news anchor to co-host of the popular show "People Are Talking." In 1984 she moved to Chicago and took over the ailing morning show, "A.M. Chicago." By September of the next year, the show was so successful that it was expanded to an hour format and renamed "The Oprah Winfrey Show." Now in syndication across the country, "The Oprah Winfrey Show" is one of the most popular television programs in history. In 1986 Winfrey founded Harpo, Inc., her own production company ("Harpo" is "Oprah" spelled backwards).

**By
Donald
Franklin Joyce**

A talented actress, Winfrey has appeared in the motion picture *The Color Purple* (1985) and in the television movie "The Women of Brewster Place" (1989).

Classical Music

When the first Africans arrived in 1619 on the eastern coast of what is now the United States, they brought with them a rich musical heritage. In the culture from which these slaves were taken, music and dance accompanied almost every public activity. Each community had professional musicians, and everyone, from the youngest to the oldest, played, sang, and danced. Because theirs was an oral tradition, they did not need sheet music to bring their songs and dances with them—they carried it all in their heads. They brought to the new world not only their songs and dances, but their love of and need for music as an integral part of daily life, and they participated in the music of their new world from the very beginning.

BLACK MUSICIANS IN EARLY AMERICA ♦ ♦ ♦ ♦ ♦ ♦ ♦ ♦ ♦ ♦ ♦ ♦

Slave Music

As slaves, the Africans assumed the lives and culture of their owners; they learned the Europeans' language, religion, and music. They sang English psalms and hymns in church as they converted to Christianity. They heard folk and popular tunes in the taverns and homes. Some slaves in the South studied with itinerant music teachers. The most talented musicians gained professional-level skills that were quickly put to use by the whites. Bonded servants and slave musicians, playing instruments such as the violin, flute, and piano, provided much of the recreational music for their masters, playing at dance balls and dancing schools. On self-sufficient plantations in the South, the most musical of the domestic slaves provided evening "entertainments." Once public concerts became possible and popular in the new world, a few talented slaves gave public concerts. The pianist Thomas "Blind Tom" Green Bethune began public concertizing while still a slave, and he continued to perform after emancipation.

Art Music in the Nineteenth Century

As a free black middle class arose in the nineteenth century and the popularity of public concerts increased, black musicians began to provide "art music" for both black and white audiences. As in white middle- and upper-class communities, genteel songs and piano pieces could be heard in the parlors of the comfortable and well-off members of the black communities; music also accompanied most public celebrations and ceremonies. As the black middle class grew, it could support more professional musicians and music educators. Singing schools and private lessons in instruments were available to anyone interested. During much of the nineteenth century, the best black artists toured throughout the United States and Europe, performing for black and white audiences alike.

The Original Colored American Opera Troupe and the Theodore Drury Colored Opera Company, both established in the second half of the nineteenth century, were the earliest long-lasting black opera companies.

In the nineteenth century, a typical "art music" concert showcased a variety of musical pieces. Songs, arias, and ensemble vocal pieces were performed in the same show as chamber, band, and orchestral numbers. The most popular singers tended to be women, including Elizabeth Taylor Greenfield, called the "Black Swan," and Matilda Sisieretta Jones, known as the "Black Patti" after the contemporary reigning white diva, Adelina Patti.

Men dominated the realm of instrumental music. Pianists included John William Boone and Samuel Jamieson in addition to Blind Tom. John Thomas Douglas, Walter F. Craig, and Edmond Dede played the violin.

Morris Brown, Jr., Robert Jones, Jacob Stans, William Appo, James Hermenway, Francis Johnson, and Aaron J. R. Connor conducted all-black orchestras, bands, and choruses; most composed music as well. The Original Colored American Opera Troupe of Washington, DC, and the Theodore Drury Colored Opera Company, both established in the second half of the nineteenth century, were the earliest long-lasting black opera companies.

♦ ♦ ♦ ♦ ♦ ♦ ♦ CLASSICAL MUSIC IN THE TWENTIETH CENTURY

During most of the nineteenth century, African-American musicians performed for both black and white audiences. Toward the end of the century, however, white audiences began to favor European performers over any American performer, and white musicians over black. Despite their obvious success in classical music, by the beginning of the twentieth century African Americans were not considered suitable as classical musicians, and white audiences accepted them only on the vaudeville and minstrel stage. Whites considered blacks unable to contribute to art music as either performers or composers. In response to composer Scott Joplin's attempt to produce his opera *Treemonisha* in New York, for example, the *New York Age* stated on March 5, 1908, "Since ragtime has been in vogue, many Negro writers have gained considerable fame as composers of that style of music. From the white man's standpoint of view … after writing ragtime, the Negro does not figure." This was the prevailing attitude for some time.

Racism and Sexism in Performance Organizations

Flutist Dorothy Antoinette Handy wrote in the preface of her *Black Women in American Bands and Orchestras* that her book "originated in the mind of a fourteen-year-old black American female who decided that she wanted to be a symphonic orchestral flutist…. She went to a New Orleans Philharmonic concert, and shortly before the end proceeded backstage from the reserved for colored section to the orchestra's first flutist. Question: 'Are you accepting any pupils?' Answer: 'Do you mean that you, a Negro, want to study flute?'" Unfortunately, this attitude has continued to reign in the second half of the century as well. In 1975, San Francisco Symphony Orchestra timpanist Elayne Jones, the only black first-chair player in a major American orchestra, filed a suit claiming contract violation on grounds of racism and sexism because she was denied tenure. She lost her case.

Conductor James DePreist rehearses with the New Philharmonic Orchestra, 1984.

Despite this opposition, African Americans have never been absent from the world of classical music. While the merits of compositions by African-American composers have been undeniable, they have often been ignored. For much of this century they have been denied entrance to this country's major metropolitan (white) symphonies, though they have constantly worked towards inclusion. William Grant Still's *Afro-American Symphony* became the first symphonic work written by a black composer to be performed by a major symphony orchestra when it was performed in 1931 by the Rochester Philharmonic Symphony. In 1933, Florence

Price became the first black female to have a symphony played by a major orchestra when the Chicago Symphony Orchestra performed her Symphony in E Minor at the Chicago World's Fair. In 1934, Price conducted her Concerto in F Minor in Chicago. In 1955, William Grant Still became the first African American to conduct a major orchestra in the deep South when he led the New Orleans Symphony Orchestra.

Black symphonic music falls into two categories: black-stream music, named after Gunther Schuller's *Third Stream,* which is serious music influenced by the composer's ethnic background; and traditional European music created by black composers. At the end of the nineteenth century, black composers became the first group of American composers to write nationalistic pieces by incorporating black traditional folk idioms into their vocal and instrumental pieces.

Until a few years ago, compositions of either style were largely unknown, but the public relations efforts and researches of Paul Freeman, Domique

Musical Styles of Black Classical Composers

de Lerma, C. Edward Thomas, and Eileen Southern have brought to light a great many first-rate symphonic compositions, both old and new. Among the best black-stream pieces are Florence Price's Symphony in E Minor (1933), William Grant Still's *Afro-American Symphony* (1931), Margaret Bonds's *Credo,* and Ornette Coleman's *Skies of America.* Examples of black symphonic music in which there is no obvious contribution from the black heritage include Chevalier de Saint-Georges's *Symphonic Concertante* (1782), Julia Perry's *Stabat Mater* (1951), and Ulysses Kay's *Markings* (1966).

Research and Recording

After years of neglect, the role of the African American in the history of music is finally being given serious attention. Rediscoveries of excellent classical pieces by African-American composers have begun to broaden the view of black music as limited to spirituals, jazz, and the blues. Studies of comprehensive musicology (the study of music in relation to the culture and society in which it exists) are beginning to focus on the unique, non-European nature of African-American music.

Several new organizations have devoted time, energy, and finances to promoting African-American creations and performances in the arts. The Afro-American Music Opportunities Association (AAMOA), in existence since 1969, was formed because of the need for more acknowledgment of black music and musicians. Since its formation, the organization's concepts have been developed by C. Edward Thomas into viable and dynamic programs that have already substantially changed American musical sociology. The AAMOA has put out its own record label for nonsymphonic repertoires starting with the release of David Baker's Sonata for Piano and String Quartet in a recorded performance that features Brazilian virtuoso Helena Freire. On March 18, 1974, the first four records of the Black Composers Series were formally released by Columbia Records. These LPs featured works by Chevalier de Saint-Georges, Samuel Coleridge-Taylor, William Grant Still, George Walker, Ulysses Kay, and Roque Cordero, under the artistic direction of Paul Freeman. This Black Composer's Series grew out of an agreement between CBS and the AAMOA for at least twelve recordings of approximately twenty black composers.

Chicago's Columbia College established the Center for Black Music Research in 1982 to support the research and performance of contemporary and historic African-American compositions.

The Center for Black Music Research, established in 1982 at Chicago's Columbia College, has actively contributed to the research publications and performances of contemporary and historic compositions. They have an ever-growing library and computer database of resources used by

Director Walter Trumbull rehearses with the Boys Choir of Harlem.

scholars all over the country. African-American classical and popular music has received more and more attention in the mainstream academic world as musicologists and ethnomusicologists have begun to focus their attention in that direction.

Black and Integrated Performance Organizations

The Symphony of the New World (1965–1976) was established by timpanist Elayne Jones and conductor Benjamin Steinberg as the first racially integrated orchestra in the country. Other founding members include cellist Kermit Moore and bassist Lucille Dixon. This orchestra served as a stepping stone for many musicians, and a number of the leading black artists in the nation have performed with it. The group has premiered many works by black composers.

In the 1970s two national black opera companies were formed. Opera/South was founded in 1970 by Sister Elise of the Catholic order of the Sisters of the Blessed Sacrament, and by members of the Mississippi Inter-Collegiate Opera Guild (Jackson State University, Utica Junior College, and Tougaloo College). In addition to staging grand opera, the company performed operas by black composers, including *Highway No. 1 USA* and *A Bayou Legend,* both by William Grant Still, and *Jubilee* and *The Juggler of Our Lady,* both by Ulysses Kay. In 1973, Sister Elise, along with Margaret Harris, Benjamin Matthews, and Wayne Sanders, organized Opera Ebony. Performers with these two companies have included conductors Leonard de Paur, Margaret Harris, and Everett Lee; pianist Way Sanders; and singers Donnie Ray Albert, William Brown, Alpha Floyed, Ester Hinds, Robert Mosely, Wilma Shakesnider, and Walter Turnbull. These companies—as well as the Houston Opera Company, which, in 1975, produced Scott Joplin's *Treemonisha*—have served as a showcase for black talent, and have launched the careers of a number of performers.

Black Representation in Major Orchestras and Opera Companies

As in other areas of American life, the civil-rights struggle continues in the realm of classical music. Programs to support young black artists, begun as a response to the civil-rights movement in the 1960s, died as a result of the economic recession of the 1970s. A 1981 survey by the National Urban League indicated that of the nearly 5,000 musicians playing regularly in fifty-six leading orchestras, only seventy were black. Only six of the 538 members of the "Big Five" orchestras—in New York, Boston, Chicago, Cleveland, and Philadelphia—were black. Few employ black conductors. The American Symphony Orchestra League published a report in 1992 with similar findings. The 146 orchestras that participated in the survey reported that of a total 8326 positions, only 133 were filled by black musicians.

In the early 1980s, the Metropolitan Opera had fifteen black artists on its roster, and the New York City Opera had eleven singers in principal roles, with two conductors and one stage director. Prior to World War II, there were no black singers in any opera house in the United States, but now they have gained acceptance almost everywhere.

THE FUTURE FOR THE BLACK CLASSICAL MUSICIAN ♦ ♦ ♦ ♦ ♦

It is impossible to know what lies in the future for African-American classical composers, conductors, and other performing artists. Gains made by blacks in orchestras during the 1970s were lost in the 1980s; the conserv-

Grace Bumbry in Verdi's
Don Carlos.

ative court and political systems of this country in the late 1980s and the early 1990s has led to a backlash. Yet the music of African Americans has been increasingly accepted and celebrated by the musical and academic worlds, and the formation of the companies mentioned above has provided an avenue for blacks to accept classical music and be accepted into it.

COMPOSERS, CONDUCTORS, INSTRUMENTALISTS, AND SINGERS ♦

Adele Addison

(1925–)

Singer

Adele Addison received her musical training at Westminster Choir College in 1946 and the University of Massachusetts in 1963. After making her recital debut at Town Hall, New York City, in 1952, she went on to perform recital tours throughout the United States and Canada. In 1963 she made a tour of the Soviet Union under a cultural exchange program.

Addison has appeared with the New England, New York City, and Washington opera companies. Her premiere performances included John La Montaine's *Fragments from the Song of Songs* with the New Haven Symphony (1959) and Poulenc's *Gloria* with the Boston Symphony (1961). She performed the soloist opening concert at the Lincoln Center's Philharmonic Hall in 1962.

Roberta Alexander

(1949–)

Singer

Opera magazine described Roberta Alexander as "a soprano who, with a range of over two octaves, rich low notes and crystalline, brilliant top notes, excellent diction and clear execution of coloratura passages, should make a name for herself"; and so she has.

She was born in Lynchburg, Virginia, grew up in Yellow Springs, Ohio and currently makes her home in Amsterdam, the Netherlands. She has a B.S. degree in music education from Central State University in Ohio and a master's degree in voice from the University of Michigan at Ann Arbor.

Her premiere with the Metropolitan Opera came in the 1983 fall season as Zerlina in *Don Giovanni.* Other Met successes were as Bess in *Porgy and Bess* and in the title role of *Jenufa.*

In the summer of 1984, she performed at the Aix-en-Provence Festival in France in Mozart's *La Finta Giardiniera,* and in 1985 she performed in Vienna as Cleopatra in Handel's *Giulio Cesare.* She has also performed in *La Boheme* in Berlin, and as Ilia in *Idomeneo.* She has performed extensively at the Netherlands Opera and the London Opera, and in America at the Santa Fe Opera and the Houston Grand Opera. In 1987 she returned to the Met, where she performed the role of Mimi in *La Boheme.*

Roberta Alexander has been praised by Opera magazine for her "range of over two octaves, rich low notes and crystalline, brilliant top notes, excellent diction and clear execution of coloratura passages."

Born in Campbell, Ohio, Betty Lou Allen studied at Wilberforce University and toured with Leontyne Price as part of the Wilberforce Sisters. She continued her musical studies at the Hartford School of Music (1950) and the Berkshire Music Center (1951), and studied voice with Sarah Peck Moore, Paul Ulanowsky, and Zinka Milanov.

Betty Lou Allen (1930–)

Educator, Singer

Allen's New York debut was in Virgil Thompson's *Four Saints in Three Acts* with the New York City Opera Company (1953), and her formal opera debut was at the Teatro Colón in Buenos Aires (1964). She has appeared as a soloist with leading orchestras and conductors, including Bernstein, Dorate, and Maazel.

Allen has served as a faculty member of such schools as the North Carolina School of the Arts, the Curtis Institute of Music in Philadelphia, and the Manhattan School of Music in New York City. She is currently the executive director and chair of the voice department at the Harlem School of the Arts in New York.

Marian Anderson (1902–1993)

Singer

At the peak of her career, Marian Anderson was regarded as the world's greatest contralto. When she made her Town Hall debut in New York on December 31, 1935, her performance was described by Howard Taubman, the *New York Times* reviewer, as "music-making that probed too deep for words."

Anderson was born on February 27, 1902 in Philadelphia. As a young choir girl, she demonstrated her vocal talents by singing parts from soprano, alto, tenor, and bass. At the age of nineteen she began studying with Giuseppe Boghetti, and four years later she appeared as soloist with the New York Philharmonic. After a short engagement with the Philadelphia Symphony Orchestra, she traveled to Europe on a scholarship granted by the National Association of Negro Musicians.

On Easter Sunday in 1939 Anderson gave what is perhaps her most memorable concert—singing on the steps of the Lincoln Memorial after having been barred from making an appearance at Constitution Hall by the Daughters of the American Revolution (an action that prompted Eleanor Roosevelt to resign in anger from the DAR).

In 1955, after years of successful concert work, she made her Metropolitan Opera debut in Verdi's *Un Ballo in Maschera*. Two years later, a State Department tour took her around the world. In September of 1958 she was named to the United States delegation to the United Nations.

In 1982, when Anderson celebrated her eightieth birthday, Grace Bumbry and Shirley Verrett sang a tribute to her at New York City's Carnegie Hall.

Thomas Jefferson Anderson was born in Coatesville, Pennsylvania. His mother was a musician, and as a teenager he toured with a jazz orchestra. He received a bachelor's degree in music from West Virginia State College in 1950 and a master's degree in education from Pennsylvania State University in 1951. Anderson went on to study at the Aspen School of Music, and in 1958 he received a Ph.D. from the University of Iowa.

Anderson was composer-in-residence with the Atlanta Symphony Orchestra on a grant from the Rockefeller Foundation during the 1969–1971 seasons. His most widely performed works have been *Chamber Symphony* (1968); *Squares* (1965), an essay for orchestra; and *Personals* (1966), a cantata for narrator, chorus, and brass ensemble. He has also written music for bands (*In Memoriam Zach Walker*), works for piano (*Watermelon*), and various compositions for solo voice and chorus.

Anderson has taught music in public school and served as a faculty member at West Virginia State College, Langston University in Oklahoma, and Tennessee State University in Maine.

Thomas Jefferson Anderson (1928–)

Composer, Educator

Martina Arroyo, a New York native, made her Metropolitan Opera debut in February 1965 in the title role of *Aida*, and has since sung engagements with opera houses in Vienna, Berlin, Buenos Aires, London, and Hamburg. In addition to operatic appearances, she has also been a frequent guest soloist with many of the world's major orchestras.

In addition to *Aida*, Arroyo's Metropolitan repertoire includes Donna Anna in *Don Giovanni*, Liu in *Turandot*, Leonora in *Il Trovatore*, Elsa in *Lohengrin*, and the title role in *Madame Butterfly*. Her public performances began in 1958 with the American premiere of Pizzetti's *Murder in the Cathedral* in Carnegie Hall. That same year she made her Metropolitan debut as the celestial voice in *Don Carlo*.

Arroyo sang at the White House in 1977, sharing the stage with Andre Previn and Isaac Stern at a dinner for twenty-six heads of state. In April 1987, she was guest artist for the New Mexico Symphony Orchestra, where she sang the overture of Verdi's *La Forza del Destino* as well as several other pieces. In 1988 she performed once again with New York's Met productions of *Turandot*, *Cavalleria Rusticana*, and *Aida*. Over the past several years, Arroyo has taught as well as performed in various summer song festivals.

Martina Arroyo (1939–)

Singer

David Nathaniel Baker, Jr. (1931–)

Composer, Educator

David Nathaniel Baker, Jr. was born in Indianapolis and obtained his bachelor's and master's degrees in music education from Indiana University. He taught music in the public schools of Indianapolis and at Indiana Central College and Lincoln University in Missouri before returning to his alma mater as a faculty member. Baker has logged considerable experience with both jazz bands and college and municipal symphony orchestras. He was a member of Quincy Jones's All-Star Jazz Orchestra, which toured Europe in 1961, and has performed with Stan Kenton, Lionel Hampton, and Wes Montgomery. Baker is currently chairman of the jazz department at the Indiana University School of Music.

Kathleen Battle (1948–)

Singer

Soprano Kathleen Battle was born in Portsmouth, Ohio, and is a graduate of the University of Cincinnati's College of Conservatory of Music, having received both bachelor's and master's degrees in music.

Battle made her Met debut in 1977 as the Shepherd in *Tannhauser* and has also been heard there as Sophie in *Werther* and Blondchen in *The Abduc-*

Kathleen Battle in a Grammy awards show performance at Radio City Music Hall in 1991.

tion from the Seraglio. The 1980–1981 season included performances in *The Italian Girl in Algiers,* as well as debuts with the Zurich Opera and the Lyric Opera of Chicago. In 1982 she received critical praise for her depiction of Rosina in the Met's production of *The Barber of Seville.*

In the 1987–1988 season, Battle returned to the Metropolitan Opera to sing the role of Zerbinetta in Strauss's *Ariadne auf Naxos.* She has since sung in major music festivals and with major orchestras, including the New York Philharmonic, Cleveland Orchestra, and Los Angeles Philharmonic.

In recent years, Battle has recorded such works as *Ariadne auf Naxos* and Mahler's Symphony No. 4. She has also recorded various Schubert Lieder and Handel arias. Battle recently joined trumpeter Wynton Marsalis in a recording of baroque arias.

Thomas Green Bethune (1849–1909)

Pianist

Thomas "Blind Tom" Bethune was born into slavery in Columbus, Georgia. Blind from birth, he was a musical prodigy. His owner, James Bethune, allowed him access to the family's piano, and realizing at once the financial possibilities, arranged for informal musical training. It soon became apparent that Tom needed only to hear a piece to be able to play it.

"Blind Tom" began performing for the profit of his owner while still a slave and a child, and he continued to tour the North and South during the Civil War. After the war, the Bethune family retained financial control over his performances through contracts. Tom performed in the U.S. and in Europe. His repertoire consisted of the usual concert fare, including serious classics by composers like Bach, Beethoven, and Chopin; fancy virtuosic pieces by composers such as Gottschalk and Liszt; improvised variations on contemporary popular ballads and arias; and his own light compositions, few of which survive today. He was said to have been able to play any one of seven thousand pieces on command. Tom retired in 1898.

Margaret Allison Bonds (1913–1972)

Composer, Pianist

Margaret Bonds grew up in an artistically and creatively active family in Chicago. Her mother, Estelle C. Bonds, an accomplished musician, invited many of the prominent musicians and artists of the time into her home. Bonds became good friends with the likes of composer Florence Price, poet Langston Hughes, singer Abbie Mitchel, and sculptor Richmond Barthe. She received her early piano lessons from her mother and composition lessons from Florence Price. While still in high school, she joined the National Association of Negro Musicians. She worked closely with such musicians as Price and Mitchel and played at dance rehearsals for Muriel Abbot.

Bonds continued her musical studies at Northwestern University in Evanston, Illinois, completing both her bachelor's and master's degrees by age twenty-one. During the 1930s, she opened her own school for dance, music, and art in Chicago and frequently performed in solo recitals and with symphony orchestras. She moved to New York in 1939 to pursue her career and study further at the Juilliard School of Music. In the 1940s and 1950s, she performed as part of a piano duo with Gerald Cook. She then left New York for Los Angeles, where she taught piano, directed the Inner City Repertory Theatre, and wrote arrangements for the Los Angeles Jubilee Singers. Bonds's many compositions include songs, symphonies, musicals, ballets, a cantata, and piano works.

Gwendolyn Bradley (1952-)

Singer

Soprano Gwendolyn Bradley was born in New York City and grew up in Bishopville, South Carolina. She was a finalist in the 1977 Metropolitan Opera National Council auditions and a graduate of the North Carolina School of the Arts. She has also attended both the Curtis Institute of Music and the Academy of Vocal Arts in Philadelphia, and she has studied with Margaret Harshaw and Seth McCoy.

Since making her professional operatic debut in 1976 with the Lake George Opera Festival as Nanetta in *Falstaff,* Bradley has been heard as Titania in *A Midsummer Night's Dream* with the Central City Opera, as Lakme with Opera/South, and as Aurelia in *Rumpelstiltskin* with the Opera Company of Philadelphia. She made her Metropolitan Opera debut as the Nightingale in the Met premiere of Ravel's *L'Enfant et les Sortilèges* in February 1981. Bradley has sung with the Philadelphia Orchestra, the Kansas City Philharmonic, and the Charleston Symphony. From 1980 to 1981 she appeared with the Los Angeles Philharmonic at the Hollywood Bowl and with the Seattle Symphony. In addition to the Metropolitan Opera she has performed with the opera companies of Philadelphia, Cleveland, and Michigan.

Mezzo-soprano Grace Bumbry is the first black performer to have sung at the Wagner Festival in Bayreuth, Germany, and one of the few singers who can boast of having been called to play a command performance at the White House. Bumbry was a guest of the Kennedys, singing at a formal state dinner opening Washington's official social season in 1962.

A native of St. Louis, Bumbry, like many black singers, had her first exposure to music in a church choir, singing with her brothers and her parents at the Union Memorial Methodist Church in St. Louis. After studying voice locally, she won a nationwide talent contest in 1954 and went on, with scholarship aid, to study successively at Boston and Northwestern universities. At the latter school, she attended master classes in opera and lieder taught by the famed singer and teacher Lotte Lehmann.

In 1959 Bumbry traveled to various European countries, performing in the operatic capitals of the world. On July 23, 1961, Wieland Wagner, grandson of Richard Wagner, shocked many traditionalists by selecting Bumbry to sing the role of Venus in *Tannhauser,* a role that conventionally calls for a figure of so-called Nordic beauty, usually a tall and voluptuous blond. Bumbry proceeded to give a performance that won acclaim from even the harshest of critics, who praised her physical radiance and brilliant singing.

In 1974 Bumbry performed with the Met in *Cavalleria Rusticana.* She has since appeared successfully with various opera companies as Dalilah, Lady Macbeth, Medea, and other great dramatic roles, which have become her specialty.

On December 6, 1981, Bumbry participated in a benefit concert at Carnegie Hall put on by Artists to End Hunger. On January 31, 1982, she appeared at Carnegie Hall again, sharing the stage with Shirley Verrett to pay tribute to Marian Anderson.

In the 1987–1988 season Grace Bumbry performed with the San Francisco Opera as Abigaille in *Nabucco,* and starred as Lady Macbeth in a new production of *Macbeth* in Los Angeles. She celebrated her twenty-fifth anniversary at the Convent Garden's Royal Opera with a series of performances of *Tosca* and appeared at the Vienna State Opera in the same role. Bumbry went to Barcelona for La Gioconda and was heard in *Cavalleria*

Grace Ann Bumbry (1937–)

Singer

Rusticana and *Don Carlos* at the Hamburg State Opera. She has also appeared as Amneris in *Aida* at the Arena di Verona.

Henry Thacker "Harry" Burleigh (1866–1949)

Arranger, Composer, Singer

Born into a poverty-stricken family, Harry Burleigh was unable to receive any formal musical training until he was an adult. At the age of twenty-six he moved from his home in Erie, Pennsylvania to New York City, where he won a scholarship to the National Conservatory of Music. After graduation, he pursued a very successful singing career that included concertizing throughout the United States and Europe. He was soloist at St. George's Protestant Episcopal Church in New York for fifty-three years, and at Temple Emanu-El for twenty-five.

As a composer and arranger, Burleigh was the first to arrange spirituals in the style of art songs, and was the first African-American composer to receive critical acclaim for his art songs. As a performer, he established the tradition of concluding recitals with a group of spirituals. His art-song compositions included settings of poetry by Robert Burns and Langston Hughes, and he composed several pieces for violin and piano. He was a member of the American Society of Composers, Authors, and Publishers (ASCAP), and sat on its board of directors. He received an honorary master's degree from Atlanta University in 1918, and an honorary doctorate from Howard University in 1920.

Frances Elaine Cole (1937–1983)

Violinist, Harpsichordist, Music Critic

Frances Cole began her musical life as a violinist. She studied at the Cleveland Institute of Music and at Miami University of Ohio, where she was concert master of the orchestra. She studied further in New York City, privately and at Columbia University Teacher's College, receiving her doctorate in 1966. During these years she played violin for the National Orchestral Association.

In the mid-1960s, as she was finishing her doctorate at Columbia, she discovered an interest in the harpsichord; she began studying the instrument at the Landowska Center in Connecticut. In 1967 she became resident harpsichordist with the Gallery Players in Provincetown, Massachusetts and started appearing on national television shows and in concerts and recitals throughout the United States and Europe.

While Cole concertized as a serious classical artist, she did not limit herself by any means. She was as well known for her humor and innovation as for her elegant musical interpretations. In 1976, for example, at an outdoor concert at Lincoln Center, she arrived dressed as Anna Magdalena Bach in a horse-drawn carriage. She played jazz with a bassist and percussionist, and sang in lounges and supper clubs under the name of Elaine Frances. In 1979 she began appearing on CBS's "Sunday Morning" as performer and music critic. Cole also served as assistant professor of music at Queens College and the Westminster Choir College, and gave workshops at many colleges and universities.

Samuel Coleridge-Taylor was noted for his choral works Hiawatha's Wedding Feast, Death of Minnehaha, *and* A Tale of Old Japan, *as well as his operas, theatrical music, and orchestral pieces.*

Samuel Coleridge-Taylor (1875–1912)

Composer

Coleridge-Taylor was one of England's most celebrated composers at the turn of the century.

Born to a doctor from Sierra Leone and a British mother, he showed musical gifts at age five, and ten years later entered the Royal College of Music in London. There he studied with Sir Charles Wood and Sir Charles Villiers Stanford. He achieved renown with the premiere of *Hiawatha's Wedding Feast.*

Coleridge-Taylor was warmly received in the United States. James Weldon Johnson and Booker T. Washington were among his friends, and he was President Theodore Roosevelt's guest at the White House. In 1901, the Coleridge-Taylor Society was organized in Washington, DC, specifically to study and perform his music.

Will Marion Cook (1869–1944)

Violinist, Composer, Conductor

Will Marion Cook wrote and directed in both popular and classical venues. He was well educated in classical genres—he entered Oberlin Conservatory when he was fifteen to study violin, studied further in Berlin between 1887 and 1889, and attended the National Conservatory of Music in New York.

In 1890 he shifted his energies from performing to conducting. He directed an orchestra in Washington, DC in 1890 and performed at the Chicago World's Fair in 1893. In 1898 he became active in writing and directing black musical comedies in New York, producing the first such show to play in a major theater for a wide audience. He organized choral societies and promoted all-black concerts. He directed the New York Syncopated Orchestra, which traveled Europe, and taught and sponsored many young and talented black musicians. In addition to his musicals, he wrote art songs, choral works, instrumental pieces, and operas.

Roque Cordero (1917–)

Composer, Educator

Roque Cordero is respected as one of Latin America's most creative talents because of his abilities as a violinist, a conductor, and a composer who incorporates popular Panamanian forms into concert music.

Born in Panama, his interests shifted from popular songwriting to classical music at the age of seventeen. Four years later he was appointed director of the Orquesta Sinfonica de la Union Musical in Panama, and he later joined the Orquesta Sinfonica de Panama as violist. In 1943 he began studying abroad. He was engaged by the University of Minnesota as Artistic Director of the Institute of Latin-American Studies, and after completing his course of study was awarded a Guggenheim fellowship. Cordero is presently music editor for the publishing company of Peer International Corporation and is professor of music at Illinois State University.

Philip Creech (1950–)

Singer

Philip Creech is a native of Hempstead, New York and a graduate of Northwestern University. Creech performed with Margaret Hillis's Chicago Symphony Chorus from 1973 to 1975 and frequently appeared as tenor soloist. Since 1976 he has sung with the Chicago Symphony, Boston Symphony, New York Philharmonic, and Cincinnati Symphony. Creech made his debut at the Salzburg Festival in 1979 singing in the Berlioz *Requiem*. He made his Metropolitan Opera debut in September 1979 as Beppe in the season's premiere of Leoncavallo's *Pagliacci*, and was heard later that season as Edmondo in the premiere and subsequent overseas telecast of the new production of Puccini's *Manon Lescaut*. Creech has also appeared at the Met as Tonio in *Pagliacci*.

Creech made his recording debut in Stravinsky's *Les Noces* with the Chicago Symphony on RCA Red Seal's *Music from Raviniar* series. He has recently recorded *Carmina Burana* with James Levine and the Chicago Symphony, a recording that was released on the DGG label and became a best seller and a Grammy award winner. Creech is also recognized as an accomplished recitalist and has sung well over one hundred recitals throughout the United States.

James Anderson DePreist (1936–)

Conductor

Born in Philadelphia, James DePreist studied piano and percussion from the age of ten, but did not decide on a musical career until he reached his early twenties. After graduating from high school, he entered the Wharton School of the University of Pennsylvania as a prelaw student, receiving a bachelor of science degree in 1958 and a master of arts degree in 1961. DePreist also studied music history, the theory of harmony, and orchestration at the Philadelphia Conservatory of Music, and he studied composition with the distinguished American composer Vincent Persichetti.

In 1962, the U.S. State Department sponsored a cultural exchange tour of the Near and Far East, engaging DePreist as an American specialist in music. During this tour, DePreist was stricken with polio, which paralyzed both of his legs, and flown home for intensive therapy. Within six months he had fought his way back to the point where he could walk with the aid of crutches and braces. Courage, determination, and talent carried him to the semifinals of the 1963 Dmitri Mitropoulos International Music Competition for Conductors.

After another overseas tour as conductor in residence in Thailand, De-Preist returned to the United States, appearing with the Minneapolis International Symphony Orchestra, the New York Philharmonic, and the Philadelphia Orchestra.

In 1964 DePreist recorded what is perhaps his most satisfying triumph, capturing first prize in the Mitropoulos International Competition. Another highlight of his career occurred on June 28, 1965, when he conducted Marian Anderson's farewell concert at Robin Hood Dell in Philadelphia.

Currently DePreist is the music director of the Oregon Symphony. He is one of a select and talented circle of conductors born and trained in America who have appeared with the nation's five premier orchestras—New York, Boston, Philadelphia, Cleveland, and Chicago. He has also been guest conductor in most of the capitals of Europe and the United States.

Chevalier de Saint-Georges (1739–1799)

Composer

Chevalier de Saint-Georges is considered the first man of African ancestry to have made a major impression on European music.

Born on the Caribbean island of Guadeloupe to an African slave mother and a French father, he displayed his talent on the violin early in life. He studied with Francois Gossec, whom he succeeded as concertmaster of the celebrated Concert des Amateurs in 1769. His musical output was enormous, including several operas, symphonies concertantes, a dozen string quartets, violin concertos, and other instrumental and vocal works.

Dean Dixon (1915–1976)

Conductor

Dixon was born in Manhattan on January 10, 1915, and graduated from DeWitt Clinton High School in 1932. Exposed to classical music by his parents (as a small boy he was regularly taken to Carnegie Hall), Dixon formed his own amateur orchestra at the Harlem YMCA while still in high school. On the basis of a successful violin audition he was admitted to the

Juilliard School, where he received his bachelor's degree in 1936; three years later he acquired his master's degree from Columbia.

The Dean Dixon Symphony Society, which he had formed in 1932, began to receive financial support from the Harlem community in 1937. In 1941, at the request of Eleanor Roosevelt, Dixon gave a concert at the Heckscher Theater. He was later signed by the musical director of NBC radio to conduct the network's summer symphony in two concerts. Two months after the NBC concerts, he made his debut with the New York Philharmonic. Dixon was the first black and, at twenty-six, the youngest musician ever to conduct the New York Philharmonic Orchestra.

Lucille Dixon began playing bass in high school and was soon studying with the New York Philharmonic's principal bassist, Fred Zimmerman. After high school, she was the second of two black women to play in the WPA-sponsored National Youth Administration Orchestra. While this group normally served as a hiring house for major United States orchestras, Dixon realized that she, as a black female, would not be hired by a symphony orchestra.

**Lucille Dixon
(Robertson)
(1923–)**

Bassist

When the NYA orchestra folded, she turned to jazz for her living. She played for two years with the Earl Hines Band, and in 1946 formed a band of her own. She did continue her classical pursuits, however. Dixon's affiliations include National Symphony of Panama, Westchester Philharmonic, Ridgefield Symphony, Scranton Symphony, and the Symphony of the New World, for which she served as manager from 1972 to 1976.

Carl Ditton received his first piano lesson from his father, who was a professional musician. He continued his studies at the University of Pennsylvania, receiving a bachelor's degree in 1909. Following graduation, he went on to become the first black pianist to make a cross-country concert tour. With the aid of an E. Azalia Hackley Scholarship, he furthered his piano studies in Munich.

**Carl Rossini Ditton
(1886–1962)**

Pianist, Singer, Composer

During the 1920s he began to study voice, and he made his concert debut in Philadelphia in 1926. He later studied voice at Juilliard, where he received an artist's diploma in 1930. That year he also received the Harmon Award for composition; his compositions include primarily art songs and arrangements of spirituals.

Mattiwilda Dobbs

(1925-)

Singer

One of the world's most gifted coloratura sopranos is Mattiwilda Dobbs. Now residing in Sweden, where she is a national favorite, Dobbs has gained international fame.

Born in Atlanta, Georgia on July 11, 1925, Dobbs graduated from Spelman College in 1946 as class valedictorian, having majored in voice training. After studying Spanish at Columbia, where she received her master's degree, she went on to Paris for two years on a Whitney fellowship.

In October 1950, competing against hundreds of singers from four continents, she won the International Music Competition held at Geneva. She made her professional debut in Paris in 1953, and then became the first black to sing a principal role at La Scala in Milan. On March 8, 1954, she made her Town Hall debut in New York in the one-act opera *Ariadne auf Naxos,* receiving a rousing ovation. One year later she repeated the success with her first concert recital on the same stage.

Dobbs has made numerous recordings, including *The Pearl Fishers* and *Zaidde,* and has toured the world with great success.

Rudolph Dunbar

(1917-1988)

Composer, Clarinetist

Born in British Guiana, Rudolph Dunbar received his musical education at the Institute of Musical Art in New York, as well as in Paris and Leipzig. He made his debut with the NBC Symphony Orchestra in New York City and conducted in Great Britain and throughout the United States. In addition to being a musical conductor, Dunbar was also a clarinetist. He is the author of *A Treatise on Clarinet Playing* and is best known for the composition *Dance of the 20th Century.*

Robert Todd

Duncan

(1903-)

Singer, Actor

Although he is primarily a teacher, Todd Duncan has made notable contributions to the world of theater and concert. Duncan was born into a well-to-do family in Danville, Kentucky on February 12, 1903. He graduated from Butler University in Indianapolis in 1925 and began a teaching career—first at a junior high school, and then in Louisville at the Municipal College for Negroes.

In 1934 he appeared in New York in a single performance of an all-black version of the opera *Cavalleria Rusticana.* On the strength of this performance alone, he was auditioned less than a year later by George Gershwin and received the role of Porgy in *Porgy and Bess*. He was such a success that he repeated his performance of the role in the 1938 and 1942 revivals of the play.

In 1940 he was a featured performer on Broadway in *Cabin in the Sky*. When the play closed, he headed for Hollywood to appear in the movie *Syncopation*.

His concert repertoire includes German lieder and French and Italian songs. Duncan retired in 1965 after singing at President Lyndon B. Johnson's inauguration. Only once has he come out of retirement: in 1972 to sing the title role of *Job* at Washington's Kennedy Center. Duncan currently teaches voice at his home in Washington, DC.

Simon Lamont Estes (1938–)

Singer

Bass-baritone Simon Lamont Estes was the first black man to sing at the Bayreuth Festival, appearing in the title role of a new production of *Der Fliegende Hollander*, a portrayal he repeated there in three subsequent seasons. A native of Centerville, Iowa, Estes attended the University of Iowa and received a full scholarship to Juilliard, studying under Sergius Kagan and Christopher West. He won the Munich International Vocal Competition in 1965 and was the silver medalist in the Tchaikovsky Competition in 1966.

Estes made his operatic debut as Ramfis in *Aida* at the Deutsche Opera Berlin and since then has appeared in most of the world's major opera houses, including La Scala, the Hamburg State Opera, the Bavarian State Opera of Munich, the Vienna State Opera, the Lyric Opera of Chicago, the San Francisco Opera, and the Zurich Opera. He made his debut at the Metropolitan Opera in 1982, foregoing the honor of singing the national anthem on baseball's opening day because it coincided with his Met debut.

Estes has appeared as soloist with most of the world's leading symphony orchestras. He has also performed recitals and orchestral engagements in numerous European cities, including Paris, Zurich, Brussels, Munich, Bonn, Madrid, and Bordeaux. His North American highlights include appearances with the Chicago Symphony Orchestra conducted by Sir George Solti, and the Montreal Symphony conducted by Charles Dutoit.

In addition to having recorded *Der Fliegende Hollander,* Estes has recorded Handel's *Messiah,* the Faure *Requiem,* Beethoven's Symphony No. 9, numerous spirituals, and highlights from *Porgy and Bess.*

Louis Moreau Gottschalk (1829–1869)

Composer, Pianist

Born in New Orleans, Louis Gottschalk was a violin prodigy at six years of age and later became a brilliant concert pianist. He was already something of a European matinee idol when he first appeared in New York on February 10, 1853, and his romantic compositions enjoyed great popularity.

Although Gottschalk went to Paris when he was thirteen to study with Halle, Stamaty, and Maleden, much of his music reflected the Creole environment of his early childhood. One of his best-known compositions, *La Bambould,* is based on the sights and sounds of New Orleans's Congo Square. His autobiographical book, *Notes of a Pianist,* provides an interesting description of his background and method of composition. Gottschalk was perhaps the first black American composer to achieve international renown. Chopin praised his debut at the Salle Pleyel in April 1844, and Berlioz, with whom he studied, applauded his "sovereign power."

Reri Grist (1932–)

Singer

Born in New York City, soprano Reri Grist received her bachelor's degree in music from Queens College in 1954. Grist first came to national attention when she performed the role of Consuela in Leonard Bernstein's *West Side Story.* This success was followed by a performance with the New York Philharmonic in Mahler's Symphony No. 4.

Considered one of America's best coloratura sopranos, Grist has sung at most of the world's great opera houses, including La Scala, Vienna State, Britain's Royal Opera, and the Metropolitan Opera. When Dr. Herbert Graf left his position as stage director of the Met in 1960 to become director of the Zurich Opera, he persuaded many operatic talents, including Grist, to accompany him there. While in Europe, Grist was asked by Stravinsky to sing under his direction in *Le Rossignol.*

In addition to a career in performance, Grist has taught voice at Indiana University and the Hochschule fur Musik in Germany.

Emma Hackley did as much to promote African-American musicians as she did to promote traditional African music. She received her musical training while growing up in Detroit, Michigan, where she studied voice and piano and began giving local recitals at an early age. She attended the University of Denver, where she received her bachelor's degree in music in 1900. In 1905 she traveled to Paris, where she continued her studies.

Hackley concertized extensively during the early years of the twentieth century, but gradually turned to developing and supporting the careers of other talented young black artists. Through recitals, concerts, lectures, and demonstrations, she raised funds for scholarships; in 1908 she established an ongoing scholarship to promote and fund study abroad. She sponsored debut recitals for young performers and helped many find good college-level teaching positions. Many of the artists she supported and promoted went on to become successful musical leaders in their own right.

Hackley founded and directed the Vocal Normal Institute in Chicago between 1912 and 1916. In the last years of her life, she organized large community concerts promoting the importance of black folk music, raising the level of public interest and pride in African-American musical heritage. So significant was her contribution that twenty years after her death, the National Association of Negro Musicians established the Hackley Collection at the Detroit Public Library for the preservation of materials relating to black musicians.

Emma Azalia Hackley (1867–1922)

Singer, Educator, Choral Director

Helen Hagen was born into a musical family—her mother played piano, and her father sang baritone. After receiving her initial musical education from her mother and the public school system in New Haven, Connecticut, in 1912 she became the first black pianist to earn a bachelor's degree in music from Yale University. She was also the first African American to win Yale's Sanford Fellowship, which permitted her to study in Europe. She earned a diploma in 1914 from the Schola Cantorum, and later received a master's degree from Columbia University Teacher's College in New York.

Between 1914 and 1918, Hagen toured in the United States; her repertoire included many of her own piano compositions. In 1918 she toured Europe, entertaining World War I servicemen; in 1919 she became the first black musician to teach in Chicago's downtown district; and in 1921 she became the first black pianist to give a solo recital in a major New

Helen Eugenia Hagen (1891–1964)

Pianist, Composer

York concert hall when she performed at Town Hall. During the 1930s she taught at Tennessee State A&M College and served as dean of music at Bishop College in Marshal, Texas. In 1935 she established the Helen Hagen Music Studio in New York City.

Dorothy Antoinette Handy (Miller) (1930–)

Flutist

Antoinette Handy began to study music as a young child under the direction of her mother, who taught her violin and piano. She went on to study at Spelman College in Atlanta, at the New England Conservatory of Music (B.M. 1952), at Northwestern University in Illinois (M.M. 1953), and the National Conservatory in Paris (Artist's Diploma 1955).

Handy has worked with many orchestras, including the Chicago Civic Orchestra (1952–1953), the International Orchestra of Paris (1954–1955), Musica Viva Orchestra of Geneva (1955), Symphony of the Air on NBC (1956), the Orchestra of America in New York (1960–1962), the Symphony of the New World (1968–1971), and the Richmond (Virginia) Symphony (1966–1976). She is a founding member of the Trio Pro Viva, which, among other activities, commissions and performs works by African-American composers.

Handy also toured widely as a concert artist, played for films and television, and has been a lecturer, consultant, project director, and radio commentator. She has taught at Florida A&M University, Tuskegee Institute, Jackson State College, and Virginia State College. She has written numerous articles for professional journals, and three books: *Black Music: Opinions and Reviews* (1974), *Black Women in American Bands and Orchestras* (1981), and *The International Sweethearts of Rhythm* (1983).

Margaret Rosezarion Harris (1943–)

Pianist, Conductor, Composer

Margaret Harris began life as a child prodigy—she gave her first concert at age three, began touring nationally when she was four, and played with the Chicago Symphony when she was ten. She studied piano and conducting at the Curtis Institute and the Juilliard School of Music, receiving her bachelor's degree in 1964 and her master's degree in 1965.

Harris's conducting career has encompassed both symphony orchestras and Broadway shows. Her Broadway credits include *Hair* (1970–1972), *Two Gentlemen of Verona* (1972–1974), *Raisin* (1974–1976), *Guys and Dolls* (1980), and *Amen Corner* (1983–1984). She has conducted major symphony orchestras in Chicago, Minneapolis, Detroit, San Diego, St.

Louis, and Los Angeles—often in these concerts she both performed and conducted her own piano concertos. She was a founding member of Opera Ebony and has served as its music director. Her compositions include two piano concerti, four musical production scores, two ballets, themes for television shows, and choral and instrumental works.

Hazel Harrison was one of the leading pianists of her day. As a child she studied with Victor Heinz, who arranged for her to study in Berlin for several years beginning in 1904. At this time, she studied with Ferruccio Busoni, gave recitals, and performed with the Berlin Philharmonic. Upon returning to the United States, she won an award that allowed her to return to Berlin from 1910 to 1914.

Hazel Harrison (1883–1969)

Pianist

When she returned again to the States, she taught in Chicago and toured throughout the country. In 1931 Harrison began teaching college—she taught at the Tuskegee Institute in Alabama (1931–1943), Howard University in Washington, DC (1934–1959), and Alabama State A&M College at Montgomery (1959–1964). She continued to concertize frequently until retirement.

Roland Hayes was born to former slave parents in Curryville, Georgia on June 3, 1887. His father, a tenant farmer, died when Hayes was twelve. Determined that her seven children would receive an education, Hayes's mother sent them to Chattanooga, Tennessee, where they set up a rotating system whereby one brother worked while the others attended school. Hayes was employed in a machine shop, but when his turn came to go to school he passed it up, continuing to supply the family income while he studied at night.

Roland Hayes (1987–1977)

Singer

In 1917 Hayes became the first black to give a recital in Boston's Symphony Hall. Three years later he traveled to London and gave a royal command performance, followed by other successes throughout Europe. His tenor voice was used to good advantage in programs blended from Negro spirituals, folk songs, operatic arias, and German lieder.

Hayes gave a well-received farewell concert at Carnegie Hall in New York on his seventy-fifth birthday in 1962. During his career he received many awards and citations, including eight honorary degrees and the NAACP's Spingarn Medal for the most outstanding achievement among blacks.

Hayes died in Boston on January 1, 1977 at the age of eighty-nine. His success in the concert field played a great part in broadening the opportunities later afforded to such singers as Paul Robeson and Marian Anderson.

Barbara Hendricks (1948-)

Singer

Barbara Hendricks was born in Stephens, Arkansas. She graduated from the University of Nebraska with a bachelor of science degree in chemistry and mathematics, then attended the Juilliard School of music and received a bachelor of music degree in voice. Hendricks made her debut in 1974 with the San Francisco Spring Opera. She has since performed with major opera companies and festivals throughout the United States and Europe, including the Boston Opera, St. Paul Opera, Deutsche Opera in Berlin, Nederlandse Operastichting, Aix-en-Provence Festival, and Glyndebourne Festival Opera. She has performed with numerous symphony orchestras, and has appeared in a film version of *La Boheme*.

Gail Hightower (1946-)

Bassoonist

Gail Hightower displayed great musical promise as a child. She attended the High School of Performing Arts in New York City. Scholarships from the New Amsterdam Musical Association and the Rockefeller Foundation, and grants from the National Endowment for the Arts, allowed her to attend the Manhattan School of Music, from which she reveived both her bachelor's and her master's degrees.

She made her debut as a recitalist at Carnegie Hall in 1979, and in 1980 she was named the NAACP Outstanding Woman in the Arts. Hightower has performed with many symphony orchestras, including the Symphony of the New World (1968–1978) and the Brooklyn Philharmonic (1979–1981; 1985). Her professional affiliations have included the Great Neck Symphony; Festival Orchestra in Siena, Italy; North Carolina School of the Arts Festival Orchestra; Urban Philharmonic (New York City and Washington, DC); Harlem Philharmonic; and the instrumental ensemble of the Dance Theater of Harlem. She currently teaches at the Aaron Copland School of Music at the Queens College of City University of New York.

Ann Stevens Hobson (1943-)

Harpist

Ann Hobson, one of the first African-American women to hold a permanent position in a major national symphony orchestra, began studying piano with her mother at an early age. She took up the harp in high school so she could play an instrument on which her mother could not tell what she was doing wrong. Early in high school she tried to attend a summer program at the Maine Harp Colony, but was rejected on the basis of her race. Several years later she tried again and was accepted. While at the colony, she met harpist Alice Chalifoux of the Cleveland Symphony Orchestra, and later transferred from the Philadelphia Musical Academy to the Cleveland Institute of Music to study with Chalifoux.

In 1966 the first harpist of the National Symphony Orchestra broke a finger; the orchestra's manager called Chalifoux, who recommended Hobson to take the place of the injured harpist. Hobson played with the group for three seasons before joining the Boston Symphony Orchestra, with which she has played ever since. Hobson's other activities have included performing with the Boston Symphony chamber players and the New England Harp Trio, and doing solo appearances with orchestras throughout the country. She has taught at the Philadelphia Musical Academy and the New England Conservatory and has conducted many clinics and workshops, always encouraging other young harpists.

Ben Holt
(1956–1990)

Singer

Born in Washington, DC, baritone Ben Holt attended the Oberlin Conservatory of Music and was a scholarship student at the Juilliard School of Music, where he worked with Sixten Ehrling, Tito Gobbi, and Manuel Rosenthal. He took Luciano Pavarotti's master classes and studied extensively with renowned pianist and coach Martin Isepp. While in the San Francisco Opera's Merola Program, in master classes of Elisabeth Schwarzkopf, he was honored with an invitation to study privately at her studio in Zurich.

Holt made his Metropolitan Opera debut during the 1985–1986 season and in 1988 made his debut with the New York City Opera in the title role of Anthony Davis's *Malcolm X*. In addition, he sang *Porgy and Bess* with the Calgary Opera in Canada, and starred in *Le Nozze di Figaro* with the Cincinnati Opera. Holt was the winner of many competitions and awards, including the Joy of Singing Competition, Oratorio Society of New York, Independent Black Opera Singers, Washington International, and D'Angelo Young Artists Competition.

Eva Jessye
(1895–1992)

Choral Conductor,
Composer

Eva Jessye, noted by *Ebony* magazine to be the "first black woman to receive international distinction as a choral director," was also the first black woman to succeed as a professional choral conductor. She began her formal training at Western University in Kansas and Langston University in Oklahoma. She taught in public schools in Oklahoma, at Morgan State College in Baltimore, and Claflin College in Orangeburg, South Carolina.

In the 1920s Jessye went to New York City, where she sang with musical shows and began organizing choirs. By 1926 she had established the Eva Jessye Choir as a successful professional venture. The group toured widely in the United States and in Europe and performed with conductors such as Ormandy, Stokowski, and Mitropoulous. In 1934 Jessye directed the choir for Virgil Thompson and Gertrude Stein's opera *Four Saints in Three Acts;* in 1935 she served as choral director for Gershwin's *Porgy and Bess.* As a composer, Jessye chose to work mainly in the spiritual tradition, and she produced many choral arrangements. Her works include the oratorios *Paradise Lost and Regained, The Life of Christ in Negro Spirituals,* and *The Chronicle of Job.*

**John Rosamond
Johnson
(1873–1954)**

Composer

J. Rosamond Johnson, brother of writer and lyricist James Weldon Johnson, was born in Jacksonville, Florida. He received his musical training at the New England Conservatory and, for a time, studied under composer Samuel Coleridge-Taylor.

Eager to pursue a career in show business, Johnson teamed up with lyricist and vaudeville entertainer Bob Cole in 1899. With lyrics supplied by his brother James, Johnson and Cole wrote numerous songs, including *Under the Bamboo Tree, Congo Love Songs, My Castle on the Nile,* and *Lift Every Voice and Sing.*

Johnson and Cole also wrote, directed, and produced several musicals, including *The Shoo-fly Regiment* in 1907 and *The Red Moon* in 1910. In addition to songwriting, Johnson edited several collections of Negro spirituals.

**Elayne Jones
(1928–)**

Timpanist

Elayne Jones began studying piano with her mother when she was six years old. When she enrolled in New York City's High School of the Performing Arts, all of the piano positions in the orchestra were taken, so she was forced to switch to a new instrument. She told the *New York Times,* "I was small and the only thing I could handle were the drums, which were small. I took a liking to them."

Jones has played with the orchestras of the New York City Ballet (1949–1952), New York City Opera (1949–1961), American Symphony Orchestra (1962–1972), Brooklyn Philharmonic (1969–1972), and Westchester Philharmonic (1969–1972). In 1972, conductor Seiji Ozawa invited her to join the San Francisco Symphony, and she became the first black female to hold a principal chair in a major symphony orchestra. When she was refused tenure in 1974, and again in 1975, she filed a suit that lasted over a year. Despite her exemplary professional record and the support of friends, colleagues, and the San Francisco public, she lost her battle.

In 1965, Jones provided the impetus for the founding of the Symphony of the New World. As she explained to the *New York Times,* when the conductor Benjamin Steinberg had money for one concert, "I suggest[ed] that he should make it have more purpose than playing one concert. He agreed that we would try to organize an orchestra of some caliber, mostly of Negroes with some white musicians." The orchestra played for eleven years, and during part of that time she also served as its president.

In addition to her symphonic work, Jones holds an extensive resumé of free-lance work that includes Broadway shows, films, and television. She has taught at the Metropolitan Music School, the Bronx Community College of the City University of New York, the Westchester Conservatory, and the San Francisco Conservatory. She has also traveled widely, giving lectures and demonstrations.

Scott Joplin (1868–1917)

Pianist, Composer

Coming from a musical family, Scott Joplin received much encouragement to study music. His father bought him a piano, and Joplin studied classical piano with a local German music teacher. When he left home, however, he could only find musical work in such venues as bars and brothels. In 1894 he settled in Sedalia, Missouri to teach piano and study theory and composition at George R. Smith College for Negroes. In 1899 he published *The Maple Leaf Rag,* which was enormously successful; his piano rags appealed greatly to the public, and within a few years he had achieved financial success with his ragtime compositions.

Joplin also composed larger works in the same style. He completed a ballet in 1899 and his first opera in 1908 (the score of which is now lost); he also wrote a second opera, *Treemonisha.* He was determined to produce this opera and see it performed, but had no luck. He personally financed the publication of the vocal score and produced a non-staged version of the opera for critics, but New York audiences were not ready for an opera about blacks by a black composer, and no one would give financial backing to a full production. After the "Ragtime Renaissance" of the early 1970s, Joplin's opera was given a world premiere in Atlanta, Georgia, and has been performed elsewhere many times, including a masterful performance by the Houston Grand Opera Company.

Ulysses Kay

(1917–)

Composer, Educator

Ulysses Kay was born in Tucson, Arizona. He attended the University of Arizona, where he received a bachelor's degree in music. He later received a master's degree in music from the Eastman School of Music at the University of Rochester. Kay also studied with Paul Hindemith at Yale and Otto Luening at Columbia. He spent the years between 1942 and 1945 in the Navy, and from 1949 to 1952 he lived in Rome, studying music as a Fulbright Fellow. Kay has taught at Boston University and the University of California at Los Angeles, and is currently professor of music at Lehman College in New York.

Although his uncle was Joseph "King" Oliver, the legendary cornet player, Kay believes that jazz is a much more limited medium than symphonic music. His works for voice, chamber groups, and orchestra include *Choral Triptych, Six Dances* (for string orchestra), *Fantasy Variations* (for orchestra), *Sinfonia in E,* and *The Boor* (an opera). He has performed and recorded throughout the United States and Europe.

Tania Justina Leon

(1944–)

Composer, Conductor

Tania Leon was born, raised, and educated in Havana, Cuba. She studied piano and composition at the Carlos Alfredo Peyrellado Conservatory, receiving a bachelor's degree in 1963 and a master's degree in 1964. She won the Young Composer's Prize from the National Council of Arts in Havana in 1966. She moved to the United States in 1967, and in 1968 she joined the Dance Theatre of Harlem as its music director and resident composer.

Leon received her introduction to conducting when the Dance Theatre attended the Spoleto Festival in the late 1960s; the director of the Dance Theatre, Arthur Mitchel, and the director of the festival, Gian-Carlo Menotti, encouraged her to conduct the festival orchestra instead of using recorded music for the dancers. When she returned to the States, she studied conducting at the Juilliard School of Music, the Berkshire Music Center at Tanglewood, and New York University, from which she received both bachelor of science and bachelor of arts degrees in 1971, and a master of science degree in 1973. She has conducted such orchestras as Genoa Symphony Orchestra, the BBC Symphony Orchestra, and the Halle Orchestra; in 1978 she was appointed Music Director and Conductor of the Brooklyn Philharmonic.

Leon's compositions bring together the rich and varied elements of her cultural heritage as an African, Cuban, and American. She has written many ballets, orchestra works, chamber pieces, and vocal works. She has taught composition at Brooklyn College, has served as the resident composer for the Lincoln Center Institute, and was the artistic director of the Composer's Forum in New York.

Henry Lewis (1932–)

Conductor, Bassist

Henry Lewis was born in Los Angeles, California and attended the University of Southern California. Between 1955 and 1957, Lewis, while stationed in Germany, directed the Seventh Army Symphony Orchestra. He made his debut as a conductor in 1972 with the New York Philharmonic and became the first black to conduct the Metropolitan Opera Orchestra. He is the founder of the Los Angeles Chamber Orchestra and the Black Academy of Arts and Letters, and has since served as guest conductor for numerous orchestras.

Dorothy Leigh Maynor (1910–)

Singer

Born in Norfolk, Virginia, Dorothy Leigh Mayner (she changed the spelling of her last name when she became a singer) was raised in an atmosphere of music and singing. She originally intended to become a home economics teacher and, with this in mind, entered Hampton Institute at the age of fourteen. She received her bachelor's degree in 1933. She was heard by the director of the Westminster Choir, who made it possible for her to receive a scholarship at Westminster Choir College in Princeton, New Jersey.

In 1935 she received her bachelor's degree in music and left for New York to study voice. Singing at the Berkshire Music Festival in 1939, she was heard by Boston Symphony Orchestra conductor Serge Koussevitzky. She has since performed with the country's major orchestras, including the New York Orchestra and the Los Angeles Symphony Orchestra. Maynor has been acclaimed by critics as one of America's leading singers.

In 1965 Maynor organized the Harlem School of the Arts in the St. James Presbyterian Church, which was pastored by her husband, the Reverend Shelby A. Rooks. In 1971 she received a doctor of humane letters from Oberlin. She was elected to the Metropolitan Opera's board of directors in 1975, becoming the first black to serve on the organization's board.

Robert McFerrin

(1921–)

Singer, Educator

Born in Marianna, Arkansas, baritone Robert McFerrin received his musical training at the Chicago Musical College, obtaining a bachelor's degree there. He sang the title role in *Rigoletto* with the New England Opera Company in 1950 and was a baritone soloist in the Lewisohn Stadium Summer Concert Series in 1954. McFerrin made his Metropolitan Opera debut in 1955, singing the role of Amonasro in *Aida*.

McFerrin has served as a guest professor of voice at Sibelius Academy in Finland and Roosevelt University in Chicago. He has also served as a member of the voice faculty at Nelson School of Fine Arts in Nelson, British Columbia, Canada.

Lena Johnson McLin

(1928–)

Composer, Conductor, Educator

Lena McLin's musical life began in the Greater Mt. Calvary Baptist Church in Atlanta, where her father was minister and her mother was music director. She received her first training in classical music from her mother, and learned traditional spirituals from her grandmother. She earned an M.A. from the American Conservatory in 1954. She has also studied at Roosevelt University in Chicago State College. In the early 1960s, she started the McLin Opera Company to give promising young artists a performing venue. She taught high school music and directed church choirs in Chicago for several decades, and helped to establish new music programs in her community. She has conducted many workshops and clinics at colleges and universities around the country; in 1972, she won the Teacher of the Year award in Chicago.

McLin's compositions are primarily sacred pieces that combine spiritual traditions with classical musical styles; as a choir director, she wrote music for her Sunday services. Her music also incorporates popular and rock idioms, and she served as the adviser on rock music for the Music Educators National Conference. Her compositions include cantatas, masses, spiritual arrangements, operas, works for piano, orchestras, and electronic music.

Leona Mitchell

(1949–)

Singer

Soprano Leona Mitchell is a native of Enid, Oklahoma, and a graduate of Oklahoma University. Mitchell has performed with the San Francisco Opera, Washington Opera Society, Houston Opera, and at the Gran Teatro del Liceo in Barcelona. Her orchestral appearances have included concerts with the Cleveland Orchestra, London Symphony, and New Jersey Symphony.

During the summer of 1980 she sang Bess in the Cleveland Orchestra Blossom Festival production of *Porgy and Bess,* and performed the same role in their subsequent recording of the work. Mitchell made her Metropolitan Opera debut as Micaela in *Carmen* in 1975, and since then she has been heard there as Lauretta in *Gianni Schicci,* Pamina in *The Magic Flute,* and Madame Lidoine in *Dialogues of the Carmelites.*

Dorothy Rudd Moore (1940–)

Composer, Singer

Dorothy Rudd Moore studied music theory and composition at Howard University, graduating magna cum laude in 1963. She studied with Nadia Boulanger at the Conservatoire de Musique in France, and at Columbia University in New York. She has taught at the Harlem School of Arts, New York University, and Bronx Community College, and has taught piano and voice privately. Her compositions have been performed throughout the United States at such eminent places as Cargnegie Hall, Town Hall, Tuly Hall, and Philharmonic Hall. She has written symphonies, songs, chamber pieces, and an opera. The *New York Times* has described her as "a gifted and creative mind at work." *Opera News* reported that in her opera *Frederick Douglass,* "Moore displays rare ability to wed musical and dramatic motion, graceful lyric inventiveness, (and) a full command of the orchestral palette."

Kermit Moore (1929–)

Cellist, Composer, Conductor

Kermit Moore started his musical career as a cellist. He studied cello at the Cleveland Institute of Music (B.M. 1951), New York University (M.A. 1952), and the Paris Conservatory (Artists Diploma, 1956). He has performed with orchestras throughout the world, including the Orchestra de la Suisse Romande, Concertgebouw of Amsterdam, National Radio Symphony of Paris, and Belgian National Orchestra. He played his debut recital at the New York Town Hall in 1949, and has since given recitals in almost every major city in the world, including Paris, Brussels, Vienna, Cologne, Hamburg, Munich, Geneva, Basel, Amsterdam, Tokyo, Seoul, New York, Boston, Chicago, and San Francisco.

In 1965, Moore co-founded the Symphony of the New World in New York; he not only performed as cellist with the group, but conducted occasionally as well. He has served as guest conductor with, among other groups, the Detroit Symphony Orchestra, Brooklyn Philharmonic, Festival Orchestra at the United Nations, Berkeley (California) Symphony, Dance Theatre of Harlem, and Opera Ebony. Moore is a member of ASCAP and was co-founder of the Society of Black Composers. His works include solo music for cello, a cello concerto, a timpani concerto, songs, arias, and various pieces for chamber ensemble.

Undine Smith Moore

(1904–1989)

Composer, Educator

Undine Smith Moore was one of the most important and influential music educators of the twentieth century, as is evident by her numerous awards and honors. She received honorary doctorates from Virginia State University in 1972, and from Indiana University in 1976. The mayor of New York City presented her with a certificate of appreciation, she received the seventh annual Humanitarian Award from Fisk University in 1973, she won the National Association of Negro Musicians Award in 1975, and in that same year Mayor Remmis Arnold of Petersburg, Virginia, proclaimed April 13th as Undine Moore Day.

Moore received her B.A. and B.M. degrees from Fisk University in Nashville, and an M.A. and professional diploma from Columbia University's Teachers College in New York. She also studied at the Juilliard School of Music, Manhattan School of Music, and Eastman School of Music in Rochester, New York. She taught at Virginia State College in Petersburg from 1927–1972, where she co-founded and directed the Black Music Center. She also served as visiting professor at numerous other schools, including Carleton College in Northfield, Minnesota; St. Benedict College in St. Joseph, Minnesota; St. Johns University in Collegeville, Minnesota; and Virginia Union University in Richmond.

As a composer, Moore wrote works for a variety of ensembles. Many of her works are for chorus, and she has also written for solo voice, piano, organ, flute, and clarinet. Her works have received much recognition, and her *Afro-American Suite,* commissioned by Antoinette Handy's Trio Pro Viva, has been performed widely. Her cantata *Scenes from the Life of a Martyr: To the Memory of Martin Luther King* received a nomination for a Pulitzer prize.

Michael Morgan

(1957–)

Conductor

Born in Washington, DC, Michael Morgan attended the Oberlin College Conservatory of Music. He pursued additional studies in the Vienna master classes of Witold Rowicki and at the Berkshire Music Center at Tanglewood, where he was a conducting fellow and student of Seiji Ozawa and Gunther Schuller. Michael Morgan appeared with the New York Philharmonic in September of 1986 in the Leonard Bernstein Young American Conductors concerts. From 1980 to 1987, he was Exxon/Arts Endowment assistant conductor of the Chicago Symphony Orchestra, where he is now an affiliate artist conductor. Previously, he was apprentice conductor of the Buffalo Philharmonic under music director Julius Rudel. Morgan has appeared as a guest conductor with many of our nation's major orchestras. He made his New York City Opera debut conducting multiple performances of *La Traviata* in New York, Wolf Trap, and Taiwan. In Europe, Morgan has led performances of the Vienna State Opera, the Deutsche Staatsoper in East Berlin, the Vienna Symphony Orchestra, Warsaw Philharmonic Orchestra, and Danish Radio Orchestra.

The many awards Morgan has earned include first prizes in the 1980 Hans Swarowsky International Conductors Competition (Vienna), the Gino Marrinuzzi International Conductors Competition (San Remo, Italy), and the Baltimore Symphony Young Conductors Competition.

Soprano Jessye Norman was born in Augusta, Georgia to a musical family. Her mother, a school teacher and amateur pianist, provided the family with piano lessons. At the age of sixteen, Norman went to Philadelphia to compete for the Marian Anderson Scholarship. She did not win this competition, but once the director of the music department at Howard University heard her sing, she was granted a full four-year scholarship.

Jessye Norman (1945–)

Singer

Norman graduated with honors from Howard in 1967 and went on to study at the Peabody Conservatory in Baltimore, Maryland and at the University of Michigan, where she received a master's degree in 1968.

In 1968, Norman entered the Bavarian Radio Corporation's International Music Competition, receiving first prize. In 1969, she made her debut with the Deutsch Opera in Berlin as Elisabeth in Wagner's *Tannhauser,* and in 1970 she made her Italian opera debut. Appearing at La Scala in Milan, Wolf Trap in Virginia, the Tanglewood Music Festival, and at the Royal Opera House in Covent Garden, England, Norman has performed with some of the world's leading orchestras.

Following a temporary leave from opera in the mid-1970s, Norman returned to the stage in 1980 in Strauss's *Ariadne auf Naxos.* She has since made numerous concert appearances and several recordings, including Berg's *Lulu Suite,* Berlioz's *Les nuits d'été* and *Romeo and Juliette,* Bizet's *Carmen,* Mahler's *Kindertotenlieder,* and a recent album entitled *Lucky to Be Me.*

Norman has received numerous awards for her work, including several Grammy awards, an Outstanding Musician of the Year award, and several honorary degrees from American universities. She is also a member of the Royal Academy of Music.

Coleridge-Taylor Perkinson (1932-)

Composer

Born in New York, Perkinson took graduate and postgraduate degrees from the Manhattan School of Music (1953, 1954) before going on to study at the Berkshire Music Center, the Mozarteum, and the Netherland Radio Union Hilversum. Becoming the first composer in residence for the Negro Ensemble Company, he wrote the music for many plays, including Peter Weiss's *Song of the Lusitanian Bogey,* Ray McIver's *God Is a (Guess What?),* and Errol Hill's *Man Better Man.* In 1965, when the Symphony of the New World was organized in New York, Perkinson was named associate conductor. His concert pieces include *Concerto for Violin and Orchestra* (1954) and *Attitudes* (1964), written for black opera star George Shirley. Perkinson has also composed music for television and radio programs, the documentary film *Cross-roads Africa,* and ballet ensembles.

Julia Perry (1924–1979)

Composer, Conductor

Julia Perry was born in Lexington, Kentucky, and raised in Akron, Ohio. She studied violin, piano, and voice as a child. In 1942, she enrolled at the Westminster Choir College in Princeton, New Jersey, studying violin, piano, voice, conducting, and composition. Even before graduating, she began publishing her compositions; *Carillon Heigh-Ho* was published in 1947. After receiving her master's degree from Westminster in 1948, she went on to attend Juilliard School of Music. In 1950, her cantata *Ruth* was premiered in New York.

Between 1951 and 1959 she lived in Europe. After studying with composer Luigi Dallapiccola at the Berkshire Music Center, she won a Guggenheim fellowship to continue studying with him in Florence and to study with Nadia Boulanger in Paris. Throughout the United States and Europe her work received acclaim. In 1954, her one-act opera *The Cask of Amontillado* was produced at Columbia University.

After her return to the States in 1959, she continued to compose music. She taught at a number of universities, including Florida A&M University in Tallahassee and the Atlanta Colleges Center. In 1955 she received the Boulanger Grand Prix award, and in 1964 she won the American Academy and National Institute of Arts and Letters award. In 1969 she received honorable mention in the ASCAP awards. Perry's compositions include *Stabat Mater* (1951) for contralto and strings, *Pastoral* (1959) for flute and strings, *Homunchulus* (1960) for soprano and percussion, and the operas *The Bottle, The Cask of Amontillado,* and *The Selfish Giant.*

While a senior at Spelman College in Atlanta studying African-American history, Evelyn Pittman committed herself to teaching black history through music. Her first work, a musical play, was produced at Spelman in 1933. During the years that she taught in the public schools in Oklahoma City (1935 to 1956), she conducted weekly broadcasts on a local radio station with her own professional group, the Evelyn Pittman Choir; she directed a 350-voice choir sponsored by the YWCA; and she directed orchestras, choirs, and operettas in the schools. She also began composing songs about black leaders, and published a collection of songs, *Rich Heritage,* in 1944.

In 1948 she went to Juilliard to study composition, then earned a master's degree from Oklahoma University in 1954. Between 1956 and 1958, she studied composition with Nadia Boulanger in Paris and completed her first opera, *Cousin Esther.* It received its first performance in Paris in 1957 and in the next few years was performed in Europe and the United States with rave reviews. She returned to public-school teaching in 1958 in New York State and continued to compose. After the assassination of Martin Luther King, Jr., in 1968, she wrote the opera *Freedom Child* in his memory and honor; when she retired, she dedicated herself to directing a touring company of *Freedom Child.* Her other compositions include choral arrangements of spirituals, and a stage work entitled *Jim Noble.*

Evelyn La Rue Pittman (1910–)

Choral Director, Composer

Karl Hampton Porter was born in Pittsburgh, Pennsylvania. While in high school, he learned to play bassoon and saxophone. He received his musical training at Carnegie-Mellon University, the Peabody Conservatory, and the Juilliard School of Music, where he studied bassoon and conducting.

Porter has organized several musical groups throughout the New York area, including the Harlem Youth Symphony, Harlem Philharmonic Orchestra, New Breed Brass Ensemble, Harlem String Quartet, and Harlem Woodwind Quintet. He has served as conductor of the Baltimore Symphony, Massapequa Symphony, and Park West Symphony, and he has been the musical director of numerous productions. Porter has taught at New York City Technical College and served as chairman of the college's Fine Arts Lecture Series.

Karl Hampton Porter (1939–)

Bassoonist, Conductor, Educator

Florence Price

(1888–1953)

Composer, Pianist

Florence Price was born in Little Rock, Arkansas and grew up in Chicago. She studied music with her mother, a talented soprano and concert pianist. In 1902 she enrolled in the New England Conservatory of Music in Boston, majoring in piano and organ. After graduating in 1907, she returned to Little Rock as a music educator, performer, and composer. In 1927, due to racial tensions, she moved to Chicago and pursued further musical education. In the early 1920s Price's compositions began to receive notice. She won the Rodman Wanamaker Foundation Award for a piano sonata and her *Symphony in E Minor;* the Chicago Symphony Orchestra premiered this work in 1933 at the Chicago World's Fair. She also presented a program of her pieces at the fair, and the Women's Symphony Orchestra of Chicago performed some of her works. In 1934 she appeared as soloist in her *Concerto in D Minor* at the Chicago Musical College and in Pittsburgh. That same year, she conducted a performance of her *Concerto in F Minor* with pianist/composer Margaret Bonds as the soloist.

Her fame grew steadily. In 1940, she performed her *Concerto in One Movement* with the WPA Symphony Orchestra in Detroit, which played her *Symphony No. 3 in C Minor* in the same program. The Forum String Quartet of Chicago and faculty members of the Music School of the University of Illinois performed some of her chamber music. The British conductor Sir John Barbirolli commissioned her to write a suite for strings, which he presented in Manchester England. Marian Anderson sang Price's *Songs to the Dark Virgin* in her second American concert tour, receiving rave reviews. In addition to her larger orchestral and chamber works, she wrote many art songs, spiritual arrangements, and choral pieces, as well as piano, organ, and violin works.

Leontyne Price

(1927–)

Singer

Born Mary Violet Leontyne Price, in Laurel, Mississippi, Price was encouraged by her parents, who were amateur musicians, to sing and play the piano at an early age. In 1949 she received her bachelor's degree from the College of Education and Industrial Arts (now Central State College) in Wilberforce, Ohio, where she had studied music education in hopes of becoming a music teacher.

Price received a scholarship to study at the Juilliard School of Music in New York City. While appearing in a student production of Verdi's *Falstaff,* she was noticed by composer and music critic Virgil Thomson, who later cast her in her first professional role in a revival of his opera *Four Saints in Three Acts.*

Between 1952 and 1954 Price performed the role of Bess in a revival of Gershwin's *Porgy and Bess*. It was during this production that she met and married her co-star, baritone William C. Warfield. The two divorced, however, in 1973, following years of separation.

In 1954 Price made her debut at New York's Town Hall. From there she went on to appear in Puccini's *Tosca* in 1955, Mozart's *The Magic Flute* in 1956, and Poulenc's *Dialogues of the Carmelites*. Between 1958 and 1960 she appeared at Verona, Vienna, Covent Garden, and La Scala. Price had become one of the world's leading sopranos.

On January 27, 1961, Price made her Metropolitan Opera debut in Verdi's *Il Trovatore*, a performance for which she received a standing ovation. She has since appeared in numerous Met productions, including Puccini's *The Girl of the Golden West* and the world premiere of Samuel Barber's *Antony and Cleopatra* in 1966.

Price has made numerous appearances at the White House, and has performed at two presidential inaugurations. In 1977 Price was awarded the San Francisco Opera medal in honor of the twentieth anniversary of her debut with the company. On April 20, 1982, Price opened the convention of the Daughters of the American Revolution in Constitution Hall with a concert honoring Marian Anderson. In 1939 Anderson had been barred from appearing in Constitution Hall by the DAR, prompting Eleanor Roosevelt to resign in anger from the organization.

Kay George Roberts (1950–)

Violinist, Conductor

Kay Roberts began her professional musical career as a violinist when she joined the Nashville Symphony during her last year in high school; she continued to play with the group until she graduated from Fisk University in 1972. In 1971 she represented the Nashville Symphony in Arthur Fiedler's World Symphony Orchestra. She received her M.M. in 1975, and her D.M.A. in 1986. She has guest conducted for many orchestras, including the Bangkok Symphony in Thailand, the Nashville Symphony Orchestra, the Mystic Valley Chamber Orchestra, and the Greater Dallas Symphony Orchestra. She became the music director of the New Hampshire Philharmonic in 1982, and the Music Director of the Cape Ann Symphony Orchestra in 1986. She has been teaching at the College of Music at the University of Lowell since 1978.

Paul Robeson
(1898–1976)

Singer, Actor

Born in Princeton, New Jersey on April 9, 1898, Paul Robeson was the son of a runaway slave who put himself through Lincoln University and later became a Presbyterian minister. Robeson entered Rutgers College (now Rutgers University) on a scholarship, and he won a total of twelve letters in track, football, baseball, and basketball. In addition to his athletic exploits, his academic ability gained him Phi Beta Kappa honors in his junior year.

In 1923, Robeson received a law degree from Columbia University, financing his schooling by playing professional football. While at Columbia, Robeson was seen by Eugene O'Neill in an amateur play. After making his professional debut in *Taboo* (1922), Robeson appeared in O'Neill's *All God's Chillun Got Wings* and *Emperor Jones*. Called upon to whistle in the latter play, Robeson sang instead, and his voice met with instant acclaim. In 1925 he made his concert debut with a highly successful program of all-African-American music. He went on to such stage successes as *Show Boat, Porgy and Bess,* and *Othello.*

A world traveler in the Soviet Union, Asia, and Europe, Robeson spoke several languages, including Chinese, Russian, Gaelic, and Spanish. Robeson's political affiliations at times tended to attract even more publicity than his artistic career. In 1950, for instance, his passport was revoked after he refused to sign an affidavit as to whether or not he had ever belonged to the Communist Party. Eight years later, the United States Supreme Court ruled that the refusal to sign such an affidavit was not valid grounds for denial of a passport. Robeson subsequently settled in London, making a number of trips to the continent (and to the Soviet Union as well) before returning to the United States in 1963.

Robeson played an active role in civil and human rights issues. He was a co-founder of the Council on African Affairs, and a member of the Joint Anti-Fascist Refugee Committee and the Committee to Aid China. Robeson died January 23, 1976 in Philadelphia, Pennsylvania.

Philippa Schuyler
(1932–1969)

Composer, Pianist

Born on August 21, 1932 in New York City, Philippa Schuyler was already playing the piano at the age of two and began composing a year later. By the time she was eight, she had some fifty compositions to her credit. Her published works include *Six Little Pieces* and *Eight Little Pieces.*

When Schuyler was twelve, her first symphonic composition, *Manhattan Nocturne,* was performed at Carnegie Hall, and the following year her scherzo *Rumpelstiltskin* was performed by the Dean Dixon Youth Orchestra, the Boston Pops, the New Haven Symphony Orchestra, and the New York Philharmonic.

In 1953 Schuyler made her debut at Town Hall in New York as a pianist. She went on to travel to some fifty countries on good will concert tours sponsored by the United States State Department.

Schuyler was considered one of America's most outstanding musical prodigies. Remembered as a mature concert pianist, she died tragically at the height of her career.

George Shirley was born April 18, 1934 in Indianapolis, and moved to Detroit in 1940. There he began giving vocal recitals in churches and decided on a musical career after playing baritone horn in a community band. In 1955 he graduated from Wayne State University in Detroit with a bachelor's degree in musical education.

**George Shirley
(1934–)**

Singer

After his discharge from the Army in 1959, he began serious vocal studies with Themy S. Georgi. In June of that year he made his operatic debut as Eisenstein in Strauss's *Die Fledermaus,* performing with the Turnau Players at Woodstock. A year later he won the American Opera Auditions, whereupon he journeyed to Milan, Italy, making his opera debut there in Puccini's *La Boheme.*

In 1961 his career was given tremendous impetus by his victory in the Metropolitan Opera auditions. Two years later he made his debut at Carnegie Hall with the Friends of French Opera, singing opposite Rita Gorr in Massenet's *La Navarraise.*

Since then, he has sung with several of the Met's leading divas, including Renata Tebaldi in *Simon Boccanegra* and Birgit Nilsson in *Salome.* In 1974, he sang the title role in Mozart's *Idomeneo* at the Glyndebourne Festival, and he has remained a favorite at the Met over the years.

William Grant Still was born in Woodville, Mississippi. Since both of his parents were musicians and his father was the town's bandmaster, he received his early musical training at home.

**William Grant Still
(1895–1978)**

Composer, Conductor

Intending to study medicine, Still enrolled at Wilberforce College but left before graduating. He began to seriously consider a career in music, and after working with various jazz musicians, including W.C. Handy and Paul Whiteman, Still enrolled at Oberlin College Conservatory of Music.

Still became the first African-American composer to have a large-scale work performed by a major American orchestra, when the Rochester Philharmonic Orchestra performed his *Afro-American Symphony* in 1931. In 1936 Still became the first African American to conduct a major American orchestra, when he conducted the Los Angeles Philharmonic in a program of his work. He was also the first African-American composer to have an opera performed by a major opera company, when the New York City Opera performed his *Troubled Island* in 1949.

Still was awarded the Harmon Award in 1928 for his contribution to black culture. He was the winner of two Guggenheim fellowships—one in 1944 and the other in 1961. In 1961, the National Federation of Music Clubs awarded him $1,500 for his composition *The Peaceful Land*. His major works include his composition *Song of a New Race,* the symphonic poem *Darker America,* the suites *Pages from Negro History* and *The American Scene,* and numerous songs and arrangements of spirituals.

Howard Swanson

(1909–1978)

Composer

Howard Swanson was born in Atlanta and raised in Cleveland, where he studied at the Institute of Music. He was taught composition by Herbert Elwell, and in 1938 he won a Rosenwald fellowship to study with Nadia Boulanger in Paris. Returning to the United States, he devoted himself to composition, and in 1950 won wide acclaim as an American composer when his *Short Symphony,* written in 1948, was performed by the New York Philharmonic with Dmitri Mitropoulos conducting. In 1952, this symphony won the New York Critics' award. One of Swanson's best-known works is the song "The Negro Speaks of Rivers," based on a poem by Langston Hughes, which Marian Anderson has sung in recital.

Swanson died in 1978. In 1979, at the St. James Presbyterian Church in New York City, a concert was given by the Triad Chorale as a memorial to him and the composer William Grant Still.

Shirley Verrett, upon her Metropolitan Opera debut in Carmen.

Born to musical family in New Orleans, Shirley Verrett moved to California at the age of five, but had no formal voice training during her childhood—largely because her father felt singing would involve his daughter in too precarious a career. Still, he offered his daughter the opportunity to sing in church choirs under his direction. She attended Ventura College, where she majored in business administration. By 1954 she was a prosperous real estate agent, but her longing for an artistic career had become so acute that she decided to take voice lessons in Los Angeles and train her sights on the concert stage anyway.

**Shirley Verrett
(1933–)**

Singer

After winning a television talent show in 1955, she enrolled at the Juilliard School on a scholarship, earning her diploma in voice some six years later. Her debut at New York's Town Hall in 1958 was not a sensational one. By 1962, however, at Spoleto, Italy, she delivered an excellent *Carmen,* and a year later she performed at Lincoln Center in New York, where her recital was said to be "simply without flaws, simply a great event in the annals of American music-making."

By 1964, her *Carmen* had improved so dramatically that the New York *Herald Tribune* critic was able to claim it as "the finest" performance "seen or heard in New York" for the past generation. Other performances in such roles as Orfeo in Gluck's *Orfeo ed Euridice,* Ulrica in Verdi's *Un Ballo de Maschera,* and Leonora in Beethoven's *Fidelio* have been met with comparable acclaim.

In 1982, Verrett appeared with Grace Bumbry in a concert honoring Marian Anderson on her eightieth birthday. Her yearly recital tours take her to the major music centers throughout the country. During the 1986–1987 season the successes for Verrett included a series of operas staged especially for her by the Paris Opera; Rossini's *Mose,* Cherubini's *Medee,* and Gluck's *Iphigenie en Tauride* and *Alceste.* She made a triumphant return to the Metropolitan Opera in 1986 as Eboli in *Don Carlo* and also starred that year in a new production of *Macbeth* with the San Francisco Opera. In the 1987–1988 season, Verrett made her long-awaited Chicago Lyric Opera debut as Lucena in *Il Trovatore.*

George Walker
(1922–)

Pianist, Educator

Born in Washington, DC, George Walker studied at Oberlin, the Curtis Institute of Music, and at the Eastman School of Music, where he completed his doctorate. His teachers included Rudolf Serkin, Giancarlo Menotti, and Robert Casadesus. Following his well-received Town Hall debut in 1945, Walker gained twenty seasons of experience touring the United States, Canada, and Europe.

Walker has served on the faculty of Smith College, Northhampton, Massachusetts, University of Colorado, University of Delaware, and the Peabody Institute of Johns Hopkins University in Baltimore, Maryland. He is currently professor of music at Rutgers University.

Baritone William Warfield was born in West Helena, Arkansas, and later moved with his family to Rochester, New York, where he attended school. The son of a Baptist minister, he received early training in voice, organ, and piano and, in 1938, while a student at Washington Junior High School, won the vocal competition at the Music Educators National Convention in St. Louis.

He studied at the Eastman School of Music and the University of Rochester, receiving his bachelor's degree in 1942.

Warfield made his debut at New York's Town Hall on March 19, 1950. After his resounding New York debut in 1950, he made an unprecedented tour of Australia under the auspices of the Australian Broadcasting Commission. A year later he made his movie debut in *Show Boat*.

Warfield has appeared on several major television shows and starred in the NBC television version of *Green Pastures*. Between 1952 and 1959 he made five international tours under the auspices of the U.S. State Department. In 1966 he appeared in a revival of the Jerome Kern–Edna Ferber classic *Showboat*. His performances as Porgy in the various revivals of *Porgy and Bess* have made him the best-known singer in this role. He was married to Leontyne Price, the brilliant opera star whom he met during a *Porgy and Bess* production.

William C. Warfield (1920–)

Singer

One of America's most gifted young pianists, Andre Watts achieved a substantial degree of fame while playing under the baton of Leonard Bernstein of the New York Philharmonic.

Born in Nuremberg, Germany, of a Hungarian mother and an American G.I. father, Andre Watts spent the first eight years of his life on Army posts in Europe before moving to Philadelphia. By the time he was nine, he was already performing as a soloist with the Philadelphia Orchestra.

At the age of seventeen, Watts appeared on television in one of Leonard Bernstein's Young People's Concerts and was a huge success. After graduating from Lincoln Preparatory School in Philadelphia, he enrolled at Baltimore's Peabody Conservatory of Music.

Andre Watts (1946–)

Pianist

On one occasion, when Glenn Gould became ill just prior to a performance with the New York Philharmonic, Bernstein chose Watts as a last-minute replacement. At the conclusion of the concerto, Watts received a standing ovation not only from the audience but from the orchestra as well.

In June 1966 Watts made his debut in London, and a month later was the soloist for the two-day Philharmonic Stravinsky Festival at Lincoln Center.

In the 1970s, Watts gave a concert in Teheran as part of the coronation festivities for the then Shah of Iran. Later, at a state dinner for Congo's President Mobutu, he was presented with the African republic's highest honor, the Order of the Zaire. Watts's other rewards include the Lincoln Center Medallion in 1971 and the National Society of Arts and Letters Gold Medal in 1982.

Felix Fowler Weir (1884–1978)

Violinist

Felix Weir began studying violin when an uncle recognized his talent and encouraged him; he played his first public concert at age eleven. He attended the Chicago Musical College and the Conservatory in Leipzig, Germany. Between 1907 and 1914 he taught in public schools in Washington, DC. In 1914 he began to perform again; he moved to New York, joined the New Amsterdam Musical Association, and played with the Clef-Club Orchestra. He formed a duo with cellist Leonard Jeter, and later a trio with pianist Olyve Jeter. In 1914 he formed the American String Quartet with cellist Jeter, violinist Joseph Lymos, and violinist Hall Johnson. In the 1920s he formed another quartet with violinist Johnson, cellist Marion Cumbo, and violinist Arthur Boyd. During the 1920s and 1930s, he also played in the orchestras for Broadway musicals and taught privately. In the 1930s he returned to public school teaching in Washington, DC.

Clarence Cameron White (1880–1960)

Violinist, Composer

Clarence Cameron White achieved success as both a violinist and composer early in life. When he was only fifteen, he performed one of his own compositions in a recital he gave in Washington, DC, and when he was seventeen, he played some of his works in recital in Chicago. White studied violin and composition at Howard University in Washington, DC, the Oberlin Conservatory of Music in Ohio, and in London, Paris, and at Juilliard. Between 1900 and 1910 White taught in the public schools in Washington and, from 1903 to 1907, headed the string program at the newly established Washington Conservatory of Music. Between 1912 and

1923, he lived and taught in Boston and concertized widely. In the 1920s and early 1930s he curtailed his touring to concentrate on composing and teaching college. In 1931 he completed his opera, *Ouanga,* and he returned to the concert circuit in the late 1930s. He composed a variety of works for violin, piano, voice, chorus, orchestra, organ, and chamber ensembles.

Olly Wilson was born in St. Louis, Missouri. While in high school, his clarinet playing earned him a scholarship to his hometown's Washington University. In 1960 Wilson received a master of music degree, with honors, from the University of Illinois, and in 1964 he received a Ph.D. from the University of Iowa.

Wilson's best-known works include the *Sextet, Three Movements for Orchestra,* and *Cetus.* Wilson's style springs from his belief that an African-American composer's "reality" is different. He draws upon a wide spectrum of music not normally regarded as part of the Euro-American tradition.

**Olly W. Wilson
(1937–)**

Composer, Educator

**By Robin
Armstrong**

Blues and Jazz

In less than a century, the remarkable American music called jazz has risen from obscure origins to become the most original form of musical expression of our times. Jazz has a long and rich ancestry, beginning with the arrival of the first Africans on American soil. Borne of the encounter between African music—including work songs, gospel, spirituals, blues, and songs for dancing—and European musical traditions, jazz has become a musical form that is loved, admired, and played all over the world.

BLACK MUSIC IN THE NINETEENTH CENTURY ♦ ♦ ♦ ♦ ♦ ♦ ♦ ♦ ♦

Ragtime and Blues

By the late nineteenth century, a dance music called ragtime had become very popular, particularly the compositions of Scott Joplin. The heavily syncopated rhythms and sprightly melodies of ragtime had a distinctly African-American flavor. About the same time, a form of black American folk music called the blues coalesced into a 12-bar pattern that made it adaptable to popular song writing. The blues has a unique harmonic quality derived from a "flattening" of the third and seventh notes of the tempered scale (creating what are called blue notes), and while seemingly simple, lends itself to infinite variation. The blues had an impact not only on jazz, but also on rock and soul, both of which would be unthinkable without the blues element.

New Orleans Jazz

Jazz was born when ragtime (primarily an instrumental music) and blues (at first primarily a vocal style) came together, and though this process was taking place in many parts of America, it was in New Orleans that the basic language of jazz was first spoken. This was due not only to the rich musical tradition of this port city (with its international atmosphere), but also because social conditions in New Orleans, while certainly not free from racist elements, were less restrictive than in other large American cities at the time. Thus, there was much contact among musicians of varied ethnic backgrounds. Many historical accounts of jazz mistakenly overemphasize the importance of the New Orleans red light district (called Storyville). While early jazz certainly was performed there, many other outlets for music-making existed, including dances, parades, carnivals, and traditional New Orleans funerals, at which a band would accompany the casket from church to cemetery with mournful strains, and then lead the march back to town with livelier music such as ragtime or jazz.

Musicians from New Orleans began to tour the United States in about 1907. Although their music made a significant impression wherever they went, their intricate style of collective improvisation, in which each instrument in the band had its own specific role, was not easily absorbed. It is another myth of jazz history that most of these early jazz players were a special breed of self-taught "naturals"; in fact, almost all of them had good basic musical training that included learning how to read music.

◆ ◆ ◆ ◆ ◆ ◆ ◆ ◆ ◆ ◆ ◆ **EARLY RECORDINGS AND IMPROVISATION**

Jazz developed almost simultaneously with the phonograph, and without the dissemination of jazz recordings, it is unlikely that jazz would have spread as quickly as it did. By studying recorded performances, musicians anywhere could learn at least the rudiments of jazz, a spontaneous music in which improvisation played a considerable role. Jazz improvisation does not mean, as is often believed, inventing music on the spot, without guidelines. It does mean adding one's own ideas to a common musical text, and taking liberties as long as they fit within a shared framework. In addition, a jazz musician's personal style is based on tonal qualities, a distinctive approach to rhythm and phrasing, and a vocabulary of melodic and thematic characteristics. Taken together, these ingredients are what makes it possible for a seasoned listener to identify who is playing in a jazz performance.

Ironically, the first New Orleans jazz to be recorded was performed by a white group, the Original Dixieland Jazz Band, in 1917. By then, black musicians had already made records, but they were not in a jazz idiom. It would take several more years for the best black New Orleans players to make records. In the meantime, however, some of them had already visited Europe, notably Sidney Bechet, the great clarinetist and soprano saxophonist who has been called the first great jazz soloist. But it was a somewhat younger musician from New Orleans, Louis Armstrong, who made the biggest impact on the future of jazz.

Armstrong was brought in 1922 to Chicago (by then the center of jazz activity) by his mentor and fellow trumpeter Joe "King" Oliver. He made his first records there, then came to New York two years later to join the band of Fletcher Henderson. Henderson's band was the first musically significant big band in jazz. While most New Orleans jazz bands used an instrumentation of trumpet, trombone, clarinet, piano, guitar (or banjo), bass (string or brass), and drums, the early big bands used three trumpets, one or two trombones, three reeds (saxophonists doubling clarinet), and rhythm section instruments. They employed written scores (called arrangements), but gave the soloists freedom to improvise their contributions.

Armstrong's arrival was a revelation to the Henderson band. His first solos on the band's records stand out like diamonds in a tin setting. What Louis brought to jazz was, first of all, his superior sense of rhythm, which made

Jazz improvisation does not mean, as is often believed, inventing music on the spot, without guidelines. It does mean adding one's own ideas to a common musical text, and taking liberties as long as they fit within a shared framework.

other players sound stiff and clumsy in comparison. He discovered the rhythmic element called "swing" that sets jazz apart from other music—a kind of rhythmic thrust that seems to float and soar. In addition, his sound on the trumpet was the biggest and most musically appealing yet heard, and he had exceptional range and powers of execution. Further, his gifts of melodic invention were so great that he can be said to have laid the foundation for jazz as a medium for personal expression by an instrumental soloist.

One of Armstrong's first Henderson colleagues to get the message was tenor saxophonist Coleman Hawkins, who soon created the first influential jazz style on his instrument. Also greatly affected was the band's chief arranger, Don Redman, who was the first to translate Armstrong's innovations to big-band arranging. Many others followed suit, especially after Armstrong, now back in Chicago, began to make records with his own studio groups, the Hot Fives and Hot Sevens.

THE JAZZ TRADITION ✦

The Twenties and Thirties

By the late-1920s, jazz had become a mainstay of American popular dance music and had spread to Europe as well. Black American musicians were touring worldwide, including such places as China and India, and wherever they went, their music made an impression. Yet there was still quite a gap between jazz at its best and the more commercially acceptable versions of it. Not until the advent of the so-called "Swing Era" in the 1930s did unadulterated jazz reach a level of popular acceptance which, thus far, remains unmatched.

This level of acceptance was primarily due to the big bands, which had reached a new height of artistic maturity. Duke Ellington, aptly called the greatest American composer, led big band music to this level of sophistication. He gradually created a perfect balance between written and improvised elements for his unique band, which included such great soloists as Johnny Hodges (alto sax), Harry Carney (baritone sax), Barney Bigard (clarinet), Cootie Williams, and Rex Stewart (trumpets). In late 1927, Ellington's band began an important engagement at Harlem's famous Cotton Club. Through appearances there, regular network radio broadcasts, and many recordings, Ellington's music was widely disseminated. His band visited Europe for the first time in 1933.

Important work was also done at this time by Redman and by Benny Carter, a brilliant multi-instrumentalist and arranger–composer. Fletcher Henderson had not previously arranged music for his band, but he began to do so in the early 1930s and soon became one of the best. Such efforts laid the foundation for the success of Benny Goodman, a white clarinetist and bandleader, who commissioned the best black arrangers and was the first white bandleader to hire black musicians.

By 1936, the Swing Era was under way. Black dance styles that developed at such places as Harlem's Savoy Ballroom swept the nation, and young people jitterbugged to the sounds of an astonishing number of excellent bands; those led by Jimmy Lunceford and Count Basie stood out among the many. The big bands spawned a host of gifted young players and brought into the limelight many giants with established reputations in the jazz community, such as Armstrong, who led his own big bands from 1929 to 1947.

World War II brought economic and social changes that affected the big bands. During the war, gasoline rationing impeded the constant touring that was a source of livelihood for the bands. After the war, the advent of television wrought fundamental changes in the ways people sought entertainment. Among the chief victims of the new stay-at-home trend was ballroom dancing. The big bands went into rapid decline, and only a handful were able to survive, among them the bands of Ellington and Basie.

The Postwar Period

Meanwhile, the music itself had also undergone fundamental changes. The singers whose popularity was first established through their work with the bands became stars in their own right. The new generation of players who had come to maturity by way of big-band experiences were eager to express themselves at greater length than most big-band work permitted, and they were coming up with new and potentially radical musical ideas.

The most advanced soloists of the Swing Era, such as Roy Eldridge (trumpet), Lester Young (tenor sax), Art Tatum (piano), and Sid Catlett (drums)

Jazz greats Ella Fitzgerald, Oscar Peterson (piano), Roy Eldridge (trumpet), and Max Roach (drums), 1952.

had been extending the rhythmic, harmonic, and technical resources of their instruments. Two young geniuses, guitarist Charlie Christian (featured with Benny Goodman) and bassist Jimmy Blanton (featured with Duke Ellington), revolutionized the language of their respective instruments.

Christian was among the many notable players who, in the early 1940s, participated in jam sessions (informal musical get-togethers) at Minton's

Playhouse, a night club in Harlem where pianist Thelonious Monk and drummer Kenny Clarke were in the regular house band. At Minton's, experimentation took place that fed into the new jazz mainstream and led to the advent of modern jazz around 1944 and 1945.

The chief creators of this new jazz language were trumpeter (and band-leader–composer) Dizzy Gillespie and alto saxophonist–composer Charlie Parker, both of whom had put in time with leading big bands. While working together in the band of pianist Earl Hines (the father of modern jazz piano style) in 1943, they began to solidify their mutually compatible ideas. When they joined forces in a small group in 1945, on records and in live performances, bebop (as the new jazz style soon was called) came into being.

Bebop

Though bebop was solidly grounded in earlier jazz styles, it seemed different to the public; the average listener often was unable to follow the intricate rhythmic and harmonic elaborations of the boppers. Furthermore, the bop musicians, unlike most of the jazz players who preceded them, were less concerned with pleasing the public than with creating music that fulfilled their artistic ambitions. (Gillespie, however, was an exception, perhaps because his irrepressible sense of humor made him a natural entertainer).

In any case, the advent of bop went hand in hand with a change in the audience for jazz. By the mid-1930s, small clubs catering to jazz connoisseurs had begun to spring up in most larger urban areas. The biggest and most famous concentration was in New York, in two blocks of West 52nd Street, which soon became known as "Swing Street." In such clubs, musicians could perform for knowledgeable listeners without making musical compromises; most of the clubs were too small for dancing, so people came strictly to listen. By this time, people all over the world had become seriously interested in jazz. Some studied and documented its origins and history; others collected, researched, and classified jazz records. Publications like *Downbeat* and *Metronome* arose, catering to musicians and serious fans. These magazines, as well as the prestigious *Esquire,* conducted polls and conferred awards; in the mid-1940s, *Esquire* presented these awards at a huge all-star jazz concert on the stage of the Metropolitan Opera House in New York.

A New Audience

Ornette Coleman's music, deeply rooted in the blues, sparked some controversy at first about its relation to jazz but was eventually accepted into the jazz tradition.

Jazz concerts had been a rarity in the 1920s. Then in 1938, Goodman staged one at Carnegie Hall, and beginning in 1943, Duke Ellington gave an annual concert there. By the late-1940s jazz concerts were regular events, among them the famous "Jazz at the Philharmonic" all-star tours. Thus, the stage was set for the acceptance of jazz not simply as music for entertainment and dancing, but as a form worthy of serious artistic consideration.

Bebop was soon succeeded by radical new forms of jazz. In 1959, a young Texas-born alto saxophonist, Ornette Coleman, brought his adventurous quartet to New York, setting off a controversy with music that seemed to have abandoned most of the harmonic and structural principles of jazz. In fact, Coleman's music was deeply rooted in the blues and in well-established improvisational jazz procedures, and in time his music was accepted as part of the jazz tradition.

By the 1960s, so-called avant-garde jazz was very much in evidence. In 1956, trumpeter Miles Davis, who had worked with Charlie Parker and had led his own very influential groups (one of which gave birth to a style known as cool jazz), hired a little-known tenor saxophonist, John Coltrane. With Coltrane, Davis introduced in 1958 a modal approach to jazz improvisation that was based on scales rather than harmonies. Coltrane soon formed his own group, which took modality much further and extended improvisation both in length and intensity. Cecil Taylor, a virtuoso of the keyboard, further stretched the boundaries of jazz. Davis

The Varied Sounds of Jazz

John Coltrane was known for his modal approach to jazz, which was based on scales rather than harmonies, and for extending improvisation both in length and intensity.

experimented with electronics and the rhythms of rock and soul. The bassist and composer Charles Mingus, deeply influenced by Ellington and Parker, found new and imaginative ways of combining written and improvised jazz. Tenor saxophonist Sonny Rollins, while remaining rooted in traditional harmonic music, expanded solo improvisation dramatically. And by the end of the 1960s, Albert Ayler, a tenor saxophonist with roots in rhythm-and-blues music, brought another new and intensely personal voice to jazz.

Born in the crucible of slavery, jazz has become the universal song of freedom. It's no coincidence that neither Adolf Hitler nor Joseph Stalin approved of jazz, and both tried unsuccessfully to banish it. Perhaps Thelonious Monk put it best when he said that "jazz and freedom go hand in hand."

When Coltrane died suddenly in 1967, jazz was at the height of its experimental, expansionist stage, much of it inspired by the social and political upheaval of the time. By then, the term "free jazz" had begun to replace "avant garde," and many young musicians were following in the footsteps of Coltrane and other innovators. But within a few years of Coltrane's death, the storm quieted. Experimentation did continue through the late-1980s, but by the early 1970s it had become clear that the period of rapid and sometimes overpowering changes in jazz had come to an end.

In its place came a period of what might be called "peaceful coexistence" of many kinds of jazz. A number of young musicians have turned to the rich tradition of jazz, among them the gifted trumpeter Wynton Marsalis (also an expert classical player) and several other remarkable musicians from New Orleans, including Wynton's brother Branford (tenor and soprano saxophones), trumpeter Terence Blanshard, and alto saxophonist Donald Harrison. These young players have rejected "fusion" with electronics and rock as well as the practices of "free jazz," instead looking to the bebop tradition and Armstrong and Ellington for inspiration.

In the late-1980s jazz musicians paid tribute to traditional jazz forms with the development of "repertory jazz," which refers to the performance of big-band compositions and arrangements. The most notable of these ensembles are the Lincoln Center Jazz Orchestra—with Wynton Marsalis as artistic director—specializing in the music of Ellington, and the Smithsonian Jazz Masterpiece Ensemble, jointly directed by David Baker and Gunther Schuller, two master musicians with classical as well as jazz training.

The many gifted players who emerged from Chicago's Association for the Advancement of Creative Music in the 1960s pursued their various approaches with stirring results, in such groups as the Art Ensemble of Chicago, the World Saxophone Quartet, and Lester Bowie's Brass Fantasy.

It is difficult to predict where jazz will go next. After a long period of innovation, the industry has reached a point where it is taking stock of its past while looking to the future. Whatever that future may bring, one thing is certain: the story of jazz is one of the most remarkable chapters in the history of twentieth-century artistic creativity.

BLUES AND JAZZ BANDLEADERS, COMPOSERS,
♦ ♦ ♦ ♦ ♦ ♦ ♦ ♦ ♦ ♦ ♦ ♦ ♦ **INSTRUMENTALISTS, AND SINGERS**

Muhal Richard Abrams (1930–)

Pianist, Composer, Bandleader

Born in Chicago, Abrams began his professional career in 1948, playing with many of the city's best musicians and bands. In 1961 he formed the Experimental Band, which soon became an informal academy for Chicago's most venturesome players. Under Abrams' quiet but firm guidance, this grew into the Association for the Advancement of Creative Music (AACM). The AACM helped young musicians perform and promote their own music, which could not be presented through established venues.

The AACM attracted future leaders of avant-garde jazz, including such musicians as Roscoe Mitchell, Joseph Jarman, Lester Bowie, Malachi Favors, and Don Moye, who would later achieve worldwide prominence as the Art Ensemble of Chicago. Although he didn't formally declare it, Abrams was the recognized leader and moral and spiritual force behind the AACM. In 1976, when the AACM musicians had come of age, Abrams moved to New York and finally began to get well-deserved national and international recognition. In 1990 he became the first recipient of the prestigious Danish "Jazzpar" Award. His work as a pianist and composer spans the entire range of the black musical tradition.

Lilian "Lil" Hardin Armstrong (1898–1971)

Pianist, Singer, Composer

Lil Armstrong was born in Memphis in 1898. She was a classically trained musician who received her music education at Fisk University. Her family moved from Memphis to Chicago around 1914 or 1915. One of her first jobs was selling sheet music in Jones music store in Chicago. It is said that she met Jelly Roll Morton while working there, and that it was Morton who influenced her style of hitting the notes "real heavy." She worked with the New Orleans Creole Jazz Band, the New Orleans Rhythm Kings, and King Oliver's Creole Jazz Band, where she met her husband Louis Armstrong. Lil and Louie were married in 1924. She played and wrote music for many of Armstrong's Hot Five and Hot Seven concerts and recordings and helped him polish his raw brilliant talent. The Armstrongs were divorced in 1938. Lil continued to play in various bands and some combos of her own. Two of her songs, "Bad Boy" and "Just for a Thrill," became big hits in the 1960s. While playing at a tribute to Louis Armstrong at Chicago's Civic Center Plaza, Lilian Armstrong collapsed and died of a heart attack on July 7, 1971.

Louis Armstrong (1901–1971)

Trumpeter

Born in New Orleans at the turn of the century, Louis Armstrong was one of the most influential and durable of all jazz artists, and quite simply one of the most famous people in the world.

On New Year's Eve in 1914, Armstrong was arrested in New Orleans for firing a pistol and sent to the Colored Waifs Home. It was there that he first learned to play the cornet. His skill increased with the experience he gained from playing in the Home's band. When he was finally released from the institution, he was already proficient enough with the instrument to begin playing for money.

Louis Armstrong acquired the nickname "Satchmo" in 1932, when he headlined a show at the London Palladium.

Befriended by his idol, King Oliver, Armstrong quickly began to develop the jazz skills that, until then, he had only been able to admire from a distance. When Oliver left for Chicago in 1919, a place opened up for Armstrong as a member of the Kid Ory band in New Orleans. In 1922 Oliver asked Armstrong to join him in Chicago as second cornet with his Creole Jazz Band. The duets between "Dippermouth" (as Armstrong was called) and "Papa Joe" (Oliver's nickname) soon became the talk of the Chicago music world.

Two years later Armstrong joined the Fletcher Henderson band at the Roseland Ballroom in New York City. In 1925 he returned to Chicago to play with Erskine Tate, switching from cornet to trumpet, the instrument he played from then on. During the next four years he made a series of recordings that profoundly influenced the course of jazz.

In 1929 Armstrong returned to New York, where, in the revue "Hot Chocolates," he scored his first triumph with the performance of a popular song (Fats Waller's "Ain't Misbehavin'"). This success was a turning point in his career. He now began to front big bands, playing and singing popular songs rather than blues or original instrumentals.

In 1932 Armstrong headlined a show at the London Palladium, where he acquired the nickname "Satchmo." From 1933 to 1935 he toured Europe, returning to the United States to film *Pennies from Heaven* with Bing Crosby. He continued to evolve from the status of musician to that of entertainer, and his singing soon became as important as his playing. In 1947 he formed a small group that was an immediate success. He continued to work in this context, touring throughout the world.

Armstrong experienced a tremendous success in 1964 with his recording of "Hello Dolly," which knocked the Beatles off the number one spot on the Top 40 list, a great feat in the age of rock. Though his health began to decline, he kept up his heavy schedule of international touring. When he died in his sleep at home in Corona, Queens, two days after his seventieth birthday, he had been preparing to resume work in spite of a serious heart attack suffered some three months before. "The music—it's my living and my life" was his motto.

Louis Armstrong's fame as an entertainer in the later stages of his extraordinary career sometimes made people forget that he remained a great musician to the end. More than any other artist, Armstrong symbolized the magic of jazz, a music unimaginable without his contribution. "You can't play a note on the horn that Louis hasn't already played," said Miles Davis, and contemporary musicians like Wynton Marsalis echo that opinion.

In 1988, after its use in the motion picture *Good Morning, Vietnam*, Armstrong's recording of "What a Wonderful World" became a surprise hit, climbing to number eleven on the *Billboard* chart. In 1992, a Louis Armstrong Archive was established at Queens College in New York. It includes his personal papers, private recordings, memorabilia, and instruments.

Count Basie is generally regarded as the leader of the best jazz band in the United States and, consequently, one of the major influences on jazz.

William "Count" Basie (1904–1984)

Pianist, Bandleader

His musical career ranges from a boyhood spent watching the pit band at the local movie theater (he later learned the organ techniques of Fats Waller by crouching beside him in the Lincoln Theater in Harlem) to his dual triumphs in 1957 when his group became the first American band to play a royal command performance for the Queen of England, and the first black jazz band ever to play at the Waldorf Astoria Hotel in New York City.

During the early 1920s Basie toured in vaudeville. Stranded in Kansas City, he joined Walter Page's Blue Devils, for whom Jimmy Rushing was the singer. After this band broke up, Basie joined Benny Moten and in 1935 formed his own band at the Reno Club in Kansas City, where a local radio announcer soon dubbed him "Count."

At the urging of critic John Hammond, Basie brought his group to New York City in 1936. Within a year he had cut his first record and was well on his way to becoming an established presence in the jazz world.

The Basie trademark was his rhythm section, which featured Basie's clean, spare piano style and outstanding soloists like Lester Young and Sweets Edison in the early years, and Lucky Thompson, J.J. Johnson, Clark Terry, and Benny Powell in the later period.

Except for the years 1950 and 1951 when he had a small group, Basie led a big band for almost forty years. Immune to changing fashion, the Basie band completed numerous global tours and successful recording engagements without ever suffering an appreciable decline in popularity.

In 1974, on his seventieth birthday, the Count was honored at a "Royal Salute" party by virtually every big name in jazz. Count Basie was honored again in 1982 at Radio City Music Hall in New York City. Among those in attendance were Dionne Warwick and Lena Horne.

Sidney Bechet
(1897–1959)

Saxophonist, Clarinetist

Sidney Bechet was the first jazz performer to achieve recognition on the soprano saxophone, and also one of the first to win acceptance in classical music circles as a serious musician.

In 1919 Bechet played in England and on the Continent with Will Marion Cook's Southern Syncopated Orchestra. Even before this, his clarinet and soprano sax had been heard in the bands of King Oliver and Freddie Keppard in his native New Orleans.

During the early 1920s Bechet made a series of records with Clarence Williams's Blue Five, worked briefly with Duke Ellington (one of his great admirers), and then returned to Europe. He came back to the United States with Noble Sissle and expanded his career, making several records.

In 1949 he moved to France, where he enjoyed the greatest success of his career. He died there in 1959. After his death, a statue of Bechet was erected in Antibes.

One of the greatest drummers in jazz, Art Blakey was also one of the field's foremost talent spotters. After early experience with Fletcher Henderson and Mary Lou Williams, he joined Billy Eckstine's band in 1944 and took part in the birth of bebop. After working with many of the greatest modern jazz musicians, he formed his own Jazz Messengers in 1954 with immediate success.

Art Blakey (1919–1990)

Drummer, Bandleader

From then on, Blakey hired and propelled to stardom a vast number of gifted players, among them Horace Silver, Lee Morgan, Freddie Hubbard, Benny Golson, Woody Shaw, Wayne Shorter, and Wynton Marsalis. Blakey had one of the most powerful beats in jazz and took part in some of the finest recordings of his time.

During his brief life, Jimmy Blanton changed the course of jazz history by originating a new way of playing the string bass. Playing the instrument as if it were a horn, he shifted it from rhythmic back-up to melodic focal point.

Jimmy Blanton (1918–1942)

Bassist

Born in St. Louis, Missouri, he played with Jeter Pillars and Fate Marable before joining Duke Ellington in 1939. Until this time the string bass rarely played anything but quarter notes in ensembles or solos, but Blanton began sliding into eighth- and sixteenth-note runs, introducing melodic and harmonic ideas that were totally new to the instrument. His skill put him in a different class from his predecessors; it made him the first true master of the bass and demonstrated the instrument's potential as a solo vehicle.

Blanton died in 1942 of tuberculosis.

Buddy Bolden, a plasterer by trade, formed in the 1890s what may have been the first real jazz band in New Orleans. By the turn of the century, his cornet playing was so popular that he was often called upon to sit in with several bands on a single evening.

Buddy Bolden (1868–1931)

Cornetist

His cornet style was the starting point for a chain of musicians from King Oliver to Louis Armstrong to Dizzy Gillespie. Because his career predates the recording of jazz, the only lasting memorial to his talent lies in the oral tradition that carries on his legend, and in the known successes of the people he influenced.

Bolden suffered from schizophrenia, and he was committed to East Louisiana State Hospital in 1907. He remained there until his death, never playing another note.

Clifford Brown (1930–1956)

Trumpeter, Composer, Bandleader

Clifford Brown's death at twenty-five in a car crash was one of jazz's great tragedies. Acclaimed as the greatest trumpet talent of his generation, Brown was on the brink of stardom as co-leader of the successful Clifford Brown–Max Roach Quintet and as a recording artist in his own right, known especially for his album with strings. He was a role model for aspiring jazz musicians—he had few vices, was raising a happy family, and was loved by all who knew him, not just for his music but for his warm and gentle personality.

He studied music at the University of Maryland, but at twenty-one was injured in a car accident that debilitated him for months. In 1952 he joined Chris Powell's R&B band (with which he made his first records), worked with the great composer–arranger Tadd Dameron, and toured Europe with Lionel Hampton's band. A year later he teamed up with Max Roach. The brilliant young trumpeter's sudden death in 1956 shocked friends and fans worldwide.

Brown was also a gifted composer; tunes like "Joy Spring" and "Dahoud" are classics, as are Brown's recordings, which still influence young musicians more than thirty-seven years after his death.

Ray Brown (Raymond Matthews) (1926–)

Bassist

Ray Brown is perhaps the most versatile bass player in jazz today and is in demand around the world. He was born in Pittsburgh in 1926. In 1951, after having worked with Dizzy Gillespie and Charlie Parker, he joined Oscar Peterson's Trio—an association that lasted fifteen years. During this time, he and Peterson produced award-winning records and were in constant demand for concerts. Since leaving Peterson in 1966, Brown has worked with many famous artists in both live and recorded performances. He also works as a record producer and personal manager.

Benny Carter made his professional debut in 1923, and seventy-one years later still ranks at the top of jazz as an instrumentalist, composer–arranger, and bandleader. In 1988 he toured Europe, visited Japan with his own band, performed in Brazil for the first time in his career, and recorded three albums. He continued at the same pace in 1993.

Admired and respected by generations of musicians, many of whom "went to school" in his bands (Sid Catlett, Miles Davis, J.J. Johnson, Max Roach, and Teddy Wilson were some), Carter helped shape the language of big-band jazz. His scoring for saxophone sections was especially influential. On the alto saxophone, he and Johnny Hodges were the pacesetters before Charlie Parker and bebop. He has few peers as a trumpeter and has composed many standards.

Carter was the first black composer to break the color barrier in the Hollywood film studios. He scored many major films and TV shows, including "M-Squad." The subject of one of the best biographies of a jazz artist (*Benny Carter: A Life in American Music*), Carter received an honorary doctorate in music from Princeton University, where he taught, in 1974.

Bennett Lester Carter (1907–)

Saxophonist, Trumpeter, Composer, Bandleader

Blinded at the age of six, Charles received his first musical training at a school for the blind in St. Augustine, Florida. He left school at the age of fifteen to play local engagements. Two years later, he formed a trio that had some success in the Northwest. In 1954 he organized a seven-piece rhythm-and-blues group.

In 1957 his first LP was released, consisting of a potpourri of instrumentals drawn from pop, gospel, and modern jazz sources. His singing and piano playing found favor particularly with a number of jazz artists who opposed what they felt was a growing tendency for jazz to become over-scored and underfelt. In Charles, they saw an artist who had restored both a sense of "soul" and instrumental "funkiness" to the jazz idiom. By the end of the 1960s, he had become one of the world's most popular performers, and he remains a star in the 1990s.

Ray Charles (1932–)

Singer, Pianist, Bandleader

Charlie Christian did for the electric guitar what Jimmy Blanton did for the bass.

Christian joined Benny Goodman in 1939 and, after only two years with the Goodman Sextet, achieved great fame as the first electric guitarist to

Charlie Christian (1916–1942)

Electric Guitarist

play single-string solos. In his after-hour activities at such Harlem clubs as Minton's, he was an early contributor to the jazz revolution that would one day come to be called bop.

In 1941 he was hospitalized with tuberculosis; he died the following year. His recordings are still an inspiration to young guitarists.

Kenny Clarke (Liaqat Ali Salaam) (1914–1985)

Drummer

Kenny Clarke was one of the "founding fathers" of the bop movement. Along with Dizzy Gillespie and Thelonious Monk, Clarke made Minton's in Harlem the late-hour haunt for musicians in the 1940s.

A pioneer in the use of drums as a solo instrument and not just a background presence, he was one of the first musicians to move away from emphasis on the bass drum. Clarke adopted a more flexible style, in which he maintained a steady rhythm on the top cymbal while "dropping bombs" with surprise bass-drum punctuations.

From a musically inclined Pittsburgh family, Clarke studied vibes, piano, and trombone as well as musical theory. His early professional experience was gained with Roy Eldridge and Edgar Hayes. (He traveled to Finland and Sweden with Hayes in 1937.)

In the early 1940s he played with Teddy Hill and then began playing at Minton's. Later he worked with Dizzy Gillespie, Coleman Hawkins, Tadd Dameron, and many others. In 1951 he toured with Billy Eckstine, and in the following year he helped organize the Modern Jazz Quartet; he stayed with the quartet for the next three years. He moved to France in 1956, where he continued to work with a number of visiting American talents, and from 1961 to 1972 he co-led a fine "big band" with Belgian pianist and arranger Frency Boland.

Ornette Coleman (1930–)

Saxophonist, Trumpeter, Violinist, Composer

Texas-born Ornette Coleman began his musical career in carnival and rhythm-and-blues bands. Fired by guitarist–singer Pee Wee Crayton for his unconventional playing style, Coleman settled in Los Angeles, making his living as an elevator operator while studying music on his own. He began to compose and sit in on jam sessions; in 1958 he made his first album. Encouraged by John Lewis, Coleman and his quartet (Don Cherry, pocket cornet; Charlie Haden, bass; Billy Higgins, drums) opened at the

Five Spot in Manhattan, stirring up great debates among jazz musicians, critics, and fans.

Coleman's music, while abandoning traditional rules of harmony and tonality, was not senseless noise, as some opponents maintained. In fact, the music of the first Coleman quartet (which made many recordings) had a strong blues feeling and was very melodic. Eventually Coleman was accepted by many of his peers. He continued to go his own way in music, creating a system he called "harmolodic" and teaching himself to play trumpet and violin. In the 1970s he composed and performed a long work for symphony orchestra and alto saxophone, "The Skies of America," and in the 1980s he formed Prime Time, a jazz-fusion band with two electric guitars and two drummers. His original quartet was triumphantly reunited at the 1989 JVC Jazz Festival and recorded again that year.

John Coltrane (or just "Trane," as he was known to many) was the last great innovator to profoundly influence the course of jazz. He first played clarinet, then alto saxophone in high school in his native North Carolina. After graduating, he moved to Philadelphia and continued to study music, winning several scholarships. After playing in a Navy band in Hawaii, he started his professional career with rhythm-and-blues bands, joining Dizzy Gillespie's big band (on alto) in 1949. When Gillespie scaled the band down to a sextet in 1951, he had Coltrane switch to tenor sax. After stints with two great but very different alto saxophonists, Earl Bostic and Johnny Hodges, Coltrane was hired by Miles Davis in 1955. At first, some musicians and listeners didn't care for what they felt was Coltrane's harsh sound, but as the Davis Quintet became the most popular jazz group of its day, Coltrane was not only accepted but began to influence younger players. He briefly left Davis in 1957 to work with Thelonious Monk and further develop what was already a highly original style. Back with Davis, he participated in the great *Kind of Blue* record dates.

John Coltrane (1926–1967)

Saxophonist, Bandleader

In 1959, while still with Davis, Coltrane composed and recorded "Giant Steps," a piece so harmonically intricate that it staggered most of his fellow saxophonists. Coltrane later formed his own quartet, including pianist McCoy Tyner, bassist Jimmy Garrison, and drummer Elvin Jones. In 1960 they recorded the song "My Favorite Things" from the musical and film *The Sound of Music* in a performance that featured Coltrane's soprano sax and lasted more than fifteen minutes. This performance became such a hit with the jazz audience that it sustained Coltrane's popularity even when he began to experiment with unusual and demanding music. The quartet became one of the most tightly knit groups in jazz history; the empathy between Coltrane and Elvin Jones was astonishing, and in their live performances, the four musicians would sometimes play for more than an hour, creating music so intense that some listeners likened it to a religious experience.

Coltrane was a deeply spiritual man. One of his masterpieces, the suite "A Love Supreme" and an accompanying poem, was his offering to God. The quartet's live recordings at the Village Vanguard and Birdland became instant classics, and Coltrane was regarded as the leading figure of the 1960s avant-garde jazz. The quartet broke up in 1966, and Coltrane searched for new modes of expression, never complacent about his work at any time in his career. His death at forty-one of liver cancer came as a shock to the jazz world. Since then, no comparably influential figure has come along. Coltrane has become a legend whose influence continues, though few have attempted to emulate the unconventional style of his later years, when he stretched the limits of his instrument.

Miles Davis (1926–1991)

Trumpeter, Bandleader

Miles Davis played a major role in the transition from the hard, aggressive stance of bop to the softer, more subtle side of jazz.

As a teenage musician in St. Louis in the early 1940s, Davis sat in with his idols Charlie Parker and Dizzy Gillespie when they passed through town with the Billy Eckstine Band.

In 1945 Davis's well-to-do dentist father sent him to the Juilliard School of Music in New York. Within a short time, Davis was working the 52nd Street clubs with Parker and Coleman Hawkins, and touring with the bands of Billy Eckstine and Benny Carter.

In 1949 Davis formed a nine-piece band, including Lee Konitz, Gerry Mulligan, John Lewis, and Max Roach. The group was short lived, but its recordings had a great impact on musicians and defined "cool" jazz.

In 1955 Davis formed a quintet with John Coltrane featured on tenor sax. Success came in the following year, when Davis made his first record with arranger Gil Evans, "Miles Ahead." This was followed by two other collaborations with Evans, "Porgy and Bess" and "Sketches of Spain," both landmarks in jazz. In 1958 came *Kind of Blue*, an album by a new sextet with Coltrane and the additions of Cannonball Adderley on alto sax and Bill Evans on piano. This album established modal improvisation in jazz and set the stage for Coltrane's explorations on his own.

Davis continued to introduce new ideas in his music and give exposure to new talent. By 1964, he had Wayne Shorter on saxophones, Herbie Hancock on piano, Ron Carter on bass, and the sensational eighteen-year-old Tony Williams on drums. This group explored unconventional musical territory, mostly in the realm of rhythmic and harmonic freedom. In 1968, however, Davis got restless again, attracted by the possibilities of electronic instruments. Hancock, Chick Corea, Joe Zawinul, and Keith Jarrett were among the keyboard players who worked with Davis during this period, starting with the album *Bitches Brew*.

Some of his many fans, and quite a few musicians, did not care for the music Davis was producing at this point, but he remained unaffected by his critics. He gradually moved further away from traditional jazz into an unclassifiable and ever-changing music that appealed to a young audience not generally interested in jazz. In the late-1970s Davis became a cult figure, and his famous reserve (he had long been known for not acknowledging applause, walking off the stand when he wasn't playing, and being a difficult interview subject) was replaced by an open manner; he began smiling more often, waving to the audience, shaking hands with those nearest the stage, and giving frequent and amiable interviews.

Eric Dolphy is greatly admired by musicians. Although his linear derivations were from Charlie Parker, his aggressive playing of the alto sax and bass clarinet had a fierce bite that stemmed from earlier jazz. His mastery of the bass clarinet has never been equaled.

Eric Dolphy

(1928–1964)

Alto Saxophonist, Clarinetist, Flutist

Dolphy was born in Los Angeles. His first recognition came when he was playing with the Chico Hamilton quintet from 1958 to 1959. In 1960, he joined Charles Mingus in New York, and in 1961 he played many club dates with trumpeter Booker Little before joining John Coltrane for some historic tours, concerts, and recordings. Dolphy also played in a group with trumpeter Freddie Hubbard and recorded with Ornette Coleman. In 1964, while on tour with Mingus, he decided to stay in Europe, where he recorded with Dutch, Scandinavian, and German rhythm sections. He died suddenly in Berlin of a heart attack possibly brought on by diabetes.

Dolphy was the winner of *Downbeat* magazine's New Star award for alto, flute, and miscellaneous instruments in 1961, and was elected to that magazine's Hall of Fame in 1965. His legacy includes many recordings for Prestige, Blue Note, Impulse, and smaller companies, both as leader and sideman.

Charles Mingus said of Dolphy that he had the "great capacity to talk in his music ... he knew the level of language which very few musicians get down to."

Roy "Little Jazz" Eldridge (1911–1989)

Drummer, Trumpeter, Singer

Born in Pittsburgh, Roy Eldridge played his first "job" at the age of seven on drums. When he was fifteen and had switched to trumpet, he ran away from home with a carnival band. After playing with some of the best bands in the Midwest, he arrived in New York in 1931, impressing the locals with his speed and range, and finding jobs with good bands. But it wasn't until his work in 1935 with Teddy Hill that he could be heard on records. By the next year, he was the star of Fletcher Henderson's band, and in 1937, he put together his own group and made some records that astounded other trumpeters. One of these trumpeters was young Dizzy Gillespie, who had been listening to Eldridge on the radio since 1935 and had tried to imitate him. By 1938, Eldridge was setting the pace for swing trumpeters, playing higher and faster than even Louis Armstrong had done, and making musical sense as well. He further impressed critics and audiences with his singing ability.

In 1941 Eldridge, now known in the world of music as "Little Jazz," took up an offer from drummer Gene Krupa to join his big band, thus becoming the first black musician to be featured in a white band not as a special attraction, but as a member of the band's section. In "Let Me Off Uptown," a duet with singer Anita O'Day, Eldridge scored a smash hit for Krupa, and his instrumental feature "Rockin' Chair" was hailed as a jazz classic. Eldridge led his own big band for a while, but joined another white band, that of Artie Shaw, in 1944. A brief stint with his own big band followed, but small groups proved more viable. By 1949, Roy was a star of "Jazz at the Philharmonic," a touring concert group of famous players including, at that time, Charlie Parker, Lester Young, and Buddy Rich. A tour with one of Benny Goodman's small groups brought him to Paris, where he stayed for a year and regained his confidence; he had been a bit shaken by the advent of bebop, and by the trumpet innovations of his former disciple Gillespie. (Rivalry aside, the two remained good friends and often recorded together.)

The 1950s marked the beginning of a long and close association with Coleman Hawkins. During this time Roy also backed Ella Fitzgerald and toured with JATP. Little Jazz led the house band at Jimmy Ryan's club in New York City for a full decade beginning in 1970, but a heart attack in 1980 put an end to his trumpet playing. He still worked occasionally as a singer and gave lectures and workshops on jazz.

Roy Eldridge comprised, in his music and personality, the essence of jazz as a music that comes straight from, and goes straight to, the heart and soul.

Ellington, nicknamed Duke in his teens for his dapper dress style and courtly manners, was born into a middle-class family in Washington, DC. After graduating from high school, he was offered an art scholarship at Pratt Institute in New York, but he'd already had a taste of bandleading and preferred to stay with music. He had some success in his hometown, mainly because he had the biggest band advertisement in the telephone book, but in 1923 he felt the urge to go to New York, where careers were made. He didn't succeed immediately (he later said that he and his friends were so broke they had to split a hot dog three ways), but by 1924 he was leading his Washingtonians at a Broadway nightclub and making his first records. That early band was only five pieces, but it had grown to ten by the time the young pianist–composer opened at the Cotton Club, the most famous Harlem night spot.

Edward Kennedy "Duke" Ellington (1899–1975)

Bandleader, Composer, Pianist

Here the unique Ellington style evolved during a five-year stay. Unlike most other bands, his played primarily his own music, though a few pop tunes were occasionally thrown in. Also unlike other bands, Ellington kept the same players with him once he'd decided that he liked their style. He had a great sense for their potential—like a great coach knows how to develop an athlete's skills—and some of Duke's bandsmen stayed with him for decades (none longer than baritone saxophonist Harry Carney, in the band from 1927 until the end). Many became stars in their own right (Johnny Hodges, alto sax; Cootie Williams, trumpet; Barney Bigard, clarinet), but somehow they always sounded better with Ellington, who knew just how to write for what he called their "tonal personalities." Ellington's scoring for the band was also strictly his own, and other arrangers found it hard to copy him.

Unlike other bandleaders, Duke Ellington tended to keep the same players with him— some for decades—once he'd decided he liked their style.

By 1933, Ellington was ready for his first European tour; performing in London and Paris, the band, whose many recordings had prepared the way, was enthusiastically received. Back home, the band had already appeared in films (and would soon make more), and they had received valuable exposure on radio and on records (Ellington was among the first musicians to truly understand the importance of records, and to realize that making good ones required something different from playing in public). In 1935, deeply touched by the death of his mother, Ellington composed "Reminiscing in Tempo," his longest work to that date; most of his songs were tailored to the time limit of a little over three minutes imposed by the 78 rpm technology.

The band reached a first peak in 1940, when almost all of the musicians had been aboard for many years. Two exceptions, tenor Ben Webster and bassist Jimmy Blanton, who both joined in 1939, were of key importance to the music. Billy Strayhorn, also a newcomer, didn't play in the band but quickly became essential to Ellington as an associate composer–arranger. Strayhorn spent the rest of his life with Duke and his men. A second peak was reached in 1956, when the band gave a tremendous performance at the Newport Jazz Festival, which fortunately was recorded; the album, highlighted by "Crescendo and Diminuendo in Blue," featuring twenty-seven choruses by tenorman Paul Gonsalves, became the best-selling Ellington record of all—and Duke made more records than any other jazz artist. It was Duke's success as a composer of popular songs that allowed him to keep the big band going through five decades; included among his hits are "Solitude," "Mood Indigo," "Sophisticated Lady," "Satin Doll," and "Don't Get Around Much Any More." All began as instrumentals. Ellington's major longer works include "Black, Brown and Beige," "Harlem," "Such Sweet Thunder," and "Far East Suite," the last two in collaboration with Strayhorn.

Ellington and his astonishing creations have been an inspiration to generations of musicians, most recently to Wynton Marsalis, who has done much to keep the Elllington legacy in the forefront of American music both in his own composing and in his efforts to get Ellington's music performed live (with the Lincoln Center Jazz Ensemble, for example). There can be no doubt that Duke Ellington (who was also a brilliant pianist) will stand as one of the greatest composers of the twentieth century.

James Reese Europe

(1881-1919)

Bandleader

James Reese Europe was born in Mobile, Alabama in 1881, and he later moved to New York. In 1906 he organized the New Amersterdam Musical Association and in 1910 formed the Clef Club orchestra.

During World War I, Europe directed the 369th Infantry Regimental Band, which performed throughout France and was a major force in the development of jazz in that country. Following his return to the United States, Europe toured the country with his band. In 1919 he was fatally stabbed by a member of his band while on tour.

Ella Fitzgerald has emerged as the top female vocalist in virtually every poll conducted among jazz musicians and singers. No other vocalist has been so unanimously acclaimed. She is fondly known as "The First Lady of Song."

Ella Fitzgerald
(1918–)

Singer

Discovered in 1934 by drummer–bandleader Chick Webb at an amateur contest at Harlem's Apollo Theater in New York City, she cut her first side with Webb a year later. In 1938, she recorded "A Tisket, A Tasket," a novelty number that brought her commercial success and made her name widely known among the general public. Among musicians, Fitzgerald's reputation rests on her singular ability to use her voice like an instrument, improvising effortlessly in a style filled with rhythmic subtleties.

For more than fifty years Ella Fitzgerald has been the leading jazz interpreter of popular song.

Detroit-born Tommy Flanagan came to New York in the mid-1950s as part of the "Motor City" invasion of gifted jazzmen (along with fellow pianist Barry Harris; trumpeters Thad Jones and Donald Byrd; and guitarist Kenny Burrell, among others) and soon was in demand for recordings and "live" dates with all the great names in modern jazz. A long stint as Ella Fitzgerald's accompanist and musical director (a role he also filled, much more briefly, with Tony Bennett) kept Flanagan out of the limelight, but since the mid-1970s, as leader of his own fine trios and as a prolific recording artist in the United States, Europe, and Japan, he has assumed his rightful place as one of the greatest living masters of jazz piano.

Tommy Flanagan
(1930–)

Pianist

A keyboard artist who played and composed by ear in the tradition of the founding fathers of jazz, Erroll Garner won the international acclaim of jazz lovers, music critics, and the general public. Strong and bouncy left-hand rhythms and beautiful melodies are the trademarks of his extremely enjoyable music. He was the best-selling jazz pianist in the world.

Erroll Garner
(1921–1977)

Pianist, Composer

Born in Pittsburgh, Garner grew up in a musical family and began picking out piano melodies before he was three years old. He started taking piano lessons at six, but his first and only piano teacher gave up on him when she realized he was playing all his assignments by ear instead of learning to read notes. At seven, he began playing regularly on Pittsburgh radio station KDKA. He dropped out of high school to play with a dance band, and first came to New York in 1939 as an accompanist for nightclub singer Ann Lewis. In 1946 he recorded "Laura," which sold a half million copies, and his fame began to grow. On March 27, 1950 he gave a solo recital at Cleveland's Music Hall, and in December of that year he gave a concert at New York's Town Hall. Gradually recitals and recording sessions took precedence over nightclub performances.

Garner's most famous composition, "Misty," was a big hit for Johnny Mathis and Sarah Vaughan. His unique piano style has often been copied but never equaled.

**Dizzy Gillespie
(1917–1993)**

Trumpeter, Bandleader

Dizzy Gillespie and Charlie Parker were the co-founders of the revolutionary movement in jazz during the 1940s—the phenomenon known as bop. The role each played in this revolution has been a subject of considerable debate. Billy Eckstine, whose band at one time included both Gillespie and Parker, defined Parker's role more as instrumentalist, while Gillespie acted more as writer and arranger. Whatever their particular contributions were, however, it cannot be disputed that the sum total of their ideas brought about a change in jazz that continues to be felt today.

Gillespie received his early musical training in his native South Carolina. After moving to Philadelphia in 1935 and gaining more professional experience there, he joined the Teddy Hill band, replacing his early idol Roy "Little Jazz" Eldridge.

He toured Europe with Hill in 1939, and when he returned to New York to play with Cab Calloway, his bop experimentation was already beginning to develop and his career as arranger began. After working with Ella Fitzgerald, Benny Carter, Charlie Barnet, Earl Hines, and others, he joined Eckstine's band in 1944 and started his own jazz band the next year.

Gillespie toured Europe, the Middle East, and Latin America with big bands and quintets subsidized by the U.S. State Department. He ultimately became a revered elder statesman of jazz.

Born in Los Angeles to a prominent physician whose patients included famous jazz musicians, Dexter Gordon joined Lionel Hampton's newly formed big band in 1940. He was with Louis Armstrong in 1944, and later that year joined the Billy Eckstine Band. After freelancing in New York, he returned home and in 1946 recorded a "The Chase," a "tenor battle" with Wardell Gray, which became one of the biggest modern jazz hits. He teamed up with Gray on and off until 1952, after which he temporarily disappeared from the jazz spotlight.

Gordon made a major comeback in the early 1960s with a series of much-acclaimed recordings. In 1962 he settled in Copenhagen, and the Danish capital became his headquarters for the next fourteen years, though he made brief playing visits to the United States. In 1977 he came home for good, forming his own group and winning many new fans. In 1986 he starred in the French feature film *Round Midnight,* in which his portrayal of a character based on Lester Young and Bud Powell won him an Oscar nomination for best actor. In 1988 he began work on an autobiography.

Dexter Gordon was the premier tenor saxophone stylist of bebop, but his strong, swinging music transcends categorization. He greatly influenced the young John Coltrane.

Johnny Griffin was born in Chicago and has played with a number of prominent jazz personalities over the years. Among them have been Lionel Hampton, Art Blakey, Thelonious Monk, and Eddie Lockjaw Davis. Griffin, like many Chicago musicians, preferred to stay and play in the Windy City, and much of his early musical development took place there. In December 1962, he moved to Europe and played all over the continent. He lived in Paris in the late-1960s and later moved to the Netherlands, where he owned a farm. In the late-1970s, Griffin moved back to the United States, celebrating the occasion with outstanding concerts and recordings with his friend and fellow saxophonist Dexter Gordon.

Lionel Hampton was the first jazz musician to feature the vibes, an instrument that has since come to play a vital role in jazz. His first recorded effort with the instrument was in 1930 on "Memories of You," with the Les Hite band in California that included Louis Armstrong.

Hampton later left Hite's band to form his own Los Angeles group. When Benny Goodman heard him in 1936, he hired him to play on a record

**Dexter Gordon
(1923–1989)**

Saxophonist, Bandleader

**Johnny Griffin
(1928–)**

Saxophonist

**Lionel Hampton
(1909–)**

Vibraphonist, Pianist,
Bandleader

Lionel Hampton and his orchestra.

date with Teddy Wilson and Gene Krupa, and then persuaded him to join the quartet on a permanent basis.

Hampton played with the Goodman Quartet until 1940, the year he formed his own big orchestra. The following year, his band scored its first big hit, "Flyin' Home."

Hampton has enjoyed great success since then, and continued to tour the world even after celebrating his eightieth birthday in 1989. Hampton helped to launch the careers of many well-known musicians, dozens of whom got their start in his band.

Herbie Hancock (1940-)

Keyboardist, Composer, Bandleader

Herbie Hancock was born in Chicago. He initially became known as a pianist, though he has also turned to electronic music as a vehicle of communication, experimenting with the electric guitar, electric bass, electric piano, echoplex, phase shifter, and synthesizer. From 1963 to 1968, he traveled and played with Miles Davis, establishing himself as a composer and instrumentalist of the first rank. While with Davis, Hancock recorded with numerous other groups and became firmly established as a major jazz figure. He has won many awards, including *Downbeat* Jazzman of the Year in 1974 and *Cash Box* and *Playboy* Awards of the Year in 1974. Hancock has also written film scores and television specials.

Although he began as a cornetist and bandleader in the 1890s, W.C. Handy's fame as the "Father of the Blues" rests almost entirely on his work as a composer.

After studying at Kentucky Musical College, Handy toured with an assortment of musical groups, becoming the bandmaster of the Mahara Minstrels in 1896.

In 1909, during a political campaign in Memphis, Handy wrote "Mr. Crump," a campaign song for E. H. "Boss" Crump. Three years later, the song was published as the "Memphis Blues."

In 1914 Handy published his most famous song, "St. Louis Blues," and that same year wrote "Yellow Dog Blues." Others that have become perennial favorites are "Joe Turner Blues" (1915); "Beale Street Blues" (1916); "Careless Love" (1921); and "Aunt Hagar's Blues" (1922).

In the 1920s Handy became a music publisher in New York. Despite his failing sight, he remained active until his death in 1958. His songs extended beyond the world of jazz to find their way into the field of popular music. Their popularity continues unabated today.

William Christopher Handy (1873–1958)

Trumpeter, Composer, Bandleader

Until Coleman Hawkins came along, the tenor saxophone was not seriously considered as a suitable jazz vehicle. The full, rich tone that Hawkins brought to the tenor has helped make it one of the most vital instruments in the contemporary jazz ensemble.

When Hawkins took up the tenor at the age of nine, he had already had four years of training on piano and cello. He continued his studies at Washburn College in Topeka, Kansas, and in 1922 toured with Mamie Smith's Jazz Hounds. In 1924 he began a ten-year stint with Fletcher Henderson's band.

Hawkins left Henderson in 1934 to tour England and the Continent, recording with Django Reinhardt, Benny Carter, and others. When he returned to the United States in 1939, he recorded with his own band his biggest hit, "Body and Soul."

Coleman Hawkins (1904–1969)

Saxophonist

Unlike many of his contemporaries, Hawkins was open to the experimentation of the young musicians of the 1940s. In 1944, for example, he formed an all-star band for the first bop record session, and he gave help and encouragement to Dizzy Gillespie, Charlie Parker, Thelonious Monk, and others he admired.

With the advent of the "cool school," Hawkins's popularity temporarily declined, but the power of his style was ultimately recognized, and he is now considered a major figure in modern jazz.

**Roy Haynes
(1925–)**

Drummer, Bandleader

Boston-born Roy Haynes is one of the originators and greatest exponents of modern jazz drumming. Turning professional in his late teens, he went on the road with Luis Russell's big band, then joined Lester Young's sextet, with which he established his reputation. Settling in New York, he worked with Charlie Parker and Dizzy Gillespie, then toured for several years in Sarah Vaughan's trio.

Other important associates include Stan Getz, Gary Burton, Thelonious Monk, and John Coltrane. Haynes recorded prolifically with these and many others, and also did recordings as leader of his own groups, including the "Hip Ensemble." Haynes is both a fantastic soloist and a creative ensemble drummer. His foot is undoubtedly the fastest ever, and his playing has an elegance that is reflected in his stylish appearance—he was once chosen by *Esquire* magazine as one of America's ten best-dressed men. Never out of date, Haynes in his sixties teamed up with such modernists as Pat Metheny and Chick Corea, and he consistently picks young players for his group.

**Fletcher Henderson
(1897–1952)**

Bandleader,
Arranger, Pianist

Born in Georgia, Fletcher Henderson came to New York in 1920 to study chemistry. To earn spending money, he took a job as house pianist and musical director for Black Swan, the first record company owned and operated by blacks. Chemistry soon took a back seat, and in 1924 he was persuaded by some of his recording studio colleagues to audition with a band for a new club. The band got the job and soon graduated to the Roseland Ballroom on Broadway, where they played for eight years, also touring and making hundreds of records.

The Henderson band was the first big band to play interesting jazz, and it was the starting point for some of the greatest stars of the day, among them

The Fletcher Henderson
Orchestra, 1927.

Louis Armstrong, Coleman Hawkins, and Benny Carter. It was the arranger and saxophonist Don Redman who shaped the band's early style. When he left in 1928, Carter and others, including Fletcher's younger brother Horace (also a pianist and arranger) took over. It was not until 1933 that Fletcher himself began to write full time for his band; he had such a talent for arranging that he soon became one of the architects of swing. Ironically, just as he hit his stride as a writer, his band fell on hard days, and for a brief while he gave it up and became a freelance arranger, contributing significantly to the library of the newly formed Benny Goodman Band.

Though he began leading again soon, and had such greats as Ben Webster and Roy Eldridge in his bands, he never again achieved the success that he had known in the 1920s.

One of the foremost tenor stylists of the post-Coltrane era, Joe Henderson studied music at Wayne State University in Detroit, where he played with visiting stars like Sonny Stitt and had his own group in 1960. After military service, he came to New York where he co-led a band with trumpeter Kenny Dorham, then joined Horace Silver in 1964 and Herbie Hancock in 1969. Since the 1970s he has led his own groups and continued to develop an original and influential solo style.

Joe Henderson
(1937–)
Saxophonist, Composer

Among his compositions are "Recordame," "Tetragon," and "Isotope." He won a Grammy award in 1993 for his album of Billy Strayhorn compositions.

**Earl "Fatha" Hines
(1903–1983)**

Pianist, Bandleader

Except for increased technical proficiency, the piano style of Earl "Fatha" Hines barely changed from what it was in the late-1920s.

Hailing from Pittsburgh, Hines grew up in a musical home: his father played the trumpet and his mother played the organ. Hines originally planned a concert career, but he was soon caught up in the world of jazz. Forming his own trio while still in high school, he began to play in local clubs before moving on to Chicago in 1925.

While there, he made a brilliant series of records with Louis Armstrong's Hot Five, and he soon became known as "the trumpet-style pianist." The intricacy of his style was well beyond that of his contemporaries, but served as a touchstone for a succeeding generation of pianists.

In 1928, Hines formed his own band at the Grand Terrace in Chicago. For the next twenty years, this band served as a proving ground for many great instrumentalists and innovators of the period (from Bud Johnson and Trummy Young in the early era to Dizzy Gillespie and Charlie Parker in the later years).

From 1948 to 1951, Hines worked with Armstrong again, and played a long engagement in San Francisco. In 1963 a New York recital revitalized his career, and he enjoyed great success in Europe, Japan, and the United States until his death.

**Milton J. Hinton
(1910–)**

Bass

Milt Hinton was born in Vicksburg, Mississippi and is considered one of the greatest bass players. He has played with many top jazz artists, including Cab Calloway, Count Basie, Louis Armstrong, Teddy Wilson, and Benny Goodman. Hinton has appeared in concerts throughout the world and on numerous television shows, and has made more records than any other jazz musician. He is also an accomplished photographer and writer whose autobiography, *Bass Lines,* appeared in 1988.

**Billie Holiday
(1915–1959)**

Singer

Billie Holiday, dubbed "Lady Day" by Lester Young, was one of the greatest jazz singers of all time.

While still a young girl, she moved from Baltimore (her hometown) to New York City, and in 1931 she began her singing career in an assortment of Harlem night spots. In 1933 she cut her first sides with Benny Goodman. From 1935 to 1939 she established her reputation with a series of records made with Teddy Wilson. Holiday also sang with the bands of Count Basie and Artie Shaw.

In such classic records as "Strange Fruit" and her own "God Bless the Child," she departed from popular material to score her greatest artistic triumphs, depicting the harsh reality of southern lynchings and the personal alienation she had experienced.

At one time addicted to drugs and alcohol, she wrote in her 1956 autobiography *Lady Sings the Blues* that "All dope can do for you is kill you—and kill you the long, slow, hard way." The subject of a feature film, several books, and videos, Billie Holiday is still a powerful force in music decades after her untimely death.

Howlin' Wolf (1910–1976)

Singer, Harmonica Player

Blues singer and harmonica player Howlin' Wolf was born Chester Arthur Burnett in West Point, Mississippi. He learned to play the harmonica from blues musician Sonny Boy Williamson and made his first recording in 1950; his baying style of singing won him the name Howlin' Wolf. His best-known recordings include "Moanin' at Midnight," "Poor Boy," and "My Country Sugar Mama."

Jean-Baptiste "Illinois" Jacquet (1933–)

Saxophonist, Bandleader

Born in Louisiana and raised in Texas, the man who contributed to making the tenor sax the most popular jazz horn began as an altoist; it was Lionel Hampton who made him switch to tenor when he joined Hampton's new big band in 1942. Soon thereafter, Jacquet recorded his famous solo on "Flyin' Home" and made both his own and the Hampton band's name.

After stints with Cab Calloway and Count Basie, Jacquet joined the Jazz at the Philharmonic touring group, in which he starred in tenor "battles" with Flip Phillips and others. He soon formed his own swinging little band and became a mainstay in the international jazz circuit, a position he still occupies in the 1990s. He formed a successful big band in the 1980s that has toured Europe and recorded; the European tour and other incidents in Jacquet's life as a musician are part of the documentary film *Texas Tenor*, which premiered at the 1992 JVC Jazz Festival.

Jacquet was one of the first to "overblow" the tenor sax, reaching high harmonics that were dismissed by some as a circus stunt but appealed to audiences; eventually, of course, such overblowing became part of the instrument's vocabulary, as in the later work of John Coltrane and the style of David Murray.

J. J. Johnson
(1924–)
Trombonist, Bandleader

J.J. Johnson is the unchallenged master of the modern jazz trombone. He is the first musician to have adapted this instrument to the demanding techniques called for by bop.

Early in his career, Johnson displayed such skill in performing high-speed and intricate solos that those who knew him only from records found it hard to believe that he was using a slide—and not a valve—trombone.

Johnson spent the 1940s with the bands of Benny Carter, Count Basie, and Dizzy Gillespie. During the those years, his trombone was as widely imitated as the trumpet and alto of Gillespie and Parker.

In the 1950s Johnson retired for a time, only to return as partner of fellow trombonist Kai Winding in the Jay and Kai Quintet. This group enjoyed great success.

Johnson's ability as a composer has been widely praised. In 1959 he performed several of his works with the Monterey Festival Orchestra. He has also composed for films and TV and has been active as a teacher.

James P. Johnson
(1894–1955)
Pianist, Composer

James Johnson is less well known than his more famous protégé, Fats Waller, but he made a substantial contribution to the fields of jazz piano and popular show music.

Johnson was the master of the "stride piano," an instrumental style that derives its name from the strong, striding playing of the left hand. "Stride piano" came into its own during the 1920s, particularly in conjunction with the phenomenon known as the "rent party." Such a party was held for the purpose of raising rent money, and involved the payment of an admission fee that entitled a patron to food, drink, conviviality, and a stride piano session. Duke Ellington and Count Basie were among the many who sharpened their skills in the rent-party training ground.

Johnson was also an early bridge between the worlds of jazz and Broadway. Numbered among his song hits are "If I Could Be With You," "Charleston," and "Runnin' Wild."

The youngest of the remarkable Jones brothers (see Hank and Thad Jones) broke in with bands in Detroit (near his hometown, Pontiac, Michigan), came to New York in the 1950s, and worked with such notables as J.J. Johnson, Sonny Rollins, and Donald Byrd before joining John Coltrane's quartet in 1960.

**Elvin Jones
(1927–)**

Drummer, Bandleader

With this group—the most influential of its time—Elvin Jones astonished musicians and listeners with his awesome independence of limbs (he could keep four rhythms going at once), amazing drive (nothing seemed to tire him out, no matter how fierce the tempo), and ability to respond immediately to Coltrane's furious flow of ideas.

Jones left Coltrane when the saxophonist added another drummer to his group (no doubt influenced by his new wife, the pianist Alice McLeod). He soon led his own groups, which have generally featured fine saxophonists; in 1992, Coltrane's son Ravi joined Jones. One of jazz's master drummers, Jones integrated the drums with the front-line (melody) players to a further extent than anyone had done before, while always maintaining the pulse.

The eldest of the three Jones brothers was raised near Detroit, Michigan, where he began his professional career. He came to New York in 1944 and worked and recorded with the great trumpeter and singer Hot Lips Page. His brilliant keyboard technique and skill as both soloist and accompanist soon found him in the company of such giants as Coleman Hawkins and Charlie Parker. He toured with Jazz at the Philharmonic and became Ella Fitzgerald's accompanist.

**Hank Jones
(1918–)**

Pianist

Settling into studio work in New York, Hank Jones became one of the most-recorded jazz musicians—he is to piano what Milt Hinton and George Duvivier were to the bass. From the 1970s on, Jones began to do more work in clubs and on tour, and to record more as a soloist and trio leader. His group is often billed as "The Great Jazz Trio," with various star bassists and drummers.

In the 1990s, Jones is still at the head of the pack when it comes to great jazz piano.

Thad Jones
(1923–1986)

Cornetist, Trumpeter, Composer, Arranger, Bandleader

The middle brother of the gifted Jones family, in his early teens Thad played in a band led by brother Hank, and in the early 1950s he was in a band that included Elvin. Coming to New York in 1954, he was quickly discovered by Charles Mingus, who recorded him for his Debut label and hailed him as the greatest jazz trumpeter (though Thad always preferred the cornet) since Dizzy Gillespie. Thad joined Count Basie's band that same year, staying for almost a decade. During this time he honed his writing skills, but he wasn't heard very much in solo. He did play a solo, however, on Basie's biggest instrumental hit, "April in Paris."

In New York in 1963, Jones joined forces with the great drummer Mel Lewis to co-lead what began as a rehearsal band but soon became the most talked-about new big band in jazz. As the Thad Jones–Mel Lewis Jazz Orchestra, it gave new life to the language of big-band jazz as Jones blossomed as a composer and arranger of music that was swinging but fresh. (Perhaps his best-known composition, however, is the beautiful ballad "A Child Is Born.") The band held together until 1979, when Jones moved to Denmark and Mel took over, keeping much of Jones's work alive. Jones led his own bands in Scandinavia, then came home in 1985 to briefly lead the Count Basie Band, returning to Denmark in ill health six months prior to his death in August 1986.

B. B. King (1925–)

Singer, Guitarist, Bandleader

B.B. King is one of the most successful artists in the history of the blues. His career started when, as a boy of fourteen in Indianola, Mississippi, he met a preacher who played the guitar. King soon owned his own guitar; he bought it for eight dollars, paid out of meager wages he earned working in the cotton fields. From that time on, King spent his spare time singing and playing the guitar with other budding musicians in the town, and listening to blues guitarists who came to Indianola clubs. In the early 1940s, he used to travel to a nearby town to play on street corners. Sometimes he'd come home with as much as twenty-five dollars.

After World War II, King hitchhiked to Memphis where a relative who was a musician got him a performing job at the 16th Street Grill. He was paid twelve dollars a night, plus room and board, five nights a week. King then found a spot on a newly opened radio station in Memphis called

WDIA. He played ten minutes each afternoon, then became a disc jockey. The station named him "The Boy from Beale Street," and thereafter Riley B. King was known as "B.B."

King's first record was made in 1949 for RPM. He had a number-one record on the rhythm-and-blues charts in 1950 and has been known nationally ever since. A change of managers led to a new direction away from the "chitlin' circuit" and into prestigious "pop"-oriented clubs, colleges, and the fast-growing field of pop festivals.

A series of personal appearances on major television shows increased his popularity. King toured Europe for the first time in 1969, starting at the Royal Albert Hall in London and continuing through England, France, Germany, Switzerland, Denmark, and Sweden. Returning to the United States, he joined a fourteen-city tour with the Rolling Stones. Twenty years later, he toured with the Stones again.

At first called "gimmicky" by critics, Roland Kirk proved to be one of the most exciting jazz instrumentalists. His ability to play a variety of instruments was matched only by the range of his improvisational styles; he often switched in the middle of a number from a dissonant exploration to a tonal solo based on a conventional melody.

Rahsaan Roland Kirk (1936–1977)

Composer, Flutist, Saxophonist

Born in Columbus, Ohio, Kirk was technically blind, able to see nothing but light from infancy. Educated at the Ohio State School for the Blind, he began picking up horns at the age of nine. At nineteen, while touring with Boyd Moore, he started experimenting with playing more than one instrument at a time. Finding obscure horns like the stritch and the manzello, he worked out a technique for playing three-part harmony through the use of false fingering.

In 1960 Ramsey Lewis helped Kirk get his first important recording date (with Argo Records). The following year he played with Charles Mingus's group, and later that year he went on the international circuit.

Among his many compositions are "Three for Dizzy"; "Hip Chops"; "The Business Ain't Nothin' but the Blues"; "From Bechet, Byas & Fats"; and "Mystical Dreams."

**John Lewis
(1920–)**

Pianist, Composer,
Bandleader

John Lewis has become an international force in the world of jazz as an arranger, conductor, composer, and instrumentalist.

Raised in a middle-class environment in Albuquerque, New Mexico, Lewis studied music and anthropology at the University of New Mexico until 1942. After three years in the Army, he went to New York City and soon became pianist and arranger with Dizzy Gillespie's band. Two years later at Carnegie Hall, Gillespie's band performed Lewis's first major work, "Toccata for Trumpet and Orchestra."

After a European tour with Gillespie, Lewis returned to the United States to play with Lester Young and Charlie Parker, and to arrange music for Miles Davis. In 1952, after finishing his studies at the Manhattan School of Music, Lewis founded the group upon which a major part of his reputation rested: the Modern Jazz Quartet (MJQ). Though it briefly disbanded in 1974, the MJQ was still together in 1993.

Lewis has never confined his creativity to the MJQ but has assumed a variety of roles, from being a conductor in Europe and Japan to being music director of the highly acclaimed Monterey Jazz Festival.

**Abbey Lincoln
(1940–)**

Singer

Born in Chicago as Anna Marie Wooldridge, Lincoln graduated from Kalamazoo Central High School in Kalamazoo, Michigan. She later studied music for a number of years in Hollywood under several prominent vocal and dramatic coaches.

She began her professional career in Jackson, Michigan in 1950. Since then she has performed in movies (*Nothing but a Man*), made many records (*Abbey Is Blue, Straight Ahead*), played prominent clubs, and appeared on national television. She has been hailed by many outstanding black jazz performers, including Coleman Hawkins, Benny Carter, and Charles Mingus, as a singer to be classed with Billie Holiday.

**Melba Liston
(1926–)**

Arranger, Trombonist

Melba Liston, who has played with the greatest names in jazz, is one of very few female trombonists. Born in Kansas City, Missouri in 1926, Liston's family later moved to California. Her musical history began in 1937, in a youth band under the tutelage of Alma Hightower. Liston continued her trombone studies, in addition to music composition, throughout high

school. She got work with the Los Angeles Lincoln Theater upon gradua-
tion. She met bandleader Gerald Wilson on the night club circuit, and he
introduced her to Dizzy Gillespie, Count Basie, Duke Ellington, Charlie
Parker, and many others. By the late-1940s, she was playing alongside
John Coltrane and John Lewis in Gillespie's band, and later toured with
Billie Holiday as her assistant musical director and arranger.

When the Big Band era waned, Liston jumped off the music circuit and returned to California, where she passed a Board of Education examination
and taught for four years. She was coaxed back into performing by Gillespie, and during the next twenty years she led an all-female jazz group,
toured Europe with Quincy Jones, and did arrangements for Ellington,
Basie, Gillespie, and Diana Ross. In 1974, she went to Jamaica to explore
reggae. When she returned to the United States in 1979, she formed
Melba Liston and Company, a band that revived swing and bebop and
featured contemporary compositions, many of which were her own. She
is regarded as a brilliant and creative arranger and an exceptional trombonist by her peers.

Jimmy Lunceford (1902–1947)

Bandleader

"The Lunceford style" was one that influenced many bandleaders and
arrangers up to the 1950s. The Lunceford band reigned alongside those of
Duke Ellington, Count Basie, and Benny Goodman as a leading and influential big jazz orchestra in the 1930s.

A native of Fulton, Missouri, Lunceford received his B.A. at Fisk University and later studied at City College in New York. After having become
proficient on all reed instruments, Lunceford began his career in 1927 as
a bandleader in Memphis. By 1934, he was an established presence in the
field of jazz. During the next decade, the Lunceford band was known as
the best-disciplined and most showmanly black jazz ensemble in the nation and featured a host of brilliant instrumentalists.

The Lunceford vogue faded after 1943, by which time the band was already experiencing charges in personnel. Lunceford died of a heart attack
in 1947 while the band was on tour.

Branford Marsalis
(1960–)

Saxophonist, Bandleader

Fourteen months older than his brother Wynton, Branford has gained equal fame, in part due to his wide exposure as bandleader for the "Tonight" show, a position that began when Jay Leno became the show's host. Marsalis has also performed beyond the jazz arena in a mid-1980s stint with Sting, for example, and in small roles in several feature films.

Marsalis is a gifted player whose many recordings, including some as sideman with brother Wynton, show him to be a warm and consistently inventive soloist and an imaginative leader–organizer. Though he is more inclined to adapt himself to contemporary surroundings than Wynton, he is also solidly grounded in the jazz tradition.

Wynton Marsalis
(1961–)

Trumpeter, Bandleader

Born into a musical family in New Orleans (his father, Ellis Marsalis, is a prominent pianist and teacher), Wynton Marsalis was well schooled in both the jazz and classical traditions. At seventeen, he won an award at the prestigious Berkshire Music Center for his classical prowess; a year later, he left the Juilliard School of Music to join Art Blakey's Jazz Messengers.

After touring and recording in Japan and the United States with Herbie Hancock, he made his first LP (in 1981), formed his own group, and toured extensively on his own. Soon after, he made a classical album and in 1984 became the first instrumentalist to win simultaneous Grammy awards as best jazz and best classical soloist, with many other awards to follow. He also received a great deal of media coverage—more than any other serious young musician in recent memory.

A brilliant virtuoso of the trumpet with total command of any musical situation, Marsalis has made himself a potent spokesperson for the highest musical standards in jazz, to which he is firmly and proudly committed. He has urged young musicians to acquaint themselves with the rich tradition of jazz and to avoid the pitfalls of "crossing over" to pop, fusion, and rock. His own adherence to these principles and his stature as a player has made his words effective. He has composed music for films and ballet and is a co-founder of the Lincoln Center Jazz Ensemble.

Carmen McRae
(1922–)

Singer, Pianist

Born in Brooklyn in 1922, McRae's natural talent on the keyboards won her numerous music scholarships. During her teen years, she carefully studied the vocal style of Billie Holiday and incorporated it into her own style. A highlight of her career came when Holiday recorded one of McRae's compositions, "Dream of Life." After finishing her education,

McRae moved to Washington, DC, and worked as a government clerk by day and a nightclub pianist–singer by night. In the early 1940s she moved to Chicago to work with Benny Carter, Mercer Ellington, and Count Basie. By 1954 she had gained enough attention through her jazz and pop recordings to be dubbed a "new star" by *Downbeat* magazine. Since then, she has made many records, toured worldwide, and become one of jazz's most acclaimed singers.

Arizona-born Mingus grew up in the Watts area of Los Angeles. Starting on trombone and cello, he eventually settled on the bass and studied with Red Callender, a noted jazz player, and Herman Rheinschagen, a classical musician. He also studied composition with Lloyd Reese. Early in his professional career he worked with Barney Bigard in a band that included the veteran New Orleans trombonist Kid Ory, and he toured briefly in Louis Armstrong's big band; he also led his own groups and recorded with them locally. After a stint in Lionel Hampton's band, which recorded his interesting composition "Mingus Fingus," he joined Red Norvo's trio, with which he came to New York in 1951.

Charles Mingus (1922–1979)

Bassist, Composer, Bandleader

Settling there, he worked with many leading players, including Dizzy Gillespie and Charlie Parker, and he founded his own record label, Debut. He also formed his first of many so-called jazz workshops, in which new music, mostly written by himself, was rehearsed and performed. Mingus believed in spontaneity as well as discipline, and often interrupted his band's public performances if the playing didn't measure up. Some musicians refused to work with him after such public humiliations, but there were some who thought so well of what he was trying to do that they stayed with him for years. Drummer Dannie Richmond was with Mingus from 1956 to 1970 and again from 1974 until the end. Other longtime "Mingusians" include trombonist Kimmy Knepper; pianist Jaki Byard; saxophonists Eric Dolphy, Booker Ervin, John Handy, and Bobby Jones; and trumpeter Jack Walrath.

Mingus's music was as volatile as his temper, filled with ever-changing melodic ideas and textures, and shifting, often accelerating, rhythmic patterns. He was influenced by Duke Ellington, Art Tatum, and Charlie Parker, and his music often reflected psychological states and his views on social issues—Mingus was a staunch fighter for civil rights, and wrote such protest pieces as "Fables of Faubus," "Meditations on Integration," and "Eat That Chicken." He was also steeped in the music of the Holiness Church

Known as a strict musical disciplinarian, Charles Mingus wrote and performed angry, humorous, passionate music that ranks with the greatest in jazz.

("Better Git It in Your Soul," "Wednesday Night Prayer Meeting") and in the whole range of the jazz tradition ("My Jelly Roll Soul," "Theme for Lester Young," "Gunslinging Bird," "Open Letter to Duke"). Himself a virtuoso bassist, he drove his sidemen to their utmost, often with vocal exhortations that became part of a Mingus performance. He composed for films and ballet and experimented with other forms; his most ambitious work, an orchestral suite called "Epitaph," lasts more than two hours and was not performed in full until years after his death. He died of amiotrophic lateral sclerosis, a disease with which he struggled valiantly, composing and directing (from a wheelchair) until just before his death. Mingus was often in financial trouble and once was evicted from his home, but he also received a Guggenheim fellowship in composition and was honored by President Jimmy Carter at a White House jazz event in 1978.

At its best, Mingus's music—angry, humorous, always passionate—ranks with the greatest in jazz. He also wrote a strange but interesting autobiography, *Beneath the Underdog* (1971). A group called Mingus Dynasty continued to perform his music into the 1990s, and in 1992 a Mingus Big Band performed weekly in New York City.

Along with Charlie Parker and Dizzy Gillespie, Thelonious Monk was a vital member of the jazz revolution that took place in the early 1940s. Some musicians (among them Art Blakey) have said that Monk actually predated his more renowned contemporaries. Monk's unique piano style and his talent as a composer made him a leader in the development of modern jazz.

Thelonious Monk (1917–1982)

Pianist, Composer

Aside from brief work with the Lucky Millender Band, Coleman Hawkins, and Dizzy Gillespie, Monk generally was the leader of his own small groups. He has been called the most important jazz composer since Duke Ellington. Many of his compositions ("Round Midnight," "Ruby My Dear") have become jazz standards.

Monk was unique as both an instrumentalist and a composer, maintaining his musical integrity and his melodic originality. He died in Englewood, New Jersey in 1982.

Jelly Roll Morton, with characteristic arrogance, claimed to have invented jazz, and he was quite possibly the first real composer of the genre.

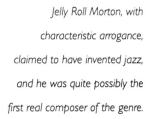

Ferdinand "Jelly Roll" Morton (1890–1941)

Composer, Pianist, Bandleader

Morton, born in New Orleans, claimed (in 1938) that he had "invented" jazz in 1902. That claim was made at the height of the Swing Era, and the few who remembered Morton paid little attention to his boast. However, Alan Lomax, a folklorist at the Library of Congress, was sufficiently intrigued, and he urged Morton to make a recording of his life story, interspersed with fine piano playing, for Lomax's archives. Morton was then living in Washington, DC, managing an obscure night club. He had made his last commercial records in 1930.

In the mid-1920s, Morton made some wonderful records for Victor, the leading label of that day, under the name Jelly Roll Morton and with his Red Hot Peppers. Most were his own compositions, all were his arrangements, and they showed that he was a major talent—quite possibly the first real composer in jazz, if not the inventor of the music. The 1920s were the peak decade in Morton's up-and-down career. He was a much-in-demand pianist in his hometown while still in his teens, working in the Storyville "houses." Restless and ambitious, he hit the road, working in vaudeville, hustling pool, running gambling halls, occasionally playing piano, and traveling as far as Alaska and Mexico. He finally settled in Chicago in 1923, made his first records, worked for a music publisher, and with characteristic arrogance, let everybody know that he was the greatest.

In 1927 he moved to New York, still with a Victor contract but no longer doing as well, and when big band swing came to the fore, Jelly's career took a dive. But after the Library of Congress sessions, Victor was persuaded to record him again, and he was briefly back in the spotlight. Failing health and restlessness led him to drive to California to be with a female companion. But the trip made him ill, and he died in his fiftieth year, just before a revival of interest in traditional jazz that would have given him the break he needed.

In 1992 a musical, *Jelly's Last Jam,* opened with great success on Broadway. It was loosely based on Morton's life and featured new arrangements of his music.

Theodore "Fats" Navarro (1923–1950)

Trumpeter

Fats Navarro was born in Key West, Florida. He started on trumpet at age thirteen, and also played tenor sax. Navarro was first heard nationally as a member of Andy Kirk's band in 1943. In 1944 Dizzy Gillespie recommended him to Billy Eckstine, with whom he played for eighteen months. From 1947 to 1948 Fats played with Illinois Jacquet, Lionel Hampton, and Coleman Hawkins. He worked with Tadd Dameron from 1948 to 1949. Navarro, a victim of drug addiction, was ranked with Dizzy Gillespie and Miles Davis as one of the greatest modern jazz trumpeters.

Joseph "King" Oliver (1885–1938)

Cornetist

Joe Oliver first earned the sobriquet "King" in 1917 after establishing himself as the best cornetist against the likes of Freddie Keppard, Manuel Perez, and a host of other early New Orleans jazz musicians. Oliver soon teamed up with Kid Ory and organized what was to become the leading jazz band in New Orleans.

During the Storyville era, Oliver met and befriended Louis Armstrong. Lacking a son of his own, Oliver became Armstrong's "unofficial father," sharing with him the musical knowledge which he had acquired over the years. In return, Armstrong treated him with great respect, referring to him as "Papa Joe."

With the end of the Storyville era, Oliver left and Armstrong replaced him in Ory's band. By 1922, Oliver summoned Armstrong to Chicago to play in his Creole Jazz Band as second cornetist. In 1923 the Creole Jazz Band made the first important recordings by a black jazz group.

The work of Oliver and Armstrong put Chicago on the jazz map of the United States. However, changing tastes caused Oliver's music to decline in popularity, and by the time he moved to New York in 1928, his best years were behind him.

Beginning in 1932, Oliver toured mainly in the South before ill health forced him to give up music. He died in Savannah, Georgia, where he worked in a poolroom from 1936 until his death in 1938.

Edward "Kid" Ory (1886–1973)

Trombonist, Bandleader

Kid Ory's musical career is in many ways emblematic of the story of jazz itself. They both reached a high point in New Orleans during the first two decades of this century. They both moved north during the 1920s, only to lapse into obscurity in the 1930s before being revived in the next two decades.

Ory was the best known of the so-called tailgate trombonists. He led his own bands in New Orleans and Los Angeles until 1924, when he moved to Chicago to play with King Oliver, Jelly Roll Morton, and others. In 1926, with Louis Armstrong, he recorded his famous composition "Muskrat Ramble."

He returned to the West Coast in 1929, and after playing for a time with local bands, he retired to run a successful chicken ranch until 1939. In the 1940s he gradually returned to music with Barney Bigard, Bunk Johnson, and other New Orleans notables. He toured Europe successfully in 1956 and again in 1959, and spent his final years comfortably in Hawaii.

Charlie "Bird" Parker (1920–1955)

Saxophonist

The influence of Charlie Parker on the development of jazz has been felt not just in the realm of the alto saxophone, but in the whole spectrum of jazz ideas. The astounding melodic, harmonic, tonal, and rhythmic innovations he introduced have made it impossible for any jazz musician from the mid-1940s to the present to develop a musical style without reflecting some of Parker's influence, whether it is acknowledged or not.

Parker left school at sixteen to become a professional musician in Kansas City, his hometown, where he eventually joined pianist Jay McShann, with whom he recorded his first sides. At this time Parker met Dizzy Gillespie. The two men had independently formulated similar ideas about the direction of jazz, and they co-founded the bop movement some four years later.

In the early 1940s, Parker played with the bands of Earl Hines, Cootie Williams, and Andy Kirk, as well as the original Billy Eckstine band—the first big band formed expressly to feature the new jazz style in its solos and arrangements.

In 1945 Parker cut a series of remarkable sides with Gillespie that put bebop on the map. Although Parker was revered by a host of younger musicians, his innovations were at first met with a great deal of opposition from traditionalist jazz musicians and critics.

In 1946, Parker, addicted to heroin, suffered a breakdown and was confined to a state hospital in California. Six months later he was back recording with Erroll Garner. From this point until his death from a heart attack in 1955, he confined most of his activity to working with a quintet, but he also recorded and toured with a string section and visited Europe in 1949 and 1950. He made his final public appearance in 1955 at Birdland, the club that had been named in his honor.

Oscar Peterson began classical study of the piano at the age of six in his native Canada, and in less than a decade was playing regularly on a local radio show in Montreal.

Oscar Peterson (1925–)

Pianist

In 1944 he became a featured soloist with Johnny Holmes, leader of one of the top bands in Canada, and his reputation soon spread throughout the U.S. jazz realm. He resisted offers from Jimmy Lunceford and others to tour the States, but in 1949 he was persuaded by Norman Granz to come to New York City for a Carnegie Hall appearance. The following year he began to record and to tour the United States with Jazz at the Philharmonic.

The original group he formed used bass (Ray Brown) and guitar (Barney Kessel, Herb Ellis), but when Ellis left in 1958, Peterson hired drummer Ed Thigpen to fill out the trio.

A phenomenal technician, Peterson has remained at the head of the jazz piano class, though he cut back on his schedule of concerts and recordings by the late-1980s.

Oscar Pettiford
(1922–1960)

Bassist

Oscar Pettiford was the leading bassist in the modern era of jazz. Building his own style on the foundation established by Jimmy Blanton, Pettiford achieved renown as the most technically capable and melodically inventive bassist in the jazz world of the late-1940s.

Pettiford was born on an American Indian reservation and raised in Minneapolis, Minnesota. Until he was nineteen, he toured with the family band (consisting of his father and eleven children) and was well known in the Midwest. In 1943 Charlie Barnet heard him in Minneapolis and hired him to team up with bassist Chubby Jackson.

Pettiford left Barnet later that year to lead his own group on 52nd Street, and he also played with Coleman Hawkins, Duke Ellington, and Woody Herman.

Pettiford's fame grew during the 1950s through his recordings and his tours of Europe and the Orient. In 1958 he settled permanently in Europe, where he continued to work until his death in Copenhagen in 1960.

Earl "Bud" Powell
(1924–1966)

Pianist, Composer

Along with Charlie Parker, Dizzy Gillespie, and Thelonious Monk, Bud Powell was one of the founding fathers of modern jazz. A piano prodigy, he had his first big-time job with trumpeter Cootie Williams's big band in 1943, and he became involved in the "birth of bebop" at Minton's Playhouse in Harlem and on 52nd Street.

The first to transfer the melodic, harmonic, and rhythmic innovations of bop to the piano keyboard, he set the style for modern jazz piano. Although he suffered recurrently from mental instability from his early twenties until the end of his life, Powell exhibited long stretches of musical brilliance. He lived in Paris from 1959 to 1964, frequently working with his old friend Kenny Clarke. He died soon after, and more than five thousand people attended his funeral in Harlem. One of Powell's finest compositions and performances is "Un Poco Loco."

Ma Rainey, the "Mother of the Blues," enveloped the 1920s with her powerful, message-oriented blues songs, and she is remembered as a genuine jazz pioneer. Born Gertrude Pridgett in Columbus, Georgia, Rainey gave her first public performance as a twelve year old at the local Springer Opera House. At age eighteen she married singer–dancer William "Pa" Rainey, and the duo embarked on a long entertainment career. Around 1912 Rainey introduced a teenaged Bessie Smith into her act, a move that was later seen as having a major impact on blues–jazz singing styles. Ten years later, Rainey was recording with Fletcher Henderson, Louis Armstrong, and Coleman Hawkins and racking up the biggest record sales of that era for Paramount Records. She stopped recording in 1928 but continued to tour the South for a few more years. She retired from singing in 1935 and, until her death four years later, managed the two theaters she owned in Georgia. Her powerful and communicative voice lives on in the more than one hundred recordings she made in her lifetime, singing of the many facets of black experience.

Dewey Redman has spent most of his life in search of a greater knowledge of his instrument, the tenor saxophone. He constantly reevaluates his relationship to his music.

Born in Ft. Worth, Texas, he started playing the clarinet when he was twelve, taking private lessons briefly for six months before he turned to self-instruction. At fifteen he got a job with an eight-piece band that performed in church as the minister passed the collection plate.

At Prairie View A&M College, Dewey teamed up with a piano and a bass player to work in local clubs, found a spot in the Prairie View "swing" band, and graduated in 1953 with a degree in industrial arts and a grasp on a new instrument he had worked with in college, the saxophone.

After a stint in the Army, Dewey obtained a master's degree in education at North Texas State University. He then taught school and directed school bands in west and south Texas.

In 1959 he moved to Los Angeles, where he found the music scene to be very cliquish, and then to San Francisco. He remained there for seven years, studying music and working out his own theories on chord progressions, improvisation, and technique. In 1967 Dewey went to New

Gertrude "Ma" Rainey (1886–1939)

Singer

Dewey Redman (1931–)

Saxophonist

York City and fell in with Ornette Coleman, who brought him into his group with Dave Izenson on bass and Denardo Coleman on drums.

By 1973, Dewey was dividing his playing time between solo efforts, gigs with Ornette Coleman and Keith Jarrett, and the composition of *Peace Suite,* dedicated to the late Ralph Bunche. Later he co-founded the group Old and New Dreams. His son Joshua emerged as one of the finest young tenor saxophonists of the early 1990s.

Don Redman (1900–1964)

Saxophonist, Composer

The first composer–arranger of consequence in the history of jazz, Don Redman was known in the 1920s as a brilliant instrumentalist on several kinds of saxophones. He also made many records with Bessie Smith, Louis Armstrong, and other top-ranking jazz artists.

Born in Piedmont, West Virginia, Redman was a child prodigy who played trumpet at the age of three, joined a band at six, and later studied harmony, theory, and composition at the Boston and Detroit conservatories. In 1924 he joined Fletcher Henderson's band as lead saxophonist and staff arranger, and in 1928 became leader of McKinney's Cotton Pickers.

During most of the 1930s Redman led his own band, which was regarded as one of the leading black orchestras of the day and the first to play a sponsored radio series. He also wrote for many other prominent bands, black and white.

In 1951 Redman became musical director for Pearl Bailey. From 1954 to 1955, he appeared in a small acting role in *House of Flowers* on Broadway. He continued to arrange and record until his death in 1964.

Maxwell Roach (1925–)

Percussionist, Composer

Brooklyn-born Max Roach was one of the key figures in the development of modern jazz. He was in the first group to play bebop on 52nd Street in New York, led by Dizzy Gillespie from 1943 to 1944, and later worked with Charlie Parker's finest group from 1947 to 1948. In 1954 he joined the brilliant young trumpeter Clifford Brown as co-leader of the Clifford Brown–Max Roach Quintet. After Brown's untimely death in a car crash, Roach began to lead his own groups of various sizes and instrumentation (including interesting work with solo and choral voices, an all-percussion band, and a jazz quartet combined with a string quartet). His many compositions include *We Insist—Freedom Now*. This suite, written with singer Abbey Lincoln (who was his wife at the time), was one of the first jazz works with a strong and direct political and social thrust.

A phenomenally gifted musician with a matchless percussion technique, Roach developed the drum solo to new heights of structural refinement; he has been an influence on every drummer to come along since the 1940s. A professor of music at the University of Massachusetts since 1972, Roach in 1988 became the first jazz artist to receive a MacArthur fellowship, the most prestigious (and lucrative) award in the world of arts and letters. His daughter, Maxine, is a violinist, and they have worked and recorded together.

Theodore Walter "Sonny" Rollins (1929–)

Saxophonist, Bandleader

Born and raised in New York City, Sonny Rollins made his recording debut at nineteen, in such fast company as J.J. Johnson and Bud Powell. Distinctively personal from the start, his style developed through work with Thelonious Monk, Powell, Art Blakey, and Miles Davis. In 1955 he joined the Clifford Brown–Max Roach Quintet. Later in the decade he took two years off from active playing to study and practice. When he reappeared at the helm of his own quartet in 1961, he surprised even those who knew the quality of his work with the power and conviction of his playing.

Since then, though briefly overshadowed by John Coltrane, Rollins has been the unchallenged master of modern jazz tenor saxophone, with a sound and style completely his own. He often draws on his West Indian heritage for melodic and rhythmic inspiration and is one of the undisputed masters of extended improvisation, often playing all by himself as his group "lays out" in amazement—a feeling shared by his listeners.

Jimmy Rushing (1903–1972)

Singer

The song "Mister Five by Five," written in tribute to Rushing, is an apt physical description of this singer, who was one of the greatest male jazz and blues singers.

Rushing played piano and violin as a boy, but he entered music professionally as a singer in the after-hours world of California in 1925. After that, Rushing was linked with several leading bands and musicians: Walter Page from 1927 to 1928; Benny Moten in 1929; and from 1936 to 1949 he was a mainstay of the famed Count Basie Band.

Rushing formed his own small group when he left Basie and in the ensuing years worked most often as a "single." Following the revival of the blues in the mid-1950s, Rushing regained widespread popularity.

His nightclub and festival engagements were always successful, and his world tours, on his own and also with Benny Goodman, earned him critical acclaim and commercial success. His style has endured across four decades of jazz largely due to its great warmth, a sure, firm melodic line, and a swinging use of rhythm. Late in life, he appeared in a featured acting role in Gordon Parks's film *The Learning Tree.*

Bessie Smith (1894–1937)

Singer

They called her "The Empress of the Blues," and she had no peers. Her magnificent voice, dramatic sense, clarity of diction, and incomparable timing and phrasing set her apart from the competition and made her appeal to lovers of both jazz and blues. Her first record, "Down Hearted Blues," sold more than a million copies in 1923, when only Caruso and Paul Whiteman were racking up those kind of figures.

By then, Bessie Smith had been singing professionally for fifteen years, but records by black singers had only been made since 1920, and usually by less earthy singers. She already had a large following and had appeared in big shows, so the timing was right—not least for Columbia Records, which she pulled out of the red. Before long she was backed by the best jazz players, including Louis Armstrong, and by 1925 she starred in her own touring show, which traveled in a private Pullman car. By 1927 she was the highest paid black artist in the world, and in 1929 she made a short film, *St. Louis Blues,* that captures for posterity some of her magnetism as a stage performer. But tastes in music were changing rapidly, and though Smith added more popular songs to her repertory and moved with the times, the Depression nearly killed the jazz and blues record business. In 1931 Columbia dropped her, and she was soon touring as a "single."

John Hammond brought her back to the studios in 1933. Her records were wonderful, her singing as powerful and swinging as ever, but these recordings didn't sell and turned out to be her last. She still found plenty of work on the traveling circuit, but the money was not what it had been in the 1920s. On the road early one morning in Mississippi, she was fatally injured in a collision. For years, there was a misconception that she died because a white hospital refused to treat her. In fact, she was treated in a black hospital, but she had lost too much blood to survive.

In 1968 Columbia reissued all of her records, then did so again on compact disc in the 1990s, with very positive results.

Born in Dayton and raised in Pittsburgh, Strayhorn early on showed an unusually sophisticated gift for writing both music and lyrics. While still in his teens he wrote "Lushlife," which was one of several songs he showed to Duke Ellington in 1938. A year or so later, Strayhorn, who was also a gifted pianist, joined the Ellington entourage in New York. Ellington first thought of him as a lyricist (something he was always looking for) but soon found out that Strayhorn also had a knack for arranging.

Billy Strayhorn (1915–1967)

Composer, Arranger, Pianist

Before long the two had established a working relationship that remains unique in the history of music—a collaboration so close that they were often unsure of who had written which part of a given composition. Each man did continue to work on his own, however, and among the many Strayhorn-signed contributions to Ellington's repertoire are such standouts as "Take the A Train," "Passion Flower," "Chelsea Bridge," "Rain Check," and "Blood Count"—the latter written in the hospital as Strayhorn was dying of cancer.

Self-effacing and modest to a fault, Strayhorn stayed out of the limelight. But musicians and serious Ellington fans knew just how much he contributed to the band's work during his lifetime.

Considered a wizard on the keyboard, Art Tatum, who was nearly blind from birth, was noted for the musical imagination he brought to life by his exceptional facility. Harmonically, he matched the boppers in sophistication—young Charlie Parker took a job as dishwasher in a club where Tatum worked so he could hear him every night. Rhythmically, he anticipated modern jazz developments and could play rings around anyone, regardless of their instrument.

Art Tatum (1909–1956)

Pianist

Though Tatum enjoyed a full career, recording prolifically—mostly as a soloist but also as leader of a trio (with electric guitar and bass, patterned on Nat King Cole's)—his career came a bit too soon to benefit from the acceptance that later came to jazz as a concert hall music. The concert hall, in which he rarely had the chance to perform, was Tatum's ideal medium. As it was, he often played "after hours" for the edification of fellow musicians, as a challenger to newer players, and to better his own skills, setting seemingly impossible tempos or picking tunes with the toughest "changes."

Billy Taylor
(1921–)

Pianist,
Composer, Educator

Few musicians have done more to promote jazz than Billy Taylor, who has been instrumental in attaining proper respect and recognition for African-American music. In the 1950s he began contributing articles to major magazines like *Esquire,* and he appeared on what was then known as "educational" television. He was at that time already well established as a pianist on the New York scene, having arrived in the Big Apple shortly after graduating from Virginia State College in 1942. Taylor became a regular on "Swing Street," and later he was the house pianist at Birdland. He started leading his own trios in 1951.

Taylor earned a doctorate in music education from the University of Massachusetts in 1975; his dissertation was later published as "Jazz Piano: History and Development," and became the text for a course offered on National Public Radio. Taylor led an eleven-piece band for television's "David Frost Show" from 1969 to 1972, was founder and director of the program "Jazz Alive" on NPR, and has been a regular on CBS-TV's "Sunday Morning" since 1981. He has served on several boards and panels, notably the prestigious National Council on the Arts.

Cecil Taylor
(1929–)

Pianist, Composer

Cecil Taylor, Ornette Coleman, and John Coltrane—each completely different from the other—are the leading figures of avant garde jazz (later known as "free jazz," perhaps a more fitting term). Of these, Taylor is the farthest removed from the blues and swing roots of jazz. He is a music unto himself—a fantastic virtuoso of the piano, with staggering energy and endurance, and astonishing improvisatory abilities.

He attended New England Conservatory but says he learned more from listening to Ellington; another early influence was Bud Powell. He made his first recording (with Steve Lacy on soprano sax) in 1956; the following year he appeared at the Newport Jazz Festival and was recorded there. Settling in New York City (he was born on Long Island), Taylor often struggled due to lack of work and acceptance but continued to go his own musical way, making interesting if infrequent recordings. In the mid-1960s he experimented with larger frameworks for his playing, recording with the Jazz Composers Orchestra. In the early 1970s he briefly taught at various universities. Meanwhile, he had gained a following in Europe and Japan, and in the 1980s found work more frequently and did a spate of recordings, including some brilliant solo efforts. He also teamed for concerts with Mary Lou Williams and with Max Roach. In 1988 he was featured in a month-long festival of concerts and workshops in Berlin; some of the results were issued in a lavish boxed set of eleven compact discs. Around the same time, Taylor, always fascinated by dance (which he sometimes included in his performances), participated in a concert with the famous ballet star Mikhail Baryshnikov. In 1992 Taylor received a MacArthur fellowship—one of the greatest awards an artist can receive.

McCoy Tyner (1938–)

Pianist,
Composer, Bandleader

The Philadelphia-born pianist came to fame when he joined John Coltrane's quartet in 1960. Prior to that, Tyner's most important job was with the Art Farmer–Benny Golson Jazztet. During his five years with Coltrane, Tyner developed a unique two-handed, densely harmonic style and became one of the most widely admired and imitated pianists in jazz.

As leader of his own groups of various sizes—from trios to an unusual big band—Tyner has continued to develop as a musician of great originality and integrity.

Sarah Vaughan (1924–1990)

Singer

Her voice was of such beauty, range, and power, her ear so sure, her musicality so rare that Sarah Vaughan could have become an opera star. Fortunately for jazz lovers, she went the way of jazz and brought joy to her listeners from the time she started singing professionally in 1943.

She had begun singing and accompanying the choir on piano in church in her native Newark, New Jersey, and she had sung pop songs at high school parties when, on a dare, she entered the Wednesday night amateur contest at Harlem's famed Apollo Theater. As in a fairy tale, Billy Eckstine happened to be backstage. He ran out front as soon as he heard her voice, and later recommended Vaughan to his boss, bandleader Earl Hines. Hines came, heard her sing, and hired her—and she did win the amateur contest, which meant a week's work at the Apollo. Charlie "Bird" Parker and Dizzy Gillespie were both in the Hines band at the time, although they and Vaughan left Hines when Eckstine decided to start his own band. By 1945 Vaughan had made her first records under her own name, and she was the only singer to record with Bird and Dizzy together.

A year later she started her solo career. Though she had some big pop hits during her long and rich career, she never strayed from jazz for long. Incredibly, as she got older, she got better, losing none of her amazing top range and adding to the bottom range, while her mastery of interpretation continued to improve. Her fans called her "The Divine One."

Thomas "Fats" Waller (1904–1943)

Composer, Pianist, Singer, Bandleader

Weighing in at over three hundred pounds and standing more than six feet tall, Tom Waller, a preacher's son born in Greenwich Village, came by his nickname naturally. He was, as one of his many good friends said, "all music." His father wanted him to follow in his footsteps, but Fats liked the good times that came with playing the piano well, which he could do almost from the start. At fifteen he turned professional, backing singers in Harlem clubs and playing piano for silent movies. Wherever he went, people loved him, and he loved to spread joy. Few pianists have been able to match his terrific beat. He was also a master of the stride piano style. He loved to play Bach, especially on the organ, and he was the first to play the organ as a jazz instrument. In Paris in 1932, world-famous Marcel Dupré invited Fats to play the organ at Notre Dame.

Waller's talent for writing songs soon became evident. His first and biggest hit was "Ain't Misbehavin'" in 1929; others include "Honeysuckle Rose," "Blue Turning Gray Over You," and "The Jitterbug Waltz." He also wrote "London Suite" for solo piano.

Waller was a great performer on the new medium of the 1920s—the radio. He had a constant line of patter to go along with his great piano and carefree singing. He also made it to Hollywood. His finest medium, however, was recorded music. With his small group and the occasional big band, he cut more than five hundred sides between 1934 and his untimely death at thirty-nine in 1943. His personality came across on records, and no matter how trite the tune, he turned it into a jazz gem. Unfortunately, Waller suffered from ill health in the midst of a successful and productive career, partly due to his huge appetite and excessive drinking. He had just finished filming *Stormy Weather,* and his first complete Broadway musical was becoming a hit, when he died of pneumonia on a cold December night.

Dinah Washington's style defies categorization, but it is seen as laying the groundwork for numerous rhythm-and-blues and jazz artists. Like many black singers, Washington got her start singing gospel—in her case, at St. Luke's Baptist Church on Chicago's South Side. She toured churches with her mother, playing the piano and singing solos, until opportunity beckoned in the form of an amateur talent contest at Chicago's Regal Theater. Her triumphant performance there led to shows at local nightclubs, and in 1943 the nineteen-year-old singer successfully auditioned for a slot in Lionel Hampton's band. She was soon discovered by composer and critic Leonard Feather, and together Washington and Feather created several chart toppers, including "Baby Get Lost," "Salty Papa Blues," "Evil Gal Blues," and "Homeward Bound." She gained legendary status with "What a Difference a Day Makes" and "Unforgettable." Washington proved to be such a versatile artist that she was acclaimed by blues, jazz, gospel, pop, and rhythm-and-blues audiences alike. Aretha Franklin dedicated one of her early albums to Washington, labelling it simply "Unforgettable."

**Dinah Washington
(1924–1963)**

Singer

Born in Kansas City, Kansas (some sources say Missouri), Ben Webster was at first a pianist but switched to saxophone in his late teens. He worked with the family band led by Lester Young's father and with many other midwestern bands, and came to New York in 1931 with Benny Moten (whose pianist was Count Basie). After gaining a name among musicians as one of the most gifted disciples of Coleman Hawkins, he made many records and toured with several prominent bands, including those of Fletcher Henderson, Cab Calloway, and Teddy Wilson.

**Ben Webster
(1909–1973)**

Saxophonist

But it was when he joined Duke Ellington in 1939 that Webster really blossomed and became an influential jazz musician. When he left Ellington in 1943, he led his own small groups, recorded prolifically, and also became one of the first black musicians to join a network radio musical staff. In 1964 he left for what had been planned as a brief visit to Europe, but he never returned home. Settling in Copenhagen, he spent the final decade of his life as a revered and beloved elder statesman of jazz. During this period, his always masterful ballad playing ripened to full maturity, and his sound, ranging from a whisper to a gruff roar, became one of the unsurpassed landmarks of classic jazz.

Mary Lou Williams
(1910–1981)

Pianist,
Composer, Arranger

Most women who have achieved fame in jazz have been singers, including Bessie Smith and Betty Carter. A singular exception to this rule was Mary Lou Williams, dubbed the "First Lady of Jazz."

Born in Atlanta and raised in Pittsburgh, Mary Elfrieda Scruggs had already performed in public at the age of six and was a professional by thirteen. Three years later she married saxophonist John Williams, with whom she made her record debut. When he joined Andy Kirk's band she took over the group. Soon she was writing arrangements for Kirk, and in 1931 she became the band's pianist and musical director.

Though she also wrote for Benny Goodman and other bands, she stayed with Kirk until 1942, helping to make the band one of the swing era's best. Settling in New York, she led her own groups (sometimes all female) and began to compose longer works, including the "Zodiac Suite," performed at Town Hall in 1946. A champion of modern jazz, she gave advice and counsel to such rising stars as Dizzy Gillespie and Thelonious Monk. Williams lived in England and France from 1952 to 1954. When she returned home she retired from music for three years, but was coaxed out by Gillespie. Resuming her career, she toured widely, wrote several religious works (including a Jazz Mass performed at St. Patrick's Cathedral), and in 1977 became artist-in-residence and teacher of jazz history and performance at Duke University, a position she held until her death. As pianist, composer, and arranger, Mary Lou Williams ranks with the very best.

Theodore Wilson
(1912–1986)

Pianist, Bandleader

Teddy Wilson's father taught English and his mother was head librarian at Tuskegee Institute. He turned to music as a career while studying printing in Detroit in 1928. He was befriended by the great Art Tatum, played in Louis Armstrong's big band, and was brought to New York by Benny Carter in 1933.

Two years later he began to make a series of records—which became classics—often with Billie Holiday and always with the greatest musicians of the time. Meanwhile, he was becoming famous as the first black jazzman to be featured with a white band, playing with the Benny Goodman Trio and Quartet. His marvelously clear, harmonically impeccable piano style was a big influence on the pianists of the swing era. His own big band, formed in 1939, was excellent but not a commercial success. From 1940 on, he mostly led small groups or appeared as a soloist, touring worldwide and making hundreds of records. Even after he became seriously ill, he continued to perform until a week before his death. Two of his three sons are professional musicians.

Blues singer and guitarist Muddy Waters was born Morganfield McKinley in Rolling Fork, Mississippi. He began playing guitar at the age of seventeen. He moved to Chicago when he was twenty-eight, and in 1947 he began to record commercially. He was best known for such songs as "I'm Your Hoochie Coochie Man," "Got My Mojo Working," "Tiger in Your Tank," and "Manish Boy."

Muddy Waters (1915–1983)

Guitarist, Singer

It was Lester Young who gave Billie Holiday the name "Lady Day" when both were with Count Basie, and it was Lady Day in turn who christened Lester Young "President" (later shortened to "Prez").

Lester "Prez" Young (1909–1959)

Saxophonist

Young spent his youth on the carnival circuit in the Midwest with his musical family, choosing to concentrate on the tenor saxophone, one of the many instruments he was able to play.

When Young took over Coleman Hawkins's chair in Fletcher Henderson's orchestra, he was criticized for not having the same style as his predecessor. As a result of this, he returned to Kansas City to play first with Andy Kirk, and then with Count Basie from 1936 to 1940. During the Basie years Young surpassed Hawkins as the vital influence on the tenor saxophone. Hardly a tenor man from the mid-1940s through the 1950s achieved prominence without building on the foundations laid by Lester Young.

Young suffered a complete breakdown in 1955 but made a comeback the next year. He died within hours of returning from a long engagement in Paris.

By Dan Morgenstern

*P*opular Music

Since the turn of the twentieth century, black music—whether gospel,

rhythm and blues, soul, funk, or rap—has shaped American popular music.

More recently, its impact can be heard in the emergence of world music

coming out of Africa, South America, and the Caribbean Islands. From the

church to the concert stage, thousands of gifted African-American singers

and musicians have bestowed upon America and the world a gift of un-

bounded spirit.

GOSPEL: THE ROOT OF POPULAR MUSIC ♦ ♦ ♦ ♦ ♦ ♦ ♦ ♦ ♦ ♦ ♦ ♦

The foundation of twentieth-century black popular music is rooted in the sounds of several folk styles, including black minstrel and vaudeville tunes, blues, and ragtime. The music of the African-American church, however, has played one of the most significant roles in the evolution of black popular music.

Inextricably bound to the spirituals sung by slaves, the gospel style came to dominate the black religious experience in America. By the turn of the century, gospel music had reached popularity as black religious songwriters began to publish their own compositions. One of the earliest and most influential of these writers was Charles Albert Tindley, a Maryland-born Methodist preacher, who was responsible for writing several gospel music classics. His song "I'll Overcome Someday" resurfaced more than a half decade later as "We Shall Overcome," the anthem of the 1960s civil-rights movement. Tindley's 1905 composition "Stand by Me" became a major hit for singer Ben E. King and the Drifters during the 1960s.

Tindley's music subsequently influenced Thomas A. Dorsey, whose talents as a religious songwriter, accompanist, and choir director earned him the title "the father of gospel music." Before dedicating his life to the Baptist church, Dorsey spent his youth as an itinerant blues pianist, performing under the name Georgia Tom. Like other bluesmen/preachers such as the Reverend Gary Davis, Blind Willie McTell, and Gatemouth Moore,

Thomas Dorsey with his group the Wandering Syncopators, 1923.

Dorsey performed both secular and religious music. In 1928, for example, he not only co-wrote the blues hit "Tight Like That" with guitarist Hudson "Tampa Red" Whitaker, but also composed his first gospel song, "If You See My Savior Tell Him You Saw Me."

Four years later, Dorsey abandoned his career as a blues and jazz pianist to devote himself to a form of religious music that historian Michael W. Harris describes as a gospel–blues style melding black religious and popular music into a unique and passionate form of gospel. During the Great Depression, Dorsey's new style of gospel served as an uplifting spiritual release from the pervasive poverty experienced in the black community. The performance of two of Dorsey's songs at the 1930 National Baptist Convention created a wave of enthusiasm for gospel across the nation. In the following year, Dorsey organized the world's first gospel choir. In 1932, he began a forty-year career as choir director at Chicago's Pilgrim Baptist Church. During his stay at Pilgrim Baptist, he launched the golden age of gospel music (c. 1945–1960), training and accompanying singers from Sallie Martin to Mahalia Jackson.

The advent of the phonograph around the turn of the century helped to heighten the popularity of gospel music. The distribution of records helped break down the musical isolation imposed upon blacks since slavery, allowing them to reach audiences outside their own communities. Recorded by the Victor label in 1902, the Jubilee and camp meeting shouts of the Dwinddie Colored Quartet appeared as one of the first black recordings. In the 1920s, black religious music became popular with the race record (a title designating the segregated sale of African-American recordings). By 1924, Paramount Records sponsored its own Jubilee singers, and within three years Columbia Records began to send engineers into the field to record the richly complex harmonies of gospel quartets. Also popular were recorded sermons backed by occasional musical instruments, and evangelistic guitars, known commonly as "jack legs," which brought street-singing gospel blues to a wider audience.

Gospel and the Recording Industry

After a decline in recordings by evangelists during the 1930s and early 1940s, gospel music experienced an immense rise in popularity as hundreds of independent recording labels appeared after World War II. During the 1940s, numerous gospel quartets went on the road as full-time professionals, while thousands more sought work on weekends. Dressed in flowing robes and fashionably designed dress suits, quartets incorporated dance routines and expressive shouts into their performances. Throughout the postwar period male gospel groups like the Five Blind Boys from Mississippi, the Mighty Clouds of Joy from Los Angeles, and the Sensational Nightingales from Memphis sang *a capella* (without instruments) on numerous recordings.

THE RISE OF RHYTHM AND BLUES ♦ ♦ ♦ ♦ ♦ ♦ ♦ ♦ ♦ ♦ ♦ ♦ ♦ ♦ ♦

As black veterans returned home from the World War II, they found not only a new gospel sound, but an exciting blues style being played by small combos: jump blues. With its roots in boogie woogie and the blues–swing arrangements of artists like Count Basie, Cab Calloway, Louis Jordan, and Lucky Millinder, this new blues style acquired an enormous following in black urban communities across the country. Unlike the swing-era big bands, jump blues groups featured fewer horns and a heavy rhythmic approach marked by a walking boogie bass line, honking saxophone solos, and a two–four drum pattern. Among the greatest exponents of postwar jump blues were guitarist T–Bone Walker, saxophonist Eddie "Cleanhead" Vincent, and blues shouter Big Joe Turner.

Soon many jump blues ensembles began to feature singers versed in a smooth gospel-influenced vocal style. In 1949 the popularity of this style led *Billboard Magazine* to change its black pop chart title to rhythm and blues, thus coining the name of this new music. Just as gospel emerged from blues and religious spirituals and hymns, rhythm and blues drew upon gospel, electric urban blues, and swing jazz to create a vibrantly modern sound appealing to the younger generation of postwar blacks. Some of the early recordings exemplifying the gospel influence on rhythm and blues were Cecil Grant's 1945 hit "I Wonder," Roy Brown's 1947 classic "Good Rocking Tonight," and Wynonie Harris's 1949 disc "All She Wants to Do Is Rock."

It was not long before this kind of raw-edged rhythm and blues emerged from hundreds of independent recording labels that appeared across the country in the postwar era. With the increased availabilty of rhythm and blues recordings, a handful of black radio disc jockeys became locally famous as the first promoters and salesmen of this music. Bringing their

Louis Jordan had a profound impact on the emergence of rhythm and blues.

colorful street language to the airwaves, pioneer black DJs such as Al Benson and Vernon Winslow not only helped to popularize rhythm and blues, but set the trend for modern pop radio.

In the early 1950s, numerous gospel quartets and street corner singing groups set out to establish careers in the black popular music scene. Influenced by gospel music and the secular singing of groups like the Inkspots, vocal groups appeared who performed complex harmonies in *a*

R&B and the Black Church

capella style. As they would for rap artists in decades to come, street corners in urban neighborhoods became training grounds for thousands of young aspiring African-American artists. This music, known as doo-wop, first arrived on the scene with the formation of the Ravens in 1945. Not long afterward, there followed a great succession of doo-wop groups. One of these, the Orioles, scored a nationwide hit in 1953 with "Crying in the Chapel"—a song that, for the first time in black popular music, walked an almost indistinguishable line between gospel and mainstream pop music. In the same year, Billy Ward formed the Dominoes, featuring lead singer Clyde McPhatter, the son of a Baptist minister.

In the wake of the success of these vocal groups, numerous gospel singers left the church to become pop music stars. In 1952, for example, the Royal Sons became the Five Royales, the Gospel Starlighters (with James Brown), and finally the Blue Flames. Five years later, a young gospel singer named Sam Cooke landed a number-one pop hit with "You Send Me," a song that achieved popularity among both black and white audiences.

The strong relationship between gospel and rhythm and blues was evident in the music of more hard-edged R&B groups like Hank Ballard and the Midnighters. Maintaining a driving blues-based sound, Ballard's music, while featuring gospel-based harmonies, retained secular themes, as evidenced in his 1954 hit "Work With Me Annie." However, the capstone of gospel R&B appeared in the talents of Georgia-born pianist and singer Ray Charles, who in 1954 hit the charts with "I Got a Woman," which was based upon the gospel song "My Jesus Is All the World to Me." Charles's 1958 recording "What I'd Say" is famed for its call-and-response pattern, which directly resembled the music in Holiness churches.

Rock and Roll   The rise of white rock and roll around 1955 served to open the floodgates for thousands of black R&B artists longing for a nationwide audience. A term applied to black R&B and its white equivalents during the mid-1950s, rock and roll represented a label given to a music form by the white media and marketplace in order to attract a mass multi-racial audience. As black music writer Nelson George explained, naming this music rock and roll "dulled down the racial identification and made young white consumers of Cold War America feel more comfortable." Taken from a term common among the Delta and electric blues cultures, rock and roll was actually rhythm and blues rechristened with a more "socially acceptable" title.

Chuck Berry revolutionized rhythm and blues by featuring the guitar as a lead instrument, rather than a rhythm instrument.

Thus, the majority of R&B performers never made the distinction be-tween rhythm and blues and rock and roll. One R&B artist who estab-lished a prosperous career in rock and roll was New Orleans–born pianist Antoine "Fats" Domino. Although he had produced a great amount of strong R&B material before his career in rock and roll, Domino did not hit the charts until 1955 with "Ain't That a Shame," followed by the classics "Blueberry Hill," "I'm Walkin," and "Whole Lotta Loving." Another R&B pianist/singer to enter the rock and roll field was Little Richard Pennimen, a former Pentecostal gospel singer whose career in pop music began in 1956 with the hit "Tutti Frutti." Before entering a Seventh Day Adventist seminary in 1959, Little Richard produced a string of hits: "Long Tall Sally," "Rip It Up," "The Girl Can't Help It," and "Good Golly Miss Molly."

In 1955, as Fats Domino's New Orleans style R&B tunes climbed the charts, a young guitarist from St. Louis named Chuck Berry achieved na-tionwide fame with the country-influenced song "Maybelleine," which reached number five on the charts. Backed by bluesman Muddy Waters's rhythm section, "Maybelleine" offered a unique form of R&B, combining white hillbilly, or rockabilly, with jump blues; Berry revolutioned R&B by featuring the guitar as a lead, rather than a rhythm, instrument. Modeled after his blues–guitar mentor T–Bone Walker, Berry's double-string guitar bends and syncopated up-stroke rhythm created a driving backdrop for his colorfully poetic tales of teenage life. A very eclectic and creative musician, Berry incorporated the sounds of urban blues, country, calypso, Latin, and even Hawaiian music into his unique brand of R&B. His classic "Johnny B. Good," recorded in 1958, became a standard in almost every rock and roll band's repertoire, including 1960s rock guitar hero Jimi Hendrix.

BLACKS AND COUNTRY MUSIC ◆ ◆ ◆ ◆ ◆ ◆ ◆ ◆ ◆ ◆ ◆ ◆ ◆ ◆ ◆ ◆

Berry was not the only African American to take an interest in country music. Ray Charles's crossover into country music in the early 1960s caused controversy in many circles. In 1959, Charles recorded "I'm Moving On," a country tune by Hank Snow. Despite opposition, Charles went on to record a fine collection of songs in 1962 entitled *Modern Sounds in Country Music*. Filled with soulful ballads and backed by colorful string sections, the session produced two classic numbers: "You Don't Know Me" and "I Can't Stop Loving You." Its popularity spawned the 1963 sequel *Modern Sounds in Country Music: Volume 2* that produced several more hits, including Hank Williams's "Your Cheating Heart" and "Take These Chains From My Heart."

Unlike other mainstream black country artists, Charles's renditions remained immersed in his unique gospel–blues sound. Before Charles's entrance into the country music field there had been many African-American country artists, but it was not until 1965, when Charley Pride arrived on the country music scene with his RCA recordings "Snakes Crawl at Night" and "Atlantic Coastal Line," that a black artist emerged as a superstar in the country tradition. Pride's songs were so steeped in the country tradition that many radio listeners were astounded when they found out his racial identity. With the arrival of Pride, there appeared other black country artists like Linda Martel from South Carolina, O. B. McClinton from Mississippi, and Oklahoma-born Big Al Downing and Stoney Edwards. The most noted of these artists, Edwards recorded two nationwide hits in 1968 with Jesse Winchester's "You're on My Mind" and Leonard Cohen's "Bird on a Wire."

Ray Charles is one of the world's most popular musicians.

♦ ♦ ♦ ♦ ♦ ♦ ♦ ♦ ♦ ♦ ♦ ♦ ♦ ♦ ♦ **SOUL: THE MIRROR OF A DECADE**

The most dominant form of black popular music of the 1960s emerged under the powerful gospel-influenced rhythm and blues style known as soul. As music historian Peter Guralnick wrote, soul music was a "brief flowering" of a distinctly southern-inspired black music that "came to its own no earlier than 1960," crossed over by 1965 or 1966, and, despite lingering traces of its influence throughout the culture, was spent as a controlling force by the early 1970s. Since it paralleled the 1960s civil-rights and black-power movements, soul embodied a sense of racial pride and independence. Such themes are evident in the soul music of Curtis Mayfield, an artist whom Nelson George describes as "black music's most unflagging Civil Rights activist." Mayfield's "People Get Ready" (1965), "We're a Winner" (1965), and "Choice of Color" (1969) represented messages of racial advancement and social change.

Although racial pride played an important role in the rise of soul, one of its main attributes was its relationship to the music of the black church—

"Godfather of Soul"

James Brown.

for there existed, during the 1960s, a distinct pattern among the careers of soul artists. Many African-American artists, for instance, after establishing a career in gospel music, became R&B and then soul artists. Among the artists who followed this pattern were soul singers Solomon Burke, Wilson Pickett, and Otis Redding.

One could say soul was the intensification of the gospel influence in popular black music. Soul artists from Joe Tex to "Lady of Soul" Aretha Franklin cultivated and refined a burningly passionate form of singing filled with gospel-influenced shouts and screams. With the incorporation of the electric bass, which replaced the acoustic bass featured on most of the R&B music of the 1940s and 1950s, these singers were provided with a modern pulsing rhythm that inspired them, and the entire band, to re-shape the sound of black music.

In 1965, when Otis Redding hit the charts with the ballad "I've Been Loving You Too Long" and Wilson Pickett released the recording "Midnight Hour," a dynamic veteran of the gospel and rhythm and blues circuit named James Brown climbed the charts with the powerful soul number "Out of Sight." A self-created legend, Brown was soul music's uncompromising individualist. As "Soul Brother No. 1," he achieved commercial success with his legendary 1963 LP *Live at the Apollo,* a record many critics believe best captures his explosive onstage energy. Throughout the 1960s, Brown astounded audiences with his ability to lead a full horn and rhythm section through spontaneous changes in the musical form by a sudden gesture or a quick vocal command. Later in the decade, Brown and his powerful rhythm section, the Famous Flames, produced a number of classic soul numbers such as the 1967 recordings "Papa's Got a Brand New Bag" and "Cold Sweat," and the 1968 racial–political statement "I'm Black and I'm Proud." The "James Brown Sound" not only had a profound impact on the development of funk and jazz fusion, but it also helped shape the sound of African popular music.

During the 1960s, as soul music gained a mass following in the black community, a black-owned and family-run Detroit record company emerged as one of the largest and most successful African-American business enterprises in America. In 1959, Berry Gordy, a Detroit entrepreneur, songwriter, and modern jazz enthusiast, established the Motown Record Corporation.

With its headquarters located in a modest two-story home, the company proudly displayed a sign on its exterior reading Hitsville USA. Taking advantage of the diversity of local talent, Gordy employed Detroit-based contract teams, writers, producers, and engineers. Motown's studio became a great laboratory for technological innovations, advancing the use of echo, multi-tracking, and over-dubbing. In the studio, Gordy employed the city's finest jazz and classical musicians to accompany the young singing talent signed to the company.

Unlike the soul music emerging in studios like Stax Records in Memphis and Muscle Shoals Sounds in Alabama, Motown's music was also marketed at the white middle class; Gordy called his music "The Sound of Young America," and he sought to produce glamorous and well-groomed acts. "Blues and R&B always had a funky look to it back in those days," explained Motown producer Mickey Stevenson. "We felt that we should have a look that the mothers and fathers would want their children to follow."

Thus, Motown set out to produce a sound that it considered more refined and less "off-key" than the music played by mainstream soul and blues

Motown: The Capital of Northern Soul

"Blues and R&B always had a funky look to it back in those days," explained Motown producer Mickey Stevenson. For Motown, he added, "we felt that we should have a look that the mothers and fathers would want their children to follow."

artists. In its early years of operation, Motown retained an R&B influence as evidenced in songs like the Marvelettes' "Please Mister Postman" (1961), Mary Wells's "You Beat Me to the Punch" (1962), and Marvin Gaye's "Pride and Joy" (1963).

One of the main forces responsible for the emergence of a unique "Motown sound" appeared in the production team of Brian and Eddie Holland, and Lamont Dozier, or H–D–H, as they came to be known. Utilizing the recording techniques of Phil Spector's "wall of sound," the H–D–H team brought fame to many of Motown's "girl groups" such as Martha and the Vandellas and the Supremes, featuring Diana Ross.

During 1966–1967, H–D–H began to use more complex string arrangements based upon minor chord structures. This gave rise to what has been referred to as their "classical period." As a result, many Motown songs reflected the darker side of lost love and the conditions of ghetto life. This mood was captured in such songs by the Four Tops as "Reach Out, I'll Be There," "Burnadette," and "Seven Rooms of Gloom."

After the Holland–Dozier–Holland team left Motown in 1968, the company, faced with numerous artistic and economic problems, fell into a state of decline. A year later, Gordy signed the Jackson Five, the last major act to join the label before its demise. The Jacksons landed thirteen consecutive hit singles, including "ABC" and "I'll Be There." In 1971 Gordy moved the Motown Record Corporation to Los Angeles, where the company directed its efforts toward making films. Through the late 1970s and early 1980s, Motown continued to sign such acts as the Commodores, Lionel Richie, and DeBarge. But in 1984, Gordy entered into a distribution agreement with MCA records and eventually sold Motown to an entertainment conglomerate.

THE ARCHITECTS OF FUNK ♦ ♦ ♦ ♦ ♦ ♦ ♦ ♦ ♦ ♦ ♦ ♦ ♦ ♦ ♦ ♦ ♦ ♦

Upon the waning of Motown in the 1970s, a new African-American music style appeared that met the demands for a harder-edged dance music. The origins of what became funk can be traced to several sources: the music of James Brown, the rhythm patterns invented by New Orleans

Jimi Hendrix redefined the sound of the electric guitar.

drummer Ziggy Modeliste, and the slapping electric bass style of Sly and the Family Stone member Larry Graham. Funk capitalized on the modern guitar styles of Jimi Hendrix and Johnny "Guitar" Watson. It also brought the synthesizer to the forefront of pop music, which gave funk a textual and rhythmic quality unlike the music played by the soul bands of the 1960s.

By the 1970s a number of groups played in the funk idiom, including soul veterans Curtis Mayfield and the Isley Brothers, and Maurice White's Earth, Wind, and Fire. Under George "Funkenstein" Clinton, there appeared a series of aggregate bands bearing the titles Parliment, Funkadelic, Bootsy's Rubber Band, the Horny Horns, and the Brides of Funkenstein, to name a few. Blending psychedelic guitar lines, complex chord work, and vocal distortion, Parliment–Funkadelic created a gritty funk style that sought to counter the sounds of the 1970s disco craze.

Other bands to join the funk scene were Kool and the Gang, the Ohio Players, and the Commodores. Although less abrasive in style than Parliment–Funkadelic, these groups retained a soul-influenced sound in an era when the commercial sounds of disco dominated the popular music scene.

RAP: A VOICE FROM THE SUBCULTURE ♦ ♦ ♦ ♦ ♦ ♦ ♦ ♦ ♦ ♦ ♦ ♦ ♦

While funk sold millions of records and received extensive radio airplay in the mid-1970s, rap music emerged within a small circle of New York artists and entertainers. In neighborhoods in Upper Manhattan and the South Bronx, disc jockeys at private parties discovered how to use "little raps" between songs to keep dancers on their feet. From behind the microphone, DJs created a call-and-response pattern with the audience. Taking advantage of their status as master of ceremonies, they often boasted of their intellectual or sexual prowess. "Soon a division of labor emerged," explains musical historian Jefferson Morley. "DJs concentrated on perfecting the techniques of manipulating the turntables, while masters of ceremonies (MCs or rappers) concentrated on rapping in rhymes." Through the use of a special stylus, rappers moved records back and forth on the turntable to create a unique rhythmic sound, known within the rap culture as needle rocking.

Long before the modern rap, or hip-hop, culture appeared, however, there were African-American artists who performed in a rap-style idiom. In 1929, for instance, New York singer–comedian Pigmeat Markham gave performances representative of an early rap style.

Rap music is also rooted in the talking jazz style of a group of ex-convicts called the Last Poets. During the 1960s, this ensemble of black intellectuals rapped in complex rhythms over music played by jazz accompanists. Last Poets member Jalal Uridin, recording under the name Lightning Rod, released an album entitled *Hustler's Convention*. Backed by the funk band Kool and the Gang, Uridin's recording became very influential to the early New York rappers.

One of the first New York rap artists of the early 1970s was Jamaican-born Clive Campbell, a.k.a. Cool Herc. A street DJ, Herc developed the art of sampling, the method of playing a section of a recording over and over in order to create a unique dance mix. Others to join the New York scene were black nationalist DJ Africa Bambaataa from the southeast Bronx and Josep Saddler, known as Grandmaster Flash, from the central Bronx. Flash formed the group Grandmaster Flash and the Three MCs (Cowboy, Kid Creole, and Melle Mel). Later he added Kurtis Blow and Duke Bootee, who founded the Furious Five.

Rap music did not reach a broad audience, however, until 1980, when the Sugar Hill Gang's song "Rapper's Delight" received widespread radio airplay. As rap groups assembled during the decade, they began to use their art to describe the harsh realities of inner-city life. Unlike early rap music, which was generally upbeat and exuberant in tone, the rap style of the 1980s exhibited a strong sense of racial and political consciousness. Toward the end of the decade, rap came to express an increasing sense of racial militancy. Inspired by the Nation of Islam and the teachings of martyred race leader Malcolm X, rap groups like Public Enemy turned their music into a voice supporting black power. Public Enemy's second LP, *It Takes a Nation of Millions to Hold Us Back,* sold over one million copies. Their song "Fight the Power" appeared in director Spike Lee's film *Do the Right Thing.* The group's third album, *Fear of a Black Planet,* was released in 1990. While it is a statement against "western cultural supremacy," explained group member Chuck D., it is also "about the coming together of all races" in a "racial rebirth."

Long before modern rap or hip-hop appeared, some African-American artists performed in a rap-style idiom. In 1929, for instance, New York singer–comedian Pigmeat Markham gave performances representative of an early rap style.

Women have also played a role in the shaping of rap music. Rap artists such as Queen Latifah and the group Salt-N-Pepa represent a growing number of female rappers who speak for the advancement of black women in American society. Queen Latifah has emerged as critic of male dominance in the music industry and the sexist image of women presented by some male rap artists.

Aside from the issues of racial protest, rap has generally been associated, especially in the mass popular culture, with themes regarding misogyny, sexual exploits, and youth culture. In other instances, rap seeks to educate young listeners about the dangers of inner-city life. But regardless of its style or message, rap is the voice of young African Americans. Like the music of its predecessors, rap is filled with artistic energy and descriptions of the human experience. "Rap is no fad," contends renowned producer Quincy Jones, "and it's not just a new kind of music. It's a whole new subculture that's been invented by the disenfranchised."

COUNTRY, GOSPEL, RAP, RHYTHM AND BLUES, AND SOUL MUSICIANS ✦

**Nicholas Ashford
(1943–)**

**Valerie Simpson
(1948–)**

Singers, Songwriters

One of the most enduring songwriting teams to emerge from Motown has been Nicholas Ashford and Valerie Simpson. For over a quarter of a century, the team has written hit songs for artists from Ray Charles to Diana Ross.

Nicky Ashford was born in Fairfield, South Carolina, on May 14, 1943, and Valerie Simpson was born in the Bronx section of New York City on August 26, 1948. The two met in the early 1960s while singing in the same choir at Harlem's White Rock Baptist Church. With Ashford's gift for lyrics and Simpson's exceptional gospel piano and compositional skills, the two began to write for the staff of Scepter Records in 1964. Two years later, their song "Let's Go Get Stoned" became a hit for Ray Charles.

In 1962 Ashford and Simpson joined Motown's Jobete Music, where they wrote and produced hit songs for Marvin Gaye and Tammi Terrell, including "Ain't Nothing Like the Real Thing," "Good Loving Ain't Easy to

Come By," and the "Onion Song." Next they worked with Diana Ross, who had just set out to establish a solo career, producing such hits as "Remember Me," "Reach Out (and Touch Somebody's Hand)," and an updated version of "Ain't No Mountain High Enough."

Ashford and Simpson's success as songwriters led them to release their own solo recording *Exposed* in 1971. After signing with Warner Brothers in 1973, they recorded a number of hit LPs: *Is It Still Good to Ya* (1978), *Stay Free* (1979), *A Musical Affair* (1980), and their biggest seller, *Solid,* in 1985. More recently, the singing and songwriting duo have collaborated on projects with producer Quincy Jones and artists like Gladys Knight and Chaka Khan.

One of the most sophisticated soul divas to emerge in the 1980s, Anita considers herself "a balladeer" dedicated to singing music rooted in the tradition of gospel and jazz. Inspired by her idols Mahalia Jackson, Sarah Vaughan, and Nancy Wilson, Baker brings audiences a sincere vocal style that defies commercial trends and electronic overproduction.

Anita Baker
(1958–)

Singer

Born in Detroit, Baker was raised in a single-parent, middle-class family. She first sang in storefront churches, where it was common for the congregation to improvise on various gospel themes. After graduating from Central High School, Baker sang in the Detroit soul/funk group Chapter 8. Although Chapter 8 recorded the album *I Just Want to Be Your Girl* for the Ariola label, the group's lack of commercial success caused it to disband, and for the next three years Baker worked as a receptionist in a law firm.

In 1982, after signing a contract with Beverly Glen, Baker moved to Los Angeles and recorded the critically acclaimed solo album *Songstress.* Following a legal battle with Glen, Baker signed with Elecktra and recorded her debut hit album *Rapture* in 1986. As the album's executive producer, Baker sought "a minimalist approach" featuring simple recording techniques that captured the natural sounds of her voice. The LP's single "Sweet Love" brought Baker immediate crossover success. Baker's follow-up effort, the multi-platinum-selling *Giving You the Best I Got,* is considered one of the finest pop music albums of the 1990s. Her third effort, *Compositions,* recorded in 1990, featured a number of notable back-up musicians, including Detroit jazz guitarist Earl Klugh. The winner of five Grammys, two NAACP Image awards, and two American Music awards, Baker brings audiences music of eloquence and integrity that sets her apart from most of her contemporaries.

Chuck Berry

(1926–)

Singer, Songwriter,
Guitarist

Chuck Berry was the first guitar hero of rock and roll, and his 1950s juke-box hits remain some of the most imaginative poetic tales in the history of popular music. Influenced by blues artists like T–Bone Walker and the picking styles of rockabilly and country musicians, Berry's solo guitar work brought the guitar to the forefront of R&B. His driving ensemble sound paved the way for the emergence of bands from the Beach Boys to the Rolling Stones.

Born on October 18, 1926, in San Jose, California, Charles Edward Anderson Berry was raised in a middle-class neighborhood on the outskirts of St. Louis. Berry first sang gospel music at home and at the Antioch Baptist Church. Although Berry was drawn to the sounds of bluesmen such as Tampa Red, Arthur Crudup, and Muddy Waters, he did not become serious about music until he was given a guitar by local R&B musician Joe Sherman. Taken by the sounds of R&B, Berry formed a trio with Johnny Jones on piano and Ebby Harding on drums. Hired to play backyard bar-becues, clubs, and house parties, the trio expanded their repertoire to include blues, Nat "King" Cole ballads, and country songs by Hank Williams.

By 1955 the twenty-eight-year-old Berry had become a formidable R&B guitarist and singer. While in Chicago, Berry visited a club to hear his idol, Muddy Waters, perform. At the suggestion of Waters, Berry visited Chess Studios where he eventually signed with the label. Berry's first hit for Chess was "Maybelline," a country song formerly entitled "Ida May." In 1956 Berry continued on a path toward superstardom with the hits "Roll Over Beethoven," "Oh Baby Doll," "Rock and Roll Music," and the guitar anthem "Johnny B. Goode."

Released from the Indiana Federal Prison in 1964 after serving a sentence for violating the Mann Act, Berry resumed his musical career, recording "Nadine" and "No Particular Place to Go." Since the 1970s, Berry has continued to record and tour. Berry's 1972 release of the novelty tune "My Ding-a-Ling" became his best-selling single. In 1988 Taylor Hackford paid tribute to the guitar legend in his film *Hail! Hail! Rock 'n Roll.*

Bobby Brown

(1966–)

Singer

Savvy and street smart, singer Bobby Brown possesses a charismatic charm that has earned him numerous million-selling records. A founding member of the Boston-based group New Edition, Brown remained with the group from 1984 to 1987. His solo debut album, *Kind of Strange,* featured the single "Girlfriend." Brown's second release, *Don't Be Cruel,* produced the single "Don't Be Cruel" and the video hits "My Prerogative" and "Every Little Step."

In 1990 Brown embarked on a worldwide tour after playing a small role in the box office smash film *Ghostbusters II*. In July of 1992 Brown married singer/actress Whitney Houston in a star-studded ceremony. Aside from maintaining a burgeoning music career, Brown is the owner of B. Brown Productions and his own private recording studio.

James Brown's impact on American and African popular music has been of seismic proportion. His explosive onstage energy and intense gospel and R&B-based sound earned him numerous titles such as "The Godfather of Soul," "Mr. Dynamite," and "The Hardest Working Man in Show Business." During the 1960s and early 1970s, Brown's back-up group emerged as one of the greatest soul bands in the history of modern music, one that served as a major force in the development of funk and fusion jazz.

James Brown (1933–)

Singer, Bandleader

Born in Barnell, South Carolina on May 3, 1933, Brown moved to Augusta, Georgia at the age of four. Although he was raised by various relatives in conditions of economic deprivation, Brown possessed an undaunted determination to succeed at an early age. When not picking cotton, washing cars, or shining shoes, he earned extra money by dancing on the streets and at amateur contests. In the evening, Brown watched shows by such bandleaders as Louis Jordan and Lucky Millinder.

At fifteen, Brown quit school to take up a full-time music career. In churches, Brown sang with the Swanee Quartet and the Gospel Starlighters, which soon afterward became the R&B group the Flames. During the same period he also sang and played drums with R&B bands. Brown toured extensively with the Flames, performing a wide range of popular material, including the Five Royales' "Baby Don't Do It," the Clovers' "One Mint Julep," and Hank Ballard and the Midnighters' hit "Annie Had a Baby."

In 1956 Brown's talents caught the attention of Syd Nathan, founder of King Records. In the same year, after signing with the Federal label, a subsidiary of King, Brown recorded "Please Please Please." After the Flames disbanded in 1957, Brown formed a new Flames ensemble, featuring former members of Little Richard's band. Back in the studio the following year, Brown recorded "Try Me," which became a Top-50 pop hit. On the road, Brown polished his stage act and singing ability, producing what became known as the "James Brown Sound."

After the release of "Out of Sight," Brown's music exhibited a more polyrhythmic sound as evidenced in staccato horn bursts and contrapuntal bass lines. Each successive release explored increasingly new avenues of popular music. Brown's 1967 hit "Cold Sweat" and the 1968 release "I Got the Feeling" not only sent shock waves through the music industry, they served as textbooks of rhythm for thousands of aspiring musicians. In 1970 Brown disbanded the Flames and formed the JBs, featuring Bootsy Collins. The group produced a string of hits like "Super Bad" and "Sex Machine." Among Brown's more recent and commercially successful efforts was the 1988 hit "Living in America," which appeared on the soundtrack of the film *Rocky IV*.

Shirley Caesar (1938-)

Singer

The leading gospel singer of her generation, Shirley Caesar was born in Durham, North Carolina, in 1938. One of twelve children born to gospel great "Big Jim" Caesar, Shirley sang in church choirs as a child. By age fourteen, Caesar went on the road as a professional gospel singer, touring the church circuit on weekends and during school vacations. Known as "Baby Shirley," Caesar joined the Caravans in 1958. Featured as an opening act in the show, Caesar worked the audience to a near fever pitch. When Inez Andrews left the Caravans in 1961, Caesar became the featured artist who provided crowds with powerful performances of such songs as "Comfort Me," "Running for Jesus," and "Sweeping Through the City."

After leaving the Caravans in 1966, Caesar formed her own group, the Shirley Caesar Singers. Her sheer energy and pugnacious spirit made her one of the reigning queens of modern gospel. Her first album, *I'll Go,* remains one of her most critically acclaimed. In 1969 she released a ten-minute sermonette with the St. Louis Choir, which earned her a gold record.

Reverend James Cleveland (1932-1991)

Singer, Pianist, Composer

Known by such titles as "King James" and the "Crown Prince," the Reverend James Cleveland emerged as a giant of the postwar gospel music scene. Likened to the vocal style of Louis Armstrong, Cleveland's raw bluesy growls and shouts appeared on more recordings than those of any other gospel singer of his generation.

Born on December 5, 1932, in Chicago, Illinois, James Cleveland first sang gospel under the direction of Thomas Dorsey at the Pilgrim Baptist Church. Inspired by the keyboard talents of gospel singer Roberta Martin, Cleveland later began to study piano. In 1951 Cleveland joined the Gospelaires, a trio that cut several sides for the Apollo label. With the Caravans, Cleveland arranged and performed on two hits: "The Solid Rock" and an uptempo reworking of the song "Old Time Religion."

By the mid-1950s, Cleveland's original compositions had found their way into the repertoires of numerous gospel groups, and he was performing with such artists as the Thorn Gospel Singers, Roberta Martin Singers, Mahalia Jackson, the Gospel Allstars, and the Meditation Singers. In 1960 Cleveland formed the Cleveland Singers, featuring organist and accompanist Billy Preston. The smash hit "Love of God," recorded with the Detroit-based Voices of Tabernacle, won Cleveland nationwide fame within the gospel community. Signing with the Savoy label, Cleveland and keyboardist Billy Preston released a long list of classic albums, including *Christ Is the Answer* and *Peace Be Still*. As a founder of the Gospel Workshop of America in 1968, Cleveland organized annual conventions that brought together thousands of gospel singers and songwriters. A year later he helped found the Southern California Community Choir.

In 1972 he was reunited with former piano understudy Aretha Franklin, who featured Cleveland as a guest artist on the album *Amazing Grace*. A recipient of the NAACP Image Award, Cleveland also acquired a honorary degree from Temple Baptist College. Although the commercial gospel trends of the 1980s had caused a downturn in Cleveland's career, he continued to perform the gutsy blues-based sound that brought him recognition from listeners throughout the world. Cleveland died February 9, 1991, in Los Angeles, California.

Nat "King" Cole (1919–1965)

Singer, Pianist

Nat Cole was born on March 17, 1919, in Montgomery, Alabama (the family name was Coles, but Cole dropped the "s" when he formed the King Cole Trio years later). When he was five the family moved to Chicago, and he was soon playing piano and organ in the church where his father served as minister. While attending Phillips High School Cole formed his own band, and he also played with small combos, including one headed by his brother Edward, a bassist.

In 1936 Cole joined the touring company of *Shuffle Along*. After the show folded, he found work in small clubs in Los Angeles. In 1937 the King

Cole Trio was formed when the drummer in his quartet failed to appear for a scheduled performance. That same year, Cole made his singing debut when a customer insisted he sing "Sweet Lorraine" (a number he later recorded with great success).

Cole's first record was made in 1943, "Straighten Up and Fly Right," which sold more than 500,000 copies. Over the years, one hit followed another in rapid succession—"Paper Moon," "Route 66," "I Love You for Sentimental Reasons," "Chestnuts Roasting on an Open Fire," "Nature Boy," "Mona Lisa," "Too Young," "Pretend," "Somewhere Along the Way," "Smile," and many others. Cole died of cancer in 1965.

Natalie Cole

(1950–)

Singer

With five gold records and her star on Hollywood Boulevard, Natalie Cole has emerged since the 1980s as a major pop music star.

Natalie Cole was born on February 6, 1950, in Los Angeles, California, the second daughter of jazz pianist and pop music legend Nat "King" Cole. During the early 1970s Cole performed in nightclubs while pursuing a degree in child psychology at the University of Massachusetts. In 1975 she recorded her first album, *Inseparable,* at Curtis Mayfield's Curtom Studios. Her other albums include *Thankful* (1978), *I'm Ready* (1983), *Dangerous* (1985), *Everlasting* (1987), and *Good to Be Back* (1989). In 1991 Cole released a twenty-two-song collection of her father's hits. The album, which contains a re-mixed version of the original title track "Unforgettable," features a duet between Cole and her father and earned her a Grammy award for record of the year and album of the year.

Sam Cooke

(1931–1964)

Singer, Songwriter

Sam Cooke's sophisticated vocal style and refined image made him one of the greatest pop music idols of the early 1960s. One of the first gospel artists to cross over into popular music, Cooke produced songs of timeless quality, filled with human emotion and spiritual optimism.

Born in Clarksdale, Mississippi, on January 2, 1931, Sam Cooke grew up the son of a Baptist minister in Chicago, Illinois. At the age of nine, Cooke, along with two sisters and a brother, formed a gospel group called the Singing Children. While a teenager, he joined the gospel group the Highway QCs, which performed on the same bill with nationally famous gospel acts.

By 1950 Cooke replaced tenor Rupert H. Harris as lead singer for the renowned gospel group the Soul Stirrers. Cooke's first recording with the Soul Stirrers, "Jesus Gave Me Water," was recorded for Art Rupe's Specialty label. Although the song revealed the inexperience of the twenty-year-old Cooke, it exhibited a quality of immense passion and heightened feeling. Under the pseudonym Dale Cooke, Sam recorded the pop song "Loveable" in 1957. That same year, in a session for producer Bumps Blackwell on the Keen label, Cooke recorded "You Send Me," which climbed to number one on the rhythm and blues charts. On the Keen label, Cooke recorded eight more consecutive hits, including "Everyone Likes to Cha Cha Cha," "Only Sixteen," and "Wonderful World," all of which were written or co-written by Cooke.

After his contract with the Keen label expired in 1960, Cooke signed with RCA and was assigned to staff producers Hugo Peretti and Luigi Creatore. In August, Cooke's recording "Chain Gang" reached the number-two spot on the pop charts. Under the lavish production of Hugo and Luigi, Cooke produced a string of hits such as "Cupid" in 1961, "Twistin' the Night Away," in 1962, and "Another Saturday Night" in 1963. Early in 1964, Cooke appeared on the "Tonight Show," debuting two songs from his upcoming LP, which included the gospel-influenced composition "A Change Is Gonna Come." On December 11, Cooke checked into a three-dollar-a-night motel, where he demanded entrance into the room of the night manager, a woman. After a brief physical struggle, the manager fired three pistol shots, which mortally wounded Cooke. The singer left behind a catalogue of classic recordings and more than one hundred original compositions, including the hit "Shake," which was posthumously released in 1965.

Andrae Crouch
(1942–)

Singer, Pianist

An exponent of a modern pop-based gospel style, Andrae Crouch became one of the leading gospel singers of the 1960s and 1970s. Born on July 1, 1942, in Los Angeles, California, Crouch grew up singing in his father's Holiness Church. Along with his brother and sister, Crouch formed the Crouch Trio, which performed at their father's services as well as on live Sunday-night radio broadcasts. In the mid-1960s Crouch was discovered by white Pentecostal evangelists and subsequently signed a contract with Light, a white religious record label.

During the late 1960s Crouch, inspired by the modern charismatic revival movement, began adopting street-smart language and informal wardrobe.

After forming the Disciples in 1968, Crouch recorded extensively and toured throughout the United States and Europe. His California style of gospel music combines rock, country music, and soul with traditional gospel forms. Since the 1970s Crouch's back-up groups have incorporated both electronic and acoustic instruments, including synthesizers. Over the last three decades Crouch has written numerous songs, many of which have become standards in the repertoire of modern gospel groups. Among his most famous songs are "I Don't Know Why Jesus Loved Me," "Through It All," and "The Blood Will Never Lose Its Power."

Fats Domino (1928–)
Singer

Antoine Domino was born on February 26, 1928, in New Orleans. As a teenager, Domino received piano lessons from Harrison Verret. In between playing night clubs, Domino worked at a factory and mowed lawns around New Orleans. At age twenty he took a job as a pianist with bassist Billy Diamond's combo at the Hideaway Club.

In 1949, while playing with Diamond's group, Domino was discovered by producer and arranger David Bartholomew, a talent scout, musician, and producer for the Imperial label. During the following year, Domino hit the charts with the autobiographical tune "Fat Man." After the release of "Fat Man," he played on tour backed by Bartholomew's band.

Although Domino released a number of sides during the early 1950s, it was not until 1955 that he gained national prominence with the hit "Ain't That a Shame." In the next six years, Domino scored thirty-five top hits with songs like "Blueberry Hill" (1956), "Blue Monday" (1957), "Whole Lotta Lovin'" (1958), and "I'm Walkin'" (1959). Domino's recording success led to his appearance in several films in the 1950s, including *The Girl Can't Help It, Shake Rattle and Roll, Disc Jockey Jamboree*, and *The Big Beat*.

After Domino's contract with Imperial expired in 1963 he signed with ABC, where he made a number of commercial recordings. In 1965 Domino moved to Mercury and then to Reprise in 1968. In the early 1970s, Domino began to tour with greater regularity than he had during the peak of his career. Today Domino continues to tour and make occasional television appearances.

Born in Asheville, North Carolina, on February 10, 1939, Roberta Flack moved to Washington, DC with her parents at the age of nine. Three years later she studied classical piano with prominent African-American concert musician Hazel Harrison. After winning several talent contests Flack won a scholarship to Howard University, where she graduated with a bachelor's degree in music education. During the early 1960s Flack taught music in the Washington, DC public school system.

While playing a club date in 1968 Flack was discovered by Les McCann, whose connections resulted in a contract with Atlantic Records. Flack's first album, *First Take,* appeared in 1970 and included the hit song "The First Time Ever I Saw Your Face." Throughout the 1970s Flack landed several hits, such as "Killing Me Softly with His Song" and "The Closer I Get to You," a duet with Donny Hathaway. In the early 1980s, Flack collaborated with Peabo Bryson to record the hit "Tonight I Celebrate My Love for You." More recently Flack has been involved in educational projects, and in 1988 she recorded the album *Oasis.*

"Writing in the start of the '90s, it's easy to forget that a quarter century ago there was no one singing like Aretha Franklin," wrote Jerry Wexler. "Today, pop music is rich with glorious voices, females in Aretha's mold." During the 1960s, the collaboration of Franklin and Atlantic Records producer Jerry Wexler brought forth some of the deepest and most sincere popular music ever recorded. As Queen of Soul, Franklin has reigned supreme for the last three decades. Her voice brings spiritual inspiration to her gender, race, and the world.

Daughter of the famous Reverend Charles L. Franklin, Aretha was born on March 25, 1942, in Memphis, Tennessee. Raised on Detroit's east side, Franklin sang at her father's New Bethel Baptist Church. Although she began to study piano at age eight, Franklin refused to learn what she considered juvenile and simple tunes. Thus, she learned piano by ear, occasionally receiving instruction from individuals like the Reverend James Cleveland. Franklin's singing skills were modeled after gospel singers and family friends, including Clara Ward, and R&B artists like Ruth Brown and Sam Cooke.

At fourteen, Franklin quit school to go on the road with her father's Franklin Gospel Caravan, a seemingly endless tour in which the family traveled thousands of miles by car. After four years on the road, Aretha

Roberta Flack (1939–)

Singer, Pianist

Aretha Franklin (1942–)

Singer, Pianist, Songwriter

traveled to New York to establish her own career as a pop artist. In 1960 she signed with Columbia Records talent scout John Hammond, who described her as an "untutored genius, the best singer ... since Billie Holiday." Her six-year stay at Columbia, however, produced only a few hits and little material that suited Franklin's unique talents.

In 1966 Franklin signed with Atlantic Records and, in the following year, recorded a session for producer Jerry Wexler that resulted in the hit "I Never Loved a Man (The Way That I Loved You)." That same year, Franklin's career received another boost when her reworking of Otis Redding's song "Respect" hit the charts. Franklin's first LP *I Never Loved a Man* was followed by a succession of artistically and commercially successful albums: *Aretha Arrives, Lady Soul, Aretha Now!,* and *This Girl's in Love with You.* Her prominence grew so great that Franklin appeared on the cover of *Time* magazine in 1968.

During the 1970s Franklin continued to tour and record. In 1971 she released the live LP *Aretha Live at the Filmore West,* backed by the horn and rhythm section of Tower of Power. Her next release, *Amazing Grace,* featured the Reverend James Cleveland and the Southern California Community Choir. In 1980 she appeared in the film *The Blues Brothers.* Five years later Franklin scored her first big commercial success in over a decade with the album *Who's Zooming Who?,* featuring the single "Freeway of Love." In 1988 she released a double live LP *One Lord, One Faith*—an effort dedicated to her father, who had passed away the previous year.

Marvin Gaye
(1939–1984)

Singer, Songwriter

The son of a Pentecostal minister, Marvin Gay was born on April 29, 1939, in Washington, DC (the final "e" on his surname was not added until the early 1960s). Raised in a segregated slum-ridden section of Washington, DC, Gaye experienced a strict religious upbringing. As Gaye later recalled: "Living with my father was like living with a king, a very peculiar, changeable, cruel, and all-powerful king." Thus Gaye looked to music for release. Around the age of three, he began singing in church. While attending Cardoza High School, Gaye studied drums, piano, and guitar. Uninspired by his formal studies, Gaye often cut classes to watch James Brown and Jackie Wilson perform at the Howard Theatre.

Soon afterward, Gaye served a short time in the Air Force, until obtaining a honorable discharge in 1957. Returning to Washington, DC, Gaye joined the doo-wop group the Marquees. After recording for Columbia's subsidiary label, Okeh, the Marquees moved to the Chess/Checker label where they recorded with Bo Diddley. Although the Marquees performed their own compositions and toured regularly, they failed to gain popularity. It was not until they were introduced to Harvey Fuqua, who was in the process of reforming the Moonglows, that the Marquees attracted notice in the pop music world. Impressed by their sound, Fuqua hired the Marquees to form a group under the new name Harvey and the Moonglows. Still under contract at Chess, Fuqua brought the Moonglows to the company's studio in Chicago to record the 1959 hit the "Ten Commandments of Love."

In 1960 Fuqua and Gaye traveled to Detroit, where Fuqua set up his own label and signed with Motown's subsidiary, Anna. After a stint as a back-up singer, studio musician, and drummer in Smokey Robinson's touring band, Gaye signed a contract with Motown as a solo artist. Released in 1962, Gaye's first album was a jazz-oriented effort entitled *The Soulful Moods of Marvin Gaye*. With his sights on a career modeled after the ballad singer Frank Sinatra, Gaye was not enthusiastic when Motown suggested he record a dance record of rhythm and blues material. Nevertheless, Gaye recorded the song "Stubborn Kind of Fellow" in 1962, which entered the top-ten R&B charts. This was followed by a long succession of Motown hits, such as "Hitch Hike," "Pride and Joy," "Can I Get a Witness," and "Wonderful One."

Motown's next projects for Gaye included a number of vocal duets, the first of which appeared with singer Mary Wells on the 1964 album *Together*. In collaboration with singer Kim Weston, Gaye recorded the 1967 hit LP *It Takes Two*. His most successful partnership, however, was with Tammi Terrell. During their two-year association Gaye and Terrell recorded, under the writing and production team of Ashford and Simpson, such hits as "Ain't No Mountain High Enough," "Your Precious Love," and "Ain't Nothing Like the Real Thing."

Back in the studio as a solo act, Gaye recorded the hit "Heard It Through the Grapevine." With his growing success, Gaye achieved greater creative independence at Motown, which led him to co-produce the 1971 hit album *What's Going On,* a session producing the best-selling singles "What's Going On," "Mercy Mercy (The Ecology)," and "Inner City Blues (Make Me Wanna Holler)."

After his last LP for Motown, *In Our Lifetime,* Gaye signed with CBS Records in April 1981, and within the next year released the album *Mid-*

night Lover, featuring the Grammy award–winning hit "Sexual Healing." On Sunday, April 1, 1984, Gaye was shot dead by his father in Los Angeles, California. Despite his public image, Gaye had suffered from years of inner conflict and drug abuse. "This tragic ending can only be softened by the memory of a beautiful human being," described long-time friend Smokey Robinson. "He could be full of joy sometimes, but at others, full of woe, but in the end how compassionate, how wonderful, how exciting was Marvin Gaye and his music."

**Berry Gordy, Jr.
(1929–)**

Songwriter, Producer,
Entrepreneur

From assembly line worker to impresario of the Motown Record Corporation, Berry Gordy, Jr. emerged as the owner of one of the largest black-owned businesses in American history. A professional boxer, songwriter, producer, and businessman, Gordy is a living legend, a self-made man who, through his determination and passion for music, helped to create one of the most celebrated sounds of modern music.

The seventh of eight children, Berry Gordy was born on November 28, 1929, in Detroit, Michigan. Berry Gordy, Sr., the owner of a grocery store, a plastering company, and a printing shop, taught his children the value of hard work and family unity. Despite his dislike for manual labor, Berry possessed a strong desire to become commercially successful. After quitting high school to become a professional boxer, Berry won several contests before leaving the profession in 1950. A year later Gordy was drafted in the Army, where he earned a high school equivalency diploma.

Upon returning from a military tour of Korea in 1953, Berry opened the 3–D Record Mart, a jazz-oriented retail store. Forced into bankruptcy, Berry closed the store in 1955 and subsequently took a job as an assembly line worker at Ford Motor Company. His nightly visits to Detroit's thriving jazz and R&B scene inspired Gordy to take up songwriting. In 1957 one of Gordy's former boxing colleagues, Jackie Wilson, recorded the hit "Rite Petite," a song written by Berry, his sister Gwen, and Billy Davis. Over the next four years, the Berry–Gwen–Davis writing team provided Wilson with four more hits, "To Be Loved," "Lonely Teardrops," "That's Why (I Love You So)," and "I'll Be Satisfied."

By 1959 Billy Davis and Gwen Gordy founded the Anna label, which distributed material through Chess Records in Chicago. Barret Strong's recording of "Money (That's What I Want)," written by Gordy and Janie Bradford, became the label's biggest-selling single. With background as a writer and producer with the Anna label, Gordy decided to start his own company. In 1959, he formed Jobete Music Publishing, Berry Gordy, Jr. Enterprises, Hitsville USA, and the Motown Record Corporation. Employing a staff of local studio musicians, writers, and producers, Berry's label scored its first hit in 1961 with Smokey Robinson's "Shop Around." By the mid-1960s Gordy had assembled a wealth of talent, including the Supremes, the Four Tops, the Marvelettes, Marvin Gaye, and Stevie Wonder.

In 1971 Gordy relocated the Motown Recording Corporation to Los Angeles. Although most of the original acts and staff members did not join the company's migration to the West Coast, Gordy's company became one of the country's top black-owned businesses. Throughout the 1970s and 1980s, Motown continued to produce motion pictures and artists like the Jackson Five, the Commodores, Lionel Richie, Rick James, and DeBarge. In 1982 Gordy, faced with financial problems, signed a distribution agreement with MCA. Gordy's induction into the Hall of Fame in 1988 brought recognition to a giant of the recording industry who helped transform the sound of popular music.

Born on August 20, 1942, in Covington, Tennessee, Issac Hayes moved to Memphis at age seven, where he heard the sounds of blues and country-western, and the music of idol Sam Cooke. Through the connections of saxophonist Floyd Newman, Hayes began a career as a studio musician for Stax Records in 1964. After playing piano on a session for Otis Redding, Hayes formed a partnership with songwriter Dave Porter, which was responsible for supplying a number of hits for Carla Thomas, William Bell, and Eddie Floyd.

Issac Hayes (1942–)

Singer, Pianist, Producer

The first real break for the Hayes–Porter team came when they were recruited to produce the Miami-based soul duo Sam Prater and Dave Moore. In the span of four years, Hayes and Porter succeeded in making Sam and Dave the hottest-selling act for Stax, producing such hits as "Hold On I'm Coming," "Soul Man," and "I Thank You!" It was the "raw rural southern" sound, recalled Hayes, that made these recordings some of the finest pop hits of the 1960s.

During this period Hayes and Porter continued to perform in a group that established them as an underground legend in the Memphis music scene. In the late 1960s Hayes's solo career emerged in an impromptu fashion, when a late-night session with drummer Al Jackson and bassist Duck

Dunn prompted Stax to release his next effort. Hot Buttered Soul went double platinum in 1969. Its extended rap–soul version of the country song "By the Time I Get to Phoenix" set a trend for the disco/soul sound of the 1970s. Following the release of the albums *To Be Continued* and *The Issac Hayes Movement*, Hayes recorded the soundtrack for the film *Shaft* and the album *Black Moses*.

Hayes left the Stax label to join ABC in 1974. To promote his career Hayes recorded the disco albums *Chocolate Chip, Disco Connection*, and *Groove-a-thon*. In 1977 the commercial downturn in Hayes's career forced him to file bankruptcy. His last gold record *Don't Let Go* was released on the Polydor label in 1979. In recent years Hayes has appeared on television shows and in such films as the futuristic thriller *Escape from New York*.

Jimi Hendrix
(1942–1970)

Guitarist, Songwriter

When Jimi Hendrix arrived on the international rock music scene in 1967, he almost single-handedly redefined the sound of the electric guitar. Hendrix's extraordinary approach has shaped the course of music from jazz fusion to heavy metal.

On November 25, 1942, in Seattle, Washington, Johnny Allen Hendrix was born to an enlisted Army soldier and a teenage mother. Four years later, Johnny Allen was renamed James Marshall Hendrix. Because of his mother's fondness for night club life and his father's frequent absences, Hendrix was a lonely, yet creative, child. At school he won several contests for his science fiction–based poetry and visual art. At the age of eight, Hendrix, unable to afford a guitar, strummed out rhythms on a broom. Eventually, he graduated to a fabricated substitute made from a cigar box, followed by a ukelele, and finally an acoustic guitar that his father purchased.

By the late 1950s Hendrix began to play in local bands in Seattle. While a teenager he played along with recordings by blues artists like Elmore James and John Lee Hooker. After a twenty-six-month stint (1961–1962) in the 101st Airborne Division, Hendrix played in the Nashville rhythm and blues scene with bassist Billy Cox. For the next three years, Hendrix performed under the name Jimi James, backing up acts such as Little Richard, Jackie Wilson, Ike and Tina Turner, and the Isley Brothers.

In 1964 Hendrix moved to New York City where he performed in various Greenwich Village clubs. While in New York he formed the group Jimi

James and the Blue Flames. After being discovered by producer and manager Chas Chandler, the former bassist with the Animals, Hendrix was urged to leave for England. Arriving in England in 1966, Hendrix, along with bassist Noel Redding and drummer Mitch Mitchell, formed the Jimi Hendrix Experience. In 1967, after touring Europe, the trio hit the charts with a cover version of the Leaves' song "Hey Joe." In the same year, the group released the ground-breaking album *Are You Experienced.*

In 1968 the Experience recorded *Axis Bold as Love,* which led to extensive touring in the United States and Europe. On the Experience's next LP, *Electric Ladyland,* Hendrix sought to expand the group's trio-based sound. A double record effort, *Electric Ladyland* featured numerous guest artists such as keyboardists Steve Winwood and Al Kooper, saxophonist Freddie Smith, and conga player Larry Faucette. The record also contained "All Along the Watchtower," a song written by Hendrix's musical and poetic idol Bob Dylan.

After the Experience broke up in 1969, Hendrix played the Woodstock Music and Arts Festival with the Gypsy Sons and Rainbows, featuring bassist Billy Cox. Along with drummer Buddy Miles, Hendrix and Cox formed the Band of Gypsys, and in 1970 the group released an album under the same title. Months later, Mitchell replaced Miles on drums. In August, the Mitchell–Cox line-up played behind Hendrix at his last major performance held at England's Isle of Wight Festival. On September 18, 1970, Hendrix died in a hotel room in England.

Whitney Houston (1963–)

Model, Singer, Actress

A Grammy award winner whose face has graced the covers of magazines from *Glamour* to *Cosmopolitan,* Whitney Houston emerged as one of the most vibrant popular music talents during the 1980s.

Born on August 9, 1963, Houston grew up in East Orange, New Jersey. As a member of the New Hope Baptist Choir, she made her singing debut at age eleven. Later, Houston appeared as a back-up singer on numerous recordings, featuring her mother Cissy Houston and cousin Dionne Warwick. Despite her success as a fashion model, Houston found the profession "degrading" and subsequently quit in order to seek a career in music.

By age nineteen, Houston received several recording contract offers. In 1985 she released her debut album on the Arista label entitled *Whitney*

Houston which produced four hits: "Saving All My Love for You," "You Give Good Love," "How Will I Know," and "The Greatest Love of All."

Houston's second LP, *Whitney,* appeared in 1987. Like her first effort, it produced a number of hits, including "I Wanna Dance with Somebody," "Didn't We Almost Have It All," "So Emotional," "Where Do Broken Hearts Go?," and "Love Will Save the Day." Following the success of her second record, Houston released *One Moment in Time* (1988) and the slickly produced *I'm Your Baby Tonight* (1990). In 1992 Houston married singer Bobby Brown and made her acting debut in the film *The Bodyguard,* co-starring Kevin Costner.

Ice Cube

Singer, Actor

Behind his gangster image, rapper Ice Cube is a serious artist dedicated to racial advancement and black pride. A staunch spokesperson for black nationalism, Ice Cube looks upon his music as a means of launching a "mental revolution" to awaken African-American youths to the value of education and the creation of private black economic enterprises.

Born Oshea Jackson, Ice Cube grew up in the west side of south-central Los Angeles. While in the ninth grade Jackson wrote his first rhyme in typing class. Prompted by his parents to pursue an education after high school, he attended a one-year drafting course at Phoenix Institute in 1988. In the following year, Ice Cube achieved great commercial success as a member of N.W.A. One of the group's founding members, Ice Cube wrote and co-wrote most of the material for N.W.A.'s first two albums. Ice Cube's authoritative baritone won him a legion of fans for his N.W.A. rap anthem "Gangsta Gangsta."

After leaving N.W.A., Ice Cube released his solo album *AmeriKKKa's Most Wanted* in 1990, which went gold within three months. During the same year, Ice Cube also made his acting debut in director John Singleton's film *Boyz N the Hood,* in which he gave a powerful performance in the role of Doughboy. Since his work with N.W.A., Ice Cube has moved increasingly toward the role of a racial spokesperson and cultural leader. "My records are my thoughts," explained Ice Cube. "I'm trying to evolve to the point where I can do just straight political records."

The youngest child of a family of talented children, Janet Jackson is a tremendously energetic performer whose singing and dance styles have reached immense popularity around the world. Born on May 16, 1966, in Gary, Indiana, Janet Jackson began performing with her brothers at age six, doing impressions of famous stars like Mae West and Cher. She made her first professional singing debut at one of the Jackson Five's shows in the Grand Hotel in Las Vegas. Before she was ten years old, Jackson was spotted by television producer Norman Lear, which resulted in her guest appearances on such television shows as *Fame, Good Times,* and *Diff'rent Strokes.*

In 1982 Jackson's debut album for the A&M label, *Janet,* contained only a few minor hits. Teamed with producers Jimmy Jam and Terry Lewis, Jackson released her more commercially successful LP *Dream Street.* Her 1986 release *Control* scored six hit singles, including "What Have You Done for Me Lately," "Nasty," "When I Think of You," "Control," "Let's Wait Awhile," and "Pleasure Principle." Under the direction of Jam and Lewis, Jackson released the dance-oriented album *Janet Jackson's Rhythm Nation 1814* in 1989, which went quadruple platinum. Among the record's numerous singles were "Miss You Much," "Come Back to Me," and "Black Cat."

After an extensive world tour in 1990, Jackson left the A&M label to sign a contract with Virgin Records in 1991, which guaranteed her an advance of fifty million dollars.

Mahalia Jackson was hailed as the world's greatest gospel singer, and her rich contralto voice became a national institution. Through live performances, recordings, and television appearances, Jackson elevated gospel music to a level of popularity unprecedented in the history of African-American religious music.

The third of six children, Jackson was born on October 26, 1912, in New Orleans, Louisiana. Growing in New Orleans, Jackson absorbed the sounds of parade music and brass bands. She later discovered the blues, a music labeled the "devil's music" by regular church-goers, and listened secretly to recordings of singers like Mamie Smith and Bessie Smith.

In 1927, at the age of thirteen, Jackson moved to Chicago where she joined the Greater Salem Baptist Church. Two years later, Jackson met the gospel musician and songwriter Thomas A. Dorsey, who invited her to

**Janet Jackson
(1966–)**

Singer

**Mahalia Jackson
(1912–1972)**

Gospel Singer

sing at the Pilgrim Baptist Church. In 1937 Jackson recorded four sides for the Decca label, including the song "God's Gonna Separate the Wheat from the Tares."

Jackson's big break came in 1947 when she released gospel music's first million-selling record "Move on Up a Little." In 1949 her song "Let the Holy Ghost Fall on Me" won the French Academy's Grand Prix du Disque. Soon afterward, she toured Europe and recorded the gospel hit "In the Upper Room." During the 1960s, Jackson became a musical ambassador. Not only did she perform at the White House and at London's Albert Hall, but she sang at the 1963 March on Washington, as well as at Martin Luther King, Jr.'s funeral ceremony in 1968.

On January 27, 1972, Jackson died of a heart condition in Chicago. At her funeral at Great Salem Baptist, some forty-five thousand mourners gathered to pay their respects to a woman who brought gospel music into the hearts and homes of millions of listeners.

Michael Jackson (1958-)

Singer, Composer

From child singing star with the Jackson Five to his success as a solo performer in the 1980s, Michael Jackson has amassed the largest following of any African-American singer in the history of popular music.

The fifth of nine children, Michael Jackson was born on August 29, 1958, in Gary, Indiana. As a child, Michael, along with his brothers Tito, Jermaine, Jackie, and Marlon, formed the Jackson Five. Under the tutelage of their father, Joe, the five boys learned to sing and dance. On weekends the family singing group traveled hundreds of miles to perform at amateur contests and benefit concerts.

After two years on the road, the group landed an audition with Motown records. Upon signing with the label in 1969, the Jackson Five hit the charts with the number-one hit "I Want You Back," a song arranged and produced by Berry Gordy, Jr. On recordings and television shows, Michael's wholesome image and lead vocal style attracted fans from every racial and age group. Between the group's stay at Motown from 1969 to 1975, the Jackson Five scored thirteen consecutive top-twenty singles such as "ABC," "The Love You Save," and "I'll Be There."

During his years as lead vocalist for the Jackson Five, Michael had signed a separate contract with Motown in 1971 and pursued a solo career that produced the hits "Got to Be There" in 1971, "Ben" in 1972, and "Just a Little Bit of You" in 1975. While cast in the role of the scarecrow in the 1975 Motown film *The Wiz*, Jackson met producer Quincy Jones, who later collaborated with him to record the 1979 hit LP *Off the Wall*, on the Epic label. Two years later, guided by the production skills of Jones, Jackson recorded the biggest-selling album of all time, *Thriller*. "All the brilliance that had been building inside Michael Jackson for twenty-five years just erupted," commented Jones. "I was electrified, and so was everybody on the project." In 1985 Jackson co-wrote the song "We Are the World" for the African famine relief fund. After Jackson joined Jones to produce the LP *Bad* in 1987, he led the most commercially successful tour in history.

Winner of twenty Grammy awards, and the writer of over fifty-two film scores, Quincy Jones is popular music's quintessential musician/producer. Aside from performing trumpet with the likes of jazzmen Lionel Hampton and Dizzy Gillespie, Jones has produced artists from Frank Sinatra to Michael Jackson.

Quincy Jones (1933–)

Trumpeter, Arranger, Producer

Quincy Jones was born on March 14, 1933, in Chicago, Illinois. At age ten, Jones moved to Bremerton, Washington. As a member of Bump Blackwell's Junior Orchestra, Jones performed at local Seattle social functions. In 1949 Jones played third trumpet in Lionel Hampton's band in the local Seattle club scene. After befriending jazz bassist Oscar Pettiford, Jones established himself as an able musician and arranger.

From 1950 to 1953 Jones performed as a regular member of Hampton's band, and he subsequently toured the United States and Europe. During the mid-1950s Jones began to record jazz records under his own name. In 1956 he toured the Middle East and South America with the United States State Department Band headed by Dizzy Gillespie.

In 1961 Jones was appointed musical director at Mercury Records. In search of new musical horizons, Jones began to produce popular music, including Leslie Gore's 1963 hit "It's My Party." Jones's growing prestige at Mercury led to his promotion to vice president of the company, marking the first time an African-American had been placed in an executive position at a major label. During this time, Jones also began to write and record film scores. In 1967 he produced the music score for the movie *In the Heat of the Night*. He also produced the music score for Alex Haley's television mini-series *Roots* and co-produced the film *The Color Purple* with Steven Spielberg. After his production of the 1978 Motown-backed film *The Wiz*, Jones went on to produce the film's star, Michael Jackson, on such recordings as the 1979 release *Off the Wall* and the 1985 record-breaking hit *Thriller*. Jones's 1990 release *Back on the Block* has been praised by critics and is no doubt a sign of Jones's continuing role in the future development of African-American popular music.

Louis Jordan

(1908–1975)

Singer, Alto-Saxophonist,
Bandleader

Louis Jordan led one of the most popular and influential bands of the 1940s. The shuffle boogie rhythm of his jump blues ensemble, the Tympany Five, had a profound impact on the emergence of rhythm and blues. As guitarist Chuck Berry admitted, "I identify myself with Louis Jordan more than any other artist." For it was Jordan's swinging rhythms, theatrical stage presence, and songs about everyday life that made him a favorite among musicians and listeners throughout the 1940s.

Born in Brinkley, Arkansas, on July 8, 1908, Jordan was the son of a bandleader and music teacher. He received his music education in the Brinkley public schools and the Baptist College in Little Rock. Jordan's early music career as a clarinetist included stints with the Rabbit Foot Minstrels and Ruby Williams's orchestra. Soon after moving to Philadelphia in 1932, Jordan joined Charlie Gains' group; sometime around 1936 he joined drummer Chick Webb's band.

After Webb's death in 1938, Jordan started his own group. Because Jordan performed for both white and black audiences, he learned to "straddle the fence," as he put it, by playing music ranging from blues to formal dance music. Signing with Decca records during the same year, Jordan began a recording career, which produced a string of million-selling recordings by the early 1940s, such as "Is You Is or Is You Ain't (My Baby)," "Choo Choo Ch' Boogie," "Saturday Night Fish Fry," and "Caledonia." In addition to working with artists like Louis Armstrong, Bing Crosby, and Ella Fitzgerald, Jordan appeared in several films, such as the 1949 release *Shout Sister Shout*.

Although failing to achieve the success he experienced during the 1940s, Jordan fronted a big band in the early 1950s. During the 1960s and 1970s, he continued to tour the United States, Europe, and Asia. His career came to an end in 1975 when he suffered a fatal heart attack in Los Angeles.

As a member of the Temptations in the 1960s, Eddie Kendricks, with his articulate, soulful falsetto, provided Motown with a number of pop music classics. Kendricks's gospel music background "enabled him to bring an unusual earnestness to the singing of love lyrics," wrote music historian David Morse. "He can be compared only with Ray Charles in his ability to take the most threadbare ballad and turn it into a dramatic and completely convincing statement."

Born on December 17, 1939, in Birmingham, Alabama, Kendricks grew up with close friend and Temptations member Paul Williams. In 1956 Kendricks and Williams quit school and traveled northward to become singing stars in the tradition of their idols Clyde McPhatter and Little Willie John. In Detroit, Kendricks and Williams formed the doo-wop singing group the Primes, which performed at talent contests and house parties. In 1961 the Primes recorded the songs "Mother of Mine" and the dance tune "Check Yourself" for Berry Gordy's short-lived Miracle label.

Upon the suggestion of Berry Gordy, the Primes changed their name to the Temptations, and after adding David Ruffin as lead vocalist, they set out to become one of the most successful groups on the Motown label. Throughout the decade, Kendricks sang lead on several songs including the classics "My Girl" in 1965, "Get Ready" in 1966, and "Just My Imagination (Running Away With Me)" in 1972.

In June of 1971, Kendricks pursued a solo career and eventually recorded two disco-influenced hits "Keep on Truckin'" in 1973, and "Boogie Down" in 1974. Kendricks's career soon fell into decline. Unable to find material to suit his unique artistic sensibility, Kendricks switched record labels several times before reuniting with the Temptations in 1982. After the reunion, Kendricks performed with the Temptations on the Live Aid broadcast and on the album *Live at the Apollo Theater with David Ruffin and Eddie Kendricks*. In 1987 Ruffin and Kendricks signed a contract with RCA and recorded the aptly titled LP *Ruffin and Kendricks*. Stricken by lung cancer, Kendricks died in October 1992.

Born May 28, 1944, in Atlanta, Georgia, Gladys Knight was raised in a family that valued education and the sounds of gospel music. At age four, Knight began singing gospel music at the Mount Moriah Baptist Church. When she was eight, Knight won first prize on the television program "Ted Mack's Amateur Hour" for a rendition of the song "Too Young." Be-

**Eddie Kendricks
(1939–1992)**

Singer

**Gladys Knight
(1944–)**

Singer

tween the years 1950–1953, Knight toured with the Morris Brown Choir of Atlanta, Georgia. Around this same time, Knight joined her sister Brenda, brother Merald, and cousins William and Eleanor Guest to form a local church singing group. In 1957 the group took the name the Pips upon the suggestion of cousin and manager James "Pips" Woods.

Two years later Langston George and Edward Patten replaced Brenda Knight and Eleanor Guest. Though Gladys periodically left the group, she rejoined in 1964. After recording for several record labels, the Pips finally signed with Motown's subsidiary, Soul. Despite the lack of commercial success, the group released a number of fine recordings under the supervision of Motown's talented production staff, including Norman Whitfield and Ashford & Simpson. In 1967 the group released the single "I Heard It Through the Grapevine," which reached number two on the Billboard charts. Following a long string of hits on Motown, the Pips signed with the Buddah label in 1973, releasing the album *Imagination,* which provided the group with two gold singles, "Midnight Train to Georgia" and "I've Got to Use My Imagination."

By the late 1970s the group, faced with legal battles and contract disputes, began to fall out of popular vogue. For three years the group was barred from recording or performing together. As a result of an out-of-court settlement in 1980, the Pips signed a new contract with CBS, where they remained until 1985. Joined by Dionne Warwick and Elton John, Knight recorded the Grammy award–winning gold single "That's What Friends Are For" in 1986. Released in 1988, the title cut of the Pip's *Love Overboard* album became their biggest-selling single in decades. That same year, Knight recorded the theme for the James Bond film *License to Kill.* Released on the MCA label, Knight's 1991 album *Good Women* features guest stars Patti Labelle and Dionne Warwick.

Little Richard
(1932–)
Singer, Pianist

Flamboyantly dressed, with his hair piled high in a pompadour, Little Richard is a musical phenomenon, an entertainer hailed by pop superstar Paul McCartney as "one of the greatest kings of rock 'n' roll." Richard's image, mannerisms, and musical talent set the trend for the emergence of modern popular music performers from Jimi Hendrix to Prince.

One of twelve children, Richard Wayne Penniman was born on December 5, 1932, in Macon, Georgia. As a child in Macon, Richard heard the sounds of gospel groups, street musicians, and spiritual-based songs emanating from homes throughout his neighborhood. Nicknamed the "War Hawk" for his unrestrained hollers and shouts, Richard's voice projected with such intensity that he was once asked to stop singing in church. Richard's first song before an audience was with the Tiny Tots, a gospel group featuring his brothers Marquette and Walter. Later Richard sang with his family in a group called the Penniman Singers, who appeared at churches, camp meetings, and talent contests.

In high school Richard played alto saxophone in the marching band. After school he took a part-time job at the Macon City Auditorium where he watched the bands of Cab Calloway, Hot Lips Page, Lucky Millinder, and Sister Rosetta Thorpe. At age fourteen, Richard left home to become a performer in Doctor Hudson's Medicine Show. While on the road he joined B. Brown's Orchestra as a ballad singer, performing such compositions as "Good Night Irene" and "Mona Lisa." Not long afterward, he became a member of the traveling minstrel show of Sugarfoot Sam from Alabam.

Richard's first break came in 1951 when the RCA label recorded him live on the radio, producing the local hit "Every Hour." Traveling to New Orleans with his band the Tempo Toppers, Richard's group eventually played the Houston rhythm and blues scene, where he attracted the attention of Don Robey, president of Peacock Records. After cutting some sides for the Peacock label, Richard sent a demo tape to Art Rupe's Los Angeles–based Specialty label. Under the direction of Specialty's producer Bumps Blackwell, Richard recorded the 1956 hit "Tutti Frutti" at J&M Studios in New Orleans. Richard's subsequent sessions for Specialty yielded a long list of classic hits such as "Long Tall Sally," "Lucille," "Jenny, Jenny," and "Keep a Knocking." In 1957 Richard appeared in the films *Don't Knock Rock* with Billy Haley and *The Girl Can't Help It* starring Jane Mansfield.

In the following year, Richard quit his rock and roll career to enter the Oakland Theological College in Huntsville, Alabama. From 1957 to 1959 Richard released several gospel recordings and toured with artists like Mahalia Jackson. In 1962 Richard embarked on a rock and roll tour of Europe with Sam Cooke. A year later Richard hired an unknown guitarist, Jimi Hendrix, who went under the pseudonym of Maurice James. In Europe Richard played on the same bills as the Beatles and the Rolling Stones.

By the 1970s, Richard pursued a career as a full-fledged evangelist and performer. In 1979 he set out on a nationwide evangelist tour. In the following decade, he appeared in the film *Down and Out in Beverly Hills* and recorded "Rock Island Line" on the tribute LP to Leadbelly and Woody Guthrie, called *Folkways: A Vision Shared.* Richard's continuing activity in show business represents the inexhaustible energy of a singer who had a profound impact on the careers of artists like Otis Redding, Eddie Cochran, Richie Valens, Paul McCartney, and Mitch Ryder.

Living Color

Rock group

Winner of several international rock awards, Living Color has been hailed by critics and listeners as one of the finest African-American crossover bands in modern music. Not since Jimi Hendrix or Parliment has a group attracted so much praise for its top-rate musicianship and hard-edged sound.

Originally formed as a trio in 1984, Living Color included drummer and Berkeley College of Music graduate Will Calhoun, bassist and New York City College music graduate Muzz Skillings, and guitar veteran of New York's avant garde music scene Vernon Reid. After adding singer Corey Glover, the band recorded its debut album *Vivid* in 1988. Aside from touring small New York clubs and college campuses, Living Color opened for such acts as Robert Palmer, Billy Bragg, and Anthrax. Released in 1990, the group's next LP, *Times Up,* produced the Grammy award-winning hit "Cult of Personality," which received extensive airplay and regular rotation on MTV.

The group's 1993 release *Stain* features bassist Doug Wimbish, who joined the group after Skilling's departure in December 1991. Defying the commercial dominance of the popular music scene, Living Color often appears at small nightclubs and impromptu performances around the New York area. In its effort to enter the modern rock scene, Living Color has made the transition on its own terms, creating music promoting social awareness while exploring new artistic avenues. "Rock is a black originated art form," explained drummer Will Calhoun, "we're just carrying on the tradition."

Curtis Mayfield

(1942-)

Singer, Songwriter, Producer

Born on June 3, 1942, in Chicago, Illinois, Curtis Mayfield learned to sing harmony as a member of the Northern Jubilee Singers and the Traveling Souls Spiritualist Church. In 1957 Mayfield joined the Roosters, a five-man doo-wop singing group led by his close friend Jerry Butler. Renamed the Impressions, the group released the 1958 hit "Your Precious Love," featuring Butler's resonant baritone and Mayfield's wispy tenor. But in the following year, Butler left the group to pursue a solo career. In search of material, Butler collaborated with Mayfield to write the hit songs "He Will Break Your Heart" and "I'm a-Telling You."

In 1960 Mayfield recruited Fred Cash to take Butler's place in the newly reformed Impressions. In the next year the Impressions hit the charts with the sensual soul tune "Gypsy Women." In collaboration with Butler, Mayfield also established the Curtom Publishing Company. With the loss of original members Richard and Arthur Brooks, the three remaining members of the Impressions, Mayfield, Cash, and Sam Goodman, continued to perform as a trio. Under the direction of jazz musician/arranger Johnny Pate, the Impressions recorded "Sad Sad Girl" and the rhythmic gospel-based song "It's Alright," released in 1963.

Also during this time, Mayfield wrote a number of songs for his Chicago contemporaries including "Monkey Time" for Major Lance, "Just Be True," for Gene Chandler, and "It's All Over Now," for Walter Jackson. Writing for the Impressions, however, Mayfield turned to more socially conscious themes reflecting the current of the civil-rights era. Mayfield's finest message or "sermon" songs were "People Get Ready" (1965), "We're a Winner" (1968), and "Choice of Colors" (1969).

After leaving the Impressions in 1970, Mayfield released his debut album *Curtis.* On his 1971 LP *Curtis Live!,* Mayfield was accompanied by a tight four-piece back-up group that included guitar, bass, drums, and percussion. Mayfield composed the score for the 1972 hit film *Superfly.* The soundtrack became Mayfield's biggest commercial success, providing him two hits with the junkie epitaph "Freddie's Dead," and the wah-wah guitar funk classic "Superfly." Despite his commercial success, Mayfield spent the remainder of the decade in collaboration with other artists, working on such projects as the soundtrack for the film *Claudine,* featuring Gladys Knight and the Pips, and the production of Aretha Franklin's 1978 album *Sparkle.*

Throughout the next decade, Mayfield continued to record such albums as *Love Is the Place* in 1981, and *Honesty* in 1982. Joined by Jerry Butler and newcomers Nate Evans and Vandy Hampton, the Impressions reunited in 1983 for a thirty-city anniversary tour. In 1983 Mayfield released the LP *Come in Peace With a Message of Love.* But in August of 1990, while performing at an outdoor concert in Brooklyn, New York, Mayfield received an injury that left him paralyzed from the neck down. In the following year, Mayfield's contributions to popular music were recognized when the Impressions were inducted into the Rock and Roll Hall of Fame.

MC Hammer
(1962–)

Singer

One of seven children, rapper MC Hammer, who now performs as Hammer, was born Stanley Kirk Burrell in Oakland, California. As a child growing up in government-aided housing, Hammer danced in neighborhood streets and parks. At age four he became enthralled with music after watching a television appearance of James Brown. Throughout his early years in Oakland, Hammer wrote original poems and commercial jingles. After obtaining a college degree in communications, Hammer served three years in the Navy and sought a career as a professional baseball player. In church he formed a religious rap duo called the Holy Ghost Boys. Hammer's album *Feel My Power*, released on his own private label Bustin Records, sold over 60,000 copies. Upon signing with Capitol Records, Hammer re-released the album in 1988 under the title *Let's Get It Started*.

Hammer's big commercial breakthrough came with his 1990 album *Hammer Don't Hurt 'Em*, which sold five million copies. By establishing his own company, Bust It Productions, Hammer has set out to employ black ex-convicts to give them a "fair shot" at becoming productive members of the community. He has also worked with African-American inner-city school children. "I make an active role model to kids," relates Hammer. "They need people to show them there's another way."

Charley Pride
(1939–)

Singer

The first African-American superstar of country music, Charley Pride is a three-time Grammy winner whose supple baritone voice has won him international fame.

Born on March 18, 1939, in Slege, Mississippi, Charley Pride grew up listening to late-night radio broadcasts of the Grand Ole Opry. Although he taught himself guitar at age fourteen, Pride soon turned his attention to a professional baseball career. At age sixteen, he left the cotton fields of Slege for a stint in the Negro American baseball league. During his baseball career, Pride sang on public address systems and in taverns. In 1963 country singer Red Sovine heard Pride and arranged for him to attend an audition in Nashville a year later. This led to a recording contract with the RCA label, which produced the 1964 hit "Snakes Crawl at Night."

Throughout the 1960s Pride toured incessantly, appearing at concert dates and state fairs, as well as on radio and television. In 1967 Pride made his debut at the Grand Ole Opry, and within the same year hit the charts with singles "Does My Ring Hurt Your Finger?" and "I Know One." By the time he received the Country Music Award for Entertainer of the Year in 1971, Pride had already achieved tremendous success as a major figure in the American popular cultural scene.

During the 1980s, Pride not only continued to find success as a music star, but he also became a successful entrepreneur. Making his home on a two hundred forty–acre estate in north Dallas, Texas, Pride emerged as a majority stockholder in the First Texas Bank and part owner of Cecca Productions.

The son of a jazz pianist, Prince Rogers Nelson was born on June 7, 1958, in Minneapolis, Minnesota. By age fourteen Prince taught himself to play piano, guitar, and drums. Drawn to many forms of rock and soul, Prince explained that he never grew up in one particular culture. "I'm not a punk, but I'm not an R&B artist either—because I'm a middle-class kid from Minnesota."

Prince (1958–)

Singer, Songwriter, Producer

It was his eclectic taste that led to Prince's creation of the Minneapolis sound. After forming the band Grand Central in high school in 1973, Prince renamed the group Champagne and eventually recruited the talents of Morris Day. In 1978 Prince signed with Warner Brothers and recorded his debut album, *For You.* His follow-up album, *Prince,* featured the hit "I Wanna Be Your Lover." Rooted in the music of Sly and the Family Stone and Jimi Hendrix, Prince's third LP, *Dirty Mind,* was released in 1980.

Two years later, Prince achieved superstardom with his album *1999,* an effort that was followed by a spectacular tour comprised of Prince and the Revolution, the Time, and the bawdy girl trio Vanity 6. Prince's 1984 film soundtrack *Purple Rain,* which received rave reviews for Prince's portrayal of a struggling young musician, grossed sixty million dollars at the box office in the first two months of its release. Near the end of 1985 Prince established his own record label, Paisley Park, the warehouse/studio located in the wooded terrain of Chanhassen, Minnesota. The same year, Prince released the album *Around the World in a Day,* featuring the hit singles "Raspberry Beret," "Paisley Park," and "Pop Life."

Prince's next film project, *Under the Cherry Moon,* filmed in France, was completed under his direction. The soundtrack *Parade: Music From Under the Cherry Moon* produced a number of hit singles, including "Kiss" and "Mountains." After reforming the Revolution, Prince released *Sign of the Times* in 1987, which included a duet with Sheena Easton, "I Could Never Take the Place of Your Man." Following the LP *Lovesexy,* Prince recorded several songs that appeared on the soundtrack for the film *Batman.* This was followed by another film soundtrack, *Graffiti Bridge,* in 1990.

In September 1992, Prince signed a six-album contract with Warner Brothers. Backed by his new first-rate ensemble, the New Power Generation, Prince embarked on a nationwide tour in April, 1993, which proved the most impressive since his commercial breakthrough in the early 1980s. Prince has not only become an owner of his own nightclub, the Grand Slam, he has contributed a set of original music to the Joffrey Ballet's production of *Billboards,* which opened in January 1993 to rave reviews.

Public Enemy

Rap group

As spokesmen of racial pride and proponents of militant public activism, Public Enemy have redefined the sound and the lyrical message of rap music.

The formation of Public Enemy centered around Adelphi University in Long Island, New York, where the group's founder Carlton Ridenhour, a.k.a. Chuck D., a graphic design major, joined fellow students Hank Shocklee and Bill Stephney at radio station WBAU. First appearing on Stephney's radio show, Ridenhour soon hosted his own three-hour program. Modeled after New York Knicks announcer Marv Albert, Ridenhour's powerful rap voice attracted a number of loyal followers. Ridenhour soon recruited the talents of William Drayton (a.k.a. Flavor Flav), Norman Rodgers (a.k.a. Terminator X), and Richard Griffin (a.k.a. Professor Griff) to form Public Enemy.

In 1987 Public Enemy released the debut album *Yo! Bum Rush the Show,* which sold over 400,000 copies. Two years later Professor Griff, the group's "minister of information," was fired by Chuck D. for making anti-Semitic comments. Under the leadership of Chuck D., the group went on to record the song "Fight the Power" for director Spike Lee's film *Do the Right Thing.* The group's second album, *It Takes a Nation of Millions to Hold Us Back,* became a million seller.

In a departure from their earlier work, Public Enemy's 1990 release *Fear of a Black Planet* featured themes regarding a world struggle for the advancement of the black race. The LP *Apocalypse '91: The Enemy Strikes Black* is a startling statement of social and racial consciousness. In 1992 Public Enemy recorded and toured with the heavy metal band Anthrax. The group also appeared on extensive concert tours with such acts as Ice–T, the Geto Boys, and Queen Latifah.

Born Dana Owens, rap artist Queen Latifah was raised in East Orange, New Jersey, and began performing in high school as the human beat box for the rap group Ladies Fresh. In 1989 she launched her solo recording career with the album *All Hail the Queen*. Her other recordings include *Nature of a Sista'*, featuring the single "Latifah Had It Up 2 Here," and her recent release, *Black Reign*.

**Queen Latifah
(1970–)**

Singer, Actress

Latifah now manages the careers of other rap artists through her New Jersey–based Flavor Unit Records and Management Company, for which she is the CEO. In addition, Latifah is currently appearing in her own television show, "Living Single," with co-stars Kim Fields, Erika Alexander, and Kim Coles, on the Fox Television Network. She has also made appearances on "Fresh Prince of Bel-Air," and in such films as *House Party II* and *Jungle Fever*.

Born on September 9, 1941, in Dawson, Georgia, Otis Redding moved with his parents at age three to the Tindall Heights housing project in Macon. In grade school Redding played drums and sang in a church gospel group, and a few years later he learned the vocals and piano style of his idol, Little Richard. Quitting school in the tenth grade, Redding went on the road with Little Richard's former band, the Upsetters. But Redding's first professional break came when he joined Johnny Jenkins and the Pinetoppers. Redding's debut single was a Little Richard imitation tune, "Shout Bamalama." Accompanying Jenkins to a Stax studio session in Memphis, Redding was afforded some remaining recording time. Backed by Jenkins on guitar, Steve Cropper on piano, Lewis Steinburg on bass, and Al Jackson on drums, Redding cut "Hey Hey Baby" and the hit "These Arms of Mine."

**Otis Redding
(1941–1967)**

Singer, Songwriter

Signed to the Stax label, Redding released the 1963 album *Pain in My Heart*. Backed by members of Booker T. and the MGs, Redding's follow-up LP *Otis Blue (Otis Redding Sings Soul)* featured the 1965 hit "Respect." In the next year, Redding broke attendance records at shows in Harlem and Watts. After releasing a cover version of the Rolling Stones' song "Satisfaction" in 1966, Redding embarked on a European tour that included his appearance on the British television show "Ready Steady Go!"

In August 1966, Redding established his own record company, Jotis, which was distributed through the Stax label. Following a few commercially unsuccessful ventures, Redding recorded singer Arthur Conley, who provided the label with the million-selling single "Sweet Soul Music." Redding's recordings "Try a Little Tenderness" and the vocal duet "Tramp," featuring Carla Thomas, hit the charts in 1967. On June 16 Redding, backed by the MGs, performed a stunning high-paced set at the Monterey Pop Festival. On December 10, Redding's career came to an tragic end when the twin engine plane carrying him to a concert date in Wisconsin crashed in Lake Monona, just outside Madison. As if in tribute, Redding's song "Sitting on the Dock of the Bay," released a few weeks after his death, became his first gold record.

**Lionel Richie
(1949–)**

Singer, Songwriter, Pianist

Lionel Brockman Richie was born on June 20, 1949, on the campus of Tuskegee Institute in Alabama. Richie's grandmother Adelaide Foster, a classical pianist, became his music instructor and introduced him to the works of Bach and Beethoven. While a freshman at the Tuskegee Institute, Richie formed the Mighty Mystics who, along with members of the Jays, became the Commodores. Combining gospel, classical, and country-western music, the Commodores emerged as a formidable live act throughout the 1960s and 1970s. After signing with the Motown label, the group landed its first hit in 1974 with the song "Machine Gun." In 1981 Richie recorded the hit theme song for Franco Zefferelli's film *Endless Love.*

A year later Richie released his first solo album, *Lionel Richie,* which featured the hits "Truly," "You Are," and "My Love." His follow-up release *Can't Slow Down* produced five more hits: "All Night Long (All Night)," "Running with the Night," "Hello," "Stuck on You," and "Penny Lover." In collaboration with Michael Jackson, Richie co-wrote "We Are the World" for USA for Africa, the famine relief project organized and produced by Quincy Jones. In 1985 Richie received an Oscar nomination for best original song for his composition "Say You, Say Me." A year later Richie's third album, *Dancing on the Ceiling,* provided him with the hits "Dancing on the Ceiling," "Love Will Conquer All," "Ballerina Girl," and "Se La."

Proclaimed by Bob Dylan as one of America's greatest poets, Smokey Robinson is a pop music legend who has risen to fame as a brilliant songwriter, producer, and singer. His instantly recognizable falsetto voice continues to bring Robinson gold records and a legion of loyal fans.

William Robinson, Jr. was born in Detroit, Michigan, on February 19, 1940. After his mother died when he was ten years old, Robinson was raised by his sister. Nicknamed "Smokey" by his uncle, Robinson was a bright student who enjoyed reading books and poetry. A reluctant saxophone student, Robinson turned his creative energy to composing songs, which he collected in a dime store writing tablet. While attending Detroit's Northern High School in 1954, Robinson formed the vocal group the Matadors, which performed at battle-of-the-band contests and at recreation centers.

Robinson's introduction to Berry Gordy in 1957 resulted in the Matadors' first record contract with George Goldner's End label. Upon joining the newly formed Motown label in 1960, the group changed their name, upon the suggestion of Gordy, to the Miracles. Although the Miracles' debut album failed to attract notice, they provided Motown with its first smash hit, "Shop Around," in 1961, a song written and co-produced by Robinson.

In close collaboration with Gordy, Robinson spent the following decade as one of Motown's most integral singers and producers. With the Miracles he recorded such hits as "You Really Got a Hold on Me" in 1963, "Tracks of My Tears" in 1965, "I Second That Emotion" in 1967, and "Tears of a Clown" in 1970. As a writer, he provided the label with hits like "My Guy" for Mary Wells, "I'll Be Doggone" for Marvin Gaye, and "My Girl" for the Temptations.

In 1972 Robinson left the Miracles to launch a solo career. Despite the moderate success of his records during the disco craze of the 1970s, Robinson continued to perform and record. In 1979 Robinson experienced a comeback with the critically acclaimed hit "Cruisin." Three years later, Robinson appeared on the NBC–TV special "Motown 25: Yesterday, Today, and Tomorrow." Between 1986 and 1991, Robinson released five more albums, including *Smoke Signals, One Heartbeat,* and *Love, Smokey.*

Smokey Robinson (1940–)

Singer, Songwriter, Producer

Diana Ross makes her last appearance with the Supremes, Cindy Birdsong (left) and Mary Wilson (center), 1970.

**Diana Ross
(1944–)**

Singer, Actress

One of six children, Diana Ross was born in Detroit, Michigan, on March 26, 1944. An extremely active child, Ross swam, ran track, and sang in church. In 1959 she joined the Primetes, a group comprised of Mary Wilson, Florence Ballard, and Barbara Martin. After failing to attract notice on the Lupine label, the group auditioned for Berry Gordy, Jr., who signed them to Motown. Upon the suggestion of Berry, the group changed its name to the Supremes. Released in 1961, the group's song "I Want a Guy," featuring Ross on lead vocals, failed to attract notice. Not long afterward, following Martin's departure, the trio continued to record with Ross on lead vocal.

The Supremes did not find commercial success on the Motown label until 1964, when they were placed under the guidance of the Holland–Dozier–Holland production team. In 1964 H–D–H turned out the Supremes' first smash hit, "Where Did Our Love Go?", followed by numerous others, such as "Baby Love" in 1964, "I Hear a Symphony" in 1965, "You Can't Hurry Love" in 1966, and "Reflections" in 1967. With preferential treatment by Gordy, Ross became the dominant figure of the group. By the mid-1960s, Ross's emerging talent prompted Gordy to bill the group as Diana Ross and the Supremes.

In 1970 Ross left the Supremes to launch her solo career. Her debut album *Diana Ross* featured the writing and production talents of Ashford & Simpson, an effort that included the hit "Reach Out and Touch (Somebody's Hand)." A year later she made her film debut in the Motown-sponsored movie *Lady Sings the Blues,* for which she won an Oscar nomination for her biographical portrayal of jazz singer Billie Holiday. Her role in the 1975 Motown-backed film *Mahogany* brought her not only an Oscar nomination, but the number-one selling single "Do You Know Where You're Going To." In 1978 Ross starred in the film version of *The Wiz,* the last full-scale motion picture to be backed by Motown.

After leaving Motown in 1981, Ross signed a twenty million dollar contract with the RCA label. Her debut album, *Why Do Fools Fall in Love?,* went platinum. This was followed by four more LPs for RCA, including *Silk Electric* in 1982, *Swept Away* in 1984, and *Eaten Alive* in 1985. Two years later, Ross left RCA to sign with the London-based EMI label, which produced the albums *Red Hot Rhythm 'n Blues* and *Working Overtime* in 1987, and *Greatest Hits, Live* in 1990. Today Ross not only continues to enjoy popularity around the world, she has achieved tremendous success as the owner of her own multi-million-dollar corporation Diana Ross Enterprises.

Tina Turner (1939–)

Singer

With a music career spanning over thirty years, Tina Turner has come to be known as the "hardest-working woman in show business." From soul music star to rock goddess, Turner is revered for her show-stopping vocal style and energetic stage act.

Born Annie Mae Bullock on November 25, 1939, in Brownsville, Tennessee, Turner moved to Knoxville with her parents at age three. Turner first sang in church choirs and at local talent contests. After moving with her mother to St. Louis at age sixteen, Turner met pianist Ike Turner,

Tina Turner performs at the 1985 Grammy award presentation, where she won three Grammies.

leader of the R&B group the Kings of Rhythm. Hired by the band to sing at weekend engagements, Annie Bullock married Ike Turner in 1958 and took the stage name Tina Turner. When the band's scheduled session singer failed to appear at a recording session in 1960, Tina stepped in to record the R&B song "Fool in Love," which became a million-seller.

With a major hit behind them, the Turners formed the Ike and Tina Turner Revue, complete with the Iketes. Major international success came for the Turners in 1966 when producer Phil Spector combined his "wall of sound" approach with an R&B sound to record the hit "River Deep, Mountain High." Subjected to years of physical abuse by her husband, Turner divorced Ike in 1976 and set out on a solo career. That same year she co-starred in The Who's rock opera film *Tommy* as the Acid Queen.

In 1984 Turner's career skyrocketed with the commercial success of the album *Private Dancer*, which featured the hit singles "What's Love Got to Do With It?" and "Better Be Good." Turner's sensuously vibrant image soon appeared on high-budget videos, on magazine covers, and in films such as the 1985 release *Mad Max 3: Beyond the Thunderdome*, in which she played the tyrannical Aunty Entity. With the immense commercial success of her 1989 album *Foreign Affair*, Turner closed out the decade as one of the most popular singers on the international music scene.

Luther Vandross
(1951–)

Singer, Composer, Producer

One of the premier pop artists of the 1980s, Luther Vandross is responsible for the emergence of a new school of modern soul singers. Born in New York on April 20, 1951, Vandross was the son of a gospel singer and a big band vocalist. Vandross received his musical education by listening to recordings of Aretha Franklin and the Supremes. In high school Vandross formed numerous singing groups. Throughout the 1970s, he was great as a background singer, performing with such artists as David Bowie, Carly Simon, and Ringo Starr. He also sang advertising jingles, such as AT&T's theme "Reach Out and Touch."

Following the release of his first album, *Never Too Much*, in 1981, Vandross was called upon to sing duets with a number of pop artists, including Aretha Franklin and Dionne Warwick. As a successful writer and producer, Vandross has released eight million-selling albums, including the 1990 release *Best of Love*, which went multi-platinum.

Mary Wells

(1943–1992)

Singer

Born and raised in Detroit, Michigan, Mary Wells started her music career as a featured soloist in her high school choir. After attracting the notice of Berry Gordy, Jr. at age seventeen, Wells signed a contract with Motown in 1959. With Smokey Robinson as her main producer and writer, Wells scored a number of hits such as "I Don't Want to Take a Chance," in 1961, "You Beat Me to the Punch" in 1962, and "My Guy" in 1964. In the same year, she recorded the album *Together* with Marvin Gaye, and she toured England with the Beatles.

At the peak of her career, Wells left the Motown label to become an actress. After relocating in Los Angeles, she signed a contract with Twentieth Century–Fox records. Unfortunately, Wells could never find a producer who equaled Robinson's ability to record her material. Her debut single in 1965, "Use Your Head," achieved only modest commercial success. In the 1970s Wells left music to raise her children. For a brief period she was married to Cecil Womack, brother of the R&B great Bobby Womack.

During the 1980s Wells returned to music, performing on the oldies circuit. In 1985 she appeared in "Motown's 25th Anniversary" television special. Diagnosed as having cancer of the larynx in August 1990, Wells, without medical insurance to pay for treatment, lost her home. Not long afterward, the Rhythm and Blues Foundation raised over $50,000 for Wells's hospital costs. Funds were also sent by artists like Bruce Springsteen, Rod Stewart, and Diana Ross. Despite chemotherapy treatments, Wells died on July 30, 1992, and was buried at Forest Lawn Memorial Park in Los Angeles.

Jackie Wilson

(1934–1984)

Singer

Between 1958 and 1963, Jackie Wilson reigned as one of the most popular R&B singers in America. Dressed in sharkskin suits and sporting a process hairstyle, Wilson exhibited a dynamic stage performance and a singing range that equaled his contemporaries James Brown and Sam Cooke.

Jack Leroy Wilson was born on June 9, 1934, in Detroit, Michigan. Wilson's mother sang spirituals and gospel songs at Mother Bradley's Church. As a youngster, he listened to the recordings of the Mills Brothers, Ink Spots, and Louis Jordan. In high school he became a boxer, and at age sixteen he won the American Amateur Golden Gloves Welterweight title. But upon the insistence of his mother, Wilson quit boxing and pursued a career in music. While a teenager, Wilson sang with the Falcons in local clubs and at talent contests held at the Paradise Theater. He also worked in a spiritual group with later members of Hank Ballard's Midnighters.

In 1953 Wilson replaced Clyde McPhatter as lead singer of the Dominoes. Wilson's only hit with the Dominoes was the reworking of the religious standard "St. Theresa of the Roses." Upon the success of the recording, Wilson signed a contract as a solo artist with the Brunswick label. Wilson's 1957 debut album *Rite Petite* featured the hit title track song, which was written by songwriters Berry Gordy, Jr. and Billy Taylor. The songwriting team of Gordy and Taylor also provided Wilson with the subsequent hits "To Be Loved" in 1957, "Lonely Teardrops" in 1958, and "That's Why I Love You So," and "I'll Be Satisfied" in 1959.

During the early 1960s, Wilson performed and recorded numerous adaptations of classical music compositions in a crooning ballad style. This material, however, failed to bring out the powerful talent of Wilson's R&B vocal style. Although Wilson's repertoire contained mostly supper-club standards, he did manage to produce the powerful pop classics "Dogging Around" in 1960 and "Baby Workout" in 1963. Teamed with writer/producer Carl Davis, Wilson also recorded the hit "Whispers" and the R&B masterpiece "Higher and Higher" in 1967.

Following Wilson's last major hit, "I Get the Sweetest Feeling," in 1968, he performed on the oldies circuit and on Dick Clark's "Good Ol' Rock 'n' Roll Revue." In 1975 Wilson suffered a serious heart attack on stage at the Latin Casino in Cherry Hill, New Jersey. Forced into retirement, Wilson spent his last eight years in a nursing home until his death on January 21, 1984.

Mary Wilson (1944–)

Singer

Mary Wilson's musical career, which began with the Motown supergroup the Supremes, represents an American success story. Born on March 6, 1944, in Greenville, Mississippi, Wilson moved to Detroit at age eleven. Raised in the Brewster–Douglas housing project on the city's east side, Wilson learned to sing by imitating the falsetto voice of Frank Lyman. Along with Barbara Martin and Betty Travis, Wilson formed the Primetes. Upon the departure of Travis, another neighborhood girl named Diana Ross joined the group. Appearing at talent shows and sock-hops, the Primetes went on to win first prize at the 1960 Detroit/Windsor Freedom Festival talent contest. Although the Primetes cut two singles on the Lupine label featuring Wilson on lead vocal, they failed to achieve commercial success.

On January 15, 1961, sixteen-year-old Wilson and Primete members Diana Ross, Florence Ballard, and Barbara Martin signed with the Motown label as the Supremes. Wilson's effort to win the lead vocal spot, however, soon gave way the dominance of Diana Ross. Released in 1964, the group's first gold single "Where Did Our Love Go?" made Wilson and the Supremes overnight celebrities. Between 1964 and 1968 Wilson sang background vocals on a number of hits, including "Baby Love," "You Can't Hurry Love," and "Reflections." Until leaving the group in 1976, Wilson also sang such recordings as "Love Child," "I'm Living in Shame," and "Someday We'll Be Together."

In 1983 Wilson was briefly reunited with the Supremes on the television special "Motown's 25th Anniversary." Making her home in Los Angeles, Wilson occasionally appears on the oldies circuit and at small Supremes revival shows.

The Winans

Gospel singing group

Detroit's first family of gospel music, the Winans have won a number of Grammy awards for their infectious modern pop gospel sound. David Jr., Michael, and twins Marvin and Carvin first sang at their great-grandfather's Zion Congregational Church of Christ on Detroit's east side; their father, minister and singer David Winan, Sr., first organized the quartet.

While attending Mumford High School, the group attracted large crowds at school talent contests. Originally called the Testimonials, the quartet released two locally produced albums, *Love Covers* in 1977 and *Thy Will Be Done* in 1978.

Upon being discovered by gospel singer Andrae Crouch, the group released its first national debut album *Introducing the Winans* in 1981, which was nominated for a Grammy award. The follow-up 1983 LP *Long Time Coming* also received a Grammy nomination. After changing record companies two years later, the Winans released *Let My People Go* on Quincy Jones's Qwest label. Known to join secular pop artists in collaborative singing projects, the Winans featured Michael McDonald on their 1987 release *Decisions*. They also sang back-up on Anita Baker's hit single "Ain't No Need to Worry," and provided vocal tracks for Michael Jackson's song "Man in the Mirror," featured on his *Bad* LP.

In 1992 the Winans appeared at "Culturefest 92" in West Africa. A year later they were invited to sing at President Bill Clinton's inauguration festivities. Known as funky gospel, the Winans' music features electric keyboards, guitar, and bass, as well as saxophone accompaniment. "In today's world, you have to have some type of beat to draw people," related Carvin. "You catch the young people with that first. The words will seep in at one point."

Popular music's genius composer and singer Stevie Wonder has remained at the forefront of musical change. His colorful harmonic arrangements have drawn upon jazz, soul, pop, reggae, and rap-derived new jack rhythms. Wonder's gift to pop music is his ability to create serious music dealing with social and political issues while at the same time revealing the more deeply mysterious nature of the human experience.

Stevie Wonder (1950–)

Singer, Pianist, Composer

Steveland Morris Judkins was born on May 13, 1950, in Saginaw, Michigan. Raised in Detroit, Steveland Morris first sang in the church choir. But the music that attracted him most was the sounds of Johnny Ace and B.B. King, which he heard on late-night radio programs. By age eight Wonder learned to play piano, harmonica, and bongos. Through the connections of Miracles member Ronnie White, Wonder auditioned for Berry Gordy, Jr., who immediately signed the thirteen-year-old prodigy and gave him the stage name of Little Stevie Wonder. After releasing his first singles "Thank You (For Loving Me All the Way)" and "Contract of Love," Wonder scored a number-one hit with "Fingertips Part 2" in 1963. In the following year Wonder hit the charts with the song "Hey Harmonica Man."

With the success of his recording career, Wonder began to tour more frequently. Motown's arrangement to assign Wonder a tutor from the Michigan School for the Blind allowed him to continue his education while on the road. In 1964 he performed in London with the Motown Revue, a package featuring Martha and the Vandellas, the Supremes, and the Temptations. Wonder's subsequent recording of the punchy R&B single "Uptight (Everything's All Right)" became a smash hit in 1966. Wonder's growing commercial success at Motown brought him greater artistic freedom in the studio. In collaboration with Clarence Paul, Wonder produced a long succession of hits, including Bob Dylan's "Blowing in the Wind" in 1966, "I Was Made to Love Her" in 1967, and "For Once in My Life" in 1968.

After recording the album *Signed, Sealed & Delivered* in 1970, Wonder moved to New York, where he founded Tarus Production Company and

Black Bull Publishing Company, both of which were licensed under Motown. With complete control over his musical career, Wonder began to write lyrics containing social and political issues. Through the use of overdubbing, he played most of the instruments on his recordings, including the guitar, bass, horns, percussion, and brilliant chromatic harmonica solos. His three creative albums, *Music from My Mind, Talking Book,* and *Inversions,* all feature Wonder's tasteful synthesizer accompaniment.

Released in 1979, Wonder's *Journey Through the Secret Life of Plants* was an exploratory musical soundtrack for a film documentary. In 1984 Wonder's soundtrack for the film *Woman in Red* won him an Academy award for best song for "I Just Called to Say I Love You." A year later, Wonder participated in the recording of "We Are the World" for USA for Africa, the famine relief project. Wonder's 1985 album *Square Circle* produced the hit singles "Part Time Lover" and "Overjoyed." In 1987 he released *Characters,* followed by *Conversation Piece* in 1990, which contains songs like "Greenhouse" and "Legal Drug Dealer" that address current social issues.

By John Cohassey

Fine and Applied Arts

"The constructive lessons of African art are among the soundest and most needed of art creeds today. They offset with equal force the banalities of sterile, imitative classicism and the superficialities of literal realism. They emphasize intellectually significant form, abstractly balanced design, formal simplicity, restrained and unsentimental emotional appeal. Moreover, Africa's art creed is beauty in use, vitally rooted in the crafts, and uncontaminated with the blight of the machine. Surely the liberating example of such art will be as marked an influence in the contemporary work of Negro artists as it has been in that of the leading modernists: Picasso, Modigliani, Matisse, Epstein, Lipchitz, Brancusi and others too numerous to mention."

This comment, made over sixty years ago during the height of the Harlem Renaissance by Alain Locke, one of America's foremost art critics, underscores the promise displayed by African Americans throughout their history in the United States. The substantial contributions of African-American artists have been achieved in the face of numerous obstacles. Blacks in the United States and Europe were long cut off from the rich artistic heritage of Africa. As Locke points out, "the liberating example" of African art was used by white Europeans long before it reached African Americans.

SUPPORT FOR BLACK ARTISTS ♦ ♦ ♦ ♦ ♦ ♦ ♦ ♦ ♦ ♦ ♦ ♦ ♦ ♦ ♦ ♦ ♦ ♦

From colonial times to the present, black artistic talent has been encouraged and recognized on a very limited basis by reigning establishments and connoisseurs in the United States, though some white institutions, such as the Rosenwald Fund in the early twentieth century, did subsidize promising black artists. More support came later from the Harmon, Rockefeller, Guggenheim, and Whitney Foundations and from government programs, such as the Works Progress Administration (which later became the Works Projects Administration) and the National Endowment for the Arts. State Arts Councils, formed in the 1960s and 1970s, have also provided grants for artists. The need for support, however, has always exceeded the available sponsorships.

Early African-American themes and expressions—whether related to slave, sharecropper, or ghetto life—have rarely been regarded as prime moneymakers by leading curators of the art world. Until very recently, few blacks attained the economic security and leisure essential to the patronage of artists. Art history books include the contributions of one or two African-American artists and very little about African art, although images of blacks abound: in Egyptian tomb paintings, on Greek vase paintings, in Roman frescoes and mosaics, in Medieval illuminated manuscripts, and in Gothic sculpture. If Africans were subjects, might not they also have been artists?

BLACK ARTISTS IN EUROPE ♦ ♦ ♦ ♦ ♦ ♦ ♦ ♦ ♦ ♦ ♦ ♦ ♦ ♦ ♦ ♦ ♦ ♦

Two black artists in seventeenth-century Europe have been documented. They are Juan de Pareja and Sebastian Gomez. Pareja was a slave, apprentice, and pupil of the great master Velasquez. Many of Pareja's works were of such a quality that they were mistakenly accepted as Velasquez's own and hung in the great museums and mansions of western Europe. Today, Pareja's paintings, properly credited to him, hang in the Dulwich Gallery in London, the Prado in Madrid, the Munich Gallery, and the Hermitage in Leningrad. Pareja's talent was recognized in his lifetime and in 1652 he was manumitted by King Philip IV.

Sebastian Gomez, a servant of Murillo, was discovered painting secretly at night in his master's studio after Murillo's pupils had departed. Murillo made Gomez his student, and eventually Gomez, known as The Mulatto of Murillo, became famous for paintings and murals in Seville.

Although Pareja and Gomez were black artists, their genius was nurtured in a European setting and tradition. Cut off from their African heritage, they naturally worked in the same style and format as their white contemporaries. Their paintings were devoted to the religious themes and aristocratic portraits desired by the art world of that era.

◆ ◆ ◆ ◆ ◆ ◆ ◆ INTERPRETATIONS OF EUROPEAN TRADITIONS

The only African-American artist in colonial America to have left a historical record was Scipio Morehead. Morehead's artistic endeavors appear to have been aided by two prominent women who lived in Boston where he was a slave: the wife of his clergyman master, the Reverend John Morehead, who was a patron of arts, and poet Phillis Wheatley, who was herself a slave. Morehead's style is in keeping with the period—it is classically allegorical, resembling the work of Romney and Reynolds, British masters of the era. Although no major work is known to have survived, the small extant portrait of Phillis Wheatley is believed to be Morehead's work.

Certainly there were many black artists and craftspeople in the eighteenth century who did not achieve historical recognition. Fortunately, as scholars have more of a desire to understand the nature and development of the American culture, a more multi-ethnic pattern is beginning to emerge with the basic foundation being Western European, African, and Native American cultures. Records indicate that skilled blacks interested in buying their freedom worked as painters, silversmiths, cabinet and coach makers, ornamentalists, and shipwrights. Eugene Warbourg, for example, a black sculptor from New Orleans, became well known for his ornamental gravestones and eventually went to study in Europe. Bill Day, a celebrated carpenter who owned slaves in his shop, has gained recognition for his interior design as well as his furniture.

Much of the colonial iron work and metal work on eighteenth century mansions, churches, and public buildings was created and executed by

Newspaper Boy, *Edward Mitchell Bannister, 1869.*

blacks and occasionally reached heights that can be classified as fine art. The artists and artisans, however, are not known.

Emerging African-American artists in the eighteenth and nineteenth centuries found that their cultural roots were not recognized. To become professionals they had to simulate European artistic styles. Many were trained by white artists, and they traveled to Europe to study and receive validation. Their works received some degree of popular acceptance, but racism kept them out of the mainstream. Most continued to work in the United States in spite of their status. Some were able to overcome immense obstacles and win recognition for their art, including Edward Mitchell Bannister, Robert Duncanson, Meta Warrick Fuller, Joshua Johnston, Edmonia Lewis, and Henry Ossawa Tanner.

In 1991, the Philadelphia Museum of Art organized a retrospective of the works of its native son, Henry Ossawa Tanner.

Some African-American artists attempted to escape the classical tradition into which they were confined, and painted themes closer to their heritage and existence. Some fine portraits of black freedmen were painted by talented but obscure black artists in the rural South during the period from 1870 through the early part of the twentieth century. Henry Ossawa Tanner's paintings in the 1880s of poor blacks, for example, belong to this little-known school of African-American art.

The turn of the century brought few changes in the approach of most African-American artists to their work. They continued to look toward Western Europe for their themes and development of expression, and there was little emphasis given to demonstrating an ethnic consciousness. Two important developments in art helped to push black artists towards cultural and social awareness and a visual aesthetic: the 1913 Armory Show of works by European cubist and modernist painters revealed an interest in, and the influence of, African art forms; and the mainstream American art world developed an interest in genre subjects. These movements toward social realism and abstract formalism in art opened the doors to new interpretations and values in artistic expression.

During the period of transition from 1900 to the 1920s, many black artists continued to express themselves in imitative styles. They felt that the interest in African-American culture was sincere in Europe, and many traveled there to study. New trends emerged, demonstrating expressions of personal dignity and ethnic awareness. The artists of this period—Palmer Hayden, Archibald Motley, Malvin Gray Johnson, William Edouard Scott, Meta Warrick Fuller, and Laura Wheeler Waring—were among the major contributors to this new awareness.

◆ ◆ ◆ ◆ ◆ ◆ ◆ ◆ ◆ ◆ ◆ ◆ ◆ ◆ ◆ ◆ ◆ ◆ **THE HARLEM RENAISSANCE**

The new respect for negritude and the African idiom that began to manifest itself after World War I is evidenced by cultural activities and organizations that developed in major American cities during the 1920s.

From Karamu House, a center for cultural activities founded in 1915 in Cleveland, came such artists as Hughie Lee-Smith, Zell Ingrams, Charles Sallee, Elmer Brown, William E. Smith, and George Hulsinger. In 1924, the Spingarn Awards were established. Three years later, the Harmon Foundation was established by philanthropist William E. Harmon to aid African-American artists. The foundation offered financial awards and exhibitions and encouraged the growth of art education programs in many black institutions throughout the country. The Harmon Foundation became one of the major organizations involved in the perpetuation and presentation of African-American art in the United States and continued to exist until the mid-1960s. Howard University established its first art gallery, under the directorship of James V. Herrings, in 1930.

The 1930s brought the depression and the Works Progress Administration. Black artists abandoned by the white philanthropists of the 1920s were rescued by the WPA. Aaron Douglas, Augusta Savage, Charles Alston, Hale Woodruff, and Charles White created murals and other works for public buildings under this program. In 1939, the Baltimore Museum Show, the first exhibition of African-American artists to be held in a southern region, presented the works of Richmond Barthe, Malvin Gray Johnson, Henry Bannarn, Florence Purviance, Hale Woodruff, Dox Thrash, Robert Blackburn, and Archibald Motley. The Harlem Art Center and the Chicago South Side Community Art Center also began with the help of the WPA.

Representation of the African-American culture through art became an important goal in the first three decades of the twentieth century. At the

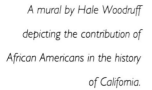

Facing History: The Black Image in American Art 1710–1940 was a major exhibit curated by Guy C. McElroy, who also wrote a catalogue that included an essay by Henry Louis Gates, Jr. It was shown in Washington, DC, at the Corcoran Gallery of Art, and in New York at the Brooklyn Museum in 1990.

A mural by Hale Woodruff depicting the contribution of African Americans in the history of California.

urging of Alain Locke, W.E.B. DuBois, and others, creative artists began collaborating in literature, music, theater, and art to increase awareness of their cultural heritage. Aaron Douglas was considered the leading painter of "The Negro Renaissance." Active in New York from 1923 to 1925, Douglas was the first of his generation to depict visual symbols—stylized African figures with overlays of geometric forms—that created a sense of movement and rhythm. The idea spread from Harlem's boundaries— where many black intellectuals and artists from the Caribbean and else-where had settled—throughout the United States. This concept, while promoting ethnic awareness and pride, also counteracted the stereotypes and shallow interpretations prevalent in the popular culture.

♦ ♦ ♦ ♦ ♦ ♦ ♦ ♦ ♦ ♦ ♦ ♦ ♦ ♦ ♦ ♦ ♦ ♦ ♦ POST-DEPRESSION ART

During this period, black artists continued to depict the American social and political landscape in their works. World War II brought a sense of urgency to the search for equality; the integration of the armed services fostered hope for equality in all facets of American life. Seeking greater cultural and professional opportunities as well as communities of African-American intellectuals and artists, many blacks migrated from the South to urban areas in the North. This migration was documented by artists such as Romare Bearden, Benford Delaney, Jacob Lawrence, and Hughie Lee-Smith.

The influence of the previous decades became evident in the proliferation of muralist art. In her book *Art: African American,* Samella Lewis notes that exterior murals are an important aspect of African architectural traditions. Charles Alston, John Biggers, Jacob Lawrence, and Charles White became important muralists during this period. Inspired by Mexican mural artists (who advocated social change through their art), African-American artists were especially drawn to the themes, bold forms, and bright colors of such artists as Diego Rivera, David Alfero Siqueiros, and Jose Clemente Orozco.

Like their successful white counterparts, African-American artists were conscious of the need to study the history, aesthetics, and formal qualities of art. Many continued to go abroad to Paris, Rome, and, before World

The Seattle Museum launched a major retrospective in 1986 of the work of Jacob Lawrence—often referred to as the "Dean of Black Painters."

1954 National Conference of Artists attendees (from left to right) Jimmy Mosley, Samella Lewis, F. Spellman, Phillip Hampton, Venola Jennings, Juanita Moulon, James Porter, Eugene Brown, and Hayward Oubre.

War II, Germany. Most, however, stayed in the United States and attended classes either at universities such as Columbia, Ohio State, and Pennsylvania State, or at professional art schools such as the Art Institute of Chicago, the New York Art Students' League, and the Philadelphia Academy of Art. Black educational institutions such as Fisk, Hampton, Howard, Morehouse, and Tuskegee emphasized art education as a means of survival, as well as the basis for continuing a future cultural aesthetic in the visual arts.

"Some historians and critics," Lewis notes, "have erroneously assumed that African-American artists are unfamiliar with the formalized techniques of Western aesthetics." Beginning in the 1940s, more African Americans were being awarded degrees in art than ever before. Some turned to abstraction, non-objective art (Delilah Pierce), and expressive forms as seen in many works by Norman Lewis, who for a time was a part of the group known as the Action Painters (Jackson Pollock, a major European-American artist, was also part of this group). Romare Bearden studied Cubism, as did Aaron Douglas. These artists were aware of the African roots of this art form long before American critics began writing about the significant influence of African art on the abstractionist painters of the twentieth century.

The end of World War II and the beginning of the dismantling of the Jim Crow segregation laws in the South were provocative subjects for artists in the 1940s and 1950s. The period was marked by social unrest as barriers to racial equality slowly broke down, and social and political expressions dominated African-American art. Many artists considered it imperative to document, inspire, and champion the "cause." Several artists, however, felt that art should be separate from race and politics. Horace Pippin, William Edmonson, and Clementine Hunter, who were self-taught individuals, and E. Simms Campbell, a cartoonist and successful pictorial journalist for *Esquire* and the *New Yorker*, were among them.

♦ ♦ ♦ ♦ THE SEARCH FOR AN AFRICAN-AMERICAN IDENTITY

The search for a black identity and the expression of militancy were the most pervasive themes of black art in the 1960s. Emotions could not always be contained on canvas, channeled into familiar forms, or exhibited in traditional settings. Art literally took to the streets of the ghetto to meet with, appeal to, and celebrate the people, as was richly illustrated in Chicago and Detroit murals.

In 1972, African-American and Hispanic teenagers in New York City created a colorful art form, "wall graffiti," to express their loyalty and pride. The content of wall graffiti is often merely the name of a street gang, the nickname of the painter, or the name of the street where the painter lives. Some of the paintings, however, depict extravagant scenes with cartoon characters and flamboyant lettering. Toward the end of the 1970s and well into the 1980s this graffiti style became very popular and acquired value in the art market. Several of the young street artists, particularly Jean-Michel Basquiat, were welcomed into the mainstream art world and made into superstars.

In 1989, the Dallas Museum organized Black Art: Ancestral Legacy, *an exhibit that explored the impact of African culture on artists in the African diaspora, particularly the Caribbean and the United States.*

Some mainstream artists, such as Keith Haring, adopted the graffiti style and made it their own, and galleries such as the Paula Cooper Gallery opened their doors to this new and defiant art. Choreographer Twyla Tharp designed a ballet for the Joffrey Company called "Deuce Coupe" that shows dancers moving against a background provided by boys spray painting on sheets of paper hung from the ceiling.

In the early 1990s, multimedia art forms (initially developed in the 1960s and 1970s; expanded by video and computers in the 1980s) came to the forefront. Artists combining traditional expressive modes (painting, printmaking, sculpture) with dance, drama, and other performance arts were finding alternative exhibition spaces as well, including the natural environment, factories, and school buildings. Traditional materials were often replaced by stones, hair, elephant dung, twigs, bricks, and found objects. Words, symbols, and numbers as images have acquired a new emphasis in much of this experimental art.

AFRICAN-AMERICAN EXHIBITIONS ♦ ♦ ♦ ♦ ♦ ♦ ♦ ♦ ♦ ♦ ♦ ♦ ♦

In 1992 the Wadsworth Atheneum in Hartford, Connecticut, opened its African-American Gallery, which is believed to be the first in the country in a major museum, with an exhibit from the National Museum of American Art, Free Within Ourselves: African-American Art in the Collection of the National Museum of American Art.

During the late 1960s and early 1970s, leading mainstream museums began responding to demands made by African-American artists to hire African-American scholars as curators and administrators. At a time of intensive demonstrations, Kynaston McShine, a young West Indian who had already established his reputation as a curator at the Jewish Museum, moved on to become the assistant curator of painting and sculpture at the Museum of Modern Art. Howardena Pindell, who had just begun her career at the Museum of Modern Art as the assistant curator of drawings and prints, later became the associate curator, and in 1980 resigned from that position to pursue her career as an artist. This progress, however, was not satisfactory to the artists who demonstrated and wrote letters demanding that more jobs be made available to black art historians.

In 1968, Gylbert Coker became the first African American to be hired at the Guggenheim Museum in an administrative trainee position. She later worked at the Museum of Modern Art as cataloguer in the museum's registration department. In 1976, she received the Rockefeller Fellowship in Museum Education and spent one year at the Metropolitan Museum of Art. The following year she became the curator of the Studio Museum in Harlem, where she set up their registration department and organized such important events as the Bob Thompson Exhibition and the Hale Woodruff Retrospective, before leaving to pursue a career as a free-lance critic and curator. In 1980 and again in 1982, Coker co-directed *Art Across the Park,* an outdoor exhibition created by the artist David Hammons. The project was so popular that several groups in New York imitated the concept. It was the first large-scale exhibit that openly encouraged all artists to take part, and it was at this time that the term *multi-ethnic* was coined.

The second African American to work at the Guggenheim in an administrative position was Cheryl McClenny. She went on to direct the Museum Collaborative Programs for the city of New York and, in 1978, became an administrator with the National Endowment for the Arts in Washington, DC. In 1980, she was appointed director of the Philadelphia Museum of Art.

Two important African-American contributors to art scholarship—Faith Weaver and Horace Brockington—graduated from the Museum Studies Program at the Whitney Museum. After completing the program, Weaver taught American Art History at the School of Visual Arts. Brockington gained recognition for his exhibition *Another Generation* for the Studio Museum in Harlem in 1978, which set the stage for *African-American Abstraction,* presented two years later at P.S. 1, an alternative art center. The Brooklyn Museum opened its Community Gallery and hired Henri Ghent, who began to organize some very important events, including several African-American exhibitions that were sent to Europe.

The Metropolitan Museum of Art in New York City boasted the largest community art program. There, people like Randy Williams, Florence Hardney, Dolores Wright, Cathy Chance, and Lowery Sims actively presented the art works of African-American and other minority artists to the Metropolitan Museum's audience. By 1977, Lowery Sims was made the museum's first African-American assistant curator in the Twentieth-Century Art department, under the curatorial guidance of Henry Geldzahler; she later became the associate curator under William Leiberman.

Depression, *Jacob Lawrence,* 1950.

Regina Perry was invited by the Metropolitan Museum of Art in 1976 to produce an exhibition called *Selections of Nineteenth-Century Afro-American Art*. The exhibition highlighted, for the first time, many early African-American portrait painters and landscape artists, and it even made attempts to document some important slave artifacts and put them into an aesthetic rather than sociological perspective. Also in 1976, Lowery Sims put together an exhibition of selected works by twentieth-century African-American artists from the museum's collection for the Bedford-Stuyvesant Restoration Corporation. Three years later Sims mounted another exhibition of African-American paintings from the twentieth-century collection.

The Newark Museum of Art in New Jersey held its first black art exhibition in 1944. The exhibition included the works of Richmond Barthe, Romare Bearden, and William Edmonson. Thirty years later, in 1974, the museum presented its second African-American art exhibit, *Black Artists: Two Generations*. The curator was Paul Waters.

By the 1990s mainstream museums across the country, including the Seattle Museum in Washington, the Dallas Museum in Texas, the Brooklyn Museum in New York, the Corcoran Gallery of Art in Washington, DC, and the Wadsorth Atheneum in Hartford, Connecticut, were sponsoring major exhibits of African-American artists' works or displaying collections and artifacts designed to appeal to black audiences.

ARCHITECTURE AND THE APPLIED ARTS ♦ ♦ ♦ ♦ ♦ ♦ ♦ ♦ ♦ ♦ ♦

Architecture   Africans brought to America many skills in such crafts as metalwork, woodcarving, masonry, and toolmaking. They built dwellings in Virginia and other parts of the Americas resembling the rondavels found in Mali, Africa. These round brick slave quarters were topped with conical roofs and date from the eighteenth century. In the nineteenth century they built homes now called "shotgun houses," a part of the legacy from the Yoruba people of Western Africa. These mostly urban houses, which came to Louisiana by way of Haiti, were narrow frame dwellings with two or more rooms, measuring in width from 10 to 14 feet, and varying in length from 22 to 65 feet, with ceilings from 6 to 12 feet in height. Slaves also built many mansions and public buildings, including a courthouse in Vicksburg, Mississippi, which later became a museum.

Like African painters at this time, black craftspeople in the eighteenth and nineteenth centuries who were interested in technology and art sought to copy their European counterparts, and were trained as slave labor or apprentices. They too, in time, began to do original works in wood, wrought iron (later cast iron), and other metals.

The first black to receive a degree from the Massachusetts Institute of Technology (in 1892) was Robert Taylor, who opened the first school of architecture in an African-American school at Tuskegee Institute. In 1901, John A. Lankford, the first recorded African-American architect to have an office, designed and built the Pythian Building, constructed entirely by African Americans. The first African American to be accepted in the American Institute of Architects was Paul R. Williams, in 1926. In 1966, Norma Merrick Sklarek became the first African-American woman to be offered a fellowship at the American Institute of Architects.

Today more than eight hundred registered architects in the United States are African American. The major schools of architecture in predominantly African-American universities include Florida A&M University in Tallahassee, Florida; Hampton University in Hampton, Virginia; Howard University in Washington, DC; Morgan State University in Baltimore, Maryland; Prairie View A&M University in Prairie View, Texas; Southern University in Baton Rouge, Louisiana; Tuskegee University in Tuskegee, Alabama; and the University of the District of Columbia in Washington, DC.

In 1991, New York architect Jack Travis edited African-American Architects in Current Practice, a study of thirty-three outstanding African-American architects, which includes a chronology of African-American architects since 1868 by Vinson McKenzie of Auburn University.

The Applied Arts: Crafts, Illustration, Fashion Design, and Automobile Design

The artistic heritage of African Americans encompasses dressmaking and tailoring, quilting, weaving, silversmithing, engraving, and ceramic production, as well as jewelrymaking, stitchery, stained-glass, blown glass, mosaics, and enameling. Many slaves learned their crafts in Africa. As these skills were discovered, the slave masters put these skilled workers to use and trained their slaves in new skills as needed.

The twentieth century saw a revival of crafts and functional art, and many artists—including quilters Faith Ringgold and Michael Cummings—began to employ traditional crafts methods and materials in their work, until the line between art and craft virtually disappeared.

Stephen Burrows (here shown with models in 1979) is one of many African-American fashion designers.

In illustration, the graphic artists Jerry Pinkney and Larry Johnson are examples of successful African Americans who have used their skills for designing postage stamps, drawing editorial cartoons, and illustrating children's books and other publications.

African-American artists in fashion design include Stephen Burrows, Gordon Henderson, and Willi Smith. Historically, some household slaves were excellent dressmakers and tailors who turned these skills into self-supporting businesses after becoming free men and women.

Emeline King and Edward T. Welburn are successful artists in the field of automobile design. In contrast to the nineteenth century, careers in industrial design are now sought by trained artists who combine engineering studies with art.

♦ ♦ ♦ ♦ ♦ ♦ ♦ ♦ ♦ ♦ ♦ ♦ ♦ ♦ ♦ ♦ ♦ ♦ **MUSEUMS AND GALLERIES**

The 1960s saw a great many radical changes in social and cultural aspects of the United States. African Americans throughout the country were demanding political, social, and cultural recognition. No longer satisfied with the limited support of such philanthropic organizations as the Harmon Foundation, these artists looked for alternative forms of exposure. In response, numerous galleries, community art centers, and community art galleries developed.

In 1969, Nigel Jackson, a former artist turned administrator, established the Acts of Art Gallery in New York City to provide exhibition space for contemporary artists. A non-profit organization, the gallery was dedicated to promoting these artists and providing them with the opportunity to attract collectors interested in their work. Largely because of the political volatility of the period and the gallery's aggressive action policy, in 1971 the Acts of Art Gallery became the center for the controversial "Whitney Rebuttal Show."

The Studio Museum in Harlem began in 1969 under the direction of Edward Spriggs. Set up as a place for artists who needed working space, it eventually branched out into a cultural center where the artists could display their work, meet other artists and art supporters, and hold concerts, panel discussions, and other art-related activities. By 1972, the Studio Museum in Harlem had become the cultural center of New York for the African-American community.

In addition, the Lewis H. Michaux Book Fair took place for three years at the Studeo Museum (1976–1979) under the direction of special program coordinator David Jackson. Lewis Michaux was a legend in the world of bookselling, having established a bookstore on 125th Street and Lenox Avenue that became a world-renowned landmark for people who were inter-

Two artists work with clay.

ested in literature by or about African Americans, Africans, Caribbeans, and South Americans. The store, called the National Memorial African Book Store, opened in 1930 and continued to exist for the next forty-four years.

While under the directorship of Edward Spriggs, the museum began celebrating the holiday Kwanzaa; at this time the museum opened its doors to the entire neighborhood to share in dancing, singing, and eating with the artists. Dancer Chuck Davis led the dancing, ending with the whole room filled with guests dancing.

By 1980, the museum had grown out of its second floor loft space and moved into an old office building on 125th Street and 7th Avenue. The new space provided the museum with additional exhibition galleries, larger office areas, and space for its growing collection and the artist-in-residence program.

Just Above Midtown Gallery was the first organization to move into the gallery district in New York City. Established in 1976, it set up its operation base in a modest space on 57th Street in midtown Manhattan. Under the directorship of Linda Bryant, the organization presented many of the leading contemporary artists of the 1970s including David Hammons, Senga Nengudi, Randy Williams, and Howardena Pindell. Placing the African-American artists in direct competition with mainstream American artists was the objective of Bryant, her board, and her artists. No longer could art critics refuse to review these works because they could not get to Harlem, Queens, or Brooklyn. But the cost of running a gallery took its toll, and to continue operations Bryant turned the gallery into a non-profit organization, adding educational programs for young artists, music concerts, performance programs, slide reviews, and lectures.

By the end of 1979, Just Above Midtown moved from 57th Street to a larger space on Franklin Street in the Tribeca section of New York. At this time the gallery changed its name to the Just Above Midtown/Downtown Alternative Art Center, and opened its doors to vanguard, new-wave artists.

The Schomburg Center for Research in Black Culture of the New York Public Library is one of the most widely used research facilities in the world devoted to the preservation of materials on black life. The Center's collections first won international acclaim in 1926 when the personal collection of the distinguished black scholar and bibliophile Arthur A. Schomburg was added to the Division of Negro Literature, History, and Prints of the 135th Street branch of the New York Public Library. Schomburg served as the curator in the Negro Division from 1932 until his death in 1938. Renamed in his honor in 1940, the collection grew steadily through the years. In 1972, it was designated as one of the Research Libraries of the New York Public Library and became the Schomburg Center for Research in Black Culture. Today, the Schomburg Center is the guardian of over five million items, and provides services and programs for constituents from the United States and abroad.

The Cinque Gallery in New York was the concept of three distinguished artists—Romare Bearden, Norman Lewis, and Ernest Crichlow. The gallery, which opened in 1969, was named after the famous African Joseph Cinque, who in 1839 led a successful revolt aboard the slave ship *Amistad,* won his freedom, and returned to Africa. It was the wish of Bearden, Crichlow, and Lewis to establish an exhibition space specifically for

Arthur A. Schomburg's personal collection, which he donated to the New York Public Library in 1926, included more than 5,000 volumes, 3,000 manuscripts, 2,000 etchings and paintings, and several thousand pamphlets. The collection was named in his honor.

young African-American artists who needed to learn the process of being a professional artist. By the end of the 1970s it was decided that the gallery doors be opened to all new and emerging artists regardless of age.

The Weusi Ya Nambe Yasana Gallery, also in New York, was one of the few cooperative community galleries to come out of the late 1960s. Housed in a brownstone in Harlem, the gallery was established to present the art work of its members. Headed by Ademola Olagebefola, the organization's other members included Otto Neals, Kay Brown, and Jean Taylor.

Genesis II was one of the alternative profit-making galleries that emerged out of the 1960s. Like many of its kind, the gallery functioned out of dealers' apartments to reduce overhead expenses. The dealer invited his or her clients to come view the works in a living environment, so that they might better appreciate the art work. Also, at these gatherings clients had the opportunity to meet other collectors as well as the artist and talk in detail about the work. The concept proved valuable for many African-American artists who needed to develop supporting collectors and to establish a real market for their work.

The New Muse in Brooklyn began in the late 1960s, offering the African-American Brooklyn community the same kinds of art programs presented at the Studio Museum. In addition to the art programs, the New Muse also offered lessons in jazz with bassist Reggie Workman, who headed the program.

The Store Front Museum in Queens was established to satisfy the artistic needs of its community. Offering art classes in painting and drawing, its focus leaned more toward the performing arts—dancing and drama. Harlem's Benin Gallery, focusing on photography, opened its doors in 1976.

The Hatch-Billops Studio began in New York in 1968 as an organization designed to present multi-ethnic plays, performances, and exhibitions. By 1973, the studio began collecting third-world memorabilia. Based on the understanding that no one will protect or present a group's history the way that group would, the collection became incorporated in 1975. Camille Billops and her husband Jim Hatch began taping the personal histories of some black theater artists. Today the collection houses more than six hundred taped interviews and panel and media events about or by artists. This collection is one of the most complete reference centers focusing on African-American art—visual, literary, and theatrical.

In Los Angeles, Samella Lewis, a painter, art historian, and professor at Claremont College, founded the Contemporary Craft Center. Alonzo and Dale Davis established and directed the Brockman Gallery, a nonprofit gallery showing contemporary African-American art and the work of other minority artists.

In Chicago, the Du Sable Museum was established in 1961 under the directorship of Margaret Burroughs to provide the South Side community with an art center. The museum grew out of an art center that was established under the WPA during the depression.

In Boston, the museum of the National Center of Afro-American Artists, begun in 1969 under the curatorship of Edmond Barry Gaither, is a multi-media art center featuring dance, theater, visual arts, film, and educational programs.

In Washington, DC, the Museum of African Art, formerly known as the Frederick Douglass Institute, was established in 1964 and for twenty years existed in a Victorian row house on Capitol Hill, nestled in the shadow of the United States Supreme Court. The house had belonged to Frederick Douglass, a former slave who became an advisor to President Abraham Lincoln. In 1984, the Museum of African Art was moved to the Smithsonian Institute, while the house on Capitol Hill retained the name Frederick Douglass Institute and became solely devoted to early African-American art and memorabilia. The Museum of African Art was established to promote and familiarize Americans with the artistic heritage of Africa; today it includes a large and extensive collection devoted exclusively to African art and culture. One of the largest and most diverse of its kind in the United States, the collection consists of some 65,000 works, including traditional carvings, musical instruments, and textiles, with particular emphasis on works from Nigeria, Ghana, Liberia, the Ivory Coast, and Zaire. In the transition, the Smithsonian has also acquired the Eliot Elisofon Photographic Archives, which contain some 150,000 slides and motion pictures available to the public.

The Smith-Mason Gallery Museum, located in Washington, DC, is a four-story Victorian house established in 1968 to present its permanent collection, which features paintings, sculptures, and graphics of African-American and Caribbean artists. The works remain on permanent display.

FINE AND APPLIED ARTISTS ♦ ♦ ♦ ♦ ♦ ♦ ♦ ♦ ♦ ♦ ♦ ♦ ♦ ♦ ♦ ♦ ♦ ♦ ♦

Charles Alston
(1907–1972)

Painter, Sculptor, Muralist

It was with his murals that painter Charles Alston insured his fame and established his reputation as a black American artist of importance.

Born in Charlotte, North Carolina in 1907, Alston studied at Columbia University in New York, receiving B.A. and M.A. degrees. He was later awarded several fellowships and grants to launch his painting career.

Alston's paintings and sculpture are in such collections as those of IBM and the Detroit Institute of Arts. His murals depicting the history of medicine adorn the facade of Harlem Hospital in New York. Alston was a member of the National Society of Mural Painters. His notable works include *Exploration and Colonization* (1949); *Blues with Guitar and Bass* (1957); *Blues Song* (1958); *School Girl* (1958); *Nobody Knows* (1966); *Sons and Daughters* (1966); and *Frederick Douglass* (1968).

Benny Andrews
(1930–)

Painter

Born in Madison, Georgia on November 13, 1930, Andrews studied at Fort Valley State College in Georgia and later at the University of Chicago. He was awarded a B.F.A. from the Art Institute of Chicago in 1958. During his career he has taught at the New York School of Social Research, the City University of New York, and Queens College in New York. His works have appeared in exhibitions around the country, including the Boston Museum of Fine Arts, the Martha Jackson Gallery in New York City, and other museums and galleries too numerous to list.

Most notably, Andrews directed the Visual Arts Program for the National Endowment for the Arts from 1982 to 1984. He has directed the National Arts Program since 1985, offering children and adults an opportunity to exhibit and compete for prizes in many cities across the country.

Andrews's other honors include an honorary doctorate from the Atlanta School of Art, 1984; a John Hay Whitney fellowship, 1965–1967; a grant from the New York Council on the Arts, 1971; an NEA fellowship, 1974; a Bellagie fellowship from the Rockefeller Foundation, 1987; and a painting fellowship from the National Endowment for the Arts, 1986. His notable works include *The Family; The Boxer; The Invisible Man; Womanhood; Flora;* and *Did the Bear.*

Born in Nova Scotia, Bannister was the son of a West Indian man and an African-American woman. Both parents died when he was very young. Bannister moved to Boston in the early 1850s, where he learned to make solar plates and worked as a photographer.

Edward Mitchell Bannister (1828–1901)

Painter

Influenced by the Barbizon style popular at the time, Bannister's paintings convey his love of the quiet beauty of nature and his pleasure in picturesque scenes with cottages, cattle, dawns, sunsets, and small bodies of water. In 1871, Bannister moved from Boston to Providence, Rhode Island, where he lived until his death. He was the only nineteenth-century African-American artist who did not travel to Europe to study art, believing that he was an American and that he wished to paint as an American. Bannister became one of the most outstanding artists in Providence in the 1870s and 1880s, and in 1880 became one of seven founders of the Providence Art Club, which was later known as the Rhode Island School of Design. His notable works include *After the Storm; Driving Home the Cows;* and *Narragansett Bay.*

Born in 1901 in Bay St. Louis, Mississippi, Barthe was educated at the Art Institute of Chicago from 1924 to 1928. He studied under Charles Schroeder and Albin Polasek. Barthe's first love was painting, but it was through his experiments with sculpture that he began initially to gain critical attention in 1927. His first commissions were busts of Henry Ossawa Tanner and Toussaint L'Ouverture. The acclaim resulting from them led to a one-man show in Chicago and a Rosenwald fellowship for study in New York City.

Richmond Barthe (1901–1989)

Sculptor

Barthe's work has been exhibited at several major American museums. The Metropolitan Museum of Art in New York City purchased *The Boxer* in 1943. In 1946 he received the first commission given to a black for a bust of Booker T. Washington for New York University's Hall of Fame. A year later he was one of the committee of fifteen artists chosen to help modernize sculpture in the Catholic churches of the United States.

Barthe held membership in the National Academy of Arts and Letters. He died March 6, 1989 at his home in Pasadena, California at the age of eighty-eight. His notable works include *Singing Slave; Maurice Ens; Lot's Wife;* and *Henry O. Tanner.*

Jean-Michel Basquiat (1960–1988)

Painter

In a brief, tragic career, Jean-Michel Basquiat gained attention from wealthy collectors as a young artist discovered by Andy Warhol and promoted by other art consultants. He was raised in Brooklyn and attracted the New York art world with his trendy personal appearance (tangled dreadlocks) and his flair as a musician and artist at the age of eighteen. His works are autobiographical and deliberately "primitive" in style. In February 1985 he was featured on the cover of the *New York Times Magazine,* shoeless but wearing a suit, shirt, and tie.

The Whitney Museum of American Art in New York City owns many of the six hundred works Basquiat produced, reportedly valued in the tens of millions of dollars (indicative of the excesses of the 1980s). The Whitney Museum mounted a retrospective exhibit of his work, from October 23, 1992, to February 14, 1993.

Basquiat began his career illegally spray painting images on buildings throughout the city, and he has said that his subject matter was "royalty, heroism and the streets." Basquiat reportedly died of a drug overdose. His notable works include *Self Portrait as a Heel #3; Untitled (History of Black People); Hollywood Africans;* and *CPRKR* (in honor of Charlie Parker).

Romare Bearden (1914–1988)

Painter, Collagist

Romare Bearden was born in Charlotte, North Carolina. His family moved to Pittsburgh and later to Harlem. Bearden studied with George Grosz at the Art Students League and later, on the G.I. Bill, went to Paris where he met Matisse, Joan Miró, and Carl Holty. A product of the new generation of African Americans who had migrated from the rural areas of the South to the urban areas of the North, Bearden's work reflected the era of industrialization. His would become the visual images that would reflect the city life, the music (jazz), and the city people. Bearden's earlier works belonged to the school of social realism, but after his return from Europe his images became more abstract.

In the 1960s, Bearden changed his approach to picture-making and began to make collages, soon becoming one of the best known collagists in the

Pepper Jelly Lady, *Romare Bearden, 1980.*

world. His images are haunting montages of his memories of past experiences, and of stories told to him by other people. They are for Bearden "an attempt to redefine the image of man in terms of the black experience." His notable works include *Street Corner; He Is Arisen; The Burial; Sheba;* and *The Prevalence of Ritual.*

John Biggers
(1924–)

Painter

John Biggers has been a leading figure in social realism as a painter, sculptor, printmaker, and teacher, as well as an outstanding surrealistic muralist.

Born in Gastonia, North Carolina in 1924, Biggers has derived much of his subject matter from the contributions made by blacks to the development of the United States. While teaching at Texas Southern University, Biggers has become a significant influence on several young black painters.

Some of his most powerful pieces have been created as a result of his study trips to Africa: *The Time of Ede, Nigeria,* a series of works done in the 1960s, are prime examples. His notable works include *Cradle; Mother and Child; The Contributions of Negro Women to American Life and Education;* and *Shotgun, Third Ward, #1.*

Camille Billops
(1933–)

Sculptor, Photographer,
Filmmaker

A sculptor of note in the art and retailing world, Camille Billops was born in California, graduated from California State College in 1960, and then studied sculpture on the West Coast under a grant from the Huntington Hartford Foundation. In 1960, she had her first exhibition at the African Art Exhibition in Los Angeles, followed in 1963 by an exhibit at the Valley Cities Jewish Community Center in Los Angeles. In 1966, she participated in a group exhibition in Moscow. Since then, her multifaceted artistic talents, which include poetry, book illustration, and jewelry making, have earned the praise of critics throughout the world, particularly in Sri Lanka and Egypt, where she has lived and worked.

Billops has also taught extensively. In 1975, she was active on the faculties of the City University of New York and Rutgers at Newark, New Jersey. In addition, she has conducted special art courses in the New York City jail (the Tombs) and in 1972 lectured in India for the United States Information Service on black American artists. She participated in an exhibit at the New York Cultural Center in 1973.

Billops is a printmaker, filmmaker, and photographer who has also been active in the mail-art movement, which has made art more accessible to the public. She has written articles for the *New York Times, Amsterdam News,* and *Newsweek.*

She has received grants for film from such institutions as the New York State Council on the Arts, in 1987, 1988, and 1989; and the New York Foundation for the Arts, in 1989.

In 1992, Billops won the prestigious Grand Jury Prize for Best Documentary at the Sundance Film Festival with *Finding Christa*, an edited combination of interviews, home movies, still images, and dramatic acting. Her notable works include *Tenure; Black American; Portrait of an American Indian* (all three are ceramic sculptures); and *Year after Year* (a painting).

Robert Blackburn (1921–)

Printmaker

Robert Blackburn was born in New York City. He studied at the Harlem Workshop, the Art Students League, and the Wallace Harrison School of Art. His exhibits include *Art of the American Negro,* 1940; *Contemporary Art of the American Negro,* 1966; exhibits in New York's Downtown Gallery and the Albany Museum; and numerous print shows in the United States and Europe. His work is represented in the Library of Congress, the Brooklyn and Baltimore museums, and the Atlanta University Collections. He is a member of the art faculty of Cooper Union.

Along with his other accomplishments, in 1949 he founded the Printmaking Workshop as an artist-run cooperative. In 1971, it was incorporated as a non-profit printmaking studio for work in lithography, etching, relief, and photo-processes. The workshop, a magnet for third-world and minority artists that reflects Blackburn's warmth and encouraging personalty, remains a haven for artists "to turn out prints for the love of it" and to do anything from experimental hodgepodge to polished pieces. In 1988, Bob Blackburn and the Printmaking Workshop were given the Governor's Art Award for making "a significant contribution to the cultural life of New York State." His notable works include *Boy with Green Head* and *Negro Mother.*

Selma Burke (1900–)

Sculptor, Educator

Selma Burke is an artist whose career has spanned more than sixty years. She was born in Mooresville, North Carolina and received her training as a sculptor at Columbia University in New York. She also studied with Maillol in Paris and with Povoley in Vienna. World War II interrupted her work in Europe and she returned to the United States to continue her artistic and humanitarian pursuits. She is best known for her relief sculpture rendering of Franklin Delano Roosevelt that was minted on the American dime.

Founder of the Selma Burke Art Center in Pittsburgh, Pennsylvania, she has taught and supported numerous artists from the period of the depression through the present day.

The Pearl S. Buck Foundation Woman's Award was given to Burke in 1987 for her professional distinction and devotion to family and humanity. Her notable works include *Falling Angel; Peace;* and *Jim.*

Stephen Burrows
(1943-)

Fashion Designer

Stephen Burrows was born September 15, 1943 in Newark, New Jersey. He studied at his grandmother's knee as a boy and started making clothes at quite a young age. He later studied at the Philadelphia Museum College of Art and the Fashion Institute of Technology in New York City.

With a partner, he opened a boutique in 1968. He worked for Henri Bendel from 1969 to 1973 and returned to Bendel's in 1977. From 1974 to 1977 he and a partner ran a Seventh Avenue firm.

Known for his unique color combinations, he used patches of cloth for decorative motifs in the 1960s. His top-stitching of seams in contrasting threads and top-stitched hems, known as "lettuce hems" because of their fluted effect, were widely copied. His designs show an inclination toward asymmetry and a preference for soft, clinging, easy-moving fabrics such as chiffon and matte jersey. His clothes were adopted readily by disco dancers, for whom he designed clothing in natural fabrics with non-constricting, light, and airy qualities. He won a Coty American Fashion Critics' Award in 1974 and a special Coty Award in 1977.

Elizabeth Catlett
(1915-)

Sculptor, Painter

The granddaughter of North Carolina slaves, Elizabeth Catlett was raised in northwest Washington, DC. As a young woman she attempted to gain admission into a then all-white art school, Carnegie Institute of Technology in Pittsburgh, Pennsylvania. She was refused entry and instead went to Howard University and graduated as an honor student in 1937. In 1940, she went on to study at the University of Iowa, where she became the first of their students to receive an M.F.A.

Her exhibition history dates back to 1937 and includes group and solo presentations at all the major American art museums as well as institutions in Mexico City, Moscow, Paris, Prague, Tokyo, Beijing, Berlin, and Havana. Catlett's public sculpture can be found in Mexico City, Mexico; Jackson, Mississippi; New Orleans, Louisiana; Washington, DC; and New York City. Her work is represented in the permanent collection of over twenty museums throughout the world. The artist resides in Cuernavaca, Mexico.

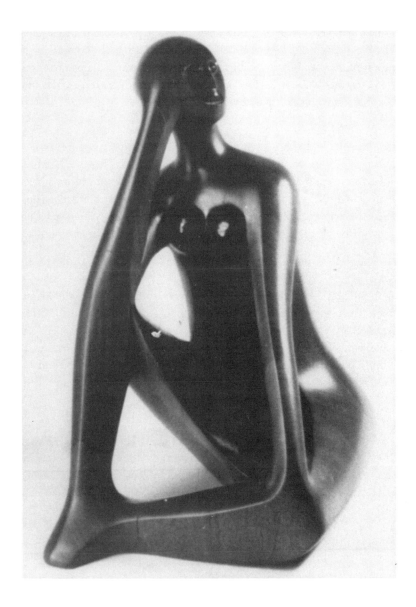

Woman Resting,

Elizabeth Catlett

Catlett accepted teaching positions at various black colleges to earn a living, but by 1946 she had moved to Mexico, where she eventually settled. Always a champion of the oppressed—concerned with the documentation of economic, social, and political themes—Catlett became deeply involved with the civil-rights movement, and it greatly affected her philosophy of life and art. Between 1941 and 1969, Catlett won eight prizes and honors, four in Mexico and four in America. Her notable works include *Black Unity* (1968); *Target Practice* (1970); *Mother and Child* (1972); and *Woman Resting* (1981).

Dana Chandler

(1941–)

Painter

Dana Chandler is one of the most visible, outspoken, and provocative black painters on the American scene. Chandler's huge, colorful black power murals can be spotted throughout the ghetto area of Boston, a constant reminder of the resolve and determination displayed by the new breed of young black urban dwellers.

"All this stuff whites are buying," Chandler says, "tells the black man a lot about where the white community is at, namely, nowhere." Chandler's easel works are bold and simple. One, *The Golden Prison*, shows a black man with a yellow and red striped flag "because America has been yellow and cowardly in dealing with the black man." *Freddie Hampton's Door* shows a bullet-splintered door bearing a stamp of U.S. government approval.

Born in Lynn, Massachusetts, Chandler received his B.S. from the Massachusetts College of Art in 1967. Chandler is currently a professor in the Art Department at Simmons College in Boston, Massachusetts. His notable works include *Fred Hampton's Door; Martin Luther King, Jr. Assassinated; Death of Uncle Tom; Rebellion '68; Dynamite; Death of a Bigot;* and *The Golden Prison.*

Robert Colescott

(1925–)

Painter

Robert Colescott was born in California in 1925. He received his B.A. in 1949 from the University of California and his M.A. in 1952 from the same university. In 1953, Colescott studied in Paris with Fernand Leger. His exhibitions include the Whitney Museum of American Art 1983 Biennial; the Hirshhorn Museum and Sculpture Garden in Washington, DC, 1984; and the Institute of Contemporary Art at the University of Pennsylvania in 1985.

His works are displayed in the Metropolitan Museum of Art, the Portland Art Museum, the Delaware Museum of Art, the Baltimore Museum of Art, and the University of Massachusetts's fine art collection.

A controversial artist criticized by both African-American groups and traditionalists, Colescott's work questions the "heroic" and "pushes the standards of taste." He has substituted black figures in place of white figures in famous European paintings as he explores racism and sex in his works, along with other taboos and stereotypes. His notable works include *Homage to Delacroix: Liberty Leading the People; Eat Dem Taters; Shirley*

Temple Black and Bill Robinson White; The Power of Desire; and *The Desire for Power.*

Born in Kentucky in 1947, Conwill spent three years studying for the priesthood. His Catholic upbringing plays a part in his art, which draws from American and African myths and religions. In his explorations, he generally uses non-traditional materials, such as latex substituted for canvas. The environments that he builds, paints, and fills with real chalices, candlesticks, carpet, or sand are works to which he adds his own personal iconography as well as some ancient symbols. Notable works include *The Cakewalk Manifesto; Passion of St. Matthew; East Shout;* and *JuJu Funk.*

Houston Conwill (1947–)

Performance Artist, Environmental Artist

Emilio Cruz was born in New York in 1938. His education includes work at the Art Students' League under Edwin Dickinson, George Grosz, and Frank J. Reilly. Cruz has exhibited widely since 1959, and his recent exhibits have included the Anita Shapolsky Gallery in 1986 and 1991; The Studio Museum in Harlem in 1987; the Portland Museum of Art in 1987; the Rhode Island School of Design in 1987; the Gwenda Jay Gallery in Chicago in 1991; and G.R. N'namdi Gallery in Birmingham, Michigan, in 1991.

An artist whose works are narrative and formalistic, emphasizing color and forms as the dominant elements, Cruz combines these two theoretical approaches often with figurative subjects.

His awards include the Cintas Foundation fellowship, 1965–66; the John Hay Whitney fellowship, 1964–65; and the Walter Gutman Foundation Award, 1962. His notable works include *Silver Umbrella; Figure Composition 6;* and *Striated Voodoo.*

Emilio Cruz (1938–)

Painter

Roy DeCarava is an urban man. His existence in New York City prepared him for his destined work as a photographer. He began as a commercial artist in 1938 by studying painting at Cooper Union. This was followed by classes at the Harlem Art Center from 1940 to 1942, where he concentrated on painting and printmaking. By the mid-1940s, he began to use photography as a convenient method of recording ideas for his paintings. In 1958, DeCarava gave up his commercial work and became a full-time freelance photographer. Edward Steichen, a very important photographer

Roy DeCarava (1919–)

Photographer

at this time, began to study his work and suggested that he apply for a Guggenheim fellowship. Winning the award allowed DeCarava the financial freedom to take his pictures and tell his story. One of DeCarava's photographs from this body of work appeared in Steichen's exhibition, "Family of Man," at the Museum of Modern Art. Later, Langston Hughes worked with DeCarava to create the book *Sweet Flypaper of Life.*

DeCarava has worked as a photographer for *Sports Illustrated* and taught photography at Hunter College, New York. His work can be found in many important collections throughout the country, among them the Andover Art Gallery of Andover-Phillips Academy, Massachusetts; the Art Institute of Chicago; Atlanta University; Belafonte Enterprises, Inc., in New York; the Center for Creative Photography at the University of Arizona; the Corcoran Gallery of Art in Washington, DC; the Harlem Art Collection in the New York State Office Building; the Lee Witkin Gallery in New York; the Menil Foundation in Houston, Texas; Houston's Metropolitan Museum of Fine Arts; New York's Museum of Modern Art; Olden Camera in New York; Joseph E. Seagram & Sons in New York; and the Sheldon Memorial Art Gallery at the University of Nebraska.

Beauford Delaney

(1910–1979)

Painter

Born in Knoxville, Tennessee, Beauford Delaney was described by his elder brother Samuel as a "remarkably dutiful child." His father, the Reverend Samuel Delaney, and his mother, Delia Johnson Delaney, understood and recognized Beauford's artistic talent, as well as that of his brother Joseph, and they encouraged them to develop their skills. For Beauford Delaney, recognition came by way of an elderly white artist of Knoxville, Lloyd Branson. Branson gave him lessons and after a time urged him to go to a city where he might study and come into contact with the art world.

In 1924, Beauford Delaney went to Boston to study at the Massachusetts Normal School, later studying at the Copley Society, where he took evening courses while working full-time at the South Boston School of Art. From Boston, Delaney moved on to New York.

Delaney took on the life of a bohemian in New York, living in the Village in coldwater flats. Much of his time was spent painting the portraits of the personalities of the day, such as Louis Armstrong, Ethel Waters, and Duke Ellington. In 1938, Beauford Delaney gained national attention when *Life Magazine,* in an article on "negroes," featured a photograph of him surrounded by a group of his paintings at the annual outdoor exhibition in Washington Square in New York. In 1945, Henry Miller wrote the essay "The Amazing and Invariable Beauford Delaney," which was later reprinted in *Remember to Remember*. The essay describes Delaney's bohemian life-style in New York during the 1940s and 1950s.

In the 1950s, Delaney left New York with the intention of studying in Rome. Taking the *Ile de France*, he sailed to Paris, next visiting Greece, Turkey, and Northern Italy—but he never got to Rome. Returning to Paris for one more visit, Delaney began to paint, make new friends, and create a social life filled with the famous and the soon-to-be-famous, like James Baldwin, who at that time had not yet become a renowned novelist. Paris was to become Delaney's permanent home.

By 1961, Delaney was producing paintings at such an intense rate that the pressure began to wear upon his strength, and he suffered his first mental collapse. He was confined to a clinic in Vincennes, and his dealer and close friends began to organize his life, hoping to relieve some of the pressure, but it was of little use. For the rest of his life, Delaney was to suffer sporadic breakdowns and by 1971 was back in a sanitarium, where he remained until his death in 1979.

Delaney's numerous exhibitions included the Artists Gallery in New York, 1948; the Roko Gallery in New York, 1950–1953; the Musée d'Art Moderne in Paris, 1963; the American Negro Exposition in Chicago, 1940; and Newark Museum, 1971. His work can be found in the collections of the Whitney Museum of American Art, New York; the Newark Museum, New Jersey; and Morgan State College in Baltimore, Maryland. Notable works include *Greene Street; Yaddo; Head of a Poet;* and *Snow Scene*.

Aaron Douglas (1899–1988)

Painter

Born in Topeka, Kansas in 1899, Aaron Douglas achieved considerable eminence as a muralist, illustrator, and academician. As a young man, Douglas studied at the University of Nebraska, Columbia University Teachers College, and l'Academie Scandinave in Paris. He had one-person exhibits at the universities of Kansas and Nebraska and also exhibited in New York at the Gallery of Modern Art. In 1939, Douglas was named to the faculty of Fisk University and later became head of its Department of Art.

In 1992, Fisk opened a new gallery in his memory. Douglas is considered the most important painter and illustrator of the "Negro Renaissance" that is now known as the Harlem Renaissance. His notable works include murals at Fisk and in the Countee Cullen Branch of the New York City Public Library, and illustrations in books by Countee Cullen, James Weldon Johnson, Alain Locke, and Langston Hughes. Marian Anderson and Mary McLeod Bethune are among the many African Americans he painted or rendered in charcoal.

David Clyde Driskell

(1931–)

Painter, Historian

Born in Eatonton, Georgia, Driskell studied at Howard University and Catholic University of America, where he received an M.A. in 1962. He also studied at the Skowhegan School of Painting and Sculpture and the Netherlands Institute for History of Art. He has taught at Talladega College, Fisk University, the Institute for African Studies of the University of Ife in Nigeria, and the University of Maryland at College Park.

Immediately after the death of Alonzo Aden, Driskell was asked to direct the gallery housing the important Barnett–Aden collection of African-American art. He has curated and mounted important exhibitions, including the impressive *200 Years of African-American Art,* shown at major museums across the country.

A recipient of many awards, including the John Hope Award and prizes from the Danforth Foundation, American Federation of Arts, and Harmon Foundation, Driskell has exhibited at the Corcoran Art Gallery, National Museum, and Rhodes National Gallery in Salisbury, Rhodesia. Notable works include *Movement; The Mountain; Still Life with Gateleg Table;* and *Shango Gone.*

Robert Duncanson

(1817–1872)

Painter

Robert Duncanson was the son of an African-American woman and a Scottish-Canadian man. Born in upstate New York, he was to spend much of his childhood in Canada. At some point in his youth, he and his mother moved to Mt. Healthy, Ohio, where in 1840 the Western Freedmen's Aid Society, an anti-slavery group, raised funds to send him to Glasgow, Scotland, to study art. Returning to Cincinnati three years later, Duncanson advertised in the local newspaper as the proprietor of a daguerreotype studio. Even though he had begun gaining a reputation as a painter, he continued to work at his daguerreotype until 1855, when he started to devote all of his time to his painting. Like many landscape artists of this time, Duncanson traveled around the United States, drawing his compositions from the images of nature before him. In 1853, he made his second trip to Europe—this time to visit Italy, France, and England.

Duncanson was painting during and after the Civil War era, though with the exception of his painting *Uncle Tom and Eva,* he made no attempts to present the turmoil that was taking place in America or the social pressures that he experienced. In September 1872, Duncanson, while at the height of his success, suffered a severe mental breakdown and ended his life on December 21 in the Michigan State Retreat in Detroit. His notable works include murals in the Taft Museum and *Bishop Payne.*

William Edmonson was a stonecutter and self-taught sculptor who was born in Nashville, Tennessee. He supported himself working as a hospital orderly at Baptist Hospital and through other menial jobs. His work was discovered by Mrs. Meyer Dahl-Wolfe, who had an extensive private collection, and who brought him to the attention of the Museum of Modern Art. In an exhibition of self-taught artists, his work was received extremely well. In 1937 he was the first African American to have a one-person exhibit at the museum. Private collectors and museums have purchased his few sculptures, which are vigorously executed and original.

William Edmonson (1882–1951)

Sculptor

Inspired by biblical passages, Edmonson engraved tombstones and worked on his sculpture, which he did in limestone, at the home he shared with his mother and sister. He continued to live alone and work there after their deaths, until he died in 1951. Notable works include *Choir Girls; Lion;* and *Crucifixion.*

Elton Fax stands among America's leading fine artists and illustrators. He is also a noted essayist. Both his drawings and his writings reflect a proud interest in the African legacy of American blacks.

Elton Fax (1909–)

Illustrator, Writer

Born in Baltimore, he graduated from Syracuse University with a B.F.A. in 1931. He taught at Claflin University from 1935 to 1936, and was an instructor at the Harlem Community Art Center from 1938 to 1939. His work has been exhibited at the Baltimore Art Museum, 1939; American Negro Exposition, 1940; the Metropolitan Museum of Art; and Visual Arts Gallery, New York, 1970. Examples of his work hang in some of the nation's best university collections, including Texas Southern, the University of Minnesota, and Virginia State University.

Publications by Fax are *Africa Vignettes; Garvey; Seventeen Black Artists;* and *Black Artists of the New Generation. The Portfolio Black and Beautiful*

Elton Fax is one of America's leading fine artists and illustrators, as well as a noted essayist.

features his art work, and he has written *Hashar* about the life of the people of Soviet Central Asia and Kazakhstan. His notable works include *Steelworker; Ethiopia Old & New; Contemporary Black Leaders;* and *Through Black Eyes.*

Meta Vaux Warrick Fuller (1877–1968)

Sculptor

Meta Vaux Warrick Fuller was a part of the transitional period between the artists who chose to simulate Euro-American subjects and styles and the later periods to follow. Her African-American figures in *The Wretched,* exhibited at the Paris Salon in 1903 and 1904, did not suit popular tastes, but they were sincere expressions of the talented artist.

Born in 1877 in Philadelphia and educated at the School of Industrial Art and the Pennsylvania Academy, Fuller's interest in sculpture led her to study with Charles Grafly and with Rodin at the Academie Colarossi in Paris. She was the first African-American woman to become a professional artist.

She married and settled in the Boston area where, in 1910, most of her works were destroyed by fire. The Boston Art Club and the Harmon Foundation exhibited her works, and today representative pieces of her sculpture can be found in the Cleveland Museum.

Mississippi-born Sam Gilliam produces hanging canvases that are laced with pure color pigments rather than shades or tones. The artist bunches these pigments in weird configurations on drooping, drapelike canvases, giving the effect, in the words of *Time* magazine, of "clothes drying on a line." His canvases are said to be "like nobody else's, black or white."

**Sam Gilliam
(1933–)**

Painter

Gilliam received his M.A. from the University of Louisville, and was awarded National Endowment of Humanities and Arts grants. He has had one-man and group shows at the Washington Gallery of Modern Art; Jefferson Place Gallery; Adams-Morgan Gallery in Washington, DC; the Art Gallery of Washington University in St. Louis, Missouri; the Speed Museum in Louisville; the Philadelphia Museum of Art; the Museum of Modern Art; the Phillips Collection and Corcoran Gallery of Art, both in Washington, DC; the San Francisco Museum of Art; the Walker Art Center in Minneapolis; and the Whitney Museum of American Art. He is represented in the permanent collection of over forty-five American museums.

Gilliam has also been represented in several group exhibitions, including the First World Festival of Negro Arts in Dakar, Senegal (1966), "The Negro in American Art" at UCLA (1967), and the Whitney Museum's American Art Annual (1969).

In 1980, Sam Gilliam was commissioned, with thirteen other artists, to design an art piece for installation in the Atlanta, Georgia Airport Terminal, one of the largest terminals in the world and the first to install contemporary artwork on its walls for public viewing. His notable works include *Watercolor4* (1969); *Herald* (1965); *Carousel Change* (1970); *Mazda* (1970); and *Plantagenets Golden* (1984).

Richard Hunt was born in Chicago and began his formal career after studying at the School of the Art Institute of Chicago, where he received a number of awards.

**Richard Hunt
(1935–)**

Painter, Sculptor

After graduating in 1957, Hunt was given the James Nelson Raymond Traveling Fellowship. He later taught at the School of the Art Institute of

Chicago and at the University of Illinois. From 1962 to 1963, he pursued his craft while under a Guggenheim fellowship.

Hunt's solo presentations have appeared at the Cleveland Museum of Art; Milwaukee Art Center; Museum of Modern Art; Art Institute of Chicago; Springfield Art Museum in Massachusetts; Indianapolis Museum of Art; and a U.S.I.S.-sponsored show throughout Africa that was organized by the Los Angeles Museum of African American Art. Hunt sits on the board of governors at the School of the Art Institute of Chicago and the Skowhegan School of Painting and Sculpture; he is a commissioner at the National Museum of American Art in Washington, DC; and he serves on the advisory committee at the Getty Center for Education in the Arts in Malibu.

His works are in the New York Museum of Modern Art; the Cleveland Museum of Art; the Art Institute of Chicago; Hirshhorn Museum in Washington, DC; the Museum of 20th Century Art in Vienna, Austria; the National Museum of Art in Washington, DC; the Albright Knox Gallery in Buffalo, New York; and Howard University. His notable works include *Man on a Vehicular Construct* (1956); *Linear Spatial Theme* (1962); *The Chase* (1965); and *Arching* (1986).

**Larry Johnson
(1949–)**

Painter, Illustrator,
Editorial Cartoonist

Born in Boston, Massachusetts, Larry Johnson attended Boston schools and the School of the Boston Museum of Fine Arts. He became a staff illustrator at *The Boston Globe* in 1968, where he covered many assignments, including courtroom sketches, sports events, entertainment, editorial sports cartoons and drawings, and other features. Johnson is now nationally syndicated through Universal Press Syndicate.

Barry Gaither, director of the National Center of African-American artists in Boston, says, "Johnson's works can be divided horizontally between commercial illustration and fine art, and vertically between drawings and paintings in acrylics and watercolor." In addition to working for the *Globe,* Johnson worked for the now defunct *National Sports Daily* and has designed book jackets for Little Brown. Commissioned by Pepsi-Cola, the *Old Farmer's Almanac,* the National Football League, *Fortune,* and others, he has left the *Globe* to freelance and run his own company, Johnson Editions, a producer of fine arts prints and other multiples, such as greeting cards. Johnson was awarded the Associated Press Editorial Cartoon Award in 1985. His notable works include *Island Chisel; Rainbow;* and *Promises.*

Born in Detroit, Michigan, Johnson attended the University of Michigan, where he received a B.F.A. in 1973 and an M.F.A. in 1974. He teaches at the Center for Creative Studies at the College of Art and Design in Detroit, Michigan.

His works are in many collections, including the Detroit Institute of Arts; Osaka University Arts, Japan; Johnson Publishers and The Masonite Corp., Chicago; Sonnenblick-Goldman Corp., New York; Taubman Co., Inc., Bloomfield Hills, Michigan; and St. Paul Co., St. Paul, Minnesota.

Commissions have included *Urban Wall Murals,* Detroit, 1974; New Detroit Receiving Hospital, 1980; and Martin Luther King Community Center. Johnson has exhibited at major institutions, including the Whitney Museum of American Art Biennial, 1973; National African-American Exhibit, Carnegie Institute, Pittsburgh, Pennsylvania; National Academy of Design, Henry Ward Ranger National Invitational, 1977.

Among his awards are the Andrew W. Mellon Foundation grant, 1982 and 1984; and a recognition award from the African-American Music Art Association.

Lester L. Johnson (1937–)

Painter, Educator

Sargent Johnson, who three times won the Harmon Foundation's medal as the nation's outstanding black artist, worked in stylized idioms—heavily influenced by the art forms of Africa—in sculpture, mural bas-reliefs, metal sculpture, and ceramics.

Born in Boston, he studied at the Worcester Art School and moved west to the San Francisco Bay area in 1915, where his teachers were Beniamino Bufano and Ralph Stackpole. He exhibited at the San Francisco Artists Annual, 1925–1931; the Harmon Foundation, 1928–1931 and 1933; the Art Institute of Chicago, 1930; Baltimore Museum, 1939; and the American Negro Exposition in Chicago, 1940. He was the recipient of numerous awards and prizes.

From the beginning of his career he spoke of his sculpture as an attempt to show the "natural beauty and dignity of the pure American Negro" and wished to present "that beauty not so much to the white man as to the Negro himself. Unless I can interest my race, I am sunk." His notable

Sargent Johnson (1888–1967)

Sculptor

works include *Sammy; Esther; Golden Gate Exposition Aquatic Park Murals;* and *Forever Free.*

William H. Johnson (1901–1970)

Painter

William H. Johnson was a pioneer black modernist whose ever-developing work went from abstract expressionist landscape and flower studies influenced by Van Gogh, to studies of black life in America, and finally to abstract figure studies in the manner of Rouault.

Born in Florence, South Carolina, he studied at the National Academy of Design; the Cape Cod School of Art, under Charles Hawthorne; in southern France from 1926 to 1929; and in Denmark and Norway from 1930 to 1938. His exhibits include Harmon Foundation (which awarded him a gold medal in 1929); Aarlins, Denmark, 1935; the Baltimore Museum, 1939; and the American Negro Exposition in Chicago, 1940. He produced one-person shows in Copenhagen in 1935 and at New York's Artists Gallery in 1938. His notable works include *Booker T. Washington; Young Man in Vest; Descent from the Cross;* and *On a John Brown Flight.*

Joshua Johnston (c. 1765–1830)

Painter

Active between 1789 and 1825, Joshua Johnston is the first known black portrait painter from the Baltimore area. At least two dozen paintings have been attributed to this artist, who was listed as a "free house-holder of colour, portrait painter." He was listed in the Baltimore directories in various studio locations.

It is believed Johnston may have been a former slave of Charles Wilson Peale, the artist who is known for having started a drawing school in Maryland in 1795; or Johnston may have simply known the artist and his works. In either case, Johnston was most likely self-taught. A portraitist in the true style of the period, his work now seems quaint and sensitive. Only one black subject has been attributed to him, *Portrait of a Cleric.* Notable works include *Portrait of Adelia Ellender; Portrait of Mrs. Barbara Baker Murphy;* and *Portrait of Sea Captain John Murphy.*

Ben Jones (1942–)

Painter, Sculptor

Ben Jones was born in Patterson, New Jersey, and studied at the School of Visual Arts; New York University, where he received an M.A.; Pratt Institute; the University of Science & Technology, Ghana; and the New School of Social Research.

A professor of Fine Arts at Jersey City State College, Jones lives in New York. His sculptures (made during the height of the Black Art Movement in 1970) were cast in plaster from living models and painted in brightly colored patterns, as if inspired by traditional African symbols. Images of masks, and arms and legs arranged in multiples or singly, seem to have roots in African ceremony ritual and magic.

His pieces are in such collections as the Newark Museum; Studio Museum in Harlem; Howard University; and Johnson Publications in Chicago. His exhibits have included the Museum of Modern Art; Studio Museum in Harlem; the Black World Arts Festival in Lagos, Nigeria; Newark Museum; and Fisk University in Nashville, Tennessee.

Jones's awards have included grants from the National Endowment for the Arts, the New Jersey Arts Council, and Delta Sigma Theta Sorority. His notable works include *Five Black Face Images; High Priestess of Soul;* and *Untitled (6 Arms).*

A native of Detroit, Michigan and the daughter of a Ford Motor Company employee, Emeline King acquired an ambition at an early age to design cars. King is a designer at the Ford Motor Company's Mustang studio.

Emeline King

Automobile Designer

King joined the company in 1983 after she graduated from Wayne State University, where she majored in industrial design. She also studied in Detroit at the Center for Creative Studies. The Art Center College of Design in Pasadena, California awarded her a bachelor of science degree in transportation.

Born in 1917 in Atlantic City, New Jersey, Jacob Lawrence received his early training at the Harlem Art School and the American Artist School. His rise to prominence was ushered in by his series of biographical panels commemorating important episodes in African-American history. Capturing the essential meaning behind a historical moment or personality, Lawrence has created several series, each consisting of dozens of small paintings that depict a particular event in American history, such as *The Migration Series* ("...and the Migrants keep coming"), which traces the migration of the African American from the South to the North, or the events of a person's life (e.g., Toussaint L'Ouverture and John Brown). A narrative painter, Lawrence relates the "philosophy of Impressionism" in his work.

**Jacob Lawrence
(1917–)**

Painter

Jacob Lawrence stands beside one of his paintings at the Institute of Modern Art in Boston, 1945.

Lawrence is a visual American historian. His paintings record the African American in trade, theater, mental hospitals, neighborhoods, or running in the Olympic races. Lawrence's works are found in such collections as the Metropolitan Museum of Art, the Museum of Modern Art, the Whitney Museum of American Art, the National Museum of American Art, and the Wadsworth Atheneum in Hartford, Connecticut.

Lawrence lives in Seattle, Washington. His notable works include *The Life of Toussaint L'Ouverture* (forty-one panels; 1937); *The Life of Harriet Tubman* (forty panels; 1939); and *The Negro Migration Northward in World War* (sixty panels; 1942).

Hughie Lee-Smith
(1915-)
Painter

Hughie Lee-Smith was born in 1915 in Eustis, Florida. He studied at Wayne State University, where he received his B.S. in art education. He later attended the Cleveland Institute of Art, where he was awarded the Gilpin Players Scholarship; the Art School of the Detroit Society of Arts and Crafts; and John Huntington Polytechnic Institute. From childhood he was encouraged to pursue his art, and he has enjoyed a long and productive career.

His paintings often depict decaying ghetto environments in the state of revitalization. His subjects seem to suggest desolation or alienation, but balloons or waving banners in the scene counter the mood in their expression of hope and gaiety.

Lee-Smith's one-person shows and exhibitions are too numerous to list. He has received more than a dozen important prizes, including the Founders Prize of the Detroit Institute of Arts (1953), Emily Lowe Award (1957, 1985), Ralph Fabri Award, Audubon Artists, Inc. (1982), Binny and Smith Award (1983), and Len Everette Memorial Prize, Audubon Artists, Inc. (1986). He is a member of the Allied Artists of America; the Michigan Academy of the Arts, Sciences & Letters; and the Artists Equity Association. His notable works include *Portrait of a Sailor; Old Man and Youth; Waste Land; Little Diana;* and *Aftermath.*

Edmonia Lewis was America's first black woman artist and also the first of her race and gender to be recognized as a sculptor. Born in 1845 in up-state New York, she was the daughter of a Chippewa Indian woman and a free black man. From 1859 to 1863, under the patronage of a number of abolitionists, she was educated at Oberlin College, the first American college to admit women into an integrated environment.

After completing her schooling, Lewis moved to Boston, where she studied with Edmund Brackett and did a bust of Colonel Robert Gould Shaw, the commander of the first black regiment organized in the state of Massachusetts during the Civil War. In 1865 she moved to Rome, where she soon became a prominent artist. Returning to the United States in 1874, she fulfilled many commissions, including a bust of Henry Wadsworth Longfellow that was executed for the Harvard College Library.

Her works are fine examples of the neo-classical sculpture that was fashionable during her lifetime. It is believed that she died in Rome in 1890. Notable works include *Hagar in the Wilderness; Forever Free;* and *Hiawatha.*

Edmonia Lewis (1845–1890)

Sculptor

Norman Lewis was born in New York City in 1909. Lewis studied at Columbia University. He also studied under Augusta Savage, Raphael Soyer, Vaclav Vytacil, and Angela Streater. During the Great Depression he taught art through the Federal Art Project from 1936 to 1939 at the Harlem Art Center. He received a Carnegie International Award in painting in 1956 and has had several one-person shows at the Willard Gallery in New York.

As one of the artists to develop the abstract movement in the United States, Lewis participated in many group shows in such institutions as the

Norman Lewis (1909–1979)

Painter

Whitney Museum of American Art, the Metropolitan Museum of Art, and the Art Institute of Chicago. His notable works include *Arrival and Departure* and *Heroic Evening*.

Ionis Bracy Martin

(1936–)

Painter, Printmaker, Educator

Born in 1936 in Chicago, Illinois, Ionis Martin attended the Junior School of the Art Institute of Chicago before going to Fisk University, where she studied with Aaron Douglas and earned her B.S. in 1957. Martin received an M.Ed. degree from the University of Hartford in 1969 and an M.F.A. from Pratt Institute in Brooklyn, New York, in 1987. She is a trustee of the Wadsworth Atheneum, co-founder of the Artists Collective (with Jackie McLean, Dollie McLean, Paul Brown, and Cheryl Smith), co-trustee and chairman of the Ella Burr McManus Trust for the Alfred E. Burr Sculpture Mall, and a member of advisory board of the CRT Craftery Gallery in Hartford, Connecticut.

Exhibiting widely in the Hartford area, Martin has also exhibited in New York, Massachusetts, Fisk University in Nashville, and the University of Vermont. Among her many prizes and honors are a grant from the Connecticut Commission on the Arts (1969); a graduate fellowship in printmaking from Pratt Institute (1981); and a Summer-Six Fellowship from Skidmore College (1987).

A teacher at Weaver and Bloomfield High Schools since 1961, and a lecturer in African-American Art at Central Connecticut State University since 1985, Martin also lectures on and demonstrates serigraphy. Her notable works include *Mother and Child; Allyn's Garden; Gran' Daddy's Garden;* and *Little Women of the Amistad: Series.*

Geraldine

McCullough

(1928–)

Sculptor

Geraldine McCullough's steel and copper abstraction *Phoenix* won the George D. Widener Gold Medal at the 1964 exhibition of the Pennsylvania Academy of Fine Arts. Other distinguished artists who had won the same honor include Jacques Lipchitz and Theodore Roszak. Of further note is the fact that this was her first showing in a major national exhibition.

A native of Arkansas, McCullough has lived in Chicago since she was three and is a 1948 graduate of the Art Institute there. She also studied at the University of Chicago, DePaul University, Northwestern University, and the University of Illinois.

McCullough taught at Wendell Phillips High School in Chicago and at Rosary College in River Forest, Illinois. Currently, she works and resides in Oak Park, Illinois. She has received many awards and commissions. Her works are represented in collections at Howard University; in Oak Park, Illinois; the Oakland, California museum; and many others. Her notable works include *Bessie Smith; View from the Moon; Todd Hall Front; Atomic Rose; Phoenix;* and *Martin Luther King.*

Evangeline Montgomery was born in New York City. She received her B.F.A. from the California College of Arts and Crafts; she also studied with Jane Leland at Los Angeles City and State Colleges.

Evangeline J. Montgomery (1933–)

Jeweler, Photographer, Sculptor

Known for her metal boxes, incense burners, and jewelry, Montgomery has also been awarded prizes for her photography. Her works are in collections at the Oakland Museum and the University of Southern Illinois.

Active with many organizations, Montgomery has served on the San Francisco Art Commission; the National Conference of Artists; the advisory board for Parting Ways Ethnohistory Museum; the board of directors at the Museum of the National Center of Afro-American Artists; the American Museums Association; and the board of directors for the Washington, DC Arts Center.

Her awards have included a Smithsonian Fellowship and a museum grant from the National Endowment for the Arts. Among her notable works are *Ancestor Box 1* and *Justice for Angela Davis.*

Archibald Motley touched on many topics and themes in his work, but none was more gratifying to him than his candid depictions of black Americans.

Archibald Motley (1891–1980)

Painter

Born in New Orleans, Motley's artistic talent was apparent by the time he attended high school. His father wanted him to become a doctor, but Archibald insisted on art and began formal education at the Art Institute of Chicago, earning his living by working as a day laborer. During this time Motley came in contact with the drifters, scavengers, and hustlers of society, who are now immortalized in his street scenes. His genre scenes are highly stylized and colorful and are often associated with the Ash-Can school of art, which was popular in the 1920s.

Archibald Motley with one of his paintings, 1932.

In 1928 Motley had a one-person show at the new galleries in downtown New York and became the first artist, black or white, to make the front page of the *New York Times*. He was awarded a Guggenheim fellowship in 1929 and studied in France. He was the recipient of a Harmon Foundation award for an early portrait. His notable works include *The Jockey Club*; *The Plotters*; *Parisian Scene*; *Black Belt*; and *Old Snuff Dipper*.

John Wilfred Outterbridge (1933–)

Sculptor, Photographer, Painter

John Wilfred Outterbridge was born in Greenville, North Carolina. He studied at Agricultural and Technical University, Greensboro, North Carolina; the Chicago Art Academy; the American Academy of Art, Chicago; and the Art Center School of Design, Los Angeles. He has taught at California State University and Pasadena Art Museum. Outterbridge is currently director of the Watts Towers Art Center in Los Angeles.

Outterbridge's sculptures are assemblages constructed from discarded materials. Some of his works are tributes to African ancestors and to their descendants in Los Angeles at the Watts Towers Art Center and in other communities. Outterbridge is known for making and helping others create "Street Art," a combination of painting, relief sculpture, and construction that incorporates words and symbols expressing community goals and social ideas.

Outterbridge was featured in *Black Artists on Art*, Volume I. His notable works include *Shoeshine Box; Mood Ghetto;* and *Ethnic Heritage Group.*

Gordon Parks (1912–)

Photographer, Composer, Writer, Director

Parks was born on November 30, 1912 in Fort Scott, Kansas. After the death of his mother, Parks went to St. Paul, Minnesota to live with relatives. While there he attended Central and Mechanical Arts high schools. Despite having fond childhood memories of his father on the family farm, Parks had a dysfunctional upbringing that lasted into young adulthood. Parks worked at a large variety of jobs including janitor, busboy, and semi-pro basketball player. Always interested in the arts, Parks also tried sculpting, writing, and touring with a band, but these artistic endeavors were largely without focus.

In 1933 Parks joined the Civilian Conservation Corps, and in the late 1930s, while working as a railroad porter, he became interested in photography as a medium on which he could finally focus his considerable artistic talents. After purchasing a used camera, Parks worked as a freelance photographer and as a photo-journalist. In 1942 he became a correspondent for the Farm Security Administration, and from 1943 to 1945 he was a correspondent for the Office of War Information. After the war he worked for Standard Oil Company of New Jersey, and in 1948 he became a staff photographer for *Life* magazine. He soon achieved national acclaim for his photographs, and in the mid-1950s he began doing consulting work on Hollywood productions. In the 1960s Parks began doing television documentaries, and in 1966 he published his biography, *A Choice of Weapons.*

Parks is also the author of *The Learning Tree* (1963); *Born Black* (1971); *Gordon Parks: Whispers of Intimate Things* (1971); *Moments without Proper Names* (1975); *To Smile in Autumn* (1979); and *Voices in the Mirror* (1991). In 1968 Parks produced, directed, and wrote the script and music for the movie production of *The Learning Tree.* Parks also directed and scored the movies *Shaft* (1971) and *Shaft's Big Score* (1972).

Parks is a recipient of the NAACP's Spingarn Award (1972); the Rhode Island School of Design's Presidents Fellow Award (1984); and Kansan of the Year (1986); and in 1988 President Ronald Reagan presented him with the National Medal for the Arts.

Parks is a member of the NAACP, Urban League, Newspaper Guild, and Association of Composers and Directors.

Marion Perkins
(1908-1961)

Sculptor

Born in Marche, Arkansas, Perkins was largely a self-taught artist. He reportedly began scupturing by whittling bars of soap, and his early works were composed while he tended a newspaper stand on Chicago's South Side. He later studied privately with Simon Gordon, and the two men became close friends.

Perkins's work has been exhibited at the Art Institute of Chicago; American Negro Exposition (1940); Xavier University; and Rockland College, Illinois (1965). As artist in residence at Jackson State College in Mississippi, where much of his sculpture his housed, Perkins founded a scholarship fund for art students.

Marion Perkins shapes a semi-abstract African head from a piece of marble.

Born in Philadelphia, Howardena Pindell received her education at Boston University, where she earned a B.F.A. in 1965, and Yale University, where she obtained her M.F.A. in 1967. She first gained national recognition for her artistic skills in 1969 with the exhibition "American Drawing Biennial XXIII" at the Norfolk Museum of Arts and Sciences in Virginia. By the mid-1970s, Pindell's work began appearing in such exhibitions as "Eleven Americans in Paris" at the Gerald Piltzer Gallery, Paris, 1975; "Recent Acquisitions; Drawings" at the Museum of Modern Art, New York, 1976; and "Pindell: Video Drawings" at the Sonja Henie Onstad Foundation, Oslo, Norway, 1976.

Around this same time, Pindell began to travel around the world as a guest speaker. Some of her lectures included "Current American and Black American Art: A Historical Survey" at Madras College of Arts and Crafts, Madras, India, 1975; and "Black Artists, U.S.A.," Academy of Art, Oslo, Norway, 1976. She is currently a professor of art at State University of New York at Stony Brook.

Her work is part of the permanent collection in over thirty museums, including the Brooklyn Museum; High Museum in Atlanta; Newark Museum; Fogg Museum in Cambridge, Massachusetts; Whitney Museum of American Art; Museum of Modern Art; and the Metropolitan Museum of Art. Pindell has received two National Endowment for the Arts Fellowships and a Guggenheim Fellowship.

**Howardena Pindell
(1943–)**

Painter

Born in Philadelphia, Jerry Pinkney studied at the Philadelphia Museum College of Art. Pinkney has exhibited in illustrator shows throughout the country and is best known for his illustrations for children's books and textbooks.

From his studio in his home in Croton-on-Hudson, New York, Pinkney has been a major contributor to the United States Postal Service's stamps in the Black Heritage Series. Benjamin Bannecker, Martin Luther King, Jr., Scott Joplin, Jackie Robinson, Sojourner Truth, Carter W. Woodson, Whitney Moore Young, Mary McLeod Bethune, and Harriet Tubman stamps were designed by Pinkney, a Citizens' Stamp Advisory Committee member.

A recipient of many honors, he has earned acclaim for his illustrations in children's books. For example, *The Talking Eggs,* written by Robert San

**Jerry Pinkney
(1939–)**

Illustrator

Souci, was designated a Caldecott Medal honor book (Pinkney's second such honor), received a Coretta Scott King Honor Book Award, was named an American Library Association Notable Book, and won the Irma Simonton Black Award from the Bank Street College of Education.

Pinkney has worked in Boston as a designer and illustrator. He is one of the founders of Kaleidoscope Studio in Boston, where he also worked for the National Center of Afro-American Art. For a while he was a visiting critic for the Rhode Island School of Design. He has taught at Pratt Institute, the University of Delaware, and in the art department at the State University of New York at Buffalo. His notable works include *The Tales of Uncle Remus*, published by Dial Books; *Call It Courage*, written by Armstrong Sperry and published by Aladdin Books; and *Self Portrait*.

Horace Pippin
(1888–1946)

Painter

Horace Pippin has been ranked in the company of Henri Rousseau because of his accomplishment as a self-taught artist. Pippin was born in 1888 in West Chester, Pennsylvania, and painted steadily from 1920 until his death in 1946. Among his most vivid portrayals on canvas are the battle scenes that he remembered from his own experience in World War I, during which he was wounded and partially paralyzed.

Pippin's earliest works are designs burned into wood with a hot poker; to accomplish this, he had to guide his right arm with his left hand. He did not complete his first oil painting until 1930—after working on it for three years. He painted scenes of family reunions, Biblical stories, and historical events. His notable works include *John Brown Goes to a Hanging; Flowers with Red Chair; The Den; The Milk Man of Goshen; and Dog Fight Over the Trenches*.

James A. Porter
(1905–1971)

Art Historian, Painter

James A. Porter was a painter of considerable scholarship who also earned acclaim as a writer and educator. Born in Baltimore, he studied at Howard University, where he earned a B.S. in 1927; the Art Students League in New York; the Sorbonne in Paris; and New York University, where he received his M.A. He was awarded numerous travel grants that enabled him to study African and European art firsthand.

Among his ten one-person shows are exhibits at Port-au-Prince, Haiti, 1946; Dupont Gallery, Washington, DC, 1949; and Howard University, 1965. His works are in the collections of Howard University; Lincoln

University, Missouri; Harmon Foundation; IBM; and others. He was the author of the classic *Modern Negro Art* (1943) and numerous articles, making him the first African-American art historian.

In 1953 he became chairman of the Department of Art and director of the Gallery of Art at Howard University, a position he held until his death. He was a delegate to the UNESCO Conference on Africa, held in Boston in 1961, and to the International Congress of African Art and Culture in Salisbury, Southern Rhodesia, in 1962. In 1965, at the twenty-fifth anniversary of the founding of the National Gallery of Art, he was named "one of America's Most Outstanding Men of the Arts." His notable works include *On a Cuban Bus; Portrait of F. A. as Harlequin; Dorothy Porter;* and *Nude.*

Martin Puryear was born in Washington, DC. He attended Catholic University of America and received an M.F.A. from Yale University in 1971; he has studied in Sweden and worked in Sierra Leone with the Peace Corps from 1964 to 1966.

**Martin Puryear
(1941–)**

Sculptor

Representing the United States in the 1989 Sao Paulo Biennial in Brazil, he received first prize. His work has been described as post-minimalist, but it really defies categorizing. Puryear executes his large pieces in wood and metal.

Puryear was the only black artist in the contemporary section of the exhibit "Primitivism in Twentieth-Century Art: Affinity of the Tribal and Modern," at the Museum of Modern Art in 1984. His other exhibits include Brooklyn Museum, 1988–1989, the Whitney Biennial, 1989, and New York Galleries, since 1987.

Puryear studied in Japan in 1987 on a Guggenheim Fellowship. His notable works include *For Beckwith; Maroon Desire;* and *Sentinel.* Recent works (since 1985) have been untitled.

Committed to a revolutionary perspective both in her political subject matter and her unconventional aesthetic, Faith Ringgold is a symbolic expressionist whose stark paintings are acts of social reform directed toward educating her audience. Her most intense focus has been upon the problems of being black in America. Her works highlight the violent tensions

**Faith Ringgold
(1930–)**

Painter, Fiber Artist

that tear at American society, including discrimination suffered by women.

Born in Harlem in 1934, she was raised by parents who made sure she would enjoy the benefits of a good education. She attended the City College of New York, receiving her B.S. in 1955 and her M.F.A. in 1959. She is a professor of Art at the University of California at San Diego.

Her boldly political work has been well-received and widely shown. She has had several one-person shows, the first in 1968, and her paintings are included in the collections of the Chase Manhattan Bank; the Museum of Modern Art; the Bank Street College of Education; and the Solomon R. Guggenheim Museum.

In 1972, Ringgold became one of the founders of the Women Students and Artists for Black Liberation, an organization whose principal goal is to make sure that all exhibitions of black artists give equal space to paintings by men and women. She donated a large mural depicting the roles of women in American Society to the Women's House of Detention in Manhattan.

Aesthetically, she believes that "black art must use its own color, black, to create its light, since that color is the most immediate black truth." Her most recent paintings have been an attempt to give pictorial realization to this vision.

Her first quilt, *Echoes of Harlem, Tar Beach* was completed in 1980. In 1991 she illustrated and wrote a children's book, *Tar Beach*. Notable works include *The Flag Is Bleeding; Flag for the Moon; Die Nigger; Mommy & Daddy;* and *Soul Sister, Woman on a Bridge*.

Betye Saar
(1926-)

Painter, Sculptor

Betye Saar was born in California in 1926. She went to college, got married, and raised her children—all while creating artwork made of discarded pieces of old dreams: postcards, photographs, flowers, buttons, fans, and ticket stubs. Her motifs range from the fetish to the everyday object. In 1978 Saar became one of a select group of American female artists to be discussed in a documentary film entitled *Spirit Catcher: The Art of Betye Saar*. It appeared on WNET-13 in New York as part of the series "The Originals: Women in Art." Her exhibitions include an installation piece especially designed for the Studio Museum in Harlem in 1980, and several one-person exhibitions at the Monique Knowlton Gallery in New York in 1981.

Saar studied at Pasadena City College, the University of California (where she received her B.F.A.), Long Beach State College, the University of Southern California, San Fernando State College, and Valley State College, California. She was a teacher at Hayward State College in California, and she has exhibited throughout the United States. Her notable works include *The Vision of El Cremo; Africa; The View from the Sorcerer's Window;* and *House of Gris Gris,* a mixed-media installation (with daughter Alison Saar).

A leading sculptor who emerged during the Negro Renaissance, Augusta Savage was one of the artists represented in the first all-black exhibition in America, sponsored by the Harmon Foundation at International House in New York City. In 1939, her symbolic group piece *Lift Every Voice and Sing* was shown at the New York World's Fair Community Arts Building.

Augusta Savage (1900–1962)

Sculptor

Savage was born in Florida and studied at Tallahassee State Normal School, at Cooper Union in New York City, and in France as the recipient of Carnegie and Rosenwald fellowships. She was the first black to win acceptance to the National Association of Women Painters and Sculptors.

In the 1930s she taught in her own School of Arts and Crafts in Harlem and helped many of her students take advantage of WPA projects for artists during the depression. Her notable works include *Lift Every Voice and Sing; The Chase; Black Women; Lenore; Gamin; Marcus Garvey;* and *W.E.B. DuBois.*

Born in Philadelphia, Pennsylvania, Searles studied at Fleicher Art Memorial of the Penn Academy of Fine Arts from 1968 to 1972. His works have been exhibited at the Dallas, Brooklyn, Philadelphia, Reading, High, Milwaukee, Whitney, and Harlem Studio Museums; Columbia University; and many other galleries and museums.

Charles Searles (1937–)

Painter, Educator

Searles has traveled to Europe and Africa. He has taught at the Philadelphia College of Art, the Philadelphia Museum Art Studio, University of

Gamin, *Augusta Savage, 1930.*

the Arts, Brooklyn Museum Art School, Jersey State College, and Bloomfield College in New Jersey.

He was commissioned to execute several murals, including the U.S. General Service Administration interior; *Celebration* (1976) for the William J.
Green Federal Building; *Play Time* (1976) for Malory Public Playground; a
wall sculpture for the Newark, New Jersey Amtrak station (1985); and the
Dempsy Service Center wall sculpture (1989).

His works are in the collections of the Smithsonian Institute in Washington, DC; the New York State Office Building; the Philadelphia Museum of Art; the Federal Railroad Administration; Ciba-Gigy, Inc.; Dallas Museum of Art; Montclair Art Museum; Phillip Morris, Inc.; and Howard University.

The human figure, color, and rhythmic patterns dominate his paintings. His notable works include *Cultural Mix; Rhythmic Forms; Play Time;* and *Celebration.*

Lorna Simpson (1960–)

Photographer, Conceptual Artist

Simpson was born in Brooklyn, New York, and attended the School of Visual Arts, where she received her B.F.A. in 1982. She received her M.F.A. from the University of California at San Diego in 1985. Her works are concerned with language and words, especially those with double and contradictory meanings, and stereotypes and cliches about gender and race.

Simpson is among the new young photographers who have broken into the mainstream of conceptual art; her work has been shown at the Museum of Modern Art and the Wadsworth Atheneum. She is on the advisory board of the New Museum in New York City, and also on the board of Artists Space.

Her works have been exhibited in the Just Above Midtown Gallery, at Mercer Union in Toronto, and in the Wadsworth Atheneum Museum's Matrix Gallery. Her works are owned by the Atheneum and other museums. Her notable works include *Outline; Guarded Conditions;* and *Untitled ("prefer/refuse/decide").*

Norma Merrick Sklarek (1928–)

Architect

Sklarek was born on April 15, 1928 in New York City, and studied architecture at Barnard College of Columbia University, where she received a B.A. in 1950. In 1954 she became the first African-American woman to be licensed as an architect in New York state.

She worked for Skidmore, Owens, Merrill from 1955 to 1960, then moved on to Gruen and Associates in Los Angeles, California, where she worked for the next twenty years. Sklarek was licensed in California in 1962, became a fellow of the American Institute of Architects in 1966 (the first black woman to achieve this honor), and eventually was elected vice president of the California chapter of the American Institute of Architects.

Since 1985, Sklarek has been a partner in the firm Siegel, Sklarek, Diamond, which is, according to Brian Lanker in *I Dream a World*, "the largest woman-owned architectural firm in the United States." Her notable works include the American Embassy in Tokyo; the Courthouse Center in Columbus, Indiana; City Hall in San Bernardino, California; and Terminal One in Los Angeles International Airport.

Moneta Sleet, Jr.

(1926–)

Photographer

Moneta Sleet was born February 14, 1926, in Owensboro, Kentucky. He studied at Kentucky State College under Dr. John Williams, a family friend who was dean of the college and an accomplished photographer. After Sleet served in World War II, Williams offered him the opportunity to set up a photography department at Maryland State College in 1948. By 1950, Sleet had moved to New York, where he obtained a master's degree in journalism.

In 1969, Sleet became the first African American to win a Pulitzer Prize in photography. Although employed by *Ebony*, he was eligible for the award because his photograph of Coretta Scott King at her husband's funeral was picked up by a wire service and published in daily newspapers throughout the country.

Sleet has won awards from the Overseas Press Club of America, National Urban League, and the National Association of Black Journalists. His work has appeared in several group exhibitions at museums, including the Studio Museum in Harlem and the Metropolitan Museum of Art. In 1970, solo exhibitions were held at the City Art Museum of St. Louis and at the Detroit Public Library.

Willi Smith

(1948–1987)

Fashion Designer

Born in 1948 in Philadelphia, Pennsylvania, Willi Smith studied at the Parsons School of Design on a scholarship, and his work became popular during the 1960s. He was known for his designer wear for men and women, made from natural fibers, that was fun, cross-seasonal, and affordable. His line of clothes, known as Willi-Wear, consisted of sportswear pieces that mixed readily with his own designs as well as those of others. Smith was known for an innovative mixing and matching of plaids, stripes, and vivid colors. Smith had his clothes manufactured in India, traveling there several times a year to supervise the making of his functional and practical collections.

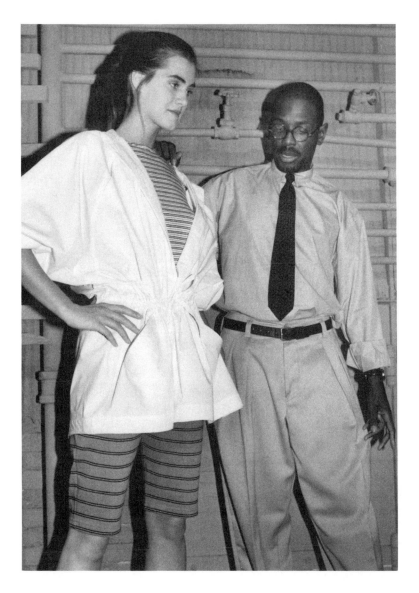

Designer Willi Smith looks at a model wearing his drawstring bicycle pants and anorak parka, 1986.

In 1983 Willi Smith received the Coty American Fashion Critics Award for Women's Fashion. He died in 1987.

Born in Brooklyn, New York, Stevens received a B.F.A. from Ohio University in 1962 and an M.F.A. from Kent State University in 1969.

An active member of AFRI-COBRA—a group exploring the aesthetics of African-American art, including representations of the human figure,

Nelson Stevens
(1938–)

Muralist, Painter, Graphic Artist

bright colors, African-inspired patterns, text, letters, and other symbols relating to the black experience—he is also a member of the National Conference of Artists.

Stevens is a professor of art at the University of Massachusetts in Amherst. He has exhibited at the National Center of Afro-American Artists in Boston; the Studio Museum in Harlem; Howard University; and Kent State University. His notable works include *Madonna and Child* for the 1993 calendar *Art in the Service of the Lord; Malcolm—King of Jihad;* and *A Different Kind of Man.*

Henry Ossawa Tanner (1859–1937)

Painter

Alain Locke called Henry Ossawa Tanner the leading talent of the "journeyman period" of black American art. Born in Pittsburgh in 1859, Tanner chose painting rather than the ministry as a career, overcoming the strong objections of his father, an African Methodist Episcopal bishop. After attending the Pennsylvania Academy of Fine Arts, he taught at Clark University in Atlanta, supplementing his salary by working as a photographer. Some of Tanner's most compelling work—such as *The Banjo Lesson* (1890)—was produced during this period, with Tanner emerging as the most promising black artist of his day.

In 1891, however, Tanner abandoned black subject matter and left the United States for Paris, where he concentrated on religious themes. In 1896, his *Daniel in the Lion's Den,* a mixture of realism and mystical symbolism, won honorable mention at the Paris Salon. The following year,

Abraham's Oak, Henry Ossawa Tanner, 1905.

the French government purchased his *Resurrection of Lazarus.* In 1900 Tanner received the Medal of Honor at the Paris Exposition, and the Lippincott Prize.

Tanner died in 1937. His notable works include *Flight into Egypt; The Annunciation; Thankful Poor;* and *The Sabot Makers.*

Alma W. Thomas (1891–1978)

Painter

Born in Columbus, Georgia, Alma Thomas moved to Washington, DC with her family when she was a teenager. She enrolled at Howard University and in 1924 was the first graduate of its art department. In 1934 she received her M.A. from Columbia University. She later studied at American University.

Retiring after a thirty-eight-year teaching career in public schools, Thomas concentrated solely on her painting. She is best known for her non-objective, mosaic-like works that emphasize color, pattern, and space. The optical relationships of her colors in flat shapes create the illusion of three-dimensional forms, enlivening the painted surfaces with movement and pulsating rhythms. It is this later work that brought her many prizes and awards.

Her works are in the collections of the National Museum of American Art at the Smithsonian Institute, Howard University, Concord Gallery, Metropolitan Museum, La Jolla Museum, and private corporations. Her notable works include *The Eclipse; Arboretum Presents White Dogwood; Elysian Fields; Red Sunset;* and *Old Pond Concerto.*

Bob Thompson (1937–1966)

Painter

With the death of Bob Thompson in 1966, the art world experienced the loss of an outstanding African-American painter—a man who had studied extensively in the United States and traveled widely in Europe and North Africa, living in Paris (1961–1962), Ibiza (1962–1963), and Rome (1965–1966).

Born in Louisville, Kentucky, Thompson studied at the Boston Museum School in 1955 and later spent three years at the University of Louisville. In 1960, Thompson participated in a two-person show at Zabriskie Gallery and two years later received a John Hay Whitney Fellowship. For the next few years, Thompson had several one-person exhibitions in New

York and Chicago. His work was also seen in Spain. He died in Rome at the age of twenty-nine.

Thompson's work is in several permanent collections around the country, including the Chrysler Museum in Provincetown, Massachusetts. In 1970, Thompson's work was featured in the African-American Artist exhibition at the Boston Museum of Fine Arts. His notable works include *Ascension to the Heavens; Untitled Diptych; The Dentist* (1963); and *Expulsion and Nativity* (1964).

James Van Der Zee
(1886–1983)

Photographer

James Van Der Zee was born on June 29, 1886, in Lenox, Massachusetts. His parents had moved there from New York in the early 1880s after serving as maid and butler to Ulysses S. Grant, who then resided on 34th Street in New York City. The second of six children, James grew up in a family of creative people. Everybody painted, drew, or played an instrument, so it was not considered out of the ordinary when, upon receiving a camera in 1900, Van Der Zee became interested in photography.

By 1906 Van Der Zee had moved to New York, married, and taken odd jobs to support his growing family. In 1907 he moved to Phoetus, Virginia, where he worked in the dining room of the Hotel Chamberlin in Old Point Comfort, Virginia. During this time he also worked as a photographer on a part-time basis. In 1909 he returned to New York.

By 1915, Van Der Zee had a photography job as assistant in a small concession in the Gertz Department Store in Newark, New Jersey. With the money he saved from this job he was able to open his own studio in 1916, on 135th Street. World War I had begun and many young soldiers came to the studio to have their pictures taken. Over the course of a half-century, James Van Der Zee recorded the visual history of Harlem. His subjects included Marcus Garvey, Daddy Grace, Father Divine, Joe Louis, Madame Walker, and many other famous African Americans.

In 1969, the exhibition "Harlem On My Mind," produced by Thomas Hoving, then director of the Metropolitan Museum of Art, brought Van Der Zee international recognition. Van Der Zee died in 1983.

Born in 1887 in Hartford, Connecticut, this portrait painter and illustrator received her first training at the Pennsylvania Academy of Fine Arts, where she studied for six years. In 1914, she won the Cresson Memorial Scholarship, which enabled her to continue her studies at the Academie de la Grande Chaumière in Paris.

Waring returned to the United States as an art instructor at Cheyney State Teachers College in Pennsylvania, eventually becoming head of the art department there. Her work, particularly portraiture, has been exhibited at several leading American art galleries. In 1927 she received the Harmon Award for achievement in fine art. For the Harmon Foundation in the 1940s, Waring, along with Betsy Graves Reyneau, completed a set of twenty-four repaintings of a variety of their works entitled *Portraits of Outstanding Americans of Negro Origin*.

Waring was also the director in charge of the black art exhibits at the Philadelphia Exposition in 1926 and was a member of the national advisory board of Art Movements, Inc. She died in 1948. Her notable works include *Alonzo Aden; W. E. Burghardt DuBois; James Weldon Johnson;* and *Mother and Daughter*.

Laura Wheeler Waring (1887-1948)

Painter

Carrie Mae Weems was born in Portland, Oregon and earned her B.F.A. from the California Institute of the Arts in 1981 and her M.F.A. from the University of California at San Diego in 1984. She also received an M.A. in African-American folklore from the University of California at Berkeley.

A young artist who explores stereotypes, especially of black women, Weems has exhibited widely in the last few years. Formerly a photo-documentarian, Weems also teaches film-making and photography at Hampshire College in Amherst, Massachusetts. Her new works are "about race, gender, class and kinship."

She has exhibited at the Rhode Island School of Design and Wadsworth Atheneum in Hartford, Connecticut. Her notable works include *Mirror, Mirror; Black Woman with Chicken; High Yella Girl; Colored People; Family Pictures and Stories;* and *Ain't Jokin'*.

Carrie Mae Weems (1953-)

Photographer, Conceptual Artist

1993 Oldsmobile Achieva SC, designed by Edward Welburn.

Edward T. Welburn

(1950–)

Automobile Designer

Chief designer of automobiles at the Oldsmobile Exterior II Studio for General Motors, Edward T. Welburn put one of the outstanding car designs on the market with the 1992 Achieva model. Welburn graduated from Howard University and from the Skip/Barber School for Auto Race Drivers. He has been in the automobile design arena for twenty years.

Before moving to the Oldsmobile Exterior II Studio in 1989, Welburn worked in the Advanced Design Studio, the Buick Exterior Studio, and the 1975 Oldsmobile Exterior Studio, where he worked on the Cutlass Supreme design. His design was the prototype for the Cutlass Ciera and Calis in 1978.

In 1985, the Indianapolis 500 pace car was designed by a team on which he served. Welburn won the Industrial Designers Society of America Award for Design Excellence for his part in the design for *Oldsmobile Aerotech* in 1992.

Charles White

(1918–1979)

Painter

White was an eminent exponent of social art. The subject matter of his paintings were the notable achievements of famous American blacks, as well as the suffering of the lowly and anonymous.

White was born in 1918 in Chicago and was influenced as a young boy by Alain Locke's critical review of the Harlem Renaissance, *The New Negro*. At the age of twenty-three, White received a Rosenwald fellowship that enabled him to work in the South for two years, during which time he painted a celebrated mural depicting the contribution of black Americans to democracy. It is now the property of Hampton Institute in Virginia.

The bulk of White's work is done in black and white, a symbolic motif that he felt gave him the widest possible purview. His notable works include *Let's Walk Together; Frederick Douglass Lives Again; Women;* and *Gospel Singer.*

Paul Revere Williams (1894–1980)

Architect

Williams was born in Los Angeles, California, and graduated from the University of California at Los Angeles. He later attended the Beaux Arts Institute of Design in Paris; he received honorary degrees from Howard, Lincoln, and Atlanta Universities as well as Hampton Institute.

Williams became a certified architect in 1915, and after working for Reginald Johnson and John Austin, distinguished designers and architects, he opened his own firm in 1923. Williams was known as America's "architect to the stars." Williams designed a total of 3,000 buildings, including some four hundred homes for such celebrities as Cary Grant, Barbara Stanwyk, William Holden, Frank Sinatra, Betty Grable, Bill "Bojangles" Robinson, and Bert Lahr.

In 1926 he was the first black to become a member of the American Institute of Architects. He served on the National Monument Commission, an appointee of President Calvin Coolidge. His notable works include Los Angeles County Airport; Palm Springs Tennis Club; and Saks Fifth Avenue at Beverly Hills.

William T. Williams (1942–)

Painter

Born in Cross Creek, North Carolina, Williams avoids labels and association with any particular movement or school. He studied at a community college and later at Pratt Institute in Brooklyn, New York. He received his M.F.A. from Yale University in 1968.

Critics have viewed Williams's work in terms of comparison to Joseph Albers and the Bauhaus traditions from Europe. Williams's own statements about his work point to such subjects as the city, architecture, tension, things in flux, order from disorder, Africa, and the United States.

He has exhibited in the Studio Museum in Harlem, Wadsworth Atheneum, the Art Institute of Chicago, the Whitney Museum of American Art, and elsewhere. His notable works include *Elbert Jackson L.A.M.F. Port II; Big Red for N.C.;* and *Buttermilk.*

John Wilson

(1922–)

Painter, Printmaker

Born in Boston, Wilson studied at the Boston Museum of Fine Arts; Fernand Leger School in Paris; the Institute Politecnico in Mexico City; and elsewhere. He has been a teacher at Boston Museum and the Pratt Institute, and is currently teaching at Boston University.

His numerous exhibits include the Albany Institute; the Library of Congress National and International Print Exhibits; Smith College; Carnegie Institute; and the American International College in Springfield, Massachusetts. His work is represented in the collections of the Museum of Modern Art; the Schomburg Collection; the Department of Fine Arts of the French Government; Atlanta University; and Bezalel Museum in Jerusalem. His notable works include *Roxbury Landscape* (oil, 1944); *Trabajador* (print, 1951); and *Child with Father* (graphic, 1969).

Hale Woodruff

(1900–1979)

Painter, Muralist

Hale Woodruff's paintings were largely modernist landscapes and formal abstractions, but he has also painted rural Georgia scenes evocative of the "red clay" country. Born in Cairo, Illinois, he graduated from the John Herron Art Institute in Indianapolis. Encouraged by a bronze award in the 1926 Harmon Foundation competition, Woodruff went to Paris to study at both the Academie Scandinave and the Academie Moderne, as well as with Henry Ossawa Tanner.

In 1931 he became art instructor at Atlanta University, and five years later he accepted a similar post at New York University. In 1939 he was commissioned by Talladega College to do *The Amistad Murals,* an episodic depiction of a slave revolt.

In 1948, Woodruff teamed with Charles Alston to work on the Golden State Mutual Life Insurance Company Murals in California, which presented the contribution of African Americans to the history of California's development. Woodruff's last mural assignment came in 1950 when he developed the series of mural panels for Atlanta University entitled "The Art of the Negro."

Hale Woodruff died in 1979, having created a body of work with styles that moved from figurative, to impressionistic, to a brief exploration of cubist visual concepts, to a comfortable move into the abstract style. Woodruff became one of America's strongest mural painters. His notable works include *Ancestral Remedies; The Little Boy;* and *The Amistad Murals.*

Richard Yarde was born in Boston, Massachusetts. He studied at the School of the Museum of Fine Arts and at Boston University, where he earned his B.F.A. in 1962 and his M.F.A. in 1964. He has taught at Boston University and has received numerous awards for his art, including Yaddo fellowships, 1964, 1966, and 1970; McDowell Colony awards, 1968 and 1970; and the Blanche E. Colman Award, 1970.

Richard Yarde

(1939–)

Painter

The Boston Museum of Fine Arts, Wadsworth Atheneum, Rose Art Museum, National Museum of African-American Artists, and Studio Museum in Harlem have all exhibited his works. He has held one-person shows at numerous galleries and universities. His works are in many collections, such as the Wadsworth Atheneum in Hartford, Connecticut. His notable works include *The Stoop; Passage Edgar and I; The Corner;* and *Paul Robeson as Emperor Jones.*

By

Ionis Bracy Martin

Science and Medicine

The earliest African-American scientists and inventors are largely unknown, their contributions to America buried in anonymity. While Benjamin Banneker's eighteenth-century successes in timepieces and urban planning are known and applauded, numerous achievements of seventeenth- and eighteenth-century blacks in architecture, agriculture, and masonry cannot be identified. While historians increasingly recognize that blacks had a significant impact on the design and construction of plantations and public buildings in the South, and that rice farming in the Carolinas might not have been possible without the efforts of blacks, the individuals who spearheaded these accomplishments remain unknown.

EARLY SCIENTISTS AND INVENTORS ♦ ♦ ♦ ♦ ♦ ♦ ♦ ♦ ♦ ♦ ♦ ♦ ♦ ♦

Henry Blair, who patented his seed planter in 1834, was probably the first African American to receive a patent. Since the race of patent-seekers was rarely noted, however, other black inventors may simply have been overlooked.

Prior to the Civil War, in one of history's most absurd bureaucratic fiats, slaves could neither be granted patents nor could they assign patents to their masters. The underlying theory was that since slaves were not citizens, they could not enter into contracts with their owners or the government. As a result, the efforts of slaves were dismissed or, if accepted, credited entirely to their masters. One can only speculate on the part blacks actually played in significant inventions. One such area of speculation concerns the grain harvester of Cyrus McCormick. Jo Anderson, one of McCormick's slaves, is believed to have played a major role in the creation of the McCormick harvester, but available records are insufficient to determine the degree of Anderson's importance in the invention.

The inventions of free blacks, however, were recorded. The first black granted a patent was probably Henry Blair in 1834 for a seed planter. But again, records fail the historian, for the race of patent-seekers was rarely noted. Blair may well have had numerous predecessors. Many inventions by blacks, including Augustus Jackson's invention of ice cream in 1832, were not patented.

The Reconstruction era marked an unleashing of the creativity that had been suppressed in blacks during generations of slavery. Between 1870 and 1900, at a time when some eighty percent of African-American adults in the United States were illiterate, blacks were awarded several hundred patents. Notable among these were the shoe last (Jan Matzeliger, 1883); a machine for making paper bags (William Purvis, 1884); assorted machinery-lubricating equipment (Elijah McCoy, beginning in 1872); an automatic railroad car coupler (Andrew Beard, 1897); and the synchronous multiplex railroad telegraph (Granville Woods, 1888).

SCIENTISTS AND INVENTORS IN THE TWENTIETH CENTURY ♦ ♦

The contributions of black scientists are better known than those of black inventors, partly because of the recognition awarded George Washington Carver, an agricultural scientist who, incidentally, refused to patent most of his inventions. African-American scientists contributed enormously to

Agricultural scientist George Washington Carver derived products from the peanut and the soybean, which liberated the South from an excessive dependence on cotton.

the knowledge of blood plasma, open heart surgery, and cortisone, all vital aspects of modern health care.

The achievements of black inventors and scientists of the mid-twentieth century have been obscured by reasons more complex than blatant racial prejudice, among them the displacement of the individual inventor by government and corporate research and development teams; individuals, whatever their race, receive less recognition under this system. The people

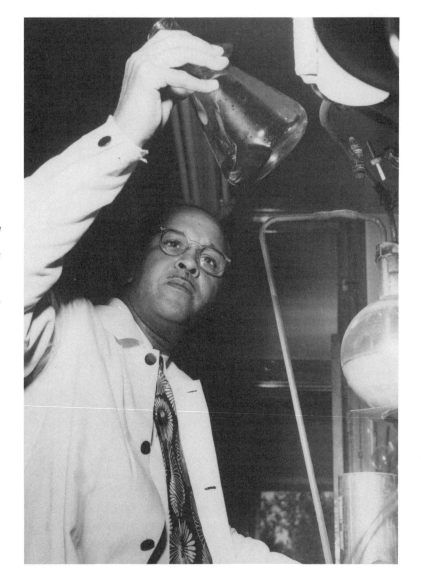

In 1935 Percy Julian synthesized the drug physostigmine, which is used today to treat glaucoma, and he later perfected a method for producing sterols, from which cortisone is derived.

behind such modern inventions as the computer, television, heart pacer, and laser are relatively obscure while such names as Bell, Edison, and Marconi are taught to every schoolchild.

In recent years, an increasing number of black students have demonstrated an interest in science—even more so since the death of Major Robert H. Lawrence, America's first black astronaut. African-American scientists and engineers are an integral part of the National Aeronautics and Space Administration (NASA). In the corporate world and academia,

Astronauts Guion Bluford (seated), Ronald McNair (left), and Frederick Gregory at Johnson Space Center in Houston, Texas, 1978.

African-American scientists and engineers are playing a substantial role in the development of solid state devices, high-powered and ultra fast lasers, hypersonic flight, and elementary particle science.

The number of African-American manufacturing and servicing firms in various computer and engineering fields continues to grow. In academia today there are more African-American science and technology faculty members, college presidents, and school of engineering deans than in the recent past. Many of these academics are serving in the country's major educational institutions.

ENGINEERS, MATHEMATICIANS, PHYSICIANS, SCIENTISTS ♦ ♦ ♦

Archie Alexander
(1887–1958)

Engineer

Born in Ottumwa, Iowa, Archie Alexander graduated from the University of Iowa in 1912 with a B.S. in civil engineering. After working for a bridge construction firm, he founded his own business, and in the next eleven years completed contracts amounting to $4,500,000. Alexander's firm was responsible for building the Tidal Basin Bridge in Washington, DC, and the heating plant at the University of Iowa.

Benjamin Banneker
(1731–1806)

Astronomer,
Mathematician

Benjamin Banneker was born in Ellicott, Maryland. His mother was a free woman and his father was a slave who eventually purchased his own freedom.

At the age of twenty-one, Banneker constructed a clock based on a pocket watch he had seen, calculating the ratio of the gears and wheels and carving them from wood. The clock operated for more than forty years.

Banneker's aptitude for mathematics and knowledge of astronomy enabled him to predict the solar eclipse of 1789. Within a few years, he began publishing an almanac that contained tide tables, data on future eclipses, and a listing of useful medicinal products and formulas. The almanac, which was the first scientific book published by an African American, appeared annually for more than a decade.

In 1771 Banneker served as a surveyor on the six-person team that helped lay out the base lines and initial boundaries for Washington, DC. When the chairman of the committee, Major Pierre Charles L'Enfant, abruptly resigned and returned to France with his plans, Banneker was able to reproduce the plans in their entirety.

While working in an Alabama railroad yard, Beard saw men lose hands and arms in accidents occurring during the manual coupling of railroad cars. The system involved the dropping of a metal pin into place when two cars came together. Men were often caught between cars and crushed to death during this split-second operation. Beard's invention, the "Jenny Coupler" (patent 594,059), was an automatic device that secured two cars by merely bumping them together. In 1897 Beard received $50,000 for an invention that has since prevented countless injuries and deaths.

Andrew Jackson Beard (c.1850–1910)

Inventor

Jim Beckwourth was born in 1798 near Fredericksburg, Virginia. His father was a landowner and member of a prominent Virginia family; his mother was an African-American woman, possibly a slave.

James Pierson Beckwourth (1798–1866)

Explorer

The family moved to a farm near St. Charles, Missouri in 1806 and Jim attended school in St. Louis from 1810 to 1814. He was apprenticed to a St. Louis blacksmith but soon decided to head west. As with many other events in Beckwourth's life, there are conflicting stories concerning the dissolution of the apprenticeship.

In 1824 Beckwourth joined a westward-bound fur trapping and trading expedition under the leadership of William Henry Ashley. Beckwourth soon became known as a man of many adventures and exploits. Although the basis of these stories are factual, many, with Beckwourth's approval, have been greatly exaggerated. Nevertheless, he undoubtedly embodied the spirit of the legendary mountain men of the American West.

In 1827, while still engaged in the fur trade, he married a Blackfoot Indian woman. In 1829 he took refuge from a debt collector by hiding with the Crow Indians, where he married again. Beckwourth claims he was made a Crow chief in recognition of his fighting prowess against the Blackfoot Indians.

By 1837 Beckwourth was with the United States Army in Florida serving as a scout during the Seminole wars. He soon returned to the Rocky Mountains, married a woman in New Mexico, and in 1842 opened a trading post near what is now Pueblo, Colorado. Between 1844 and 1850 he fought in the California uprising against Mexico and in the Mexican-American War.

In 1850 he joined the California gold rush and while in the Sierra Nevadas discovered a mountain pass that now bears his name. He made the gap more passable, opened an inn, and by 1851 was guiding wagon trains through the pass.

In 1856, with the help of ghostwriter T. D. Bonner, Beckwourth published his memoirs, entitled *Life and Adventures of James P. Beckwourth, Mountaineer, Scout and Pioneer.* Beckwourth traveled to St. Louis and Kansas City, where the popularity of his book enhanced his reputation and he was regarded as a celebrity.

He returned to Denver, married again, opened a trading post, and was charged with and acquitted of manslaughter. Tiring of city life, he signed on with the Army as a scout and fought the Cheyenne Indians. Beckwourth probably died of food poisoning on or around September 25, 1866, while riding to a Crow encampment. Accounts of the Crow Indians intentionally poisoning him are generally dismissed as false.

Henry Blair

(1804–1860)

Inventor

On October 14, 1834, Henry Blair of Maryland was granted a patent for a corn-planting machine; two years later, he received a second patent for a similar device used in planting cotton.

In the registry of the patent office, Blair was designated "a colored man"— the only instance of identification by race in these early records. Since slaves could not legally obtain patents, Blair was evidently a free man and is probably the first black inventor to receive a United States patent.

Guion Stewart

Bluford, Jr.

(1942–)

Astronaut

Bluford was born November 22, 1942 in Philadelphia. He graduated with a B.S. from Pennsylvania State University in 1964. He then enlisted in the United States Air Force and was assigned to pilot training at Williams Air Force Base in Arizona. Bluford served as a fighter pilot in Vietnam and flew 144 combat missions, sixty-five of them over North Vietnam. Attaining the rank of lieutenant colonel, Bluford received an M.S. from the Air Force Institute of Technology in 1974 and a Ph.D. in aeronautical engineering in 1978.

In 1979 Bluford was accepted in NASA's astronaut program as a mission specialist. On August 30, 1983, with the lift-off of the STS-8 Orbiter *Chal-*

lenger, Bluford became the first African American in space. He flew two other space shuttle missions—in 1985 and 1991—for a total of 314 hours in space. Bluford retired from NASA in 1993 to pursue a career in private industry.

Bluford has won numerous awards, including the Distinguished National Science Award given by the National Society of Black Engineers (1979), NASA Group Achievement Award (1980, 1981), NASA Space Flight Medal (1983), and the NAACP Image Award in 1983. Some of his military honors include the National Defense Service Medal (1965), Vietnam Campaign Medal (1967), Air Force Commendation Medal (1972), Air Force Meritorious Service Award (1978), and the USAF Command Pilot Astronaut Wings (1983).

Charles Frank Bolden, Jr. (1946–)

Astronaut

Charles Bolden, Jr., a graduate of the United States Naval Academy and the University of Southern California, has a bachelor of science degree in electrical science and a master of science degree in systems management.

Bolden began his career as a second lieutenant in the United States Marine Corps, becoming a naval aviator by 1970. In 1973, he flew more than 100 sorties while assigned in Thailand. Upon his return to the United States, Bolden began a tour as a Marine Corps selection and recruiting officer. In 1979 he graduated from the United States Naval Test Pilot School and was assigned to the Naval Test Aircraft Directorates.

Bolden was selected as an astronaut candidate by NASA in May 1980, and in July 1981 completed the training and evaluation program—making him eligible for assignment as a pilot on space shuttle flight crews. Bolden has logged more than 270 hours in space. He has served as pilot for the STS-31 Hubble Space Telescope mission and commander for the STS-45 mission. He has been awarded the Defense Superior Service Medal, the Defense Meritorious Service Medal, the Air Medal, and the Strike/Flight Medal.

Marjorie Lee Browne (1914–)

Mathematician

Browne was born September 9, 1914 in Memphis, Tennessee. She received a B.S. in mathematics from Howard University in 1935, an M.S. from the University of Michigan in 1939, and a Ph.D. in mathematics, again from the University of Michigan, in 1949.

Browne taught at the University of Michigan in 1947 and 1948. She accepted the post of professor of mathematics at North Carolina Central University in 1949 and became department chairperson in 1951.

Browne's doctoral dissertation dealt with topological and matrix groups, and she has been published in the *American Mathematical Monthly*. She was a fellow of the National Science Foundation in 1958–1959 and again in 1965–1966. Browne belongs to the American Mathematical Society, the Mathematical Association of America and the Society for Industrial and Applied Mathematics.

George E. Carruthers (1940–)

Physicist

George Carruthers is one of two naval research laboratory scientists responsible for the *Apollo* 16 lunar surface ultraviolet camera/spectrograph, which was placed on the moon in April 1972. Carruthers designed the instrument, while William Conway adapted the camera for the lunar mission. The spectrographs, obtained from eleven targets, include the first photographs of the ultraviolet equatorial bands of atomic oxygen that girdle the earth.

Carruthers, born and raised on Chicago's South Side, built his first telescope at the age of ten. He received his Ph.D. in physics from the University of Illinois in 1964, the same year that he started employment with the Navy. Carruthers is the recipient of the NASA Exceptional Scientific Achievement medal for his work on the ultraviolet camera/spectrograph.

George Washington Carver (1864–1943)

Agricultural Scientist

George Washington Carver devoted his life to research projects connected primarily with southern agriculture. The products he derived from the peanut and the soybean revolutionized the economy of the South by liberating it from an excessive dependence on cotton.

Born a slave in Diamond Grove, Missouri, Carver was only an infant when he and his mother were abducted from his owner's plantation by a band of slave raiders. His mother was sold and shipped away, but Carver was ransomed by his master in exchange for a race horse.

While working as a farm hand, Carver managed to obtain a high school education. He was admitted as the first black student of Simpson College, Indianola, Iowa. He then attended Iowa Agricultural College (now Iowa

State University) where, while working as the school janitor, he received a degree in agricultural science in 1894. Two years later he received a master's degree from the same school and became the first African American to serve on its faculty. Within a short time his fame spread, and Booker T. Washington offered him a post at Tuskegee.

Carver revolutionized the southern agricultural economy by showing that three hundred products could be derived from the peanut. By 1938, peanuts had become a $200 million industry and a chief product of Alabama. He also demonstrated that one hundred different products could be derived from the sweet potato.

Although he held three patents, Carver did not patent most of his many discoveries made while at Tuskegee, saying, "God gave them to me, how can I sell them to someone else?" In 1938 he donated over $30,000 of his life's savings to the George Washington Carver Foundation and willed the rest of his estate to the organization so his work might be carried on after his death.

For fifty-one years W. Montague Cobb was a member of the Howard University Medical School faculty, and thousands of medical and dental students have studied under his direction. At Howard, he built a collection of more than 600 documented skeletons and a comparative anatomy museum in the gross anatomy laboratory.

W. Montague Cobb (1903–)

Physician, Medical Editor

As editor of the *Journal of the National Medical Association* for twenty-eight years, he developed a wide range of scholarly interests evidenced by the nearly seven hundred published works under his name in the fields of medical education, anatomy, physical anthropology, public health, and medical history.

He was the first African American elected to the presidency of the American Association of Physical Anthropologists, and he served as chairman of the anthropology section of the American Association for the Advancement of Science. Among his many scientific awards is the highest award given by the American Association of Anatomists. For thirty-one years he has been a member of the board of directors of the NAACP, and for many years he served as the board's president.

He has received many honorary degrees, as well as earning a B.A. from Amherst College, an M.D. from Howard University, and a doctorate from Case Western Reserve.

Elbert Frank Cox
(1895–1969)

Mathematician

Cox was born in Evansville, Indiana on December 5, 1895. He received his B.A. from Indiana University in 1917 and his Ph.D. from Cornell University in 1925. His dissertation dealt with polynomial solutions and made Cox the first African American to be awarded a doctorate in pure mathematics.

Cox was an instructor at Shaw University from 1921 to 1923, a professor in physics and mathematics at West Virginia State College from 1925 to 1929, and an associate professor of mathematics at Howard University from 1929 to 1947. In 1947 he was made full professor.

Cox was a Brooks Fellow and an Erastus Brooks Fellow, and he belonged to the Mathematical Society and the Physical Society. Cox died in 1969.

Ulysses Grant
Dailey
(1885–1961)

Surgeon

Ulysses Grant Dailey served for four years (1908–1912) as surgical assistant to Dr. Daniel Hale Williams, founder of Provident Hospital and noted heart surgeon.

Born in Donaldsonville, Louisiana, Dailey graduated in 1906 from Northwestern University Medical School, where he was appointed a demonstrator in anatomy. He later studied in London, Paris, and Vienna, and in 1926 set up his own hospital and sanitarium in Chicago. His name soon became associated with some of the outstanding achievements being made in anatomy and surgery.

For many years an associate editor of the *Journal of the National Medical Association,* Dailey traveled around the world in 1933 under the sponsorship of the International College of Surgeons, of which he was a founder fellow.

In 1951 and again in 1953, the U.S. State Department sent him to Pakistan, India, Ceylon, and Africa. A year later he was named honorary consul to Haiti.

Using techniques already developed for separating and preserving blood, Charles Drew explored further the field of blood preservation, and applied research procedures to clinical work, leading to the founding of blood banks just prior to World War II.

Born in Washington, DC, Drew graduated from Amherst College in Massachusetts, where he received the Messman Trophy for having brought the most honor to the school during his four years there. He was not only an outstanding scholar but the captain of the track team and a star halfback on the football team.

After receiving his medical degree from McGill University in 1933, Drew returned to Washington, DC, to teach pathology at Howard. In 1940, while taking his D.Sc. degree at Columbia University, he wrote a dissertation on "banked blood" and soon became such an expert in this field that the British government called upon him to set up the first blood bank in England.

During World War II, Drew was appointed director of the American Red Cross blood donor project. Later, he served as chief surgeon at Freedmen's Hospital in Washington, DC, as well as professor of surgery at Howard University Medical School from 1941 to 1950. He was killed in an automobile crash in 1950.

Charles Richard Drew (1904–1950)

Physician,
Blood Plasma Researcher

Glanville attended Smith College from 1941 to 1946 and earned a B.A. and an M.A. in mathematics. She received a Ph.D. from Yale University in 1949, thereby becoming the first African-American woman to be awarded a Ph.D. in pure mathematics.

Glanville's first teaching position was as an instructor at New York University (1949–1950). She moved to Fisk University where she was an assistant professor, and then to the University of Southern California as a lecturer, where she remained from 1961 to 1973. Since then she has been an associate professor at California State University. Glanville is the author of *Theory of Applications of Math for Teachers*.

Evelyn Boyd Glanville (1924–)

Mathematician

Gregory was born January 7, 1941 in Washington, DC. He is the nephew of the late Dr. Charles Drew, noted African-American blood plasma specialist. Under the sponsorship of U.S. Representative Adam Clayton Powell, Gregory attended the United States Air Force Academy and graduated

Frederick Drew Gregory (1941–)

Astronaut

with a B.S. in 1964. In 1977 he received an M.S.A. from George Washington University.

Gregory was a helicopter and fighter pilot for the USAF from 1965 to 1970 and a research and test pilot for the USAF and NASA in 1971. In 1978 he was accepted into NASA's astronaut program. In 1985 he went into space aboard the Spacelab 3 *Challenger* Space Shuttle as a pilot.

Gregory belongs to the Society of Experimental Test Pilots, the Tuskegee Airmen, the American Helicopter Society, and the National Technical Association.

He has won numerous medals and awards, including the Meritorious Service Medal, the Air Force Commendation Medal, two NASA Space Flight Medals, and the Distinguished Flying Cross (twice). He is also the recipient of George Washington University's Distinguished Alumni Award, NASA's Outstanding Leadership Award, and the National Society of Black Engineers' Distinguished National Scientist Award.

Gregory is with NASA's astronaut program at the Johnson Space Center in Houston, Texas, and is a colonel in the USAF.

Lloyd Augustus Hall

(1894–)

Chemist

As the chief chemist and director of research for Griffith Laboratories of Chicago, Lloyd Hall discovered curing salts for the preserving and processing of meats, thus revolutionizing the meat-packing industry. He has more than 100 patents registered for processes used in the manufacturing and packing of food, especially meat and bakery products.

An honor graduate in science from East High School of Aurora, Illinois, Hall went on to receive a B.S. in pharmaceutical chemistry from Northwestern University. He continued his training with graduate work at the University of Chicago and University of Illinois, then embarked on his unique and fruitful career.

Henson was born August 8, 1866 in Charles County, Maryland, near Washington, DC. He attended school in Washington for six years but at the age of thirteen signed on as a cabin boy on a ship headed for China. Henson worked his way up to seaman while he sailed over the world's oceans. Tiring of life at sea, Henson took a job in a Washington, DC clothing store. While there he met Nicaragua-bound United States Navy surveyor Robert Edward Peary. He was hired on the spot as Peary's valet. Henson was not pleased to be a personal servant, but he felt his new position offered future opportunities.

Peary eventually developed an interest in arctic exploration. After numerous trips to Greenland between 1893 and 1905, Peary became convinced that he could become the first man to stand at the North Pole. Henson accompanied Peary on these trips to Greenland and became an integral part of Peary's plans.

In 1906, along with a number of Inuits, Peary and Henson set out from Greenland on their first attempt to reach the North Pole. They came within 160 miles of their goal but were forced to turn back because unseasonably warm weather had created open sheets of water that could not be traversed by dogsled.

Undaunted, Peary and Henson tried again in 1909. Although Peary was undoubtedly the driving force of these expeditions, he was increasingly reliant on Henson. Henson's greatest asset was his knowledge of the Inuit language and his ability to readily adapt to their culture. He was also an excellent dog driver and possessed a physical stamina that Peary lacked due to leukemia. Henson felt that he was serving the black race by his example of loyalty, fortitude, and trustworthiness.

By the end of March 1909 they were within 150 miles of their goal. Henson, because of his strength, would break trail and set up camp for the night, while Peary followed. On April 6, Henson thought he had reached the pole. When Peary arrived later he asserted that they were three miles short. After a brief rest they both set out together and stopped when they thought they were in the area of the North Pole. There have been conflicting theories ever since as to who was the first man to reach the top of the world.

In 1912 Henson wrote *A Negro at the North Pole*, but the book aroused little interest. He took work as a porter and then as a customs official in New

Matthew Alexander Henson (1866–1955)

Explorer

York. By the 1930s, however, Henson began receiving recognition for his contributions to arctic exploration. In 1937 he was the first African American elected to the Explorers Club in New York. In 1945 he and other surviving members of the expedition received the Navy Medal. In the early 1950s Henson also received public recognition from President Dwight Eisenhower.

Henson died in 1955 and was buried in New York. In 1988 his remains were exhumed and buried with full military honors at Arlington National Cemetery next to the grave of Robert Peary.

William A. Hinton

(1883–1959)

Medical Researcher

One of the world's foremost authorities on venereal disease, William A. Hinton is responsible for the development of the Hinton test, a reliable method for detecting syphilis. He also collaborated with Dr. J. A. V. Davies on what is now called the Davies-Hinton test for detection of this same disease.

Born in Chicago, Hinton graduated from Harvard in 1905. He finished his medical studies at Harvard Medical School in three years, graduating in 1912. For three years after graduation, he was a voluntary assistant in the pathological laboratory at Massachusetts General Hospital. This was followed by eight years of laboratory practice at the Boston Dispensary and at the Massachusetts Department of Public Health. In 1919 Hinton was appointed lecturer in preventive medicine and hygiene at Harvard Medical School, where he served for thirty-four years while continuing to work at the Boston Dispensary. In 1949, he was the first person of color to be granted a professorship at Harvard.

In 1931, at the Boston Dispensary, Hinton started a training school for poor girls so that they could become medical technicians. From these classes of volunteers grew one of the country's leading institutions for the training of technicians.

Though he lost a leg in an automobile accident, Hinton remained active in teaching and at the Boston Dispensary Laboratory, which he directed from 1916 to 1952. He died in Canton, Massachusetts in 1959.

Born in Washington, DC, Shirley Ann Jackson graduated as valedictorian of her class from Roosevelt High School in 1964. In 1968 she received a bachelor of science degree from Massachusetts Institute of Technology. She stayed at M.I.T. for her doctorate studies, and in 1973 she became the first African-American woman in the United States to earn a Ph.D. in physics.

Jackson has worked as a member of the technical staff on theoretical physics at AT&T Bell Laboratories, as a visiting scientist at the European Organization for Nuclear Research in Geneva, and as a visiting lecturer at the NATO International Advanced Study Institute in Belgium. She is currently employed at the AT&T Bell Laboratories in New Jersey, where she now specializes in scattering and low energy physics.

**Shirley Ann Jackson
(1946–)**

Physicist

Mae Jemison was born October 17, 1956 in Decatur, Alabama; her family moved to Chicago when she was three. She attended Stanford University on a National Achievement Scholarship and received a B.S. in chemical engineering and a B.A. in Afro-American studies in 1977. She then enrolled in Cornell University's medical school and graduated in 1981. Her medical internship was at the Los Angeles County/University of Southern California Medical Center in 1982. She was a general practitioner with the INA/Ross Loos Medical Group in Los Angeles until 1983, followed by two years as a Peace Corps medical officer in Sierra Leone and Liberia. Returning to the United States in 1985, she began working for CIGNA Health Plans, a health maintenance organization in Los Angeles.

**Mae C. Jemison
(1956–)**

Astronaut, Physician

In 1987 Jemison was accepted in NASA's astronaut program. Her first assignment was representing the astronaut office at the Kennedy Space Center in Cape Canaveral, Florida. On September 12, 1992, when the space shuttle *Endeavor* lifted off, Jemison was aboard and became the first African-American woman in space. She served aboard the *Endeavor* as a science specialist.

In 1988 Jemison won the Science and Technology Award given by *Essence* magazine, and in 1990 she was Gamma Sigma Gamma's Woman of the Year. In 1991 she earned a Ph.D. from Lincoln University.

Jemison resigned from NASA in 1993 to pursue personal goals related to science education and minorities.

Mae Jemison, formerly a general practitioner and Peace Corps medical officer, was accepted in NASA's astronaut program in 1987. In September of 1992, Jemison became the first African-American woman in space as a science specialist aboard the space shuttle Endeavor.

Frederick McKinley Jones (1892–1961)

Technician

In 1935, Frederick McKinley Jones built the first automatic refrigeration system for long-haul trucks. Later, the system was adapted to various other carriers, including railway cars and ships.

Previously, foods were packed in ice, a system whereby even slight delays led to spoilage. Jones's new method instigated a change in the eating habits and patterns of the entire nation and allowed for the development of food production facilities in almost any geographic location.

Jones was born in Cincinnati. His mother died when he was a boy and he moved to Covington, Kentucky, where he was raised by a priest until he was sixteen. When he left the rectory, Jones worked as a pin boy, mechanic's assistant, and finally, as chief mechanic on a Minnesota farm. He served in World War I, and in the late 1920s his fame as an adept mechanic spread when he developed a series of devices to adapt silent movie projectors into sound projectors.

Jones also developed an air conditioning unit for military field hospitals, a portable x-ray machine, and a refrigerator for military field kitchens. During his lifetime, a total of sixty-one patents were issued in Jones's name.

Born in Montgomery, Alabama, Julian attended DePauw University in Greencastle, Indiana. He graduated Phi Beta Kappa and was valedictorian of his class. Throughout college Julian lived in the attic of a fraternity house where he worked as a waiter. For several years, Julian taught at Fisk and Howard universities, as well as at West Virginia State College, before attending Harvard and the University of Vienna.

In 1935 Julian synthesized the drug *physostigmine,* which is used today in the treatment of glaucoma. He later headed the soybean research department of the Glidden Company and then formed Julian Laboratories in order to specialize in the production of sterols, which he extracted from the oil of the soybean. The method perfected by Julian in 1950 eventually lowered the cost of sterols to less than twenty cents a gram, and ultimately enabled millions of people suffering from arthritis to obtain relief through the use of cortisone, a sterol derivative.

In 1947 Julian was awarded the Spingarn Medal, and in 1968 he was awarded the Chemical Pioneer Award by the American Institute of Chemists.

**Percy Lavon Julian
(1898–1975)**

Chemist

**Ernest Everett Just
(1883–1941)**

Biologist

Born in Charleston, South Carolina, Ernest Just received his B.A. with high honors from Dartmouth in 1907 and his Ph.D. from the University of Chicago in 1916.

A member of Phi Beta Kappa, Just received the Spingarn Medal in 1914 and served as associate editor of *Physiological Zoology,* the *Biological Bul-*

letin, and the *Journal of Morphology.* Between 1912 and 1937, Just published more than fifty papers on fertilization, parthenogenesis, cell division, and mutation. In 1930 he was one of twelve zoologists to address the International Congress of Zoologists, and he was elected vice president of the American Society of Zoologists.

Samuel L. Kountz
(1931–1981)

Surgeon

Born in Lexa, Arkansas, Samuel Kountz graduated third in his class at the Agricultural, Mechanical and Normal College of Arkansas in 1952. He pursued graduate studies at the University of Arkansas, earning a degree in chemistry. Senator J. W. Fulbright, whom he met while a graduate student, advised Kountz to apply for a scholarship to medical school. Kountz won the scholarship on a competitive basis and was the first black to enroll at the University of Arkansas Medical School in Little Rock. Through his research, Kountz discovered that large doses of the drug *methylprednisolone* could help reverse the acute rejection of a transplanted kidney. The drug was used for a number of years in the standard management of kidney transplant patients.

In 1964, working with Dr. Roy Cohn, one of the pioneers in the field of transplantation, Kountz made medical history by transplanting a kidney from a mother to a daughter—the first transplant between humans who were not identical twins. At the University of California in 1967, Kountz worked with other researchers to develop the prototype of a machine that is now able to preserve kidneys up to fifty hours from the time they are taken from the body of a donor. The machine, called the Belzer Kidney Perfusion Machine, was named for Dr. Folkert O. Belzer, who was Kountz's partner.

Kountz died in 1981 after a long illness contracted on a trip to South Africa in 1977.

Lewis Howard
Latimer
(1848–1928)

Inventor, Engineer

Lewis Howard Latimer was employed by Alexander Graham Bell to make the patent drawings for the first telephone, and later went on to become chief draftsman for both the General Electric and Westinghouse companies.

Born in Chelsea, Massachusetts, on September 4, 1848, Latimer enlisted in the Union Navy at the age of fifteen, and began studying drafting upon completion of his military service. In 1881, he invented a method of making carbon filaments for the Maxim electric incandescent lamp. He also supervised the installation of electric light in New York, Philadelphia, Montreal, and London for the Maxim-Weston Electric Company. In 1884, he joined the Edison Company.

Air Force Major Robert H. Lawrence, Jr. was the first African-American astronaut to be appointed to the Manned Orbiting Laboratory. Lawrence was a native of Chicago, and while still in elementary school he became a model airplane hobbyist and a chess enthusiast. Lawrence became interested in biology while at Englewood High School in Chicago. As a student at Englewood, Lawrence excelled in chemistry and track. When he graduated, he placed in the top 10 percent of the class.

Lawrence entered Bradley University, joining the Air Force Reserve Officers' Training Corps. There he attained the rank of lieutenant colonel, thus becoming the second highest ranking cadet at Bradley. Lawrence was commissioned a second lieutenant in the United States Air Force in 1956 and soon after received his bachelor's degree in chemistry. Following a stint at an air base in Germany, Lawrence entered Ohio State University through the Air Force Institute of Technology as a doctoral candidate.

Lawrence died in 1967 when his F-104D Starfighter jet crashed on a runway in a California desert.

Robert H. Lawrence, Jr. (1935–1967)

Astronaut

Arthur Logan was born in Alabama in 1909. When he was ten his family moved to New York City, where he received his middle school and high school education. After attending Williams College in Williamstown, Massachusetts, he went to medical school at Columbia University College of Physicians and Surgeons, graduating in 1934. Wishing to work among his people, Logan interned at Harlem Hospital and was affiliated with the hospital for the rest of his life.

In addition to his many years of medical service to Harlem residents and others, Logan also headed New York City's Council Against Poverty in 1965 at the request of Robert F. Wagner, then mayor of the city.

Logan was a board member of New York City's Health and Hospital Corporation, as well as a longtime activist in the civil-rights movement and a

Arthur C. Logan (1909–1973)

Physician

strong supporter of a wide range of community causes. He was active with the National Urban League and the NAACP Legal Defense Fund, and he was an intimate friend of Martin Luther King, Jr., Whitney Young, and Roy Wilkins. His home in New York was often a meeting place for major figures of the civil-rights movement in the 1960s.

Miles Vandahurst Lynk

(1871–1956)

Physician

Miles Vandahurst Lynk, M.D., was born on June 3, 1871 near Brownsville, Tennessee. He was founder, editor, and publisher of the first black medical journal, the *Medical and Surgical Observer,* first published in December 1892. At the age of nineteen, Lynk received his M.D. from Meharry Medical College. Lynk was one of the organizers of the first black national medical association, which later became known as the National Medical Association. He also founded and was president of the School of Medicine at the University of West Tennessee.

Jan Matzeliger

(1852–1889)

Inventor

Born in Paramaribo, Dutch Guiana, Matzeliger found employment in the government machine works at the age of ten. Eight years later he immigrated to the United States, settling in Philadelphia where he worked in a shoe factory. He later moved to New England, settling permanently in Lynn, Massachusetts.

The Industrial Revolution had by this time brought the invention of machines to cut, sew, and tack shoes, but none had been perfected to last a shoe. Matzeliger lost little time in designing and patenting just such a device, which he refined over the years so that it could adjust a shoe, arrange the leather over the sole, drive in the nails, and deliver the finished product—all in one minute's time.

Matzeliger's patent was subsequently bought by Sydney W. Winslow, who established the United Shoe Machine Company. The continued success of this business resulted in a 50 percent reduction in the price of shoes across the nation, doubled wages, and improved working conditions for millions of people dependent on the shoe industry for their livelihood.

Between 1883 and 1891, Matzeliger received five patents on his inventions, all of which contributed to the shoe-making revolution. His last patent was issued in September 1891, two years after his death.

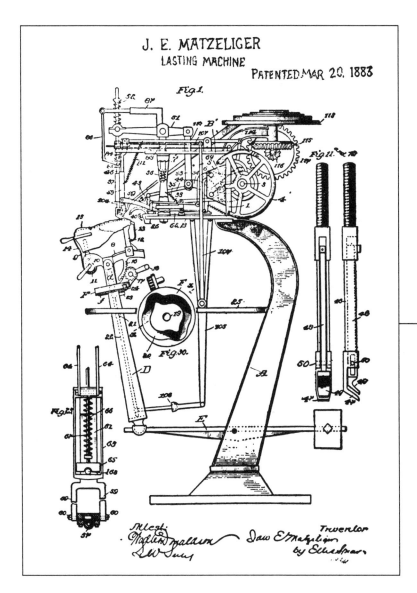

Drawings for Matzeliger's shoe lasting machine.

Matzeliger died at the age of thirty-seven, long before he had the chance to realize a share of the enormous profit derived from his invention. In fact, he never received any money for his patents. Instead, he was issued stock in the United Shoe Machine Company that did not become valuable until after his death.

Elijah McCoy

(1844–1918?)

Inventor

Elijah McCoy's inventions were primarily connected with the automatic lubrication of moving machinery. Perhaps his most valuable design was the "drip cup," a tiny container filled with oil whose flow to the moving parts of heavy-duty machinery was regulated by means of a "stopcock." The drip cup was a key device in perfecting the overall lubrication system used in large-machine industry today.

Born in Canada, McCoy moved to Ypsilanti, Michigan after the Civil War, and over the next forty years acquired some fifty-seven patents for devices designed to streamline his automatic lubrication process.

Ronald E. McNair

(1950–1986)

Astronaut

Ronald McNair was graduate of North Carolina A&T State University with a B.S. in physics. He also received a Ph.D. in physics from the Massachusetts Institute of Technology. He was presented an honorary doctorate of laws from North Carolina A&T in 1978.

McNair was working in optical physics when, in 1978, he was selected by NASA to train as an astronaut. In August 1979, he completed a one-year training and evaluation period that made him eligible for assignment as mission specialist on space shuttle flight crews. He presented papers in the areas of lasers and molecular spectroscopy and gave many presentations in the United States and Europe. He was the second African American to orbit the earth on a NASA mission.

McNair was aboard the flawed shuttle *Challenger* that exploded shortly after lift-off from Cape Kennedy and plunged into the waters off the Florida coast in January 1986. The shuttle had a crew of seven persons, including two women, a mission specialist, and a teacher-in-space participant.

Garrett A. Morgan

(1877–1963)

Inventor

The value of Garrett Morgan's "gas inhalator" was first acknowledged during a successful rescue operation of several men trapped two hundred feet below the surface of Lake Erie after a tunnel explosion in the Cleveland Waterworks. During the emergency, Morgan, his brother, and two other volunteers—all wearing inhalators—were the only men able to descend into the smoky, gas-filled tunnel to save several workers from asphyxiation.

Orders for the Morgan inhalator soon began to pour into Cleveland from fire companies all over the nation, but when Morgan's racial identity be-

Ronald McNair, a mission specialist who was the second African American to orbit the earth on a NASA mission, was aboard the flawed shuttle Challenger that exploded shortly after lift-off from Cape Kennedy in January of 1986.

came known, many of them were canceled. In the South, it was necessary for Morgan to have a white man demonstrate his invention. During World War I the Morgan inhalator was transformed into a gas mask used by combat troops.

Born in Paris, Kentucky, Morgan moved to Cleveland at an early age. His first invention was an improvement on the sewing machine, which he sold for $150. In 1923, having established his reputation with the gas inhalator, he was able to command a price of forty thousand dollars from the General Electric Company for his automatic traffic signal.

Morgan died in Cleveland, the city that had awarded him a gold medal for his devotion to public safety.

Norbert Rillieux

(1806–1894)

Inventor

Norbert Rillieux's inventions were of great value to the sugar-refining industry. The method formerly used required gangs of slaves to ladle boiling sugarcane juice from one kettle to another—a primitive process known as "the Jamaica Train."

In 1845, Rillieux invented a vacuum evaporating pan (a series of condensing coils in vacuum chambers) that reduced the industry's dependence on gang labor and helped manufacture a superior product at a greatly reduced cost. The first Rillieux evaporator was installed at Myrtle Grove Plantation, Louisiana, in 1845. In the following years, factories in Louisiana, Cuba, and Mexico converted to the Rillieux system.

A native of New Orleans, Rillieux was the son of Vincent Rillieux, a wealthy engineer, and Constance Vivant, a slave on his plantation. Young Rillieux's higher education was obtained in Paris, where his extraordinary aptitude for engineering led to his appointment at the age of twenty-four to instructor of applied mechanics at L'Ecole Centrale. Rillieux moved to Paris permanently in 1854, securing a scholarship and working on the deciphering of hieroglyphics.

When his evaporator process was finally adopted in Europe, he returned to inventing with renewed interest—applying his process to the sugar beet. In so doing, he cut production and refining costs in half.

Rillieux died in Paris on October 8, 1894, leaving behind a system that is universally used throughout the sugar industry and in the manufacture of soap, gelatin, glue, and many other products.

Lewis Temple

(1800–1854)

Inventor

The toggle harpoon invented by Lewis Temple vastly improved the whaling methods of the nineteenth century, more than doubling the catch for this leading New England industry.

Little is known of Temple's early background, except that he was born in Richmond, Virginia in 1800 and had no formal education. As a young man he moved to New Bedford, Massachusetts, then a major whaling port. Finding work as a metal smith, Temple modified the design of the whaler's harpoon, and in the 1840s manufactured a new version of the harpoon that allowed lines to be securely fastened to the whale. Using the "toggle harpoon," whalers soon entered a period of unprecedented prosperity. Temple, who never patented his harpoon, died destitute.

A pioneer in open heart surgery, Daniel Hale Williams was born in Holidaysburg, Pennsylvania. His father died when he was eleven, and his mother deserted him after apprenticing him to a cobbler. He later worked as a roustabout on a lake steamer and as a barber before finishing his education at the Chicago Medical College in 1883.

Daniel Hale Williams (1856–1931)

Surgeon

Williams opened his office on Chicago's South Side at a time when Chicago hospitals did not allow African-American doctors to use their facilities. In 1891 Williams founded Provident Hospital, which was open to patients of all races.

At Provident Hospital on July 10, 1893, Williams performed the operation that earned him renown in the medical field. A patient was admitted to the emergency ward with a knife wound in an artery lying a fraction of an inch from the heart. With the aid of six staff surgeons, Williams made an incision in the patient's chest and operated successfully on the artery.

For the next four days, the patient, James Cornish, lay near death, his temperature far above normal and his pulse dangerously uneven. The crisis period soon ended, and three weeks later, Williams performed minor surgery to remove fluid from Cornish's pleural cavity. After recuperating for another month, Cornish fully recovered and was able to leave the hospital.

Williams was instrumental in the forming of the Medico-Chirurgical Society and the National Medical Association. In 1913 he was inducted into the American Board of Surgery at its first convention. Williams died in 1931 after a lifetime devoted to his two main interests—the NAACP and the construction of hospitals and training schools for black doctors and nurses.

**Granville T. Woods
(1856–1910)**

Inventor

Born in Columbus, Ohio, Woods attended school until he was ten. He was first employed in a machine shop, and he continued to improve his mechanical aptitude by working on a railroad in 1872, in a rolling mill in 1874, and later by studying mechanical engineering at college. In 1878, Woods became an engineer aboard the *Ironsides*, a British steamer, and within two years was handling a steam locomotive on the D&S Railroad.

In 1887, Woods patented the most advanced of his many inventions—the Synchronous Multiplex Railway Telegraph. This device, designed to avert accidents, kept each train informed of the whereabouts of the train immediately ahead of or behind it by enabling communication between stations from moving trains.

Woods marketed this product, and others that followed, through his own company. The patent files in Washington, DC show Woods to have been an extremely prolific inventor. In the twenty-year span between 1879 and 1899, no less than twenty-three separate inventions bear his name. In 1887 alone, he registered seven separate inventions with the patent office, all of them connected with the ingenious railway communications system he devised.

S*ports*

The untimely AIDS-related death of Arthur Ashe in 1993 robbed the black community of a pioneering sports hero who was also one of the most passionate and articulate spokesmen for minority athletes. Ashe—the first black American man to win Wimbledon, the U.S. Open, and a Grand Slam of tennis—spent his entire career protesting unjust racial practices in the sporting world. His outstanding accomplishments notwithstanding, Ashe was distressed by the discrimination he faced in his own career and by what he perceived as racist hiring and promotional tactics throughout collegiate and professional sports. As a tennis star, and later as an author and newspaper columnist, he called for equal opportunity in all aspects of athletic endeavor.

The concerns Ashe voiced have become critical issues as the $70 billion-a-year business of American sports moves toward the twenty-first century. The dilemma is obvious: although black players predominate on the field in a number of professional and amateur sports, minorities are grossly underrepresented in the business of managing, owning, and running teams.

CURRENT ISSUES ✦

Grass-roots entreaties to increase minority hiring in sports have ranged from demonstrations led by the Reverend Jesse Jackson to threats of player boycotts to assure more minority coaches. The message is becoming clear: Equal opportunity employment must be extended to all areas of professional and amateur athletics, from locker room to boardroom.

The 1990s have witnessed the flowering of a grass-roots movement to spark more minority hiring in the vast sports industry. A 1992 *Sporting News* magazine poll identifying the 100 most important people in sports named only six blacks. Although 75 percent of the players in the NBA were black in 1992, only two head coach positions belonged to minorities. The same scenario held true for football—60 percent of the players in the NFL were black in 1992; two head coaches were black. Professional baseball has even seen a decline in the number of black players on the field. PGA golf tournaments are still held at private clubs with all-white memberships. Hockey, tennis, and horse racing have included only minimal numbers of blacks.

The situation is much the same at the amateur level. Black athletes have excelled at the Olympic Games, but a vast majority of collegiate coaches, trainers, and athletic directors are white. Blacks are also scarce among the ranks of referees, umpires, play-by-play announcers, and agents.

Interestingly, professional boxing—that most brutal of sports—has the best record for integration throughout its ranks. Not only are many of the fighters minorities, but many of the trainers, managers, and promoters are as well. The flamboyant Don King, long a fixture in the sport, was one of the members of the *Sporting News*'s list of the most important figures in organized athletics.

Black attendance at sporting events has declined dramatically in recent years. In 1992 it was estimated that only 5 percent of paying customers for major league baseball were black. The glamorous arenas that serve as stages for athletic competition—many of them equipped with luxury sky boxes and packed with season ticket–holders—have been described by some as exclusive "country clubs" existing only to amuse the nation's wealthiest citizens. Many sports franchises sponsor community outreach programs, but these do little to attract minority customers to the ball park.

Gains have been made, however. As president of baseball's National League, Bill White holds one of the sport's most influential positions. Professional basketball had four black general managers in 1992: Elgin Baylor of the Los Angeles Clippers, Bernie Bickerstaff of the Denver Nuggets,

Shortly before his death in February of 1993, tennis great Arthur Ashe wrote, "We as African Americans will continue our cultural emphasis on sports participation, and we will make our mark in new areas."

Wayne Embry of the Cleveland Cavaliers, and Willis Reed of the New Jersey Nets. Art Shell of the Los Angeles Raiders and Dennis Green of the Minnesota Vikings are the first two black head coaches in professional football since 1923. Track coach Bob Kersee had a hand in the Olympic medals won by his wife, Jackie Joyner-Kersee, and his sister-in-law, Florence Griffith Joyner. Agent W. Jerome Stanley negotiated a $16.5 million contract for Reggie Lewis of the Boston Celtics in 1990. Perhaps most important, Peter C. B. Bynoe and Bertram Lee became the first black managing partners of a major sports franchise—basketball's Denver Nuggets.

No one would dare argue, as baseball executive Al Campanis did in 1987, that blacks lack the "necessities" to manage or run sports teams. In fact, according to findings released by the Center for the Study of Sport and Society at Northeastern University, professional sport outstrips the wider American society in non-discriminatory hiring practices. A "report card" issued by the university gave society at large a "D" grade overall while the National Basketball Association averaged a "B," the National Football League a "B," and Major League Baseball a "C." The study took into consideration the vast number of black athletes and their salaries compared to those of their white teammates.

It is these athletes themselves who stand poised to transform not only organized sports, but society as well. Outside the entertainment industry, no other profession has supplied so many well-known and well-loved figures to the American public. No other industry could ever offer more opportunities for blacks to become role models, national heroes, or spokespersons for social causes. For instance, the discovery that basketball star Earvin "Magic" Johnson of the Los Angeles Lakers was infected with the AIDS virus did more to advance public knowledge of the disease than a decade of prior publicity had done.

Arthur Ashe was not prone to optimism about the future of blacks in the business sector of sports, but even he saw some chance of improvement by decade's end. In an *Ebony* essay published in August of 1992, just a few months before his death, he wrote: "We as African-Americans will continue our cultural emphasis on sports participation, and we will make our mark in new areas." Ashe's words, like his life, should be inspiring for generations to come.

BASEBALL ✦

Prior to 1947, professional baseball was segregated, and blacks played in the Negro Leagues. These leagues provided the only opportunities for several generations of extremely talented and dedicated minority ball players. A surge in the popularity of baseball after World War II helped pave the way for black participation in the formerly all-white major leagues. Brooklyn Dodger second baseman Jackie Robinson broke the color barrier in 1947 and went on to be named rookie of the year.

Josh Gibson was reputed to be the greatest hitter ever in the Negro baseball leagues of the 1930s.

Robinson and other early black major leaguers faced widespread hostility from fans and second-class treatment in the Jim Crow South. Nevertheless, blacks began to stream into professional baseball, breaking records that had previously been held by white superstars. By the 1970s, blacks were on the rosters of every team in the league and were joined in increasing numbers by talented players from all parts of Latin America. Today minority players—including those of color from the Caribbean and elsewhere—comprise some 20 percent of all major league positions.

Frank Robinson became the first black manager of a major league team in 1974, and since then a half dozen other African Americans have managed on the major league level.

A number of black athletes have risen to prominence in baseball. Hank Aaron holds the record for most career home runs. Ricky Henderson set a single-season record for stolen bases. Willie Mays is acclaimed as the game's greatest center fielder. Frank Robinson was the only player ever to win an MVP award in both the National and American leagues and was the first black named manager of a major league franchise. In 1993, two-time National League MVP Barry Bonds became the highest-paid baseball player of all time with a contract that will pay more than $7 million per year.

Black participation in major league baseball peaked in the 1970s and has declined since. One factor sparking the change is the closing of inner-city baseball programs and urban Little Leagues due to lack of financial support. The economic situation has become so desperate in some American cities that even scholastic athletic programs are threatened with cutbacks or dissolution.

Its declining black membership notwithstanding, major league baseball has made modest strides toward equal opportunity employment in the many franchise front offices. Frank Robinson became the first black manager in 1974, and since then a half dozen other blacks have managed on the major league level. Bill White, a former All Star, was named president of the National League in 1988. From his office on Park Avenue in New York City, White negotiates labor agreements, oversees league expansion, dispenses fines and suspensions, and enforces league rules. Teams employing blacks in high executive positions include the Baltimore Orioles, the Boston Red Sox, the Atlanta Braves, the Los Angeles Dodgers, and the Houston Astros.

Nevertheless, the percentage of black participation in baseball's business management lags far behind the percentage of minority players in major league baseball, and it has become the target of a grass-roots movement for equal opportunity. Jesse Jackson's Rainbow Commission for Fairness in Athletics has planned demonstrations outside major league ballparks and training facilities in order to remind both executives and fans that blacks— long superstars on the field—want to make a wider mark on the game.

♦ **BASKETBALL**

Professional basketball began to integrate in 1951, when the Boston Celtics drafted Chuck Cooper and the New York Knicks hired Nat "Sweetwater" Clifton. By the late 1960s, most of the sport's biggest stars were minorities—men like Bill Russell, Wilt Chamberlain, Kareem Abdul-Jabbar, Elvin Hayes, and Willis Reed. These and other talented athletes helped transform the game from a relatively polite and static affair to a fast-breaking, physical, high-speed contest.

Black players won more and more roster positions as the 1970s progressed. Athletes such as Abdul-Jabbar, Julius "Dr. J" Erving, Moses Malone, Bob McAdoo, and Wes Unseld helped further the evolution of the modern professional basketball game. By the 1980s, black dominance of the sport was assured with the arrival of Earvin "Magic" Johnson, Patrick Ewing, Michael Jordan, Clyde Drexler, Charles Barkley, and Shaquille O'Neil.

A full three-quarters of all NBA players are black. This reality was vividly reflected in the composition of the first American Olympic basketball team composed of professional players. Of the twelve men asked to represent the nation at the 1992 Olympic Games, only two were white. The celebrated "Dream Team" won the gold medal easily.

Basketball was also one of the first major sports to hire black head coaches. Bill Russell was the first, in 1966. At one time, as many as a half dozen NBA head coaches were black, but by 1992 the number had declined to two. As many as twenty-four head coaches were hired and fired between 1990 and 1992—not one of them black. Disgruntled players have threatened a game-by-game boycott if more minority coaches are not hired by decade's end.

The scenario is not entirely bleak in the NBA, however. The Denver Nuggets are partially owned and fully run by a black man, Colorado businessman Bertram Lee. Basketball was the only sport in 1992 to feature black general managers, with four in the position representing the Los Angeles Clippers, the Denver Nuggets, the Cleveland Cavaliers, and the New Jersey Nets.

Of all sports, basketball seems to offer the brightest future for minority hiring. A generation of superstar players will soon retire with enough

Kareem Abdul-Jabbar was one of basketball's biggest star players by the late 1960s. Here he leaps over Detroit Pistons player Rick Mahorn in 1989 during the final game of his 20-year NBA career.

Michael Jordan and the Chicago Bulls after an NBA championship.

wealth to purchase controlling shares in franchises. This is a stated goal of Magic Johnson, who retired in 1992 after testing positive for the HIV virus, and a possible goal of Michael Jordan as well.

The vast popularity of basketball in America transcends any racial boundaries. The best players are not just black heroes; they are American heroes. As such they have an enormous power to shape public opinion, especially among the young. This power is displayed in everything from athletic shoe advertising to literacy programs and AIDS awareness, and it is likely to remain a vital force well into the twenty-first century.

◆ **FOOTBALL**

Unlike the other major American sports, professional football began as an integrated entertainment. Blacks played alongside whites on the gridiron until 1930. Then for fifteen years the sport was all white. In 1945 a handful of black players were recruited, including Woodrow Strode of the Los Angeles Rams and Ben Willis of the Cleveland Browns.

Slowly the number of black roster players increased as the 1950s progressed. Then, in 1957, the history of the NFL was forever changed by the arrival of Jim Brown. Brown, a superstar for the Cleveland Indians, led the league in rushing for eight of his nine years in football and established a new career rushing record. By the time his tenure on the field came to an end in 1966, other black players had emerged as stars, among them Chicago Bears running back Gayle Sayers, and New York Giants safety Emlen Tunnel.

One stumbling block remained for black football players: three key positions were quietly considered "white only": middle linebacker, center, and quarterback. In the interests of winning games, however, these artificial boundaries inevitably fell. Willie Lanier of the Kansas City Chiefs became the first in a long line of black All-Star middle linebackers. Quarterback James Harris of the Los Angeles Rams became the first black starter at his position in the 1970s. Centers Ray Donaldson of the Indianapolis Colts and Dwight Stephenson of the Miami Dolphins both turned in long careers as starters in the 1980s.

Black stars also redefined football's defensive game in the 1970s. The process began with the "Purple People Eaters" of the Minnesota Vikings

Eric Dickerson of the Los Angeles Raiders.

defensive line—including Carl Eller, Allan Page, and Jim Marshal. It extended through the Los Angeles Rams' "Fearsome Foursome," which included Rosey Grier, David "Deacon" Jones, and Lamar Lundy. Possibly the best-known unit, however, is the Pittsburgh Steelers' "Steel Curtain," including "Mean" Joe Greene, L. C. Greenwood, and Dwight White, who helped the Steelers win four Super Bowls.

The 1980s witnessed an explosion of black talent. Chicago Bears running back Walter Payton did the unthinkable when he broke Jim Brown's rushing record in 1984. Jerry Rice grabbed an all-time record 101 touchdown receptions and helped the San Francisco 49ers win two Super Bowls. Doug Williams overcame injuries to quarterback the underdog Washington Redskins to a Super Bowl victory in 1988. Two teams featured black starting quarterbacks: Warren Moon of the Houston Oilers and Randall Cunningham of the Philadelphia Eagles. By 1990 blacks comprised a full 60 percent of the 1,316 players in the NFL.

The coaching ranks have been slow to integrate but are finally showing some progress. Art Shell of the Los Angeles Raiders became the first black head coach of the modern era in 1990. Dennis Green assumed the head-coaching duties for the Minnesota Vikings in 1992. Professional football has also added three black coaches to the important positions of offensive and defensive coordinators. Executives in the NFL acknowledge that more progress must be made to promote black coaches. That promotion process should also affect the woeful record for minority coaching on the collegiate level, long a source of frustration for talented blacks in football.

As with basketball, football players' salaries have risen dramatically since the mid-1980s—a result of player-directed lawsuits and strikes. Front office personnel are more willing than ever to listen and respond to star players' demands, a fact that may lead to profound changes in NFL management by the twenty-first century.

♦ **BOXING**

Black athletes have been boxing professionally since colonial times. They have virtually dominated the sport since the 1930s, especially in the most

Joe Frazier knocks down Jimmy Ellis, 1970.

popular heavyweight division. Joe Louis held the world heavyweight title for a record eleven years and eight months in the 1930s and 1940s, and the American public cheered for middleweight champion Sugar Ray Robinson when he demolished German opponent Max Schmeling prior to World War II. Henry Armstrong held three world titles at once—featherweight, lightweight, and welterweight—during the Great Depression.

Louis, Robinson, and Armstrong were stars in what is considered the first Golden Age of blacks in boxing. A new Golden Age was ushered in on March 8, 1971, when Muhammad Ali and Joe Frazier drew the sport's first multimillion-dollar gate. Ali, a national figure since winning an Olympic gold medal in 1960, was one of the first athletes to exploit his position to comment on American political and social events. Almost singlehandedly he transformed boxing from a second-rank endeavor to a top-drawing entertainment.

No serious white contender has risen in boxing's heavyweight division since the days of Ali. Other divisions, too, have featured stellar black

Evander Holyfield, heavyweight champion in 1991.

fighters. During the 1970s and 1980s fans were thrilled by middle- and welterweight match-ups between Sugar Ray Leonard, Marvin Hagler, and Thomas Hearns. When Ali was no longer able to defend his heavyweight crown, new challengers such as Larry Holmes and Leon Spinks ascended to the championship ranks.

As purses for major boxing events inched into the neighborhood of $100 million per match in the mid-1980s, a new generation of fighters arose.

Marvin Hagler celebrates his undisputed world middleweight championship after knocking out Thomas Hearns.

"Iron" Mike Tyson, a tough youngster from Brooklyn, became the best-known heavyweight champion since Ali and the wealthiest boxer of all time. His tumultuous reign ended with a knockout by Buster Douglas, who in turn lost to Evander Holyfield. Holyfield was unseated in 1992 by Riddick Bowe, another citizen of the same Brooklyn projects where Tyson had grown up. Unlike the combative Tyson, Bowe earned a reputation for professionalism and social activism as he spoke against apartheid policies in South Africa, and for the need for more sports programs in the nation's ghettos. In 1993, Holyfield defeated Bowe, once again becoming the heavyweight champion.

A top boxer like Riddick Bowe can conceivably earn as much as $100 million for less than a dozen major ring events. The advent of pay-per-view television and cable network sponsorship has led to soaring profits for the sport and its practitioners.

Professional boxing features well-known black figures in all realms of the sport. Bowe, for instance, employs black trainers, including the well-known Eddie Futch, and a black manager, Rock Newman. Entrepreneur Don King is both the most famous and the wealthiest boxing promoter of the modern era. His powerful position in boxing's ranks—and his ability to ingratiate himself with champion after champion—assure him continued success in his field.

Boxing is a brutal and dangerous sport, but it demands years of specialized training, rigorous conditioning, and singular dedication. The public appetite for major boxing events will continue to provide ample opportunities for talented athletes from all over the world.

◆ **WOMEN IN SPORTS**

American sporting history has been greatly enriched by the activities of a number of talented black women athletes. From the championships won by tennis star Althea Gibson to the gold medals earned by Jackie Joyner-Kersee, women have achieved both fame and power from athletic endeavor.

High jumper Alice Coachman became the first black woman to win an Olympic gold medal. She earned the gold at the 1948 Olympic Games in London, paving the way for generations of American athletes to come. Other Olympic medal winners include Wilma Rudolph, who overcame a serious disability to snatch three gold medals in the 1960 Olympics; Florence Griffith Joyner, who won a phenomenal three gold medals and one silver medal for track events at the 1988 Olympics; Debi Thomas, the first black woman to win an Olympic medal in figure skating with a bronze showing at the 1988 Olympics; and Jackie Joyner-Kersee, an Olympic champion in the grueling heptathlon competition and the long jump.

A 1992 *Sporting News* magazine list of the 100 most powerful Americans in sports included the name Anita DeFrantz. DeFrantz, who won a bronze medal for competitive rowing in the 1976 Olympics, is the first African-American member of the International Olympic Committee. DeFrantz will play a crucial role in the planning of the 1996 Olympic Games in Atlanta, Georgia, and other international events as well.

One of the best-known black heroines in sports is Althea Gibson. During the crisis years of the civil-rights era in the late 1950s, Gibson made her mark by winning a Grand Slam tennis tournament in 1956, two Wimbledon titles in 1957 and 1958, and the United States Lawn Tennis Association national singles championships in 1957 and 1958. Gibson was the first African American to gain top honors in professional tennis, and her performance paved the way for subsequent stars such as Arthur Ashe and Zina Garrison.

Florence Griffith Joyner won a phenomenal three gold medals and one silver medal in track events at the 1988 Olympic Games.

Althea Gibson makes a low return on her way to victory in 1957, when she became the first black ever to win a Wimbledon title.

The increased political clout of women has brought about changes in attitudes toward competitive sports. While women may never achieve parity in funding for their athletic programs on college campuses and in public schools, a federal mandate has been issued to try to bridge the gap. The issue will become more crucial as increasing numbers of women who have played competitive sports encourage their children to engage in athletics.

♦ ♦ ♦ ♦ ♦ ♦ ♦ ♦ ♦ ♦ ♦ ♦ ♦ ♦ AFRICAN-AMERICAN ATHLETES

Born in Mobile, Alabama on February 5, 1934, Aaron first played sandlot ball as a teenager. He later played for a team called the Black Bears, but soon thereafter signed a $200-per-month contract with the Indianapolis Clowns of the Negro American League.

Hank Aaron (1934–)

Baseball Player

In June of 1952, Aaron was purchased by the Boston Braves. The following season, playing for Jacksonville, his .362 average led the South At-

Hank Aaron, pictured here in 1970, hit more home runs than any other player in major league history.

lantic League. This led to a promotion to the Braves, then based in Milwaukee, and the beginning of his brilliant major league career in 1954.

Aaron enjoyed perhaps his finest season in 1957, when he was named Most Valuable Player and led his team to a world championship. His stats that year included a .322 average, 44 homers, 132 runs batted in, and 118 runs scored.

Aaron hit more home runs than anyone else in the history of major league baseball. He attained this plateau with his second home run of the 1974 season, a shot that marked his 715th career round-tripper and thus broke the previous record of 714, which had been held by Babe Ruth. Aaron finished that season with 20 homers and brought his career mark to a total of 733. He completed his career with a total of 755 home runs.

Over his career, Aaron won a pair of batting titles and hit over .300 in 12 seasons. He won the home run and RBI crowns four times apiece, hit 40 or more homers eight times, and hit at least 20 for 20 consecutive years, a National League record. In addition, he was named to 20 consecutive all-star teams.

In January 1982, Aaron received 406 of 415 votes from the Baseball Writers Association as he was elected into the Baseball Hall of Fame.

Abdul-Jabbar was born Ferdinand Lewis Alcindor, Jr. In high school, at 7'1/2" tall, he was easily the most sought after basketball player, particularly after he established a New York City record of 2,067 points and 2,002 rebounds, leading Power Memorial High School to three straight championships. Power won 95 and lost only six games during Lew Alcindor's years with the team; 71 of these victories were consecutive.

Kareem Abdul-Jabbar (1947–)

Basketball Player

Abdul-Jabbar combined great height with catlike moves and a deft shooting touch to lead UCLA to three consecutive NCAA Championships. Twice, as a sophomore and a senior, he was chosen as the top collegiate player in the country. He finished his career at UCLA as the ninth all-time collegiate scorer, accumulating 2,325 points in 88 games for an average of 26.4 points per game. After leading UCLA to its third consecutive NCAA title, Abdul-Jabbar signed a contract with the Milwaukee Bucks for $1.4 million.

In his rookie season, 1969–1970, he led the Bucks, a recently established expansion club, to a second-place finish in the Eastern Division, only a few games behind the division winners, the New York Knickerbockers. Abdul-Jabbar won personal acclaim for his outstanding play in the 1970 NBA All-Star game, combining with the Knicks' Willis Reed to lead the East to victory. After being voted Rookie of the Year, he went on to win the scoring championships in 1971 and 1972. He was one of the keys to the Bucks' world championship in 1971. In 1973, he finished second in scoring with a 30.2 point average, but he had become dissatisfied with life in Milwaukee. At the end of the 1974–1975 season he was traded to the L.A. Lakers. Abdul-Jabbar enjoyed a very successful career with the Lakers, leading the team to NBA championships in 1980, 1982, 1985, 1987, and 1988.

A serious person both on and off the court, Abdul-Jabbar is a convert to the Hanafi Muslims. Greatly influenced by the life and struggles of Malcolm X, he believes that the Islamic religion (as distinct from the nationalistic Black Muslims) and determined effort have much to offer for a good life.

Abdul-Jabbar announced his retirement after the 1988–89 season, one year after the Lakers had won back-to-back World Championships.

Muhammad Ali

(1942–)

Boxer

Born Cassius Clay in Louisville, Kentucky, Ali started boxing because he thought it was "the quickest way for black people to make it." After winning the 1960 Olympic gold medal as light-heavyweight, he turned professional. In 1963 he converted to Islam, though the faith strongly disapproves of boxing, and changed his name. A year later, Ali won the world heavyweight championship by knocking out Sonny Liston.

Nine successful title defenses followed before Ali's famous war with the Army began. Refusing to serve in the armed forces during the Vietnam War, Ali maintained that it was contrary to Muslim tenets. Stripped of his title and banned from boxing in the United States, Ali faced prison, but he refused to back down and was finally vindicated by the United States Supreme Court in 1970.

Coming back to the ring after a three-and-a-half year layoff, he worked his way up for another title shot. His biggest matches along the way were Superfights I and II against Joe Frazier, in which Ali suffered his first loss, and, in a return match, evened the score.

Few fans gave Ali a chance against heavyweight champion George Foreman when they met in Zaire on October 30, 1974. A four-to-one underdog at ring time, Ali amazed the boxing world, knocking out his stronger, younger opponent. After regaining the crown, Ali knocked out Chuck Wepner and Ron Lyle, and decisioned Joe Bugner.

In December of 1981, Muhammad Ali entered the ring and lost a bout against Canadian heavyweight Trevor Berbick. It was a rare occasion and an inauspicious end to a career for a fighter who had won the heavyweight title three times.

As he gets older Ali's personal dedication to helping black people everywhere becomes increasingly more generous, and he now places special emphasis on setting a good example for black youth.

The only fighter ever to hold three titles at the same time is Henry Armstrong, who accomplished this feat on August 17, 1938, when he added the lightweight championship to the featherweight and welterweight titles that he had won earlier.

Armstrong was born on December 12, 1912 in St. Louis, Missouri. In 1929, while fighting under the name of Melody Jackson, he was knocked out in his professional debut in Pittsburgh. Two weeks later, however, he won his first fight. For the next eight years he traveled from coast to coast, fighting all comers until he was finally given a shot at the featherweight title on October 20, 1937, when he defeated Petey Sarron.

Less than a year later, on May 31, 1938, Armstrong picked up his second title with a decision over welterweight champion Barney Ross. Within three months he gained his own triple crown, winning a decision over lightweight champion Lou Ambers. Armstrong was inducted into the Black Athletes Hall of Fame in 1975.

Henry Armstrong (1912–1988)

Boxer

Born in 1943 in Richmond, Virginia, Ashe learned the game at the Richmond Racket Club, which had been formed by local black enthusiasts. Dr. R. W. Johnson, who had also served as an adviser and benefactor to Althea Gibson, sponsored Ashe's tennis career, spending thousands of dollars and a great deal of time with him.

By 1958, Ashe reached the semifinals in the under-fifteen division of the National Junior Championships. In 1960 and 1961 he won the Junior Indoors Singles title. Even before he finished high school, he was ranked 28th in the country.

In 1961 Ashe entered UCLA on a tennis scholarship. He was on his way to winning the U.S. Amateur Tennis Championship and the U.S. Open Tennis Championship, in addition to becoming the first black man ever named to a Davis Cup Team.

In 1975 Ashe was recognized as one of the world's great tennis players, having defeated Jimmy Connors at Wimbledon as well as taking the World Championship Tennis (WCT) singles title over Bjorn Borg. At Wimbledon he defeated Connors 6–1, 5–7, 6–4.

Arthur Ashe (1943–1993)

Tennis Player

In 1979, at the age of thirty-five, Ashe suffered a heart attack. Following quadruple bypass heart surgery, he retired from playing tennis. He began writing a nationally syndicated column and contributed monthly articles to *Tennis* magazine. He wrote a tennis diary, *Portrait in Motion*, his autobiography *Off the Court*, and the book *Advantage Ashe*. In addition, he compiled the historical work *A Hard Road to Glory: A History of the African-American Athlete*.

Ashe was named captain of the U.S. Davis Cup team in 1981. He was a former president and active member of the board of directors of the Association of Tennis Professionals, and a co-founder of the National Junior Tennis League. Late in his career, he also served as a television sports commentator.

In April 1992, Ashe announced that he had contracted AIDS as the result of a tainted blood transfusion during heart-bypass surgery. He died on February 6, 1993.

Elgin Baylor

(1934–)

Basketball Player

Born in Washington, DC, Elgin Baylor first became an All American while attending Spingarn High School. While at Seattle University he was a college All American. In 1959 Baylor made a sensational professional debut with the Minneapolis Lakers; he became the first rookie to be named most valuable player in the All-Star Game. That same year he was named to the All-League team, setting a scoring record of 64 points in a single game.

After five years as a superstar, Baylor injured his knee during a 1965 playoff game against the Bullets. Constant work brought him back to competitive form, but he never reached his former greatness. His career point total of 23,149 is fourth highest in NBA history, and his field goal average of 27.4 is second. His best year was 1961–1962, when he averaged 38.2 points a game. When he retired in 1968, Baylor had made the All-Pro first team nine times and had played eight consecutive All-Star games.

Baylor was inducted into the Black Athletes Hall of Fame in 1975, and the Basketball Hall of Fame in 1976.

Jim Brown

(1936–)

Football Player

James Nathaniel Brown was born February 17, 1936, on St. Simon Island, Georgia, but his family moved to Manhasset, Long Island, New York, when he was seven. While at Manhasset High School he became an outstanding competitor in baseball, football, track and field, basketball, and lacrosse; following graduation he had a choice of 42 college scholarships, as well as professional offers from both the New York Yankees and the Boston Braves. Brown chose Syracuse University, where he gained national recognition. An All-American performer in both football and lacrosse, he turned down the opportunity to compete in the decathlon at the 1956 Olympic Games, since it would have conflicted with his football schedule. He also spurned a three-year $150,000 offer to become a professional fighter.

Brown's 1957 entry into professional football with the Cleveland Browns was emblematic of the manner in which he would dominate the game in the decade to come. He led the league in rushing, paced Cleveland to a division championship, and was unanimously named rookie of the year. Brown broke rushing and scoring records in both single-season and lifetime totals, and he was All-League fullback virtually every season. His records include most yards gained—lifetime 12,312—and most touchdowns—lifetime 106. He was voted Football Back of the Decade for 1950–1960.

Brown announced his retirement in the summer of 1966, deciding to devote his time to a budding movie career and to the improvement of black business. He has made several films, including *Rio Conchos, The Dirty Dozen,* and *100 Rifles*. In addition to his movie-making activities, he is president and founder of Amer-I-Can.

Roy Campanella (1921-1993)

Baseball Player

Born in Philadelphia, Campanella began playing semi-professional baseball at the age of fifteen with the Bacharach Giants. In 1945 Campanella turned down the opportunity to become the first black in the major leagues, when he mistakenly understood Branch Rickey's offer to be a contract with a rumored black team in Brooklyn. A few days later, he learned from Jackie Robinson that the offer had involved the possibility of playing with the Brooklyn Dodgers of the National League.

In 1946 Campanella was signed by the Dodgers. Before the year was out, however, Campanella was brought up to Brooklyn. Over the next eight years, the Dodger star played with five National League pennant winners and one world championship team. He played on seven consecutive National League All-Star teams (1949–1955).

Roy Campanella (right) with Sammy Hughes, 1942.

In January 1958, Campanella's career was ended by an automobile accident, which left him paralyzed and confined to a wheel chair. In March 1975, he was inducted into the Black Athletes Hall of Fame.

Wilt Chamberlain

(1936–)

Basketball Player

Chamberlain was born in Philadelphia on August 21, 1936. By the time he entered high school, he was already 6'11". When he graduated from high school, he had his choice of 77 major colleges and 125 smaller schools. He chose Kansas University but left after his junior year with two years of All-American honors behind him.

Before joining the NBA in 1959 Chamberlain played with the Harlem Globetrotters. Although dominating the sport with the Philadelphia 76ers (1959–1967) and with the Los Angeles Lakers (1968–1972), Chamberlain was a member of only two championship teams, Philadelphia (1961) and Los Angeles (1972). For his gargantuan effort in defeating the Knicks in the latter series, including playing the final game with both hands painfully injured, he was voted MVP. At the start of the 1974 season, he left the Lakers to become player–coach of the San Diego Conquistadors (ABA) for a reported $500,000 contract.

Wilt Chamberlain holds most of the major basketball records: for single games, most points (100); most field goals made (36); most free throws (28); and most rebounds (55). His career records are most rebounds (23,924); highest scoring average (30.1); most points (31,419); most field goals made (12,681); and most free throws attempted (11,862).

Born Robert Lee Elder in Washington, DC, Elder first picked up golf as a caddie at the age of fifteen. After his father's death during World War II, Elder and his mother moved to Los Angeles, where he met the famed black golfer Ted Rhodes. He was later drafted by the United States Army, where he sharpened his skills as captain of the golf team.

Following his discharge from the Army, he began to teach golf. In 1962 he debuted as a professional, winning the national title of the United Golf Association, a black organization. Elder had played seventeen years with the United Golf Association prior to his participation in the PGA, participating in close to fifty tournaments. He debuted with the PGA in November 1967, finishing one stroke out of the money. In thirty PGA tournaments, Elder earned $38,000; he was the first black professional golfer to reach $1 million in earnings.

Lee Elder

(1934–)

Golfer

Erving was born in Hempstead, Long Island, on February 22, 1950. As a player at Roosevelt High School, Erving made the All-County and All–Long Island teams. He was awarded an athletic scholarship to the University of Massachusetts, but after completing his junior year he left college, hired the services of a management firm, and signed a $500,000 contract for four years with the Virginia Squires of the ABA. Voted rookie of the year in 1972, he renegotiated his contract and eventually signed with the New Jersey Nets for $2.8 million for four years.

In his first season with the Nets (1973), he led the league in scoring for the second consecutive year and paced his team to the ABA championship. After being traded to the 76ers, Erving became a favorite with Philadelphia fans, leading the 76ers to the NBA championship in 1983. Between his combined seasons with the two teams, he became the thirteenth player to score 20,000 points. Erving retired following the 1986–1987 season.

Julius "Dr. J"

Erving (1950–)

Basketball Player

Althea Gibson was born in Silver, South Carolina, but raised in Harlem, where she learned to play paddle tennis. After her paddle tennis days, she entered and won the Department of Parks Manhattan Girls' Tennis Championship. In 1942 she began to receive professional coaching at the interracial Cosmopolitan Tennis Club, and a year later won the New York State Negro Girls Singles title. In 1945 and 1946, she won the National Negro Girls Singles championship, and in 1948 she began a decade of domination of the same title in the women's division.

Althea Gibson

(1927–)

Tennis Player

A year later Gibson entered Florida A&M University, where she played tennis and basketball for the next four years. In 1950 she was runner-up for the National Indoor Championship, and that same year became the first black to play at Forest Hills. The following year she became the first black to play at Wimbledon. In 1957 Gibson won the Wimbledon singles crown, and she teamed with Darlene Hard to win the doubles championship as well. In 1957 and 1958, Gibson won the U.S. Open Women's Singles title.

Gibson has served as a recreation manager, a member of the New Jersey State Athletic Control Board and the Governor's Council on Physical Fitness, and as a sports consultant. She is also the author of a book, *I Always Wanted to Be Somebody.*

Reggie Jackson
(1946–)

Baseball Player

Because of his outstanding performance in the early fall, Reggie Jackson became known as "Mr. October." During his years with the Oakland Athletics and New York Yankees, Jackson captured or tied 13 World Series records to become baseball's greatest record holder for the fall classic. Reggie Jackson ranks among baseball's crop of players with proven superstar ability. His temperament, long reported to be as explosive and dynamic as his skill with the bat, gave him the drive to reach the top.

Born in Wynecote, Pennsylvania, he followed his father's encouragement to become an all-around athlete while at Cheltenham High School, where he ran track, starred at halfback, and batted .550. An outstanding football and baseball collegian at Arizona State University, he left after his sophomore year to join the Athletics (then located in Kansas City).

In 1968, his first full season with the Athletics, he hit 29 homers and batted in 74 runs, but made 18 errors and struck out 171 times, the second worst seasonal total in baseball history. After playing a season of winter ball under Frank Robinson's direction, Jackson was back on track. His performance continued to improve, and in 1973 he batted .293, led the league in home runs (32), RBIs (117), and slugging average (.531), and was selected most valuable player.

While with the Oakland Athletics, Jackson participated in three straight World Series: 1972, 1973, and 1974. Later, with the New York Yankees, Jackson participated in the World Series of 1977, 1978, and 1981. In 1977 he was named series MVP after hitting five home runs, three in the crucial sixth and deciding game.

The first of the big money free agents, Jackson hit 144 homers, drove in 461 runs, and boosted his total career home runs to 425 while with the Yankees. In January 1982, after an often stormy tenure in New York, he signed with the California Angels. Jackson retired as an active player in 1987, and he has occasionally served as a commentator on baseball broadcasts. He has also devoted more time to his collection of antique cars.

Johnson was born August 14, 1959 in Lansing, Michigan. He attended Everett High School and in 1974 made their varsity basketball team as a guard. It was while playing for Everett that he picked up the nickname "Magic" because of his ball-handling abilities. While in high school Johnson made the All-State Team and for three years was named the United Press International Prep-Player of the Year in Michigan.

Earvin "Magic" Johnson, Jr. (1959–)

Basketball Player

In 1977 Johnson enrolled at Michigan State University and played college ball until 1979, when he was selected by the LA Lakers in the National Basketball Association draft. Johnson played with the Lakers until his forced retirement in 1991 when he tested positive for HIV, the virus that is closely associated with acquired immunodeficiency syndrome (AIDS).

Throughout his college and professional career Johnson was an outstanding basketball player who brought much excitement, goodwill, and admiration to the game. He was the recipient of many awards and was chosen to play on many post-season all-star teams, including All–Big Ten Team (1977), NCAA Tournament's Most Outstanding Player, NCAA All-Tournament Team, Consensus All-American (1979), NBA Finals' Most Valuable Player, NBA All-Star Team, NBA All-Rookie Team (1980), All-NBA Team (1982–1989, 1991), Seagrams Seven Crowns of Sports Award, NBA Finals Most Valuable Player (1982), Schick Pivotal Player Award (1984), NBA Most Valuable Player (1987, 1989, 1990), Sporting News NBA Player of the Year, Allstate Good Hands Award, NBA Finals Most Valuable Player (1987), and NBA All-Star Game's Most Valuable Player (1990).

Since retiring from professional basketball Johnson continues to make appearances on the court, including playing on the United States Olympic Basketball Team in 1992 and playing in the 1992 NBA All-Star Game, where he won another most valuable player award.

**Jack Johnson
(1878–1946)**

Boxer

Jack Johnson became the first black heavyweight champion after winning the crown from Tommy Burns in Sydney, Australia, on December 26, 1908.

Johnson was born in Galveston, Texas in 1878, the son of a school janitor. He was so tiny as a boy that he was nicknamed "Li'l Arthur," a name that stuck with him throughout his career. As a young man, he "hoboed" around the country, making his way to Chicago, Boston, and New York, and learning the fighting trade by working out with veteran professionals whenever he could. When he finally got his chance at the title, he had already been fighting for nine years and had lost only three of approximately 100 bouts.

With his victory over Burns, Johnson became the center of a bitter racial controversy, as the American public clamored for the former white champion, Jim Jeffries, to come out of retirement and recapture the crown. When the two fought on July 4, 1910 in Reno, Nevada, Johnson knocked out Jeffries in the fourteenth round.

In 1913, Johnson left the United States because of legal entanglements. Two years later he defended his title against Jess Willard in Havana, Cuba, and was knocked out in the twenty-sixth round. His career record was 107 wins, 6 losses. Johnson died in 1946 in an automobile crash in North Carolina. He was inducted into the Boxing Hall of Fame in 1954.

**Michael Jordan
(1963–)**

Basketball Player

Michael Jordan was born in Brooklyn, New York and attended the University of North Carolina. As a rookie with the Chicago Bulls, Jordan was named to the All-Star team during the 1985 season. A skilled ball-handler and a slam-dunk artist, in 1986 he became the second NBA player in history to score more than 3,000 points in a single season.

Jordan was the NBA's individual scoring champ from 1987 through 1991. He was also named the NBA's most valuable player at the end of the 1987–88 season. In 1991 Jordan led the Chicago Bulls to their first NBA Championship and was the league's most valuable player. Under Jordan's leadership, the Bulls experienced repeat NBA championships in 1992 and 1993. In the autumn of 1993, Jordan announced his retirement from basketball.

Michael Jordan was the NBA's individual scoring champ from 1987 to 1991, and he led the Chicago Bulls to three consecutive NBA championships beginning in 1991.

In 1992 Jordan played for the United States Olympic Basketball team, which captured the gold medal in Barcelona, Spain. He is the founder of the Michael Jordan Celebrity Golf Classic, which raises funds for the United Negro College Fund.

Born in Los Angeles, Florence Griffith started in track at an early age. She first attended California State University at Northridge, but later transferred with her coach Bob Kersee when he moved to UCLA. She married 1984 Olympic gold medalist Al Joyner in 1987.

Florence Griffith Joyner (1959–)

Track and Field Athlete

At the 1984 Olympic Games she won a silver medal. She returned to the Olympic Games in 1988, winning gold medals in the 100-meter, 200-meter, and 400-meter relay races, and a silver medal in the 1600-meter relay race. She also set the world record for the 100-meter and 200-meter races that year.

Jackie Joyner-Kersee (1962–)

Track and Field Athlete

Often touted as the world's greatest female athlete, Jackie Joyner-Kersee won two gold medals at the 1988 Olympic Games and a gold and a bronze medal at the 1992 Games.

A native of East St. Louis, Illinois, she studied previous outstanding women athletes and soon teamed with her husband, coach Bob Kersee, to pursue her dreams of success in the field of competition. Prior to winning the 1988 gold medal, she participated in the 1984 Olympics and came away with a silver medal for the heptathlon despite a torn hamstring muscle.

The only woman to gain more than 7,000 points in the heptathlon four times, she set a world record for the grueling two-day event with 7,215 points at the 1988 Olympic trials prior to the competition itself. Joyner-Kersee also earned another gold medal in the heptathlon and a bronze medal in the long jump at the 1992 Olympic Games in Barcelona, Spain.

Carl Lewis (1961–)

Track and Field Athlete

In the 1984 Olympic Games in Los Angeles, Carl Lewis became the first athlete since Jesse Owens in 1936 to win four gold medals in Olympic competition.

Olympic champion Jackie Joyner-Kersee is widely considered the world's greatest female athlete.

In 1984 Carl Lewis became the second athlete—and the first since Jesse Owens in 1936—to win four gold medals in Olympic competition.

An often controversial track and field performer, the New Jersey native went into the 1984 competition with the burden of tremendous expectations as the result of intense pre-Olympics publicity. He did not set any Olympic records, even as a gold medalist, and found that his statements regarding training and drug use were often the subject of public concern.

Lewis went to the 1988 Olympics in Seoul, South Korea, hoping to duplicate his four gold-medal wins, and he was the subject of widespread interest as he faced off against his arch-rival, Canadian Ben Johnson.

Lewis won gold medals in the long jump and the 100-meter dash—though the latter prize came after Ben Johnson was disqualified following the race when he tested positive for steroid use—and a silver medal in the 200-meter dash. At the 1992 Olympics in Barcelona, Spain, Lewis won a gold medal for the long jump.

Joe Louis

(1914–1981)

Boxer

Joe Louis held the heavyweight championship for more than 11 years, longer than anyone else, and defended the title more often than any other heavyweight champion. His 25 title fights were more than the combined total of the eight champions who preceded him.

Born in a sharecropper's shack in Chambers County, Alabama, in 1914, Louis moved to Detroit as a small boy. Taking up boxing as an amateur, he won 50 out of 59 bouts (43 by knockout), before turning professional in 1934. He quickly gained a reputation in the Midwest.

In 1935 Lewis came east to meet Primo Carnera, a former boxing champion who was then staging a comeback. Louis knocked out Carnera in six rounds, earning his nickname "The Brown Bomber." After knocking out ex-champion Max Baer, Louis suffered his lone pre-championship defeat at the hands of Max Schmeling, the German title holder who knocked him out in the twelfth round. Less than a month later, Louis knocked out another former champion, Jack Sharkey, in three rounds. After defeating a number of other challengers, he was given a title fight with Jim Braddock on June 22, 1937. He stopped Braddock in the eighth round and began the long championship reign that was to see him defending his crown as often as six times in six months.

One of Louis's greatest fights was his 1941 come-from-behind, thirteenth-round knockout of Billy Conn. After winning a disputed decision over Joe Walcott in 1947, Louis knocked out the Jersey challenger six months later, then went into retirement. Joe Louis died April 12, 1981 at the age of sixty-seven.

Willie Mays

(1931–)

Baseball Player

During his 21 seasons with the San Francisco Giants, Willie Mays hit more than 600 home runs. Besides being a solid hitter, Mays also has been called the game's finest defensive outfielder and perhaps its best baserunner as well.

Willie Mays slides across home plate, 1956.

Born in Fairfield, Alabama on May 6, 1931, Mays made his professional debut on July 4, 1948, with the Birmingham Black Barons. He was signed by the New York Giants in 1950 and reached the major leagues in 1951, in time to become the National League's Rookie of the Year with 20 home runs, 68 RBIs, and the sensational fielding that contributed to his team's pennant victory.

After two years in the Army, Mays returned to lead the Giants to the World Championship in 1954, gaining recognition as the league's most valuable player for his 41 homers, 110 RBIs, and .345 batting average.

When the Giants moved to San Francisco, Mays continued his phenomenal home-run hitting and led his team to a 1962 pennant. A year later, *Sport* magazine named him "the greatest player of the decade." He won the MVP award again in 1965, after hitting 52 home runs and batting .317.

Traded to the New York Mets before the 1972 season, he continued to play outfield and first base. At the end of the 1973 season, his records included 2,992 games (third on the all-time list), 3,283 hits (seventh), and 660 home runs (third). Willie Mays is one of only seven ballplayers to have hit four home runs in one game. After acting as a coach for the Mets, Mays left baseball to pursue a business career. He was elected to the Baseball Hall of Fame in 1979.

Willie O'Ree

(1935–)

Hockey Player

Born in Fredericton, New Brunswick, Canada, William Eldon O'Ree began playing hockey as a child. In 1956 he signed with the Quebec Aces. In 1958 he made his debut with the Boston Bruins, becoming the first black hockey player in the National Hockey League—only thirteen blacks have played in the NHL since the league's creation. From 1958 to 1980 O'Ree played for various major and minor league hockey teams, including the Ottawa Canadiens, San Diego Gulls, and San Diego Hawks. O'Ree retired in 1980.

Jesse Owens

(1913–1980)

Track and Field Athlete

The track and field records Jesse Owens set have all been eclipsed, but his reputation as one of the first great athletes with the combined talents of a sprinter, low hurdler, and broad jumper has hardly diminished with the passing of time.

Born James Cleveland Owens in Danville, Alabama, Jesse and his family moved to Ohio when he was still young; the name "Jesse" derived from the way a teacher pronounced his initials, "J.C."

In 1932, while attending East Technical High School in Cleveland, Owens gained national fame with a 10.3 clocking in the 100-meter dash. Two years later Owens entered Ohio State University, and for the next four years he made track history, becoming universally known as "The Ebony Antelope." While competing in the Big Ten Championships at Ann Arbor, Michigan, on May 25, 1935, Owens had what has been called "the greatest single day in the history of man's athletic achievements." In the space of about 70 minutes, he tied the world record for the 100-yard dash and surpassed the world record for five other events, including the broad jump, the 220-yard low hurdles, and the 220-yard dash.

In 1936, at the Berlin Olympics, Owens won four gold medals—at that time the most universally acclaimed feat in the history of the Games. When Adolf Hitler refused to present him with the medals he had won in the various competitions, Owens's fame became even more widespread as a result of the publicity.

Leroy Robert

"Satchel" Paige

(1906–1982)

Baseball Player

Long before Jackie Robinson broke the color barrier of "organized baseball," Satchel Paige was a name well known to the general sports public. As an outstanding performer in "Negro baseball," Paige had become a legendary figure whose encounters with major league players added considerable laurels to his athletic reputation.

Jesse Owens (center) accepts the gold medal at the 1936 Olympic Games in Berlin, Germany.

Paige was born in Mobile, Alabama in July 1906. He began playing semi-professional ball while working as an iceman and porter. In the mid-1920s he became a professional player with the Birmingham Black Barons, and later, while playing at Chattanooga, he acquired the nickname "Satchel" because of his "satchel-sized feet."

For the next two decades Paige compiled a phenomenal record. In 1933 he won 31 games and lost four. Paige also dominated winter ball in Latin America during the 1930s. In 1942 Paige led the Kansas City Monarchs to victory in the Negro World Series, and four years later he helped them to the pennant by allowing only two runs in 93 innings, a performance that included a string of 64 straight scoreless innings.

In 1948, when he was brought up to the major leagues, Paige was well past his prime, but he still was able to contribute six victories in Cleveland's pennant drive. Four years later, while pitching for the St. Louis Browns, he was named to the American League All-Star squad.

Until the 1969 baseball season, Paige was primarily active on the barn-storming circuit with the Harlem Globetrotters and a host of other exhibition teams. In 1969 the Atlanta Braves, in an attempt to make Paige eligible for baseball's pension plan, signed him to a one-year contract as coach. Paige died in June 1982.

Walter Payton
(1954–)

Football Player

When Walter Payton retired as a running back for the Chicago Bears after the 1986 season, he was the National Football League's all-time leading rusher, having broken a record held for many years by Jim Brown.

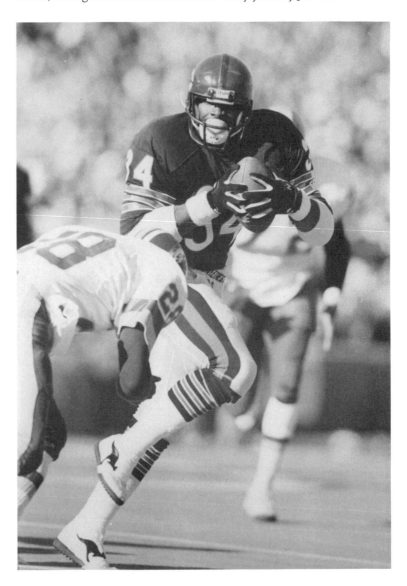

Upon his retirement in 1987, Walter Payton was the NFL's all-time leading rusher.

A graduate of Jackson State University, Payton played his entire career in Chicago and received numerous awards. Nicknamed "Sweetness," he broke O.J. Simpson's single game rushing record after gaining 275 yards during a game with the Minnesota Vikings in 1977. Seven years later, he surpassed Jim Brown's career rushing record of 12,312 yards during a game with the New Orleans Saints.

Willis Reed

(1943–)

Basketball Player

A native of Louisiana, Willis Reed spent his boyhood picking cotton around his hometown of Bernice. He attended Grambling College, where he was discovered by Red Holzman, the chief scout for the New York Knicks. Reed led the Knicks in scoring and rebounding on his way to becoming rookie of the year in 1965.

In 1970, when the Knicks won their first NBA Championship, Reed received three separate MVP awards—one for the regular season, one for the All-Star game, and one for the playoffs.

At 6'9" and 240 pounds, Reed was not big for a center. Nonetheless, he was named to the All-Star team his first seven seasons. In 1973 he led the Knicks to their second NBA title and was again named most valuable player. Unfortunately, knee problems ended his career. In 1981 Reed was elected to the National Memorial Basketball Hall of Fame.

Frank Robinson

(1935–)

Baseball Player
and Manager

Frank Robinson was major league baseball's first black manager. Named to the head post of the Cleveland Indians in 1975, Robinson exhibited the same cool, confident demeanor that served him well during an 18-year career as a major league player.

Robinson left the Indians in 1977 and became the manager of the Rochester Red Wings, a minor league team, in 1978. In 1981 Robinson was hired by the San Francisco Giants, which he managed until 1984. He also managed the Baltimore Orioles during the late 1980s.

Born in Beaumont, Texas in 1936, Robinson moved with his family to Oakland, California at the age of five. During his teens he was a football and baseball star at McClyronds High School. After graduation in 1953, he signed with the Cincinnati Reds.

In 1956, he made a smash debut in the major leagues, hitting 38 homers and winning rookie of the year honors. Over the next eight years, he hit 259 homers and had 800 RBIs, an outstanding record, but one that was often underpublicized since Robinson played in the shadow of such greats as Willie Mays and Hank Aaron.

In 1961 Robinson was named most valuable player for leading Cincinnati to the National League pennant. Five years later, Robinson won the American League's Triple Crown and became the first player to win the MVP in both leagues. By the end of the 1973 season, he had hit .297 in 2,432 games with 2,614 hits, 1,639 runs, and 1,613 RBIs. Robinson retired as an active player in 1976 and was elected to the National Baseball Hall of Fame in 1982.

Jackie Robinson

(1919–1972)

Baseball Player

Born in Cairo, Georgia, Robinson was raised in Pasadena, California. At UCLA he gained All-American honorable mention as a halfback, but he left college in his junior year to play professional football for the Los Angeles Bulldogs. After serving as an Army lieutenant during World War II, Robinson returned to civilian life with the hope of becoming a physical education coach. To achieve this, he felt he had to make a name for himself, and for this reason he decided to spend a few seasons in the Negro baseball league.

In 1945, while he was playing with the Kansas City Monarchs, Branch Rickey of the Brooklyn Dodgers assigned him to the Montreal Royals, the team's top farm club, where he was to be groomed for a career in the majors. On April 10, 1947, the Dodgers announced that they had purchased Robinson's contract, and the following day he began his major league career. During a 10-year career, he hit .311 in 1,382 games with 1,518 hits, 947 runs, 273 doubles, and 734 RBIs. He stole home 19 times, once in World Series play. He won the National League's most valuable player award in 1949 and played on six National League pennant winners, as well as one world championship team. Robinson was inducted into the National Baseball Hall of Fame in 1962.

After his retirement from baseball, Robinson became a bank official, president of a land development firm, and a director of programs to combat drug addiction. He died on October 24, 1972 in Stamford, Connecticut.

Born Walker Smith in Detroit on May 3, 1920, he took the name Robinson from the certificate of an amateur boxer whose identity enabled him to meet the age requirements for getting a match in Michigan; the "Sugar" came from his having been dubbed "the sweetest fighter."

As a 10-year-old boy, Robinson had watched a Detroit neighbor, Joe Louis, train for an amateur boxing career. When Robinson moved to New York two years later, he began to spend most of his time at local gyms in preparation for his own amateur career. After winning all 89 of his amateur bouts and the 1939 Golden Gloves featherweight championship, he turned professional in 1940 at Madison Square Garden, fighting for the first time on a card headlined by the Fritzie Zivic–Henry Armstrong fight.

After several years of being "the uncrowned king of the welterweights," Robinson beat Tommy Bell in an elimination title bout in December 1946. He successfully defended the title for five years, and on February 14, 1951, took the middleweight crown from Jake LaMotta.

In July 1951 he lost the title to Randy Turpin, only to win it back two months later. Retiring for a time, Robinson subsequently fought a series of exciting battles with Carl "Bobo" Olsen, Carmen Basilio, and Gene Fullmer before retiring permanently, on December 10, 1965, with six victories in title bouts to his credit—more than any other fighter in history.

Suffering from diabetes, hypertension, and Alzheimer's disease, one month shy of his 69th birthday, Robinson died of apparent natural causes at the Brotman Medical Center in Culver City, California on April 12, 1989. Over his career, he won 174 of 201 professional bouts, including titles in three weight classes.

Wilma Rudolph is the only American woman runner, aside from Florence Griffith Joyner, to win three gold medals in the Olympic Games. Her performance is all the more remarkable in light of the fact that she had double pneumonia and scarlet fever as a young child and could not walk without braces until age eleven.

Born on June 23, 1940, in St. Bethlehem, Tennessee, she soon moved with her family to Clarksville. At an early age, she survived polio and scar-

"Sugar Ray" Robinson (1920–1989)

Boxer

Wilma Rudolph (1940–)

Track and Field Athlete

let fever, and was left with the use of one leg. Through daily leg massages administered in turn by different members of her family, she progressed to the point where she was able to walk with the aid of a special shoe. Three years later, however, she discarded the shoe and began joining her brother in backyard basketball games.

While a sophomore at Burt High School in Clarksville, Rudolph broke the state basketball record for girls. As a sprinter, she was undefeated in all her high school track meets.

In 1957 she enrolled at Tennessee State University and began to set her sights for the Olympic Games in Rome. In the interim, she gained national recognition in collegiate meets, setting the world record for the 200-meter dash in July 1960.

In the Olympics, she earned the title of the "World's Fastest Woman" by winning gold medals for the 100-meter dash, the 200-meter dash (Olympic record), and for anchoring the 400-meter relay (world record). She was named by the Associated Press as the U.S. Female Athlete of the Year for 1960, and also won United Press Athlete of the Year honors.

Rudolph has served as a track coach, an athletic consultant, and the assistant director of athletics for the Mayor's Youth Foundation in Chicago. She is also the founder of the Wilma Rudolph Foundation.

Bill Russell

(1934–)

Basketball Player

Bill Russell, who led the Boston Celtics to eleven titles, eight in a row, is regarded as the finest defensive basketball player in the game's history. The 6'10" star is also the first black to coach and play for a National Basketball Association team. His style of play is credited with revolutionizing basketball.

Russell was born on February 12, 1934, in Monroe, Louisiana. The family moved to Detroit when he was nine, but two years later the family continued on to Oakland, California. There, at McClyronds High School, Russell proved to be an awkward but determined basketball player who eventually received a scholarship to the nearby University of San Francisco.

In college Russell came into his own, becoming the most publicized athlete on the West Coast during his sophomore year. Over the next two years, his fame spread across the nation as he led his team to sixty consecutive victories (a collegiate record) and two straight NCAA titles.

The Celtics had never won an NBA Championship before Russell's arrival in 1957. With the help of Russell's defensive capabilities, the Celtics became one of the most successful teams in the history of professional sports, winning the world championship eight years in a row. Russell himself was named most valuable player on five separate occasions (1958, 1961–1963, 1965). In 1966, Russell became the Celtics player/coach.

After the 1968–1969 season, having led the Celtics to their eleventh NBA crown, Russell retired as both coach and player. A five-time NBA most valuable player, Russell is the NBA leader in career minutes (40,726) and second in career rebounds (21,721).

After retirement, Russell was a color commentator on NBC–TV's NBA Game of the Week. In 1974 he accepted a lucrative contract to become head coach and general manager of the Seattle Supersonics. That year, he was inducted into the Basketball Hall of Fame.

Russell left basketball for several years but returned once again to active coaching with the Sacramento Kings in 1987. In 1988, the Kings announced that Russell had accepted a position as the team's director of player personnel.

O.J. Simpson (1947–)

Football Player

Orenthal J. Simpson may have been the finest running back in pro football. Nicknamed "The Juice," he holds rushing records for most yards in a single game and most yards in a single season.

Born in San Francisco on July 9, 1947, Simpson began his football stardom at the University of Southern California, winning the Heisman Trophy in 1968. A year prior to that he was a member of the USC relay team, which set a world record of 38.6 seconds in the 440-yard run. A year after graduation, ABC Sports voted him College Player of the Decade. He signed with the Buffalo Bills in 1969, and three years later he achieved his first rushing title, gaining over 1,200 yards.

Simpson enjoyed his finest season in 1973. On opening day he rushed for 250 yards against the New England Patriots, breaking the record of 247 yards held by Willie Ellison. He gained an astonishing 2,003 yards for the entire season, surpassing the previous mark of 1,863 yards held by Jim Brown. In addition, he scored 12 touchdowns, averaged 6 yards per carry, and had more rushing yardage than 15 of the other NFL clubs. He was named player of the year and won the Jim Thorpe Trophy.

Simpson retired from football in 1978. He has appeared in several feature films and worked as a sports commentator for ABC–TV. He is currently a co-host for NBC–TV's NFL Live.

Marshall W. Taylor

(1878–1932)

Cyclist

Marshall W. "Major" Taylor became America's first black U.S. National Champion in 1899. Born in Indianapolis, the son of a coachman, he worked at a bicycle store part time as a teen. After attending his first race, his boss suggested that Major enter a couple of races. To their surprise, he won a 10-mile race and proceeded to compete as an amateur.

By the time he was sixteen, he went to work in a factory owned by a former champion, and with his new boss's encouragement, competed in races in Canada, Europe, Australia, and New Zealand.

During nearly sixteen years of competition, he won numerous championships and set several world records. Years after he retired, he met President Theodore Roosevelt, who told him that he had followed his career with admiration. Taylor is a member of the Bicycle Hall of Fame.

Bill White

(1934–)

Baseball Player and President of the National League

Born William DeKova White, he began his major league career with the New York Giants in 1956 and spent thirteen years as a player with the San Francisco Giants, St. Louis Cardinals, and the Philadelphia Phillies. During his career, White was named to the National League All-Star team six times and won seven Gold Gloves. He retired from baseball in 1969, and in 1971 joined Phil Rizzuto as a television play-by-play announcer for the New York Yankees.

By Mark Kram

On April 1, 1989, Bill White became the first black president of the National League.

Military

As with other aspects of American society, the role of black people in the nation's armed forces has been evolutionary. It was shaped by the white majority of an infant republic that embraced and later rejected slavery. Next came an adolescent "separate but equal" era of racial segregation. Finally, the United States has matured—as an increasingly multicultural society—in its understanding of race and racism. Historically, it has been a short—but humanly painful—200-year evolution.

Sadly, a nation's history is often shaped by its wars. Insofar as blacks and the United States military are concerned, the historic linkage extends from the Revolutionary War to "Operation Desert Storm." A memorial to the 5,000 black soldiers of the Revolutionary War has been planned for the Mall at Washington, DC. Ironically, that memorial of the eighteenth-century war comes after similar recognition of the nineteenth-century "Buffalo Soldiers" at Fort Leavenworth, Kansas, and of the twentieth-century Tuskegee Airmen at the United States Air Force Academy.

EARLY MILITARY PARTICIPATION ✦ ✦ ✦ ✦ ✦ ✦ ✦ ✦ ✦ ✦ ✦ ✦ ✦ ✦ ✦ ✦ ✦

Based on European experiences, the early American colonists were wary of the military. Both the Declaration of Independence and the United States Constitution reflect the fear of a large and permanent military establishment. As a result, much of early United States military history revolves around the locally recruited militia—now the National Guard of the states and territories.

Grudgingly, America's founding fathers accepted free black men for service in the Continental Army. On January 16, 1776, the Congress authorized that "free Negroes who have served faithfully in the Army at Cambridge may be reenlisted therein." By 1778, the Continental Army was racially integrated.

Integration did not last, however. Exclusion of blacks from the military became law in 1792 when Congress restricted military service to "free able-bodied white males." Six years later, the Secretary of War reiterated this law when he issued an order to the Commandant of the Marine Corps that "no Negro, mulatto or Indian is to be enlisted."

The War of 1812 was mainly fought by naval forces, and black sailors made up approximately 20 percent of Navy crews. While the Army and Marine Corps continued to exclude blacks, the Louisiana legislature authorized enlistments of free black landowners in the militia. The black troops' bravery in combat was a key factor in the American victory at the Battle of New Orleans, though it was fought after the war had officially ended.

THE CIVIL WAR (1861–1865) ✦ ✦ ✦ ✦ ✦ ✦ ✦ ✦ ✦ ✦ ✦ ✦ ✦ ✦ ✦ ✦ ✦ ✦

At the outbreak of the Civil War, the United States suffered a near-fatal blow. Led by Robert E. Lee, nearly half of the West Point–trained United States Army officer corps defected to the Confederacy. The nation had to recruit, train, and deploy an expanded military but lacked trained leaders. One result of this situation was the enactment of the Morrill Land Grant

College Act, which mandated the inclusion of a course on military science—the forerunner of today's Reserve Officers' Training Corps (ROTC).

As soon as the war began, blacks outside of the rebel territory volunteered for the Army. Expecting a short war, Secretary of War Cameron rebuffed the offers. Although some Army leaders such as Major General John C. Freemont sought to recruit blacks as soldiers, the Lincoln administration countermanded such actions. Meanwhile, the Confederacy relied on slave labor to construct fortifications and assist in related combat service support tasks. By 1862, after significant military setbacks, Congress lifted the ban on blacks in the military and approved their use as Union Army laborers.

Following the Emancipation Proclamation in September 1862, Massachusetts was permitted to organize two black regiments: the 54th and 55th Massachusetts Infantry. (The exploits of the 54th Massachusetts Infantry formed the basis of the motion picture *Glory*.) In May 1863, the severe manpower shortage forced the War Department to approve the organization of additional black regiments led by white officers. The units were designated as United States Colored Troops (USCT).

United States Colored Troops (USCT)

Following the establishment of USCT regiments, blacks fought and died in every major Civil War action. For a period, they did so being paid $3.50 per month less than white troops. In some units, black troops refused to accept the lower pay. After vigorous protests by both black and

A rifle company of black Union soldiers.

white citizens, the 1864 Army Appropriations Act approved identical pay scales for all soldiers.

The passions of the Civil War resulted in the violation of emerging doctrines of land warfare, particularly concerning the treatment of non-combatants and prisoners of war; these doctrines had arisen in Europe in the wake of the Napoleonic wars. The most serious documented breaches of land warfare law were committed by the Confederacy. In an infamous example, white Union prisoners of war at Andersonville Prison in Georgia were treated barbarically by Confederacy soldiers. Black soldiers who fell into Confederate hands were either re-enslaved or summarily killed. One of the bloodiest events orchestrated by the Confederacy is known as the "Fort Pillow Massacre." Tennessee Congressional Report No. 65, dated April 24, 1864, identified the rebel leader responsible as General Nathan Bedford Forrest; following the war, Forrest organized the Ku Klux Klan. According to the report:

> The rebels commenced an indiscriminate slaughter, sparing neither age nor sex, white or black, soldier or civilian. The officers and men seemed to vie with each other in the devilish work; men, women, and even children, wherever found, were deliberately shot down, beaten, and hacked with sabres; some of the children not more than ten years old were forced to stand up and face their murderers while being shot; the sick and wounded were butchered without mercy, the rebels even entering the hospital building and dragging them out to be shot or killing them as they lay there unable to offer the least resistance.

The Medal of Honor

This nation's highest decoration for valor, the Medal of Honor, was established by Congress on December 21, 1861. Issuance was initially limited to enlisted men of the Navy and Marine Corps, but was expanded to include the Army on July 12, 1862. On March 3, 1863, commissioned officers also became eligible for the Medal of Honor. During the Civil War, 1,523 Medals of Honor were awarded, including twenty-three for black servicemen. The first black recipient was Sergeant William H. Carney, 54th Massachusetts Infantry, for combat valor on July 18, 1863, at Fort Wagner, South Carolina.

By the end of the Civil War, more than 35,000 black troops had died— approximately 35 percent of the blacks who had served in combat.

The parents of Marine Private James Anderson, Jr. receive his Medal of Honor, awarded posthumously August 21, 1968.

United States Colored Troops had constituted 13 percent of the Union Army.

◆ ◆ ◆ ◆ ◆ ◆ ◆ ◆ ◆ ◆ ◆ ◆ ◆ THE INDIAN CAMPAIGNS (1866–1890)

Post–Civil War America had acquired a new appreciation of the importance of military power. In 1866, the 39th Congress passed legislation to

The 9th Cavalry was one of the first all-black Regular Army regiments.

"increase and fix the Military Establishment of the United States." The peacetime army included five artillery regiments, ten cavalry regiments, and forty-five infantry regiments. This legislation also stipulated that "to the six regiments of cavalry now in service shall be added four regiments, two of which shall be composed of colored men."

In addition to Henry Ossian Flipper, there were only two other nineteenth-century black graduates of West Point: John H. Alexander (1864–1894) in the class of 1887, and Charles A. Young (1864–1922) in the class of 1889. Forty-seven years passed before another black cadet graduated from the United States Military Academy.

With that new law, the nation gained its first all-black Regular Army regiments: the 9th and 10th Cavalry, and the 24th and 25th Infantry—the "Buffalo Soldiers." Although the term Buffalo Soldiers initially denoted these four post–Civil War regiments, it has been adopted with pride by veterans of all racially segregated black Army ground units of the 1866–1950 era.

A misconception perpetuated by Hollywood films involves the depiction of an all-white Army's post–Civil War westward expansion. In reality, approximately 20 percent of Army soldiers on duty in the West were black. According to Gary Donaldson in his *History of African-Americans in the Military,* "even today, few Americans realize that when the cavalry came to the rescue of white settlers in the Old West ... the rescuers, those gallant soldiers in blue, might well have been black." The heroism of black soldiers is attested to by the eighteen Medals of Honor they earned during what historians term either "The Indian Campaigns" or "The Plains War."

Black participation in the war against Native American Indians was a situation fraught with irony, both in terms of fighting another race subjugated by Anglo-Americans, and in terms of anti-black sentiment within the U.S. military. One of many painful episodes for the original "Buffalo Soldiers" was the case of Second Lieutenant Henry Ossian Flipper. Born in Thomasville, Georgia on March 21, 1856, Flipper was the first black to graduate from the United States Military Academy at West Point, New York. He ranked fiftieth among the seventy-six members of the Class of 1887, and became the only black commissioned officer in the Regular Army. Assigned initially to Fort Sill, Oklahoma Territory, Lieutenant Flipper was eventually sent to Fort Davis, Texas. He was assigned the duties routine to a newly commissioned officer, such as surveying and supervising construction projects. Flipper also acquired some combat experience fighting Apache Indians led by Chief Victoria.

In August 1881, Lieutenant Flipper was arrested and charged with failing to mail $3,700 in checks to the Army Chief of Commissary. The young lieutenant was tried by court-martial for embezzlement and conduct unbecoming an officer. He was acquitted of the first charge (the checks were found in his quarters), but convicted of the second. Upon confirmation of his sentence by President Chester Arthur, Flipper was dismissed from the service on June 30, 1882. Returning to civilian life, Flipper used his West Point education as a surveyor and engineer in working for mining companies. He also published his memoirs as well as technical books dealing with Mexican and Venezuelan laws.

Nearly a century after Flipper left West Point, a review of his record indicated that he had been framed by his fellow officers. His records were cor-

The 10th Cavalry was one of the first all-black Regular Army regiments.

rected and he was posthumously granted an honorable discharge from the Army. On the 100th anniversary of his graduation, his bust was unveiled and is now displayed in the Cadet Library at the Military Academy.

THE SPANISH-AMERICAN WAR (1898) ♦ ♦ ♦ ♦ ♦ ♦ ♦ ♦ ♦ ♦ ♦ ♦ ♦

America's "Ten Week War" with Spain marked the nation's emergence as a global colonial power. Although the United States had just completed its own "Indian Campaigns," the tension between the two nations arose from Spain's treatment of Cuba's indigenous population, which increasingly resisted autocratic Spanish rule on the island. In 1885, open rebellion by the Cuban people resulted in brutal suppression by the Spanish. The battleship *USS Maine* was sent to Cuba to protect the United States' interests there and as a reminder of America's intention to enforce the Monroe Doctrine.

On the evening of February 15, 1898, a gigantic explosion rocked the warship. It sank rapidly in Havana's harbor, killing 266 American sailors—including twenty-two blacks. The cause of the *Maine*'s sinking was undetermined, but inflamed American passions were represented by the slogan, "Remember the *Maine*, to hell with Spain."

During the Spanish-American War, African-American men served for the first time in every Army grade below general officer.

On March 29 the United States issued an ultimatum to Spain, demanding the release of Cubans from brutal detention camps, a declaration of an armistice, and preparations for peace negotiations mediated by President McKinley. The Spanish government did not comply, and on April 19 the United States Congress proclaimed Cuba free and independent. In its proclamation, Congress authorized the president to use United States troops to remove Spanish forces from Cuba.

In the annals of United States military history, the Spanish-American War was of special significance for the black officer. It was the first time black men served in all Army grades below general officer. This opportunity arose because of a geographically determined national security strategy. Separated from Europe and Asia by oceans, the United States understood that those waters provided a mobilization time cushion. Any perceived threat from either direction had to overcome United States naval power before touching the United States. Thus, the Navy became "the first line of defense." The small Regular Army was really a cadre force in charge of the recruitment, training, and deployment of volunteers—or draftees. An additional mobilization asset were the various state militia composed of part-time citizen soldiers.

The war with Spain was an expeditionary campaign requiring maritime deployment to foreign soil. It was the nation's first large-scale exposure to the complex logistics of overseas operations, an experience that would evolve into occupation duty and counter-insurgency (COIN) warfare.

The Regular Army of only 28,000 men included the all-black 9th and 10th Cavalry regiments, and the 24th and 25th Infantry regiments. All four regiments distinguished themselves during combat in Cuba. A manpower augmentation of 175,000 troops came from the federalized state militia/national guard reservoir, designated United States Volunteer Infantry (USVI).

The USVI included the nation's oldest all-black national guard unit which had its organizational roots in Chicago, Illinois. Formed in the wake of the 1871 Chicago fire, it was originally known as the Hannibal Guards. It became the 9th Battalion, an Illinois militia unit, on May 5, 1890; the unit was commanded by Major Benjamin G. Johnson, a black man. When the war erupted, other all-black militia regiments were organized: the 3rd Alabama, the 23rd Kansas, the 3rd North Carolina, the 9th Ohio, and the 6th Virginia.

Although only ten weeks long, the Spanish-American War produced six black Medal of Honor recipients: five from the 10th Cavalry, which fought as infantry in Cuba, and one to a black sailor from the USS Iowa, which fought in the waters off Santiago, Cuba.

Until it was converted to artillery battalions in World War II, the 8th Illinois was a unit commanded by a black officer; Colonel John R. Marshall was the highest-ranking black officer of the Spanish-American War, and commanded the 8th Illinois until 1914. Marshall was born on March 15, 1859, in Alexandria, Virginia. After attending public schools in Alexandria and Washington, DC, he became an apprentice bricklayer. He moved to Chicago and was appointed Deputy Clerk of Cook County. Marshall joined the Illinois National Guard, organized a battalion, and served in it as lieutenant and as major. In June 1892, he was commissioned as a colonel and assumed command of the 8th Illinois USVI Regiment. He led the regiment to Cuba, where it joined with the 23rd Kansas and 3rd North Carolina in occupation duty.

Although only ten weeks long, the Spanish-American War produced six black Medal of Honor recipients—five from the 10th Cavalry, an infantry unit in Cuba. A black sailor won the sixth medal for heroism aboard the *USS Iowa* in the waters off Santiago, Cuba. The Spanish-American War provided a small increase in the number of black Regular Army officers. Benjamin O. Davis served as a lieutenant in the 8th Illinois USVI. Upon his discharge, he enlisted on June 14, 1899 as a private in the 9th Cavalry. He was promoted to corporal, and then to sergeant major. Davis was commissioned a Regular Army second lieutenant of cavalry on February 2, 1901. Also commissioned as Regular Army officers that year were John R. Lynch and John E. Green. As the twentieth century began, the United States Army had four black commissioned officers (excluding chaplains): Captain Charles A. Young, and Lieutenants Davis, Green, and Lynch. In 1940, Davis became the nation's first black general officer (see "World War II").

WORLD WAR I ♦

During World War I Sergeant Henry Johnson of New York's 369th Infantry Regiment became the first American, black or white, to receive the French croix de guerre.

The nation's entry into World War I again raised the question of how to utilize black troops. Of the more than 400,000 black soldiers who served during the war, only about 10 percent were assigned to combat duty in two infantry divisions. The 92nd Infantry Division was composed mainly of draftees. Black men from the 8th Infantry of the Illinois National Guard and the 315th Infantry of the New York National Guard formed the 93rd Infantry Division (Provisional). The majority of black World War I soldiers were assigned to stevedore units at ports, or to labor units as quartermaster troops.

The most difficult question for the War Department was the demand that blacks be trained as commissioned officers. Initially, the idea was dismissed as ludicrous. It was said to be "common knowledge" that black men inherently lacked leadership qualities. Only through the persistence of the NAACP, the Urban League, and black newspapers like the *Chicago Defender* did the War Department policy eventually change. An all-black Officer Training School was established at Fort Dodge, near Des Moines, Iowa. On October 14, 1917, the school graduated and commissioned 639 black officers. The War Department, however, had an iron-clad rule: No black officer could command white officers or enlisted men. White supremacy was to remain ensconced in the nation's armed services.

The 369th Infantry Regiment, known as the "Harlem Hell Fighters," established the best World War I record of any United States Army infantry regiment.

One solution to the issue of utilizing black officers and soldiers was characteristic of military racism at this time: several black regiments were "attached" to the allied French Army. Colonel William Hayward, commander of New York's 369th Infantry criticized General John J. Pershing for this decision. According to Arthur W. Little in *From Harlem to the Rhine: The Story of New York's Colored Volunteers,* Colonel Hayward charged that Pershing "simply put the black orphan in a basket, set it on the doorstep of the French, pulled the bell, and went away."

Despite the imposed "orphan" status, it was the 369th Infantry Regiment (15th New York) that established the best World War I record of any United States Army infantry regiment. The 369th served for 191 consecutive days in the trenches and never lost a foot of ground to the Germans. The so-called "Harlem Hell Fighters" won their laurels while attached to the French 4th Army, using French weapons and wearing United States uniforms. In 1919, Columbia University President Nicholas Murray Butler gave *Harper's Weekly* his assessment of the 369th Infantry Regiment: "No American soldier saw harder or more constant fighting and none gave better accounts of themselves. When fighting was to be done, this regiment was there."

Black soldiers earned an impressive number of awards for combat bravery in defeating German troops. Sergeant Henry Johnson of New York's 369th Infantry Regiment was the first American, black or white, to receive the French croix de guerre. France awarded its croix de guerre to thirty-four black officers and eighty-nine black enlisted men during the war. In the 92nd Division, fourteen black officers and thirty-four black enlisted men earned the United States Army Distinguished Flying Cross (DFC). Ten officers and thirty-four enlisted men of the 93rd Division were DFC recipients.

Posthumous Medal of Honor Awarded

No Medal of Honor was awarded to a black serviceman during World War I. In 1988, the Department of the Army researched the National Archives to determine whether racial barriers had prevented the conferment of the nation's highest decoration for valor. The archives search produced evidence that Corporal Freddie Stowers of Anderson County, South Carolina had been recommended for the award. For "unknown reasons," the recommendation had not been processed. Stowers was a squad leader in Company C, 371st Infantry Regiment, 93rd Division. On September 28, 1918, he led his squad through heavy machine gun fire and destroyed the gun position on Hill 188 in the Champagne Marne Sector, France. Mortally wounded, Stowers continued to lead his men through a second trench line.

On April 24, 1991, President George Bush belatedly presented Stowers's Medal of Honor to his surviving sisters in a White House ceremony.

THE INTERWAR YEARS (1919–1940) ♦ ♦ ♦ ♦ ♦ ♦ ♦ ♦ ♦ ♦ ♦ ♦ ♦

With the end of the war, the nation generally returned to applying the "separate but equal" doctrine with a vengeance. Some senior white Army officers advocated barring enlistment or re-enlistment of blacks altogether, an action that would have eventually abolished the four black Regular Army regiments by attrition.

A focal point of the Army's anti-black sentiment was the black commissioned officer. Despite countless well-documented cases of superb combat leadership, most black officers were eliminated from active duty following World War I. Many opponents of black officers focused on their allegedly poor performance; specifically, critics attacked the black Officer Training School (OTS) class at Des Moines, Iowa. One of the severest critics was Major General Charles C. Ballou, commander of the World War I 93rd Infantry Division. Ballou emphasized in a 1920 letter that while white candidates were required to be college graduates, "only high school educations were required for ... the colored ... and in many cases these high school educations would have been a disgrace to any grammar school. For the parts of a machine requiring the finest steel, pot metal was provided."

However, there were combat-experienced white officers who held a decidedly different view of black officer training, such as Major Thomas A. Roberts. "As I understand the question," Roberts wrote in April 1920, "what the progressive Negro desires today is the removal of discrimination against him; that this can be accomplished in a military sense I believe to be largely possible, but not if men of the two races are segregated." Noting the "tremendous force of the prejudice against association between negroes and whites," Roberts declared, "my experience has made me believe that the better element among the negroes desires the removal of the restriction rather than the association itself."

As for commissioned officers, the Reserve Officers' Training Corps (ROTC) detachments at Howard and Wilberforce Universities provided the bulk of new black second lieutenants. With no allocations for black officers to attend service schools, the lack of opportunity to maintain proficiency caused considerable attrition in the number of black reserve officers. To retain their commissions, other officers took advantage of correspondence and specially organized lectures and seminars.

Major Thomas A. Roberts, a white officer, wrote in 1920:

"That [the removal of discrimination] can be accomplished in a military sense I believe to be largely possible, but not if men of the two races are segregated."

♦ **WORLD WAR II**

Less than two months after war began in Europe, the nation's preeminent black organizations, the NAACP and the Urban League, had mobilized to defeat American racial segregation as well as Axis fascism. The black community could clearly foresee that the United States would eventually ally itself with Britain and France in war against Germany, Italy, and Japan.

Military mobilization began on August 27, 1940 with the federalizing of the National Guard and activation of the Organized Reserve. When Japan attacked Pearl Harbor on December 7, 1941, there were 120,000 officers and 1,523,000 enlisted men on active duty in the Army and its Air Corps. On September 16, 1940, the nation began its first peacetime draft. By the end of World War II, the Selective Service System had inducted 10,110,104 men; 1,082,539 (10.7 percent) were black.

A minority of blacks, including Nation of Islam founder Elijah Muhammad, openly favored a Japanese victory; Muhammad's stance led to a four-year term in the United States Penitentiary at Milan, Michigan.

America's war effort required rapid expansion of both military and industrial power. Victory depended on the constant provision of ammunition, guns, planes, tanks, naval vessels, and merchant ships. The nation would have to unite to survive. Essential to the desegregation activism of the NAACP and the Urban League was the influence of black-owned weekly newspapers such as Robert S. Abbott's *Chicago Defender* and Robert Vann's *Pittsburgh Courier*. The rallying slogan was the "Double V"—victory against fascism abroad and against racial discrimination in the United States. The goal was equal opportunity in both the armed services and civilian defense industries.

Soon, the NAACP and the Urban League were joined by the black activists of the March on Washington Movement led by A. Philip Randolph of the Brotherhood of Sleeping Car Porters and Maids. Randolph predicted that upwards of 100,000 blacks would march on Washington demanding equal employment opportunities in defense plants. On June 25, 1941, a week before the scheduled march, President Franklin D. Roosevelt forestalled the protest by issuing Executive Order 8802. The president's order established a Committee on Fair Employment Practice "to provide for the full and equitable participation of all workers in defense industries, without discrimination." Of course, the executive order did not apply to the armed services.

The necessity of winning the war opened the job market to millions of black men and women who surged into defense plants, earning the same wages as their white co-workers. The war years thus brought economic upward mobility for many black civilians. Furthermore, through the postwar benefits of the G.I. Bill of Rights, the number of black college graduates and homeowners increased dramatically.

A fact that has been largely ignored is that the United States Army took its first steps toward racial integration early in World War II. The obvious waste of duplicated facilities caused the Army to operate all of its twenty-four Officer Candidate Schools as racially integrated institutions, where the primary quality sought was proven leadership capacity. The so-called "ninety-day wonders" who survived the standard three-month course were commissioned as second lieutenants in one of the twenty-four Army branches ranging from the Army Air Forces Administrative School in Miami, Florida, to the Tank Destroyer School in Camp Hood, Texas. Of course, upon graduation, black officers were only assigned to black units.

The exception in racially integrated Army officer procurement was the Army Air Force Aviation Cadet program that trained pilots, bombardiers, and navigators in a segregated environment. Ironically, black non-flying officers graduated from the integrated AAF Officer Candidates School at Miami Beach.

A total of 926 black pilots earned their commissions and wings at the segregated Tuskegee Army Air Field (TAAF) near Chehaw, Alabama. The 673 single-engine TAAF pilot graduates eventually formed the four squadrons of the 332nd Fighter Group.

Led by Lieutenant Colonel Benjamin O. Davis, Jr., a 1936 West Point graduate, the 99th Fighter Squadron was assigned to the 33rd Fighter Group commanded by Colonel William M. Meyer. The 99th's first operational mission was a June 2, 1943 strafing attack on the Italian island of Pantelleria. On this date, Captain Charles B. Hall scored the squadron's first air victory by shooting down an FW-190 and damaging an Me-109. The 99th then settled into normal operations—or so the men thought.

In September Colonel Davis was recalled to take command of the 332nd Fighter Group. That is when he and the black community discovered that the so-called "Tuskegee Experiment" was about to be declared a failure. To this effect, Colonel Meyer submitted an extremely negative letter appraising the 99th Fighter Squadron:

For the first time during World War II, the U.S. Army desegregated all twenty-four of its Officer Candidate Schools. Upon graduation, however, black officers were still assigned only to black units.

The Army Air Force (AAF)

Based on the performance of the 99th Fighter Squadron to date, it is my opinion that they are not of the fighting caliber of any squadron in this group. They have failed to display the aggressiveness and daring for combat that are necessary to a first class fighting organization. It may be expected that we will get less work and less operational time out of the 99th Fighter Squadron than any squadron in this group.

On October 16, 1943, squadron commander Davis appeared before the War Department's Committee on Special [Negro] Troop Policies to answer his group commander's allegations.

In his 1991 autobiography, written after his retirement as an Air Force lieutenant general, Davis describes the problem he faced at the Pentagon as a lieutenant colonel: "It would have been hopeless for me to stress the hostility and racism of whites as the motive behind the letter, although that was clearly the case. Instead, I had to adopt a quiet, reasoned approach, presenting the facts about the 99th in a way that would appeal to fairness and win out over ignorance and racism."

Davis presented such a convincing factual case that Army Chief of Staff General George C. Marshall ordered a G-3 [operations] study of the black squadron. The study's title, "Operations of the 99th Fighter Squadron Compared with Other P-40 Squadrons in the Mediterranean Theatre of Operations," precisely describes its contents. In his book, General Davis describes the G-3 study: "It rated the 99th according to readiness, squadron missions, friendly losses versus enemy losses, and sorties dispatched. The opening statement in the report was the clincher: 'An examination of the record of the 99th Fighter Squadron reveals no significant general difference between this squadron and the balance of the P-40 squadrons in the Mediterranean Theatre of Operations'."

On October 13, 1942, the Army activated the 100th, 301st, and 302nd Fighter Squadrons. Combined with the 99th, the four squadrons would become the 332nd Fighter Group. Colonel Robert R. Selway, Jr., a white pilot, was its initial commanding officer. With the 99th vindicated by the G-3 study, Davis assumed command of the Fighter Group at Selfridge Army Air Field in Michigan. The 332nd departed for Italy on January 3, 1944, and absorbed the 99th as its fourth squadron.

While the 99th was deployed and the 332nd was organizing, the TAAF program expanded to training two-engine B-25 pilots. While the fighter pilot fought alone, the B-25 "Mitchell" medium bomber required a five- to six-man crew that included two pilots and a bombardier-navigator. The 253 medium-bomber pilots who were trained at TAAF, as well as 393 black navigators and bombardiers from Hondo and Midland Fields in Texas, formed the nation's second black flying organization when the Army Air Force activated the four-squadron 477th Bombardment Group (Medium) in June 1943.

The 477th was plagued from the start by a shortage of enlisted aircrew members, ground technicians, and even airplanes. Fifteen months after activation, the 477th was still short twenty-six pilots, forty-three co-pilots, two bombardier-navigators, and all of its authorized 288 gunners. Moving from base to base for "operational training," the 477th logged 17,875 flying hours in one year without a major accident. Although finally earmarked for duty in the Pacific, the war ended before the 477th was deployed overseas.

As for the 332nd Fighter Group, it became famous for escorting heavy bombers. It was the only AAF fighter group that never lost an escorted bomber to enemy planes. The wartime record of the 332nd Fighter Group was 103 enemy aircraft destroyed during 1,578 combat missions. In addition to more than one hundred Distinguished Flying Crosses, the 332nd also earned three Distinguished Unit Citations.

The Tuskegee Experiment thus proved that black men could fly "state-of-the-art" aircraft, and could also conduct highly successful combat operations meeting AAF standards. The fruit of the Tuskegee Airmen's efforts would be harvested in less than three years with the 1948 racial desegregation of the United States military.

The Ground War

The World War II United States Army fielded two major black combat organizations: the 92nd Infantry Division in Europe, and the 93rd Infantry Division in the Pacific.

Both of the Divisions suffered from avoidable impediments. Just as in World War I, the 93rd Division was employed only in a fragmented manner. Major General Raymond G. Lehman's headquarters sailed from San Francisco, California on January 11, 1944; the artillery and infantry battalions and division headquarters assembled on Guadalcanal at the end of

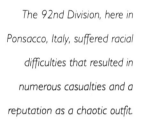

The 92nd Division, here in Ponsacco, Italy, suffered racial difficulties that resulted in numerous casualties and a reputation as a chaotic outfit.

February. As scholar Ulysses Lee observed in *The Employment of Negro Troops,* "This was the last time until the end of the war that all elements of the division were gathered in the same location." The division spent the rest of the war island-hopping, relieving units that had defeated Japanese troops. The 93rd Division World War II casualties were twelve killed in action, 121 wounded in action, and five who died later of wounds.

Elements of the 93rd Division, primarily the 24th Infantry Regiment, performed well during the 1944 Bougainville campaign. Generally, the division's performance was considered adequate and acceptable. The usual after-action comments were made concerning the lack of initiative by junior officers, but overall the 93rd Division was described as well-disciplined and having good morale.

The 92nd Infantry Division, in contrast, gained a reputation as a chaotic outfit. During its preparation for deployment overseas, elements of the 92nd Division were sprinkled across the United States. While the division headquarters were at Fort Huachuca, Arizona, subordinate units were stationed at Fort McClellan, Alabama; Camp Robinson, Arkansas; Camp Breckinridge, Kentucky; and Camp Atterbury, Indiana. The division's World War II casualty figures were vastly different than those of the 93rd Division: 548 killed in action; 2,187 wounded in action; and sixty-eight who died later of wounds. From its training in the United States through combat in Europe, the division's main problem seemed to be its commander, Major General Edward M. Almond. Many veterans of the 92nd Division continue to blame General Almond for the division's reputation and casualties.

It appears that "Ned" Almond was openly racist. In a 1984 interview retired Lieutenant General William P. Ennis, Jr. gave a "warts and all" description of Almond. As a World War II brigadier general, Ennis had commanded the corps artillery that supported the 92nd Division. According to Ennis in the *Journal of Military History*, Almond and many white Southern officers in the division were selected because "in theory, they knew more about handling Negroes than anybody else, though I can't imagine why because [Almond] just despised the ground they walked on."

The contrast of attitude at the division's various posts was amazing. While Almond denigrated the competence of black officers, Officer Candidate School (OCS) commandants generally held different views. For example, Brigadier General H. T. Mayberry, who commanded the Tank Destroyer OCS, observed in a 1945 interview that "a considerable number of young, potentially outstanding Negro officers were graduated. It was surprising—to me, at least—how high the Negroes (those who graduated) stood in the classes."

Lieutenant Colonel Robert C. Ross, a field artillery battalion commander in the 92nd Division, reported to Almond on five black officers who completed the basic artillery course. Three were made course instructors, while two were selected "as outstanding students from the entire forty-eight officers, both white and colored, from the first Officers Basic School."

One black officer, Captain Hondon B. Hargrove, was a 1938 Wilberforce University ROTC graduate. After his wartime service in the division's 597th Field Artillery Battalion, he commented that Almond did not believe that "any black, no matter what his file showed, or how much training he had, was able in an officer's position.... He firmly believed only white officers could get the best out of [Negro troops] … [and] just could not countenance black officers leading them."

General Almond established his headquarters at Viareggio, Italy on October 5, 1944. Two days later, the division's 370th Infantry Regiment began its assault on Massa. Professor Lee described the 92nd Division's major weakness: "It was a problem in faith and lack of it—the wavering faith of commanders in the ability and determination of subordinates and enlisted men, and the continuation in the minds of enlisted men of training period convictions that they could not trust their leaders." Thus, the Massa attack degenerated into chaos. In what became a major charge against the division, the men began to "melt away" from the fighting. After Massa, there were increasing cases of mutinous behavior toward both black and white officers.

In February 1945, the 92nd became the focus of serious Pentagon scrutiny. The man who examined the situation was Truman K. Gibson,

Brigadier General Benjamin Davis, Sr. pins the Distinguished Flying Cross on his son, Colonel Benjamin Davis, Jr.

Jr., a black insurance company lawyer from Chicago, and civilian aide to Secretary of War Henry L. Stimpson. In his assessment, Gibson refused to blame the victim, or to generalize about the capabilities of black soldiers based on the performance of General Almond's 92nd Division. In a March 14 news conference in Rome, Gibson maintained that "If the division proves anything, it does not prove that Negroes can't fight. There is no question in my mind about the courage of Negro officers or soldiers and any generalization on the basis of race is entirely unfounded."

On May 14, 1945, a week after Germany surrendered, Lieutenant Colonel Marcus H. Ray wrote a letter to Gibson. A fellow Chicagoan, Colonel Ray was a National Guard officer of the 8th Illinois when it was mobilized in 1940. He ended the war as commanding officer of the 600th Field Artillery Battalion of the 92nd Division. Colonel Ray closed his letter to Gibson by observing that "those who died in the proper performance of their assigned duties are our men of the decade and all honor should be paid them. They were Americans before all else. Racially, we have been the victims of an unfortunate chain of circumstances backgrounded by the unchanged American attitude as regards the proper 'place' of the Negro.... I do not believe the 92nd a complete failure as a combat unit, but when I think of what it might have been, I am heart-sick."

The most highly acclaimed black ground combat unit of World War II was the 761st Tank Battalion. As an organization, it enjoyed circumstances very different from the 92nd Division. Like the 92nd Division, commanding officers of the 761st Battalion influenced the unit's performance, but with a positive outcome. Before the United States entered World War II, some white United States Army officers favored opening opportunities for black soldiers. They rejected the dogma of their colleagues who declared that modern weaponry was "too technical" for blacks. Fortunately, one such officer became the Commanding General of Army Ground Forces.

The 761st Tank Battalion

In this post, Lieutenant General Lesley James McNair spent most of his time visiting the nationwide array of ground forces training camps. And when he visited the 761st at Camp Claiborne, Louisiana, he openly praised and encouraged the Army's first black tankers. When the 761st went ashore in France on October 10, 1944, the men believed that their outfit's existence was due mainly to McNair. (General McNair was killed by United States "friendly fire" on July 25, 1944 in France. The Joint

Chiefs of Staff National Defense University is located at Fort Lesley J. Mc-Nair, named in his honor, in Washington, DC.)

The 761st joined the 26th Division on October 31st and was welcomed by the division commander, Major General Willard S. Paul: "I am damned glad to have you with us. We have been expecting you for a long time, and I am sure you are going to give a good account of yourselves." Two days later, General George S. Patton visited and welcomed the 761st.

The 761st's initial combat was on November 8, 1944 at Athaniville, France—the first of 183 continuous days of combat for the battalion. During their advance through six European countries, the 761st proved to be a stellar combat organization. The battalion is credited with killing 6,266 enemy soldiers, and capturing 15,818. Despite its outstanding combat record, the 761st did not receive its much-deserved Presidential Unit Citation until January 24, 1978.

The veterans of the 761st still pursue a World War II mission: a posthumous Medal of Honor for Staff Sergeant Ruben Rivers, of Tecumseh, Oklahoma. Sergeant Rivers was severely wounded on November 16, 1944, when his tank ran over two mines near Guebling, France. With his lower thigh torn and his kneebone protruding, Sergeant Rivers refused evacuation. Instead, he remained with his tank and crew for three days of continuous combat. When his company was taken under fire by German heavy weapons, the company commander ordered his tanks to pull back below the crest of a hill. Sergeant Rivers's tank opened fire at the enemy and continued firing until it was hit in the turret by an armor-piercing round that killed Sergeant Rivers.

The veterans of the 761st have been acknowledged—unfortunately, not without some controversy—by the Public Broadcasting System (PBS). On Nov. 11, 1992, PBS presented an hour-long documentary called "The Liberators," focusing on the exploits of the 761st Tank Battalion. Moreover, the broadcast asserted that the 761st helped liberate the most infamous of all Nazi concentration camps—Buchenwald and Dachau. Unquestionably, the 761st did liberate some concentration camps, but the assertion that the battalion played a role in the liberation of those two specific camps has been challenged by some 761st veterans. The April 1945 after-action report of the 761st contains no entries concerning either of the two camps. Furthermore, the April 1945 location entries in the report place the 761st miles from either camp. PBS therefore withdrew "The Liberators" from further exhibition pending additional research.

Following a decade of excluding blacks from enlistment, the United States Navy in 1932 decided to accept blacks, but placed them in a separate branch of the Navy. The branch was known as the Stewards' Service, referred to in the black community as "sea-going bell hops." The 1940 Navy consisted of 170,000 men of whom 4,007 or 2.3 percent were blacks in the Stewards' Service. In addition to blacks, Navy stewards were also recruited from among Filipinos and other Asian-American populations.

The advent of World War II transformed this situation. President Franklin D. Roosevelt had served as assistant secretary of the Navy during World War I, and considered it "his branch" of the armed services. Therefore, his January 9, 1942 memo to the Navy had tremendous impact. The president noted to then-Secretary of the Navy Frank Knox: "I think that with all the Navy activities, Bureau of Navy might invent something that colored enlistees could do in addition to the rating of messman."

The Navy did relent on April 7, 1942 by announcing it would accept 14,000 black enlistees in all ratings and branches. The initial training of black sailors was conducted at the Great Lakes Naval Training Station, north of Chicago, Illinois.

It was at Great Lakes that the Navy finally made a breakthrough regarding black personnel. In January 1944, sixteen black petty officers began a special and intensive course of instruction that was conducted without public announcement. Three months later, the Navy announced the commissioning of twelve black ensigns and one warrant officer. These men are known as the Navy's "Golden Thirteen."

Shortly after the Golden Thirteen were commissioned, the Navy opened the V-12 officer training programs to black men. Among the V-12 graduates who became Navy officers in World War II were Samuel L. Gravely, Jr. and Carl T. Rowan. Gravely became the Navy's first black admiral; Rowan is now a syndicated columnist and broadcaster.

By the end of World War II, 165,000 blacks had served in the Navy; 17,000 in the Marine Corps; 5,000 in the Coast Guard; 12,000 in Construction Battalions (Sea Bees); and 24,000 in the Merchant Marine.

The Sea Services

President Franklin D. Roosevelt, urging the Navy to upgrade the status of black sailors, wrote in 1942: "I think that with all the Navy activities, Bureau of Navy might invent something that colored enlistees could do in addition to the rating of messman."

Evolution to the Inevitable

As the Allied victory of World War II approached, the highest levels of the United States government recognized that a new domestic racial era had emerged. The war to defeat fascism had indeed involved the entire United States population.

One impetus for change of military policy toward blacks was an August 5, 1945 letter from Colonel Noel F. Parrish, commander of Tuskegee Army Air Field, to Brigadier General William E. Hall, Headquarters Army Air Forces. Colonel Parrish recommended "that future policy, instead of retreating defensibly further and further, with more and more group concessions, openly progress by slow and reasonable but definite steps toward the employment and treatment of Negroes as individuals which law requires and military efficiency demands."

Although Secretary of War Henry L. Stimpson often revealed racist tendencies, his assistant, John R. McCloy, was considerably more liberal. Stimpson was succeeded by Robert P. Patterson, who adopted McCloy's suggestion for a study of future use of blacks in the military. The study was made by a board of three Army generals: Lieutenant General Alvan C. Gillem, Jr., a former corps commander; Major General Lewis A. Pick, who built the Ledo Road in Burma; and Brigadier General Winslow C. Morse, of the Army Air Force. During a six-week period, the so-called Gillem Board took testimony from more than fifty witnesses toward forming the Army's postwar racial policy. Two key individuals who worked with the Gillem Board were the two black Chicagoans who served sequentially as civilian aide to the Secretary of War: Truman K. Gibson, Jr. and the recently discharged Lieutenant Colonel Marcus H. Ray. It is noteworthy that racial desegregation of the military was driven by the considerable political and economic influence of black Chicago.

The Gillem Board's findings leaned toward more "efficient" use of Negro manpower, but did not advocate actual desegregation. That vagueness reactivated the pre-war coalition of the NAACP, the National Urban League, and the grassroots labor forces led by A. Philip Randolph.

The advent of the Cold War led to the National Security Act of 1947. One of the major elements of the new law was the establishment of the Department of Defense (DOD), with the subordinate Departments of Army, Navy, and Air Force. The other new entity created was the Central Intelligence Agency (CIA).

In the continuing movement toward desegregation of the military, 1947 brought two important black personnel shifts within the Department of Defense: Lieutenant Colonel Marcus H. Ray returned to active duty as senior advisor on racial matters in Europe. In the Pentagon, Dr. James C. Evans, a Howard University professor and Department of Army official, moved to the new post of special assistant to the Secretary of Defense. As the highest-ranking black civilian in the Department of Defense, Evans served under ten secretaries of defense until his retirement in 1970.

The demand for desegregation of the military became a key political issue in black America. As preparations for the 1948 presidential election intensified, President Harry S Truman faced a campaign against Republican Thomas E. Dewey, states' rights segregationist Strom Thurmond, and the Communist Party–supported Progressive Party of former Vice President Henry A. Wallace. In such a fragmented situation, the black vote became crucial.

By May 1948, President Truman had decided to desegregate the armed forces by an executive order. Evans guided the politically sensitive staff coordination effort through the Pentagon. In other executive branch and Capitol Hill offices, two political concessions were required. First, no deadlines would be imposed. Second, the order would not denounce racial segregation. With a final sign-off by the attorney general, President Truman issued Executive Order No. 9981, which signaled a policy to end segregation in the military.

◆ **THE KOREAN WAR**

As North Korean forces surged across the 38th parallel on June 25, 1950, only the Air Force had desegregated. The United States ground forces in Korea were savaged by the North Koreans and driven south.

The first United States victory of the Korean War was won by black soldiers of the 24th Infantry Regiment on July 20, 1950 at Yechon. Captain Charles M. Bussey, a World War II Tuskegee Airman, was the ground commander and earned a Silver Star at Yechon. Two black soldiers were awarded posthumous Medals of Honor during the Korean War: Private

First Class William Thompson and Sergeant Cornelius H. Charlton, both of the 24th Infantry Regiment.

Private First Class Thompson distinguished himself by conspicuous gallantry and intrepidity above and beyond the call of duty in action against the enemy on August 6, 1950, near Haman, Korea. While his platoon was reorganizing under cover of darkness, enemy forces in overwhelming strength launched a surprise attack on the unit. PFC Thompson set up his machine gun in the path of the onslaught and swept the enemy with fire, momentarily pinning them down and thus permitting the remainder of his platoon to withdraw to a more tenable position. Although hit repeatedly by grenade fragments and small-arms fire, he resisted all efforts of his comrades to induce him to withdraw, steadfastly remaining at his machine-gun and continuing to deliver fire until mortally wounded by an enemy grenade.

Sergeant Charlton, a member of Company C, distinguished himself in action against the enemy on June 2, 1931, near Chipo-Ri, Korea. His platoon was attacking heavily defended hostile positions on commanding ground when the leader was wounded and evacuated. Sergeant Charlton assumed command, rallied the men, and spearheaded the assault against the hill. Personally eliminating two hostile positions and killing six enemy soldiers with his rifle-fire and grenades, he continued up the slope until the unit suffered heavy casualties and was stalled. Regrouping the men, he led them forward, only to be again forced back by a shower of grenades. Despite a severe chest wound, Sergeant Charlton refused medical attention and led a third daring charge that would advance to the crest of the ridge. Observing that the remaining emplacement that had retarded the advance was situated on the reverse slope, he charged it alone and was hit again by a grenade, but raked the position with fire that eventually routed the enemy. The wounds inflicted during his daring exploits resulted in his death.

The early defeats American forces experienced in Korea prompted President Truman to replace his close friend, Secretary of Defense Louis A.

The Korean War Evolution

Between 1953 and 1961 there was a slow but steady increase in the number of black career officers. Pictured is Major Jerome Cooper, 9th Marines, in Vietnam.

Johnson, with retired General of the Army George C. Marshall, who had been Truman's secretary of state from 1947 to 1949.

One of Marshall's first acts as secretary of defense was the creation of a new entity: Office of Assistant Secretary of Defense for Manpower & Reserves, or OASD (MP&R). Marshall appointed Anna M. Rosenberg, a forty-eight-year-old New York City labor and public relations consultant, as head of this office. In 1944, she had persuaded President Franklin D. Roosevelt to have Congress enact the education provisions of the World War II G.I. Bill of Rights. Dr. James C. Evans's office of special assistant became a part of the OASD (MP&R), thereby bringing together two individuals familiar with discrimination—a Hungarian Jewish immigrant woman and a black male college professor. Known affectionately in the Pentagon as "Aunt Anna," Rosenberg and the OASD (MP&R) had responsibility for industrial and military manpower, including Selective Service System policies. Secretary Rosenberg viewed military desegregation as an impetus for civilian society reform, observing that "In the long run, I don't think a man can live and fight next to one of another race and share experiences where life is at stake, and not have a strong feeling of understanding when he comes home."

The effective implementation of Truman's Executive Order No. 9981 depended in part on black military personnel taking advantage of hard-won opportunities. The individual who was truly the mentor of the black military professional, especially black officers, was James Evans. During much of his tenure in the Pentagon, Evans's executive officer was Army

Increasing numbers of blacks entered the services and opted for full careers. Pictured are Brigadier General Frederick Davison and Captain Oliver E. Murray in Vietnam.

Colonel John T. Martin, who later was director of the Selective Service System for the District of Columbia. Commenting in 1993, Colonel Martin reflected that "James C. Evans and his associates accomplished much behind the scenes—and with no fingerprints—to advance the careers of all [black] personnel in the military."

By the end of the Korean War, racial segregation had been eliminated from the United States armed services. In the years preceding the Vietnam War, increasing numbers of blacks entered the services and opted for full careers. Between 1953 and 1961, there was a slow but steady increase in the number of black career officers in each service. This became a sophisticated form of non-civilian affirmative action.

◆ ◆ ◆ ◆ ◆ ◆ ◆ ◆ ◆ ◆ ◆ ◆ ◆ OUTSTANDING MILITARY FIGURES

Jesse L. Brown was the first black American to become a naval aviator and the first black naval officer to be killed in action during the Korean War.

Ensign Jesse L. Brown (1926–1950)

Naval Aviator

Brown was born October 13, 1926 in Hattiesburg, Mississippi. He graduated from Eureka High School in 1944 and studied engineering at Ohio State University from 1944 to 1947. In 1946 Brown joined the Naval Reserve and in 1947 became an aviation cadet.

Brown's flight training was at Pensacola, Florida, and in 1948 he became the first African American to earn the Navy Wings. In 1949 Brown was assigned to the *USS Leyte* and won the Air Medal and the Korean Service Medal for his twenty air combat missions. On December 4, 1950, he was shot down while flying air support for United States Marines at the Battle of the Chosin Reservoir. He was posthumously awarded the Purple Heart and the Distinguished Flying Cross for exceptional courage, airmanship, and devotion to duty.

In 1973 the *USS Jesse L. Brown,* a destroyer escort, was named in his honor and launched at the Avondale Shipyard at Westwege, Louisiana.

Sergeant William H. Carney

(1840–1908)

First African-American Medal of Honor Recipient

William Carney was born a slave in Norfolk, Virginia. Around 1856, Carney's father moved the family to New Bedford, Massachusetts. In 1863 Carney enlisted in the 54th Massachusetts Colored Infantry. On July 18, 1863, Carney and the 54th Massachusetts led an assault on Fort Wagner, South Carolina, during which Carney was severely wounded. On May 23, 1900, Carney was issued a Medal of Honor.

Brigadier General Benjamin O. Davis, Sr.

(1877–1970)

First African-American General, United States Army

Born in Washington, DC, Benjamin O. Davis, Sr. graduated from Howard University and joined the army in 1898 during the Spanish-American War. At the end of that war, he re-enlisted in the 9th Cavalry and was made second lieutenant in 1901. Promotions of blacks were rare in those years, but Davis rose through the officers' ranks until he was made a full colonel in 1930. During that time, in addition to his military commands, he was a professor of military science and tactics at Wilberforce and Tuskegee Universities, military attache to Liberia, and instructor of the 372nd Infantry of the Ohio National Guard. After his promotion to brigadier general and his service in World War II, he became an assistant to the inspector general in Washington, DC, until his retirement in 1948.

Among General Davis's many awards and decorations are the Distinguished Service Medal; the Bronze Star Medal; the Grade of Commander of the Order of the Star of Africa, from the Liberian government; and the French croix de guerre with palm. General Davis died on November 26, 1970.

Lieutenant General Benjamin O. Davis, Jr. (1912–)

The First African-American General, United States Air Force

Born in Washington, DC, in 1912, Davis was educated in Alabama (his father taught military science at Tuskegee), and later in Cleveland, where he graduated president of his class. Davis went on to attend Western Reserve University and the University of Chicago before accepting an appointment to the United States Military Academy in 1932. In 1936 Davis graduated 35th in his class of 276.

After serving in the infantry for five years, he transferred to the Army Air Corps in 1942 and was among the first six black air cadets to graduate from the Advanced Army Flying School.

As commander of the 99th Fighter Squadron (and later commander of the all-black 332nd Fighter Group), Davis flew sixty missions in 224 combat hours during World War II, winning several medals, including the Silver Star.

In 1957 Davis was made chief of staff of the 12th Air Force of the United States Air Forces in Europe (USAFE). In 1961 he became director of Manpower and Organization, and in 1965 he became chief of staff for the United Nations Command and United States forces in Korea. Davis was assigned as deputy commander in chief, U.S. Strike Command, in 1968. He retired from active duty in 1970.

Henry Ossian Flipper was born a slave in Thomasville, Georgia; his father, a craftsman, bought his family's freedom. Flipper attended Atlanta University and in 1873 was appointed to the United States Military Academy.

Lieutenant Henry O. Flipper (1856?–1940)

First African-American Graduate of the United States Military Academy

Flipper graduated from the academy in 1877 and was commissioned as second lieutenant and assigned to the all-black 10th Cavalry. In 1881, however, Flipper became the victim of a controversial court-martial proceeding, which cut short his career.

Flipper went on, as a civilian, to become a notable figure on the American frontier as a mining engineer and consultant and, later, as a translator of Spanish land grants. Flipper tried several times to vindicate himself, befriending such prominent Washington officials as Senator A. B. Fall of New Mexico. When Fall became Secretary of the Interior, Flipper became his assistant until the infamous Teapot Dome affair severed their relationship.

Flipper returned to Atlanta at the close of his mining career and lived with his brother, an AME bishop, until his death in 1940. His quest to remove the stain of "conduct unbecoming an officer and a gentleman" remained unfulfilled at the time of his death. Nearly a century after he left West Point, however, a review of his record indicated that he had been framed by his fellow officers. His records were corrected and he was posthumously granted an honorable discharge from the Army. On the 100th anniversary of his graduation, his bust was unveiled and is now displayed in the Cadet Library at the Military Academy.

**Vice Admiral
Samuel L. Gravely,
Jr. (1922-)**

First African-American
Admiral,
United States Navy

Gravely was born in Richmond, Virginia on June 4, 1922. He enrolled at Virginia Union University but quit school to enlist in the Navy. He received naval training at the Great Lakes facility in Great Lakes, Illinois, and the Midshipmen School at Columbia University in New York. During World War II, Gravely served aboard a submarine chaser. After the war he returned to school and received a B.A. in history in 1948.

Gravely was called back to duty in 1949 and decided to make a career of the Navy. During the Korean War he served aboard the cruiser *USS Toledo.*

Gravely was steadily promoted through the ranks, and in 1962 he accepted command of the destroyer escort *USS Falgout.* Stationed at Pearl Harbor as part of the Pacific Fleet, he became the first African American to assume command of a Navy combat ship. In 1971, while commanding the guided missile frigate *USS Jouett,* Gravely was promoted to admiral, the first African American to achieve that rank. In 1976 he was again promoted, this time to vice admiral, and placed in command of the United States Navy's 3rd Fleet, a position he held until 1978. Gravely, now retired, has also served as director of the Defense Communications Agency (1978–1980), and the executive director of education and training for the Armed Forces Communications and Electronics Association.

While in the navy Gravely received many medals, including the Legion of Merit, Bronze Star, Meritorious Service Medal, Joint Service Commendation Medal, and the Navy Commendation Medal, as well as medals for his service in three wars.

Gravely has also received numerous civilian awards, including the Founding Fathers Military Commands Award presented by the Masons (1975), the Military Headliner of the Year Award given by the San Diego Press Club (1975), and Savannah State College's Award of Excellence (1974). In 1972 Gravely received the Distinguished Virginian Award presented by the Governor of Virginia.

Appointed Commander of NORAD on August 29, 1975, Daniel "Chappie" James was the first black four-star general in United States military history. Before coming to this post, he had been a flying ace in the Korean War, had served as deputy secretary of defense, and was vice commander of military airlift command.

Born on February 11, 1920 in Pensacola, Florida, he attended Tuskegee Institute, where he took part in the Army Air Corps program. He was commissioned a second lieutenant in 1943. During the Korean War, James flew 101 combat missions in F-51 and F-80 aircraft. After the war, he performed various staff assignments until 1957, when he graduated from the Air Command and Staff College at Maxwell Air Force Base, Alabama. In 1966, he became deputy commander for operations of the 8th Tactical Fighter Wing stationed in Thailand, before promotion to commander of the 7272nd Flying Training Wing at Wheelus Air Force Base in Libya.

James became a brigadier general in 1970, and a lieutenant general in 1973. He has received numerous civilian awards as well as his military awards, which include the Legion of Merit with one oak leaf cluster, Distinguished Flying Cross, Air Medal with ten clusters, Distinguished Unit Citation, Presidential Unit Citation, and Air Force Outstanding Unit Award. In 1975 James was appointed commander in chief of NORAD/ADCOM, and was promoted to four-star general.

On February 25, 1978, James died of a heart attack at the age of fifty-eight in Colorado Springs.

General Daniel James, Jr. (1920–1978)

First African-American Four-Star General, United States Air Force

Johnson was born in 1927 at West Chester, Pennsylvania, and received nurse's training at Harlem Hospital in New York. She enlisted in the United States Army in 1955 and in 1960 joined the Army's Nursing Corps as a first lieutenant. She then went on to earn a bachelor's degree in nursing from Villanova University, a master's degree in nursing education from Columbia University, and a doctorate in education administration from Catholic University in Washington, DC.

In 1979 Johnson was promoted to brigadier general, the first African-American woman to hold that rank, and was placed in command of the Army Nurse Corps. In 1983 she retired from the service and began working for the American Nursing Association as director of its government af-

General Hazel W. Johnson (1927–)

First African-American Female General, United States Army

fairs division. In 1986 she joined the faculty of George Mason University in Virginia as a professor of nursing.

Johnson is a recipient of the Army's Distinguished Service Medal, Legion of Merit, Meritorious Service Medal, and the Army Commendation Medal with oak leaf cluster.

Sergeant Henry
Johnson
(1897–1929)

369th Infantry Regiment,
93rd Division, United
States Army

A member of the 15th National Guard of New York, which became the 369th Infantry, Henry Johnson was probably the most famous black soldier to have fought in World War I.

The 369th was the first group of black combat troops to arrive in Europe. After a summer of training, the group saw action at Champagne and fought its way to the Rhine River in Germany, receiving the croix de guerre from the French government. Johnson and another soldier (Needham Roberts) were the first Americans to receive this French medal for individual heroism in combat; Johnson was cited by the French as a "magnificent example of courage and energy." He was later promoted to sergeant.

Dorie Miller
(1919–1943)

Mess Attendant Third
Class, United States Navy

A messman aboard the *USS Arizona*, Dorie Miller had his first taste of combat at Pearl Harbor on December 7, 1941, when he manned a machine gun and brought down four Japanese planes.

Born on a farm near Waco, Texas in 1919, Miller was the son of a sharecropper and grew up to become star fullback on the Moore High School football team in his native city. At 19, he enlisted in the United States Navy, and was nearing the end of his first hitch at the time of the Pearl Harbor attack.

For his heroism, Miller was awarded the Navy Cross, which was conferred by Admiral Chester W. Nimetz, the Commander in Chief of the Pacific Fleet.

He remained a messman during the hostilities, serving aboard the aircraft carrier *Liscome Bay* and being promoted to Mess Attendant Third Class. He was killed in action in the South Pacific in December of 1943. Miller was commended for "distinguished devotion to duty, extreme courage, and disregard of his personal safety during attack."

Petersen was born March 2, 1932 in Topeka, Kansas. He attended Washington University in St. Louis and George Washington University in Washington, DC, before entering the Naval Reserve in 1951 as an aviation cadet.

General Frank E. Petersen (1932–)

First African-American General in the United States Marine Corps

General Frank E. Petersen, speaking to reporters in 1988, said that the military "far surpasses the civilian society" in combatting racial problems.

In 1952 Petersen was commissioned as a second lieutenant in the United States Marine Corps. He was a designated naval aviator and received flight training at the United States Air Station at Pensacola, Florida. He also received flight training at Corpus Christi, Texas and the Marine Corps Air Station at Santa Ana, California.

Petersen flew thirty-one air combat missions during the Korean War. In 1953 and 1954 he was assigned to the 1st Marine Aircraft Wing as its liaison officer. From 1954 to 1960 he was assigned to the Marine Corps's Santa Ana facility, and in 1968 he commanded the Marine Aircraft Group in Vietnam. In 1979 Petersen was promoted to the rank of brigadier general.

As an African-American Marine Corps officer, Petersen accomplished many firsts. He was the first African American to receive a commission as aviator, to attend the National War College, to command a tactical air squadron, and to be promoted to marine general.

Petersen is a recipient of the Distinguished Flying Cross, the Air Medal with silver star, the Korean Service Medal, the Korean Presidential Citation, the National Defense Service Medal with bronze star, and the United Nations Service Medal.

General Colin L. Powell (1937–)

First African-American Chairman of the Joint Chiefs of Staff

Powell was born in New York City on April 5, 1937 and graduated from Morris High School in 1954. In 1958 he received a B.S. in geology from City College of New York; while in college Powell was active in the ROTC program and attained the rank of cadet colonel.

Powell began his military career immediately after graduation by accepting a second lieutenant's commission in the United States Army. In 1962 he served as a military advisor in South Vietnam. Returning to the United States, Powell earned an M.B.A. from George Washington University in 1971, and in 1972 he accepted his first political appointment as White House Fellow. This led to his promotion to brigade commander in 1976 and assistant division commander in 1981.

In 1983 Powell was back in a political position, serving as military assistant to the secretary of defense. In 1987, after holding posts with the Na-

General Colin Powell with Brigade Commander Kristin Baker at the U.S. Military Academy graduation ceremony at West Point in 1990.

tional Security Council, Powell was appointed by President Ronald Reagan to the position of National Security Adviser, head of the National Security Council. In 1989 Powell took the position of chairman of the Joint Chiefs of Staff, the highest military position in the United States. From this position, Powell received international recognition as one of the chief architects of the 1991 Persian Gulf War. In the autumn of 1993, Powell retired as chairman of the Joint Chiefs of Staff.

Powell is a recipient of the Purple Heart and the Bronze Star (1963), Legion of Merit Award (1969 and 1971), Distinguished Service Medal, Soldier's Medal, and Secretary's Award (1988).

General Roscoe Robinson, Jr. (1928-)

First African-American Four-Star General, United States Army

Robinson was born on October 11, 1928, in St. Louis, Missouri. He graduated from the United States Military Academy with a bachelor's degree in military engineering. He also has a master's degree in international affairs from the University of Pittsburgh; he received further training at the National War College, the Army Command and General Staff College, and the Army's Infantry School.

After graduating from West Point, Robinson was commissioned a second lieutenant in the United States Army. He served as a personnel management officer from 1965 to 1967, and in 1968 he was promoted to commanding officer of the 82nd Airborne Division's 2nd Brigade at Fort Bragg, North Carolina. Robinson was promoted to general in 1973 and was placed in command of forces in Okinawa. In 1978 he was placed in command of the 7th Army. From 1982 to 1985 Robinson served as the United States representative to NATO. He has also held the position of executive chief of staff, United States Pacific Command. Robinson retired from active service in 1985.

Robinson has been decorated with the Silver Star with oak leaf cluster, Legion of Merit with oak leaf cluster, Bronze Star, Air Medal, Army Commendation Medal, Combat Infantryman Badge, Distinguished Flying Cross, Master Parachutist Badge, Defense Distinguished Service Medal, and Army Distinguished Medal with oak leaf cluster.

By Allen G. Harris

*I*ndex

PHOTOGRAPHY CREDITS

The Bettmann Archive: pp. **23, 99, 199, 204, 443, 457, 507, 520, 659, 660, 683**; AP/Wide World Photos: pp. **28, 44, 45, 46, 53, 54, 59, 60, 67, 74, 90, 103, 106, 107, 108, 110, 113, 116, 118, 119, 120, 134, 137, 141, 142, 143, 144, 145, 150,, 152, 154, 155, 159, 166, 168, 169, 170, 172, 173, 175, 186, 187, 188, 191, 203, 205, 211, 212, 213, 220, 221, 234, 236, 242, 244, 250, 253, 265, 267, 268, 273, 280, 287, 293, 295, 298, 300, 301, 310, 313, 314, 317, 319, 321, 326, 331, 336 bottom, 338, 339, 341, 342, 351, 355, 356, 360, 363, 366, 367, 370, 371, 373, 379, 381, 382, 383, 386, 388, 389, 390, 391, 393, 398, 400 top, 409, 415, 417, 418, 420, 421, 422, 428, 431, 433, 435, 438, 450 bottom, 468, 469, 470, 471, 484, 501, 502, 503, 516, 523, 525, 527, 538, 543, 545, 546, 549, 553, 555, 557, 559, 561, 562, 570, 571, 575, 579, 584, 586, 591, 613, 622, 638, 650, 653, 665, 675, 677, 681, 692, 693, 694, 696, 697, 698, 700, 701, 702, 708, 709, 710, 713, 714, 717, 718, 719, 720, 725, 731, 754, 759, 763**; Archive Photos: pp. **31, 85, 146, 231, 541**; Courtesy of The Prints and Photographs Division, The Library of Congress: pp. **40, 47, 67, 101**; UPI/Bettmann: pp. **49, 58, 65, 91, 115, 125, 138, 156, 190, 246, 251, 282, 333, 365, 402, 420, 482, 518, 632, 636, 647, 674, 687, 689, 716, 761**; Reuters/Bettmann: pp. **57, 130, 148, 711**; New York Amsterdam News: p. **69**; UPI/Bettmann Newsphotos: pp. **71, 93, 132, 271, 286, 532**; Schomberg Center for Research in Black Culture, The New York Public Library: pp. **78, 259**; Ace Creative Photos: p. **105**; A. Philip Randolph Institute: p. **123**; Courtesy of National Urban League: p. **126**; United Nations: pp. **165, 608**; Photograph by Andy Roy: p. **183**; Fisk University Library: p. **192**; Photograph by Bruce Griffin: p. **208**; Courtesy of Molefi Kete Asante: p. **209**; Surlock Photographers: p. **210**; Courtesy of John F. Kennedy Library: p. **216**; Archive Photos/American Stock Photos: pp. **229, 558**; The New York Public Library: pp. **245, 528**; Tony Brown Productions, Inc: p. **323**; © Mike Carpenter: p. **325**; *Black Enterprise* Magazine: p. **331**; ©1927 The Associated Publishers, Inc: p. **336 top**; Photograph by Ron Scherl: p. **359**; New York City Ballet: p. **364**; Photograph by Martha Swope Associates/Carol Rosegg: p. **396**; Archive Photos/Fotos International: p. **400 bottom**; ©1986 Island Pictures. All Rights Reserved: p. **401**; Archive Photos/David Lee: p. **419**; Archive Photos/Darlene Hammond: p. **423**; Photograph by Alix B. Williamson: p. **473**; *Downbeat*: p. **485**; Courtesy of William Morris Agency: p. **496**; © Stanley B. Burns MD and The Burns Archive: p. **504**; Springer/Bettmann Film Archive: p. **505**; Photograph by Ron Rogers, ABC/Dunhill Records: p. **512**; National Museum of American Art, Washington, D.C./Art Resource, New York: pp. **596, 615, 644, 648**; Galbreath Photo Service: p. **600**; Geoffrey Clements, New York: p. **603**; Fairchild Publications: p. **606**; General Motors Corporation, Public Relations Department: p. **652**; NASA: p. **661**; The Granger Collection, New York: p. **671**; Photograph by Carl Nesfield: p. **704**; NBC: p. **715**; National Archive: p. **732**; U.S. War Department, National Archive: pp. **737, 757**; U.S. Army: pp. **744, 752**; U.S. Air Force: p. **746**; U.S. Defense Department: p. **753**.